The Rise of the Network Society

Manuel Castells

BLACKWELL
Publishers

First published 1996
Reprinted 1997 (three times),
1998 (twice)

Blackwell Publishers Inc
350 Main Street
Malden, Massachusetts 02148, USA

Blackwell Publishers Ltd
108 Cowley Road
Oxford OX4 1JF, UK

Library of Congress Cataloging in Publication Data
Castells, Manuel.
The rise of the network society / Manuel Castells.
p. cm. — (Informational age : 1)
Includes bibliographical references and index.
ISBN 1–55786–616–3 — ISBN 1–55786–617–1 (pbk)
1. Information technology — Economic aspects. 2. Information technology — Social aspects. 3. Information society. 4. Information networks. 5. Technology and civilization. I. Title. II. Series: Castells, Manuel. Information age : 1
HC79.I55C373   1996   95–45082
303.48'33 — dc20   CIP

British Library Cataloguing in Publication Data
A CIP catalogue record for this book is available from the British Library

Printed and bound in Great Britain
by T. J. International Limited, Padstow, Cornwall

This book is printed on acid-free paper

Contents

Contents   ix

Figures

Tables

Acknowledgements

This book has been twelve years in the making, as my research and writing were trying to catch up with an object of study expanding faster than my working capacity. That I have been able to reach some form of completion, however tentative, is due to the cooperation, help, and support of a number of persons and institutions.

My first and deepest expression of gratitude goes to Emma Kiselyova, whose collaboration was essential in obtaining information for several chapters, in helping with the elaboration of the book, in securing access to languages that I do not know, and in commenting, assessing, and advising on the entire manuscript.

I also want to thank the organizers of four exceptional forums where the main ideas of the book were discussed in depth, and duly rectified, in 1994–5, in the final stage of its elaboration: the special session on this book at the 1994 Meeting of the American Anthropological Association, organized by Ida Susser; the Department of Sociology Colloquium at Berkeley, organized by Loic Wacquant; the international seminar on new world trends organized in Brasilia around Fernando Henrique Cardoso, as he was assuming the Presidency of Brazil; and the series of seminars on the book at Tokyo's Hitotsubashi University, organized by Shujiro Yazawa.

Several colleagues in several countries read carefully the draft of the book, in full or specific chapters, and spent considerable time commenting on it, leading to substantial and extensive revisions of the text. The mistakes that remain in the book are entirely mine. Many positive contributions are theirs. I want to acknowledge the collegial efforts of Stephen S. Cohen, Martin Carnoy, Alain Touraine, Anthony Giddens, Daniel Bell, Jesus Leal, Shujiro Yazawa, Peter Hall, Chu-joe Hsia, You-tien Hsing, François Bar, Michael Borrus, Harley Shaiken, Claude Fischer, Nicole Woolsey-Biggart, Bennett Harrison, Anne Marie Guillemard, Richard Nelson, Loic Wacquant, Ida Susser,

Fernando Calderon, Roberto Laserna, Alejandro Foxley, John Urry, Guy Benveniste, Katherine Burlen, Vicente Navarro, Dieter Ernst, Padmanabha Gopinath, Franz Lehner, Julia Trilling, Robert Benson, David Lyon and Melvin Kranzberg.

Throughout the last twelve years a number of institutions have constituted the basis for this work. First of all is my intellectual home, the University of California at Berkeley, and more specifically the academic units where I work: the Department of City and Regional Planning, the Department of Sociology, the Center for Western European Studies, the Institute of Urban and Regional Development, and the Berkeley Roundtable on the International Economy. They have all helped me, and my research, with their material and institutional support, and in providing the appropriate environment to think, imagine, dare, investigate, discuss and write. A key part of this environment, and therefore of my understanding of the world, is the intelligence and openness of graduate students with whom I have been fortunate to interact. Some of them have also been most helpful research assistants, whose contribution to this book must be recognized: You-tien Hsing, Roberto Laserna, Yuko Aoyama, Chris Benner, and Sandra Moog. I also wish to acknowledge the valuable research assistance from Kekuei Hasegawa at Hitotsubashi University.

Other institutions in various countries have also provided support to conduct the research presented in this book. By naming them, I extend my gratitude to their directors and to the many colleagues in these institutions who have taught me about what I have written in this book. These are: Instituto de Sociología de Nuevas Tecnologías, Universidad Autónoma de Madrid; International Institute of Labour Studies, International Labour Office, Geneva; Soviet (later Russian) Sociological Association; Institute of Economics and Industrial Engineering, Siberian Branch of the USSR (later Russian) Academy of Sciences; Universidad Mayor de San Simon, Cochabamba, Bolivia; Instituto de Investigaciónes Sociales, Universidad Nacional Autónoma de Mexico; Center for Urban Studies, University of Hong Kong; Center for Advanced Studies, National University of Singapore; Institute of Technology and International Economy, The State Council, Beijing; National Taiwan University, Taipei; Korean Research Institute for Human Settlement, Seoul; and Faculty of Social Studies, Hitotsubashi University, Tokyo.

I reserve a special thought for John Davey, Blackwell's editorial director, whose intellectual interaction and helpful criticism over more than twenty years have been precious to the development of my writing, helping me out of frequent dead ends by constantly reminding me that books are about communicating ideas, not about printing words.

Last but not least, I want to thank my surgeon, Dr Lawrence Werboff, and my physician, Dr James Davis, both from the University of California at San Francisco's Mount Zion Hospital, whose care and professionalism gave me the time and energy to finish this book, and maybe others.

March 1996   Berkeley, California

Prologue: The Net and the Self

"Do you think me a learned, well-read man?"
"Certainly," replied Zi-gong, "Aren't you?"
*"Not at all," said Confucius. "I have simply grasped one thread which links up the rest."**

Toward the end of the second millennium of the Christian Era several events of historical significance have transformed the social landscape of human life. A technological revolution, centered around information technologies, is reshaping, at accelerated pace, the material basis of society. Economies throughout the world have become globally interdependent, introducing a new form of relationship between economy, state, and society, in a system of variable geometry. The collapse of Soviet statism, and the subsequent demise of the international communist movement, has undermined for the time being the historical challenge to capitalism, rescued the political left (and Marxian theory) from the fatal attraction of Marxism–Leninism, brought the Cold War to an end, reduced the risk of nuclear holocaust, and fundamentally altered global geopolitics. Capitalism itself has undergone a process of profound restructuring, characterized by greater flexibility in management; decentralization and networking of firms both internally and in their relationships to other firms; considerable empowering of capital *vis-à-vis* labor, with the concomitant decline of influence of the labor movement; increasing individualization and diversification of working relationships; massive incorporation of women into the paid labor force, usually under

* Recounted in Sima Qian (145–ca. 89BC), "Confucius," in Hu Shi, *The Development of Logical Methods in Ancient China*, Shanghai: Oriental Book Company, 1922; quoted in Qian 1985: 125.

discriminatory conditions; intervention of the state to deregulate markets selectively, and to undo the welfare state, with different intensity and orientations depending upon the nature of political forces and institutions· in each society; stepped-up global economic competition, in a context of increasing geographic and cultural differentiation of settings for capital accumulation and management. As a consequence of this general overhauling of the capitalist system, still under way, we have witnessed the global integration of financial markets, the rise of the Asian Pacific as the new dominant, global manufacturing center, the arduous economic unification of Europe, the emergence of a North American regional economy, the diversification, then disintegration, of the former Third World, the gradual transformation of Russia and the ex-Soviet area of influence in market economies, the incorporation of valuable segments of economies throughout the world into an interdependent system working as a unit in real time. Because of these trends, there has also been an accentuation of uneven development, this time not only between North and South, but between the dynamic segments and territories of societies everywhere, and those others that risk becoming irrelevant from the perspective of the system's logic. Indeed, we observe the parallel unleashing of formidable productive forces of the informational revolution, and the consolidation of black holes of human misery in the global economy, be it in Burkina Faso, South Bronx, Kamagasaki, Chiapas, or La Courneuve.

Simultaneously, criminal activities and mafia-like organizations around the world have also become global and informational, providing the means for stimulation of mental hyperactivity and forbidden desire, along with any form of illicit trade demanded by our societies, from sophisticated weaponry to human flesh. Besides, a new communication system, increasingly speaking a universal, digital language is both integrating globally the production and distribution of words, sounds and images of our culture, and customizing them to the tastes of identities and moods of individuals. Interactive computer networks are growing exponentially, creating new forms and channels of communication, shaping life and being shaped by life at the same time.

Social changes are as dramatic as technological and economic processes of transformation. For all the difficulty in the process of transformation of women's condition, patriarchalism has come under attack, and has been shaken in a number of societies. Thus, gender relationships have become, in much of the world, a contested domain, rather than a sphere of cultural reproduction. It follows a fundamental redefinition of relationships between women, men and children, and thus, of family, sexuality, and personality.

Environmental consciousness has permeated down to the institutions of society, and its values have won political appeal, at the price of being belied and manipulated in the daily practice of corporations and bureaucracies. Political systems are engulfed in a structural crisis of legitimacy, periodically wrecked by scandals, essentially dependent on media coverage and personalized leadership, and increasingly isolated from the citizenry. Social movements tend to be fragmented, localistic, single-issue oriented, and ephemeral, either retrenched in their inner worlds, or flaring up for just an instant around a media symbol. In such a world of uncontrolled, confusing change, people tend to regroup around primary identities: religious, ethnic, territorial, national. Religious fundamentalism, Christian, Islamic, Jewish, Hindu, and even Buddhist (in what seems to be a contradiction in terms), is probably the most formidable force of personal security and collective mobilization in these troubled years. In a world of global flows of wealth, power, and images, the search for identity, collective or individual, ascribed or constructed, becomes the fundamental source of social meaning. This is not a new trend, since identity, and particularly religious and ethnic identity, have been at the roots of meaning since the dawn of human society. Yet identity is becoming the main, and sometimes the only, source of meaning in a historical period characterized by widespread destructuring of organizations, delegitimation of institutions, fading away of major social movements, and ephemeral cultural expressions. People increasingly organize their meaning not around what they do but on the basis of what they are, or believe they are. Meanwhile, on the other hand, global networks of instrumental exchanges selectively switch on and off individuals, groups, regions, and even countries, according to their relevance in fulfilling the goals processed in the network, in a relentless flow of strategic decisions. It follows a fundamental split between abstract, universal instrumentalism, and historically rooted, particularistic identities. **Our societies are increasingly structured around a bipolar opposition between the Net and the Self.**

In this condition of structural schizophrenia between function and meaning, patterns of social communication become increasingly under stress. And when communication breaks down, when it does not exist any longer, even in the form of conflictual communication (as would be the case in social struggles or political opposition), social groups and individuals become alienated from each other, and see the other as a stranger, eventually as a threat. In this process, social fragmentation spreads, as identities become more specific and increasingly difficult to share. The informational society, in its global manifestation, is also the world of Aum Shinrikyo, of American Militia,

of Islamic/Christian theocratic ambitions, and of Hutu/Tutsi reciprocal genocide.

Bewildered by the scale and scope of historical change, culture and
thinking in our time often embrace a new millenarism. Prophets of
technology preach the new age, extrapolating to social trends and
organization the barely understood logic of computers and DNA.
Postmodern culture, and theory, indulge in celebrating the end of
history, and, to some extent, the end of Reason, giving up on our
capacity to understand and make sense, even of nonsense. The
implicit assumption is the acceptance of full individualization of
behaviour, and of society's powerlessness over its destiny.

The project informing this book swims against streams of destruction, and takes exception to various forms of intellectual nihilism,
social skepticism, and political cynicism. I believe in rationality, and
in the possibility of calling upon reason, without worshipping its
goddess. I believe in the chances of meaningful social action, and
transformative politics, without necessarily drifting towards the deadly
rapids of absolute utopias. I believe in the liberating power of identity, without accepting the necessity of either its individualization or
its capture by fundamentalism. And I propose the hypothesis that all
major trends of change constituting our new, confusing world are
related, and that we can make sense of their interrelationship. And,
yes, I believe, in spite of a long tradition of sometimes tragic intellectual errors, that observing, analyzing, and theorizing is a way of
helping to build a different, better world. Not by providing the
answers, that will be specific to each society and found by social actors
themselves, but by raising some relevant questions. This book would
like to be a modest contribution to a necessarily collective, analytical
effort, already underway from many horizons, aimed at understanding our new world on the basis of available evidence and
exploratory theory.

To walk preliminary steps in this direction, we must take technology
seriously, using it as the point of departure of this inquiry; we ought
to locate this process of revolutionary technological change in the
social context in which it takes place and by which it is being shaped;
and we should keep in mind that the search for identity is as powerful
as techno–economic change in charting the new history. Then, after
saying the words, we will depart for our intellectual journey, following
an itinerary that will take us to numerous domains, and will cross
through several cultures and institutional contexts, since the understanding of a global transformation requires a perspective as global as
possible, within the obvious limits of this author's experience and
knowledge.

Technology, Society, and Historical Change

The information technology revolution, because of its pervasiveness throughout the whole realm of human activity, will be my entry point in analyzing the complexity of new economy, society, and culture in the making. This methodological choice does not imply that new social forms and processes emerge as consequences of technological change. Of course technology does not determine society.[1] Neither does society script the course of technological change, since many factors, including individual inventiveness and entrepreneurialism, intervene in the process of scientific discovery, technological innovation, and social applications, so that the final outcome depends on a complex pattern of interaction.[2] Indeed, the dilemma of technological determinism is probably a false problem,[3] since technology *is* society, and society cannot be understood or represented without its technological tools.[4] Thus, when in the 1970s a new technological paradigm, organized around information technology, came to be constituted, mainly in the United States (see chapter 1), it was a specific segment of American society, in interaction with the global economy and with world geopolitics, that materialized into a new way of producing, communicating, managing, and living. That the constitution of this paradigm took place in the United States, and to some extent in California, and in the 1970s, probably had considerable consequences for the forms and evolution of new information technologies. For instance, in spite of the decisive role of military funding and markets in fostering early stages of the electronics industry during the 1940s–1960s, the technological blossoming that took place in the early 1970s can be somehow related to the culture of freedom, individual innovation, and entrepreneurialism that grew out from the 1960s culture of American campuses. Not so much in terms of its politics, since Silicon Valley was, and is, a solid bastion of the conservative vote, and most innovators were meta-political, but in regard to social values of breaking away from established patterns of behavior, both in society at large and in the business world. The emphasis on personalized devices, on interactivity, on networking, and the relentless

[1]   See the interesting debate on the matter in Smith and Marx 1994.
[2]   Technology does not determine society: it embodies it. But neither does society determine technological innovation: it uses it. This dialectical interaction between society and technology is present in the works of the best historians, such as Fernand Braudel.
[3]   Classic historian of technology Melvin Kranzberg has forcefully argued against the false dilemma of technological determinism. See, for instance, Kranzberg's (1992) acceptance speech of the Award to Honorary Membership in NASTS.
[4]   Bijker et al. (1987).

pursuit of new technological breakthroughs, even when it apparently did not make much business sense, was clearly in discontinuity with the somewhat cautious tradition of the corporate world. The information technology revolution half-consciously[5] diffused through the material culture of our societies the libertarian spirit that flourished in the 1960s movements. Yet, as soon as new information technologies diffused, and were appropriated by different countries, various cultures, diverse organizations, and miscellaneous goals, they exploded in all kinds of applications and uses that fed back into technological innovation, accelerating the speed, broadening the scope of technological change, and diversifying its sources.[6] An illustration will help us to understand the importance of unintended social consequences of technology.[7]

As is known, the Internet originated in a daring scheme imagined in the 1960s by the technological warriors of US Defense Department Advanced Research Projects Agency (the mythical DARPA) to prevent a Soviet takeover or destruction of American communications in case of nuclear war. To some extent, it was the electronic equivalent of the Maoist tactics of dispersal of guerrilla forces around a vast territory to counter an enemy's might with versatility and knowledge of terrain. The outcome was a network architecture that, as its inventors wanted, cannot be controlled from any center, and is made up of thousands of autonomous computer networks that have innumerable ways to

[5]   There is still to be written a fascinating social history of the values and personal views of some of the key innovators of the 1970s Silicon Valley revolution in computer technologies. But a few indications seem to point to the fact that they were intentionally trying to undo the centralizing technologies of the corporate world, both out of conviction and as their market niche. As evidence, I recall the famous Apple Computer 1984 advertising spot to launch Macintosh, in explicit opposition to Big Brother IBM of Orwellian mythology. As for the countercultural character of many of these innovators, I shall also refer to the life story of the genius developer of the personal computer, Steve Wozniak: after quitting Apple, bored by its transformation into another multinational corporation, he spent a fortune for a few years subsidizing rock groups that he liked, before creating another company to develop technologies of his taste. At one point, after having created the personal computer, Wozniak realized that he had no formal education in computer sciences, so he enrolled at UC Berkeley. But in order to avoid embarrassing publicity he used another name.
[6]   For selected evidence concerning the variation of information technology diffusion patterns in different social and institutional contexts see, among other works: Guile (1985); Landau and Rosenberg (1986); Wang (1994); Watanuki (1990); Bianchi et al. (1988); Freeman et al. (1991); Bertazzoni et al (1984); Agence de L'Informatique (1986); Castells et al. (1986).
[7]   For an informed and cautious discussion of relationships between society and technology, see Fischer (1985).

link up, going around electronic barriers. Ultimately ARPANET, the network set up by the US Defense Department, became the foundation of a global, horizontal communication network of thousands of computer networks (admittedly for a computer literate elite of about 20 million users in the mid-1990s, but growing exponentially), that has been appropriated for all kinds of purposes, quite removed from the concerns of an extinct Cold War, by individuals and groups around the world. Indeed, it was via the Internet that Subcomandante Marcos, the leader of Chiapas' *zapatistas*, communicated with the world, and with the media, from the depth of Lacandon forest, during his escape in February 1995.

Yet, if society does not determine technology, it can, mainly through the state, suffocate its development. Or alternatively, again mainly by state intervention, it can embark on an accelerated process of technological modernization able to change the fate of economies, military power, and social well-being in a few years. Indeed, the ability or inability of societies to master technology, and particularly technologies that are strategically decisive in each historical period, largely shapes their destiny, to the point where we could say that while technology *per se* does not determine historical evolution and social change, technology (or the lack of it) embodies the capacity of societies to transform themselves, as well as the uses to which societies, always in a conflictive process, decide to put their technological potential.[8]

Thus, around 1400, when the European Renaissance was planting the intellectual seeds of technological change that would dominate the world three centuries later, China was the most advanced technological civilization in the world, according to Mokyr.[9] Key inventions had developed in China centuries earlier, even a millennium and a half earlier, as in the case of blast furnaces that allowed the casting of iron in China by 200BC. Also, Su Sung introduced the water clock in AD1086, surpassing the accuracy of measurement of European mechanical clocks of the same date. The iron plow was introduced in the sixth century, and adapted to wet-field rice cultivation two centuries later. In textiles, the spinning wheel appeared at the same time as in the West, by the thirteenth century, but advanced much faster in China because there was an old-established tradition of sophisticated weaving equipment: draw looms to weave silk were used in Han times.

---

[8] See the analyses presented in Castells (1988b); also Webster (1991).
[9] My discussion on China's interrupted technological development relies mainly, on the one hand, on an extraordinary chapter by Joel Mokyr (1990: 209–38); on the other hand, on a most insightful, although controversial book, Qian (1985).

The adoption of water power was parallel to Europe: by the eight century the Chinese were using hydraulic trip hammers, and in 1280 there was wide diffusion of the vertical water wheel. Ocean travel was easier for the Chinese at an earlier date than for European vessels: they invented the compass around AD960, and their junks were the most advanced ships in the world by the end of the fourteenth century, enabling long sea trips. In military matters, the Chinese, besides inventing powder, developed a chemical industry that was able to provide powerful explosives, and the crossbow and the trebuchet were used by Chinese armies centuries ahead of Europe. In medicine, techniques such as acupuncture were yielding extraordinary results that only recently have been universally acknowledged. And of course, the first information processing revolution was Chinese: paper and printing were Chinese inventions. Paper was introduced in China 1,000 years earlier than in the West, and printing probably began in the late seventh century. As Jones writes: "China came within a hair's breadth of industrializing in the fourteenth century."[10] That it did not, changed the history of the world. When in 1842 the Opium Wars led to Britain's colonial impositions, China realized, too late, that isolation could not protect the Middle Kingdom from the evil consequences of technological inferiority. It took more than one century thereafter for China to start recovering from such a catastrophic deviation from its historical trajectory.

Explanations for such a stunning historical course are both numerous and controversial. There is no place in this Prologue to enter the complexity of the debate. But, on the basis of research and analysis by historians such as Needham,[11] Qian,[12] Jones,[13] and Mokyr,[14] it is possible to suggest an interpretation that may help to understand, in general terms, the interaction between society, history, and technology. Indeed, most hypotheses concerning cultural differences (even those without implicitly racist undertones), fail to explain, as Mokyr points out, the difference not between China and Europe but between China in 1300 and China in 1800. Why did a culture and a kingdom that had been the technological leader of the world for thousands of years suddenly become technologically stagnant precisely at the moment when Europe embarked on the age of discoveries, and then on the industrial revolution?

Needham has proposed that Chinese culture was more prone than

---

[10] Jones (1981: 160), cited by Mokyr (1990: 219).
[11] Needham (1954–88, 1969, 1981).
[12] Qian (1985).
[13] Jones (1988).
[14] Mokyr (1990).

Western values to a harmonious relationship between man and nature, something that could be jeopardized by fast technological innovation. Furthermore, he objects to the Western criteria used to measure technological development. However, this cultural emphasis on a holistic approach to development had not impeded techno-logical innovation for millennia, nor stopped ecological deterioration as a result of irrigation works in Southern China, when the conser-vation of nature was subordinated to agricultural production in order to feed a growing population. In fact, Wen-yuan Qian, in his powerful book, takes exception to Needham's somewhat excessive enthusiasm for the feats of Chinese traditional technology, notwithstanding his shared admiration for Needham's monumental life-long work. Qian calls for a closer analytical linkage between the development of Chinese science and the characteristics of Chinese civilization domi-nated by the dynamics of state. Mokyr also considers the state to be the crucial factor in explaining Chinese technological retardation in modern times. The explanation may be proposed in three steps: technological innovation was, for centuries, fundamentally in the hands of the state; after 1400 the Chinese state, under the Ming and Qing dynasties, lost interest in technological innovation; and, partly because of their dedication to serve the state, cultural and social elites were focused on arts, humanities, and self-promotion *vis-à-vis* the imperial bureaucracy. Thus, what does seem to be crucial is the role of the state, and the changing orientation of state policy. Why would a state that had been the greatest hydraulic engineer in history, and had established an agricultural extension system to improve agricul-tural productivity since the Han period, suddenly become inhibited from technological innovation, even forbidding geographical explor-ation, and abandoning the construction of large ships by 1430? The obvious answer is that it was not the same state; not only because they were of different dynasties, but because the bureaucratic class became more deeply entrenched in the administration due to a longer than usual period of uncontested domination.

According to Mokyr, it appears that the determining factor for tech-nological conservatism was the rulers' fears of the potentially disruptive impacts of technological change on social stability. Numerous forces opposed the diffusion of technology in China, as in other societies, particularly the urban guilds. Bureaucrats content with the status quo were concerned by the possibility of triggering social conflicts that could coalesce with other sources of latent oppo-sition in a society that had been kept under control for several centuries. Even the two enlightened Manchu despots of the eighteenth century, K'ang Chi and Ch'ien Lung, focused their efforts on pacification and order, rather than on unleashing new development. Conversely, exploration and contacts with foreigners, beyond controlled trade and acquisition of weapons, were deemed at best unnecessary, at worst threatening, because of the uncertainty they would imply. A bureaucratic state without external incentive and with internal disincentives to engage in technological modernization opted for the most prudent neutrality, as a result stalling the technological trajectory that China had been following for centuries, if not millennia, precisely under state guidance. The discussion of the factors underlying the dynamics of the Chinese state under the Ming and Qing dynasties is clearly beyond the scope of this book. What matters for our research purpose are two teachings from this fundamental experience of interrupted technological development: on the one hand, the state can be, and has been in history, in China and elsewhere, a leading force of technological innovation; on the other hand, precisely because of this, when the state reverses its interest in technological development, or becomes unable to perform it under new conditions, a statist model of innovation leads to stagnation, because of the sterilization of society's autonomous innovative energy to create and apply technology. That the Chinese state could, centuries later, build anew an advanced technological basis, in nuclear technology, missiles, satellite launching, and electronics,[15] demonstrates again the emptiness of a predominantly cultural interpretation of technological development and backwardness: the same culture may induce very different technological trajectories depending on the pattern of relationships between state and society. However, the exclusive dependence on the state has a price, and the price for China was that of retardation, famine, epidemics, colonial domination, and civil war, until at least the middle of the twentieth century.

   A rather similar, contemporary story can be told, and will be told in this book (in volume III), of the inability of Soviet statism to master the information technology revolution, thus stalling its productive capacity and undermining its military might. Yet we should not jump to the ideological conclusion that all state intervention is counterproductive to technological development, indulging in ahistorical reverence for unfettered, individual entrepreneurialism. Japan is of course the counter-example, both to Chinese historical experience and to the inability of the Soviet state to adapt to the American-initiated revolution in information technology.

   Historically, Japan went, even deeper than China, through a period of historical isolation under the Tokugawa Shogunate (established in

<hr>

[15]   Wang (1993).

1603), between 1636 and 1853, precisely during the critical period of formation of an industrial system in the western hemisphere. Thus, while at the turn of the seventeenth century Japanese merchants were trading throughout East and Southeast Asia, using modern vessels of up to 700 tons, the construction of ships above 50 tons was prohibited in 1635, and all Japanese ports, except Nagasaki, were closed to foreigners, while trade was restricted to China, Korea, and Holland.[16] Technological isolation was not total during these two centuries, and endogenous innovation did allow Japan to proceed with incremental change at a faster pace than China.[17] Yet, because Japan's technological level was lower than China's, by the mid-nineteenth century the *kurobune* (black ships) of Commodore Perry could impose trade and diplomatic relations on a country substantially lagging behind Western technology. However, as soon as the 1868 *Ishin Meiji* (Meiji Restoration) created the political conditions for a decisive state-led modernization,[18] Japan progressed in advanced technology by leaps and bounds in a very short time span.[19] Just as one significant illustration, because of its current strategic importance, let us briefly recall the extraordinary development of electrical engineering and communication applications in Japan in the last quarter of the nineteenth century.[20] Indeed, the first independent department of electrical engineering in the world was established in 1873 in the newly founded Imperial College of Engineering in Tokyo, under the leadership of its Dean, Henry Dyer, a Scottish mechanical engineer. Between 1887 and 1892, a leading academic in electrical engineering, British professor William Ayrton, was invited to teach at the College, being instrumental in disseminating knowledge to the new generation of Japanese engineers, so that by the end of the century the Telegraph Bureau was able to replace foreigners in all its technical departments. Technology

[16] Chida and Davies (1990).
[17] Ito (1993).
[18] Several distinguished Japanese scholars, and I tend to concur with them, consider that the best Western account of the Meiji Restoration, and of the social roots of Japanese modernization, is Norman (1940). It has been translated into Japanese and is widely read in Japanese universities. A brilliant historian, educated at Cambridge and Harvard, before joining the Canadian diplomatic corps Norman was denounced as a communist by Karl Wittfogel to the McCarthy Senate Committee in the 1950s, and then submitted to constant pressure from Western intelligence agencies. Appointed Canadian Ambassador to Egypt he committed suicide in Cairo in 1957. On the contribution of this truly exceptional scholar to the understanding of the Japanese state, see Dower (1975); for a different perspective, see Beasley (1990).
[19] Matsumoto and Sinclair (1994); Kamatani (1988).
[20] Uchida (1991).

transfer from the West was sought after through a variety of mechanisms. In 1873, the Machine Shop of the Telegraph Bureau sent a Japanese clockmaker, Tanaka Seisuke, to the International Machines exhibition in Vienna to obtain information on the machines. About ten years later, all the Bureau's machines were made in Japan. Based on this technology, Tanaka Daikichi founded in 1882 an electrical factory, Shibaura Works, that, after its acquisition by Mitsui, went on to become Toshiba. Engineers were sent to Europe and to America. And Western Electric was permitted to produce and sell in Japan in 1899, in a joint venture with Japanese industrialists: the name of the company was NEC. On such a technological basis Japan went full speed into the electrical and communications age before 1914: by 1914 total power production had reached 1,555,000 kw/hour, and 3,000 telephone offices were relaying a billion messages a year. It is indeed symbolic that Commodore Perry's gift to the Shogun in 1857 was a set of American telegraphs, until then never seen in Japan: the first telegraph line was laid in 1869, and ten years later Japan was connected to the whole world through a transcontinental information network, via Siberia, operated by the Great Northern Telegraph Co., jointly managed by Western and Japanese engineers and transmitting in both English and Japanese.

The story of how Japan became a major world player in information technology industries in the last quarter of the twentieth century, under the strategic guidance of the state, is now general public knowledge, so it will be assumed in our discussion.[21] What is relevant for the ideas presented here is that it happened at the same time as an industrial and scientific superpower, the Soviet Union, failed this fundamental technological transition. It is obvious, as the preceding reminders show, that Japanese technological development since the 1960s did not happen in an historical vacuum, but was rooted in a decades-old tradition of engineering excellence. Yet what matters for the purpose of this analysis is to emphasize what dramatically different results state intervention (and lack of intervention) had in the cases of China and the Soviet Union, as compared to Japan in both the Meiji period and the post-second World War period. The characteristics of the Japanese state at the roots of both processes of modernization and development are well known, both for *Ishin Meiji*[22] and for the contemporary developmental state,[23] and

---

[21]   Ito (1994); Japan Informatization Processing Center (1994); for a western perspective, see Forester (1993).
[22]   See Norman (1940) and Dower (1975); see also Allen (1981a).
[23]   Johnson (1995).

their presentation would take us excessively away from the focus of these preliminary reflections. What must be retained for the understanding of the relationship between technology and society is that the role of the state, by either stalling, unleashing, or leading technological innovation, is a decisive factor in the overall process, as it expresses and organizes the social and cultural forces that dominate in a given space and time. To a large extent, technology expresses the ability of a society to propel itself into technological mastery through the institutions of society, including the state. The historical process through which such development of productive forces takes place earmarks the characteristics of technology and its interweaving in social relationships.

This is not different in the case of the current technological revolution. It originated and diffused, not by accident, in a historical period of the global restructuring of capitalism, for which it was an essential tool. Thus, the new society emerging from such a process of change is both capitalist and informational, while presenting considerable historical variation in different countries, according to their history, culture, institutions, and to their specific relationship to global capitalism and information technology.

Informationalism, Industrialism, Capitalism, Statism: Modes of Development and Modes of Production

The information technology revolution has been instrumental in allowing the implementation of a fundamental process of restructuring of the capitalist system from the 1980s onwards. In the process, this technological revolution was itself shaped, in its development and manifestations, by the logic and interests of advanced capitalism, without being reducible to the expression of such interests. The alternative system of social organization present in our historical period, statism, also tried to redefine the means of accomplishing its structural goals while preserving the essence of these goals: that is the meaning of restructuring (or *perestroyka*, in Russian). Yet Soviet statism failed in its attempt, to the point of collapsing the whole system, to a large extent because of the incapacity of statism to assimilate and use the principles of informationalism embodied in new information technologies, as I shall argue in this book (volume III) on the basis of empirical analysis. Chinese statism seemed to succeed by shifting from statism to state-led capitalism and integration in global economic networks, actually becoming closer to the developmental state model of East Asian capitalism than to the "Socialism with Chinese

characteristics" of official ideology,[24] as I shall also try to discuss in
volume III. Nonetheless, it is highly likely that the process of structural transformation in China will undergo major political conflicts
and institutional change in the coming years. The collapse of statism
(with rare exceptions, for example, Vietnam, North Korea, Cuba,
which are, however, in the process of linking up with global capitalism) has established a close relationship between the new, global
capitalist system shaped by its relatively successful *perestroyka*, and the
emergence of informationalism, as the new material, technological
basis of economic activity and social organization. Yet both processes
(capitalist restructuring, the rise of informationalism) are distinct,
and their interaction can only be understood if we separate them
analytically. At this point in my introductory presentation of the
book's *idées fortes*, it seems necessary to propose some theoretical
distinctions and definitions concerning capitalism, statism, industrialism, and informationalism.

It is a well-established tradition in theories of postindustrialism and
informationalism, starting with classic works by Alain Touraine[25] and
Daniel Bell,[26] to place the distinction between pre-industrialism,
industrialism, and informationalism (or postindustrialism) on a
different axis than the one opposing capitalism and statism (or collec-
tivism, in Bell's terms). While societies can be characterized along the
two axes (so that we have industrial statism, industrial capitalism, and
so on), it is essential for the understanding of social dynamics to maintain the analytical distance and empirical interrelation between
modes of production (capitalism, statism) and modes of development
(industrialism, informationalism). To root these distinctions in a
theoretical basis, that will inform the specific analyses presented in
this book, it is unavoidable to take the reader, for a few paragraphs,
into the somewhat arcane domains of sociological theory.

This book studies the emergence of a new social structure, manifested under various forms, depending on the diversity of cultures and
institutions throughout the planet. This new social structure is associated with the emergence of a new mode of development,
informationalism, historically shaped by the restructuring of the capitalist mode of production towards the end of the twentieth century.

The theoretical perspective underlying this approach postulates
that societies are organized around human processes structured by
historically determined relationships of *production, experience,* and

[24]   Nolan and Furen (1990); Hsing (1996).
[25]   Touraine (1969).
[26]   Bell (1973). All quotes are from the 1976 edition, which includes a new,
substantial "Foreword 1976."

power. Production is the action of humankind on matter (nature) to appropriate it and transform it for its benefit by obtaining a product, consuming (unevenly) part of it, and accumulating surplus for investment, according to a variety of socially determined goals. *Experience* is the action of human subjects on themselves, determined by the interaction between their biological and cultural identities, and in relationship to their social and natural environment. It is constructed around the endless search for fulfillment of human needs and desires. *Power* is that relationship between human subjects which, on the basis of production and experience, imposes the will of some subjects upon others by the potential or actual use of violence, physical or symbolic. Institutions of society are built to enforce power relationships existing in each historical period, including the controls, limits, and social contracts achieved in the power struggles.

Production is organized in class relationships that define the process by which some human subjects, on the basis of their position in the production process, decide the sharing and uses of the product in relationship to consumption and investment. Experience is structured around gender/sexual relationships, historically organized around the family, and characterized hitherto by the domination of men over women. Family relationships and sexuality structure personality and frame symbolic interaction.

Power is founded upon the state and its institutionalized monopoly of violence, although what Foucault labels the microphysics of power, embodied in institutions and organizations, diffuses throughout the entire society, from work places to hospitals, enclosing subjects in a tight framework of formal duties and informal aggressions.

Symbolic communication between humans, and the relationship between humans and nature, on the basis of production (with its complement, consumption), experience, and power, crystallize over history in specific territories, thus generating *cultures and collective identities.*

Production is a socially complex process, because each one of its elements is internally differentiated. Thus, humankind as collective producer includes both labor and the organizers of production, and labor is highly differentiated and stratified according to the role of each worker in the production process. Matter includes nature, human-modified nature, human-produced nature, and human nature itself, the labors of history forcing us to move away from the classic distinction between humankind and nature, since millennia of human action have incorporated the natural environment into society, making us, materially and symbolically, an inseparable part of this environment. The relationship between labor and matter in the process of work involves the use of means of production to act upon matter on the basis of energy, knowledge, and information. Technology is the specific form of this relationship.

The product of the production process is socially used under two forms: consumption and surplus. Social structures interact with production processes by determining the rules for the appropriation, distribution, and uses of the surplus. These rules constitute modes of production, and these modes define social relationships of production, determining the existence of social classes that become constituted as such classes through their historical practice. The structural principle under which surplus is appropriated and controlled characterizes a mode of production. In the twentieth century we have lived, essentially, with two predominant modes of production: capitalism and statism. Under capitalism, the separation between producers and their means of production, the commodification of labor, and the private ownership of means of production on the basis of the control of capital (commodified surplus), determined the basic principle of appropriation and distribution of surplus by capitalists, although who is (are) the capitalist class(es) is a matter of social inquiry in each historical context, rather than an abstract category. Under statism, the control of surplus is external to the economic sphere: it lies in the hands of the power-holders in the state: let us call them *apparatchiki* or *ling-dao*. Capitalism is oriented toward profit-maximizing, that is, toward increasing the amount of surplus appropriated by capital on the basis of the private control over the means of production and circulation. Statism is (was?) oriented toward power-maximizing, that is, toward increasing the military and ideological capacity of the political apparatus for imposing its goals on a greater number of subjects and at deeper levels of their consciousness.

The social relationships of production, and thus the mode of production, determine the appropriation and uses of surplus. A separate yet fundamental question is the level of such surplus, determined by the productivity of a particular process of production, that is by the ratio of the value of each unit of output to the value of each unit of input. Productivity levels are themselves dependent on the relationship between labor and matter, as a function of the use of the means of production by the application of energy and knowledge. This process is characterized by technical relationships of production, defining modes of development. Thus, modes of development are the technological arrangements through which labor works on matter to generate the product, ultimately determining the level and quality of surplus. Each mode of development is defined by the element that is fundamental in fostering productivity in the production process. Thus, in the agrarian mode of development, the source of increasing surplus results from quantitative increases of labor and natural resources (particularly land) in the production process, as well as from the natural endowment of these resources. In the industrial mode of development, the main source of productivity lies in the introduction of new energy sources, and in the ability to decentralize the use of energy throughout the production and circulation processes. In the new, informational mode of development the source of productivity lies in the technology of knowledge generation, information processing, and symbol communication. To be sure, knowledge and information are critical elements in all modes of development, since the process of production is always based on some level of knowledge and in the processing of information.[27] However, what is specific to the informational mode of development is the action of knowledge upon knowledge itself as the main source of productivity (see chapter 2). Information processing is focused on improving the technology of information processing as a source of productivity, in a virtuous circle of interaction between the knowledge sources of technology and the application of technology to improve knowledge generation and information processing: this is why, rejoining popular fashion, I call this new mode of development informational, constituted by the emergence of a new technological paradigm based on information technology (see chapter 1).

Each mode of development has also a structurally determined performance principle around which technological processes are organized: industrialism is oriented toward economic growth, that is toward maximizing output; informationalism is oriented towards technological development, that is toward the accumulation of knowledge and towards higher levels of complexity in information processing. While higher levels of knowledge may normally result in higher levels of output per unit of input, it is the pursuit of knowledge

[27] For the sake of clarity in this book, I find it necessary to provide a definition of knowledge and information, even if such an intellectually satisfying gesture introduces a dose of the arbitrary in the discourse, as social scientists who have struggled with the issue know well. I have no compelling reason to improve on Daniel Bell's (1973: 175) own definition of *knowledge*: "Knowledge: a set of organized statements of facts or ideas, presenting a reasoned judgment or an experimental result, which is transmitted to others through some communication medium in some systematic form. Thus, I distinguish knowledge from news and entertainment." As for *information*, some established authors in the field, such as Machlup, simply define information as the communication of knowledge (see Machlup 1962: 15). However, this is because Machlup's definition of knowledge seems to be excessively broad, as Bell argues. Thus, I would rejoin the operational definition of information proposed by Porat in his classic work (1977:2): "Information is data that have been organized and communicated."

and information that characterizes the technological production function under informationalism.

Although technology and technical relationships of production are organized in paradigms originating in the dominant spheres of society (for example, the production process, the military industrial complex) they diffuse throughout the whole set of social relationships and social structures, so penetrating and modifying power and experience.[28] Thus, modes of development shape the entire realm of social behavior, of course including symbolic communication. Because informationalism is based on the technology of knowledge and information, there is a specially close linkage between culture and productive forces, between spirit and matter, in the informational mode of development. It follows that we should expect the emergence of historically new forms of social interaction, social control, and social change.

Informationalism and capitalist *perestroyka*

Shifting from theoretical categories to historical change, what truly matters for social processes and forms making the living flesh of societies is the actual interaction between modes of production and modes of development, enacted and fought for by social actors, in unpredictable ways, within the constraining framework of past history and current conditions of technological and economic development. Thus, the world, and societies, would have been very different if Gorbachev had succeeded in his own *perestroyka*, a target that was politically difficult, but not out of reach. Or if the Asian Pacific had not been able to blend its traditional business networking form of economic organization with the tools provided by information technology. Yet the most decisive historical factor accelerating, channeling and shaping the information technology paradigm, and inducing its associated social forms, was/is the process of capitalist restructuring undertaken since the 1980s, so that the new techno-economic system can be adequately characterized as *informational capitalism*.

The Keynesian model of capitalist growth that brought unprece-

---

[28]   When technological innovation does not diffuse in society, because of institutional obstacles to such diffusion, what follows is technological retardation because of the absence of necessary social/cultural feedback into the institutions of innovation and into the innovators themselves. This is the fundamental lesson that can be drawn from such important experiences as Qing's China, or the Soviet Union. For the Soviet Union, see vol. III. For China, see Qian (1985) and Mokyr (1990).

dented economic prosperity and social stability to most market economies for almost three decades after the Second World War, hit the wall of its built-in limitations in the early 1970s, and its crisis was manifested in the form of rampant inflation.[29] When the oil price increases of 1974 and 1979 threatened to spiral inflation out of control, governments and firms engaged in a process of restructuring in a pragmatic process of trial and error that is still underway in the mid-1990s with a more decisive effort at deregulation, privatization, and the dismantling of the social contract between capital and labor that underlay the stability of the previous growth model. In a nutshell, a series of reforms, both at the level of institutions and in the management of firms, aimed at four main goals: deepening the capitalist logic of profit-seeking in capital–labor relationships; enhancing the productivity of labor and capital; globalizing production, circulation, and markets, seizing the opportunity of the most advantageous conditions for profit-making everywhere; and marshaling the state's support for productivity gains and competitiveness of national economies, often to the detriment of social protection and public interest regulations. Technological innovation and organizational change, focusing on flexibility and adaptability, were absolutely critical in ensuring the speed and efficiency of restructuring. It can be argued that without new information technology global capitalism would have been a much-limited reality, flexible management would have been reduced to labor trimming, and the new round of spending in both capital goods and new consumer products would not have been sufficient to compensate for the reduction in public spending. Thus, informationalism is linked to the expansion and rejuvenation of capitalism, as industrialism was linked to its constitution as a mode of production. To be sure, the process of restructuring had very different manifestations in areas and societies around the world, as I shall briefly survey in chapter 2: it was diverted from its fundamental logic by the military Keynesianism of the Reagan Administration, actually creating even greater difficulties for the American economy at the end of the euphoria of artificial stimulation; it was somewhat limited in Western Europe because of society's resistance to the dismantling of the welfare state and to one-sided labor market flexibility, with the

[29]   I presented years ago my interpretation of the causes of the 1970s worldwide economic crisis, as well as a tentative prognosis of avenues for capitalist restructuring. Notwithstanding the excessively rigid theoretical framework I juxtaposed to the empirical analysis, I think that the main points I made in that book (written in 1977–8), including the prediction of Reagonomics under that name, are still useful to understand the qualitative changes operated in capitalism during the last two decades (see Castells 1980).

result of raising unemployment in the European Union; it was
absorbed in Japan without dramatic changes by emphasizing productivity and competitiveness on the basis of technology and cooperation
rather than by increasing exploitation, until international pressures
forced Japan to offshore production and to broadening the role of an
unprotected, secondary labor market; and it plunged into a major
recession, in the 1980s, the economies of Africa (except South Africa
and Botswana) and Latin America (with the exception of Chile and
Colombia), when International Monetary Fund policies cut money
supply, reduced wages and imports, to homogenize conditions of
global capital accumulation around the world. Restructuring
proceeded on the basis of the political defeat of organized labor in
major capitalist countries, and the acceptance of a common economic
discipline by countries of the OECD area. Such discipline, although
enforced when necessary by the Bundesbank, the Federal Reserve
Board, and International Monetary Fund, was in fact inscribed in the
integration of global financial markets that took place in the early
1980s using new information technologies. Under conditions of
global financial integration, autonomous, national monetary policies
became literally unfeasible, thus equalizing basic economic parameters of restructuring processes throughout the planet.

  While capitalism's restructuring and the diffusion of informationalism were inseparable processes on a global scale, societies did
act/react differently to such processes, according to the specificity of
their history, culture, and institutions. Thus, to some extent it would
be improper to refer to an Informational Society, which would imply
the homogeneity of social forms everywhere under the new system.
This is obviously an untenable proposition, empirically and theoretically. Yet we could speak of an Informational Society in the same way
that sociologists have been referring to the existence of an Industrial
Society, characterized by common fundamental features in their
socio-technical systems, for instance in Raymond Aron's formulation.[30] But with two important qualifications: on the one hand,
informational societies, as they exist currently, are capitalist (unlike
industrial societies, some of which were statist); on the other hand, we
must stress the cultural and institutional diversity of informational
societies. Thus, Japanese uniqueness[31] or Spain's difference[32] are
not going to fade away in a process of cultural indifferentiation,
marching anew towards universal modernization, this time measured

---

[30]   Aron (1963).
[31]   On Japanese uniqueness in a sociological perspective, see Shoji (1990).
[32]   On the social roots of Spanish differences, and similarities, *vis-à-vis* other
countries, see Zaldivar and Castells (1992).

by rates of computer diffusion. Neither are China or Brazil going to be melted in the global pot of informational capitalism by continuing their current high-speed developmental path. But Japan, Spain, China, Brazil, as well as the United States, are and will be more so in the future, informational societies, in the sense that the core processes of knowledge generation, economic productivity, political/military power and media communication are already deeply transformed by the informational paradigm, and are connected to global networks of wealth, power, and symbols working under such a logic. Thus, all societies are affected by capitalism and informationalism, and many societies (certainly all major societies) are already informational,[33] although of different kinds, in different settings, and with specific cultural/institutional expressions. A theory of the informational society, as distinct from a global/informational economy,

---

[33] I should like to draw an analytical distinction between the notions of "information society" and "informational society," with similar implications for information/informational economy. The term information society emphasizes the role of information in society. But I argue that information, in its broadest sense, e.g. as communication of knowledge, has been critical in all societies, including medieval Europe which was culturally structured, and to some extent unified, around scholasticism, that is, by and large an intellectual framework (see Southern 1995). In contrast, the term informational indicates the attribute of a specific form of social organization in which information generation, processing, and transmission become the fundamental sources of productivity and power, because of new technological conditions emerging in this historical period. My terminology tries to establish a parallel with the distinction between industry and industrial. An industrial society (a usual notion in the sociological tradition) is not just a society where there is industry, but a society where the social and technological forms of industrial organization permeate all spheres of activity, starting with the dominant activities, located in the economic system and in military technology, and reaching the objects and habits of everyday life. My use of the terms informational society and informational economy attempts a more precise characterization of current transformations, beyond the commonsense observation that information and knowledge are important to our societies. However, the actual content of "informational society" has to be determined by observation and analysis. This is precisely the object of this book. For instance, one of the key features of informational society is the networking logic of its basic structure, which explains the use of the concept of "network society," as defined and specified in the conclusion of this volume. However, other components of "informational society," such as social movements or the state, exhibit features that go beyond the networking logic, although they are substantially influenced by such logic, as characteristic of the new social structure. Thus, "the network society" does not exhaust all the meaning of the "informational society". Finally, why, after all these precisions, have I kept *The Information Age* as the overall title of the book, without including medieval Europe in my inquiry? Titles are communicating devices. They should be user-friendly, clear enough for the reader to guess what is the real topic of the book, and worded in a fashion that does not

will always have to be attentive to historical/cultural specificity as much as to structural similarities related to a largely shared techno-economic paradigm. As for the actual content of this common social structure that could be considered to be the essence of the new informational society, I'm afraid I am unable to summarize it in one paragraph: indeed, the structure and processes that characterize informational societies are the subject matter covered in this book.

The Self in the Informational Society

New information technologies are integrating the world in global networks of instrumentality. Computer-mediated communication begets a vast array of virtual communities. Yet the distinctive social and political trend of the 1990s is the construction of social action and politics around primary identities, either ascribed, rooted in history and geography, or newly built in an anxious search for meaning and spirituality. The first historical steps of informational societies seem to characterize them by the preeminence of identity as their organizing principle. I understand by identity the process by which a social actor recognizes itself and constructs meaning primarily on the basis of a given cultural attribute or set of attributes, to the exclusion of a broader reference to other social structures. Affirmation of identity does not necessarily mean incapacity to relate to other identities (for example, women still relate to men), or to embrace the whole society under such identity (for example, religious fundamentalism aspires to convert everybody). But social relationships are defined *vis-à-vis* the others on the basis of those cultural attributes that specify identity. For instance, Yoshino, in his study on *nihonjiron* (ideas of Japanese uniqueness), pointedly defines cultural nationalism as "the aim to regenerate the national community by creating, preserving or strengthening a people's cultural identity when it is felt to be lacking, or threatened. The cultural nationalist regards the nation as the product of its unique history and culture and as a collective solidarity endowed with unique attributes."[34] Calhoun, although rejecting the historical newness of the phenomenon, has also emphasized the decisive role

---

depart excessively from the semantic frame of reference. Thus, in a world built around information technologies, information society, informatization, information superhighway, and the like (all terminologies originated in Japan in the mid-1960s – *Johoka Shakai*, in Japanese – and were transmitted to the West in 1978 by Simon Nora and Alain Minc, indulging in exoticism), a title such as *The Information Age* points straightforwardly to the questions to be raised, without prejudging the answers.

[34] Yoshino (1992: 1).

of identity in defining politics in contemporary American society, particularly in the women's movement, in the gay movement, in the civil rights movement, movements "that sought not only various instrumental goals but the affirmation of excluded identities as publicly good and politically salient."[35] Alain Touraine goes further, arguing that "in a post-industrial society, in which cultural services have replaced material goods at the core of production, *it is the defense of the subject, in its personality and in its culture, against the logic of apparatuses and markets, that replaces the idea of class struggle.*"[36] Then the key issue becomes, as stated by Calderon and Laserna, in a world characterized by simultaneous globalization and fragmentation, "how to combine new technologies and collective memory, universal science and communitarian cultures, passion and reason?"[37] How, indeed! And why do we observe the opposite trend throughout the world, namely, the increasing distance between globalization and identity, between the Net and the Self?

Raymond Barglow, in his illuminating essay on this matter, from a socio-psychoanalytical perspective, points at the paradox that while information systems and networking augment human powers of organization and integration, they simultaneously subvert the traditional Western concept of a separate, independent subject: "The historical shift from mechanical to information technologies helps to subvert the notions of sovereignty and self-sufficiency that have provided an ideological anchoring for individual identity since Greek philosophers elaborated the concept more than two millennia ago. In short, technology is helping to dismantle the very vision of the world that in the past it fostered."[38] Then he goes on to present a fascinating comparison between classic dreams reported in Freud's writing and his own patients' dreams in the high tech environment of 1990s' San Francisco: "Image of a head . . . and behind it is suspended a computer keyboard . . . I'm this programmed head!"[39] This feeling of absolute solitude is new in comparison to classic Freudian representation: "the dreamers . . . express a sense of solitude experienced as existential and inescapable, built into the structure of the world . . . Totally isolated, the self seems irretrievably lost to itself."[40] Thus, the search for new connectedness around shared, reconstructed identity.

[35]   Calhoun (1994: 4).
[36]   Touraine (1994: 168; my translation, his italics).
[37]   Calderon and Laserna (1994: 90; my translation).
[38]   Barglow (1994: 6).
[39]   Ibid.: 53.
[40]   Ibid.: 185.

However insightful, this hypothesis may be only part of the explanation. On the one hand, it would imply a crisis of the self limited to a Western individualist conception, shaken by uncontrollable connectedness. Yet the search for new identity and new spirituality is on also in the East, in spite of a stronger sense of collective identity and the traditional, cultural subordination of individual to the family. The resonance of Aum Shinrikyo in Japan in 1995, particularly among the young, highly educated generations, could be considered a symptom of the crisis of established patterns of identity, coupled with the desperate need to build a new, collective self, significantly mixing spirituality, advanced technology (chemicals, biology, laser), global business connections, and the culture of millenarist doom.[41]

On the other hand, elements of an interpretative framework to explain the rising power of identity must also be found at a broader level, in relationship to macroprocesses of institutional change, to a large extent connected to the emergence of a new global system. Thus, widespread currents of racism and xenophobia in Western Europe may be related, as Alain Touraine[42] and Michel Wieviorka[43] have suggested, to an identity crisis on becoming an abstraction (European), at the same time that European societies, while seeing their national identity blurred, discovered within themselves the lasting existence of ethnic minorities in European societies (a demographic fact since at least the 1960s). Or again, in Russia and the ex-Soviet Union, the strong development of nationalism in the postcommunist period can be related, as I shall argue in volume III, to the cultural emptiness created by 70 years of imposition of an exclusionary ideological identity, coupled with the return to primary, historical identity (Russian, Georgian), as the only source of meaning after the crumbling of the historically fragile *sovetskii narod* (Soviet people).

The emergence of religious fundamentalism seems also to be linked both to a global trend and to an institutional crisis. We know from history that ideas and beliefs of all brands are always in stock waiting to catch fire under the right circumstances.[44] It is significant that fundamentalism, be it Islamic or Christian, has spread, and will spread, throughout the world at the historical moment when global networks of wealth and power connect nodal points and valued

---

[41]   For the new forms of revolt linked to identity in explicit opposition to globalization, see the exploratory analysis undertaken in Castells, Yazawa, and Kiselyova, (1996b).

[42]   Touraine (1991).

[43]   Wieviorka (1993).

[44]   See, for instance Kepel (1993); Colas (1992).

individuals throughout the planet, while disconnecting, and excluding, large segments of societies, regions, and even entire countries. Why did Algeria, one of most modernized Muslim societies, suddenly turn to fundamentalist saviors, who became terrorists (as did their anti-colonialist predecessors) when they were denied their electoral victory in democratic elections? Why did the traditionalist teachings of Pope John Paul II find an undisputable echo among the impoverished masses of the Third World, so that the Vatican could afford to ignore the protests of a minority of feminists in a few advanced countries where precisely the progress of reproductive rights contributes to diminishing the number of souls to be saved? There seems to be a logic of excluding the excluders, of redefining the criteria for value and meaning in a world where there is shrinking room for the computer illiterate, for consumptionless groups, and for under-communicated territories. When the Net switches off the Self, the Self, individual or collective, constructs its meaning without global, instrumental reference: the process of disconnection becomes reciprocal, after the refusal by the excluded of the one-sided logic of structural domination and social exclusion.

Such is the terrain to be explored, not just declared. The few ideas advanced here on the paradoxical manifestation of the self in the informational society are only intended to chart the course of my inquiry for the reader's information, not to draw conclusions beforehand.

A Word on Method

This is not a book about books. While relying on evidence of various sorts, and on analyses and accounts from multiple sources, it does not intend to discuss existing theories of postindustrialism or the information society. There are available several thorough, balanced presentations of these theories,[45] as well as various critiques,[46] including my own.[47] Similarly, I shall not contribute, except when

---

[45] A useful overview of sociological theories on postindustrialism and informationalism is Lyon (1988). For the intellectual and terminological origins of notions of "information society," see Ito (1991a) and Nora and Minc (1978). See also Beniger (1986); Katz (1988); Salvaggio (1989); Williams (1988).

[46] For critical perspectives on postindustrialism, see, among others, Lyon (1988); Touraine (1992); Shoji (1990); Woodward (1980); Roszak (1986). For a cultural critique of our society's emphasis on information technology, see Postman (1992).

[47] For my own critique on postindustrialism, see Castells (1994, 1995, 1996).

necessary for the sake of the argument, to the cottage industry created in the 1980s around postmodern theory,[48] being for my part fully satisfied with the excellent criticism elaborated by David Harvey on the social and ideological foundations of "post-modernity,"[49] as well as with the sociological dissection of postmodern theories performed by Scott Lash.[50] I certainly owe many thoughts to many authors, and particularly to the forebears of informationalism, Alain Touraine and Daniel Bell, as well as to the one Marxist theorist who sensed the new, relevant issues just before his death in 1979, Nicos Poulantzas.[51] And I duly acknowledge borrowed concepts when I use them as tools in my specific analyses. Yet I have tried to construct a discourse as autonomous and nonredundant as possible, integrating materials and observations from various sources, without submitting the reader to the painful revisiting of the bibliographic jungle where I have lived (fortunately, among other activities) for the past 12 years.

In a similar vein, while using a significant amount of statistical sources and empirical studies, I have tried to minimize the processing of data, to simplify an already excessively cumbersome book. Therefore, I tend to use data sources that find broad, accepted consensus among social scientists (for example, OECD, United Nations, World Bank, governments' official statistics, authoritative research monographs, generally reliable academic or business sources), except when such sources seem to be erroneous (such as Soviet GNP statistics or the World Bank's report on adjustment policies in Africa). I am aware of limitations in lending credibility to information that may not always be accurate, yet the reader will realize that there are numerous precautions taken in this text, so as to form conclusions usually on the basis of convergent trends from several sources, according to a methodology of triangulation with a well-established, successful tradition among historians, policemen, and investigative reporters. Furthermore, the data, observations, and references presented in this book do not really aim at demonstrating but at suggesting hypotheses while constraining the ideas within a corpus of observation, admittedly selected with my research questions in mind but certainly not organized around preconceived answers. The methodology followed in this book, whose specific implications will be discussed in each chapter, is at the service of the overarching purpose of its intellectual endeavor: to propose some elements of an

[48]   See Lyon (1993); also Seidman and Wagner (1992).
[49]   Harvey (1990).
[50]   Lash (1990).
[51]   Poulantzas (1978: esp. 160–9).

exploratory, cross-cultural theory of economy and society in the information age, *as it specifically refers to the emergence of a new social structure*. The broad scope of my analysis is required by the pervasiveness of the object of such analysis (informationalism) throughout social domains and cultural expressions. But I certainly do not intend to address the whole range of themes and issues in contemporary societies, since writing encyclopedias is not my trade.

The book is divided into three parts that the publisher has wisely transformed into three volumes, to appear within the span of approximately one year. They are analytically interrelated, but they have been organized to make their reading independent. The only exception to this rule concerns the General Conclusion, in volume III, that is the overall conclusion of the book, and presents a synthetic interpretation of its findings and ideas.

The division into three volumes, while making the book publishable and readable, raises some problems in communicating my overall theory. Indeed, some critical topics that cut across all the themes treated in this book are presented in the second volume. Such is the case, particularly, of the analysis of women and patriarchalism, and of power relationships and the state. I warn the reader that I do not share a traditional view of society as made up of superimposed levels, with technology and economy in the basement, power on the mezzanine, and culture in the penthouse. Yet, for the sake of clarity, I am forced to a systematic, somewhat linear presentation of topics that, while relating to each other, cannot fully integrate all the elements until they have been discussed in some depth throughout the intellectual journey on which the reader is invited by this book. The first volume, in the reader's hands, deals primarily with the logic of what I call the Net, while the second (*The Power of Identity*) analyzes the formation of the Self, and the interaction between the Net and the Self in the crisis of two central institutions of society: the patriarchal family and the national state. The third volume (*End of Millennium*) attempts an interpretation of current historical transformations as a result of the dynamics of processes studied in the two first volumes. It is only at the end of the third volume that a general integration between theory and observation, linking up the analyses concerning the various domains, will be proposed, although each volume concludes with an effort at synthesizing the main findings and ideas presented in the volume. While volume III is more directly concerned with specific processes of historical change in various contexts, throughout the whole book I have tried my best to accomplish two goals: to ground analysis in observation, without reducing theorization to commentary; to diversify culturally my sources of observation *and of ideas*, as much as possible. This approach stems from my conviction that we have entered a truly multicultural, interdependent world, that can only be understood, and changed, from a plural perspective that brings together cultural identity, global networking, and multidimensional politics.

— 1 —

The Information Technology
Revolution

Which Revolution?

"Gradualism," wrote paleontologist Stephen J. Gould, "the idea that all change must be smooth, slow, and steady, was never read from the rocks. It represented a common cultural bias, in part a response of nineteenth century liberalism to a world in revolution. But it continues to color our supposedly objective reading of life's history. . . . . The history of life, as I read it, is a series of stable states, punctuated at rare intervals by major events that occur with great rapidity and help to establish the next stable era."[1] My starting point, and I am not alone in this assumption,[2] is that, at the end of the twentieth century, we are living through one of these rare intervals in history. An interval characterized by the transformation of our "material culture"[3] by the works of a new technological paradigm organized around information technologies.

By technology I understand, in straight line with Harvey Brooks and Daniel Bell, "the use of scientific knowledge to specify ways of doing

[1]   Gould (1980: 226).
[2]   Melvin Kranzberg, one of the leading historians of technology, wrote "The Information Age has indeed revolutionized the technical elements of industrial society" (1985: 42). As for its societal effects: "While it might be evolutionary, in the sense that all changes and benefits will not appear overnight, it will be revolutionary in its effects upon our society" (ibid. 52). Along the same lines of argument, see also, for instance, Perez (1983); Forester (1985); Dizard (1982); Nora and Minc (1978); Stourdze (1987); Negroponte (1995); Ministry of Posts and Telecommunications (Japan) (1995); Bishop and Waldholz (1990); Darbon and Robin (1987); Salomon (1992); Dosi et al. (1988b); Petrella (1993).
[3]   On the definition of technology as "material culture" which I consider to be the appropriate sociological perspective, see the discussion in Fischer (1992: 1–32, esp): "Technology here is similar to the idea of material culture.'

things in a *reproducible* manner."[4] Among information technologies, I
include, like everybody else, the *converging set* of technologies in
microelectronics, computing (machines and software), telecommu-
nications/broadcasting, and optoelectronics.[5] In addition, unlike
some analysts, I also include in the realm of information technologies
genetic engineering and its expanding set of developments and applications.[6] This is, first, because genetic engineering is focused on the
decoding, manipulation, and eventual reprogramming of information codes of the living matter. But also because, in the 1990s, biology,
electronics, and informatics seem to be converging and interacting in
their applications, in their materials, and, more fundamentally, in
their conceptual approach, a topic that deserves further mention
below in this chapter.[7] Around this nucleus of information technologies, in the broad sense as defined, a constellation of major
technological breakthroughs has been taking place in the last two
decades of the twentieth century in advanced materials, in energy
sources, in medical applications, in manufacturing techniques
(current or potential, such as nanotechnology), and in transportation
technology, among others.[8] Furthermore, the current process of technological transformation expands exponentially because of its ability
to create an interface between technological fields through common
digital language in which information is generated, stored, retrieved,
processed, and transmitted. We live in a world that, in the expression
of Nicholas Negroponte, has become digital.[9]

The prophetic hype and ideological manipulation characterizing
most discourses on the information technology revolution should not
mislead us into underestimating its truly fundamental significance. It
is, as this book will try to show, at least as major a historical event as
was the eighteenth-century Industrial Revolution, inducing a pattern
of discontinuity in the material basis of economy, society, and culture.
The historical record of technological revolutions, as compiled by
Melvin Kranzberg and Carroll Pursell,[10] shows that they are all

4   Brooks (1971: 13) from unpublished text, quoted with emphasis added by
Bell (1976: 29).
5   Saxby (1990); Mulgan (1991).
6   Marx (1989); Hall (1987).
7   For a stimulating, informed, although deliberately controversial, account of
the convergence between the biological revolution and the broader Information
Technology Revolution, see Kelly (1995).
8   Forester (1988); Herman (1990); Lyon and Gorner (1995); Lincoln and Essin
(1993); Edquist and Jacobsson (1989); Drexler and Peterson (1991); Lovins and
Lovins (1995); Dondero (1995).
9   Negroponte (1995).
10 Kranzberg and Pursell (1967).

characterized by their *pervasiveness*, that is by their penetration of all domains of human activity, not as an exogenous source of impact, but as the fabric in which such activity is woven. In other words, *they are process-oriented*, besides inducing new products. On the other hand, unlike any other revolution, *the core* of the transformation we are experiencing in the current revolution refers to *technologies of information processing and communication*.[11] Information technology is to this revolution what new sources of energy were to the successive Industrial Revolutions, from the steam engine to electricity, to fossil fuels, and even to nuclear power, since the generation and distribution of energy was the key element underlying the industrial society. However, this statement on the preeminent role of information technology is often confused with the characterization of the current revolution as essentially dependent on new knowledge and information. This is true of the current process of technological change, but so it is of preceding technological revolutions, as is shown by leading historians of technology, such as Melvin Kranzberg and Joel Mokyr.[12] The first Industrial Revolution, although not science-based, relied on

[11]   The full understanding of the current technological revolution would require the discussion of the specificity of new information technologies *vis-à-vis* their historical ancestors of equally revolutionary character, such as the discovery of printing in China probably in the late seventh century, and in Europe in the fifteenth century, a classical theme of communications literature. Without being able to address the issue within the limits of this book focused on the sociological dimension of technological change, let me suggest a few topics to the reader's attention. Electronic-based information technologies (including electronic printing) feature incomparable memory storage capacity and speed of combination and transmission of bits. Electronic text allows for substantially greater flexibility of feedbacks, interaction, and reconfiguration of text, as any word-processing writer will acknowledge, thus altering the process of communication itself. On-line communication, combined with flexibility of text, allows for ubiquitous, asynchronous space/time programming. As for the social effects of information technologies, I propose the hypothesis that the depth of their impact is a function of the pervasiveness of information throughout the social structure. Thus, while printing did substantially affect European societies in the Modern Age, as well as Medieval China to a lesser extent, its effects were somewhat limited because of widespread illiteracy in the population and because of the low intensity of information in the productive structure. Thus, the industrial society, by educating citizens and by gradually organizing the economy around knowledge and information, prepared the ground for the empowering of the human mind when new information technologies became available. See, for a historical comment on this earlier information technology revolution, Boureau et al. (1989). For some elements of the debate on technological specificity of electronic communication, including McLuhan's perspective, see chapter 5.

[12]   M. Kranzberg, "Prerequisites for industrialization," in Kranzberg and Pursell (1967: I. ch. 13); Mokyr (1990).

the extensive use of information, applying and developing preexisting knowledge. And the second Industrial Revolution, after 1850, was characterized by the decisive role of science in fostering innovation. Indeed, R&D laboratories appeared for the first time in the German chemical industry in the last decades of the nineteenth century.[13]

What characterizes the current technological revolution is not the centrality of knowledge and information, but the application of such knowledge and information to knowledge generation and information processing/communication devices, in a cumulative feedback loop between innovation and the uses of innovation.[14] An illustration may clarify this analysis. The uses of new telecommunications technologies in the last two decades have gone through three distinct stages: automation of tasks, experimentation of uses, reconfiguration of applications.[15] In the first two stages, technological innovation progressed through learning *by using*, in Rosenberg's terminology.[16] In the third stage, the users learned technology *by doing*, and ended up reconfiguring the networks, and finding new applications. The feedback loop between introducing new technology, using it, and developing it into new realms becomes much faster under the new technological paradigm. As a result, diffusion of technology endlessly amplifies the power of technology, as it becomes appropriated and redefined by its users. New information technologies are not simply tools to be applied, but processes to be developed. Users and doers may become the same. Thus users can take control of technology, as in the case of Internet (see chapter 5). It follows a close relationship between the social processes of creating and manipulating symbols (the culture of society) and the capacity to produce and distribute goods and services (the productive forces). For the first time in history, the human mind is a direct productive force, not just a decisive element of the production system.

Thus, computers, communication systems, and genetic decoding and programming are all amplifiers and extensions of the human mind. What we think, and how we think, become expressed in goods, services, material and intellectual output, be it food, shelter, transportation and communications systems, computers, missiles, health, education, or images. The growing integration between minds and machines, including the DNA machine, is canceling what Bruce Mazlish calls the "fourth discontinuity"[17] (the one between humans

[13]   Ashton (1948); Landes (1969); Mokyr (1990: 112); Clow and Clow (1952).
[14]   Hall and Preston (1988); Saxby (1990); Dizard (1982); Forester (1985).
[15]   Bar (1990).
[16]   Rosenberg (1982); Bar (1992).

and machines), fundamentally altering the way we are born, we live, we learn, we work, we produce, we consume, we dream, we fight, or we die. Of course, cultural/institutional contexts and purposeful social action decisively interact with the new technological system, but this system has its own, embedded logic, characterized by the capacity to translate all inputs into a common information system, and to process such information at increasing speed, with increasing power, at decreasing cost, in a potentially ubiquitous retrieval and distribution network.

There is an additional feature characterizing the information technology revolution in comparison with its historical predecessors. Mokyr[18] has shown that technological revolutions took place only in a few societies, and diffused in a relatively limited geographic area, often living in isolated space and time *vis-à-vis* other regions of the planet. Thus, while Europeans borrowed some of the discoveries that took place in China, for many centuries China and Japan adopted European technology only on a very limited basis, mainly restricted to military applications. The contact between civilizations at different technological levels often took the form of the destruction of the least developed, or of those who had predominantly applied their knowledge to non-military technology, as in the case of American civilizations annihilated by Spanish conquerors, sometimes through accidental biological warfare.[19] The Industrial Revolution did extend to most of the globe from its original West European shores during the next two centuries. But its expansion was highly selective, and its pace rather slow by current standards of technological diffusion. Indeed, even in Britain by the mid-nineteenth century, sectors that accounted for the majority of the labor force, and at least half the gross national product, were not affected by new industrial technologies.[20] Furthermore, its planetary reach in the following decades more often than not took the form of colonial domination, be it in India under the British Empire; in Latin America under commercial/industrial dependency on Britain and the United States; in the dismembering of Africa under the Berlin Treaty; or in the opening to foreign trade of Japan and China by the guns of Western ships. In contrast, new information technologies have spread throughout the globe with lightning speed in less than two decades, between the mid-1970s and the mid-1990s, displaying a logic that I propose as characteristic of this technological revolution: the immediate

[17]   Mazlish (1993).
[18]   Mokyr (1990: 293, 209 ff).
[19]   See, for instance, Thomas (1993).
[20]   Mokyr (1990: 83).

application to its own development of technologies it generates, connecting the world through information technology.[21] To be sure, there are large areas of the world, and considerable segments of the population, switched off from the new technological system: this is precisely one of the central arguments of this book. Furthermore, the speed of technological diffusion is selective, both socially and functionally. Differential timing in access to the power of technology for people, countries, and regions is a critical source of inequality in our society. The switched-off areas are culturally and spatially discontinuous: they are in the American inner cities or in the French *banlieues*, as much as in the shanty towns of Africa or in the deprived rural areas of China or India. Yet dominant functions, social groups, and territories across the globe are connected by the mid-1990s in a new technological system that, as such, started to take shape only in the 1970s.

How did this fundamental transformation happen in what amounts to an historical instant? Why is it diffusing throughout the globe at such an accelerated, if uneven, pace? Why is it a "revolution"? Since our experience of the new is shaped by our recent past, I think the answers to these basic questions could be helped by a brief reminder of the historical record of the Industrial Revolution, still present in our institutions, and therefore in our mind-set.

Lessons from the Industrial Revolution

Historians have shown that there were at least two Industrial Revolutions: the first started in the last third of the eighteenth century, characterized by new technologies such as the steam engine, the spinning jenny, the Cort's process in metallurgy, and, more broadly, by the replacement of hand-tools by machines; the second one, about 100 years later, featured the development of electricity, the internal combustion engine, science-based chemicals, efficient steel casting, and the beginning of communication technologies, with the diffusion of the telegraph and the invention of the telephone. Between the two there are fundamental continuities, as well as some critical differences, the main one being the decisive importance of scientific knowledge in sustaining and guiding technological development after 1850.[22] It is precisely because of their differences that

---

[21]   Pool (1990); Mulgan (1991).
[22]   Singer et al. (1958); Mokyr (1985). However, as Mokyr himself points out, an interface between science and technology was also present in the first Industrial Revolution in Britain. Thus, Watt's decisive improvement of the steam engine

features common to both may offer precious insights in understanding the logic of technological revolutions.

First of all, in both cases, we witness what Mokyr describes as a period of "accelerating and unprecedented technological change"[23] by historical standards. A set of macro-inventions prepared the ground for the blossoming of micro-inventions in the realms of agriculture, industry, and communications. Fundamental historical discontinuity, in an irreversible form, was introduced into the material basis of the human species, in a path-dependent process whose inner, sequential logic has been researched by Paul David and theorized by Brian Arthur.[24] They were indeed "revolutions," in the sense that a sudden, unexpected surge of technological applications transformed the processes of production and distribution, created a flurry of new products, and shifted decisively the location of wealth and power in a planet that became suddenly under the reach of those countries and elites able to master the new technological system. The dark side of this technological adventure is that it was inextricably tied to imperialist ambitions and inter-imperialist conflicts.

Yet this is precisely a confirmation of the revolutionary character of new industrial technologies. The historical ascent of the so-called West, in fact limited to Britain and a handful of nations in Western Europe as well as to their North American, and Australian offspring, is fundamentally linked to the technological superiority achieved during the two Industrial Revolutions.[25] Nothing in the cultural, scientific, political or military history of the world prior to the Industrial Revolution would explain such undisputable "Western" (Anglo-Saxon/German, with a French touch) supremacy between the 1750s and the 1940s. China was a far superior culture for most of pre-Renaissance history; the Muslim civilization (taking the liberty of using such a term) dominated much of the Mediterranean and exerted a significant influence in Africa and Asia throughout the Modern age; Asia and Africa remained by and large organized around autonomous cultural and political centers; Russia ruled in splendid

designed by Newcomen took place in interaction with his friend and protector Joseph Black, professor of chemistry at the University of Glasgow, where Watts was appointed in 1757 as "Mathematical Instrument Maker to the University," and where he conducted his own experiments on a model of the Newcomen engine (see Dickinson 1958). Indeed, Ubbelohde (1958: 673) reports that "Watt's development of a condenser for the steam, separated from the cylinder in which the piston moved, was closely linked up with and inspired by the scientific researches of Joseph Black (1728–99) the professor of chemistry at Glasgow University.'

[23]   Mokyr (1990: 82).
[24]   David (1975); David and Bunn (1988); Arthur (1989).
[25]   Rosenberg and Birdzell (1986).

isolation a vast expanse across East Europe and Asia; and the Spanish Empire, the laggard European culture of the Industrial Revolution, was the major world power for more than two centuries after 1492. Technology, expressing specific social conditions, introduced a new historical path in the second half of the eighteenth century.

This path originated in Britain, although its intellectual roots can be traced back all over Europe and to the Renaissance's spirit of discovery.[26] Indeed, some historians insist that the necessary scientific knowledge underlying the first Industrial Revolution was available 100 years earlier, ready to be used under mature social conditions; or, as others argue, waiting for the technical ingenuity of self-trained inventors, such as Newcomen, Watts, Crompton or Arkwright, able to translate available knowledge, combined with craft experience, into decisive new industrial technologies.[27] However, the second Industrial Revolution, more dependent on new scientific knowledge, shifted its center of gravity towards Germany and the United States, where the main developments in chemicals, electricity, and telephony took place.[28] Historians have painstakingly dissected the social conditions of the shifting geography of technical innovation, often focusing on the characteristics of education and science systems, or on the institutionalization of property rights. However, the contextual explanation for the uneven trajectory of technological innovation seems to be excessively broad and open to alternative interpretations. Hall and Preston, in their analysis of the changing geography of technological innovation between 1846 and 2003, show the importance of *local* seedbeds of innovation, of which Berlin, New York, and Boston are crowned as the "high technology industrial centers of the world" between 1880 and 1914, while "London in that period was a pale shadow of Berlin."[29] The reason lies in the territorial basis for the interaction of systems of technological discovery and applications, namely in the synergistic properties of what is known in the literature as "milieux of innovation."[30]

---

[26]   Singer et al. (1957).
[27]   Rostow (1975); see Jewkes et al. (1969) for the argument, and Singer et al. (1958) for the historical evidence.
[28]   Mokyr (1990).
[29]   Hall and Preston (1988: 123).
[30]   The origin of the concept of "milieu of innovation" can be traced back to Aydalot (1985). It was also implicitly present in the work by Anderson (1985); and in the elaboration by Arthur (1985). Around the same dates Peter Hall and I in Berkeley, Roberto Camagni in Milan, and Denis Maillat in Lausanne, together for a brief period with the late Philippe Aydalot, started to develop empirical analyses of milieux of innovation, a theme that, rightly so, has become a cottage research industry in the 1990s.

Indeed, technological breakthroughs came in clusters, interacting with each other in a process of increasing returns. Whichever conditions determined such clustering, the key lesson to be retained is that *technological innovation is not an isolated instance.*[31] It reflects a given state of knowledge, a particular institutional and industrial environment, a certain availability of skills to define a technical problem and to solve it, an economic mentality to make such application cost-efficient, and a network of producers and users who can communicate their experiences cumulatively, learning by using and by doing: elites learn by doing, thereby modifying the applications of technology, while most people learn by using, thus remaining within the constraints of the packaging of technology. The interactivity of systems of technological innovation and their dependence on certain "milieux" of exchange of ideas, problems, and solutions are critical features that can be generalized from the experience of past revolutions to the current one.[32]

The positive effects of new industrial technologies on economic growth, living standards, and the human mastery of a hostile Nature (reflected in the dramatic lengthening of life expectancy, which did not improve steadily before the eighteenth century) over the long run are undisputable in the historical record. However, they did not come early, in spite of the diffusion of the steam engine and new machinery. Mokyr reminds us that "per capita consumption and living standards increased little initially [at the end of the eighteenth century] but production technologies changed dramatically in many industries and sectors, preparing the way for sustained Schumpeterian growth in the second half of the 19th century when technological progress spread to previously unaffected industries."[33] This is a critical assessment that forces us to evaluate the actual effects of major technological changes in light of a time lag highly dependent on the specific conditions of each society. The historical record seems to indicate however that, in general terms, the closer the relationship between the sites of innovation, production, and use of new technologies, the faster the transformation of societies, and the greater the positive feedback from social conditions on the general conditions for further innovation. Thus, in Spain, the Industrial Revolution diffused rapidly in Catalonia, as early as the late eighteenth century,

---

[31] The specific discussion of the historical conditions for the clustering of technological innovations cannot be undertaken within the limits of this chapter. Useful reflections on the matter can be found in Mokyr (1990); and in Gille (1978). See also Mokyr (1990: 298).

[32] Rosenberg (1976, 1982); Dosi (1988).

[33] Mokyr (1990: 83).

but followed a much slower pace in the rest of Spain, particularly in Madrid and in the South; only the Basque Country and Asturias had joined the process of industrialization by the end of the nineteenth century.[34] The boundaries of industrial innovation were to a large extent coterminous with areas that were prohibited to trade with the Spanish American colonies for about two centuries: while Andalusian and Castilian elites, as well as the Crown, could live from their American rents, Catalans had to provide for themselves through their trade and ingenuity, while being submitted to the pressure of a centralist state. Partly as a result of this historical trajectory, Catalonia and the Basque Country were the only fully industrialized regions until the 1950s and the main seedbeds of entrepreneurialism and innovation, in sharp contrast with trends in the rest of Spain. Thus, specific social conditions foster technological innovation that itself feeds into the path of economic development and further innovation. Yet the reproduction of such conditions is cultural and institutional, as much as economic and technological. The transformation of social and institutional environments may alter the pace and geography of technological development (for example, Japan after the Meiji Restoration, or Russia for a brief period under Stolypin), although past history does bear considerable inertia.

A last and essential lesson from the Industrial Revolutions, that I consider relevant to this analysis, is controversial: although they both brought a whole array of new technologies that actually formed and transformed an industrial system in successive stages, at their core there was fundamental innovation in the generation and distribution of energy. R.J. Forbes, a classic historian of technology, affirms that "the invention of the steam engine is the central fact in the industrial revolution", followed by the introduction of new prime movers and by the mobile prime mover, under which "the power of the steam-engine could be created where needed and to the extent desired."[35] And although Mokyr insists on the multifaceted character of the Industrial Revolution, he also thinks that "the protestations of some economic historians notwithstanding, the steam engine is still widely regarded as the quintessential invention of the Industrial Revolution."[36] Electricity was the central force of the second revolution, in spite of other extraordinary developments in chemicals, steel, the internal combustion engine, telegraphy and telephony. This is because only through electrical generation and distribution were all the other fields able to develop their applications and be connected

[34]   Fontana (1988); Nadal and Carreras (1990).
[35]   Forbes (1958: 150).
[36]   Mokyr (1990: 84).

to each other. A case in point is the electric telegraph which, first used experimentally in the 1790s and widely in existence since 1837, could only grow into a communication network, connecting the world on a large scale, when it could rely on the diffusion of electricity. The widespread use of electricity from the 1870s onwards changed transportation, telegraphy, lighting, and, not least, factory work by diffusing power in the form of the electrical engine. Indeed, while factories have been associated with the first Industrial Revolution, for almost a century they were not concomitant with the use of the steam engine that was widely used in craft shops, while many large factories continued to use improved water-power sources (and thus were known for a long time as mills). It was the electrical engine that both made possible and induced large-scale organization of work in the industrial factory.[37] As R.J. Forbes wrote (in 1958):

> During the last 250 years five great new prime movers have produced what is often called the Machine Age. The eighteenth century brought the steam-engine; the nineteenth century the water-turbine, the internal combustion engine and the steam-turbine; and the twentieth the gas-turbine. Historians have often coined catch-phrases to denote movements or currents in history. Such is "The Industrial Revolution," the title for a development often described as starting in the early eighteenth century and extending through much of the nineteenth. It was a slow movement, but wrought changes so profound in their combination of material progress and social dislocation that collectively they may well be described as revolutionary if we consider these extreme dates.[38]

Thus, by acting on the process at the core of all processes – that is, the necessary power to produce, distribute, and communicate – the two Industrial Revolutions diffused throughout the entire economic system and permeated the whole social fabric. Cheap, accessible, mobile energy sources extended and augmented the power of the

---

[37] Hall and Preston (1988); Canby (1962); Jarvis (1958). One of the first detailed specifications for an electric telegraph is contained in a letter signed C.M. and published in *Scots Magazine* in 1753. One of the first practical experiments with an electrical system was proposed by the Catalan Francisco de Salva in 1795. There are unconfirmed reports that a single-wire telegraph, using Salva's scheme, was actually constructed between Madrid and Aranjuez (26 miles) in 1798. However, it was only in the 1830s (William Cooke in England, Samuel Morse in America) that the electric telegraph was established, and in 1851 the first submarine cable laid out between Dover and Calais (Garratt 1958); see also Mokyr (1990); Sharlin (1967).
[38] Forbes (1958: 148).

human body, creating the material basis for the historical continuation of a similar movement towards the expansion of the human mind.

The Historical Sequence of the Information Technology Revolution

The brief, yet intense history of the Information Technology Revolution has been told so many times in recent years as to render it unnecessary to provide the reader with another full account.[39] Besides, given the acceleration of its pace, any such an account would be instantly obsolete, so that between this writing and your reading (let's say 18 months), microchips will have doubled in performance at a given price, according to the generally acknowledged "Moore's law."[40] Nevertheless, I find it analytically useful to recall the main axes of technological transformation in information generation/processing/transmission, and to place them in the sequence that drifted towards the formation of a new socio-technical paradigm.[41] This brief summary will allow me, later on, to skip references to technological features when discussing their specific interaction with economy, culture, and society throughout the intellectual itinerary of this book, except when new elements of information are required.

[39]   A good history of the origins of the Information Technology Revolution, naturally superseded by developments since the 1980s, is Braun and Macdonald (1982). The most systematic effort at summarizing the developments of the Information Technology Revolution has been conducted by Tom Forester in a series of books (1980, 1985, 1987, 1989, 1993). For good accounts of the origins of genetic engineering, see Russell (1988) and Elkington (1985).

[40]   An accepted "law" in the electronics industry, originated by Gordon Moore, Chairman of Intel, the legendary Silicon Valley start-up company, today the world's largest and one of the most profitable firms in microelectronics.

[41]   The information reported in this chapter is widely available in newspapers and magazines. I extracted much of it from my reading of *Business Week, The Economist, Wired, Scientific American*, the *New York Times, El Pais* and the *San Francisco Chronicle*, which constitute my daily/weekly information staple. It also comes from occasional chats on technology matters with colleagues and friends around Berkeley and Stanford, knowledgeable about electronics and biology and acquainted with industry sources. I do not consider it necessary to provide detailed references to data of such general character, except when a given figure or quote could be hard to find.

Micro-engineering macro changes: electronics and information

Although the scientific and industrial predecessors of electronics-based information technologies can be found decades before the 1940s[42] (not the least being the invention of the telephone by Bell in 1876, of the radio by Marconi in 1898, and of the vacuum tube by De Forest in 1906), it was during the Second World War, and in its aftermath, that major technological breakthroughs in electronics took place: the first programmable computer, and the transistor, source of microelectronics, the true core of the Information Technology Revolution in the twentieth century.[43] Yet I contend that only in the 1970s did new information technologies diffuse widely, accelerating their synergistic development and converging into a new paradigm. Let us retrace the stages of innovation in the three main technological fields that, although closely interrelated, constituted the history of electronics-based technologies: microelectronics, computers, and telecommunications.

The transistor, invented in 1947 at Bell Laboratories in Murray Hill, New Jersey, by three physicists, Bardeen, Brattain, and Shockley (recipients of the Nobel Prize for this discovery), made possible the processing of electric impulses at a fast pace in a binary mode of interruption and amplification, thus enabling the coding of logic and of communication with and between machines: we call these processing devices semiconductors, and people commonly call them chips (actually now made of millions of transistors). The first step in the transistor's diffusion was taken with the invention by Shockley of the junction transistor in 1951. Yet its fabrication and widespread use required new manufacturing technologies and the use of an appropriate material. The shift to silicon, literally building the new revolution on sand, was first accomplished by Texas Instruments (in Dallas) in 1954 (a move facilitated by the hiring in 1953 of Gordon Teal, another leading scientist from Bell Labs). The invention of the planar process in 1959 by Fairchild Semiconductors (in Silicon Valley) opened up the possibility of the integration of miniaturized components with precision manufacturing.

---

[42]   See Hall and Preston (1988); Mazlish (1993).
[43]   I think that, as with the Industrial Revolutions, there will be several Information Technology Revolutions, of which the one constituted in the 1970s is only the first. Probably the second, in the early twenty-first century, will give a more important role to the biological revolution, in close interaction with new computer technologies.

Yet the decisive step in microelectronics had taken place in 1957: the integrated circuit was co-invented by Jack Kilby, a Texas Instrument engineer (who patented it), and Bob Noyce, one of the founders of Fairchild. But it was Noyce who first manufactured ICs by using the planar process. It triggered a technological explosion: in only three years, between 1959 and 1962, prices of semiconductors fell by 85%, and in the next ten years production increased by 20 times, 50% of which went to military uses.[44] As a point of historical comparison, it took 70 years (1780–1850) for the price of cotton cloth to drop by 85% in Britain during the Industrial Revolution.[45] Then, the movement accelerated during the 1960s: as manufacturing technology improved and better chip design was helped by computers using faster and more powerful microelectronic devices, the average price of an integrated circuit fell from $50 in 1962 to $1 in 1971.

The giant leap forward in the diffusion of microelectronics in all machines came in 1971 with the invention by an Intel engineer, Ted Hoff (also in Silicon Valley), of the microprocessor, that is the computer on a chip. Thus, information processing power could be installed everywhere. The race was on for ever-greater integration capacity of circuits on a single chip, the technology of design and manufacturing constantly exceeding the limits of integration previously thought to be physically impossible without abandoning the use of silicon material. In the mid-1990s, technical evaluations still give 10 to 20 years of good life for silicon-based circuits, although research in alternative materials has been stepped up. The level of integration has progressed by leaps and bounds in the last two decades. While technical details have no place in this book, it is analytically relevant to indicate the speed and extent of technological change.

As is known, the power of chips can be evaluated by a combination of three characteristics: their integration capacity, indicated by the smallest line width in the chip measured in microns (1 micron = 1 millionth of an inch); their memory capacity, measured in bits: thousands (k), and millions (megabits); and the speed of the microprocessor measured in megahertz. Thus, the first 1971 processor was laid in lines of about 6.5 microns; in 1980, it reached 4 microns; in 1987, 1 micron; in 1995, Intel's Pentium chip featured a size in the 0.35 micron range; and at the time of writing projections were for reaching 0.25 micron in 1999. Thus, where in 1971 2,300 transistors were packed on a chip the size of a thumbtack, in 1993 there were 35 million transistors. Memory capacity, as indicated by DRAM (dynamic random access memory) capacity was in 1971, 1,024

[44]   Braun and Macdonald (1982).
[45]   Mokyr (1990: 111).

bits; in 1980, 64,000; in 1987, 1,024,000; in 1993, 16,384,000; and projected in 1999, 256,000,000. As for the speed, current 64-bit microprocessors are 550 times faster than the first Intel chip in 1972; and MPUs are doubling every 18 months. Projections to 2002 forecast an acceleration of microelectronics technology in integration (0.18 micron chips), in DRAM capacity (1,024 megabits), and microprocessor speed (500+ megahertz as compared to 150 in 1993). Combined with dramatic developments in parallel processing using multiple microprocessors (including, in the future, linking multiple microprocessors on a single chip), it appears that the power of microelectronics is still being unleashed, thus relentlessly increasing computing capacity. Furthermore, greater miniaturization, further specialization, and the decreasing price of increasingly powerful chips made it possible to place them in every machine in our everyday life, from dishwashers and microwave ovens to automobiles, whose electronics, in the 1990s standard models, was more valuable than their steel.

Computers were also conceived from the mother of all technologies that was the Second World War, but they were only born in 1946 in Philadelphia, if we except the war-related tools of the 1943 British Colossus applied to deciphering enemy codes, and the German Z-3 reportedly produced in 1941 to help aircraft calculations.[46] Yet most Allied effort in electronics was concentrated in research programs at MIT, and the actual experimentation of the calculators' power, under US Army sponsorship, took place at the University of Pennsylvania, where Mauchly and Eckert produced in 1946 the first general purpose computer, the ENIAC (Electronic Numerical Integrator and Calculator). Historians will recall that the first electronic computer weighed 30 tons, was built on metal modules nine feet tall, had 70,000 resistors and 18,000 vacuum tubes, and occupied the area of a gymnasium. When it was turned on, its electricity consumption was so high that Philadelphia's lighting twinkled.[47]

Yet the first commercial version of this primitive machine, UNIVAC-1, produced in 1951 by the same team, then under the Remington Rand brand name, was extremely successful in processing the 1950 US Census. IBM, also supported by military contracts and relying partly on MIT research, overcame its early reservations about the computer age, and entered the race in 1953 with its 701 vacuum tube machine. In 1958, when Sperry Rand introduced a second-generation computer mainframe machine, IBM immediately

[46]   Hall and Preston (1988).
[47]   See the description by Forester (1987).

followed up with its 7090 model. But it was only in 1964 that IBM, with its 360/370 mainframe computer, came to dominate the computer industry, populated by new (Control Data, Digital), and old (Sperry, Honeywell, Burroughs, NCR) business machines companies. Most of these firms were ailing or had vanished by the 1990s: this is how fast Schumpeterian "creative destruction" has proceeded in the electronics industry. In that ancient age, that is 30 years ago from the time of writing, the industry organized itself in a well-defined hierarchy of mainframes, minicomputers (in fact, rather bulky machines), and terminals, with some specialty informatics left to the esoteric world of supercomputers (a cross-fertilization of weather forecasting and war games), in which the extraordinary ingenuity of Seymour Cray, in spite of his lack of technological vision, reigned for some time.

Microelectronics changed all this, inducing a "revolution within the revolution." The advent of the microprocessor in 1971, with the capacity to put a computer on a chip, turned the electronics world, and indeed the world itself, upside down. In 1975, Ed Roberts, an engineer who had created a small calculator company, MITS, in Albuquerque, New Mexico, built a computing box with the improbable name of Altair, after a character in the *Star Trek* TV series, that was the object of admiration of the inventor's young daughter. The machine was a primitive object, but it was built as a small-scale computer around a microprocessor. It was the basis for the design of Apple I, then of Apple II, the first commercially successful microcomputer, realized in the garage of their parents' home by two young school drop-outs, Steve Wozniak and Steve Jobs, in Menlo Park, Silicon Valley, in a truly extraordinary saga that has by now become the founding legend of the Information Age. Launched in 1976, with three partners and $91,000 capital, Apple Computers had by 1982 reached $583 million in sales, ushering in the age of diffusion of computer power. IBM reacted quickly: in 1981 it introduced its own version of the microcomputer, with a brilliant name: the Personal Computer (PC), that became in fact the generic name for microcomputers. But because it was not based on IBM's proprietary technology, but on technology developed for IBM by other sources, it became vulnerable to cloning, which was soon practiced on a massive scale, particularly in Asia. Yet while this fact eventually doomed IBM's business dominance in PCs, it also spread the use of IBM clones throughout the world, diffusing a common standard, in spite of the superiority of Apple machines. Apple's Macintosh, launched in 1984, was the first step towards user-friendly computing, with the introduction of icon-based, user interface technology, originally developed by Xerox's Palo Alto Research Center.

A fundamental condition for the diffusion of microcomputers was fulfilled with the development of new software adapted to their operation.[48] PC software also emerged in the mid-1970s out of the enthusiasm generated by Altair: two young Harvard drop-outs, Bill Gates and Paul Allen, adapted BASIC for operating the Altair machine in 1976. Having realized its potential, they went on to found Microsoft (first in Albuquerque, two years later moving to Seattle, home of Bill Gates' parents), today's software giant, that parlayed dominance in operating system software into dominance in software for the exponentially growing microcomputer market as a whole.

In the last 15 years, increasing chip power has resulted in a dramatic enhancement of microcomputing power, thus shrinking the function of larger computers. By the early 1990s, single-chip microcomputers had the processing power of IBM only five years earlier. Networked microprocessor-based systems, composed of smaller desktop machines (clients), served by more powerful, more dedicated machines (servers), may eventually supplant more specialized information-processing computers, such as traditional mainframes and supercomputers. Indeed, to advances in microelectronics and software we have to add major leaps forward in networking capabilities. Since the mid-1980s, microcomputers cannot be conceived of in isolation: they perform in networks, with increasing mobility, on the basis of portable computers. This extraordinary versatility, and the capacity to add memory and processing capacity by sharing computing power in an electronic network, decisively shifted the computer age in the 1990s from centralized data storage and processing to networked, interactive computer power-sharing. Not only the whole technological system changed, but its social and organizational interactions as well. Thus, the average cost of processing information fell from around $75 per million operations in 1960 to less than one-hundredth of a cent in 1990.

This networking capability only became possible, naturally, because of major developments both in telecommunication and computer networking technologies during the 1970s. But, at the same time, such changes were only made possible by new microelectronic devices and stepped-up computing capacity, in a striking illustration of the synergistic relationships in the Information Technology Revolution.

Telecommunications have been revolutionized also by the combination of "node" technologies (electronic switches and routers) and new linkages (transmission technologies). The first industrially produced electronic switch, the ESS-1, was introduced by Bell Labs in 1969. By the mid-1970s, progress in integrated circuit technologies had made possible the digital switch, increasing speed, power, and

[48]   Egan (1995).

flexibility, while saving space, energy, and labor, *vis-à-vis* analog devices. Although ATT, parent of the discoverer Bell Labs, was initially reluctant about its introduction, because of the need to amortize the investment already made in analog equipment, when in 1977 Canada's Northern Telecom captured a share of the US market through its lead in digital switching, the Bell companies joined the race and triggered a similar movement around the world.

Major advances in optoelectronics (fiber optics and laser transmission) and digital packet transmission technology dramatically broadened the capacity of transmission lines. The Integrated Broadband Networks (IBN) envisioned in the 1990s could surpass substantially the revolutionary 1970s proposals for an Integrated Services Digital Network (ISDN): while the carrying capacity of ISDN on copper wire was estimated at 144,000 bits, the 1990s IBN on optic fibers, if and when they can be realized, though at a high price, could carry a quadrillion bits. To measure the pace of change, let us recall that in 1956 the first transatlantic cable phone carried 50 compressed voice circuits; in 1995, optical fibers could carry 85,000 such circuits. This optoelectronics-based transmission capacity, together with advanced switching and routing architectures, such as the Asynchronous Transmission Mode (ATM) and Transmission Control Protocol/Interconnection Protocol (TCP/IP), are the basis of the so-called 1990s Information Superhighway, whose characteristics are discussed in chapter 5.

Different forms of utilization of the radio spectrum (traditional broadcasting, direct satellite broadcasting, microwaves, digital cellular telephony), as well as coaxial cable and fiber optics, offer a diversity and versatility of transmission technologies, that are being adapted to a whole range of uses, and make possible ubiquitous communication between mobile users. Thus, cellular telephony diffused with force all over the world in the 1990s, literally dotting Asia with unsophisticated pagers and Latin America with status-symbol cellular phones, relying on the promise (from Motorola for example) of an upcoming universal-coverage, personal communication device before 2000. Each leap and bound in a specific technological field amplifies the effects of related information technologies. Thus, mobile telephony, relying on computing power to route the messages, provides at the same time the basis for ubiquitous computing and for real-time, untethered, interactive electronic communication.

The 1970s technological divide

This technological system in which we are fully immersed in the 1990s came together in the 1970s. Because of the significance of specific historical contexts for technological trajectories, and for the particular form of interaction between technology and society, it is important to recall a few dates associated with essential discoveries in information technologies. All of them have something essential in common: while mainly based on previously existing knowledge, and developed in prolongation of key technologies, they represented a qualitative leap forward in the massive diffusion of technology in commercial and civilian applications because of their accessibility and their decreasing cost with increasing quality. Thus, the microprocessor, the key device in spreading microelectronics, was invented in 1971 and began to diffuse by the mid-1970s. The microcomputer was invented in 1975 and the first successful commercial product, Apple II, was introduced in April 1977, around the same date that Microsoft started to produce operating systems for microcomputers. The Xerox Alto, the matrix of many software technologies for 1990s personal computers, was developed at PARC labs in Palo Alto in 1973. The first industrial electronic switch appeared in 1969, and digital switching was developed in the mid-1970s and commercially diffused in 1977. Optic fiber was first industrially produced by Corning Glass in the early 1970s. Also by the mid-1970s, Sony started to produce VCR machines commercially, on the basis of 1960s discoveries in America and England that never reached mass production. And last, but not least, it was in 1969 that the US Defense Department's Advanced Research Projects Agency (ARPA) set up a new, revolutionary electronic communication network, that would grow during the 1970s to become the current Internet. It was greatly helped by the invention by Cerf and Kahn in 1974 of TCP/IP, the interconnection network protocol that ushered in "gateway" technology, allowing different types of networks to be connected.[49] I think we can say, without exaggeration, that the Information Technology Revolution, as a revolution, was born in the 1970s, particularly if we include in it the parallel emergence and diffusion of genetic engineering around the same dates and places, a development that deserves, to say the least, a few lines of attention.

Technologies of life

Although biotechnology can be traced all the way back to a 6000BC Babylonian tablet on brewing, and the revolution in microbiology to the scientific discovery of the basic structure of life, DNA's double helix, by Francis Crick and James Watson at Cambridge University in

---

[49]   Hart et al. (1992).

1953, it was only in the early 1970s that gene splicing and recombinant DNA, the technological foundation of genetic engineering, made possible the application of cumulative knowledge. Stanford's Stanley Cohen and University of California at San Francisco's Herbert Boyer are generally credited with the discovery of gene cloning procedures in 1973, although their work was based on research by Stanford's Nobel Prize winner Paul Berg. In 1975 researchers at Harvard isolated the first mammalian gene, out of rabbit hemoglobin; and in 1977 the first human gene was cloned.

What followed was a rush to start up commercial firms, most of them spin-offs from major universities and hospital research centers, clusters of such firms emerging in Northern California, New England, and Maryland. Journalists, investors, and social activists alike were struck by the awesome possibilities opened up by the potential ability to engineer life, including human life. Genentech in South San Francisco, Cetus in Berkeley, and Biogen in Cambridge, Massachusetts, were among the first companies, organized around Nobel Prize winners, to use new genetic technologies for medical applications. Agro-business followed soon; and micro-organisms, some of them genetically altered, were given an increasing number of assignments, not least to clean up pollution, often generated by the same companies and agencies that were selling the superbugs. Yet scientific difficulties, technical problems, and major legal obstacles derived from justified ethical and safety concerns slowed down the much-vaunted biotechnological revolution during the 1980s. A considerable amount of venture capital investment was lost and some of the most innovative companies, including Genentech, were absorbed by pharmaceutical giants (Hoffman-La Roche, Merck) who, better than anybody else, understood that they could not replicate the costly arrogance that established computer firms had displayed towards innovative start-ups: to buy small, innovative firms, along with their scientists' services, became a major insurance policy for pharmaceutical and chemical multinationals, to both internalize the commercial benefits of the biological revolution and to control its pace. A slowing down of this pace followed, at least in the diffusion of its applications.

However, in the late 1980s and in the 1990s a major science push, and a new generation of daring scientist entrepreneurs, revitalized biotechnology, with a decisive focus on genetic engineering, the truly revolutionary technology in the field. Genetic cloning entered a new stage when, in 1988, Harvard formally patented a genetically engineered mouse, thus taking the copyright of life away from God and Nature. In the next seven years, an additional seven mice were also patented as newly created forms of life, identified as the property of their engineers. In August 1989 researchers from the University of Michigan and Toronto discovered the gene responsible for cystic fibrosis, opening the way for genetic therapy.

In the wake of expectations generated by this discovery, the US Government decided in 1990 to sponsor and fund a $3 billion, 15-year collaborative program, coordinated by James Watson, bringing together some of the most advanced microbiology research teams to map the human genome, that is to identify and locate the 60,000 to 80,000 genes that compose the alphabet of the human species.[50] Through this and other efforts, a continuous stream of human genes related to various diseases are being identified, so that by the mid-1990s about 7% of human genes have been located, with a proper understanding of their function. This of course creates the possibility of acting on such genes, and on those identified in the future, making humankind able not only to control some diseases, but to identify biological predispositions and to intervene in such predispositions, potentially altering genetic fate. Lyon and Gorner conclude their balanced survey of developments in human genetic engineering, with a prediction and an admonition:

> We could in a few generations do away with certain mental illnesses, perhaps, or diabetes, or high blood pressure, or almost any affliction we selected. The important thing to keep in mind is that the quality of decision making dictates whether the choices to be made are going to be wise and just . . .The rather inglorious way that the scientific and administrative elite are handling the earliest fruits of gene therapy is ominous . . . We humans have evolved intellectually to the point that, relatively soon, we will be able to understand the composition, function, and dynamics of the genome in much of its intimidating complexity. Emotionally however, we are still apes, with all the behavioral baggage that the issue brings. Perhaps the ultimate form of gene therapy would be for our species to rise above its baser heritage and learn to apply its new knowledge wisely and benignly.[51]

Yet, while scientists, regulators, and ethicists debate the humanistic implications of genetic engineering, researchers-turned-business-entrepreneurs are taking the short path, setting up mechanisms for

---

[50]   On the development of biotechnology and genetic engineering, see, for instance, Teitelman (1989); Hall (1987); US Congress, Office of Technology Assessment (1991); Bishop and Waldholz (1990).
[51]   Lyon and Gorner (1995: 567).

legal and financial control of the human genome. The most daring attempt in this sense was the project initiated in 1990 in Rockville, Maryland, by two scientists, J. Craig Venter, then with the National Institute of Health, and William Haseltine, then at Harvard. Using supercomputer power, they sequenced in only five years parts of about 85% of all human genes, creating a gigantic genetic data base.[52] The problem is that they do not know, and will not know for a long time, which gene's piece is what or where it is located: their data base comprises hundreds of thousands of gene fragments with unknown functions. What is then the interest? On the one hand, focused research on specific genes may (and does in fact) use to its advantage the data contained in such sequences. But, more importantly and the main reason for the whole project, Craig and Haseltine have been busy patenting all their data, so that, literally, they may own one day the legal rights to a large portion of the knowledge to manipulate the human genome. The threat posed by such a development was serious enough that, while on the one hand they have attracted tens of millions of dollars from investors, on the other hand, a major pharmaceutical company, Merck, gave in 1994 substantial funding to Washington University to proceed with the same blind sequencing and to make the data public, so that there would be no private control of bits and pieces of knowledge which could block development of products based on a future, systematic understanding of the human genome.

The lesson for the sociologist of such business battles is not just another instance of human greed. It signals an accelerating tempo in the spread and deepening of the genetic revolution. Because of its specificity, both scientific and social, the diffusion of genetic engineering proceeded at a slower pace of development in the 1970s–1990s period than the one we observed in electronics. But in the 1990s, more open markets and greater education and research capabilities throughout the world have accelerated the biotechnological revolution. All indications point towards the explosion of its applications at the turn of the millennium, thus triggering a most fundamental debate at the now blurred frontier between nature and society.

Social context and the dynamics of technological change

Why were discoveries of new information technologies clustered in the 1970s, and mostly in the United States? And what are the conse-

[52] See *Business Week* (1995e).

quences of such timed/placed clustering for their future development and for their interaction with societies? It would be tempting to
relate directly the formation of this technological paradigm to the
characteristics of its social context; particularly if we remember that
in the mid-1970s the United States and the capitalist world were
shaken by a major economic crisis, epitomized (but not caused) by
the oil shock of 1973–4: a crisis that prompted the dramatic restructuring of the capitalist system on a global scale, actually inducing a
new model of accumulation in historical discontinuity with post-
Second World War capitalism, as I proposed in the Prologue of this
book. Was the new technological paradigm a response by the capitalist
system to overcome its internal contradictions? Or, alternatively, was
it a way to ensure military superiority over the Soviet foe, responding
to its technological challenge in the space race and nuclear weaponry?
Neither explanation seems to be convincing. While there is a historical coincidence between the clustering of new technologies and the
economic crisis of the 1970s, their timing was too close, the "technological fix" would have been too quick, and too mechanical, when we
know from the lessons of the Industrial Revolution and other
historical processes of technological change that economic, industrial, and technological paths, while related, are slow-moving and
imperfectly fitting in their interaction. As for the military argument,
the Sputnik shock of 1957–60 was answered in kind by the massive
technological build up of the 1960s, not the 1970s; and the new major
American military technology push was launched in 1983 around the
"Star Wars" program, actually using and furthering technologies
developed in the preceding, prodigious decade. In fact, it seems that
the emergence of a new technological system in the 1970s must be
traced to the autonomous dynamics of technological discovery and
diffusion, including synergistic effects between various key technologies. Thus, the microprocessor made possible the microcomputer;
advances in telecommunications, as mentioned above, enabled
microcomputers to function in networks, thus increasing their power
and flexibility. Applications of these technologies to electronics
manufacturing enhanced the potential for new design and fabrication technologies in semiconductor production. New software was
stimulated by the fast-growing microcomputer market that, in turn,
exploded on the basis of new applications and user-friendly technologies churned out from software writers' minds. And so on.

The strong, military-induced technological push of the 1960s
prepared American technology for the leap forward. But Ted Hoff's
invention of the microprocessor while trying to fulfill an order for a
Japanese hand calculator company in 1971 came out of knowledge
and ingenuity accumulated at Intel, in close interaction with the

milieu of innovation created since the 1950s in Silicon Valley. In other words, the first Information Technology Revolution clustered in America, and to some extent in California, in the 1970s, building on developments of the two preceding decades, and under the influence of various institutional, economic, and cultural factors. But it did not come out of any preestablished necessity: it was technologically induced rather than socially determined. However, once it came into existence as a system, on the basis of the clustering I have described, its development and applications, and ultimately its content, were decisively shaped by the historical context where it expanded. Indeed, by the 1980s capitalism (specifically: major corporations and governments of the club of G-7 countries) did undertake a substantial process of economic and organizational restructuring, in which new information technology played a fundamental role and was decisively shaped by the role it played. For instance, the business-led movement towards deregulation and liberalization in the 1980s was decisive in the reorganization and growth of telecommunications, most notably after the 1984 divestiture of ATT. In turn, the availability of new telecommunication networks and information systems prepared the ground for the global integration of financial markets and the segmented articulation of production and trade throughout the world, as I shall examine in the next chapter.

Thus, to some extent, the availability of new technologies constituted as a system in the 1970s was a fundamental basis for the process of socio-economic restructuring in the 1980s. And the uses of such technologies in the 1980s largely conditioned their uses and trajectories in the 1990s. The rise of the network society, which I shall attempt to analyze in the following chapters of this volume, cannot be understood without the interaction between these two relatively autonomous trends: development of new information technologies, and the old society's attempt to retool itself by using the power of technology to serve the technology of power. However, the historical outcome of such a half-conscious strategy is largely undetermined, since the interaction of technology and society depends on stochastic relationships between an excessive number of quasi-independent variables. Without necessarily surrendering to historical relativism, it can be said that the Information Technology Revolution was culturally, historically, and spatially contingent on a very specific set of circumstances whose characteristics earmarked its future evolution.

Models, Actors, and Sites of the Information Technology Revolution

If the first Industrial Revolution was British, the first Information Technology Revolution was American, with a Californian inclination. In both cases scientists and industrialists from other countries did play an important role, both in the discovery and in the diffusion of new technologies. France and Germany were key sources of talent and applications in the Industrial Revolution. Scientific discoveries originated in England, France, Germany, and Italy were at the roots of new technologies in electronics and biology. The ingenuity of Japanese companies has been critical in the improvement of manufacturing processes in electronics and in the penetration of information technologies into everyday life around the world through a flurry of innovative products, from VCRs and faxes to video games and pagers.[53] Indeed, in the 1980s Japanese companies came to dominate semiconductor production in the world market, although by the mid-1990s American companies by and large had retaken the competitive lead. The whole industry evolved towards interpenetration, strategic alliances, and networking between firms of different countries, as I shall analyze in chapter 3. This made differentiation by national origin somewhat less relevant. Yet not only were US innovators, firms, and institutions at the origins of the revolution in the 1970s, but they have continued to play a leading role in its expansion, which is likely to be sustained into the twenty-first century; although we shall undoubtedly witness an increasing presence of Japanese, Chinese, Korean, and Indian firms, as well as significant European contributions in biotechnology and telecommunications.

To understand the social roots of the Information Technology Revolution in America, beyond the myths surrounding it, I shall recall briefly the process of formation of its most notorious seedbed of innovation: Silicon Valley. As I already mentioned, it was in Silicon Valley that the integrated circuit, the microprocessor, the microcomputer, among other key technologies, were developed, and that the heart of electronics innovation has beat for four decades, sustained by about a quarter of a million information technology workers.[54] Besides, the San Francisco Bay Area at large (including other centers of innovation such as Berkeley, Emeryville, Marin County, and San Francisco itself) was also at the origins of genetic engineering and is, in the

[53]   Forester (1993).
[54]   On the history of formation of Silicon Valley, two useful, easy-reading books are Rogers and Larsen (1984) and Malone (1985).

1990s, one of the world's leading centers of advanced software, genetic engineering, and multimedia computing design.

Silicon Valley (Santa Clara County, 30 miles south of San Francisco, between Stanford and San Jose) was formed as a milieu of innovation by the convergence on one site of new technological knowledge; a large pool of skilled engineers and scientists from major universities in the area; generous funding from an assured market with the Defense Department; and, in the early stages, the institutional leadership of Stanford University. Indeed, the unlikely location of the electronics industry in a charming, semi-rural area of Northern California can be traced back to the establishment in 1951 of Stanford Industrial Park by Stanford University's visionary Dean of Engineering and Provost, Frederick Terman. He had personally supported two of his graduate students, William Hewlett and David Packard, in creating an electronics company in 1938. The Second World War was a bonanza for Hewlett-Packard and other start-up electronics companies. Thus, naturally, they were the first tenants of a new, privileged location where only firms that Stanford judged innovative could benefit from a notional rent. As the Park was soon filled, new electronics firms started to locate down freeway 101 towards San Jose.

The decisive move was the hiring by Stanford in 1956 of William Shockley, the inventor of the transistor. And this was a fortuitous development, although it reflects on the historical inability of established electronics firms to seize revolutionary microelectronics technology. Shockley had solicited the support of large companies on the East Coast, such as RCA and Raytheon, to develop his discovery into industrial production. When he was turned down he accepted Stanford's offer, mainly because his mother lived in Palo Alto, and he decided to create there his own company, Shockley Transistors, with the backing of Beckman Instruments. He recruited eight brilliant young engineers, mainly from Bell Labs, attracted by the possibility of working with Shockley; one of them, although not precisely from Bell Labs, was Bob Noyce. They were soon disappointed. While learning the fundamentals of cutting-edge microelectronics from Shockley, they were turned off by his authoritarianism and stubbornness that led the firm into dead-ends. Particularly they wanted, against his decision, to work on silicon as the most promising route to the larger integration of transistors. Thus, after only one year they left Shockley (whose firm collapsed), and created (with the help of Fairchild Cameras) Fairchild Semiconductors, where the invention of the planar process and of the integrated circuit took place in the next two years. As soon as they discovered the technological and business potential of their knowledge, each one of these brilliant engineers left

Fairchild to start his own firm. And their new recruits did the same after some time, so that one-half of the 85 largest American semiconductors firms, including today's leading producers such as Intel, Advanced Micro Devices, National Semiconductors, Signetics, and so on, can be traced back to this spin-off from Fairchild.

It was this technology transfer from Shockley to Fairchild, then to a network of spin-off companies, that constituted the initial source of innovation on which Silicon Valley, and the microelectronics revolution, were built. Indeed, by the mid-1950s Stanford and Berkeley were not yet leading centers in electronics: MIT was, and this was reflected in the original location of the electronics industry in New England. However, as soon as knowledge was available in Silicon Valley, the dynamism of its industrial structure and the continuous creation of start-up firms anchored Silicon Valley as the world's microelectronics center by the early 1970s. Anna Saxenian compared the development of electronics complexes in the two areas (Boston's Route 128 and Silicon Valley) and concluded that the decisive role was played by the social and industrial organization of companies in fostering or stymying innovation.[55] Thus, while large, established companies in the East were too rigid (and too arrogant) to constantly retool themselves towards new technological frontiers, Silicon Valley kept churning out new firms, and practicing cross-fertilization and knowledge diffusion by job-hopping and spin-offs. Late-evening conversations at the Walker's Wagon Wheel Bar and Grill in Mountain View did more for the diffusion of technological innovation than most seminars in Stanford.

A similar process took place in the development of the microcomputer, which introduced a historical divide in the uses of information technology.[56] By the mid-1970s Silicon Valley had attracted tens of thousands of bright young minds from around the world, coming to the excitement of the new technological Mecca in a search for the talisman of invention and money. They gathered in loose clubs, to exchange ideas and information on the latest developments. One of such gatherings was the Home Brew Computer Club, whose young visionaries (including Bill Gates, Steve Jobs, and Steve Wozniak) would go on to create in the following years up to 22 companies, including Microsoft, Apple, Comenco, and North Star. It was the club's reading, in *Popular Electronics*, of an article reporting Ed Roberts' Altair machine which inspired Wozniak to design a microcomputer, Apple I, in his Menlo Park garage in the summer of 1976. Steve Jobs saw the potential, and together they founded Apple, with

---

[55]   Saxenian (1994).
[56]   Levy (1984); Egan (1995).

a $91,000 loan from an Intel executive, Mike Markkula, who came in as a partner. At about the same time Bill Gates founded Microsoft to provide the operating system for microcomputers, although he located his company in 1978 in Seattle to take advantage of the social contacts of his family.

A rather similar story could be told about the development of genetic engineering, with leading scientists at Stanford, UC San Francisco and Berkeley bridging into companies, first located in the Bay Area. They would also go through frequent processes of spin-off while keeping close ties with their alma maters.[57] Very similar processes took place in Boston/Cambridge around Harvard–MIT, in the Research Triangle around Duke University and the University of North Carolina, and, more importantly, in Maryland around major hospitals, national health research institutes, and Johns Hopkins University.

The fundamental learning from these colorful stories is two-fold: the development of the information technology revolution contributed to the formation of the milieux of innovation where discoveries and applications would interact, and be tested, in a recurrent process of trial and error, of learning by doing; these milieus required (and still do in the 1990s, in spite of on-line networking) spatial concentration of research centers, higher education institutions, advanced technology companies, a network of ancillary suppliers of goods and services, and business networks of venture capital to finance start-ups. Once a milieu is consolidated, as Silicon Valley was in the 1970s, it tends to generate its own dynamics, and to attract knowledge, investment and talent from around the world. Indeed, in the 1990s Silicon Valley is witnessing a proliferation of Japanese, Taiwanese, Korean, Indian, and European companies for whom an active presence in the Valley is the most productive linkage to the sources of new technology and valuable business information. Furthermore, because of its positioning in the networks of technological innovation, the San Francisco Bay Area has been able to jump on any new development. For instance, the coming of multimedia in the mid-1990s created a network of technological and business linkages between computer design capabilities from Silicon Valley companies and image-producing studios in Hollywood, immediately labeled the "Siliwood" industry. And in a run-down corner of San Francisco, artists, graphic designers, and software writers came together in the so-called "Multimedia Gulch" that threatens to flood our living rooms with images coming from their fevered minds.

[57]   Blakely et al. (1988); Hall et al. (1988).

Can this social, cultural, and spatial pattern of innovation be extrapolated throughout the world? To answer this question, in 1988 my colleague Peter Hall and I undertook a several years' tour of the world that brought us to visit and analyze some of the main scientific/technological centers of this planet, from California to Japan, New England to Old England, Paris-Sud to Hsinchu-Taiwan, Sophia-Antipolis to Akademgorodok, Szelenograd to Daeduck, Munich to Seoul. Our conclusions[58] confirm the critical role played by milieus of innovation in the development of the Information Technology Revolution: clusters of scientific/technical knowledge, institutions, firms, and skilled labor are the furnaces of innovation in the Information Age. Yet they do not need to reproduce the cultural, spatial, institutional and industrial pattern of Silicon Valley, or for that matter, of other American centers of technological innovation, such as Southern California, Boston, Seattle, or Austin.

Our most striking discovery is that the largest, old metropolitan areas of the industrialized world are the main centers of innovation and production in information technology outside the United States. In Europe, Paris-Sud constitutes the largest concentration of high-technology production and research; and London's M4 corridor is still Britain's preeminent electronics site, in historical continuity with ordnance factories working for the Crown since the nineteenth century. The displacement of Berlin by Munich was obviously related to the German defeat in the Second World War, with Siemens deliberately moving from Berlin to Bavaria in anticipation of American occupation of that area. Tokyo-Yokohama continues to be the technological core of the Japanese information technology industry, in spite of the decentralization of branch plants operated under the Technopolis Program. Moscow-Szelenograd and St Petersburg were and are the centers of Soviet and Russian technological knowledge and production, after the failure of Khrushchev's Siberian dream. Hsinchu is in fact a satellite of Taipei; Daeduck never played a significant role *vis-à-vis* Seoul-Inchon, in spite of being in the home province of dictator Park; and Beijing and Shanghai are, and will be, the core of Chinese technological development. And so are Mexico City in Mexico, Sao Paulo-Campinas in Brazil, and Buenos Aires in Argentina. In this sense, the technological fading of old American metropolises (New York-New Jersey, in spite of its prominent role up to the 1960s; Chicago; Detroit; Philadelphia) is the exception at the international level, linked to American exceptionalism of frontier spirit, and to its endless escapism from the contradictions of built

---

[58]   Castells and Hall (1994).

cities and constituted societies. On the other hand, it would be intriguing to explore the relationship between this American exceptionalism and the indisputable American preeminence in a technological revolution characterized by the need to break mental molds to spur creativity.

Yet the metropolitan character of most sites of the Information Technology Revolution around the world seems to indicate that the critical ingredient in its development is not the newness of the institutional and cultural setting, but its ability to generate synergy on the basis of knowledge and information, directly related to industrial production and commercial applications. The cultural and business strength of the metropolis (old or new – after all, the San Francisco Bay Area is a metropolis of about 6 million people) makes it the privileged environment of this new technological revolution, actually demystifying the notion of placelessness of innovation in the information age.

Similarly, the entrepreneurial model of the Information Technology Revolution seems to be overshadowed by ideology. Not only are the Japanese, European, and Chinese models of technological innovation quite different from the American experience, but even this leading experience is often misunderstood. The role of the state is generally acknowledged as decisive in Japan, where large corporations were guided and supported by MITI for a long time, well into the 1980s, through a series of bold technological programs, some of which failed (for example, the Fifth Generation Computer), but most of which helped to transform Japan into a technological superpower in just about 20 years, as Michael Borrus has documented.[59] No start-up innovative firms and little role for universities can be found in the Japanese experience. Strategic planning by MITI and the constant interface between the *keiretsu* and government are key elements in explaining the Japanese prowess that overwhelmed Europe and overtook the US in several segments of information technology industries. A similar story can be told about South Korea and Taiwan, although in the latter case multinationals played a greater role. India's and China's strong technological bases are directly related to their military–industrial complex, under state funding and guidance.

But so was also the case for much of the British and French electronics industries, centered on telecommunications and defense, until the 1980s.[60] In the last quarter of the twentieth century, the

[59]   Borrus (1988).
[60]   Hall et al. (1987).

European Union has proceeded with a series of technological programs to keep up with international competition, systematically supporting "national champions", even at a loss, without much result. Indeed, the only way for European information technology companies to survive technologically has been to use their considerable resources (a substantial share of which comes from government funds) to make alliances with Japanese and American companies, which are increasingly their main source of know-how in advanced information technology.[61]

Even in the US it is a well-known fact that military contracts and Defense Department technological initiatives played decisive roles in the formative stage of the Information Technology Revolution, that is, between the 1940s and the 1960s. Even the major source of electronics discovery, Bell Laboratories, in fact played the role of a national laboratory: its parent company (ATT) enjoyed a government-enforced monopoly of telecommunications; a significant part of its research funds came from the US Government; and ATT was in fact forced by the Government from 1956, in return for its monopoly on public telecommunications, to diffuse technological discoveries in the public domain.[62] MIT, Harvard, Stanford, Berkeley, UCLA, Chicago, Johns Hopkins, and national weapons laboratories such as Livermore, Los Alamos, Sandia, and Lincoln, worked with and for Defense Department agencies on programs that led to fundamental breakthroughs, from the 1940s computers to optoelectronics and artificial intelligence technologies of the 1980s "Star Wars" programs. DARPA, the extraordinarily innovative Defense Department Research Agency, played in the US a role not too different from that of MITI in Japan's technological development, including the design and initial funding of the Internet.[63] Indeed, in the 1980s, when the ultra-*laissez-faire* Reagan Administration felt the pinch of Japanese competition, the Defense Department funded SEMATECH, a consortium of American electronics companies to support costly R&D programs in electronics manufacturing, for reasons of national security. And the federal government also helped the cooperative effort by major firms to cooperate in microelectronics by creating MCC, with both SEMATECH and MCC locating in Austin, Texas.[64] Also, during the decisive 1950s and 1960s, military contracts and the space program were essential markets for the electronics industry, both for the giant defense contractors of Southern California and for the

---

[61] Freeman et al. (1991); Castells et al. (1991).
[62] Bar (1990).
[63] Tirman (1984); Broad (1985); Stowsky (1992).
[64] Borrus (1988); Gibson and Rogers (1994).

start-up innovators of Silicon Valley and New England.[65] They could not have survived without the generous funding and protected markets of a US Government anxious to recover technological superiority over the Soviet Union, a strategy that eventually paid off. Genetic engineering spun off from major research universities, hospitals, and health research institutes, largely funded and sponsored by government money.[66] Thus, the state, not the innovative entrepreneur in his garage, both in America and throughout the world, was the initiator of the Information Technology Revolution.[67]

However, without these innovative entrepreneurs, such as those at the origin of Silicon Valley or of Taiwan's PC clones, the Information Technology Revolution would have had very different characteristics, and it is unlikely that it would have evolved toward the kind of decentralized, flexible technological devices that are diffusing through all realms of human activity. Indeed, since the early 1970s, technological innovation has been essentially market driven:[68] and innovators, while still often employed by major companies, particularly in Japan and Europe, continue to establish their own businesses in America and, increasingly, around the world. This gives rise to an acceleration of technological innovation and a faster diffusion of such innovation, as ingenious minds, driven by passion and greed, constantly scan the industry for market niches in products and processes. **It is indeed by this interface between macro-research programs and large markets developed by the state, on the one hand, and decentralized innovation stimulated by a culture of technological creativity and role models of fast personal success, on the other hand, that new information technologies came to blossom.** In so doing, they clustered around networks of firms, organizations, and institutions to form a new socio-technical paradigm.

The Information Technology Paradigm

As Christopher Freeman writes:

A techno-economic paradigm is a cluster of interrelated technical, organizational, and managerial innovations whose advantages are to be found not only in a new range of products and systems, but most of all in the dynamics of the relative cost

[65]   Roberts (1991).
[66]   Kenney (1986).
[67]   See the analyses gathered in Castells (1988b).
[68]   Banegas (1993).

structure of all possible inputs to production. *In each new para-digm a particular input or set of inputs may be described as the "key factor" in that paradigm characterized by falling relative costs and universal availability.* The contemporary change of paradigm may be seen as a shift from a technology based primarily on cheap inputs of energy to one *predominantly based on cheap inputs of information derived from advances in microelectronic and tele-communications technology.*[69]

The notion of the technological paradigm, elaborated by Carlota Perez, Christopher Freeman, and Giovanni Dosi, adapting the classic analysis of scientific revolutions by Kuhn, helps to organize the essence of current technological transformation as it interacts with economy and society.[70] Rather than refining the definition to include social processes beyond the economy, I think it would be useful, as a guide to our upcoming journey along the paths of social transforma-tion, to pinpoint those features that constitute the heart of the information technology paradigm. Taken together, they are the material foundation of the informational society.

The first characteristic of the new paradigm is that information is its raw material: *these are technologies to act on information,* not just infor-mation to act on technology, as was the case in previous technological revolutions.

The second feature refers to the *pervasiveness of effects of new tech-nologies.* Because information is an integral part of all human activity, all processes of our individual and collective existence are directly shaped (although certainly not determined) by the new technolog-ical medium.

The third characteristic refers to the *networking logic* of any system or set of relationships using these new information technologies. The morphology of the network seems to be well adapted to increasing complexity of interaction and to unpredictable patterns of develop-ment arising from the creative power of such interaction.[71] This

---

[69] C. Freeman, "Preface to Part II," in Dosi et al. (1988b: 10).

[70] Perez (1983); Dosi et al. (1988b); Kuhn (1962).

[71] Kelly (1995: 25–7) elaborates on the properties of networking logic in a few telling paragraphs:

> The Atom is the past. The symbol of science for the next century is the dynamical Net . . . Whereas the Atom represents clean simplicity, the Net channels the messy power of complexity . . . The only organization capable of nonprejudiced growth, or unguided learning is a network. All other topologies limit what can happen. A network swarm is all edges and there-fore open ended any way you come at it. Indeed, the network is the least structured organization that can be said to have any structure at all . . . In

topological configuration, the network, can now be materially implemented, in all kinds of processes and organizations, by newly available information technologies. Without them, the networking logic would be too cumbersome to implement. Yet this networking logic is needed to structure the unstructured while preserving flexibility, since the unstructured is the driving force of innovation in human activity.

Fourthly, related to networking but a clearly distinct feature, the information technology paradigm is based on *flexibility*. Not only processes are reversible, but organizations and institutions can be modified, and even fundamentally altered, by rearranging their components. What is distinctive to the configuration of the new technological paradigm is its ability to reconfigure, a decisive feature in a society characterized by constant change and organizational fluidity. Turning the rules upside down without destroying the organization has become a possibility, because the material basis of the organization can be reprogrammed and retooled. However, we must stop short of a value judgment attached to this technological feature. This is because flexibility could be a liberating force, but also a repressive tendency if the rewriters of rules are always the powers that be. As Mulgan wrote: "Networks are created not just to communicate, but also to gain position, to outcommunicate.'[72] It is thus essential to keep a distance between assessing the emergence of new social forms and processes, as induced and allowed by new technologies, and extrapolating the potential consequences of such developments for society and people: only specific analyses and empirical observation will be able to determine the outcome of interaction between new technologies and emerging social forms. Yet it is essential as well to identify the logic embedded in the new technological paradigm.

Then, a fifth characteristic of this technological revolution is the growing *convergence of specific technologies into a highly integrated system*, within which old, separate technological trajectories become literally indistinguishable. Thus, microelectronics, telecommunications, optoelectronics, and computers are all now integrated into informa-

---

fact a plurality of truly divergent components can only remain coherent in a network. No other arrangement – chain, pyramid, tree, circle, hub – can contain true diversity working as a whole.

Although physicists and mathematicians may take exception to some of these statements, Kelly's basic message is an interesting one: the convergence between the evolutionary topology of living matter, the open-ended nature of an increasingly complex society, and the interactive logic of new information technologies.

[72]   Mulgan (1991: 21).

tion systems. There still exists, and will exist for some time, some business distinction between chip makers and software writers, for instance. But even such differentiation is blurred by the growing integration of business firms in strategic alliances and cooperative projects, as well as by the inscription of software programs into chip hardware. Furthermore, in terms of technological system one element cannot be imagined without the other: microcomputers are largely determined by chip power, and both the design and the parallel processing of microprocessors depend on computer architecture. Telecommunications is now but one form of processing information; transmission and linkage technologies are at the same time increasingly diversified and integrated into the same network, operated by computers.[73]

Technological convergence increasingly extends to growing interdependence between the biological and microelectronics revolutions, both materially and methodologically. Thus, decisive advances in biological research, such as the identification of human genes or segments of human DNA, can only proceed because of massive computing power.[74] On the other hand, the use of biological materials in microelectronics, although still very far from a generalized application, was already at the experimentation stage in 1995. Leonard Adleman, a computer scientist at the University of Southern California, used synthetic DNA molecules, and with the help of a chemical reaction made them work according to the DNA combining logic as the material basis for computing.[75] Although research has still a long way to go toward the material integration of biology and electronics, the logic of biology (the ability to self-generate unprogrammed, coherent sequences) is increasingly being introduced in electronic machines.[76] The cutting edge of robotics is the field of learning robots, using neural network theory. Thus, at the European Union Joint Research Centre's neural network laboratory in Ispra, Italy, computer scientist Jose Millan has for years been patiently teaching a couple of robots to learn by themselves, with the hope that, in the near future, they will find a good job working in applications such as surveillance and material handling in nuclear installations.[77] The ongoing convergence between different

[73] Williams (1991).
[74] *Business Week* (1995e); Bishop and Waldholz (1990).
[75] Allen (1995).
[76] See, for an analysis of trends, Kelly (1995); for a historical perspective on the convergence between mind and machines, see Mazlish (1994); for a theoretical reflection, see Levy (1994).
[77] Millan (1996); and Kaiser et al. (1995).

technological fields in the information paradigm results from their shared logic of information generation, a logic that is most apparent in the working of DNA and in natural evolution and that is increasingly replicated in the most advanced information systems, as chips, computers, and software reach new frontiers of speed, storage capacity, and flexible treatment of information from multiple sources. While the reproduction of the human brain, with its billions of circuits and unsurpassable recombining capacity, is strictly science fiction, the boundaries of information power of today's computers are being transgressed month by month.[78]

From the observation of such extraordinary changes in our machines and knowledge of life, and with the help provided by these machines and this knowledge, a deeper technological transformation is taking place: that of categories under which we think all processes. Historian of technology Bruce Mazlish proposes the idea of the necessary

> recognition that human biological evolution, now best understood in cultural terms, forces upon humankind – us – the consciousness that tools and machines are inseparable from evolving human nature. It also requires us to realize that the development of machines, culminating in the computer, makes inescapable the awareness that the same theories that are useful in explaining the workings of mechanical contrivances are also useful in understanding the human animal – and vice versa, for the understanding of the human brain sheds light in the nature of artificial intelligence.[79]

From a different perspective, based on fashionable discourses of the 1980s on "chaos theory", in the 1990s a network of scientists and researchers converged towards a shared epistemological approach, identified by the code word "complexity". Organized around seminars held at the Santa Fe Institute in New Mexico (originally a club of high-level physicists from Los Alamos Laboratory, soon joined by a select network of Nobel Prize winners and their friends), this intellectual circle aims at communicating scientific thought (including social sciences) under a new paradigm. They focus on understanding the emergence of self-organizing structures that create complexity out of simplicity and superior order out of chaos, through several orders of interactivity between the basic elements at the origin of the process.[80] Although this project is often dismissed by mainstream

---

[78]   See the excellent prospective analysis by Gelernter (1991).
[79]   Mazlish (1993: 233).

science as a nonverifiable proposition, it is one example of the effort being made from different quarters towards finding a common ground for intellectual cross-fertilization of science and technology in the Information Age. Yet this approach seems to forbid any integrating, systemic framework. Complexity thinking should be considered as a method for understanding diversity, rather than a unified meta-theory. Its epistemological value could come from acknowledging the serendipitous nature of Nature and of society. Not that there are no rules, but that rules are created, and changed, in a relentless process of deliberate actions and unique interactions.

The information technology paradigm does not evolve towards its closure as a system, but towards its openness as a multi-edged network. It is powerful and imposing in its materiality, but adaptive and open-ended in its historical development. Comprehensiveness, complexity, and networking are its decisive qualities.

Thus, the social dimension of the Information Technology Revolution seems bound to follow the law on the relationship between technology and society proposed some time ago by Melvin Kranzberg: **"Kranzberg's First Law reads as follows: Technology is neither good nor bad, nor is it neutral."**[81] It is indeed a force, probably more than ever under the current technological paradigm that penetrates the core of life and mind.[82] But its actual deployment in the realm of conscious social action, and the complex matrix of interaction between the technological forces unleashed by our species, and the species itself, are matters of inquiry rather than of fate. I shall now proceed with such an inquiry.

[80]   The diffusion of chaos theory to a broad audience was largely due to the best-seller by Gleick (1987); see also Hall (1991). For a clearly written, intriguing history of the "complexity" school, see Waldrop (1992).

[81]   Kranzberg (1985: 50).

[82]   For an informative, casual discussion of recent developments at the crossroads of science and the human mind, see Baumgartner and Payr (1995). For a more forceful, if controversial, interpretation by one of the founders of the genetic revolution, see Crick (1994).

— 2 —

The Informational Economy and the Process of Globalization

Introduction

A new economy has emerged in the last two decades on a worldwide scale. I call it informational and global to identify its fundamental distinctive features and to emphasize their intertwining. It is *informational* because the productivity and competitiveness of units or agents in this economy (be it firms, regions, or nations) fundamentally depend upon their capacity to generate, process, and apply efficiently knowledge-based information. It is *global* because the core activities of production, consumption, and circulation, as well as their components (capital, labor, raw materials, management, information, technology, markets) are organized on a global scale, either directly or through a network of linkages between economic agents. It is informational *and* global because, under the new historical conditions, productivity is generated through and competition is played out in a global network of interaction. And it has emerged in the last quarter of the twentieth century because the Information Technology Revolution provides the indispensable, material basis for such a new economy. It is the historical linkage between the knowledge-information base of the economy, its global reach, and the Information Technology Revolution that gives birth to a new, distinctive economic system, whose structure and dynamics I shall explore in this chapter.

To be sure, information and knowledge have always been critical components of economic growth, and the evolution of technology has indeed largely determined the productive capacity of society and standards of living, as well as social forms of economic organization.[1] Yet,

---

[1] Rosenberg and Birdzell (1986); Mokyr (1990).

as argued in chapter 1, we are witnessing a point of historical discontinuity. The emergence of a new technological paradigm organized around new, more powerful, and more flexible information technologies makes it possible for information itself to become the product of the production process. To be more precise: the products of new information technology industries are information-processing devices or information processing itself.[2] New information technologies, by transforming the processes of information processing, act upon all domains of human activity, and make it possible to establish endless connections between different domains, as well as between elements and agents of such activities. A networked, deeply interdependent economy emerges that becomes increasingly able to apply its progress in technology, knowledge, and management to technology, knowledge, and management themselves. Such a virtuous circle should lead to greater productivity and efficiency, given the right conditions of equally dramatic organizational and institutional changes.[3] In this chapter I shall try to assess the historical specificity of a new informational, global economy, outline its main features, and explore the structure and dynamics of a worldwide economic system emerging as a transitional form toward the informational mode of development that is likely to characterize the coming decades.

Productivity, Competitiveness, and the Informational Economy

The productivity enigma

Productivity drives economic progress. It is by increasing the yields of output per unit of input over time that humankind eventually mastered the forces of Nature and, in the process, shaped itself as Culture. No wonder that the debate over the sources of productivity is the cornerstone of classical political economy, from the Physiocrats to Marx, via Ricardo, and remains at the forefront of that dwindling stream of economic theory still concerned with the real economy.[4] Indeed, the specific ways of increasing productivity define the structure and dynamics of a given economic system. If there is a new, informational economy, we should be able to pinpoint the historically

---

[2]   Monk (1989); Freeman (1982).
[3]   Machlup (1980, 1982, 1984); Dosi et al. (1988a).
[4]   Nelson (1994); Boyer (ed.) (1986); Arthur (1989); Krugman (1990); Nelson and Winter (1982); Dosi et al. (1988a).

novel sources of productivity that make such an economy a distinctive one. But as soon as we raise this fundamental question we sense the complexity and uncertainty of the answer. Few economic matters are more questioned and more questionable than the sources of productivity and productivity growth.[5]

Academic discussions on productivity in advanced economies ritually start with the reference to the pioneering work by Robert Solow in 1956–7 and to the aggregate production function he proposed within a strict neoclassical framework to explain the sources and evolution of productivity growth in the American economy. On the basis of his calculations he contended that gross output per man doubled in the American private nonfarm sector between 1909 and 1949, "with 87½% of the increase attributable to technical change and the remaining 12½% to increased use of capital."[6] Parallel work by Kendrick converged toward similar results.[7] However, although Solow interpreted his findings as reflecting the influence of technical change on productivity, statistically speaking what he showed was that increasing output per hour of work was not the result of adding more labor, and only slightly of adding capital, but came from some other source, expressed as a statistical residual in his production function equation. Most econometric research on productivity growth in the two decades after Solow's pathbreaking work concentrated on explaining the "residual," by finding ad hoc factors that would account for the variation in the evolution of productivity, such as energy supply, government regulation, education of the labor force, and so on, without succeeding very much in clarifying this enigmatic "residual."[8] Economists, sociologists, and economic historians, supporting Solow's intuition, did not hesitate to interpret the "residual" as being equivalent to technological change. In the most refined elaborations, "science and technology" were understood in the broad sense, namely as knowledge and information, so that the technology of management was considered to be as important as the management of technology.[9] One of the most insightful, systematic research efforts on productivity, that by Richard Nelson,[10] starts from

---

[5]   Nelson (1981).
[6]   Solow (1957: 32); see also Solow (1956).
[7]   Kendrick (1961).
[8]   See, for the USA, Denison (1974, 1979); Kendrick (1973); Jorgerson and Griliches (1967); Mansfield (1969); Baumol et al. (1989). For France, Carre et al. (1984); Sautter (1978); Dubois (1985). For international comparison, see Denison (1967) and Maddison (1984).
[9]   Bell (1976); Nelson (1981); Rosenberg (1982); Stonier (1983); Freeman (1982).
[10]   Nelson (1980, 1981, 1988, 1994) and Nelson and Winter (1982).

the widespread assumption of the central role of technological change in productivity growth, thus recasting the question about the sources of productivity to shift the emphasis toward the origins of such change. In other words, the economics of technology would be the explanatory framework for the analysis of the sources of growth. However, this analytical intellectual perspective may in fact complicate the matter even further. This is because a stream of research, particularly by the University of Sussex's Science and Policy Research Unit economists,[11] has demonstrated the fundamental role of institutional environment and historical trajectories in fostering and guiding technological change, thus ultimately inducing productivity growth. Therefore, to argue that productivity creates economic growth, and that productivity is a function of technological change, is tantamount to stating that the characteristics of society are the crucial factors underlying economic growth, by their impact on technological innovation.

This Schumpeterian approach to economic growth[12] raises an even more fundamental question concerning the structure and dynamics of the informational economy. Namely, what is historically new about our economy? What is its specificity vis-à-vis other economic systems, and particularly vis-à-vis the industrial economy?

Is knowledge-based productivity specific to the informational economy?

Economic historians have shown the fundamental role played by technology in economic growth, via productivity increase, throughout history and especially in the industrial era.[13] The hypothesis of the critical role of technology as a source of productivity in advanced economies seems also able to comprehend much of the past experience of economic growth, cutting across different intellectual traditions in economic theory.

Furthermore, the analysis by Solow, repeatedly used as the starting point of the argument in favor of the emergence of a post-industrial economy by Bell and others, *is based on data for the 1909–49 period of the American economy, namely the heyday of the American industrial economy.* Indeed, in 1950 the proportion of manufacturing employment in the US was almost at its peak (the highest point was reached in 1960), so that by the most usual indicator of "industrialism" Solow's calculations

---

[11]   Dosi et al. (1988a).
[12]   Schumpeter (1939).
[13]   Basalla (1988); Mokyr (1990); David (1975); Rosenberg (1976); Arthur (1986).

were referring to the process of expansion of the industrial economy. What is the analytical meaning of this observation? If the explanation of productivity growth introduced by the aggregate production function school is not substantially different from the results of historical analysis of the relationship between technology and economic growth over longer periods, at least for the industrial economy, does this mean that there is nothing new about the "informational" economy? Are we simply observing the mature stage of the industrial economic system whose steady accumulation of productive capacity frees labor from direct material production for the benefit of information-processing activities, as it was suggested in the pioneering work by Marc Porat?[14]

Table 2.1   Productivity rate: growth rates of output per worker; average annual percentage change by period

Country	1870–1913	1913–29	1929–50	1950–60	1960–9
Canada	1.7	0.7	2.0	2.1	2.2
France[a]	1.4	2.0	0.3	5.4	5.0
Germany[b]	1.6	-0.2	1.2	6.0	4.6
Italy[a]	0.8	1.5	1.0	4.5	6.4
Japan[c]	–	–	–	6.7	9.5
United Kingdom	1.0	0.4	1.1	1.9	2.5
United States[d]	1.9	1.5	1.7	2.1	2.6

[a] Initial year for period 1950–60 is 1954.
[b] Initial year for 1870–1913 is 1871.
[c] Initial year for 1950–1960 is 1953.
[d] Initial year for period 1870–1913 is 1871.
Historical Statistics of the United States: Colonial Times to 1970, Part 1, Series F10–16.

To answer this question, let us look at the long-term evolution of productivity growth in advanced market economies (see tables 2.1 for the so-called G-7 countries and 2.2 for the OECD countries). For the purpose of my analysis, what is relevant is the change of trends between four periods: 1870–1950, 1950–73, 1973–9, and 1979–93. Because we use two different statistical sources we cannot compare levels of productivity growth rates between the periods before and after 1969, but we can reason on the evolution of growth rates within and between periods for each source. Overall, there was a moderate rate of growth of productivity for the 1870–1950 period (never surpassing 2% for any country or subperiod, except for Canada), a high rate of growth during the 1950–73 period (always over 2%,

[14]   Porat (1977).

except for the UK) with Japan leading the charge; and a low growth rate in 1973–93 (very low for the US and Canada), always below 2% in total factor productivity, except Italy in the 1970s. Even if we account for the specificity of some countries, what appears clearly is that *we observe a downward trend of productivity growth starting roughly around the same time that the Information Technology Revolution took shape in the early 1970s.* Highest growth rates of productivity took place during the 1950–73 period when industrial technological innovations that came together as a system during the Second World War were woven into a dynamic model of economic growth. But by the early 1970s, the productivity potential of these technologies seemed to be exhausted, and new information technologies did not appear to reverse the productivity slowdown for the next two decades.[15] Indeed, in the United States, the famous "residual", after accounting for about 1.5 points of annual productivity growth during the 1960s, made no contribution at all in 1972–92.[16] In a comparative perspective, calculations by the reliable Centre d'Etudes Prospectives et d'Informations Internationales[17] show a general reduction of total factor productivity growth for the main market economies during the 1970s and 1980s. Even for Japan, the role of capital in productivity growth was more important than that of multifactor productivity for the 1973–90 period. This decline was particularly marked in all countries for service activities, where new information-processing devices could be thought to have increased productivity, if the relationship between technology and productivity were simple and direct. Evidently, it is not.

Thus, over the long term,[18] there was a steady, moderate productivity growth, with some downturns, in the period of formation of the

[15]   Maddison (1984); Krugman (1994a).

[16]   See Council of Economic Advisers (1995).

[17]   Centre d'Etudes Prospectives et d'Informations Internationales (CEPII), 1992. I have relied on key information in the 1992 report on the world economy prepared by CEPII, on the basis of the MIMOSA model of the world economy elaborated by the researchers of this leading economic research center linked to the French Prime Minister's office. Although the data base has been produced by this research center, and thus does not coincide entirely in its periodization and estimates with various international sources (OECD, US Government statistics, etc.), it is a reliable model that allows me to compare very different economic trends in the whole world, and for the same periods, without changing the data base, thus furthering consistency and comparability. However, I have also felt the necessity of relying on additional sources from standard statistical publications, which I have cited where necessary. For a presentation of the characteristics of this model, see CEPII–OFCE (1990).

[18]   Kindleberger (1964); Maddison (1984); Freeman (ed.) (1986); Dosi et al. (1988a).

Table 2.2 Productivity in the business sector: percentage changes at annual rates

	Total factor productivity[a]			Labor productivity[b]			Capital productivity		
	1960ᶜ–73	1973–79	1979–93ᵈ	1960ᶜ–73	1973–79	1979–93ᵈ	1960ᶜ–73	1973–79	1979–93ᵈ
United States	1.6	-0.4	0.4	2.2	0	0.8	0.2	-1.3	-0.5
Japan	5.6	1.3	1.4	8.3	2.9	2.5	-2.6	-3.4	-1.9
Germany[e]	2.6	1.8	1.0	4.5	3.1	1.7	-1.4	-1.0	-0.6
France	3.7	1.6	1.2	5.3	2.9	2.2	0.6	-1.0	-0.7
Italy	4.4	2.0	1.0	6.3	2.9	1.8	0.4	0.3	-0.7
United Kingdom	2.6	0.6	1.4	3.9	1.5	2.0	-0.3	-1.5	0.2
Canada	1.9	0.6	-0.3	2.9	1.5	1.0	0.1	-1.1	-2.8
Total of above countries[f]	2.9	0.6	0.8	4.3	1.4	1.5	-0.5	-1.5	-0.8
Australia	2.3	1.0	0.5	3.4	2.3	1.2	0.2	-1.5	-0.7
Austria	3.3	1.2	0.7	5.8	3.2	1.7	-2.0	-3.1	-1.5
Belgium	3.8	1.4	1.4	5.2	2.7	2.3	0.6	-1.9	-0.7
Denmark	2.3	0.9	1.3	3.9	2.4	2.3	-1.4	-2.6	-0.8
Finland	4.0	1.9	2.1	5.0	3.2	3.2	1.4	-1.6	-0.8
Greece	3.1	0.9	-0.2	9.1	3.4	0.7	-8.8	-4.2	-2.1
Ireland	3.6	3.0	3.3	4.8	4.1	4.1	-0.9	-1.2	0.2
Netherlands	3.5	1.8	0.8	4.8	2.8	1.3	0.8	0	-0.2
New Zealand	0.7	-2.1	0.4	1.6	-1.4	1.6	-0.7	-3.2	-1.4
Norway[g]	2.3	1.4	0	3.8	2.5	1.3	0	-0.3	-1.9
Portugal	5.4	-0.2	1.6	7.4	0.5	2.4	-0.7	-2.5	-0.8
Spain	3.2	0.9	1.6	6.0	3.2	2.9	-3.6	-5.0	-1.5
Sweden	2.0	0	0.8	3.7	1.4	1.7	-2.2	-3.2	-1.4
Switzerland	2.0	-0.4	0.4	3.2	0.8	1.0	-1.4	-3.5	-1.3
Total of above smaller countries[f]	3.0	0.9	1.1	5.0	2.5	2.0	-1.5	-2.8	-1.1

Total of above North American countires[f]	1.6	-0.4	0.4	2.3	0.1	0.9	0.2	-1.3	-0.7
Total of above European countries[f]	3.3	1.4	1.2	5.1	2.6	2.0	-0.7	-1.4	-0.7
Total of above OECD countries[f]	2.9	0.6	0.9	4.4	1.6	1.6	-0.7	-1.7	-0.9

[a] TFP growth is equal to a weighted average of the growth in labor and capital productivity. The sample-period averages for capital and labor shares are used as weights.

[b] Output per employed person.

[c] Or earliest year available, i.e. 1961 for Australia, Greece and Ireland; 1962 for Japan, the United Kingdom and New Zealand; 1964 for Spain; 1965 for France and Sweden; 1966 for Canada and Norway and 1970 for Belgium and the Netherlands

[d] Or latest available year, i.e. 1991 for Norway and Switzerland; 1992 for Italy, Australia, Austria, Belgium, Ireland, New Zealand, Portugal and Sweden and 1994 for the United States, Western Germany and Denmark.

[e] Western Germany

[f] Aggregates were calculated on the basis of 1992 GDP for the business sector expressed in 1992 purchasing power parities.

[g] Mainland business sector (i.e. excluding shipping as well as crude petroleum and gas extraction).

Source: OECD Economic Outlook, June 1995.

industrial economy between the late nineteenth century and the Second World War; a substantial acceleration of productivity growth in the mature period of industrialism (1950–73); and a slowing down of productivity growth rates in the 1973–93 period, in spite of a substantial increase in technology inputs and acceleration in the pace of technological change. Thus, on the one hand, we should expand the argument on the central role of technology in economic growth to past historical periods, at least for the Western economies in the industrial era. On the other hand, the pace of productivity growth in the last two decades does not seem to covariate with the timing of technological change. This could indicate the absence of substantial differences between the "industrial" and the "informational" regimes of economic growth, at least with reference to their differential impact on productivity growth, thus forcing us to reconsider the theoretical relevance of the distinction altogether. However, before surrendering to the enigma of vanishing productivity growth in the midst of one of the fastest and most comprehensive technological revolutions in history, I shall advance a number of hypotheses that could help to unveil the mystery.

First, economic historians argue that a considerable time lag between technological innovation and economic productivity is characteristic of past technological revolutions. For instance, Paul David, analyzing the diffusion of the electrical engine, showed that while it was introduced in the 1880s, its real impact on productivity had to wait until the 1920s.[19] For new technological discoveries to be able to diffuse throughout the whole economy, thus enhancing productivity growth at an observable rate, the culture and institutions of society, business firms, and the factors intervening in the production process need to undergo substantial change. This general statement is particularly appropriate in the case of a technological revolution centered around knowledge and information, embodied in symbol-processing operations that are necessarily linked to the culture of society, and to the education/skills of its people. If we date the emergence of the new technological paradigm to the mid-1970s, and its consolidation to the 1990s, it appears that society as a whole, business firms, institutions, organizations, and people, hardly had time to process technological change and decide on its uses. As a result, the new techno-economic system did not yet characterize entire national economies in the 1970s and 1980s, and could not be reflected in such synthetic, aggregate measure as the productivity growth rate for the whole economy.

However, this wise, historical perspective requires social specificity.

[19]   David (1989).

Namely, why and how *these* new technologies had to wait to deliver their promise in enhancing productivity? Which are the conditions for such enhancement? How do they differ depending on the characteristics of technology? How different is the rate of diffusion of technology, and thus its impact on productivity, in various industries? Do such differences make overall productivity dependent on the industrial mix of each country? Accordingly, can the process of economic maturation of new technologies be accelerated or restrained in different countries, or by different policies? In other words, the time lag between technology and productivity cannot be reduced to a black box. It has to be specified. So let us have a closer look at the differential evolution of productivity by countries and industries over the last two decades, restricting our observation to leading market economies, so as not to lose the thread of the argument in excessive empirical detail (see tables 2.3 and 2.4).

A fundamental observation concerns the fact that the slowdown of productivity has taken place mainly in service industries. And since these industries account for the majority of employment and GNP, its weight is statistically reflected in overall productivity growth rate. This simple remark raises two fundamental problems. The first one refers to the difficulty of measuring productivity in many service industries,[20] particularly in those that account for the bulk of employment in services: education, health services, government. There are endless paradoxes, and instances of economic nonsense, in many of the indexes used to measure productivity in these services. But even when considering only the business sector, measurement problems are substantial. For instance, in the US in the 1990s the banking industry, according to Bureau of Labor Statistics, increased its productivity by about 2% a year. But this calculation seems an underestimate, because growth in real output in banking and other financial services is assumed equal to the increase in hours worked in the industry, and therefore labor productivity is eliminated by assumption.[21] Until we develop a more accurate economic analysis of services, with its corresponding statistical apparatus, measuring productivity in many services is subject to considerable margins of error.

Secondly, under the term services are dumped together miscellaneous activities with little in common except being other than agriculture, extractive industries, utilities, construction, and manufacturing. The "services" category is a residual, negative notion,

---

[20] See the interesting effort at measuring services productivity by McKinsey Global Institute (1992). However, they focused on just five services industries which were relatively easy to measure.

[21] Council of Economic Advisers (1995: 110).

Table 2.3 Evolution of the productivity of business sectors (% average annual growth rate)

Country	1973/60[a]	1979/73	1989/79[b]	1985/79	1989/85[b]
Total factor productivity					
United States	2.2	0.4	0.9	0.6	1.4
Japan	3.2	1.5	1.6	1.5	1.6
W. Germany	3.2	2.2	1.2	0.9	1.7
France	3.3	2.0	2.1	2.1	2.0
UK[c]	2.2	0.5	1.8	1.6	2.2
Productivity of capital					
United States	0.6	-1.1	-0.5	-1.0	0.7
Japan	-6.0	-4.1	-2.6	-2.3	-3.0
W. Germany	-1.5	-1.3	-1.1	-1.8	0.0
France	-1.9	-2.5	-0.9	-1.8	0.4
UK[c]	-0.8	-1.7	0.3	-0.7	1.9
Productivity of labor (output per person/hour)					
United States	2.9	1.1	1.5	1.3	1.8
Japan	6.9	3.7	3.2	3.0	3.4
W. Germany	5.6	4.1	2.4	2.3	2.5
France	5.6	3.9	3.3	3.7	2.7
UK[c]	3.5	1.5	2.5	2.6	2.4

[a] The period starts in 1970 in Japan, 1971 in France, and 1966 in the UK.
[b] The period ends in 1988 in the United States.
[c] For the UK the work factor is measured in number of workers and not in hours worked.
Source: CEPII–OFCE, data base of the MIMOSA model.

Table 2.4 Evolution of productivity in sectors not open to free trade
(% average annual growth rate)

Country	1973/60[a]	1979/73	1989/79[b]	1985/79	1989/85[b]
Total factor productivity					
United States	1.9	0.6	-0.1	-0.1	0.0
Japan	0.1	0.3	-0.2	-0.1	-0.4
W. Germany	1.4	0.9	0.7	0.0	1.6
France	2.4	0.6	1.6	1.6	1.7
UK[c]	1.3	-0.3	1.2	0.5	2.3
Productivity of capital					
United States	0.4	-0.6	-1.2	-1.4	-0.7
Japan	-7.9	-4.5	-5.3	-4.3	-6.7
W. Germany	-2.4	-2.2	-1.6	-2.7	0.1
France	-1.7	-3.2	-0.6	-1.6	0.9
UK[c]	-1.1	-2.6	-0.1	-0.9	1.1
Productivity per person/hour					
United States	2.5	1.1	0.4	0.4	0.3
Japan	4.0	2.6	2.1	1.8	2.6
W. Germany	4.3	3.2	2.4	2.1	2.8
France	4.7	2.7	2.8	3.3	2.1
UK[c]	2.2	0.5	1.5	1.0	2.3

[a] The period starts in 1970 in Japan, 1971 in France, and 1966 in the UK.
[b] The period ends in 1988 in the United States.
[c] For the UK the work factor is measured in number of workers and not in hours worked.
Source: CEDII–OFCE, data base of the MIMOSA model.

inducing analytical confusion, as I shall argue in some detail below (chapter 4). Thus, when we analyze specific service industries we observe a great disparity in the evolution of their productivity in the last two decades. One of the leading experts in this area, Quinn, observes that "initial analyses [in the mid-1980s] indicate that measured added value in the services sector is at least as high as in manufacturing.'[22] Some service industries in the US, such as telecommunications, air transportation, and railroads, displayed substantial increases in productivity, between 4.5% and 6.8% per year for the period 1970–83. On a comparative basis, the evolution of labor productivity in services as a whole shows wide disparity between countries, increasing much faster in France and Germany than in the US and the UK, with Japan in between.[23] This indicates that the evolution of productivity in services is to a large extent dependent on the actual structure of services in each country (for example, much lower weight of retail employment in France and Germany vis-à-vis the USA and Japan in the 1970s and 1980s).

By and large, the observation of stagnant productivity in services as a whole is counterintuitive to observers and business managers, who have been witnessing staggering changes in technology and procedures in office work for more than a decade.[24] Indeed, detailed analysis of accounting methods for economic productivity reveals considerable sources of measurement error. One of the most important distortions in US calculating procedures refers to the difficulty of measuring software and R&D investment, a major item of investment goods in the new economy, yet categorized as "intermediate goods and services," and not showing up in final demand, thus lowering the actual rate of growth of both output and productivity. An even more important source of distortion is the difficulty in measuring prices for many services in an economy that has become so diversified and has submitted to rapid change in the goods and services produced.[25] In sum, it may well be that a significant proportion of the mysterious productivity slowdown results from a growing inadequacy of economic statistics to capture movements of the new informational economy, *precisely because of the broad scope of its transformation under the impact of information technology and related organizational change.*

If that is the case, manufacturing productivity, relatively easier to measure for all its problems, should offer a different picture. And this is indeed what we observe. Using the CEPII data base, for the US and

[22]   Quinn (1987: 122–7).
[23]   CEPII (1992: 61).
[24]   *Business Week* (1995f: 86–96).
[25]   Council of Economic Advisers (1995: 110).

Japan multifactor productivity in manufacturing in 1979–89 increased by an annual average of 3% and 4.1% respectively, dramatically upgrading the performance of 1973–9, *and increasing productivity at a faster pace than during the 1960s.* The UK displayed a similar trend, although at a slightly slower pace than productivity increases in the 1960s. On the other hand, Germany and France continued their slowdown in manufacturing productivity growth, with annual increases of 1.5% and 2.4% respectively in 1979–89, way below their past performance. Thus, instead of a catch-up effect on productivity in European countries *vis-à-vis* higher US productivity, we observe the opposite, maybe an indication of their technological lagging *vis-à-vis* the US and Japan. The better-than-usually-thought performance of manufacturing productivity growth in the US in the 1980s is also documented by the US Department of Labor, although the periods selected and methods used offer a lower estimate than CEPII's data base. According to its calculations, output per hour in the manufacturing sector went from 3.3% annual increase in 1963–72, to 2.6% in 1972–8, and again 2.6% in 1978–87, hardly a spectacular drop. Productivity increases in manufacturing are much more significant in the United States and Japan in the sectors that include electronics manufacturing. According to the CEPII data base, in these sectors productivity increased by 1% per year in 1973–9, but it exploded by 11% per year in 1979–87, accounting for the largest share of total increase in manufacturing productivity.[26] While Japan displays similar trends, France and Germany experienced a decline of productivity in the electronics industry, again probably as a reflection of the accumulated technological gap in information technologies *vis-à-vis* America and Japan.

So maybe after all, productivity is not really vanishing but is increasing through partly hidden avenues, in expanding circles. Technology, and the management of technology involving organizational change, could be diffusing from information technology manufacturing, telecommunications, and financial services (the original sites of technological revolution) into manufacturing at large, then into business services, to reach gradually miscellaneous service activities, where there are lower incentives for the diffusion of

---

[26]   Source: CEPII (1992); see tables 2.3 and 2.4 in this chapter, and CEPII (1992: 58–9). Data on manufacturing productivity do not coincide with those of US Bureau of Labor Statistics because of different periodization and calculation procedures. However, trends in both sources coincide in not showing a slowdown in manufacturing productivity growth during the 1980s: according to BLS data there was a stabilization of growth rates; according to CEPII data, there was an increase in growth rates.

technology and greater resistance to organizational change. This interpretation seems to be plausible in light of the evolution of productivity in the US in the early 1990s. According to some sources, in 1993 and 1994 factory productivity grew by an annual 5.4% (while real factory wages declined by 2.7%), with electronics again leading the trend.[27] Moreover, together with the diffusion of technology and new methods of management in services, this increase in manufacturing productivity pushed productivity for the whole economy between 1991 and 1994 to a level of growth of about 2% per year, more than doubling the performance of the past decade.[28] So the productivity dividend of technological revolution *could be* on its way to pay off. Yet the picture is still confusing, as data at the time of writing are insufficient to establish a trend.[29] It seems that commentary on the data may ground our understanding of the informational economy, but cannot tell the real story until we introduce some analytical tools to broaden the scope of analysis beyond the boundaries of uncertain productivity statistics.

Informationalism and capitalism, productivity and profitability

Yes, in the long term productivity is the source of the wealth of nations. And technology, including organizational and managerial technology, is the major productivity-inducing factor. But, from the perspective of economic agents, productivity is not a goal in itself. Neither is investing in technology for the sake of technological innovation. This is why Richard Nelson, in a recent paper on the matter, considers that the new agenda for formal growth theorizing should be built around the relationships between technical change, firm capabilities, and national institutions.[30] Firms and nations (or political entities of different levels, such as regions or the European Union) are the actual agents of economic growth. They do not seek technology for the sake of technology or productivity enhancement for the betterment of humankind. They behave in a given historical context, within the rules of an economic system (informational

---

[27]   Cooper (ed.) (1994: 62), using data from US Department of Labor.
[28]   Council of Economic Advisers (1995: 108).
[29]   Upward trends in productivity growth rates by the mid-1990s in the US should still be taken with a grain of salt. As the Council of Economic Advisers' Report to the President (1995) wrote: "While the evidence in favor of a slight improvement in the productivity growth trend is encouraging, it is not yet decisive. The experience of the next few years will be quite telling for this issue." Indeed.
[30]   Nelson (1994: 41).

capitalism, as I proposed above), which will ultimately reward or penalize their conduct. Thus, *firms will be motivated not by productivity, but by profitability*, for which productivity and technology may be important means, but certainly not the only ones. And *political institutions*, being shaped by a broader set of values and interests, *will be oriented, in the economic realm, towards maximizing the competitiveness of their constituent economies.* **Profitability and competitiveness are the actual determinants of technological innovation and productivity growth.** It is in their concrete, historical dynamics that we may find the clues for understanding productivity's vagaries.

The 1970s were at the same time the likely birth date of the Information Technology Revolution and a watershed in the evolution of capitalism, as I argued above. Firms in all countries reacted to actual or feared decline in profitability by adopting new strategies.[31] Some of them, such as technological innovation and organizational decentralization, while essential in their potential impact, had a relatively long-term horizon. But firms looked for shorter-term results that could show up in their bookkeeping and, for American firms, in their quarterly reports. To increase profits, for a given financial environment and with prices set by the market, there are four main ways: to reduce production costs (starting with labor costs); to increase productivity; to broaden the market; and to accelerate capital turnover.

With different emphases, depending on firms and countries, all were used during the last decade. In all of them, new information technologies were essential tools. But I propose the hypothesis that one strategy was implemented earlier and with more immediate results: the broadening of markets and the fight for market share. This is because to increase productivity without a prior expansion of demand, or the potential for it, is too risky from the investor's point of view. This is why the American electronics industry desperately needed military markets in its infant years until investments in technological innovation could pay off in a broad range of markets. And this is why Japanese firms, and after them Korean firms, used a protected market and clever targeting of industries and segments of industries at the global level as ways to build up economies of scale in order to reach economies of scope. The real crisis of the 1970s was not the oil prices shock. It was the inability of the public sector to keep expanding its markets, and thus income-generating employment, without either increasing taxes on capital or fueling inflation through additional money supply and public

[31]   Boyer (ed.) (1986); Boyer (1988a); Boyer and Ralle (1986a); Aglietta (1976).

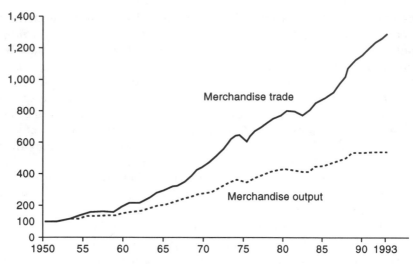

Figure 2.1   Long-term trends of world merchandise trade and
output, 1950–93 (indices and percentages)
Source: GATT (1994).

indebtedness.[32] While some short-term answers to the profitability
crisis focused on labor trimming and wage attrition, the real challenge for individual firms and for capitalism as a whole was to find
new markets able to absorb a growing productive capacity of goods
and services.[33] This is at the root of the substantial expansion of
trade relative to output, and, later, that of foreign direct investment
in the last two decades (see figure 2.1 and table 2.5). They became
the engines of economic growth throughout the world.[34] It is true
that world trade grew at a lower rate in these years than during the
1960s (because of a lower rate of economic growth overall), but the
critical figure is the relationship between the expansion of trade and
GDP growth: in 1970–80, while world's GDP grew at an annual 3.4%,
exports of merchandise trade grew at 4% per year. In 1980–92, the

---

[32]   The critique by the monetarist school on sources of inflation in the American
economy seems to be plausible. See Milton Friedman (1968). However, it omitted
the fact that expansionary monetary policies were also responsible for unprecedented, stable economic growth in the 1950s and 1960s. On this point, see my
own analysis (Castells 1980).

[33]   The old underconsumption theory, at the heart of Marxian economics, but
also of Keynesian policies, still has relevance when placed in the new context of
global capitalism. On this issue, see Castells and Tyson (1988).

[34]   I refer the reader to the excellent overview of global economic transformations by Chesnais (1994).

Table 2.5   Worldwide foreign direct investment and selected economic indicators, 1991, and growth rates for 1981–5, 1986–90

Indicator	Value at current prices, 1991 (US$ bn)	Annual growth %[a] 1981–5	1986–90
All countries[b]			
Foreign direct investment outflows	180	4	24
Foreign direct investment stock	1,800	7	16
Sales of transnational corporations	5,500[c]	2[d]	15
Gross domestic product at market prices	21,500	2	9
Gross domestic investment	4,900	0.5	10
Exports of goods and non-factor services	4,000	-0.2	12
Royalties and fees receipts	34	0.1	19
Developed countries			
Foreign direct investment outflows	177	3	24
Gross domestic product at market prices	17,200	3	10
Gross domestic investment	3,800	2	11
Exports of goods and non-factor services	3,000	2	12
Royalty and fees receipts	33	0.2	19
Developing economies			
Foreign direct investment inflows	39	-4	17
Gross domestic product at market prices	3,400	0.2	8
Gross domestic investment	800	-3	9
Exports of goods and non-factor services	930	-3	13
Royalties and fees payments	2	-1	23

[a] Growth rates were calculated at an annual compounded rate, derived from a semi-logarithmic regression equation.

[b] Data on developed and developing economies do not equal those for all countries because of the inclusion of Central and Eastern Europe in the item on "countries."

[c] For 1990.

[d] For 1982–5.

*Sources:*UNCTAD, Programme on Transnational Corporations, based on International Monetary Fund (IMF) balance-of-payments tape, retrieved in February 1993; and unpublished data provided by the World Bank, International Economics Department.

Table 2.6   Growth in the value of world exports by major product
group, 1985–93
(Billion dollars and percentage)

	Value US$ bn 1993	Average annual change (%)			
		1985–90	1991	1992	1993
World merchandise exports[a]	3,640	12.3	1.5	6.3	-0.4
Agricultural products	438	10.1	1.1	6.8	-2.1
Mining products	433	2.5	-5.0	-1.8	-2.7
Manufactures	2,668	15.5	3.0	7.9	0.1
World exports of commercial services	1,020	—	5.5	12.5	0.5

[a] Including unspecified products
Note: The statistics for commercial services and for merchandise
trade are not directly comparable because (i) the country coverage of
available data on commercial services trade is less comprehensive
than that for merchandise trade, and (ii) the data on commercial
services are subject to other sources of (primarily downward) bias.
Source: GATT (1994).

corresponding figures were 3% and 4.9%. Table 2.6 shows the substantial acceleration of world trade, when measured in value, in the
second half of the 1980s: an average annual growth of 12.3%. And
although in 1993 world trade experienced a downturn, in 1993–5 it
continued to grow at rates over 4%.[35] For nine major manufacturing
sectors considered in the CEPII model of the world economy,[36] the
proportion of internationally traded manufactured goods in total
world production was in 1973 15.3%, in 1980 19.7%, in 1988 22.2%,
and in the year 2000 should reach 24.8%. As for foreign direct
investment, scanning the globe in search of better production conditions and market penetration, according to UNCTAD's World
Investment Report, it increased at an annual rate of 4% in 1981–5,
and at a staggering 24% per year in 1986–90. The stock of foreign
direct investment reached $2 trillion in 1992. Over 170,000 affiliates
of 37,000 parent firms generated about $5.5 trillion in worldwide
sales in 1990. This figure can be put into perspective compared to $4
trillion of total world exports and nonfactor services in 1992.[37]
   To open up new markets, linking in a global network valuable

[35]   World Bank (1995); GATT (1994).
[36]   CEPII (1992: MIMOSA model).
[37]   UNCTAD (1993: 13 ff).

market segments of each country, capital required extreme mobility, and firms needed dramatically enhanced communication capabilities. Deregulation of markets and new information technologies, in close interaction, provided such conditions. The earliest and most direct beneficiaries of such restructuring were the very actors of techno-economic transformation: high-technology firms and financial corporations. The global integration of financial markets since the early 1980s, made possible by new information technologies, had a dramatic impact on the growing disassociation of capital flows from national economies. Thus, Chesnais measures the movement of internationalization of capital by calculating the percentage over GDP of crossborder operations in shares and obligations:[38] in 1980, this percentage was not over 10% in any major country; in 1992, it varied between 72.2% of GDP (Japan) and 122.2% (France), with the US standing at 109.3%.

By extending its global reach, integrating markets, and maximizing comparative advantages of location, capital, capitalists, and capitalist firms have, as a whole, substantially increased their profitability in the last decade, and particularly in the 1990s, restoring for the time being the preconditions for investment on which a capitalist economy depends.[39]

This recapitalization of capitalism may explain to some extent the uneven progress of productivity. Throughout the 1980s there was massive technological investment in the communications/information infrastructure that made possible the twin movements of deregulation of markets and globalization of capital. Firms and industries that were directly affected by such dramatic transformation (such as microelectronics, microcomputers, telecommunications, financial institutions) experienced a surge in productivity as well as in profitability.[40] Around this hard core of new, dynamic, global capitalist firms and ancillary networks, successive layers of firms and industries were

---

[38]   Chesnais (1994: 209).
[39]   For the US, a good measure of profitability, for non-financial corporations, is the after-tax profit per unit of output (the higher the ratio, the higher the profit, of course). The ratio stood at 0.024 in 1959; went down to 0.020 in 1970 and 0.017 in 1974; bounced back to 0.040 in 1978, to decline again to 0.027 in 1980. Then, since 1983 (0.048) it kept an upward trend that accelerated substantially during the 1990s: 1991, 0.061; 1992, 0.067; 1993, 0.073; third quarter 1994, 0.080. See Council of Economic Advisers (1995: 291, Table B-14).
[40]   Source: CEPII (1992). Profitability was high since the 1980s in electronics, telecommunications, and finance as a whole. However, cut-throat competition, and risky financial deals, did cause a number of setbacks and bankruptcies. Indeed, without the US government bail-out of a number of savings & loan associations, a major financial crash could have been a very serious possibility.

either integrated in the new technological system or phased out. Thus, the slow movement of productivity in national economies taken as a whole may hide contradictory trends of explosive productivity growth in leading industries, decline of obsolete firms, and persistence of low-productivity service activities. Furthermore, the more this dynamic sector constituted around highly profitable firms becomes globalized across boundaries, the less it is meaningful to calculate productivity of "national economies," or of industries defined within national boundaries. Although the largest proportion of GDP, and of employment, of most countries continues to depend on activities aimed at the domestic economy, rather than at the global market, it is indeed what happens to competition in these global markets, in manufacturing as in finance, telecommunications or entertainment, that determines the share of wealth appropriated by firms and, ultimately, by people in each country.[41] This is why, together with the search for profitability as the driving motivation of the firm, the informational economy is also shaped by the vested interest of political institutions in fostering the competitiveness of those economies they are supposed to represent.

As for *competitiveness*, it is an elusive, indeed controversial, notion that has become a rallying flag for governments and a battleground for real-life economists opposing academic model-makers.[42] Competitiveness is an attribute of economic collectives, such as countries or regions, rather than of firms, for which the traditional, and rather complex, notion of "competitive position" seems to be

[41]   The decisive role played by global competition in the economic prosperity of the nation is widely accepted all over the world, except in the United States, where, in some economists' circles, and in sectors of the public opinion, there is still the conviction that because exports only account for about 10% of GNP in the early 1990s, the country's economic health depends essentially on the domestic market (see Krugman 1994a). Although the size and productivity of the American economy does make it much more autonomous than any other country in the world, the idea of quasi-self reliance is a dangerous illusion that is in fact not shared by either business or government elites. For arguments and data concerning the critical role of global competition for the American economy, as for all economies in the world, see Cohen and Zysman (1987); Castells and Tyson (1989); Reich (1991); Thurow (1992); Carnoy et al. (1993b).

[42]   The debate over productivity versus competitiveness as keys to renewed economic growth has raged in American academic and political circles in the 1990s. Paul Krugman, one of the most brilliant academic economists in America, can be credited with triggering a necessary debate by his vigorous critique of the notion of competitiveness, unfortunately tainted and obscured by manners inappropriate to a scholar. For a sample of the debate, see Krugman (1994b). For a reply, Cohen (1994).

more adequate. One reasonable definition, by Stephen Cohen et al. states:

> Competitiveness has different meanings for the firm and for the national economy. A nation's competitiveness is the degree to which it can, under free and fair market conditions, produce goods and services that meet the test of international markets while simultaneously expanding the real incomes of its citizens. Competitiveness at the national level is based on superior productivity performance by the economy and the economy's ability to shift output to high productivity activities which in turn can generate high levels of real wages.[43]

Naturally, since "free and fair market conditions" belong to the unreal world, political agencies acting in the international economy seek to interpret such a principle in a way that maximizes the competitive advantage of firms under their jurisdiction. The emphasis here is on the *relative position of national economies* vis-à-vis *other countries*, as a major legitimizing force for governments.[44]

The strategic importance of competitiveness, both for economic policies and political ideologies, comes from two factors. On the one hand, the growing interdependence of economies, and particularly of capital markets and currencies, makes increasingly difficult the existence of genuine national economic policies. Practically all countries have to steer their economies both in cooperation and in competition with others, while the tempos of their societies and polities is unlikely to be synchronized with their economic moves. Therefore, to compete is to strengthen relative position in order to acquire greater bargaining power in the necessary negotiation process in which all political units must adjust their strategies in an interdependent system.

On the other hand, competitiveness has come to the foreground of business, governments, media, political scientists, and, lately, of economists as well, as a result of the challenge mounted by nationalist policies in the Asian Pacific to previously unchallenged domination by American companies in the international arena. That Japan first, then the Asian tigers, and finally maybe giant China could enter *en force* global competition, and win substantial market share while protecting their own markets for a long time, came as a rude awakening to American business and government.[45] It prompted a

[43] Cohen et al. (1985: 1).
[44] Tyson and Zysman (1983).
[45] Cohen (1993).

confused mobilization that soon found similar echoes in Europe, this
time against both American and Japanese competition. New technologies and the new industries associated with them were seen,
rightly, as the main tool for global competition and a good indication
of competitiveness. Therefore, programs of technological innovation
and of managerial restructuring were induced or supported by
governments, first in Asian Pacific countries, then in Europe, finally,
somehow, in the US, under the label of competitiveness policies.[46]
Their differential diffusion, their variable accuracy, and their mixed
record of success have induced distinct technological trajectories,
with equally diverse outcomes on productivity, in spite of a largely
shared technological stock.

Ultimately, the process of globalization feeds back into productivity
growth, since firms must improve their performance when faced with
stronger competition from around the world, or when they vie to win
market shares internationally. Thus a 1993 McKinsey Global Institute
Study on manufacturing productivity in the US, Japan, and Germany
found a high correlation between an index of globalization,
measuring exposure to international competition, and the relative
productivity performance of nine industries analyzed in the three
countries.[47] Thus, the linkage path between information technology,
organizational change, and productivity growth goes, to a large
extent, through global competition.

This is how firms' search for profitability and nations' mobilization
towards competitiveness induced variable arrangements in the new
historical equation between technology and productivity. In the
process, they created, and shaped, a new, global economy that may be
the most characteristic and important feature of informational
capitalism.

The repoliticization of informational capitalism

There is an additional, critical element in the economy, old and new:
the state. By integrating countries in a global economy, the specific
political interests of the state in each nation become directly linked
with the fate of economic competition for firms that are either
national or located in the country's territory.[48] In key instances of
development, governments use economic competition by their
countries' firms as an instrument of fulfillment of their national

---

[46]   Tyson (1992); Borrus and Zysman (1992).
[47]   McKinsey Global Institute (1993).
[48]   Carnoy et al. (1993b).

interest, as G.C. Allen and Chalmers Johnson have argued for Japan, and Amsdem for Taiwan and South Korea, as I have tried to suggest for the four "Asian tigers with a dragon head," or as Peter Evans has proposed in general terms, on the basis of his comparative analysis of Brazil, India, and South Korea.[49] The new form of state intervention in the economy links up, in an explicit strategy, competitiveness, productivity, and technology. The new developmental state supports technological development in their countries' industries and in their productive infrastructure as a way of fostering productivity and helping "its" firms to compete in the world market. Simultaneously, some governments have restrained as much as possible the penetration of their markets by foreign competition, thus creating competitive advantage for specific industries in their period of nurturing. In the analysis by Johnson, Tyson, and Zysman, politics and productivity become intertwined as key instruments for competitiveness.[50]

On the other hand, since the mid-1980s states all over the world have also engaged in deregulating markets and privatizing public companies, particularly in strategic, profitable sectors, such as energy, telecommunications, media, and finance.[51] In many cases, particularly in Latin America, it can be argued that liberalization and privatization have opened up investment opportunities, increased productivity in privatized companies, induced technological modernization and, ultimately, spurred economic growth overall, as was shown by the cases of Chile in the 1980s and of Brazil, Argentina, and Peru in the 1990s.[52] However, deregulation *per se* or privatization *per se* are not developmental mechanisms. Under the conditions of a globalized capitalist economy they are often prerequisites for economic growth. But countries that are left exclusively to the impulses of market forces, in a world where established power relationships of governments and multinational corporations bend and shape market trends, become extremely vulnerable to volatile financial flows and technological dependency.[53] After the immediate benefits of liberalization (for example, massive inflows of fresh capital searching for new opportunities in emergent markets) dissolve in the real economy of the country, economic shock therapy tends to substitute for

[49]   Allen (1981a); Johnson (1982, 1995); Amsdem (1979, 1989); Castells (1992); Evans (1995).
[50]   Tyson (1992); Johnson et al. (eds) (1989).
[51]   Haggard and Kaufman (eds) (1992).
[52]   Calderon and dos Santos (1995); Frankel et al. (1990), Gereffi and Wyman (eds) (1990); Massad and Eyzaguirre (1990); *Economist* (1995c).
[53]   Stallings (1993).

consumption euphoria, as Spain realized after the 1992 feasts, and Mexico and Argentina discovered in 1994–5.

Thus, surprising as it may be to emphasize the economic role of states in the age of deregulation, *it is precisely because of the interdependence and openness of international economy that states must become engaged in fostering development strategies on behalf of their economic constituencies.* Traditional economic policies managed within the boundaries of regulated national economies are increasingly ineffective, as key factors, such as monetary policy, interest rates, or technological innovation, are highly dependent on global movements. In the new, global economy, if states want to increase the wealth and power of their nations, they must enter the arena of international competition, steering their policies towards enhancing collective competitiveness of firms under their jurisdiction, as well as the quality of production factors in their territories. Deregulation and privatization may be elements of states' developmental strategy, but their impact on economic growth will depend on the actual content of these measures and on their linkage to strategies of positive intervention, such as technological and educational policies to enhance the country's endowment in informational production factors.[54] Notwithstanding the persistence of the economic ideology of out-of-this-world, unfettered markets, successful experiences of economic growth in the last two decades have often been associated with active development strategies by the state *within the context of a market economy*, particularly in the Asian Pacific, and to a lesser extent in the European Union (see volume III). The counterexample is obviously the undermining of America's competitiveness, the massive indebtedness of the United States, and the deterioration of living standards for most Americans, by the unfair, shortsighted, and ideological *laissez-faire* policies of the 1980s, as Stephen Cohen and Lester Thurow have documented.[55]

The informational, global economy is indeed a highly politicized economy. Stepped-up market competition played on a global scale takes place under conditions of managed trade. Rapid technological change combines entrepreneurial innovation with deliberate government strategies in supporting research and targeting technology. Countries that fall victims to their own ideology see their technological and economic positions rapidly deteriorate relative to others. Thus, the new economy, based upon socio-economic restructuring and technological revolution will be shaped, to some extent, according to political processes played out in and by the state.

[54]   Sagasti and Araoz (eds) (1988); Castells and Laserna (1989).
[55]   Cohen (1993); Thurow (1992).

The historical specificity of informationalism

A complex picture emerges regarding the process of historical development of the new informational economy. This complexity explains why highly aggregated statistical data cannot reflect directly the extent and pace of economic transformation under the impact of technological change. The informational economy is a distinctive socio-economic system in relationship to the industrial economy, but not because they differ in the sources of their productivity growth. In both cases, knowledge and information processing are critical elements in economic growth, as can be illustrated by the history of the science-based chemical industry[56] or by the managerial revolution that created Fordism.[57] **What is distinctive is the eventual realization of the productivity potential contained in the mature industrial economy because of the shift toward a technological paradigm based on information technologies.** The new technological paradigm changed first the scope and dynamics of the industrial economy, creating a global economy and fostering a new wave of competition between existing economic agents as well as between them and a legion of newcomers. This new competition, played out by firms but conditioned by the state, led to substantial technological changes in processes and products that made some firms, some sectors, and some areas more productive. Yet, at the same time, creative destruction did occur in large segments of the economy, also affecting disproportionately firms, sectors, regions, and countries. The net result in the first stage of the informational revolution was thus a mixed blessing for economic progress. Furthermore, the generalization of knowledge-based production and management to the whole realm of economic processes on a global scale requires fundamental social, cultural, and institutional transformations that, if the historical record of other technological revolutions is considered, will take some time. This is why the economy is informational, not just information-based, because the cultural-institutional attributes of the whole social system must be included in the diffusion and implementation of the new technological paradigm, as the industrial economy was not merely based on the use of new sources of energy for manufacturing but on the emergence of an industrial culture, characterized by a new social and technical division of labor.

Thus, while the informational/global economy is distinct from the industrial economy, it does not oppose its logic. It subsumes it

[56] Hohenberg (1967).
[57] Coriat (1990).

through technological deepening, embodying knowledge and information in all processes of material production and distribution on the
basis of a gigantic leap forward in the reach and scope of the circulation sphere. In other words: the industrial economy had to become
informational and global or collapse. A case in point is the dramatic
breakdown of the hyperindustrial society, the Soviet Union, because
of its structural inability to shift into the informational paradigm and
to pursue its growth in relative isolation from the international
economy (see volume III). An additional argument to support this
interpretation refers to the process of increasingly divergent development paths in the Third World, in fact ending the very notion of
"a Third World,"[58] on the basis of the differential ability of countries
and economic agents to link up with informational processes and to
compete in the global economy.[59] Thus, the shift from industrialism
to informationalism is not the historical equivalent of the transition
from agricultural to industrial economies, and cannot be equated to
the emergence of the service economy. There are informational agriculture, informational manufacturing, and informational service
activities that produce and distribute on the basis of information and
knowledge embodied in the work process by the increasing power of
information technologies. What has changed is not the kind of activities humankind is engaged on, but its technological ability to use as
a direct productive force what distinguishes our species as a biological
oddity: its superior capacity to process symbols.

The Global Economy: Genesis, Structure, and Dynamics

The informational economy is global. A global economy is a historically new reality, distinct from a world economy. A world economy,
that is an economy in which capital accumulation proceeds
throughout the world, has existed in the West at least since the
sixteenth century, as Fernand Braudel and Immanuel Wallerstein
have taught us.[60] **A global economy is something different: it is an
economy with the capacity to work as a unit in real time on a planetary
scale.** While the capitalist mode of production is characterized by its
relentless expansion, always trying to overcome limits of time and

---

[58]   Harris (1987).
[59]   Castells and Tyson (1988); Kincaid and Portes (eds) (1994); Katz (ed.)
(1987); Fajnzylber (1990).
[60]   Braudel (1967); Wallerstein (1974).

space, it is only in the late twentieth century that the world economy was able to become truly global on the basis of the new infrastructure provided by information and communication technologies. This globality concerns the core processes and elements of the economic system.

Capital is managed around the clock in globally integrated financial markets working in real time for the first time in history:[61] billion dollars-worth of transactions take place in seconds in the electronic circuits throughout the globe. Table 2.7 provides a measure of the phenomenal growth and dimension of transborder financial flows for major market economies: their share of GDP increased by a factor of about 10 in 1980–92. New technologies allow capital to be shuttled back and forth between economies in very short time, so that capital, and therefore savings and investment, are interconnected worldwide, from banks to pension funds, stock exchange markets, and currency exchange. Since currencies are interdependent, so are economies everywhere. Although major corporate centers provide the human resources and facilities necessary to manage an increasingly complex financial network,[62] it is in the information networks connecting such centers that the actual operations of capital take place. Capital flows become at the same time global and increasingly autonomous *vis-à-vis* the actual performance of economies.[63]

Labor markets are not truly global, except for a small but growing segment of professionals and scientists (see chapter 4), but labor is a global resource at least in three ways:[64] firms may choose to locate in a variety of places worldwide to find the labor supply they need, be it in terms of skills, costs, or social control; firms everywhere may also solicit highly skilled labor from everywhere, and they will obtain it provided they offer the right remuneration and working conditions; and labor will enter any market on its own initiative, coming from anywhere, when human beings are pushed from their homes by poverty and war or pulled towards a new life by hope for their children. Immigrant labor from all over the planet may flow to wherever jobs are, but its mobility is increasingly restricted by xenophobic movements leading to much stricter immigration controls. Indeed, citizens and politicians of affluent societies seem to be determined to keep barbarians of impoverished areas off their world, protected behind the walls of immigration authorities.[65]

---

[61]   Chesnais (1994: 206–48); Shirref (1994); Heavey (1994); *Economist* (1995b); Khoury and Ghosh (1987).

[62]   Sassen (1991).

[63]   Lee et al. (1994); Chesnais (1994: 206–48).

[64]   Sengenberger and Campbell (eds) (1994).

Table 2.7 Transborder financial flows, 1980–92 (% of GDP)[a]

Country	1980	1981	1982	1983	1984	1985	1986	1987	1988	1989	1990	1991	1992
United States	9.3	9.4	11.8	15.9	20.8	36.4	71.7	86.1	85.3	104.3	92.1	98.8	109.3
Japan	n.a.	n.a.	n.a.	n.a.	25.0	62.8	163.7	147.3	128.5	156.7	120.7	92.9	72.2
Germany	7.5	7.8	12.5	16.0	20.7	33.9	45.6	55.2	60.7	67.3	61.1	59.2	90.8
France	n.a.	n.a.	8.4	13.8	14.0	21.4	28.0	37.3	34.6	51.6	53.6	78.9	122.2
Italy	1.1	1.4	1.0	1.4	1.9	4.0	6.9	8.1	10.3	17.6	26.6	60.4	118.4
UK	n.a.	n.a.	n.a.	n.a.	n.a.	366.1	648.9	830.1	642.6	766.6	689.0	1,016.6	n.a.
Canada	9.6	8.0	7.4	10.5	15.8	26.7	40.5	58.9	39.1	54.5	64.1	81.4	111.2

[a] Estimated purchases and scales of stocks between residents and non-residents.
n.a. = not available.

Source: Bank for International Settlements, *62nd Annual Report*, 15 June 1992.

Science, technology, and information are also organized in global flows, albeit in an asymmetrical structure. Proprietary technological information plays a major role in creating competitive advantage, and R&D centers are heavily concentrated in certain areas and in some companies and institutions.[66] However, the characteristics of new productive knowledge favor its diffusion. Innovation centers cannot live in secrecy without drying up their innovative capacity. Communication of knowledge in a global network of interaction is at the same time the condition to keep up with fast advancement of knowledge and the obstacle to its proprietary control.[67] In addition, the capacity to innovate is fundamentally stored in human brains, which makes possible the diffusion of innovation by the movement of scientists, engineers, and managers between organizations and production systems.

In spite of the persistence of protectionism and restrictions to free trade, markets for goods and services are becoming increasingly globalized.[68] This does not mean that all firms sell worldwide. But it does mean that the strategic aim of firms, large and small, is to sell wherever they can throughout the world, either directly or via their linkage with networks that operate in the world market. And there are indeed, to a large extent thanks to new communication and transportation technologies, channels and opportunities to sell everywhere. This statement must be qualified, however, by the fact that domestic markets account for the largest share of GDP in most countries, and that in developing countries, informal economies, mainly aimed at local markets, constitute the bulk of urban employment. Also, some major economies, for instance Japan, have important segments (for example, public works, retail trade) sheltered from worldwide competition by government protection and by cultural/institutional insulation.[69] And public services and government institutions throughout the world, accounting for between one-third and over a half of jobs in each country, are, and will be, by and large removed from international competition. Yet, the *dominant segments and firms, the strategic cores* of all economies are deeply connected to the world market, and their fate is a function of their performance in such a market. The dynamism of domestic markets depends ultimately on the capacity of domestic firms and networks of firms to compete

[65] Baldwin-Evans and Schain (eds) (1995); Portes and Rumbault (1990); Soysal (1994).

[66] Sagasti and Alberto (1988); Soete (1991); Johnston and Sasson (1986).

[67] Castells and Hall (1994); Arthur (1985); Hall and Preston (1988); Soete (1991).

[68] Andrieu et al. (eds) (1992); Daniels (1993); Chesnais (1994: 181–206).

[69] Tyson (1992).

globally.[70] Here again, the globalization of markets has only been made possible in the late twentieth century by dramatic changes in transportation and communication technologies, for information, people, goods, and services.

However, the most important transformation underlying the emergence of a global economy concerns the management of production and distribution, and of the production process itself.[71] The dominant segments of most economic sectors (either for goods or for services) are organized worldwide in their actual operating procedures, forming what Robert Reich has labeled "the global web." The production process incorporates components produced in many different locations by different firms, and assembled for specific purposes and specific markets in a new form of production and commercialization: high-volume, flexible, customized production. Such a web does not correspond only to the vision of a global corporation obtaining its supplies from different units around the world. The new production system relies on a combination of strategic alliances and ad hoc cooperation projects between corporations, decentralized units of each major corporation, and networks of small and medium enterprises connecting among themselves and/or with large corporations or networks of corporations. These transborder production networks operate under two main configurations: in Gereffi's terminology, producer-driven commodity chains (in industries such as automobiles, computers, aircraft, electrical machinery), and buyer-driven commodity chains (in industries such as garment, footwear, toys, housewares). What is fundamental in this web-like industrial structure it that it is territorially spread throughout the world, and its geometry keeps changing, as a whole and for each individual unit. In such a structure, the most important element for a successful managerial strategy is to position a firm (or a given industrial project) in the web in such a way as to gain competitive advantage for its relative position. Thus, the structure tends to reproduce itself and to keep expanding as competition goes on, so deepening the global character of the economy. For the firm to operate in such a variable geometry of production and distribution a very flexible form of management is required, a form that is dependent on the flexibility of the firm itself and on the access to communication and production technologies suited to such flexibility (see chapter 3). For instance, to be able to assemble parts produced from very distant sources, it is necessary to have, on the one hand, a microelectronics-based

---

[70] Chesnais (1994); UNCTAD (1993); Reich (1991); Stallings (1993); Porter (1990).
[71] BRIE (1992); Dicken (1992); Reich (1991); Gereffi (1993); Imai (1990b).

precision quality in the fabrication process, so that the parts are compatible to the smallest detail of specification;[72] on the other hand, a computer-based flexibility enabling the factory to program production runs according to the volume and customized characteristics required by each order.[73] In addition, the management of inventories will depend on the existence of an adequate network of trained suppliers, whose performance was enhanced in the last decade by new technological capability to adjust demand and supply on-line.[74]

The limits to globalization

After reviewing the operation of current economic processes, it appears that the new, informational economy works on a global scale. Yet the notion of globalization has come under spirited attack, particularly from Stephen Cohen.[75] Some of the criticism is based on a commonsense, often forgotten observation: the international economy is not global *yet.* Markets, even for strategic industries and major firms, are still far away from being fully integrated; capital flows are restricted by currency and banking regulations (although the offshoring of financial centers and the prevalence of computer transactions tend to increasingly circumvent such regulations);[76] the mobility of labor is undermined by immigration controls and people's xenophobia; and multinational corporations still keep most of their assets and their strategic command centers in their historically defined "home" nations.[77] However, this is a very important objection only when dealing with economic policy issues, a concern that is marginal for the intellectual purpose of this book. If the argument is simply that the trends toward globalization are not yet fully realized, it would be only a matter of time down the historical sequence to observe in all clarity the profile of the new, global economy.

But there is something else in the critical appraisal of the notion of globalization: in its simplistic version[78] the globalization thesis ignores the persistence of the nation state and the crucial role of government in influencing the structure and dynamics of the new economy (see, in particular, the forceful critique by Stephen Cohen and the group of BRIE researchers on the matter;[79] as well as the argument by Martin

[72]   Henderson (1989).
[73]   Coriat (1990).
[74]   Gereffi and Wyman (eds) (1990); Tetsuro and Steven (eds) (1994).
[75]   Cohen (1990).
[76]   Bertrand and Noyelle (1988).
[77]   Carnoy et al. (1993).
[78]   Ohmae (1990).
[79]   Cohen (1990); BRIE (1992); Sandholtz et al. (1992).

Carnoy concerning the role of the nation state[80]). Evidence shows that government regulation and policies affect the international boundaries and structure of the global economy.[81] There is not, and there will not be in the foreseeable future, a *fully integrated*, open world market for labor, technology, goods, and services, as long as nation states (or associations of nation states, such as the European Union) exist, and as long as governments are there to foster the interests of their citizens and of firms in the territories under their jurisdiction, in the global competition. Furthermore, corporate nationality is not irrelevant to corporate behavior, as is shown by the stream of research produced by the United Nations Center on Transnational Corporations. This is quite obvious to observers from developing countries, but it is also the conclusion reached by Martin Carnoy after reviewing the literature on this question concerning multinationals in advanced economies. Japanese multinationals have been supported fully by the Japanese Government, and they have kept their main financial and technological assets at home. European multinationals have been the object of systematic support by their own governments, as well as by the European Union, both in technology and in market protection. German multinationals (such as Volkswagen) have disinvested in West European countries to undertake financially risky investments in East Germany to fulfill the national ideal of German unification.[82] American multinationals (for example, IBM) have followed the instructions of their Government, sometimes reluctantly, when it came to withholding technology or restraining trade with countries at odds with US foreign policy. Accordingly, the US Government has supported technology projects for American corporations or intervened in business transactions in the name of national security interests. Indeed, some analysts have stressed the need to protect the American microelectronics industry from Japanese unfair competition to prevent Japan from controlling strategic military inputs.[83] The US Defense Department is confronting, in some areas, the kind of military technological dependency that countries around the world, including West European nations, had been experiencing for decades *vis-à-vis* key technology held by American corporations.

Furthermore, it is rightly claimed that market penetration is not reciprocal. While the American and, to a lesser extent, European

---

[80]   Carnoy et al. (1993).
[81]   Johnson et al. (1989); Evans (1995).
[82]   UNCTAD (1993); Carnoy et al. (1993); Okimoto (1984); Johnson et al. (1989); Abbeglen and Stalk (1985); Van Tulder and Junne (1988); Dunning (ed.) (1985); Cohen (1990).
[83]   Reich (1991); Borrus (1988).

economies are relatively open markets (for trade and for foreign direct investment), the Japanese economy, as well as the Chinese, Korean, Taiwanese, Indian, or Russian economies, remain highly protected. For instance, in 1989–91 Japanese direct investment in the US amounted to 46% of total Japanese direct investment abroad, and in the European Union, to 23%. However, both US and European direct investment in Japan amounted to only about 1% of their total direct investment abroad.[84] Because the mentioned Asian economies represented over one-fifth of world markets in the early 1990s this "exception" to the formation of a world market is significant.[85]

Nevertheless, the overall, dominant trend points toward the increasing interpenetration of markets, particularly after the reasonably successful Uruguay Round of GATT, the birth of the World Trade Organization, the slow but steady progress in European unification, the signing of the North American Free Trade Agreement, the intensification of economic exchanges within Asia, the gradual incorporation of Eastern Europe and Russia into the global economy, and the growing role played by trade and foreign investment in economic growth everywhere. Furthermore, the quasi-total integration of capital markets makes all economies globally interdependent. Yet, because of the persistence of nations and national governments, and because of the role of governments in using economic competition as a tool of political strategy, boundaries and cleavages between major economic regions are likely to remain for a long period, establishing a regional differentiation of the global economy.

The regional differentiation of the global economy

The global economy is internally diversified into three major regions and their areas of influence: North America (including Canada and Mexico, after NAFTA); the European Union (particularly after some revised version of the Maastricht Treaty trickles down into policy-making); and the Asian Pacific region, centered around Japan, but with the increasing weight of South Korea, Indonesia, Taiwan, Singapore, Overseas Chinese, and, most of all, China itself, in the region's economic potential. Barbara Stallings has proposed an insightful analysis of simultaneous concentration and regionalization of the global economy, arguing that

> present data show that trade and investment are increasing *both* within the so-called triad area (the United States, Japan, and

[84] Stallings (1993).
[85] CEPII (1992).

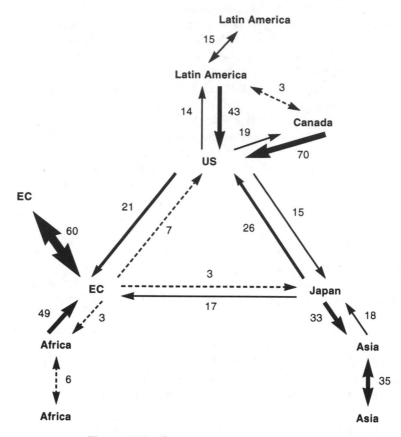

Figure 2.2   Structure of world trade, 1991
Figures are percentages of total trade (exports plus imports). Weight
of lines between trading partners indicates intensity of exchanges.
Source: International Monetary Fund, *Direction of Trade Statistics
Yearbook, 1992*, Washington, DC: IMF, 1992; elaborated by Stallings
(1993).

Europe) *and* within the three blocs. Other areas are being
marginalized in the process. . . . [The concept is] nonhegemonic
interdependence. The different types of capitalism that exist in
the three regions have given rise to differential economic performance. The result is conflict *and* cooperation, divergence *and*
convergence.[86]

From a different perspective, Lester Thurow reaches a similar con-

[86]   Stallings (1993: 21).

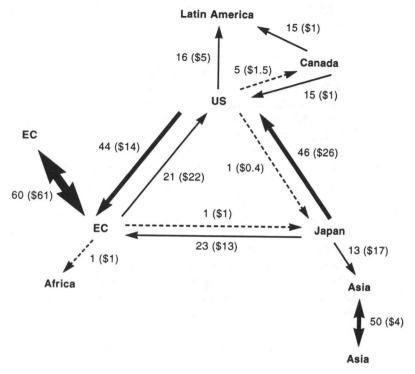

Figure 2.3   Structure of world direct foreign investment, 1989–91
(average)
Figures are percentages of total direct investment; those in
parentheses are absolute values in US$ bn. Weight of lines between
trading partners indicates intensity of exchanges.
Sources: For US: *Survey of Current Business,* August 1992; for Japan:
Ministry of Finance, unpublished data; for Europe: UNTNC: *World
Investment Report, 1992, Survey of Current Business* (inflow to US), and
IMF, *Balance of Payments Yearbook, 1992.* Other figures are estimates.
Data elaborated by Stallings (1993).

clusion, although he emphasizes the process of growing competition
between the three regions, and the undermining of American hegemony first by Japan and, in the future, by the European Union.[87]
Around this triangle of wealth, power, and technology, the rest of the
world becomes organized in a hierarchical and asymmetrically interdependent web, as different countries and regions compete to attract
capital, human skills, and technology to their shores. Stallings

---

[87]   Thurow (1992).

illustrates the argument by mapping flows of trade and foreign investment between the three centers, and between each one of them and their areas of influence, as shown in figures 2.2 and 2.3.

The notion of a regionalized, global economy is not a contradiction in terms. There is indeed a global economy because economic agents do operate in a global network of interaction that transcends national and geographic boundaries. But such an economy is not politically undifferentiated, and national governments play a major role in influencing economic processes. Yet the economic accounting unit is the global economy, because it is at such a global scale that strategic production and trade activities take place, as well as capital accumulation, knowledge generation, and information management. The political differentiation of this global system defines economic processes and shapes the strategies of competing agents. In this sense, **I consider internal regionalization to be a systemic attribute of the informational/global economy.** This is because states are the expression of societies, not of economies. **What becomes crucial, in the informational economy, is the complex interaction between historically rooted political institutions and increasingly globalized economic agents.**

The segmentation of the global economy

An additional qualification is essential in defining the contours of the global economy: *it is not a planetary economy.* In other words, the global economy does not embrace all economic processes in the planet, it does not include all territories, and it does not include all people in its workings, although it does affect directly or indirectly the livelihood of the entire humankind. While its effects reach out to the whole planet, **its actual operation and structure concern only segments of economic structures, countries, and regions, in proportions that vary according to the particular position of a country or region in the international division of labor.**[88] Furthermore, such a position can be transformed over time, placing countries, regions, and populations constantly on the move, which is tantamount to structurally induced instability. Thus, the new, global economic system is at the same time highly dynamic, highly exclusionary, and highly unstable in its boundaries. While dominant segments of all national economies are linked into the global web, segments of countries, regions, economic sectors, and local societies are disconnected from the processes of accumulation and consumption that characterize the informational/global

[88] Sengenberger and Campbell (eds); UNCTAD (1993); Portes et al. (eds) (1989); Carnoy et al. (1993); Sassen (1988); Mingione (1991).

economy. I do not pretend that these "marginal" sectors are not socially connected to the rest of the system, since there is no such thing as a social vacuum. But their social and economic logic is based upon mechanisms clearly distinct from those of the informational economy.[89] Thus, while the informational economy shapes the entire planet, and in this sense it is indeed global, most people in the planet do not work for or buy from the informational/global economy. Yet all economic and social processes do relate to the structurally dominant logic of such an economy. How and why such a connection is operated, and who and what is connected and disconnected over time is a fundamental feature of our societies that requires specific, careful analysis (see "The Rise of the Fourth World" in volume III).

The sources of competitiveness in the global economy

The structure of the global economy is produced by the dynamics of competition between economic agents and between the locales (countries, regions, economic areas) where they are situated. Such competition is played out on the basis of factors that are specific to the new, informational economy, in a global system articulated by a network based on information technologies. Four main processes determine the form and outcome of competition.

The first is *technological capacity*. Under such a notion should be included the science base of the production and management process, the R&D strength, the human resources necessary for technological innovation, the adequate utilization of new technologies, and the level of their diffusion into the whole network of economic interaction. In other words, technological capacity is not simply what results from adding up various elements, but is an attribute of a system: what I called the science–technology–industry–society system (the STIS system).[90] It refers to the appropriate articulation of science, technology, management, and production in a system of complementaries, each level being provided, by the educational system, with the necessary human resources in skills and quantity. The excellence of a given element in a given economic unit, for instance a strong science base or a long manufacturing tradition in a country, is not enough to ensure the successful adoption of a new technological paradigm based on information technologies. It is the articulation of different elements that becomes critical. This is why technological capacity can hardly be the attribute of individual firms (even giant

---

[89] I elaborated on the new processes of dualism in a comparative perspective in Castells (1990).

[90] Castells et al. (1986).

global firms such as IBM). It is related to production complexes that tend to have a territorial basis, although they connect to each other once they have established themselves in a given territory, and they diffuse and interact globally via telecommunication/transportation networks.[91] The operational expression of this production form in advanced technological systems is what BRIE researchers call the "supply base":

> By the supply base of an economy we mean the parts, components, subsystems, materials, and equipment technologies available for new product and process development, as well as the structure of relations among the firms that supply and use these elements.[92]

However, a technologically advanced "supply base" needs to be anchored in a fully fledged STIS system that acts as the provider of the components of the supply base and as the recipient of feedback effects resulting from technological learning in the production process.

Available evidence shows that competitiveness of industrial sectors in OECD countries is largely determined by the technological level of each sector. Similarly, the ability of countries to compete in the international economy is directly related to their technological potential.[93]

The second major factor influencing competitiveness is *access to a large, integrated, affluent market*, such as the European Union, the United States/North American Trade Zone or, to a lesser extent, Japan. The best competitive position is the one that enables firms to operate unchallenged within one of these large markets, and still have the possibility of access to the others with as few restrictions as possible.[94] Thus, the larger and deeper the integration of a given economic area, the greater the chances of spurring productivity and profitability for firms locating in that zone.[95] Therefore, the dynamics of trade and foreign investment between countries and macro-regions affect decisively the performance of individual firms or networks of firms.

The third factor that explains competitive performance in the global market is *the differential between production costs at the production site and prices at the market of destination* – a calculation that is more appropriate than the simplistic formula that focuses only on labor costs, since other cost factors may be as important (for example, land

[91]   Castells and Hall (1994).
[92]   Borrus and Zysman (1992: 25).
[93]   Dosi et al. (1988a); Dosi and Soete (1983); OECD (1992); Soete (1991); Castells and Tyson (1988); Tyson (1992).
[94]   Lafay and Herzog (1989).
[95]   Cecchini (1988); Spence and Hazard (1988).

costs, taxes, environmental regulations, and so on).[96] However, this factor can only affect competitiveness if the two preceding factors are integrated positively in the firm's commercial strategy. That is, the potential profit involved in lower production costs can only be realized if there is access to a large, rich market. Also, cost-price differentials are no substitute for technological capacity. Given the level of technological diffusion worldwide, a competitive strategy based on low cost still needs to operate within the information technology paradigm. The winning formula is the addition of technological/managerial excellence and production costs lower than those of competitors, lower costs and technological excellence being understood in terms relative to the characteristics of each product.[97] This observation is critical because it precludes in fact the possibility for developing countries to compete on the basis of low costs if they are not able, at the same time, to adapt their production system to the requirements of the information age.

Finally, competitiveness in the new global economy, as stated above, seems to be highly dependent on *the political capacity of national and supranational institutions to steer the growth strategy of those countries or areas under their jurisdiction,* including the creation of competitive advantages in the world market for those firms considered to serve the interests of the populations in their territories by generating jobs and income. Governments' actions are not limited to managing trade: they also may provide the necessary support for technological development and human resources training, the fundamental basis for the informational economy to work. Furthermore, government markets (for example, defense, telecommunications), and government subsidies and soft loans (for R&D, training, exports) have been critical in positioning firms in the global competition.[98] Thus, the active intervention by Japanese and South Korean governments has been decisive in fostering the competitiveness of their firms. European self-sufficiency in the critical commercial aviation industry could never have been achieved without decisive help from French, German, British, and Spanish governments to launch and sell the Airbus. The ideology of positive non-intervention practiced by the Reagan and

[96]   Cohen et al. (1985); Krugman (ed.) (1986). For an analysis of sources of competitiveness in the new global economy on the basis of experiences in the Asian Pacific, see my monograph, and the economic analyses on which I relied, most of them from Asian scholars, on the sources of economic development of Hong Kong and Singapore: Castells et al. (1990).
[97]   Katz (ed.) (1987); Dahlman et al. (1987).
[98]   Freeman (ed.) (1990); Johnson (1982); Deyo (ed.) (1987); Tyson and Zysman (1983); Castells (1989a); Evans (1995); Reich (1991); Amsdem (1989); Johnson et al. (eds) (1988); Cohen (1993).

Thatcher administrations in the midst of world turmoil wrecked the manufacturing and trade bases of both the American and British economies in the 1980s. On the other hand, the mixed record of the European Union's interventionist policies in sectors as diverse as electronics, automobiles, and agriculture shows that there are limits to governments' capacity to reverse technological or economic decline (for example, French farmers' productivity; European microelectronics manufacturing). However, such governmental efforts made it possible to help European competitiveness in some critical market segments (consumer electronics, telecommunications, aerospace, pharmaceuticals, nuclear energy, and so on), while buying time for restructuring in other sectors (automobiles, steel).

The above-mentioned factors jointly determine the dynamics and forms of competition between firms, regions, and countries in the new global economy, thus ushering in a new international division of labor.

The Newest International Division of Labor

The global economy emerging from informational-based production and competition is characterized by its *interdependence*, its *asymmetry*, its *regionalization*, the *increasing diversification within each region*, its *selective inclusiveness*, its *exclusionary segmentation*, and, as a result of all these features, an extraordinarily *variable geometry* that tends to dissolve historical, economic geography.

I shall try to assess this newest pattern of international division of labor in the late twentieth century[99] by focusing sequentially on each one of these characteristics. To support the argument I shall use, unless indicated otherwise, the same data source, to avoid problems of statistical comparability between countries and periods of time. Thus, when referring to broad areas of the global economy, data are cited from the model of the world economy 1990–2000 elaborated in 992 by Centre d'Etudes Prospectives et d'Information Internationales (CEPII), a research institution linked to the French Prime Minister's Office, working in cooperation with technical staff of the French Government's Commissariat du Plan.[100] Naturally, data for 2000 are projections from the model. Sources for other global data are the World Bank's Development Reports.

[99]　I use the term "newest international division of labor" to differentiate my analysis from the somewhat simplistic perspective introduced in the 1970s by "new international division of labor" theorists, as represented, for instance, by the powerful book by Froebel et al. (1980).
[100]　CEPII (1992).

Changing patterns of international division of labor in the informational/global economy: triad power, the rise of the Pacific, and the end of the Third World

As mentioned above, the global economy is still far from being a single, undifferentiated system. Yet the interdependence of its processes and agents has advanced at a fast pace in a short period of time. For the nine major manufacturing industrial sectors considered in CEPII's MIMOSA model, the proportion of internationally traded manufactured goods in total world production for the same manufacturing sectors in 1973 was 15.3%, in 1980 19.7%, in 1988 22.2%, and in the year 2000 should reach 28.5%. If we consider the growth of foreign investment for the same sectors, the proportion of manufacturing production under foreign control for the whole world was 13.2% in 1973, 14.7% in 1980, 16.5% in 1988, and should reach 24.8% in 2000, that is almost doubling in the last quarter of the century. Interdependence is particularly strong between Western Europe and the United States. In the year 2000 Western European companies are projected to control 14% of American manufacturing production, and American companies 16% of Western European production. As stated above, Japan is also deeply embedded in the trade and investment networks in both Western Europe and North America,[101] but in this case the level of penetration is not reciprocal, since Japan is, for the time being, less open to imports and almost closed to direct foreign investment (less than 1% of total investment).

International trade is concentrated in the exchanges between Western Europe, the United States, and the Asian Pacific, with a clear advantage for the latter region. Thus, as an illustration of the intertwining of trade flows, in 1992 the European Union exported goods and services worth $95 billion to the US and imported from America $111 billion; it exported $96 billion to the Asian Pacific, and imported $153 billion. As for the US, it exported goods and services worth $128 billion to the Pacific Rim and imported from that region a staggering $215 billion.[102] If we add financial interdependence, technology transfer, and alliances, interlockings, and joint ventures between firms, it is obvious that the core of the global economy is a tightly interdependent network between USA, Japan, and Western Europe that is becoming increasingly so, constituting what Ohmae labeled years ago "Triad Power."[103] Around this core, as argued by

[101]   Glickman and Woodward (1987); Humbert (ed.) (1990).
[102]   Sources: for Europe, German Ministry of Economy; for US, US Department of Commerce.
[103]   Ohmae (1985).

Barbara Stallings,[104] all the other areas of the world organize their economies in a multiple dependency relationship. However, patterns are changing. Japan has substantially increased its investments in Asia in recent years, as well as opening its markets to a greater extent to Asian exports, although the bulk of Japanese imports from Asia still originate from Japanese companies offshore.[105] Japan is also investing heavily in Latin America, particularly in Mexico. And South American exports in the mid-1990s are more oriented toward the European Union and the Asian Pacific than toward the United States.

The global economy is deeply asymmetric. But not in the simplistic form of a center, semi-periphery, and a periphery, or following an outright opposition between North and South; because there are several "centers" and several "peripheries," and because both North and South are so internally diversified as to make little analytical sense in using these categories.[106] Still, a group of countries that corresponds, approximately, to the membership of the Organization for Economic Cooperation and Development (OECD), concentrates an overwhelming proportion of technological capacity, capital, markets, and industrial production. If we add to the OECD the four newly industrialized countries of Asia, in 1988 the three major economic regions represented 72.8% of world's manufacturing production, and in 2000 their share should still amount to 69.5%, while the population of these three regions in 2000 would only be 15.7% of world population. The concentration of resources is even greater at the core of the system, in the G-7 countries, particularly in terms of technology, skills, and informational infrastrcture, key determinants of competitiveness. Thus, in 1990 the G-7 countries accounted for 90.5% of high-technology manufacturing in the world, and were holding 80.4% of global computing power.[107] The differential in human resources is critical: while the world average of scientific and technical manpower in 1985 was 23,442 per million population, the actual figure for developing countries was 8,263; for developed countries, 70,452; and for North America, 126,200, that is more than 15 times the level of developing countries. As for R&D expenditures, while North America accounted for 42.8% of the world's total in 1990, Latin America and Africa *together* represented less than 1% of the same total.[108]

[104]   Stallings (1993).
[105]   Doherty (ed.) (1995); Cohen and Borrus (1995b).
[106]   Coutrot and Husson (1993); Harris (1987).
[107]   US National Science Board (1991).
[108]   UNESCO (1990).

Thus, the new competitive paradigm, based on technological capacity,[109] while inducing interdependency in the new global economy, has also reinforced dependency in an asymmetrical relationship that, by and large, has reinforced patterns of domination created by previous forms of dependency throughout history.

However, this apparent historical continuity must be corrected by observing processes of diversification taking place both in the so-called "North" and in the so-called "South" under the impact of the factors of competitiveness I presented above. First of all, a dramatic realignment in the distribution of capital, technology, and manufacturing capacity has taken place among the three dominant regions in the last third of the century, to the benefit of the Asian Pacific Region (see figure 2.4). Adding the newly industrialized Asian countries to Japan to form the "developed Asia" region, such a region is poised to become the largest industrial region of the world, with 26.9% of world manufacturing in the year 2000, against 24.6% for Western Europe, and just 18% for North America. And this is without counting China, whose rapid growth and technological modernization will make it a major economic power before long. Furthermore, the importance of manufacturing in developed Asia, extrapolating on the basis of current tendencies, would be particularly significant in electronics, the critical sector for the informational economy, and may also take the lead in automobile manufacturing.[110]

In addition, if we include in the picture the growing linkages between Japan and the "four tigers" with China and the South East Asian region, what seems to be emerging at the turn of century is a powerful, semi-integrated Asian Pacific economy that has become a major center of capital accumulation in the world.[111] The Asian Pacific economy is internally differentiated among at least five distinct networks of economic power: the Japanese corporations; the Korean corporations; American multinational corporations, particularly in electronics and finance, established in the area for many years; the powerful networks of ethnic Chinese capital, connecting Hong Kong, Taipei, Singapore, and "overseas" Chinese business groups (often operating through Hong Kong), all of them with direct linkages to China, forming what observers are calling "the China Circle"; the

---

[109]   Foray and Freeman (eds) (1992).
[110]   CEPII (1992); Guerrieri (1991); Mortimore (1992); Bergsten and Noland (eds) (1993).
[111]   Urata, in Bergsten and Noland (1993); Soesastro and Pangestu (eds) (1990); Ernst (1994b); *Business Week* (1994c); Bergsten and Noland (1993); Ernst and O'Connor (1992); Ernst, in Doherty (ed.) (1995).

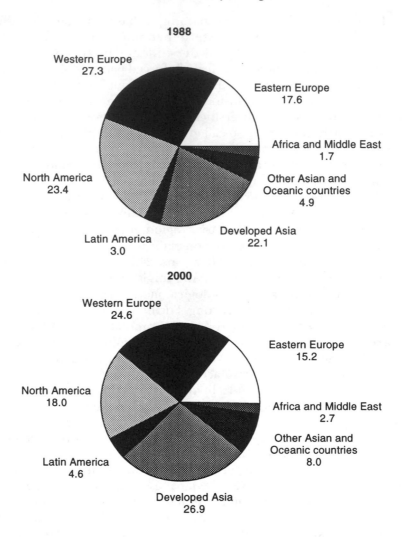

Figure 2.4   Share by region of the world's manufacturing
production: 2000 projections (%)
Source: CEPII calculations from the Industrie 2000 model and the
CHELEM and PIM data bases.

Chinese Government and Chinese provincial and local governments, with their diversified financial and industrial interests.[112]

Indeed, the rapid incorporation of China's new market economy into the global system is the economic miracle of the last decade. China's GDP grew at an average rate of 9.4% in 1980–91, and at a rate of 12.8% in 1992, and 13.4% in 1993.[113] During the same period, China's exports increased over 11% per year on average. Foreign direct investment in China grew from under $1billion in 1983 to $26 billion in 1993, making China the second-largest investment host country in the world after the US. Of this investment 70% came from Hong Kong and Taiwan, giving substance to the notion of the "China circle." You-tien Hsing has analyzed the social and political linkages created between Taiwanese and Hong Kong investors and local and provincial officials in Southern China: this is the true face of new Chinese capitalism.[114]

The economic power accumulated in the Asian Pacific region, even without counting Japan, is staggering. In 1993, East Asian governments had foreign currency reserves of $250 billion, three times those of Japan. In addition, private corporations outside Japan were holding another $600 billion in cash reserves. Savings were expected to increase by $550 billion per year during the 1990s, so that by the year 2000 the gross domestic product of East Asia (including China) could reach $2 trillion, and surpass Japan.[115] According to another calculation, taking together China, Hong Kong, and Taiwan (which would correspond to the stricter definition of the "China circle"), in 1993 the three economies together were approaching two-thirds of Japanese GDP.[116] An indirect and substantial impact of China's entry into the Asian economy has been the reaction by South East Asian countries, particularly Indonesia and Thailand, to stimulate their growth and to open up their economies to offer alternatives to foreign investment.[117] Vietnam and the Philippines are following this example.[118]

Thus, if we consider together the lasting technological and economic power of Japan, the sustained process of economic growth and international integration of China, the explosion of investment by Japanese, ethnic Chinese, and Korean firms in the East and South

[112] Sung (1994); Naughton (1994); Hsing (1994).
[113] Jia (1994).
[114] Hsing (1996).
[115] *Business Week* (1993).
[116] Estimates by Jia (1994: 3).
[117] Tan Kong Yam (1994).
[118] *Economist* (1995d).

East Asia region, the meaning of the "North" in the new global economy is definitively blurred. The emergence of Asian Pacific fast-growth capitalism is, with the end of the Soviet Empire and the process of European unification, one of the most important structural changes taking place in the world at the turn of the century. Although I shall analyze the historical roots and social consequences of this process in some detail (see "Towards the Pacific Era?" in volume III), it is important to trace back the possibility of such a phenomenon to the structural trends that, in my hypothesis, constitute the source of competitiveness in the new global economy. Among them, the ability of these countries to use new information technologies, both in processes and in products, to reverse the established pattern of the international division of labor, mainly on the base of en-dogenous processes, since American multinationals played a minor role in the process, with the exception of Malaysia and Singapore. The openness of the global economy, enabling access to major markets, and the role of governments, steering their countries' competitive-ness in the global, capitalist economy; altogether, the recentering of capital accumulation and high technology manufacturing around the Asian Pacific is a process of historical proportions whose shockwaves in the rest of the world, and particularly in Western Europe and North America, were only starting to be felt in the early 1990s.[119]

This process of extreme diversification of development trajectories is also visible at the other end of the global economy, the so-called "South," to the point that Nigel Harris was proven to be correct when announcing "the end of the Third World."[120] To be sure, there is wide-spread poverty and human suffering throughout the planet, and it will unfortunately continue to be so in the foreseeable future.[121] Indeed, there is a growing polarization of income at the world level, as shown in the calculations of the CEPII model on the evolution of GDP per capita by world areas in 1960–2000. Yet, there is also increasing differ-entiation of economic growth, technological capacity, and social conditions between areas of the world, between countries, within countries, and even within regions. Thus, South Asia, and particularly some areas of India, in the 1990s started upon a process of fast economic growth and integration into the global economy, improving over the moderate performance of the previous decade: in

[119] For an overview of the process, see Appelbaum and Henderson (eds) (1992); and Fouquin et al. (1992); Martin (1987); Wade (1990); Amsdem (1992).
[120] Harris (1987).
[121] Rodgers (ed.) (1995); Nayyar (1994); Baghwati and Srinivasan (1993); ILO-ARTEP (1993); Lachaud (1994); Lustig (1995); Tchernina (1993); Islam (1995).

the 1980s, South Asia's GDP per capita increased at an average annual rate of 3.2% (5.5% in GDP growth), contrasting to the meager 0.6% per capita growth during the 1970s. After the economic crisis of 1990, India went into a new policy of internationalization and liberalization of its economy that induced an economic boom around areas such as Ahmedabad, Bombay, Bangalore (a new node in the world's electronics industry), and New Delhi. However, economic quasi-stagnation continues in most rural areas, as well as in some major metropolitan centers such as Calcutta. Furthermore, social inequality and a new brand of unrestrained capitalism keep the majority of the Indian population, including in the most dynamic urban centers, in miserable living conditions. Sub-Saharan Africa is projected to continue to stagnate at a subhuman level. Latin America as a whole has hardly recovered from the social costs inflicted by the "lost decade" of the 1980s, in spite of its dynamic integration into the global economy in the mid-1990s. Most of the ex-Soviet Empire countries for the remaining years of the century will still be catching up with their standards of living in the 1960s. And even Asia as a whole, while experiencing substantial growth (about 6% per year on average during the 1980s, most likely to be improved in the 1990s), will still remain at an abysmal distance from living standards of developed regions, with the obvious exceptions of Japan and the four Asian tigers.

Nevertheless, there is a substantial process of development under way for millions of people in some areas, particularly in China, home of one-fifth of the world's population, but also in most of Asia (over two-thirds of humankind), and in major Latin American countries. By development I mean, for the sake of this analysis, the simultaneous process of improvement in living standards, structural change in the productive system, and growing competitiveness in the global economy. While theorizing on postindustrialism we are experiencing, toward the end of the twentieth century, one of the largest waves of industrialization in history, if we use a simple indicator such as the absolute number of manufacturing workers, at its peak in 1990 (see figure 2.5) and growing: in the Pearl River Delta alone at least 6 million new manufacturing jobs were created in the last decade. On the other hand, some rural regions of China, India, and Latin America, entire countries around the world, and large segments of the population everywhere are becoming irrelevant (*from the perspective of dominant economic interests*) in the new pattern of international division of labor, and thus they are being socially excluded.[122] To enter

[122]   Rodgers et al. (eds) (1995).

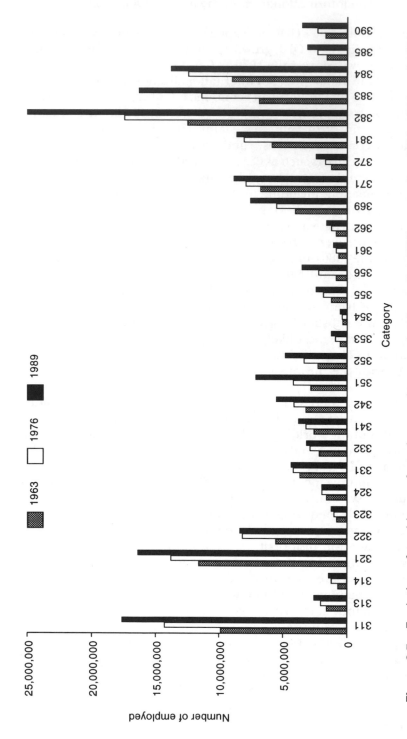

Figure 2.5 Evolution of world manufacturing employment, by three-digit ISIC categories, 1963, 1976, and 1989
Source: UNIDO; elaborated by Wieczorek (1995).

the complexity of this process of development, I shall examine sequentially the contradictory trends experienced by Latin America in the last two decades, and the structural logic that threatens to exclude most of Africa from the global economy.

Sources of growth and stagnation in the international division of labor: the changing fortunes of Latin America

Latin America, whose economic stagnation in the 1980s has been repeatedly contrasted to the East Asian development saga,[123] is a much more diversified and dynamic reality than the image presented by the dogmatic version of dependency theory.[124] Indeed, until the mid-1970s Latin America's major countries' growth rates were not far away from those of East Asia (see table 2.8). It was the "lost decade" of the 1980s, as a consequence of the debt crisis and of deterioration in terms of trade, that set back Latin America.[125] Even countries with high export performances such as Brazil had to use their earnings to cover their financial obligations, being forced to cut imports and public spending at a critical moment when international competition and technological revolution required the modernization of the productive structure.

Taking the long-term view, it is possible to say that Latin America has struggled in the half-century after the Second World War to make the transition along three distinct, albeit overlapping, models of development.[126] The first model was based on exports of raw materials and agricultural products, within the traditional pattern of unequal exchange, trading primary commodities for manufactured goods and know-how from most advanced regions in the world. The second

[123]   Gereffi (1989); Evans (1987).

[124]   Dependency theory has played a decisive role in the study of development by transforming and diversifying a theoretical paradigm dominated until the 1960s by modernization theory, based on an ethnocentric approach, often irrelevant to historical reality in developing countries. Fernando Henrique Cardoso and Enzo Faletto (1969) were the intellectual source of the most productive, sensitive approach to the analysis of the relationship between dependency and development. However, at about the same time, a dogmatic brand of dependency theory spread all over the world, and particularly in Latin America, oversimplifying issues and reducing the complexity of development process to the sheer dynamics of foreign domination. The best-known author of what I consider to be the dogmatic dependency school is Andre Gunder Frank (1967), a most honorable scholar, yet carried away by his ideological commitment. For an intelligent, up-to-date discussion on dependency theory, see Lidia Goldenstein (1994).

[125]   Sainz and Calcagno (1992); Frischtak (1989).

[126]   Bradford (ed.) (1992); Fajnzylber (1988); Kuwayama (1992); Castells and Laserna (1989).

Table 2.8 Latin America: gross domestic product, by type of expenditure, at constant 1980 prices

	1950–65	1965–74	Annual growth rates[a] 1974–80	1980–5	1985–90	1950–90
Gross domestic product	5.3	6.2	5.1	0.3	1.8	4.8
Private consumption	4.7	6.5	5.5	-0.4	1.8	4.7
General government consumption	4.7	7.0	5.2	1.9	1.7	4.9
Gross domestic investment	5.0	8.9	4.7	-8.7	-0.2	4.7
Exports	6.3	3.7	4.7	5.5	5.8	4.5
Imports	3.1	8.7	5.7	-9.5	6.0	4.3

[a] Calculated by regression.
Source: ECLAC, on the basis of official data.

model was based on import-substitution industrialization, along the policies designed and implemented by United Nations–CEPAL economists (most notably Raul Prebisch and Anibal Pinto), counting on the expansion of protected domestic markets. The third was based on an outward development strategy, using comparative cost advantages to win market shares in the global economy, trying to imitate the successful path of Asia's newly industrialized countries. I argue, for the sake of simplicity, that the first model deteriorated in the 1960s, the second was exhausted by the end of the 1970s, and the third failed by and large in the 1980s (with the exception of Chile, to be considered), leaving the 1990s as a critical period of restructuring in the relationship of Latin America to the new, global economy. I also propose the idea that such failures were determined by the combined effect of transformations taking place in the informational/global economy and of the institutional inability of most Latin American countries to adapt to such transformations.[127] Reactions to structural decline in the 1990s, with different timing for different countries, led to a growing diversification between Latin American economies, as each society looked for a specific form of incorporation into the increasingly intrusive global economy. Because this analysis is critical to understanding the differential dynamics of new global economy, I shall go in some detail into Latin America's changing pattern of dependency and development in the last three decades.

The first model of development, the most traditional form of commercial dependency, was exhausted from the 1960s onwards as a result of the structural transformation of world trade and production. For the world as a whole, the part of non-energy primary commodities in total trade in 1970 was only 16%, while for Latin America it was over 48%. Indeed, up to the 1980s, for all Latin American countries, with the major exception of Brazil, primary commodities represented more than 50% of their exports. This dependency on primary exports put Latin America at a disadvantage in the world economy because of three main reasons: the constant deterioration in terms of trade of primary products relative to manufactured goods; the increasing productivity in agricultural production in the most developed economies, leading to lower prices and decreasing demand in world markets; technological change that induced gradual substitution of synthetic products and advanced materials for traditional raw materials, also reducing their consumption via the recycling of used metals.

The weakness of economies that were dependent on low-priced

---

[127] Fajnzylber (1983); Touraine (1987); Stallings and Kaufman (eds) (1989); Calderon and Dos Santos (1989, 1995).

primary commodity exports was a key argument for a government-supported, import-substitution industrialization strategy in protected domestic markets. Indeed, traditional sources of revenue were dwindling, and competition in the open economy was considered to be hopeless against the technological and financial power of firms in dominant countries. Although these policies were initiated in the 1930s and 1940s, as a response to the 1930s crisis, they expanded considerably in the 1960s with a substantial flow of foreign direct investment, mainly from the US, aimed at domestic markets. In addition to import-substitution industrialization, in the case of three major countries (Brazil, Mexico, and Argentina), exports also grew substantially in the 1960s and 1970s, particularly in primary resource-intensive sectors. These policies were quite successful in Latin America up to the mid-1970s, albeit at a price of generating high (but not hyper) inflation: GDP for the whole region grew at an average annual rate of 5.3% in 1950–65, and at 6.2% in 1965–74. Average annual growth of manufacturing exports in 1970–80 was a robust 11.9%, lower than but not too far from the 15.95% of the four Asian tigers in the same period.[128] The exhaustion of the import-substitution industrialization model came as a consequence of various factors, against the background of the technological and economic restructuring that took place in the world economy from the mid-seventies onwards. It will be easier to recall this process in historical sequence.

The decline of the primary commodity export model, with the exception of oil exporting countries, depleted government reserves on which the economy depended for its imports. The two oil shocks (1974, 1979) forced a realignment in the external sector. Eroded by rampant inflation, domestic demand started to fall, shrinking the basis for import substitution as an accumulation strategy. The resulting social tensions brought an end by the late 1960s to most of the social alliances that had been at the root of Latin American populist states, and opened the way for a variety of military regimes that introduced, more often than not, widespread corruption and inefficiency, besides political repression and social inequity. Yet the economic difficulties experienced by the import-substitution model could have been coped with, in due time, except for the intervention of external factors directly linked to the dynamics of the new global economy. After all, the Asian Pacific countries, including Japan, Taiwan, and South Korea, went in the 1950s and 1960s through a prolonged period of import-substitution policies in highly protected

[128]   World Bank (1994).

markets, until their industries were ready for the gradual assault on the world economy. What decisively twisted the development process in Latin America were the massive, irresponsible indebtedness of the late 1970s and the monetary policies designed to deal with the debt crisis in the 1980s.

Much has been written on the origins and processes that led to the debt crisis, in Latin America and in other areas of the world, and much of this writing is straightforwardly ideological, both by dogmatic leftist critics,[129] and by orthodox neoclassical economists.[130] Yet the story is relatively simple.[131] In a nutshell, there was a surplus of petrodollars to be recycled in the global financial markets at the very moment when advanced economies were in the worst recession since the 1930s and low interest rates were yielding negative returns in real terms. Private international banks, particularly in the US, saw the opportunity to lend to Latin American governments, particularly to those who were oil-rich and therefore potentially solvent. But they were not particularly picky: any government wanting a major loan could obtain it, the banks counting on the possibility of applying political pressures on the Latin governments if they were to default, as eventually happened.

Governments used loans in a variety of ways, often unproductive, sometimes extravagant: Argentina's military dictators used the money to buy military hardware to try to take the Malvinas from Britain, helping on the way Thatcher's political career; Mexico's Lopez Portillo and many of the Mexican state companies indulged in greater than usual corruption, succeeding in creating the largest debt in Mexican history precisely during the years of the boom in oil prices, production and exports; Venezuela sank much of the money in unprofitable public corporations, particularly in steel and petrochemicals, ruining the country for the benefit of technocrats running such corporations; Banzer's Bolivia used public money to expand public expenditure with little productive impact, and to support export-oriented private investment in the lowlands, setting the stage for the growing of coca and the illegal processing of cocaine; perhaps only Brazil tried to invest at least some of the loans in rebuilding the country's industrial and communications infrastructure, yet in the

[129]   Payer (1974).
[130]   Feldstein et al. (1987).
[131]   The interpretation of the debt crisis presented here is, naturally, my responsibility alone. However, I have relied on analyses and information from several sources, among which: Stallings (1992); French-Davis (ed.) (1983); Arancibia (1988); Schatan (1987); Griffith-Jones (1988); Calderon and Dos Santos (1995); Sunkel (ed.) (1993).

midst of wasteful management practices by a confused military regime. Thus, the convergence of interests between irresponsible lending by private financial firms, mainly from the United States, and the misuse of loans by Latin American governments created a financial time bomb that exploded in 1982 when Mexico renounced the payment of its debt.

The stage was set for the second act of the drama: enter the international lending institutions, spearheaded by the International Monetary Fund (IMF).[132] With their economies in financial bankruptcy, major Latin American countries were confronted with a choice: either sever their damaged ties with the global economy; or else accept a profound restructuring of their economies, strictly following the policies designed for each country by the IMF on behalf of the creditors' club. Few governments dared to resist.[133] And those who tried, did so from such a weak position, relying on unrealistic demagoguery without real political support, that they rapidly sank into disgrace, Peru's Alan Garcia being the clearest example of such a doomed strategy. Thus, with the acquiescence of entrapped governments, IMF-inspired economists went to work on the restructuring of Latin America during the 1980s. While the principles of neoclassical, free-trade orthodoxy were proclaimed relentlessly (ignoring the diversity of economic theories and experiences, and thus the impudence of *any* orthodoxy), two measures became the centerpiece of all new policies, and one simple goal presided over the overall strategy. The two measures were: (a) control of inflation, particularly by sharply reducing government spending, imposing fiscal austerity, tightening credit and money supply, and lowering real wages; and (b) privatization of as much as possible of the public sector, particularly its most profitable companies, offering them up to foreign capital bidding. The fundamental goal pursued through these measures was

[132]   Stallings (1992); Siddell (1987); Gwin and Feinberg (1989); Haggard and Kaufman (eds) (1992).

[133]   Brazil showed the world in 1993 that international debt payments can be negotiated directly with the creditor banks without the intervention of the International Monetary Fund. The then Finance Minister Fernando Henrique Cardoso reached an agreement in New York with Brazil's main creditors without involving IMF in the negotiations, thus avoiding losing his freedom in economic policy. I do not think that this freedom to maneuver, and to design a policy having in mind the specific conditions of the country, is unrelated to the spectacular success of Cardoso's *Plan Real* in controlling inflation in 1994. To be sure, not all countries have the weight of Brazil to help them escape IMF's diktat. However, the astonishing case of Russia's submissiveness to IMF's policies (in exchange for meager aid), in spite of its power as a nation, shows that a government's self-confidence is a major factor in managing processes in the new global economy.

to homogenize the macroeconomic features of Latin America, aligning them with those of the open, global economy. Thus, investment could come in from, and go out to, anywhere in the world, free trade could proceed, and production could be transferred to whatever location in the region. In the process, interest on the outstanding debt could be paid by increasingly competitive economies. Although the immediate goal of these policies was to avoid massive default on international loans, thus avoiding a major crisis for international banking, the ultimate design of the debt-induced restructuring of Latin America was to incorporate the continent into the new, global economy, or at least the most productive, potentially dynamic segments of the economy of each country. Thus, the sequence went from irresponsible lending to irresponsible spending, then to a monetarist diktat by IMF and the creditors' club, which entrusted a capable, well-intentioned alliance of democrats and technocrats to take their countries into the high seas of the global economy.

In fact, in spite of all the hype on Latin America at the moment of writing, it did not exactly work out the way it was supposed to do. The strategic aim of the restructuring program was to make Latin American economies competitive in the new world economy, which implied their ability to compete in manufacturing exports. Yet the precondition for such competitiveness was the technological modernization of Latin America's productive base.[134] Without such technological capacity, the exports of the region could increase on the basis of cost-cutting strategies at the low end of manufacturing goods, but could never rise to competitive exports of high-value manufactured goods. Yet the modernization of technological infrastructure (from telecommunications to R&D, and the training of human resources) required massive public and private investment at the very moment when austerity policies and cuts in spending left Latin American governments and companies without resources.[135] Furthermore, companies and affluent individuals looked to their own survival, placing their savings in the international financial networks, so that in the 1980s the net transfer of private capital out of Latin America was larger than the region's total debt.[136] As for the evolution of trade, following Paolo Guerrieri's careful statistical analysis of Brazil, Mexico, and Argentina,[137] during the 1970s and until the debt crisis of the early 1980s exports grew faster than the world average,

[134]   Bradford (ed.) (1994); Fajnzylber (1990); Katz (1994); Katz (ed.) (1987); Castells and Laserna (1989).
[135]   Massad (1991).
[136]   Sainz and Calcagno (1992).
[137]   Guerrieri (1994).

Table 2.9 Shares of Latin American NIEs in world exports, 1970–90[a]

	1970	1976	1979	1982	1984	1986	1988	1990
Total trade	1.99	1.94	2.10	2.89	3.51	2.69	2.41	2.13
Agricultural products	5.84	5.62	5.21	4.91	5.63	5.02	4.18	5.23
Fuels	0.04	0.56	1.70	5.70	6.34	4.15	3.98	3.94
Other raw materials	4.50	7.57	6.38	9.18	8.65	5.01	5.17	9.80
Food industries	6.63	6.87	7.14	7.00	8.89	8.03	7.98	5.62
Traditional products	1.02	1.40	1.53	1.34	2.09	1.93	1.52	1.18
Primary resource-intensive products	0.61	0.57	0.75	1.99	3.28	2.94	3.52	2.58
Scale-intensive products	0.60	0.76	1.12	1.43	2.06	1.76	2.12	1.84
Specialized supplier products	0.32	0.58	0.83	0.90	1.32	1.41	1.00	0.92
Science-based products	0.43	0.56	0.65	0.80	1.40	1.94	1.17	0.97
Others	10.32	10.31	7.59	6.66	7.61	1.87	0.46	0.67

[a]The ratio of Latin American NIEs' exports to world exports in each product group; percentage shares in values.
Source: SIE-World Trade data base; elaborated by Guerrieri (1994).

and the share of world exports for the three countries increased by 76%. In contrast, during the 1980s the whole region suffered industrial stagnation, and world export share of the three countries declined by 39%. At the root of the decreasing competitiveness of Latin American economies lies, according to Guerrieri, in line with a number of Latin American economists, the inability of countries and firms to transform their technological basis in a context where manufacturing exports had become critical for economic growth. Thus, on the one hand, for the three countries the share of manufactures in exports increased from 25.6% of total exports in early 1970s to about 55% in late 1980s. But the picture becomes troublesome when analyzing differential growth of manufacturing exports by sectors. Following Guerrieri's typology, and observing his data for Mexico, Brazil, and Argentina (see table 2.9), growth of manufacturing exports was concentrated in primary resource-intensive products and food industries (in the case of Brazil, also in scale-intensive products, such as automobiles). On the other hand, science-based products (for example, electronics, specialty chemicals) and specialized-supplier products (such as mechanical engineering), sectors with higher value added and with the highest rate of growth in world trade, not only had a modest role in total exports, but decreased substantially their competitiveness in the second half of the 1980s. The policies of the 1980s reversed in fact the reduction in technological dependency attained by Latin America in the 1970s.[138] Decreasing technological capacity affected negatively the whole productive structure, undermining productivity and competitiveness in strategic sectors, because of the interdependent nature of technological linkages in the informational economy. According to Guerrieri:

> In the case of Latin American newly industrialized economies, these technological linkages among firms and sectors either were absent or performed very poorly, especially during the past decade [1980s]. This weak technological interdependence has greatly contributed to the substantial deterioration of the long-term competitive position of the three Latin American economies.[139]

The net result of the 1980s restructuring policies for Latin America was economic retardation and a painful social crisis.[140] Sharply

---

[138]   Guerrieri (1994); Katz (1994).

[139]   Guerrieri (1994: 198).

[140]   Sainz and Calcagno (1992); CEPAL (1990b); for an example of the increase of poverty in dynamic Latin American metropolitan areas, see the analysis of Sao Paulo in SEADE Foundation (1995). Sources for growth data are World Bank's Development Reports.

Table 2.10 Shares of major Latin American countries in world exports, 1970–90

	Mexcio			Brazil			Argentina			Chile		
	1970 -3	1979 -82	1987 -90	1970 -3	1979 -82	1987 -90	1970 -3	1979 -82	1987 -90	1970 -3	1979 -82	1987 -90
Total trade	0.455	0.943	0.815	1.023	1.143	1.135	0.573	0.475	0.330	0.300	0.238	0.255
Agricultural products	1.260	1.143	1.345	1.850	1.223	1.770	2.290	2.815	1.495	0.108	0.318	0.668
Fuels	0.018	3.603	4.173	0.050	0.043	0.000	0.000	0.000	0.033	0.005	0.000	0.000
Other raw materials	1.193	1.523	1.753	3.600	6.073	5.385	0.078	0.080	0.080	1.698	1.730	2.823
Food industries	0.853	0.338	0.538	3.408	4.973	4.190	3.178	2.158	2.030	0.123	0.340	0.498
Traditional products	0.430	0.223	0.350	0.673	0.938	0.838	0.228	0.288	0.190	0.023	0.063	0.078
Primary resource-intensive products	0.503	0.450	0.725	0.160	0.805	1.925	0.043	0.313	0.285	2.500	1.483	1.553
Scale-intensive products	0.288	0.255	0.650	0.225	0.855	1.115	0.168	0.198	0.195	0.033	0.048	0.043
Specialized supplier products	0.058	0.138	0.298	0.205	0.663	0.583	0.133	0.148	0.088	0.003	0.013	0.008
Science-based products	0.208	0.113	0.535	0.140	0.523	0.503	0.130	0.093	0.073	0.005	0.015	0.005
Others	0.858	1.193	0.175	8.590	5.658	0.350	0.085	0.033	0.013	0.003	0.030	0.295

Source: SIE-World Trade data base; elaborated by Guerrieri (1994).

contrasting with past experience in this century, characterized by steady economic growth, in 1980–91 Latin America's per capita GDP experienced a negative average annual rate of growth (–0.3%). To be sure, with the major exception of Brazil, inflation came gradually under control: the dead do not move. And the economies of major countries, when measured on a per capita basis, were almost dead during the 1980s decade (although Brazil, consistent with its character, still went up and down): per capita GDP in 1990 in major countries was below or barely at the level of 1982, with the exception of Colombia and Chile. These exceptions must be taken into consideration. Colombia performed very well during the 1980s, both in terms of growth and in controlling inflation. The explanation, notwithstanding protests from Colombia's official economists, is very simple: precisely during the 1980s it became a key center of capital accumulation and trade management for one of the most flourishing industries in the world, cocaine production and distribution.[141] I shall analyze in detail this new form of incorporation into the global economy (see volume III).

As for Chile, the quintessential model of free-trade ideologists (initially advised in the 1970s by the so-called "Chicago boys" and supported by the International Monetary Fund under the Pinochet dictatorship), it is indeed a successful case of transition to a new strategy of export-driven growth.[142] Yet it is often misunderstood because, seen from the perspective of the 1990s, Chilean development mixed sequentially two very different models of growth:[143] the first one, under General Pinochet's dictatorship (1974–89), went through a crisis in 1980–2, and met serious difficulties by the late 1980s. The second model, under conditions of political democracy in the 1990s, may represent the chance for sustained economic growth in the new global economy. The two Chilean models are in fact representative of divergent paths for the future of Latin America. Thus, because of the confusion created in international circles by making Chile the show case of Latin American economic development while mixing substantially different economic policies, I find it necessary to recall some of the features of this unique experience.

Chile's economic performance during the 1980s has been overstated by self-serving discourses of the International Monetary Fund and other free marketeers. Check the data: Chile's average annual growth rate of GNP per capita in 1980–9 was 1.0%. For the whole period of the dictatorship, between 1974 and 1989, Chilean GDP grew

[141]   Handinghaus (1989); Garcia Sayan (ed.) (1989); Arrieta et al. (1991).
[142]   Fontaine (1988); CEPAL (1986, 1994); Sainz and Calcagno (1992).
[143]   Foxley (1995). For data on Chile, see MIDEPLAN (1994).

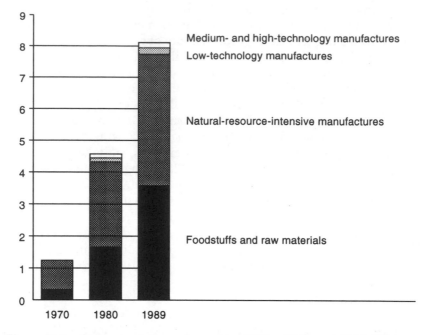

Figure 2.6   Chile: evolution of exports, 1970, 1980, and 1989 (US$ bn)
The classification is based on the Standard International Trade
Classification (SITC) at the three-digit level in line with the criteria
used by ECLAC in *El comercio de manufacturas de América Latina:
Evolución y estructura 1962–1989* (LC/R.1056, Santiago, Chile,
September 1991) and in *Interindustry Trade: A comparison between
Latin America and some industrial countries* (LC/R.1101, Santiago,
Chile, November 1991).
Source: Estimates on the basis of primary data from the Latin American
and Caribbean External Trade Data Bank (BADECEL); Statistics and
Projections Division, ECLAC.

at an average annual rate of 3%, certainly improving on Latin
America's dismal performance in the 1980s, but hardly comparable
to East Asian growth rates. Annual inflation in the 1980s was, on
average, over 20%, comparing favorably with neighbors sick from
hyperinflation, but still disturbing for international standards. As for
exports, while they grew at a high rate (10.4% per year) in the 1970s,
their growth was halved (to 5.2% annual average) in 1980–91.
Furthermore, table 2.10, calculated by Guerrieri from his world data
base, provides surprising information: Chile's share of world exports
in 1987–90, after one and a half decades of growth, was lower than its
share during the Allende government in 1970–3. The first reason for
such a fact is very obvious: total world trade grew faster than Chile's.

The second reason is less apparent and more important: it concerns the structure of Chilean trade. As shown in table 2.10, while Chilean exports performed very well in agricultural products and food industries, they remained stagnant in high value-added science-based products and specialized-supplier products. Exports were concentrated in two categories: foodstuffs and raw materials (copper, wood products, produce, wine, and so on); and natural-resource-intensive manufactures (such as fishmeal, canned seafood, paper pulp, farmed fish) (see figure 2.6). The share of manufactured goods in exports was very small: indeed, Chile, unlike the Asian Pacific countries that it likes to imitate, suffered a severe deindustrialization process, particularly during the 1970s: in 1982 per capita manufacturing GDP had fallen to 69% of the 1972 level, and risen to 93% in 1990. GNP per capita in 1990 was still under $2,000. As for the benefits of economic growth for the Chilean people, the percentage of GDP that went into wages decreased from 42.7% in 1970 to 33% in 1985, so that between 1982 and 1989 real wages declined slightly, and the purchasing power of minimum wages fell substantially. As a result, in 1987, 44.7% of the population was living under the poverty level, with 17% being in conditions of extreme misery.[144] Yet with all these caveats, Chile did better than the rest of Latin America during the "lost decade" of the 1980s. Why so? The critical element in spurring economic growth was the surge in exports: they went from 12% of GDP in 1974 to 32% in 1989. The conditions for this performance were linked to five main factors:

(a) until the end of the 1980s, a ruthless authoritarian government allowed for very low labor costs and, most importantly, for a natural-resource economy, for an absolute lack of environmental controls that made Chilean products highly competitive in sectors where the compliance with environmental regulations is a major obstacle to quick profits[145] (for example, Chilean fishmeal processing was made easy by allowing firms to gobble up entire fish banks off the coast and send them to the mixer without any further procedure);
(b) the existence of a very strong Chilean agro-business bourgeoisie, with the capital and entrepreneurial skills to take on the world market on the basis of their learning of technology. A good example of this strategy is the development of Chilean fish farming, a booming exports sector, on the basis of imitating Norwegian technology;

---

[144]   Sainz and Calcagno (1992); Foxley (1995).
[145]   Collado (1995); Quiroga Martinez (ed.) (1994).

(c) major support by international lending institutions, and particularly by the International Monetary Fund, committed to make Chile a show case for trade-driven development in the new open, world economy;

(d) substantial foreign direct investment (almost $1 billion per year in 1983–90), encouraged by Chile's credibility with the international institutions;

(e) and also, ironically, the persistence of a strong revenue-generating public sector under Pinochet allowed the Chilean Government to keep receiving the necessary revenue to proceed with its infrastructural development projects, in spite of the restriction of imports linked to tight monetary policy. CODELCO, the monopoly of copper production in Chile nationalized under Allende, was not privatized under Pinochet and kept feeding the Chilean Government and through it, Chilean business. In ardent free-marketeer Chile, public-sector investment as a percentage of GDP grew from 4.7% in 1982 to 8% in 1987.[146])

However, by the late 1980s the "neo-liberal" Chilean model was reaching its limits. On the one hand, widespread poverty and stagnation of average real wages restricted the domestic market to a growing, but relatively small affluent middle class. On the other hand, the outward orientation of the economy required enhancement of technological capacity, including information and commercial networking in external markets, to ensure the transition into higher value-added markets. Besides, the growing opposition of a traditionally democratic Chilean society to dictator Pinochet was inducing political instability, creating potential risks for essential foreign investment. In the last period of the Pinochet regime, economic growth was reduced to 3%, the investment rate fell below 18% of GDP, and inflation hit an annual rate of 30% at the end of 1989.

The new, democratically elected government that took over in Chile in March 1990 aimed at consolidating growth in an open economy, while engaging in income redistribution and fostering social programs to improve living conditions, ensure social stability, and broaden domestic markets. The four years of President Aylwin's administration were rather successful on most fronts. GDP growth increased at an average annual rate of 7% in 1990–3, again driven by exports that increased their share of GDP from 32% to 35%. But the key difference from previous policies was that real wages increased 4% per year, the minimum wage rose by 24%, income redistribution substantially improved, and the percentage of the population under

---

[146]   Sainz and Calcagno (1992: 22, n. 6).

the poverty level decreased to 32.7% of the total, while the government engaged in a large-scale housing program. Inflation was reduced at about 12% per year by 1993. Two policies were critical in this overhauling of the shaky Chilean miracle: on the one hand, a social pact between government, business, and labor unions that gave the government room, and time, to maneuver; on the other hand fiscal reform that substantially increased tax revenues, providing the resources for increased social expenditure and the beginning of modernization of the technological infrastructure. Unfortunately, environmental policies, while rewritten into politically correct language in official statements, continued to be bent for the sake of the profitability of a natural-resources-based export economy. Chile still faces a structural problem, related to its weak technological basis, that would need improvement to shift into higher value-added exports, particularly if Chile joins NAFTA. Yet it may be able to make its full transition to the new model of competition in an open economy thanks to its attractiveness to foreign investment. Indeed, competent economic management, the recovery of democratic stability, and its entrepreneurial class have made Chile a favorite destination of foreign investment. The headstart of Chile in the new model of development during the 1990s could be rewarded by its incorporation into the global economic networks just on time to offset the effects of the exhaustion of its model of exports based on extensive, and somewhat destructive, exploitation of natural resources.

There is a key lesson to be drawn from the Chilean experience. After the crumbling of the import-substitution model, under the pressures of the global economy enacted by international private banks and the IMF, Latin American economies could only survive in a new form of incorporation to the global economy in which the export capacity of the economy and the ability to attract foreign investment are the critical factors. Chile, in its two-stage sequence, showed the feasibility, but also the social and environmental costs, of such strategy.

On the other hand, Mexico was the country that took the boldest step in the direction of the new outward-oriented model, fully integrating itself into the North American economy.[147] As a result, even before the signing of NAFTA, Mexico received over $28 billion in 1990–1, and an additional $35 billion foreign investment in 1992, accounting for over a half of total foreign investment in Latin America. An expanding manufacturing base, beyond the *maquiladoras* enclaves, is transforming Mexico into an industrial platform to sell in

---

[147] Martinez and Farber (1994); Skezely (1993); Pozas (1993); Rogozinski (1993); Randall (ed.) (1992); Cook, Middlebrook, and Molinar (eds) (1994).

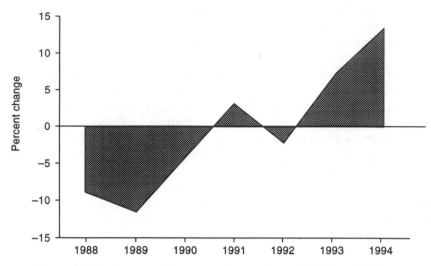

Figure 2.7   Peru: percentage change in total GDP, 1988–94
Source: Banco Central de Reserva.

the integrated North American market industrial goods produced in Mexico at lower costs, and with similar productivity levels, than in the United States.[148] Exports from Mexico accounted in 1992 for almost a quarter of its GDP. However, Mexico's trade deficit, its extreme dependence on global capital flows, and the sensitivity of financial flows to the political context of the country, plunged Mexico into a devastating financial crisis in 1994, a crisis that brought down the dollar after the US came to the rescue of a Mexican economy that is now inextricably linked with that of its powerful neighbor.[149]

Latin America, with all the singularities of such a diverse continent, was in the 1990s in the process of being integrated into the new global economy, albeit, again, in a subordinate position. Discounting Chile and Mexico, exports for the whole region, representing about 15% of GDP in 1980, accounted for 20.6% of GDP in 1992. Foreign investment has poured into some countries, particularly Mexico, Chile, Brazil, and Argentina since the early 1990s.[150] Even Peru, which was literally in a process of economic disintegration during the 1980s, spectacularly reversed its decline in 1993–5 (see figure 2.7), under the impact of massive foreign direct investment flows and fast expanding trade, once President Fujimori established some sort of political stability and imposed the "Fujishock" to regain the good

[148]   Shaiken (1990).
[149]   *Business Week* (1995b).
[150]   Bradford (ed.) (1994).

reputation with IMF that the country had lost under Alan Garcia.[151] That about 60% of the Peruvian population remains below the poverty level does not undermine the importance of the fact that a country that in 1992 was 30% below its GDP per capita level of a decade earlier, became in 1994 the country with the highest rate of growth in the world (12%).

However, since massive foreign investment, both in stocks and in real estate assets, is an essential part of new economic dynamism in Argentina, Peru, Bolivia, Mexico, and to some extent Brazil, we may be observing an artificial increase of the wealth of these economies, by labeling as investment what is basically a transfer in ownership of existing assets, particularly in privatized state companies in strategic sectors. Thus, some of the region's new prosperity could be a financial mirage, subject to reversible capital flows relentlessly scanning the planet for short-term profitability, as well as for positioning in strategic sectors (such as telecommunications). The competitiveness of export-oriented economies, including Brazil, is hampered by the technological gap which Latin America still suffers, Furthermore, the social and environmental devastation of IMF-inspired policies of the 1980s[152] has not been reversed by a new model of economic growth that gives priority to fiscal austerity and external competitiveness over any other criteria. Therefore, widespread poverty shrinks potential domestic markets, forcing economies to survive in the global competition by cutting costs on labor, social welfare, and environmental protection.

Yet overall, after the painful restructuring of the 1980s, Latin America in the 1990s has been incorporated into the new global economy, with dynamic segments in all countries being immersed in the international competition for selling goods and attracting capital. The price of this incorporation has been very high:[153] a substantial proportion of the Latin American population has been excluded from such dynamic sectors, both as producers and consumers. In some cases people, cities and regions are reconnected through the local informal economy and the outward-oriented criminal economy (see "The criminal global economy" in volume III). This is why the

---

[151]   Chion (1995).
[152]   Nelson (ed.) (1990, 1992); see the literature review on poverty in Latin America in the 1980s and 1990s, in Faria (1995); for processes of environmental destruction linked to the new pattern of growth advocated by IMF, see Vaquero (ed.) (1994).
[153]   For a collective reflection by distinguished Latin American intellectuals on the new historical course of development, see the three volumes of the symposium held in Mexico in 1991: Coloquio de Invierno (1992).

future of Latin America, and its actual form of incorporation into the informational/global economy, will depend on the relative weight of two opposed models of development: one closer to Pinochet's Chile, based on absolute exploitation of population and devastation of the environment, to support cut-throat competition in external markets; or a different one, closer to that of democratic Chile in the 1990s, linking up external competitiveness, social well-being, and expansion of the internal market, on the basis of redistribution of wealth and stepped-up technological/managerial modernization. Indeed, it is this latter model that mirrors the reality of East Asian development experiences that are often proposed as role models to Latin America.

Two processes of economic restructuring, under way in the mid-1990s, will decide the fate of Latin America through the early twenty-first century. The first is the successful integration of Mexico, but also of Chile, and later on, of other economies, in NAFTA. For all the painful consequences that such integration implies for both American workers and Mexican peasants, mobility of capital, labor, and technology within such a large, dynamic, integrated economic area will foster investment, bypass some of the wasteful closets of government corruption, open up new markets, and stimulate tech-nological diffusion. Furthermore, one-sided dependency will be more difficult to operate under the complexity created by the new regional economy. The feasibility of NAFTA will, however, depend on the capacity of Mexico to democratize the state and to redistribute wealth among the population at large.

The second process is the project of economic restructuring and social reform undertaken by President Cardoso in Brazil in 1995. Brazil is the economic and technological powerhouse of Latin America, and the tenth largest economy in the world. But it is also one of the most unequal countries on the planet, and a giant weakened by the illiteracy and lack of education of a substantial proportion of its population.[154] With labor aristocracy and populist politicians blocking the reforms, and business elites entrenched in a tradition of claiming government subsidies and illegally exporting profits, the chances of success are uncertain. However, if by the beginning of the twenty-first century Brazil has proceeded with the technological overhauling of its productive structure, with some improvement in income distribution and with a large-scale program of public invest-ment in education and health it could become a substantial component of the global economy and carry along the development path much of Latin America. Yet neither in Brazil or Mexico will

[154]   SEADE (1995); *Economist* (1995c).

a successful incorporation in the new, informational economy guarantee the integration of their people, many of whom could become, as my co-author Fernando Henrique Cardoso, in his former incarnation, wrote in 1992, "not even considered worth the trouble of exploitation; they will become inconsequential, of no interest to the developing globalized economy."[155]

The dynamics of exclusion from the new global economy: Africa's fate?

The dynamics of social exclusion of a significant proportion of the population as a result of new forms of inclusion of countries in the global economy operates on a larger scale in the case of Africa.[156] Because of the importance of the matter, both in human terms and for understanding the uneven logic of the new economy, I shall analyze this process in some detail in another volume, in what I consider to be one of the most relevant chapters in this book (see "The rise of the Fourth World" in volume III). Yet it is necessary to include an overview of Africa's recent economic evolution for any understanding of the new global economy. It is precisely the feature of this new economy: that it affects the whole planet either by inclusion or exclusion in the processes of production, circulation, and consumption, that have become at the same time globalized and informationalized.

Thus, the exhaustion of the model of primary-commodity production, due to the deterioration in the terms of trade, led most African countries, and particularly the countries of Sub-Saharan Africa, to virtual economic bankruptcy in the 1970s.[157] In 1970 the proportion of primary commodities in total exports was over 52% for Sub-Saharan Africa and over 70% for Northern Africa. Worldwide restructuring, based on manufacturing trade and foreign direct investment, during the 1970s made increasingly difficult the continuation of the traditional trade model on which most African economies operated. African governments, as in the case of Latin America, tried a conversion to industrialization and commercially oriented agriculture, and to do so, they borrowed heavily from the lending-happy international banks.[158] But the conditions of competitiveness in the new informational, global economy were too far away

[155]   Cardoso (1993: 156).
[156]   CEPII (1992); Lachaud (1994); Sandbrook (1985); Illiffe (1987); Ungar (1985); Jamal (1995).
[157]   Leys (1987, 1994); Ghai and Rodwan (eds) (1983).
[158]   Brown (1992).

from what could be accomplished in the short term by rather primitive economies that were by and large still committed to the trade channels of the old and new (USSR) colonial powers. When the oil shock of 1979 and the rise in interest rates provoked their financial bankruptcy, most African economies came under the direct control of policies of international financial institutions that imposed liberalization measures supposedly aimed at generating trade and investment. The fragile African economies did not resist the shock. Even the jewel of the former French colonial crown, the Ivory Coast, sank into economic disintegration:[159] after having grown at a hefty 6.6% per year in the 1970s, it turned into negative growth (annual average rate of –0.5%) in 1980–91; in fact, on a per capita basis, its GDP regressed at a rate of –4.6% per year during the 1980s. The competitive position of African countries in international trade was not brilliant in the 1960s, but deteriorated dramatically after the intervention of international financial institutions in African economic policies (see appendix to this chapter): the share of Sub-Saharan Africa in world trade of manufactured goods in 1970 was just 1.2%, but it went down to 0.5% in 1980, and to 0.4% in 1989.[160] Furthermore, the primary commodities trade also collapsed: from 7.2% of world trade of primary goods in 1970, it went down to 5.5% in 1980, and to 3.7% in 1989. Furthermore, the damage done to the agricultural production of Africa was even greater than the data show. While liberalization policies were not able to attract investment or improve competitiveness, what they did was to destroy large sectors of agricultural production for local markets, and in some cases, subsistence agriculture.[161] As a result, African countries were left without defense against the impact of bad harvests. When drought struck in Central and Eastern Africa, widespread famine followed (the Sahel, Ethiopia, Sudan), aggravated by civil wars and banditry induced by the heritage of surrogate military confrontation between the superpowers (Ethiopia, Somalia, Angola, Mozambique). Because states, as intermediaries between their countries and the meager resources transferred from abroad, were the main source of income, control of the state became a matter of survival.[162] And because tribal and ethnic networks were the safest bet for people's support, the fight to control the state (often equated to control of the military) was organized around ethnic cleavages, reviving centuries-old hatred and prejudice:

[159] Glewwe and de Tray (1988).
[160] CEPII (1992).
[161] Durufle (1988); African Development Bank (1990).
[162] Bayart (1992); Rothchild and Chazan (eds) (1988); Wilson (1991); Davidson (1992); Leys (1994).

genocidal tendencies and widespread banditry are rooted in the political economy of Africa's disconnection from the new, global economy.

North African economies, because of their proximity to Europe geographically, demographically, and economically, did not suffer as much as the rest of Africa during the restructuring process. They found new forms of insertion in the European economy through the export of workers (remittances from emigrants is one of the most important items in their balance of payments),[163] and the beginning of a strategy of exporting low-priced manufactured goods, particularly Morocco (4.2% annual growth of manufacturing production in the 1980s). Still, the Soviet-style industrialization process of Algeria collapsed because of the limits of the domestic market, Egypt saw its 1970s strong growth halved during the 1980s, and Tunisia (the modernized example of the region in the eyes of international institutions) grew at a meager 1.1% per capita annual GDP in 1980–91. In the 1990s, widespread poverty and mechanisms of social exclusion were prevailing in much of the Maghreb and the Machreq.[164]

Overall, the systematic logic of the new global economy does not have much of a role for the majority of the African population in the newest international division of labor. Most primary commodities are useless or low priced, markets are too narrow, investment too risky, labor not skilled enough, communication and telecommunication infrastructure clearly inadequate, politics too unpredictable, and government bureaucracies inefficiently corrupt (since no official international criticism has been heard about other bureaucracies equally corrupt but still efficient, for example, in South Korea until the presidency of Kim Young Sam). Under such conditions, the only real concern of the "North" (particularly of Western Europe) was the fear of being invaded by millions of uprooted peasants and workers unable to survive in their own countries. This is why international aid was channeled to African countries in the hope of still taking advantage of some valuable natural resources and with the purpose of preventing massive famines that could trigger large-scale migrations. Yet what can be said of the experience of the transition of Africa into the new global economy is that *structural irrelevance* (from the systems point of view) is a more threatening condition than dependency. Such structural irrelevance was revealed when policies of adjustment were imposed on Africa during the 1980s, in the wake of the debt crisis, applying abstract formulae to specific historical conditions: under the dominance of free market conditions, internationally and

---

[163] Choucri (1986).
[164] Bedoui (1995).

domestically, most of Africa ceased to exist as an economically viable entity in the informational/global economy.

This is why the most hopeful prospects for future development in Africa come from the potential role that could be played by the new, democratic, black-majority South Africa, with strong economic and technological linkages to the global economy. The stability and prosperity of South Africa, and its willingness and capacity to lead its neighbors as *primus inter pares*, offers the best chance to avoid the human holocaust that threatens Africa, and through Africa, the sense of humanity in all of us.

The last frontier of the global economy: the segmented incorporation of Russia and the ex-Soviet republics

The restructuring of the international economy has been further complicated by the disintegration of the Soviet Empire, and by the eventual incorporation of the broken pieces of former command economies into the global market economy. The collapse of communism and of the Soviet Union are major historical events that I consider to be directly related to the structural difficulties of the statist mode of production in making the transition to the informational mode of development (see volume III). But whatever the origins of such a phenomenon, the integration of resulting economic ruins into the global economy is the last frontier for the expansion of capitalism. These economies can hardly survive without linkages to the world system of circulation of capital, commodities, and technology. Indeed, their transition to the market economies, operated with the support (but not much help) from advanced capitalist countries and international financial institutions, means primarily the implementation of macroeconomic policies enabling foreign capital and foreign trade to operate in the ex-command economies. The sheer size of these economies, their educated population, their strong scientific basis, and their immense reserves of energy and natural resources will substantially impact the world's economic system. In the long term, a critical contribution of this area to the global economy could be to add a dynamic market of 400 million consumers, thus providing outlets for the excess capacity being accumulated in the high-technology productive structures of the West, particularly in Western Europe. However, such a long-term view would require a process of economic growth to make these consumers solvent enough to pay for their consumption, on a scale large enough to make the market significant. Yet, since the late 1980s, ex-command economies are posting negative growth rates, and the estimate is that, in the best though unlikely scenarios, they could only recover their modest standards of living of 1980 by the year 2000.[165] In fact, it appears that for Russia and the ex-Soviet republics economic deterioration could continue well into the twenty-first century.[166] Thus, the process of incorporation of the ex-Soviet Empire into the global economy is highly complex, and requires careful consideration. While not being able fully to address the issue within the limits of this chapter, I shall briefly sketch what seem to be the main trends developing in the 1990s.[167]

Eastern European countries are being annexed, by bits and pieces, into the European Union area of influence, particularly through German investment and trade (see "The unification of Europe" in volume III). The Baltic states are developing a close relationship to Scandinavian countries, and their small size and high level of education could make them potential subcontracting sites for Western European high-technology industries, in addition to their current role as import–export platforms for Russian trade. As for the other ex-Soviet republics, and particularly for Ukraine, their form of incorporation in the global economy will largely follow the path of the new, capitalist Russia.

Western fears and hopes about the immediate economic impact of post-Soviet Russia never materialized. The 25 million Russians who, according to a report for the Commission of the European Union, were supposed to invade Europe after the collapse of their economy and the granting of freedom to travel abroad, stayed home. Emigration was by and large limited to Jewish people (but much less than anticipated), and to hundreds of thousands, not millions (through 1995), mainly scientists and skilled professionals. Total direct foreign investment in 1990–4 posted a modest total of US$5 billion or $3 billion, depending upon estimates. This figure may be

---

[165] CEPII (1992).

[166] Khanin (1994).

[167] This section is mainly based on my ongoing field-work research on the crisis of the Soviet Union and the process of social transformation in Russia, from 1989 to the present. Specifically, more recent information comes from field-work and interviews conducted, jointly with Emma Kiselyova, in June and July 1995 in Khabarovsk, Sakhalin, Novosibirsk, and Moscow. Key ideas and information were obtained from interviews and conversations with several leading economists of the Russian Academy of Sciences, including Valery Kuleshov, Gregory Khanin, Galina Kovalyova, and Valery Kryukov from the Novosibirsk's Institute of Economics and Industrial Engineering, and Alexander Granberg, director of SOPS Institute in Moscow. Naturally, the responsibility for the analysis presented here is exclusively mine, since I have interpreted in my own terms the substance of our conversations. For a different view on Russian economic transition, seen from an informed, orthodox economic perspective, see Aslund (1995).

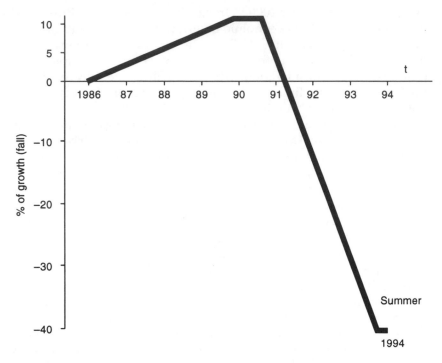

Figure 2.8   Changes in industrial production in Russia from 1986 to
second half 1994 (approximate scale)
Base level for comparison: early 1970s.
Source: Kuleshov (1994).

compared to the $26 billion of foreign investment in China just in
1993, or to $63 billion of foreign investment in Mexico in 1990–2.
Foreign trade shrank in 1991–3 (exports were in 1993 at 86% of their
1991 level, and imports went down to 61% of the 1991 level),
although both exports and imports increased in 1994 (increase of
9.1% in exports, and 5.1% in imports over 1993 by November 1994),
and were on their way to similar increases in 1995 at the time of writing. Yet the one fulfilled prediction was that of fast
internationalization of the Russian economy: in November 1994,
exports represented about 25% of Russian GDP and imports about
17%, thus making the proportion of the external sector over GDP
about twice as high as in the US.[168]

---

[168]   Source: data from various Russian sources, compiled and cited by Kur'yerov
(1994, 1995a, 1995b). See also Economist Intelligence Unit (1995).

The reason for such an apparent paradox (fast internationalization of the economy in spite of declining exports and imports and meager foreign investment) is sadly simple: the collapse of the Russian economy, with stunning negative rates in GDP growth (see figure 2.8).[169] Thus, GDP fell by 29% in 1992/1991, and by 12% in 1993/92. Material production fell by 63% between 1989 and 1993. Total investment in the economy fell by 15% in 1991, by 40% in 1992, and by 16% in 1993. Fall in investment was much greater in manufacturing, so that by 1994 it was estimated that 60% of industrial machinery was used up since, according to a survey, in 1993 only a quarter of company managers were ready to invest in new equipment. In agriculture, investment fell by a factor of 7 between 1991 and 1993. The overall rate of accumulation in the economy (*dolya nakopleniya osnovnykh fondov*) decreased by 33.8% in 1989, by 32% in 1992, and by 25.8% in 1993.[170] In spite of official optimism in 1995, independent academic economists reported the continuation of the decline in production in agriculture and the construction industry.[171] Additional manufacturing decline was considered likely because of lack of markets, obsolescence of equipment, and the high level of indebtedness of most enterprises.[172] By the mid-1990s the military-industrial sector, the heart of Soviet industry, was essentially wrecked; science and technology institutions were in shambles; production of oil and gas in some important areas, particularly in Tyumen, was disorganized and still declining; and transportation and telecommunications infrastructures were in desperate need of equipment and repairs.[173] As for the country's financial situation, Russian foreign debt in 1993 represented 64% of Russian GDP and 262% of annual exports. It was projected to reach US$130 billion by the end of 1995.[174]

Thus, it is because the Russian economy as a whole is in a process of disintegration and decline that its external sector becomes a relatively bright spot. The small segments of the economy that link up with global processes and markets are the most dynamic and those which feed the wealth being accumulated in an equally small segment of the

---

[169] Kuleshov (1994). Figure 2.8 is elaborated by Kuleshov on a different statistical basis than that of Kur'yerov data cited in the text. However, both sources, and both authors, converge in assessing a steep decline of Russian production since during the first half of the 1990s.
[170] Kur'yerov (1994).
[171] Professor Valery Kuleshov, interview, Novosibirsk, July 1995.
[172] Professor Gregory Khanin, interview, Novosibirsk, July 1995.
[173] Castells and Natalushko (1993); Natalushko, personal communication, Moscow, July 1995; Schweitzer (1995); Kryukov (1994).
[174] Kur'yerov (1994).

Table 2.11   Foreign trade of Russia (including trade with CIS countries), 1995

	Volume[b]	Value (US$ m)	% of level in same period of 1994[a]
Exports of principal goods, January–June 1995			
Crude oil (million tons)	58.9	6,259	99
Oil products (million tons)	19.4	1,939	92
Natural gas (billion m³)	98.4	6,625	105
Coal	12.4	404	121
Coke	527	27.6	73
Iron ores & concentrates	6,965	129	118
Cast iron	1,307	162	73
Ferro-alloys	197	191	76
Copper	187	457	147
Aluminium unprocessed	986	1,430	88
Nickel	60.7	515	137
Round timber (thousand m³)	6,841	457	101
Saw-timber (thousand m³)	1,839	284	73
Plywood (thousand m³)	287	82.5	88
Cellulose	631	439	154
Newsprint	488	242	161
Ammonia	1,880	230	97
Methanol	491	160	86
Nitrogen fertilizers	3,714	420	111
Potash fertilizers	2,379	165	149
Rubber synthetic	191	219	122
Fish frozen	588	486	88
Machinery, equipment	—	1,756	82
Imports of principal goods January–May 1995			
Grain	—	151	55
Sugar, incl. raw sugar	1,027	422	109
Meat frozen	321	455	127
Chicken frozen	262	224	147
Butter	126	223	135
Sunflower oil	111	107	336
Citrus fruits	281	155	84
Coffee	10.8	53.4	92
Tea	—	133	123
Medicines	—	386	86
Clothing, knitted and textile	—	269	62
Leather shoes (million pairs)	12.1	88.1	64
Non-ferrous metals	—	234	85
Pipes	455	243	85
Machinery and equipment	—	6,111	137

[a] Comparison refers to volume except when no data are available; otherwise, to value.
[b] Volume is in thousands of tons unless otherwise stated.
Source: Kur'yerov (1995b).

population, formed by *nomenklatura* leaders turned capitalists, mafia-related businesses, new daring entrepreneurs, and a growing group of young professionals with the skills to operate the connection between Russia and the global economy.

Thus, after years of decline, exports are on the rise, but they are increasingly concentrated in the fuel and energy sector (accounting for about 50% of total exports), natural resources, and raw materials[175] (see table 2.11). Share of machinery and equipment in exports, already at a low 6.7% of total in 1993, fell even further, to 5.2% in 1994. As a result, Russia has become increasingly dependent on Siberia and the Far East: almost two-thirds of its exports originate in this area. As for the structure of imports, it also displays the trends of a deteriorating economy increasingly oriented towards its survival: in 1994 the share of machinery imports went down from 33% to 30%, while the share of food imports (in spite of a good harvest) increased from 23% to 33%. Imports of poultry from America, including the famous "Bush's legs,"[176] accounted for a substantial proportion of food imports.

The other major linkage developing between the global economy and the Russian economy is portfolio investment by foreign capital. Indeed, foreign capital is considered to account for about 80% of transactions on the Russian stock exchange. The main reason for such interest is that Russian companies' shares were hugely undervalued during the phase of accelerated privatization accomplished by the Russian Government in 1992–5.[177] According to some sources, through 1994 about $11 billion have been committed (though not invested as yet) in shares of companies in sectors such as oil and gas, electronics and telecommunications, leisure and hotels, transportation equipment and shipping, and real estate. These investments not only may pay off in the future, when and if a giant Russian market economy starts working, but they have already revalued the acquired assets by three to ten times.[178] A case in point is Gazprom, the giant gas consortium, managing 40% of the world's natural gas reserves, privatized, but still under control of Russian state holdings. In 1994,

---

[175]   Kovalyova (1995); Kur'yerov (1995a and b); Castells, Granberg and Kiselyova (1996a, in progress).

[176] In the early 1990s, as an expression of American support, President Bush stepped up subsidized exports of frozen food and poultry to Russia. Thus, in many Russian homes, the only meat seen for months were chicken drumsticks, quickly named by people "Bush's legs," in fact a sign of appreciation, with a little ironic twist. In 1995, the Russian government argued that some of their poultry imports presented a health risk.

[177]   Denisova (1995); Stevenson (1994).

[178]   *Economist* (1994b); Denisova (1995).

the stock market valued its reserves at three-tenths of $1 per barrel of oil equivalent, compared with $10.30 for British Gas:[179] whoever bought its shares is sure to make a hefty profit in not such a long time. Thus, most of this portfolio investment aims more at financial speculation than at reconstructing the Russian economy. Russian interests, and particularly company managers and government *apparatchiki* who presided over the privatization process, kept the most valuable property under their control, yet devalued stocks of privatized companies in order to offer substantial profits to foreign partners in exchange for instant cash, most often kept in bank accounts abroad.

Foreign direct investment in production is proceeding with extraordinary precautions in the situation of legal uncertainty, bureaucratic arbitrariness, and safety concerns that characterize Russia's wild capitalism. Even in the potentially profitable oil and gas sector, prudence is the rule. Our own research on investment by American and Japanese companies in the most promising offshore oil and gas drilling in Sakhalin[180] shows that, while substantial investment could come from these companies (about $25 billion in 20 years), firm commitments await the final passage of special legislation that would guarantee entire freedom of movement for capital and management of production to foreign companies. In contrast, huge gas reserves in Western Siberia appear to be less attractive to foreign direct investment because of the need to rely on Russian controls for production and transportation of gas. In other words: foreign capital approaches to Russia aim at taking advantage of energy and natural resources, as well as of good financial deals, while being as little involved as possible in the Russian economy and setting up its own operating infrastructure. On the other hand, Russian government and Russian business strategy seems to be to attract foreign capital to prepackaged deals, without relinquishing control except when there is no alternative (for example, lack of technology and equipment for offshore drilling).

Yet understanding the dynamics of Russian transition to the market economy, including its connection to the global economy, lies in what is fundamentally at stake in this transition: primitive accumulation of capital on a gigantic scale. Or, in less analytical terms, the pillage of Russia's wealth, as the old class of *apparatchiki* strives to become fully fledged partners of global capitalism, sometimes by using unruly methods. Indeed, a non-negligible fraction of new business elites are sometimes connected to various criminal economy networks,

---

[179]   Stevenson (1994).
[180]   Castells, Granberg, and Kiselyova (1996a, in progress).

probably the most internationalized sector of the Russian economy. Iurii Sukhotin, using several sources, estimated that in 1992 criminal business income in Russia accounted for about 14.5% of Russian GDP. Since then, the proportion has probably increased.[181] While the process of primitive accumulation goes on, and as long as the struggle continues between different groups and persons to appropriate individually what was state property through a largely biased privatization process blessed by the world's financial institutions, nothing can be settled, investment can hardly proceed, and the real economy continues to decline. Indeed, survival mechanisms and petty commodity trade are the staple of daily life for most Russian people. The quasi-informal kiosk economy as the basis for trade, and cultivation at dachas for self-subsistence are the real pillars of Russia's transition to the market economy.[182] Limited linkages to the international economy, overwhelmingly concentrated in Moscow and St Petersburg and connected to a few nodes from Nizhni-Novgorod to Khabarovsk, through Yekaterinburg, Tomsk, and Novosibirsk, constitute the dynamic pole of the new economy, making a few hundred millionaires (in dollars) and a few thousand billionaires (in rubles) as the living proof of success on the wildest capitalist frontier.

In the mean time, living standards for the large majority of the population continue to decline, and, together with a catastrophic environmental heritage, have prompted the spectacular rise of mortality rates in Russia, reversing for the first time a worldwide historical trend towards increasing life expectancy.[183] There is a growing polarization between small segments of Russia that are being fully globalized and the majority of people who are being drawn into an increasingly primitive, local economy, often submitted to racketeering and violence. Such a tendency may trigger unpredictable social responses and help the political chances of a populist, ultra-nationalist movement. In 1995, a celebrated joke in Russian intellectual circles attributed *perestroyka* to a genial design by Andropov to relegitimize communism among the Russian people after a few years of experiencing capitalism. I doubt memories are so

---

[181]   Handelman (1995); Voshchanov (1995); *Commersant Weekly* (1995); Sukhotin (1994).

[182]   Kuleshov (1994).

[183]   Male life expectancy in Russia in 1990 was 64 years, compared with 72 years for American men. But it dropped further to 57 years in 1994, putting Russia at a lower level than Egypt or Bolivia. Infant mortality rate increased by 15% per year in 1992–4. In 1994, the death rate in Russia reached 15.6 per 1,000 people, an increase of about 30% since 1992 (death rate in the US was 9 per 1,000). See Specter (1995).

short in Russia. However, I do not think either that the social segmentation and social exclusion implicit in the logic of the new global economy can proceed further in Russia without being challenged.

In April 1992 the Advisory Committee to the Russian Government on the Social Problems of the Transition, which I chaired, delivered a confidential report to the Acting Prime Minister and Deputy Prime Ministers,[184] in which we wrote:

> A market economy does not operate outside of an institutional context. The key task for the Reform Movement in Russia today is to build the institutional context in order to create the conditions necessary for a market economy. Without such structures the market economy cannot develop beyond petty speculation and one shot looting. That is to say, a functioning, or productive market economy is fundamentally different from the simple task of transferring assets from the state and the old nomenklatura to their successors. . . . This social, political, and institutional infrastructure includes many elements, such as: laws, rules, codes, and procedures for resolving conflicts, for determining responsibility, for defining property, for defining and bounding property rights. [It is also necessary] to generate quickly a widespread conviction that those rules are indeed the rules governing economic life, and not just pieces of paper. For that to happen, a functioning public administration is needed. The market is not a substitute for the state: it is a complement. Without it the market cannot work.

The report was praised by the then Russian leaders, yet was not very influential in policy-making. A few months later, our duly warned interlocutors, Gaidar and Burbulis, were evicted from the government. A year later, tanks were necessary to promulgate a new constitution. Two years later, Zhirinovsky and the communists scored

---

[184]   In January 1992, the Prime Minister's Office of the first democratic government of post-Soviet Russia asked me to organize an international advisory committee of leading social scientists to help the Russian Government to manage social problems during the transition period. I accepted the task, and a Committee comprising Fernando Henrique Cardoso, Martin Carnoy, Stephen S. Cohen, Alain Touraine, and me went to work on the matter. During 1992 we/I had several meetings with Russian leaders in Moscow (including a closed-door, two full days meeting of the whole committee with Gaidar, Burbulis, Shokhin, and their staff in March 1992). We wrote a report, and several working notes, all confidential, although I decided that the short paragraph quoted in this book does not compromise international security. For press reports on the activities of this Committee, which faded away by the end of 1992 after Gaidar's resignation, see *Izvestia*, 1 April 1992: 2, and 9 July 1992: 1.

major wins in parliamentary elections. Three years later, in 1995, the
communists won in the parliamentary elections. In 1994, an in-depth
assessment of the Russian economy published in *EKO*, the prestigious
economics journal of the Siberian Academy of Sciences, concluded
that

> there is an obvious and evidently final failure of government's
> economic policy, with its one-sided accent on financial stabiliz-
> ation, with disregard of interests of material production, with an
> excessively simplified, and politicized approach to problems of
> market development, and with its primitive understanding
> of role and functions of the state in the market economy.[185]

Yet the apparent inattention to obvious warnings can be easily
explained in terms of social interests served by this economic policy.
The segmented incorporation of Russia to the global economy, a
fundamental matter for the future structure and dynamics of this
economy, is taking place not according to the a-historical logic of
markets, but to historically determined processes that, as in the
origins of capitalism in other latitudes, were motivated by greed and
imposed by force.

The Architecture and Geometry of the Informational/Global Economy

I can now sum up the structure and dynamics of the new global
economy emerging from the historical interaction between the rise of
informationalism and capitalist restructuring.

**The structure of this economy is characterized by the combination
of an enduring architecture and a variable geometry.** The architecture
of the global economy features an asymmetrically interdependent
world, organized around three major economic regions and increasingly polarized along an axis of opposition between productive,
information-rich, affluent areas, and impoverished areas, economically devalued and socially excluded. Between the three dominant
regions, Europe, North America, and the Asian Pacific, the latter
appears to be the most dynamic yet the most vulnerable because of its
dependence upon the openness of the markets of the other regions.
However, the intertwining of economic processes between the three
regions makes them practically inseparable in their fate. Around each
region an economic hinterland has been created, with some countries

[185] Kur'yerov (1994: 7, translation by E. Kiselyova). For an alternative view on
the Russian economic record, with which I disagree, see the informed book by
Aslund (1995).

being gradually incorporated into the global economy, usually through the dominant regions that are their geographic neighbors: North America for Latin America; the European Union for Eastern Europe, Russia, and the South Mediterranean; Japan and the Asian Pacific for the rest of Asia, as well as for Australia and New Zealand, and maybe for the Russian Pacific, Eastern Siberia and Kazakhstan; Africa, while still dependent on ex-colonial economic networks, seems to be increasingly marginalized in the global economy; the Middle East is, by and large, integrated into the global networks of finance and energy supply, although highly dependent on the avatars of the world's geopolitics.

To be sure, there is nothing automatic in the emergence of such a world economic order: Russia is likely to emerge as a power on its own and could link up with Japan, providing much-needed energy and natural resources, once Japanese nationalism is ready to settle the Kuriles dispute; Kazakhstan has strong connections with American oil companies, and with South Korean *chaebol*; MERCOSUR[186] exports more to Europe than to North America, and Chilean markets are increasingly in the Asian Pacific; China is linking up with the ethnic Chinese networks in the Pacific rather than with Japan, most likely constituting in the future a formidable, economic subregion with more capital and labor than the Japanese-centered area; South Korea is not, by any means, an appendage of Japan, and is becoming a major world player in high-technology industries. The "South" is increasingly differentiated internally, and some of its fragments are being incorporated into the "North" over time; for example, Indonesia is being drawn into the dynamic waters of the Asian Pacific economy, both through Japanese and through ethnic Chinese investments. Even Africa is not necessarily sentenced to poverty: as mentioned above, the new democratic, black-majority-ruled South Africa could be the industrial, financial, and technological magnet of the Southern African subcontinent, maybe linking up with Angola, Namibia, Mozambique, Botswana, and Zimbabwe to form a viable subregional entity. Yet, in spite of all the complexity of this pattern, there is a basic architecture, inherited from history, that frames the development of the global economy.

However, this is not the whole story. Within this visible architecture there are dynamic processes of competition and change that infuse a variable geometry into the global system of economic processes.

---

[186]   MERCOSUR is the trade association between Brazil, Argentina, Uruguay, and Paraguay, that represents the embryo of a future South American Common Market. In 1995, the largest share of MERCOSUR exports went to the European Union.

Indeed, the evolution that I have recalled somewhat schematically in the preceding pages shows the emergence of a new pattern of international division of labor, characteristic of the global economy. What I call the newest international division of labor is constructed around four different positions in the informational/global economy: the producers of high value, based on informational labor; the producers of high volume, based on lower-cost labor; the producers of raw materials, based on natural endowments; and the redundant producers, reduced to devalued labor. The differential location of such different types of labor also determines the affluence of markets, since income generation will depend upon the capacity to create value incorporated in each segment of the global economy. The critical matter is that these different positions do not coincide with countries. *They are organized in networks and flows, using the technological infrastructure of the informational economy.* They feature geographic concentrations in some areas of the planet, so that the global economy is not geographically undifferentiated. Yet the newest international division of labor does not take place between countries but between economic agents placed in the four positions I have indicated along a global structure of networks and flows. In this sense, all countries are penetrated by the four positions indicated because all networks are global in their reality or in their target. Even marginalized economies have a small segment of their directional functions connected to the high-value producers network, at least to ensure the transfer of whatever capital or information is still accumulated in the country. And certainly, the most powerful economies have marginal segments of their population placed in a position of devalued labor, be it in New York,[187] in Osaka,[188] in London,[189] or in Madrid.[190]

Because the position in the international division of labor does not depend, fundamentally, on the characteristics of the country but on the characteristics of its labor (including embodied knowledge) and of its insertion into the global economy, changes may occur, and indeed do, in a short time span. Actions by governments and by entrepreneurial sectors of societies are critical in this matter. The newest international division of labor is organized on the basis of labor and technology, but is enacted and modified by governments and entrepreneurs. The relentlessly variable geometry that results from such processes of innovation and competition struggles with the historically produced architecture of the world economic order, inducing the creative chaos that characterizes the new economy.

[187]   Mollenkopf and Castells (eds) (1991).
[188]   Sugihara et al. (1988).
[189]   Lee and Townsend (1993).
[190]   Leal (1993).

Appendix: Some methodological comments on adjustment policies in Africa and their evaluation

In 1993, the World Bank's Development Vice-Presidency conducted a study aimed at responding to criticisms of its adjustment policies in Africa. Indeed the record, in the words of the World's Bank Development Vice-President and Chief Economist "raised troubling questions about the extent and efficacy of the policy reform efforts" (World Bank 1994a xi). The study, published in 1994, intended to provide evidence on the economic benefits of adjustment policies recommended by the Bank. It received wide publicity in the media, as well as in development forums, as proof of the rightful attitude of international institutions in advocating macroeconomic adjustment policies in spite of the social and political costs of such policies. Because of the relevance of this matter, and of this report, to the debate on development and underdevelopment in the new global economy, I believe it can be helpful to challenge the empirical evidence presented in it, at the price of going into some petty details concerning the use of statistics in justifying failed policies. Within the limits of this note, I shall simply point to faulty procedures, inviting the reader to judge by checking the report. To simplify the matter, I am not introducing different data sources, but taking at face value (a nonobvious approach) data as presented.

In a nutshell, the procedure followed by the authors of the report was to classify 26 Sub-Saharan countries according to their good or bad behavior on macroeconomic policies into three groups: large improvement in macroeconomic policies, small improvement, and deterioration. The terminology of course suggests that economic improvement, measured by rates of variation in GDP per capita, would follow broadly within the same groupings. Then for each country and group of countries their percentage of average annual GDP growth is compared for two periods: 1981–6 (before adjustment policies) and 1987–91 (after adjustment policies). Although countries as a whole did not improve much (0.5 percentage points of difference between periods), the difference in percentage points by group shows that "good policy countries" fared somewhat better than "small improving policy countries" (median of 1.8 points difference versus 1.5), and much better than the "deteriorating policy countries" (median of –2.6) (see World Bank 1994a: 138, table 5.1).

I argue that the conclusion that "There are rewards to adjustment, as countries that have come further in implementing good policies –

particularly good macroeconomic policies – have enjoyed a resurgence of growth" (Vice-President's foreword, p. xi) is inaccurate and misleading as stated, and overall is based on a statistical artifact. It is inaccurate as stated because two out of the six "good policy countries," according to World Bank criteria, actually decreased their rate of growth between periods: Burkina Faso by 1.7 points, and The Gambia by 0.8 of a point. It is misleading because the highest performing country of all 26, Mozambique, which improved its growth rate by 7.6 points, is ranked deep down in the "bad policy countries" group of the report. It is also misleading because the three highest performers, Nigeria, Ghana, and Tanzania, improved their rate to a large extent because they were coming from substantially negative rates of growth in the preceding period (–4.6%, –2.4%, –1.7%), which was also the case for Mozambique. And it is a statistical artifact because the calculations by group (median and mean) are biased by groupings in widely different sizes for each group (six good policy countries, nine medium policy countries, and eleven bad policy countries).

It works like this: if you have 26 countries in a generally bad situation, and you group together eleven as "deteriorating" and six under "good policy," it will be more difficult for the eleven-member pool than for the six-member pool to show a good mean value, simply because more "low values" will go into the eleven member-pool by simple statistical probability.

Let us change the procedure, and group the countries by their actual performance in improving the growth rate. Let us now take the top one-third of the distribution, that is eight countries (cutting, by the natural break point of the curve, between 2.2 and 1.6). What kind of countries do we find in such a group of "economic performers"? Using World Bank categories: three "good policy countries" (Nigeria, Ghana, and Tanzania), three "small improvement" countries, and two "deterioration" countries (Mozambique and Sierra Leone, both among the top six). This is hardly the basis for a significant correlation, let alone for drawing conclusions about development policies. Indeed, if we rank 26 countries in two scales, one of improvement in GDP per capita, and another of obedience to adjustment policies, the two rankings differ considerably.

The report does calculate a linear regression between policy and GDP growth, which is shown to be significant, but only after controlling the equation to eliminate the effect of the growth rate before adjustment, since its authors acknowledge that countries which were doing particularly poorly are more likely to experience an improvement (p. 140), thus voiding of meaning such a calculation. If we eliminate from the "good six" group, countries that were doing badly in the first period (Nigeria, Ghana, and Tanzania), the whole group disappears since, as stated, the growth rate of two others in fact decreased, so that the only star, at the end, would be Zimbabwe, displaying a staggering performance from 0.3% growth to 1.0% growth.

In the final analysis, it is difficult to understand why the authors of the report go through all this pain to prove their point, gearing up to the ultimate policy goal of improving export performance as the development tool in the global economy, only to find in their regression analysis that "the terms-of-trade effect is not significant and generally has the wrong sign (improved terms of trade slows growth)" (p. 140). Never mind, the authors have an answer: "This result reflects the peculiarities of the short time period under study and should not be taken to contradict the well-established positive relation in the long run between growth and the terms of trade" (p. 140). But "the peculiarities of the short time period under study" do not deter the authors from taking less negative trends of growth as proof of goodness of adjustment policies. This is how decisions are taken, and legitimized *ex post*, in the wonderland of international financial institutions.

— 3 —

The Network Enterprise: The Culture, Institutions, and Organizations of the Informational Economy

Introduction

The informational economy, as with all historically distinctive forms of production, is characterized by its specific culture and institutions. Yet culture, in this analytical framework, should not be considered as a set of values and beliefs linked to a particular society. What characterizes the development of the informational, global economy is precisely its emergence in very different cultural/national contexts: in North America, in Western Europe, in Japan, in the "China circle," in Russia, in Latin America, as well as its planetary reach, affecting all countries, and leading to a multi-cultural framework of reference. Indeed, the attempts to propose a theory of "cultural economics" to account for new development processes on the basis of philosophies and mentalities (such as Confucianism), particularly in the Asian Pacific,[1] have not resisted the scrutiny of empirical research.[2] But the diversity of cultural contexts where the informational economy emerges and evolves does not preclude the existence of a common matrix of organizational forms in the processes of production, consumption, and distribution. Without such organizational arrangements, neither technological change, state policies, nor firms' strategies would be able to come together in a new economic system. I contend, along with a growing number of scholars, that cultures manifest themselves fundamentally through their embeddedness in institutions and organizations.[3] By organizations I understand specific

[1] Berger (1987); Berger and Hsiao (eds) (1988).
[2] Hamilton and Biggart (1988); Biggart (1991); Clegg (1990); Whitley (1993); Janelli (1993).
[3] Granovetter (1985); Clegg (1992); Evans (1995).

systems of means oriented to the performance of specific goals. By institutions I understand organizations invested with the necessary authority to perform some specific tasks on behalf of society as a whole. The culture that matters for the constitution and development of a given economic system is the one that materializes in organizational logics, using Nicole Biggart's concept: "By organizational logics I mean a legitimating principle that is elaborated in an array of derivative social practices. In other words, organizational logics are the ideational bases for institutionalized authority relations."[4]

My thesis is that the rise of the informational economy is characterized by the development of a new organizational logic which is related to the current process of technological change, but not dependent upon it. It is the convergence and interaction between a new technological paradigm and a new organizational logic that constitutes the historical foundation of the informational economy. However, this organizational logic manifests itself under different forms in various cultural and institutional contexts. Thus, in this chapter I shall try to account at the same time for the commonality of organizational arrangements in the informational economy, and for their contextual variety. In addition, I shall examine the genesis of this new organizational form and the conditions of its interaction with the new technological paradigm.

Organizational Trajectories in the Restructuring of Capitalism and in the Transition from Industrialism to Informationalism

The economic restructuring of the 1980s induced a number of reorganizing strategies in business firms.[5] Some analysts, particularly Piore and Sabel, argue that the economic crisis of the 1970s resulted from the exhaustion of the mass-production system, constituting a "second industrial divide" in the history of capitalism.[6] For others, such as Harrison and Storper,[7] the diffusion of new organizational forms, some of which had already been practiced in some countries or firms for many years, was the response to the crisis of profitability in the process of capital accumulation. Others, like Coriat[8] suggest a

---

[4]   Biggart (1992: 49).
[5]   Harrison (1994); Sengenberger and Campbell (eds) (1992); Williamson (1985).
[6]   Piore and Sabel (1984).
[7]   Harrison (1994).
[8]   Coriat (1990).

long-term evolution from "Fordism" to "post-Fordism," as an expression of a "grand transition," the historical transformation of the relationships between, on the one hand, production and productivity, and on the other hand, consumption and competition. But in spite of the diversity of approaches there is coincidence in four fundamental points of the analysis:

(a) whichever the causes and the genesis of the organizational transformation, there was from the mid-1970s onwards a major divide (industrial or otherwise) in the organization of production and markets in the global economy;
(b) organizational changes interacted with the diffusion of information technology but by and large were independent, and in general preceded the diffusion of information technologies in business firms;
(c) the fundamental goal of organizational changes, in various forms, was to cope with the uncertainty caused by the fast pace of change in the economic, institutional, and technological environment of the firm by enhancing flexibility in production, management, and marketing;
(d) many organizational changes were aimed at redefining labor processes and employment practices, introducing the model of "lean production" with the objective of saving labor, by the automation of jobs, elimination of tasks, and suppression of managerial layers.

However, these sweeping interpretations of major organizational changes in the last two decades display an excessive tendency to merge in one single evolutionary trend various processes of change that are in fact different, albeit interrelated. In a parallel analysis to the notion of technological trajectories,[9] I propose to consider the development of different organizational trajectories, namely specific arrangements of systems of means oriented toward increasing productivity and competitiveness in the new technological paradigm and in the new global economy. In most cases, these trajectories evolved from industrial organizational forms, such as the vertically integrated corporation and the independent small business firm, that had become unable to perform their tasks under the new structural conditions of production and markets, a trend that became fully apparent in the crisis of the 1970s. In other cultural contexts, new organizational forms emerged from preexisting ones that had been pushed aside by the classical model of industrial organization, to find

---

[9]   Dosi (1988).

new life in the requirements of the new economy and in the possibilities offered by new technologies. Several organizational trends evolved from the process of capitalist restructuring and industrial transition. They must be considered separately before proposing their potential convergence in a new kind of organizational paradigm.

From mass production to flexible production

The first, and broader, trend of organizational evolution that has been identified, particularly in the pioneering work by Piore and Sabel, is the **transition from mass production to flexible production, or from "Fordism" to "post-Fordism"** in Coriat's formulation. The mass-production model was based on productivity gains obtained by economies of scale in an assembly-line-based, mechanized process of production of a standardized product, under the conditions of control of a large market by a *specific organizational form: the large corporation structured on the principles of vertical integration, and institutionalized social and technical division of labor.* These principles were embedded in the management methods known as "Taylorism" and "scientific organization of work," methods adopted as guidelines by both Henry Ford and Lenin.

When demand became unpredictable in quantity and quality, when markets were diversified worldwide and thereby difficult to control, and when the pace of technological change made obsolete single-purpose production equipment, the mass-production system became too rigid and too costly for the characteristics of the new economy. A tentative answer to overcome such rigidity was the flexible production system. It has been practiced and theorized in two different forms: first, as flexible specialization, in the formulation of Piore and Sabel, on the basis of the experience of the Northern Italian industrial districts, when "production accommodates to ceaseless change without pretending to control it"[10] in a pattern of industrial craft, or customized production. Similar practices have been observed by researchers in firms performing advanced services, such as banking.[11]

Yet industrial management practice in recent years has introduced another form of flexibility: dynamic flexibility in the formulation of Coriat, or high-volume flexible production in the formula proposed by Cohen and Zysman, also shown by Baran to characterize the transformation of the insurance industry.[12] High-volume flexible

---

[10]   Piore and Sabel (1984: 17).
[11]   Hirschhorn (1985); Bettinger (1991); Daniels (1993).
[12]   Coriat (1990: 165); Cohen and Zysman (1987); Baran (1985).

production systems, usually linked to a situation of growing demand for a given product, combine high-volume production, permitting economies of scale, and customized, reprogrammable production systems, capturing economies of scope. New technologies allow for the transformation of assembly lines characteristic of the large corporation into easy-to-program production units that can be sensitive to variations in the market (product flexibility) and in the changes of technological inputs (process flexibility).

Small business and the crisis of the large corporation: myth and reality

A second, distinct trend emphasized by analysts in recent years, is *the crisis of the large corporation, and the resilience of small and medium firms as agents of innovation and sources of job creation.*[13] For some observers, the crisis of the corporation is the necessary consequence of the crisis of standardized mass production, while the revival of customized, craft production and flexible specialization is better enacted by small businesses.[14] Bennett Harrison has written a devastating empirical critique of this thesis.[15] According to his analysis, based on data from the United States, Western Europe, and Japan, large corporations have continued to concentrate a growing proportion of capital and markets in all major economies; their share of employment has not changed in the last decade, except in the UK; small and medium firms remain by and large under the financial, commercial, and technological control of large corporations; he also contends that small businesses are less technologically advanced, and less able to innovate technologically in process and in product than larger firms. Furthermore, on the basis of the work of a number of Italian researchers (Bianchi and Belussi, particularly) he shows how the archetype of flexible specialization, the Italian firms in the industrial districts of Emilia Romagna during the early 1990s, went through a series of mergers, and either came under the control of large corporations or became large corporations themselves (for example, Benetton), or else were unable to keep up with the pace of competition if they remained small and fragmented, as in the Prato district.

Some of these statements are controversial. The work by other researchers points to somewhat different conclusions.[16] For instance,

[13] Weiss (1988); Sengenberger et al. (eds) (1990); Clegg (1990).
[14] Piore and Sabel (1984); Lorenz (1988); Birch (1987).
[15] Harrison (1994).
[16] Weiss (1988, 1992).

the study by Schiatarella on Italian small firms suggests that small businesses have outperformed large firms in job creation, profit margins, investment per capita, technological change, productivity, and value added. Friedman's study on Japanese industrial structure even pretends that it is precisely this dense network of small and medium subcontracting enterprises which lies at the root of Japanese competitiveness. Also the calculations by Michael Teitz and collaborators, years ago, on California's small businesses pointed at the enduring vitality and critical economic role of small businesses.[17]

In fact, we must separate the argument concerning the shift of economic power and technological capability from the large corporation to small firms (a trend that, as Harrison argues, does not seem to be supported by empirical evidence) from the argument referring to the decline of the large, vertically integrated corporation as an organizational model. Indeed, Piore and Sabel foresaw the possibility of survival of the corporate model through what they called "multinational Keynesianism," that is the expansion and conquest of world markets by corporate conglomerates, counting on growing demand from a rapidly industrializing world. But to do so, corporations did have to change their organizational structures. Some of the changes implied the growing use of subcontracting to small and medium businesses, whose vitality and flexibility allowed gains in productivity and efficiency for large corporations, as well as for the economy as a whole.[18]

Thus, at the same time, it is true that small and medium businesses appear to be forms of organization well adapted to the flexible production system of the informational economy, and it is also true that their renewed dynamism comes under the control of large corporations that remain at the center of the structure of economic power in the new global economy. We are not witnessing the demise of powerful, large corporations, but we are indeed observing the crisis of the traditional corporate model of organization based on vertical integration, and hierarchical, functional management: the "staff and line" system of strict technical and social division of labor within the firm.

[17] Schiatarella (1984); Friedman (1988); Teitz et al. (1981).
[18] Gereffi (1993).

"Toyotism": management–worker cooperation, multifunctional labor, total quality control, and reduction of uncertainty

A third development concerns *new methods of management,* most of them originating in Japanese firms,[19] although in some cases they were experimenting within other contexts, for example in Volvo's Kalmar complex in Sweden.[20] The substantial success in productivity and competitiveness obtained by Japanese automobile firms has been attributed to a large extent to this managerial revolution, so that in the business literature "Toyotism" is opposed to "Fordism" as the new winning formula adapted to the global economy and to the flexible production system.[21] The original Japanese model has been widely imitated by other companies, as well as transplanted by Japanese firms to their foreign locations, often leading to a substantial improvement in the performance of these firms *vis-à-vis* the traditional industrial system.[22] Some elements of this model are well known:[23] the *kan-ban* (or "just in time") system of supplies, by which inventories are eliminated or reduced substantially through delivery from the suppliers to the production site at the exact required time and with the characteristics specified for the production line; "total quality control" of products in the production process, aiming at near-zero defects and best use of resources; workers' involvement in the production process, by using team work, decentralized initiative, greater autonomy of decision on the shop floor, rewards for team performance, and a flat management hierarchy with few status symbols in the daily life of the firm.

Culture may have been important in generating "Toyotism" (particularly the consensus-building, cooperative model of team work) but it is certainly not a determinant for its implementation. The model works equally well in Japanese firms in Europe, and in the United States, and several of its elements have been successfully adopted by American (GM-Saturn) or German (Volkswagen) factories. Indeed, the model was perfected by Toyota engineers over a period of 20 years, after its first, limited introduction in 1948. To be able to generalize the method to the whole factory system, Japanese engineers studied the control procedures used in American supermarkets to assess stock on their shelves, so it could be argued that "just in time"

---

[19]   Nonaka (1990); Coriat (1990); Durlabhji and Marks (eds) (1993).
[20]   Sandkull (1992).
[21]   Cusumano (1985); McMillan (1984).
[22]   Wilkinson et al. (1992).
[23]   Coriat (1990); Aoki (1988); Dohse et al. (1985).

is to some extent an American mass-production method, adapted to flexible management by using the specificity of Japanese firms, particularly the cooperative relationship between management and workers.

The stability and complementarity of relationships between the core firm and the suppliers' network are extremely important for the implementation of this model: Toyota maintains in Japan a three-tier network of suppliers embracing thousands of firms of different sizes.[24] Most of the markets for most of the firms are captive markets for Toyota, and the same can be said of other major firms. How different is this from the structure of divisions and departments in a vertically integrated corporation? Most of the key suppliers are in fact controlled or influenced by financial, commercial or technological undertakings, belonging either to the parent firm or to the overarching *keiretsu*. Under such conditions, are we not observing a system of planned production under the premise of relative market control by the large corporation? Thus, what is important in this model is the vertical disintegration of production along a network of firms, a process that substitutes for the vertical integration of departments within the same corporate structure. The network allows for greater differentiation of the labor and capital components of the production unit, and probably builds in greater incentives and stepped-up responsibility, without necessarily altering the pattern of concentration of industrial power and technological innovation.

The performance of the model relies also on the absence of major disruptions in the overall process of production and distribution. Or, to put it in other words, it is based on the assumption of the "five zeros": zero defect in the parts; zero mischief in the machines; zero inventory; zero delay; zero paperwork. Such performances can only be predicated on the basis of an absence of work stoppages and total control over labor, on entirely reliable suppliers, and on adequately predicted markets. **"Toyotism" is a management system designed to reduce uncertainty rather than to encourage adaptability.** The flexibility is in the process, not in the product. Thus, some analysts have suggested that it could be considered as an extension of "Fordism,"[25] keeping the same principles of mass production, yet organizing the production process on the basis of human initiative and feedback capacity to eliminate waste (of time, work, and resources) while maintaining the characteristics of output close to the business plan. Is this

[24] Friedman (1988); Weiss (1992).
[25] Tetsuro and Steven (eds) (1994).

really a management system well fitted to a global economy in constant swirl? Or, as Stephen Cohen likes to say, "Is it too late for 'just in time'?"

In fact, the truly distinctive character of Toyotism, as distinct from Fordism, does not concern relationships between firms, but between management and workers. As Coriat argued, in the international seminar convened in Tokyo to debate the question "Is Japanese Management Post-Fordism?," in fact, "it is neither pre- nor post-Fordist, but an original and new way of managing the labor process: the central and distinctive feature of the Japanese path was to de-specialize the professional workers and, instead of scattering them, to turn them into multi-functional specialists."[26] A distinguished Japanese economist, Aoki, also emphasizes labor organization as the key to the success of Japanese firms:

> The main difference between the American firm and the Japanese firm may be summarized as follows: the American firm emphasizes efficiency attained through fine specialization and sharp job demarcation, whereas the Japanese firm emphasizes the capability of the workers' group to cope with local emergencies autonomously, which is developed through learning by doing and sharing knowledge on the shopfloor.[27]

Indeed, some of the most important organizational mechanisms underlying productivity growth in Japanese firms seem to have been overlooked by Western experts of management. Thus, Ikujiro Nonaka,[28] on the basis of his studies of major Japanese companies, has proposed a simple, elegant model to account for the generation of knowledge in the firm. What he labels "the knowledge-creating company" is based on the organizational interaction between "explicit knowledge" and "tacit knowledge" at the source of innovation. He argues that much of the knowledge accumulated in the firm is made out of experience, and cannot be communicated by workers under excessively formalized management procedures. And yet the sources of innovation multiply when organizations are able to establish bridges to transfer tacit into explicit knowledge, explicit into tacit knowledge, tacit into tacit, and explicit into explicit. By so doing, not only is worker experience communicated and amplified to increase the formal body of knowledge in the company, but also knowledge generated in the outside world can be incorporated into the tacit

[26]   Coriat (1994: 182).
[27]   Aoki (1988: 16).
[28]   Nonaka (1991); Nonaka and Takeuchi (1994).

habits of workers, enabling them to work out their own uses and to improve on the standard procedures. In an economic system where innovation is critical, the organizational ability to increase its sources from all forms of knowledge becomes the foundation of the innovative firm. This organizational process, however, requires the full participation of workers in the innovation process, so that they do not keep their tacit knowledge solely for their own benefit. It also requires stability of the labor force in the company, because only then does it become rational for the individual to transfer his/her knowledge to the company, and for the company to diffuse explicit knowledge among its workers. Thus, this apparently simple mechanism, the dramatic effects of which in enhancing productivity and quality are shown in a number of case studies, in fact engages a profound transformation of management–labor relationships. Although information technology does not play a prominent role in Nonaka's "explicit analysis," in our personal conversations we shared the thought that on-line communication and computerized storage capacity have become powerful tools in developing the complexity of organizational links between tacit and explicit knowledge. Yet this form of innovation preceded the development of information technologies, and was, in fact, for the last two decades "tacit knowledge" of Japanese management, removed from the observation of foreign managerial experts, but truly decisive in improving performance of the Japanese firms.

Interfirm networking

Let us now turn to consider two other forms of organizational flexibility in the international experience, characterized by interfirm linkages. These are *the multidirectional network model enacted by small and medium businesses* and *the licensing–subcontracting model of production under an umbrella corporation*. I shall briefly describe these two distinct organizational models that have played a considerable role in the economic growth of several countries in the last two decades.

Small and medium enterprises, as I wrote, in concurrence with Bennett Harrison's argument, are often under the control of subcontracting arrangements or financial/technological domination from large corporations. Yet they also frequently take the initiative in establishing networking relationships with several large firms and/or with other small and medium enterprises, finding market niches and co-operative ventures. Besides the classical example of the Italian industrial districts, a good case in point is represented by Hong Kong's manufacturing firms. As I argued in my book on Hong Kong, on the basis of work by Victor Sit and other researchers of the Hong Kong scene,[29] its export success was based, for a long period between the late 1950s and the early 1980s, on domestic small businesses networks competing in the world economy. Over 85% of Hong Kong manufacturing exports up to the early 1980s originated from Chinese family-based firms, of which 41% were small enterprises employing fewer than 50 workers. In most cases they did not subcontract to larger firms, but exported through the network of Hong Kong's import–export firms – also small, also Chinese, and also family-based – that numbered 14,000 in the late 1970s. Networks of production and distribution formed, disappeared, and reformed on the basis of the variations in the world market, through the signals transmitted by flexible intermediaries often using a network of "commercial spies" in the main world markets. Very often the same person would be entrepreneur or salaried worker at different points in time, according to the circumstances of the business cycle and his own family needs.

Taiwan's exports during the 1960s came also mainly from a similar small and medium enterprise system, although in this case the traditional Japanese trading companies were the main intermediaries.[30] Granted, as Hong Kong prospered, many of the small enterprises merged, refinanced, and grew bigger, sometimes linking up with large department stores or manufacturers in Europe and America, to become their surrogate producers. Yet the, by then, medium-large businesses subcontracted much of their own production to firms (small, medium, and large) across the Chinese border in the Pearl River Delta. By the mid-1990s, somewhere between six and ten million workers, depending upon the estimates used, were involved in Guandong province in these subcontracting production networks.

Taiwanese companies took an even more complex circuit. In order to produce in China, taking advantage of low labor costs, social control, and China's export quotas, they set up intermediary firms in Hong Kong. These firms linked up with local governments in Guandong and Fujian provinces, setting up manufacturing subsidiaries in China.[31] These subsidiaries put out work to small shops and homes in the surrounding villages. The flexibility of such a system allowed it to capture cost advantages in different locations, to diffuse technology throughout the system, to benefit from various supports from various governments, and to use several countries as export platforms.

In a very different context, Ybarra found a similar networking

[29]   Castells et al. (1990); Sit et al. (1979); Sit and Wong (1988).
[30]   Gold (1986).
[31]   Hsing (1996).

production pattern among small and medium footwear, textile, and toy-making enterprises in the Valencia region of Spain.[32] There are numerous examples of such horizontal networks of enterprises in other countries and industries, as reported in the specialized literature.[33]

A different kind of production network is the one exemplified by the so-called "Benetton Model," the object of much commentary in the business world, as well as of some limited but revealing research, particularly that by Fiorenza Belussi and by Bennett Harrison.[34] The Italian knitwear firm, a multinational enterprise grown from a small family business in the Veneto region, operates on the basis of licensing commercial franchises, reaching about 5,000 stores in the whole world, for the exclusive distribution of its products under the strictest control of the core firm. On-line feedback is received by the center from all distribution points, triggering resupply of stock, as well as defining market trends in shapes and colors. The network model is also effective at the production level by putting out work to small firms and homes in Italy and other Mediterranean countries, such as Turkey. This type of network organization is an intermediate form of arrangement between vertical disintegration through the subcontracting arrangements of a large firm and the horizontal networks of small businesses. It is a horizontal network, but based on a set of core-periphery relationships, both on the supply and on the demand side of the process.

Similar forms of horizontal business networks integrated vertically by financial control have been shown to characterize direct sales operations in America, as researched by Nicole Biggart, and to inform the decentralized structure of many business consulting firms in France, organized under an umbrella of quality control.[35]

Corporate strategic alliances

A sixth organizational pattern emerging in recent years refers to *the intertwining of large corporations* in what has come to be known as strategic alliances.[36] Such alliances are very different from the traditional forms of cartels and other oligopolistic agreements, because they concern specific times, markets, products, and processes, and they do not exclude competition in all the areas (the majority)

[32]   Ybarra (1989).
[33]   Powell (1990).
[34]   Belussi (1992); Harrison (1994).
[35]   Biggart (1990b); Leo and Philippe (1989).
[36]   Imai (1980); Gerlach (1992); Ernst (1995); Cohen and Borrus (1995b).

not covered by the agreements.[37] They have been particularly relevant in high-technology industries, as the cost of R&D has skyrocketed and access to privileged information has become increasingly difficult in an industry where innovation is the main competitive weapon.[38] Access to markets and capital resources is often exchanged for technology and manufacturing skills; in other cases joint efforts by two or more companies are undertaken to develop a new product or refine a new technology, often under the sponsorship of governments or public agencies. In Europe, the European Union has even forced companies from different countries to cooperate as a condition of receiving subsidies, as was the case with Philips, Thomson-SGS, and Siemens in the microelectronics JESSI program. Small and medium firms receive European Union and EUREKA program support for R&D on the basis of establishing joint ventures between firms of more than one country.[39] The structure of high-technology industries in the world is an increasingly complex web of alliances, agreements, and joint ventures in which most large corporations are interlinked. Such linkages do not preclude stepped-up competition. Rather, strategic alliances are decisive instruments in this competition, with today's partners becoming tomorrow's foes, while collaboration in a given market is in sharp contrast to the ferocious struggle for market share in another region of the world.[40] Furthermore, because large corporations are the tip of the pyramid of a vast network of subcontracting arrangements, their patterns of alliance and competition involve also their subcontractors. Often, practices such as securing supplies from subcontracting firms or barring access to a network are competitive weapons used by firms. Reciprocally, subcontractors use whatever margin of freedom they have to diversify their clients and hedge their bets, while absorbing technology and information for their own use. This is why proprietary information and technological copyright are so critical in the new global economy.

In sum, the large corporation in such an economy is not, and will no longer be, self-contained and self-sufficient. The arrogance of the IBMs, the Philips, or the Mitsuis of the world has become a matter of cultural history.[41] Their actual operations are conducted with other firms: not only with the hundreds or thousands of subcontracting and ancillary enterprises, but with the dozens of relatively equal partners

---

[37]   Dunning (1993).
[38]   Van Tulder and Junne (1988); Ernst and O'Connor (1992); Ernst (1995).
[39]   Baranano (1994).
[40]   Mowery (ed.) (1988).
[41]   Bennett (1990).

with whom they cooperate and compete at the same time in this new brave economic world where friends and foes are the same.

The horizontal corporation and global business networks

The corporation itself has changed its organizational model, to adapt to the conditions of unpredictability ushered in by rapid economic and technological change.[42] *The main shift can be characterized as the shift from vertical bureaucracies to the horizontal corporation.* The horizontal corporation seems to be characterized by seven main trends: organization around process, not task; a flat hierarchy; team management; measuring performance by customer satisfaction; rewards based on team performance; maximization of contacts with suppliers and customers; information, training, and retraining of employees at all levels.[43] This transformation of the corporate model, particularly visible in the 1990s in some leading American companies (such as ATT), follows the realization of the limits of the "lean production" model attempted in the 1980s. This "lean model" (justifiably called by its critics "lean and mean") was fundamentally predicated on labor savings, by using a combination of automation, computerized worker control, "putting out" work, and retrenchment of production. In its most extreme manifestation, it created what has been labelled the "hollow corporation," that is a business specialized in intermediation between financing, production, and market sales, on the basis of an established trade mark or industrial image. A direct expression of capitalist restructuring to overcome the crisis of profitability of the 1970s, the "lean production" model reduced costs but also perpetuated obsolete organizational structures rooted in the logic of the mass-production model under the conditions of oligopolistic market control. To maneuver in the new global economy, characterized by an endless flurry of new competitors using new technologies and cost-cutting capabilities, the large corporations had to become primarily more effective rather than more thrifty. The networking strategies added flexibility to the system, but they did not solve the problem of adaptability for the corporation. To be able to internalize the benefits of network flexibility the corporation had to become a network itself and dynamize each element of its internal structure: this is in essence the meaning and the purpose of the "horizontal corporation" model, often extended in the decentralization of its units and in the growing autonomy given to each of these units, even allowing them

[42]   Drucker (1988).
[43]   *Business Week* (1993); *Business Week* (1995).

to compete against each other, albeit within a common overall strategy.[44]

Ken'ichi Imai is probably the organizational analyst who has gone the furthest in proposing and documenting the thesis of the transformation of corporations into networks.[45] On the basis of his studies of Japanese and American multinational corporations, he argues that the process of internationalization of business activity has proceeded along three different strategies for firms. The first, and most traditional, refers to a multidomestic market strategy for companies investing abroad from their national platform. The second targets the global market, and organizes different company functions in different locations, which are integrated within an articulated, global strategy. The third strategy, characteristic of the most advanced economic and technological stage, is based on cross-border networks. Under this strategy, on the one hand, companies relate to a variety of domestic markets; on the other hand, there is an exchange of information between these various markets. Rather than controlling markets from the outside, companies try to integrate their market shares and market information across borders. Thus, in the old strategy, foreign direct investment aimed at taking control. Under the most recent strategy, investment is geared toward the construction of a set of relationships between companies in different institutional environments. Global competition is greatly helped by "on the spot information" from each market, so that designing strategy in a top-down approach will invite failure in a constantly changing environment and with highly diverse market dynamics. Information coming from specific time and space is the crucial factor. Information technology allows simultaneously for the decentralized retrieval of such information and for its integration into a flexible system of strategy-making. This cross-border structure allows small and medium businesses to link up with major corporations, forming networks that are able to innovate and adapt relentlessly. Thus, *the actual operating unit becomes the business project, enacted by a network*, rather than individual companies or formal groupings of companies. Business projects are implemented in fields of activity, which can be product lines, organizational tasks, or territorial areas. Appropriate information is critical to companies' performance. And the most important information, under new economic conditions, is that processed between companies, on the basis of experience received from each field. Information circulates through networks: networks between companies, networks within

---

[44]   Goodman, Sproull, and Associates (1990).
[45]   Imai (1990a).

companies, personal networks, and computer networks. New information technologies are decisive in allowing such a flexible, adaptive model to actually work. For Imai, this cross-border network model, closer to the experience of Japanese corporations than to that of American companies, which are generally sticking to the old model of a unified global strategy, is at the root of competitiveness of Japanese firms.

Provided the large corporation can reform itself, transforming its organization into an articulated network of multifunctional decision-making centers, it could actually be a superior form of management in the new economy. The reason for this is that the most important management problem in a highly decentralized, extremely flexible structure is the correction of what organizational theorist Guy Benveniste calls "articulation errors." I agree with his definition: "Articulation errors are the partial or total lack of fit between what is wanted and what is available."[46] With the increasing interconnectedness and extreme decentralization of processes in the global economy, articulation errors become more difficult to avoid, and their micro- and macroeconomic impacts have greater intensity. The flexible production model, in its different forms, maximizes the response of economic agents and units to a fast-changing environment. But it also increases the difficulty of controlling and correcting articulation errors. The large corporations, with adequate levels of information and resources, could handle such errors better than fragmented, decentralized networks, provided they use adaptability on top of flexibility. This implies the capacity of the corporation to restructure itself, not simply by eliminating redundancy, but by allocating reprogramming capabilities to all its sensors while reintegrating the overarching logic of the corporate system into a decision-making center, working on-line with the networked units in real time. Many of the debates and experiments concerning the transformation of large-scale organizations, be they private or public, business-oriented or mission-oriented, are attempts to combine flexibility and coordination capabilities, to ensure both innovation and continuity in a fast-changing environment. The "horizontal corporation" is a dynamic and strategically planned network of self-programmed, self-directed units based on decentralization, participation, and coordination.

[46]   Benveniste (1994: 74).

The crisis of the vertical corporation model and the rise of business networks

These different trends in the organizational transformation of the informational economy are relatively independent of each other. The formation of subcontracting networks centered in large enterprises is a different phenomenon from the formation of horizontal networks of small and medium businesses. The web-like structure of strategic alliances between large corporations is different from the shift toward the horizontal corporation. Workers' involvement in the production process is not necessarily reduced to the Japanese model based also on *kan-ban* and total quality control. These various trends interact with each other, influence each other, but they all are different dimensions of a fundamental process: the process of disintegration of the organizational model of vertical, rational bureaucracies, characteristic of the large corporation under the conditions of standardized mass production and oligopolistic markets.[47] The historic timing of these various trends is also different, and the time sequence of their diffusion is extremely important to the understanding of their social and economic meaning. For instance, *kan-ban* originated in Japan in 1948, and was designed by Ono Taiichi, a former labor union staff member, who became a Toyota manager.[48] "Toyotism" was gradually adopted by the Japanese automobile firms at a historical moment (the 1960s) when they still did not represent a competitive threat to the rest of the world.[49] "Toyotism" was able to develop by taking advantage of two specific mechanisms historically available to Toyota: its control over labor and its total control over a huge network of suppliers that were external to the firm but internal to the *keiretsu*. When in the 1990s Toyota had to offshore some of its production, it was not always possible to reproduce the *kan-ban* model (it was not in the symbolic NUMMI plant of Toyota-GM in Fremont, California). Thus "Toyotism" is a transitional model between standardized, mass production and a more efficient work organization characterized by the introduction of craft practices, as well as by workers' and suppliers' involvement, in an assembly-line based, industrial model.

Thus, what emerges from the observation of major organizational changes in the last two decades of the century is not a new, "one best way" of production, but the crisis of an old, powerful but excessively rigid model associated with the large, vertical corporation, and with

---

[47]   Vaill (1990).
[48]   Cusumano (1985).
[49]   McMillan (1984).

oligopolistic control over markets. A variety of models and organizational arrangements emerged from this crisis, prospering or failing according to their adaptability to various institutional contexts and competitive structures. As Piore and Sabel conclude in their book:

> Whether our economy is based on mass production or on flexible specialization are open questions. The answers will depend in part on the capacity of nations and social classes to envision the future that they want.[50]

Yet recent historical experience has already provided some of the answers concerning the new organizational forms of the informational economy. Under different organizational arrangements, and through diverse cultural expressions, they are all based in networks. **Networks are the fundamental stuff of which new organizations are and will be made.** And they are able to form and expand all over the main streets and back alleys of the global economy because of their reliance on the information power provided by the new technological paradigm.

Information Technology and the Network Enterprise

The new organizational trajectories I have described were not the mechanical consequence of technological change. Some of them preceded the rise of new information technologies. For instance, as mentioned, the *kan-ban* system was first introduced in Toyota in 1948, and its implementation did not require on-line electronic linkages. Instructions and information were written on standardized cards posted at different working points, and exchanged between suppliers and factory operators.[51] Most of the workers' involvement methods experimented with by Japanese, Swedish, and American companies, required a change of mentality rather than a change in machinery.[52] The most important obstacle in adapting the vertical corporation to the flexibility requirements of the global economy was the rigidity of traditional corporate cultures. Furthermore, at the moment of its massive diffusion, in the 1980s, information technology was supposed to be the magic tool to reform and change the industrial corporation.[53] But its introduction in the absence of fundamental organizational change in fact aggravated the problems of bureau-

---

[50]   Piore and Sabel (1984: 308).
[51]   McMillan (1984); Cusumano (1985).
[52]   Dodgson (ed.) (1989).
[53]   Kotter and Heskett (1992); Harrington (1991).

cratization and rigidity. Computerized controls are even more paralyzing than traditional face-to-face chains of command in which there was still place for some form of implicit bargaining.[54] In the 1980s in America, more often than not, new technology was viewed as a labor-saving device and as an opportunity to take control of labor, not as an instrument of organizational change.[55]

Thus, organizational change happened, independently from technological change, as a response to the need to cope with a constantly changing operational environment.[56] Yet, once it started to take place, the feasibility or organizational change was extraordinarily enhanced by new information technologies. As Boyett and Conn write:

> The ability of large American companies to reconfigure themselves to look and act like small businesses can, at least in part, be attributed to the development of new technology that makes whole layers of managers and their staffs unnecessary.[57]

The ability of small and medium businesses to link up in networks among themselves and with large corporations also became dependent on the availability of new technologies, once the networks' horizon (if not their daily operations) became global.[58] True, Chinese business had been based on networks of trust and cooperation for centuries. But when in the 1980s they stretched out across the Pacific, from Tachung to Fukien, from Hong Kong to Guandong, from Jakarta to Bangkok, from Hsinchu to Mountain View, from Singapore to Shanghai, from Hong Kong to Vancouver, and, above all, from Taipei and Hong Kong to Guangzhou and Shanghai, only reliance on new communication and information technologies allowed them to work on an ongoing basis, once the family, regional, and personal codes established the basis for the rules of the game to be followed up in their computers.

The complexity of the web of strategic alliances, of subcontracting agreements, and of decentralized decision-making for large firms would have been simply impossible to manage without the development of computer networks;[59] more specifically, without powerful microprocessors installed in desktop computers linked up via digitally switched telecommunication networks. This is a case in which organizational change induced to some extent the technological trajectory.

[54]   Hirschhorn (1985); Mowshowitz (1986).
[55]   Shaiken (1985).
[56]   Cohendet and Llerena (1989).
[57]   Boyett and Conn (1991: 23).
[58]   Shapira (1990); Hsing (1996).
[59]   Whightman (1987).

If the large, vertical corporations had been able to continue to operate successfully in the new economy, the crisis of IBM, Digital, Fujitsu, and of the mainframe computer industry in general might not have happened. It was because of the networking needs of new organizations, large and small, that personal computers and computer networking underwent an explosive diffusion. And because of the massive need for the flexible, interactive manipulation of computers, software became the most dynamic segment of the industry and the information-producing activity that is likely to shape processes of production and management in the future. On the other hand, it was because of the availability of these technologies (due to the stubbornness of innovators in Silicon Valley resisting the "1984" model of informatics) that networking became the key for organizational flexibility and business performance.[60]

Bar and Borrus have shown, in a stream of important research papers, that information networking technology jumped by a quantum leap in the early 1990s, due to the convergence of three trends: digitization of the telecommunications network, development of broadband transmission, and a dramatic increase in the performance of computers connected by the network, performance that was in turn determined by technological breakthrough in microelectronics and software. Then, computer interactive systems that had been limited until then to Local Area Networks, became operational in Wide Area Networks, and the computer paradigm shifted from the mere linkage between computers to "cooperative computing," regardless of the location of the interacting partners. Qualitative advances in information technology, not available until the 1990s, allowed the emergence of fully interactive, computer-based, flexible processes of management, production, and distribution, involving simultaneous cooperation between different firms and units of such firms.[61]

On the other hand, Dieter Ernst has shown that the convergence between organizational requirements and technological change has established networking as the fundamental form of competition in the new, global economy. Barriers to entry in the most advanced industries, such as electronics or automobiles, have skyrocketed, making it extremely difficult for new competitors to enter the market by themselves, and even hampering large corporations' ability to open up new product lines or to innovate their own processes in accordance with the pace of technological change.[62] Thus, co-

[60]   Fulk and Steinfield (eds) (1990); *Business Week* (1996).
[61]   Bar and Borrus (1993).
[62]   Ernst (1994b).

operation and networking offer the only possibility to share costs, and risks, as well as to keep up with constantly renewed information. Yet networks also act as gatekeepers. Inside the networks, new possibilities are relentlessly created. Outside the networks, survival is increasingly difficult. Under the conditions of fast technological change, networks, not firms, have become the actual operating unit. In other words, through the interaction between organizational crisis and change and new information technologies a new organizational form has emerged as characteristic of the informational/global economy: the **network enterprise**.

To define more precisely the network enterprise, I need to recall my definition of organization: a system of means structured around the purpose of achieving specific goals. I would add a second analytical distinction, adapted (in a personal version) from Alain Touraine's theory.[63] In a dynamic, evolutionary perspective there is a fundamental difference between two types of organizations: organizations for which the reproduction of their system of means becomes their main organizational goal; and organizations in which goals, and the change of goals, shape and endlessly reshape the structure of means. I call the first type of organizations bureaucracies; the second type, enterprises.

On the basis of these conceptual distinctions, I propose what I believe to be a potentially useful (non-nominalist) definition of the network enterprise: **that specific form of enterprise whose system of means is constituted by the intersection of segments of autonomous systems of goals.** Thus, the components of the network are both autonomous and dependent *vis-à-vis* the network, and may be a part of other networks, and therefore of other systems of means aimed at other goals. The performance of a given network will then depend on two fundamental attributes of the network: its *connectedness*, that is its structural ability to facilitate noise-free communication between its components; its *consistency*, that is the extent to which there is sharing of interests between the network's goals and the goals of its components.

Why is the network enterprise the organizational form of the informational/global economy? One easy answer would be predicated on an empiricist approach: it is what has emerged in the formative period of the new economy, and it is what seems to be performing. But it is intellectually more satisfying to understand that this performance seems to be in accordance with the characteristics of the informational economy: the successful organizations are those able to generate knowledge and process information efficiently; to

[63] Touraine (1959).

adapt to the variable geometry of the global economy; to be flexible enough to change its means as rapidly as goals change, under the impact of fast cultural, technological, and institutional change; and to innovate, as innovation becomes the key competitive weapon. These characteristics are indeed features of the new economic system we have analyzed in the preceding chapter. In this sense, **the network enterprise makes material the culture of the informational/global economy: it transforms signals into commodities by processing knowledge.**

Culture, Institutions, and Economic Organization: East Asian Business Networks

Forms of economic organization do not develop in a social vacuum: they are rooted in cultures and institutions. Each society tends to generate its own organizational arrangements. The more a society is historically distinct, the more it evolves in isolation from other societies, and the more its organizational forms are specific. However, when technology broadens the scope of economic activity, and when business systems interact on a global scale, organizational forms diffuse, borrow from each other, and create a mixture that responds to largely common patterns of production and competition, while adapting to the specific social environments in which they operate.[64] This is tantamount to saying that the "market logic" is so deeply mediated by organizations, culture, and institutions that economic agents daring to follow an abstract market logic, as dictated by neoclassical economics orthodoxy, would be at a loss.[65] Most firms do not follow such logic. Some governments do, out of ideology, and they end up losing control over their economies (for example, the Reagan Administration in the US in the 1980s, or the Spanish Socialist Government in the early 1990s). In other words: market mechanisms change over history and work through a variety of organizational forms. The critical question is then: Which are the sources of market specificity? And such a question can only be answered by comparative studies of economic organization.

A major stream of research in comparative organizational theory has shown the fundamental differences in firms' organization and behavior in contexts very different from the traditional Anglo-Saxon pattern embedded in property rights, individualism, and separation

[64]   Hamilton (1991).
[65]   Abolaffia and Biggart (1991).

between state and enterprises.[66] The focus of much of this research has been on the East Asian economies, an obvious choice because of the astounding performance of such economies in the last quarter of the twentieth century. The findings of organizational research on East Asian economies are extremely important for a general theory of economic organization, for two reasons.

First, it can be shown that patterns of business organization in East Asian societies are produced by the interplay of culture, history, and institutions, with the latter being the fundamental factor in the formation of specific business systems. Furthermore, as expected in the institutionalist theory of economics, such patterns present common trends, linked to cultural similarity, as well as very distinct features that can be traced to major differences in institutions, as a result of specific historical processes.

Secondly, the fundamental common trend of East Asian business systems is that they are based on networks, albeit on different forms of networks. The building block of such systems is not the firm or the individual entrepreneur, but networks or business groups of different kinds, in a pattern that, with all its variations, tends to fit with the organizational form that I have characterized as the network enterprise. If this is the case, and if the informational/global economy is better suited to the network form of business organization, then East Asian societies, and their organizational forms of economic activity, would have a distinctive comparative advantage in global competition, because such an organizational model is embedded in their culture and institutions. Their historical specificity would tend to converge with the sociotechnical logic of the informational paradigm. The historical record supports such a hypothesis: East Asian economies and firms have adapted more rapidly than any other area of the world to the new technologies and to the new forms of global competition, actually altering the balance of world trade and capital accumulation in favor of the Asian Pacific in only 30 years (see chapter 2). But I must introduce a word of caution: historical coincidence does not mean structural causality. Aren't we repeating the same ethnocentric mistake of the neoclassical paradigm, arguing for "one best way" of universal value, this time from another cultural source? To discuss this issue we need to consider, simultaneously, the historical specificity of cultures, the historical trajectories of institutions, the structural requisites of the informational paradigm, and the forms of competition in the global economy. It is in the interplay of these different social domains that we can find some tentative answers on "the spirit of informationalism."

---

[66]   Clegg and Redding (eds) (1990).

A typology of East Asian business networks

Let us first set forth the record on the formation, structure, and dynamics of East Asian business networks. Fortunately, this is a subject that has received sufficient attention in social research,[67] and in which I can rely on the systematic efforts of comparative analysis and theorization by the leading social scientists in this field, Nicole Woolsey Biggart and Gary Hamilton,[68] in addition to my own research work in the Asian Pacific between 1983 and 1995.

The organized network of independent firms is the prevailing form of economic activity in the market economies of East Asia. There are three distinctive, basic types of networks, each one of them characterizing Japanese, Korean, and Chinese businesses.[69]

Japan

In Japan, business groups are organized around networks of firms that mutually own each other (*kabushiki mochiai*), and whose main companies are run by managers. There are two sub-types of these networks:[70]

(a) horizontal networks based on intermarket linkages among large firms (*kigyo shudan*). These networks reach out across a variety of economic sectors. Some of them are the heirs of the *zaibatsu*, the giant conglomerates that led Japanese industrialization and trade before the Second World War, prior to their formal (and ineffective) dissolution during the American occupation. The three largest old networks, are Mitsui, Mitsubishi, and Sumitomo. After the war three new networks were formed around major banks: Fuyo, Dao-Ichi Kangin, and Sanwa. Each one of the networks has its own sources of financing, and competes in all main sectors of activity;

(b) vertical networks (*keiretsu*), built around a *kaisha*, or large specialized industrial corporation, comprising hundreds, and even thousands, of suppliers and their related subsidiaries. Main *keiretsu* are those centered around Toyota, Nissan, Hitachi, Matsushita, Toshiba, Tokai Bank, and Industrial Bank of Japan.

These stable business groups practically control the core of the Japanese economy, organizing a dense network of mutual obligations, financial interdependency, market agreements, personnel transfer,

[67]   Whitley (1993).
[68]   Biggart (1991); Hamilton and Biggart (1988); Biggart and Hamilton (1992); Hamilton (1991).
[69]   Hamilton et al. (1990).
[70]   Gerlach (1992); Imai and Yonekura (1991); Whitley (1993).

and information sharing. A critical component of the system is the General Trading Company (*sogo shosha*) for each network, which acts as a general intermediary between suppliers and consumers, and adjusts inputs and outputs.[71] It is the system integrator. Such a business organization works as a flexible unit in the competitive market, allocating resources to each member of the network as it sees fit. This also makes it extremely difficult for any external firm to penetrate markets. This specific economic organization explains to a large extent the problems that foreign firms meet in penetrating the Japanese market, since all operations must be established anew, and suppliers refuse to serve other customers unless their parent *kaisha* agrees with the deal.[72]

Labor practices and work organization reflect this hierarchical network structure.[73] At the core, large companies offer their workers lifetime employment, reward systems based on seniority, and cooperation with firm-based unions. Team work and autonomy of task performance is the rule, counting on workers' commitment to the prosperity of their company. Management is involved at the shop-floor level, and they share facilities and working conditions with manual workers. Consensus-building is sought through a number of procedures, from the organization of work to symbolic action such as the singing of a corporate anthem to start the day.[74]

On the other hand, the more that firms are in the periphery of the network, the more labor is considered expendable and exchangeable, most of it being accounted for by temporary workers and part-time employees (see chapter 4). Women and poorly-educated youth are the bulk of such peripheral labor.[75] Thus, networked business groups lead both to flexible cooperation and to highly segmented labor markets that induce a dual social structure, mainly organized along gender lines. Only the relative stability of the patriarchal Japanese family integrates both ends of the social structure, downplaying the trends towards a polarized society – but only for as long as Japanese women can be kept in subservience, both at home and at work.[76]

Korea

The Korean networks (*chaebol*), although historically inspired by the Japanese *zaibatsu*, are far more hierarchical than their Japanese

---

[71]   Yoshino and Lifson (1986).
[72]   Abegglen and Stalk (1985).
[73]   Koike (1988); Clark (1979); Durlabhji and Marks (eds) (1993).
[74]   Kuwahara (1989).
[75]   Jacoby (1979); Shinotsuka (1994).
[76]   Chizuko (1987); Chizuko (1988); Seki (1988).

counterparts.[77] Their main distinctive trend is that all firms in the network are controlled by a central holding company owned by an individual and his family.[78] In addition, the central holding company is backed by government banks and by government-controlled trading companies. The founding family keeps tight control by appointing members of the family, regional acquaintances, and close friends to top managerial posts throughout the *chaebol*.[79] Small and medium businesses play a minor role, unlike in the Japanese *keiretsu*. Most of the firms of the *chaebol* are relatively sizable, and they work under the coordinated initiative of the top, centralized management of the *chaebol*, often reproducing the military style that their government backers brought to it, particularly after 1961. *Chaebol* are multisectoral, and their managers are transferred from one sector of activity to another, thus ensuring unity of strategy, and cross-fertilization of experience. The four largest Korean *chaebol* (Hyundai, Samsung, Lucky Gold Star, and Daewoo) figure today among the world's largest economic conglomerates, and together accounted in 1985 for 45% of all South Korean gross domestic product. *Chaebol* are largely self-sufficient entities, only dependent on government. Most contractual relations are internal to the *chaebol*, and subcontracting plays a minor role. Markets are shaped by the state, and developed by competition between *chaebol*.[80] Mutual obligation networks external to the *chaebol* are rare. Internal *chaebol* relations are a matter of discipline down the network, rather than of cooperation and reciprocity.

Labor policies and practices also fit this authoritarian pattern. There is, as in Japan, a sharp segmentation of labor markets between core workers and temporary workers, depending on the centrality of the firm in the *chaebol*.[81] Women play a much reduced role, since patriarchalism is even more intense in Korea than in Japan,[82] and men are reluctant to let women work outside the household. But core workers do not receive the same kind of commitment to long-term employment and working conditions from their firms.[83] Neither are they expected to commit themselves by taking the initiative. They are mainly supposed to fulfill the orders they receive. Unions were state-controlled and were kept subservient for a long period. When in the 1980s democracy made substantial gains in Korea, the unions'

[77]   Steers et al. (1989).
[78]   Biggart (1990a).
[79]   Yoo and Lee (1987).
[80]   Kim (1989).
[81]   Wilkinson (1988).
[82]   Gelb and Lief Palley (eds) (1994).
[83]   Park (1992).

growing independence was met with confrontational tactics from *chaebol* leaders, leading to a highly conflictual pattern of industrial relations,[84] a trend that belies the racist ideology about Asian labor's supposedly obedient attitude, sometimes mistakenly attributed to Confucianism.

However, while distrust of workers is the rule, trust is a fundamental feature between different levels of management in the Korean networks, to the point that such trust is mainly embedded in kinship relationships: in 1978, 13.5% of the directors of the largest 100 *chaebol* were part of the owner's family, and they were in control of 21% of top management positions.[85] Additional managerial positions are generally held by persons trusted by the owner's family on the basis of direct knowledge, enforced by mechanism of social control (local social networks, family networks, school networks). However, the interests of the *chaebol* are paramount, even in relationship to the family. If there is a contradiction between the two, government makes sure that *chaebol*'s interests, not individuals' or families' concerns, prevail.[86]

China

The Chinese business organization is based on family firms (*jiazuqiye*), and cross-sectoral, business networks (*jituanqiye*), often controlled by one family. Although most of the detailed research available concerns the formation and development of business networks in Taiwan,[87] empirical evidence, as well as my personal knowledge, allow for an extrapolation of such a pattern to Hong Kong and to overseas Chinese communities in South-East Asia.[88] Interestingly enough, similar networks seem to be at work in the fast process of market-driven industrialization in South China, if we extend the networks' reach to include among them the officials of local government.[89]

The key component of Chinese business organization is the family.[90] Firms are family property, and the dominant value concerns the family, not the firm. When the firm prospers, so does the family. Thus, after enough wealth has been accumulated, it is divided among family members who invest in other businesses, most often unrelated to the activity of the original firm. Sometimes, the pattern of creation

---

[84]   Koo and Kim (1992).
[85]   Shin and Chin (1989).
[86]   Amsdem (1989); Evans (1995).
[87]   Hamilton and Kao (1990).
[88]   Sit and Wong (1988); Yoshihara (1988).
[89]   Hsing (1994); Hamilton (1991).
[90]   Greenhalgh (1988).

of new businesses, as the family increases its wealth, is intragenera-
tional. But if this does not happen in the life of the founder of the
firm, it will after his death. This is because, unlike in Japan and Korea,
the family system is based on patrilineage and equal inheritance
among the sons, and thus each son will receive his share of the family
assets, to start a business of his own. Wong, for instance, considers that
successful Chinese businesses go through four phases in three generations: emergent, centralized, segmented, and disintegrative, after
which the cycle starts all over again.[91] In spite of frequent intrafamily
rivalries, personal trust is still the basis for business deals, beyond and
aside from legal–contractual rules. Thus, families prosper by creating
new firms in any sector of activity deemed profitable. Family-based
firms are linked by subcontracting arrangements, exchange of investment, sharing of stock. Firms are specialized in their trade, families
are diversified in their investments. Connections between firms are
highly personalized, fluid, and changeable, unlike the long-term
commitment patterns of Japanese networks. Sources of finance tend
to be informal (family savings, loans from trusted friends, revolving
credit associations, or other forms of informal lending, such as
Taiwan's "curb market").[92]

In such a structure, management is highly centralized and authoritarian. Middle management, not being part of the family, is
considered only as a transmission belt; and workers' loyalty is not
expected, since the workers' ideal is to start their own businesses, and
thus they are suspect as future competitors. Commitments are short-
term, which undermines long-range planning strategies. On the other
hand, the extreme decentralization and flexibility of such a system
allows for fast adjustments to new products, to new processes, and to
new markets. Through alliances between families, and their corresponding networks, capital turnover is accelerated, and allocation of
resources is optimized.

The weak point in these small-scale Chinese business networks is
their inability to undertake major strategic transformations, requiring
for instance R&D investment, knowledge of world markets, large-scale
technological modernization, or offshoring of production. I shall
argue below, unlike some observers of Chinese business, that the state,
particularly in Taiwan but also in other contexts, such as Hong Kong
and certainly in China, has provided this critical strategic backing for
Chinese networks to prosper in the informational/global economy
beyond their profitable, but limited, local horizon. The ideology of
entrepreneurial familism, rooted in an ancestral distrust of the state

[91] Wong (1985).
[92] Hamilton and Biggart (1988).

in Southern China, cannot be taken at face value, even it if shapes, to a large extent, the behavior of Chinese businessmen.

Entrepreneurial familism was only part of the success story of Chinese business networks, albeit the substantial one. Another element was the Chinese version of the developmental state, in Taiwan, Hong Kong, or China. Under different forms, the state, after so many historic failures, had the intelligence finally to find the formula to support Chinese entrepreneurialism, based on familistic, trustworthy, information relationships, without suffocating its autonomy, once it became clear that the lasting glory of Chinese civilization was in fact dependent upon the relentless vitality of selfishly bustling families. It is probably not by accident that the convergence between families and the state occurred in the Chinese culture at the dawn of the informational/global age, when power and wealth depend more on network flexibility than on bureaucratic might.

Culture, organizations, and institutions: Asian business networks and the developmental state

Thus, East Asian economic organization, without question the most successful in world competition in the last third of the twentieth century, is based on business networks, both formal and informal. But there are considerable differences between the three cultural areas where these networks have arisen. As Nicole Biggart and Gary Hamilton put it, within the network Japanese firms enact a communitarian logic, Korean firms a patrimonial logic, and Taiwanese firms a patrilineal logic.[93]

Both the similarities and differences of East Asian business networks can be traced back to the cultural and institutional characteristics of these societies.

The three cultures intermixed over centuries, and were deeply permeated by philosophical/religious values of Confucianism and Buddhism, in their various national patterns.[94] Their relative isolation from other areas of the world until the nineteenth century reinforced their specificity. The basic social unit was the family, not the individual. Loyalty is due to the family, and contractual obligations to other individuals are subordinated to familistic "natural law." Education is of central value, both for social ascension and for personal enhancement. Trust and reputation, within a given network

[93]   Hamilton and Biggart (1988).
[94]   Whitley (1993).

of obligation, are the most valued qualities, and the most severely
sanctioned rule in case of failure.[95]

Although the shaping of organizational forms by cultural attributes
is sometimes too indeterminate an argument, because of its lack of
specificity, it would seem that the commonality of network forms in
East Asia can be related to these common cultural trends. If the unit
of economic transaction is not the individual, property rights take
second place to family rights. And if the hierarchy of obligations is
structured along mutual trust, stable networks have to be established
on the basis of such trust, while agents external to these networks will
not be treated equally in the market place.

But if culture fosters the commonality of network business patterns,
institutions seem to account for their substantial differences while, at
the same time, reinforcing their networking logic. The fundamental
difference between the three cultures concerns the role of the state,
both historically and in the process of industrialization. In all cases,
the state preempted civil society: merchant and industrial elites came
under the guidance, alternatively benevolent and repressive, of the
state. But in each case, the state was historically different and played
a different role. At this point in the argument, I must set a distinction
between the role of state in history and the performance of the
contemporary, developmental state.[96]

In recent history, the substantial difference was between the
Japanese state[97] and the Chinese state.[98] The Japanese state not only
molded Japan, but also Korea and Taiwan under its colonial domination.[99] Since the Meiji period it was an agent of authoritarian
modernization, but working through, and with, clan-based business
groups (the *zaibatsu*), some of which (Mitsui, for instance) can be
traced back to merchant houses linked to powerful feudal lords.[100]
The Japanese imperial state set up a modern, insulated technocracy
that sharpened its skills in the preparation of the Japanese war
machine (the immediate ancestor of MITI was the Ministry of
Munitions, core of the Japanese military industry).[101] It is only when
we introduce this particular institutional setting that we understand
the precise workings of culture on organizations. For instance,
Hamilton and Biggart show the institutional background of

95   Baker (1979); Willmott (ed.) (1972).
96   Biggart (1991); Wade (1990); Whitley (1993).
97   Beasley (1990); Johnson (1995).
98   Feuerwerker (1984).
99   Amsdem (1979, 1985, 1989, 1992).
100   Norman (1940).
101   Johnson (1982).

the cultural explanation usually provided for Japanese consensus-building in the work process through the notion of *Wa* or harmony. *Wa* searches for the integration of the world order, through the subordination of the individual to the group practices. But Biggart and Hamilton refuse to accept the direct determination of Japanese management practices as the cultural expression of *Wa*. They argue that such organizational arrangements result from an industrial system, fostered and enforced by the state, that finds support for its implementation in the elements of traditional culture, the building materials with which institutions work to produce organizations. As they write, citing Sayle, "the Japanese government does not stand apart from or over the community: it is rather the place where *Wa* deals are negotiated."[102] Thus, business groups in Japan, as was historically the case in the areas of Japanese influence, tend to be organized vertically, around a core corporation with direct access to the state.

The Chinese state had a very different relationship to business, and particularly to business in Southern China, the fundamental source of Chinese entrepreneurialism. Both in the last decades of the imperial state and in the brief period of the Kuomintang state in China, business was at the same time abused and solicited, seen as a source of income rather than as an engine of wealth. This led, on the one hand, to the harmful practices of excessive taxation and lack of support for industrialization; on the other hand, to favoritism for some business groups, thus breaking the rules of competition. Reactions to this state of affairs led Chinese business to stay away from the state as much as possible, building on a secular fear imposed on southern entrepreneurial Chinese by their northern conquerors. Such a distance from the state emphasized the role of family, as well as of local and regional connections, in setting up business transactions, a trend that Hamilton shows can be dated back to the Qin dynasty.[103]

Without a reliable state enforcing property rights, you do not need to be Confucian in order to place your trust in kin rather than in a legal contract on paper. Significantly enough, it was the active involvement of the state in the West in enforcing property rights, as North has shown,[104] and not the lack of state intervention, that became the critical factor in organizing economic activity along market transactions between free individual agents. When the state did not act to create the market, as in China, families did it on their own, bypassing

[102] Hamilton and Biggart (1988: 72).
[103] Hamilton (1984, 1985).
[104] North (1981).

the state and embedding market mechanisms in socially constructed networks.

But the dynamic configuration of East Asian business networks, able to take on the global economy, came in the second half of the twentieth century, under the decisive impulse of what Chalmers Johnson labeled the developmental state.[105] To extend this fundamental concept, which originated in Johnson's study of the role of MITI in the Japanese economy, to the broader experience of East Asian industrialization, I used in my own work a somewhat modified definition of the developmental state.[106] A state is developmental when it establishes as its principle of legitimacy its ability to promote and sustain development, understanding by development the combination of steady high rates of economic growth and structural change in the economic system, both domestically and in its relationship to the international economy. This definition is misleading, however, unless we specify the meaning of legitimacy in a given historical context. Most political theorists remain prisoners of an ethnocentric conception of legitimacy, related to the democratic state. But not all states have attempted to ground their legitimacy on the consensus of the civil society. The legitimacy principle may be exercised on behalf of the society-as-it-is (in the case of the democratic state), or on behalf of a societal project carried on by the state, as self-proclaimed interpreter of the "historical needs" of the society (the state as social "vanguard," in the Leninist tradition). When such a societal project involves a fundamental transformation of the social order, I refer to it as a revolutionary state, based on revolutionary legitimacy, regardless of the degree of internalization of such legitimacy by its subjects, for example the Communist Party state. When the societal project carried forward by the state respects the broader parameters of social order (although not necessarily of a specific social structure, for example an agrarian society), I consider it to be a developmental state. The historical expression of this societal project in East Asia took the form of the affirmation of national identity, and national culture, building or rebuilding the nation as a force in the world, in this case by means of economic competitiveness and socioeconomic improvement. Ultimately, for the developmental state economic development is not a goal, but a means: the means of implementing a nationalist project, superseding a situation of material destruction and political defeat after a major war, or, in the

[105]   Johnson (1982, 1995).
[106]   Castells (1992). Chalmers Johnson, in his latest book (1995) converged on my redefinition of the developmental state, accepting it as a further refinement of his theory, which it is.

case of Hong Kong and Singapore, after the severance of their ties
with their economic and cultural environment (communist China,
independent Malaysia). Along with a number of researchers,[107] I have
empirically argued in several writings that at the roots of the rise of
Asian Pacific economies lies the nationalist project of the developmental state. This is now generally acknowledged in the case of Japan,
Korea, and Singapore. There is some debate on the matter in the case
of Taiwan, although it does seem to fit the model.[108] And I raised a few
eyebrows when I extended the analysis to Hong Kong, albeit with due
specifications.[109]

I cannot go into the empirical detail of this debate in the framework of this text. It would take the analysis of Asian business too far
away from the focus of this chapter, namely the emergence of the
network enterprise as the prevailing organizational form in the information economy. But it is possible and useful for the sake of the
argument to show the correspondence between the characteristics of
state intervention in each East Asian context and the variety
of network forms of business organization.

In Japan, government guides economic development by advising
business on product lines, export markets, technology, and work organization.[110] It backs its guidance with powerful financial and fiscal
measures, as well as with selective support for strategic R&D programs.
At the core of government industrial policy was (is) the activity of the
Ministry of International Trade and Industry, MITI, that periodically
elaborates "visions" for Japan's development trajectory, and sets up
the industrial policy measures that are necessary to implement the
desirable course along this trajectory. The crucial mechanism in
ensuring that private business broadly follows government's policies
relies on financing. Japanese corporations are highly dependent on
bank loans. Credit is channeled to the banks of each major business
network by the Central Bank of Japan, under instructions from the
Finance Ministry, in coordination with MITI. Indeed, while MITI took
responsibility for strategic planning, real power in the Japanese
government always lay in the Finance Ministry. Furthermore,
much of the lending funds comes from postal savings, a massive
supply of available finance controlled by the Ministry of Posts and

---

[107]   Deyo (ed.) (1987); Wade (1990); Johnson (1982, 1985, 1987, 1995); Gold
(1986); Amsdem (1989, 1992); Appelbaum and Henderson (eds) (1992); Evans
(1995).
[108]   Amsdem (1985); Gold (1986).
[109]   Castells et al. (1990).
[110]   Johnson (1982, 1995); Johnson et al. (eds) (1989); Gerlach (1992).

Telecommunications. MITI targeted specific industries for their competitive potential, and provided a number of incentives, such as tax breaks, subsidies, market and technology information, and support for R&D and personnel training. Until the 1980s, MITI also enforced protectionist measures, insulating specific industries from world competition during their nurturing period. Such long-standing practices have created a protectionist inertia that survives to some extent after the formal abolition of restrictions on free trade.

Government's economic intervention in Japan is organized around the autonomy of the state *vis-à-vis* business, and to a large extent *vis-à-vis* the political party system, although the conservative Liberal Democratic Party ruled uncontested until 1993. Recruitment of the top-level bureaucracy on the basis of merit, most often from Tokyo University graduates and particularly from the Law School, and always from elite universities (Kyoto, Hitotsubashi, Keio, and so on), ensures a tight social network of highly professional, well-trained, and largely apolitical technocrats, who constitute the actual ruling elite of contemporary Japan. Furthermore, only about 1% of these high-level bureaucrats reach the top of the hierarchy. The others in the later stage of their career take well-paid jobs either in para-public sector institutions, in corporate business, or in mainstream political parties, thus ensuring the diffusion of the values of the bureaucratic elite among the political and economic agents who are in charge of implementing government's strategic vision of Japan's national interests.

This form of state intervention, based on consensus, strategic planning, and advice, largely determines the organization of Japanese business in networks, and the particular structure of such networks. Without a centralized planning mechanism to allocate resources, Japan's industrial policy can only be effective if business itself is tightly organized in hierarchical networks that can carry out the guidelines issued by MITI. Such coordinating mechanisms have very concrete expressions. One of them is the *shacho-kai*, or monthly meetings, that bring together the presidents of the core companies of a major intermarket network. These meetings are occasions to build social cohesion in the networks, in addition to carrying out the directives that are signaled by government's formal or informal communications. The actual structure of the network also reflects the type of government intervention: financial dependency on government-approved loans gives a strategic role to the main bank (or banks) of the network; international trade restrictions and incentives are channeled through the general trading company of each network which works as a system integrator, both between the members of the network and between the network and MITI. Thus, for a firm to break the discipline of government's industrial policy is tantamount to excluding itself from the network, being cut off from access to financing, technology, and import-export licensing. Japan's strategic planning, and the centralized network structure of Japanese business are but two faces of the same model of economic organization.

The connection between government policy and business organization is even more evident in the case of the Republic of Korea.[111] Yet it is important to notice that the developmental state in Korea was not characteristic of Korea during the 1950s. After the war, Syngman Rhee's dictatorship was a corrupt regime, playing simply the role of a vassal government of the United States. It was the nationalistic project of the Park Chung Hee regime, after the 1961 military coup, that set up the bases for a state-led process of industrialization and competition in the world economy, enacted by Korean business on behalf of the interests of the nation and under the strict guidance of the state. The Park government aimed at creating the equivalent of the Japanese *zaibatsu*, on the basis of existing large Korean companies. But because the resulting networks were forced into existence by the state they were even more centralized and authoritarian than their Japanese predecessors. To achieve its design, the Korean government closed the domestic market to international competition and practiced an import-substitution policy. As soon as Korean firms started to operate, it targeted the enhancement of their competitiveness, and favored an export-oriented strategy along a trajectory of increasingly capital- and technology-intensive industries, with specific goals outlined in five-year economic plans established by the Economic Planning Board, the brain and engine of Korea's economic miracle. In the vision of the Korean military, to be competitive Korean firms had to be concentrated in large conglomerates. They were forced to do so by government's control of the banking system, and of the export-import licenses. Both credit and licences were selectively given to firms on condition of joining a *chaebol*, since government's privileges were accorded to the central firm (owned by a family) in the *chaebol*. Business was also explicitly requested to finance government's political activities, as well as to pay in cash for any special favors obtained from top-level bureaucrats, generally military officers. To enforce strict business discipline, the Park government did not relinquish control over the banking system. Thus, unlike in Japan, Korean *chaebol* were not financially independent until the 1980s. Labor policies were also shaped by military-induced authoritarianism, with

[111] Amsdem (1989); Evans (1995); Jacobs (1985); Lim (1982); Jones and Sakong (1980).

the unions being directly under government control to make sure that they would be purged of any communist influence. These labor policies led to the ferocious repression of any independent labor organization, thus destroying the possibility of consensus-building in the work process of Korean industry.[112] The military state origin of *chaebol* was certainly more influential in shaping the authoritarian and patrilineal character of Korean business networks than the Confucian tradition of rural Korea.[113]

The interaction between state and business is far more complex in the case of Chinese family firms, rooted in centuries-old distrust of government interference. And yet government planning and policy have been a decisive factor in Taiwan's economic development.[114] Not only does Taiwan have the largest public enterprise sector of the capitalist Asian Pacific (amounting to about 25% of GDP up to the late 1970s), but government guidance was formalized in successive four-year economic plans. As in Korea, control of banks and of export–import licenses were the main instruments for the implementation of government's economic policy, also based on the combination of an import-substitution policy and export-oriented industrialization. Yet, unlike in Korea, Chinese firms did not depend primarily on bank credits but, as mentioned above, relied on family savings, credit cooperatives, and informal capital markets, largely autonomous from the government. Thus, small and medium-size enterprises thrived on their own, and established the horizontal, family-based networks I have described. The intelligence of the KMT state, having learned from its historical mistakes in 1930s Shanghai, was to build on the foundations of these dynamic networks of small enterprises, many of them in the rural fringes of the metropolitan areas, sharing farming and craft industrial production. However, it is doubtful that these small enterprises would have been able to compete on the world market without critical, strategic support from the state. Such support took three main forms: (a) subsidized health and education, public infrastructure, and income redistribution, on the basis of a radical agrarian reform; (b) attraction of foreign capital, via tax incentives, and the establishment of the first export-processing zones in the world, thus ensuring linkages, subcontracting and enhancement of quality standards for Taiwanese firms and workers that came into contact with foreign companies; (c) decisive government support for R&D, technology transfer, and diffusion. This latter point was particularly critical to enable Taiwanese firms to climb up

[112]   Kim (ed.) (1987).
[113]   Janelli (1993).
[114]   Amsdem (1979, 1985); Gold (1986); Kuo (1983); Chen (1979).

the ladder of the technological division of labor. For instance, the process of diffusion of advanced electronics technology, at the origin of the expansion of the most dynamic sector of Taiwan's industry in the 1980s, PC clone manufacturing, was directly organized by the government in the 1960s.[115] The government acquired the license for chip design technology from RCA, together with the training of Chinese engineers by the American company. Relying on these engineers, the government created a public research center, ETRI, that kept up to date with developments in the world's electronic technology, emphasizing its commercial applications. Under government directives, ETRI organized enterprise seminars to diffuse, at no cost, the technology it was generating among Taiwanese small firms. Furthermore, ETRI engineers were encouraged to leave the Institute after a few years, and were provided with government funding and technology support to start up their own businesses. Thus, although in more traditional industries government support in Taiwan was more indirect than in South Korea or Japan, what is characteristic is that productive interaction was found between government and business networks: networks continued to be family-based and relatively small in the size of their firms (although there are also major industrial groups in Taiwan, for example Tatung); but government policies assumed the coordinating and strategic planning functions when it was necessary for such networks to broaden and upgrade the scope of their activities in products, processes, and markets.

The story is more complex in the case of Hong Kong, but the outcome is not too dissimilar.[116] The basis of the export-oriented industrial structure of Hong Kong was made from small and medium businesses that originated mainly from family savings, starting with 21 industrialists' families who emigrated from Shanghai after the communist revolution. But the colonial government aimed at making Hong Kong into a showcase for the successful implementation of British benevolent colonialism, and in the process also tried to make the Territory self-sufficient in its finances in order to put off pressures for decolonization from the Labour Party back home. To do so behind the ideological screen of "positive nonintervention" (eagerly consumed by the Milton Friedmans of the world) the Hong Kong "cadets," career civil servants from the British Colonial Service, introduced an active developmental policy, half by design, half by accident.[117] They strictly controlled the distribution of textile and garment export

[115] Castells et al. (1990); Wong (1988); Chen (1979); Lin et al. (1980).
[116] Castells (1989c); Castells and Hall (1994).
[117] Miners (1986); Mushkat (1982); Lethbridge (1978).

quotas among firms, allocating them on the basis of their knowledge of competitive capabilities. They built a network of government institutions (Productivity Center, Trade Council, and so on) to diffuse information about markets, technology, management, and other critical matters throughout the networks of small enterprises, thus accomplishing the coordinating and strategic functions without which such networks would never have been able to tap into the markets of the US and of Commonwealth countries. They built the largest public housing program in the world in terms of the proportion of the population housed in its premises (later it became second to Singapore, after Singapore had imitated the formula). Not only were there thousands of factories in high-rise buildings (called "flatted factories") paying low rents as an integral part of the public housing program, but the subsidy of the program substantially lowered labor costs, and the safety net it provided made it possible for workers to venture into starting their own businesses without excessive risk (seven starts on average before succeeding). In Taiwan, the rural dwelling and the family plot of land, resulting from the persistence of farming in the industrial areas, was the safety mechanism that allows for movements back and forth between self-employment and salaried employment.[118] In Hong Kong, the functional equivalent was the public housing program. In both cases, networks of small businesses could emerge, disappear, and re-emerge under a different form because there was a safety net provided by family solidarity and a peculiar colonial version of the welfare state.[119]

A similar form of linkage between supportive government and family-based business networks seems to be emerging in the process of export-oriented industrialization in Southern China in the 1990s.[120] On the one hand, Hong Kong and Taiwanese manufacturers tapped into the regional networks of their villages of origin in Guandong and Fukien provinces to create subsidiaries and to establish subcontractors, in order to offshore the low end of their manufacturing production (for example, in shoes, plastics, or consumer electronics). On the other hand, such production networks can only exist on the basis of the support of provincial and local governments, which provide the necessary infrastructure, enforce labor discipline, and act as intermediaries between management, labor, and export firms. As Hsing writes in concluding her pioneering

---

[118]   Chin (1988).
[119]   Schiffer (1983).
[120]   Hsing (1994, 1996); Hamilton (1991).

effort of research on Taiwanese manufacturing investment in Southern China:

> The new pattern of foreign direct investment in the rapidly industrializing regions of China is characterized by the dominant role played by small and medium-sized investors and their collaboration with low-level local authorities in new production sites. The institutional basis that maintains and enhances the flexibility of their operations is a network form of production and marketing organizations, as well as the increasing autonomy of the local governments. Of equal importance, the cultural affinity of overseas investors and their local agents, including local officials and local workers, facilitates a much smoother and faster process of establishing transnational production networks.[121]

Thus, the form of Chinese business networks is also a function of the indirect, subtle, yet real and effective form of state intervention in the process of economic development in various contexts. However, a process of historical transformation may be under way, as Chinese business networks have grown extraordinarily in wealth, influence, and global reach. Interestingly enough, they continue to be family-based, and their interlocking seems to reproduce the early forms of networking between small entrepreneurs. But they are certainly powerful enough to bypass directives from government in Taiwan, in Hong Kong, and for that matter, in other South-East Asian countries, with the exception of the strong Singaporean state. Chinese business networks, while keeping in essence their organizational structure and cultural dynamics, appear to have reached a qualitatively larger size, one that allows them finally to be set free from the state.[122] But such a perception might be an illusion linked to a period of historical transition; because what is looming on the horizon is the gradual linkage between powerful Chinese business networks and the multilayered structure of the mainland Chinese state. Indeed, the most profitable investments of Chinese businesses are already taking place in China. When and if such linkage takes place, the autonomy of Chinese business networks will be tested, as will be the ability of a developmental state constructed by a Communist Party to evolve into a form of government able to steer without subduing the flexible, family-based, network enterprises. If such convergence takes place, the world's economic landscape will be transformed.

Thus, the observation of East Asian business networks shows the

[121]   Hsing (1996: 307).
[122]   Mackie (1992b, 1992b).

cultural and institutional sources of such organizational forms, both in their common features and in their significant differences. Let us now return to the general analytical implications of this conclusion. Are such networking forms of economic organization able to develop in other cultural/institutional contexts? How does contextual variation influence their morphology and performance? What is common to the new rules of the game in the informational/global economy, and what is specific to particular social systems (for example, East Asian business systems, the "Anglo-Saxon model," the "French Model," the "Northern Italian model," and so on)? And the most important question of all: How will the organizational forms of the late industrial economy, such as the large multi-unit corporation, interact with the emerging network enterprise in its various manifestations?

Multinational Enterprises, Transnational Corporations, and International Networks

The analysis of East Asian business networks shows the institutional/cultural production of organizational forms. But it also shows the limits of the market-driven theory of business organizations, ethnocentrically rooted in the Anglo-Saxon experience. Thus, Williamson's influential interpretation[123] of the emergence of the large corporation as the best way to reduce uncertainty and minimize transaction costs by internalizing transactions within the corporation, simply does not hold when confronted with the empirical evidence of the spectacular process of capitalist development in the Asian Pacific, based on networks external to the corporation.[124]

Similarly, the process of economic globalization based on network formation seems also to contradict the classical analysis by Chandler[125] that attributes the rise of the large multi-unit corporation to the growing size of the market, and to the availability of communications technology that enables the large firm to take hold on such a broad market, thus reaping economies of scale and scope, and internalizing them within the firm. Chandler extended his historical analysis of the expansion of the large firm in the US market to the rise of the multi-national enterprise as a response to the globalization of the economy, this time by using enhanced information technologies.[126] In most of

---

[123]   Williamson (1985).
[124]   Hamilton and Biggart (1988).
[125]   Chandler (1977).
[126]   Chandler (1986).

the literature of the last 20 years it seems as if the multinational enterprise, with its divisional, centralized structure, was the organizational expression of the new, global economy.[127] The only debate on the matter was between those who argued for the persistence of the national roots of the multinational enterprise,[128] and those who considered the new forms of enterprise as truly transnational corporations, having superseded in their vision, interests, and commitments any particular country, regardless of their historical origin.[129] Yet empirical analyses of the structure and practice of large corporations with a global scope appear to show that both visions are outdated and should be replaced by the emergence of international networks of firms, and of subunits of firms, as the basic organizational form of the informational/global economy. Dieter Ernst has summarized a substantial amount of available evidence concerning the formation of interfirm networks in the global economy, and considers that most economic activity in leading industries is organized around five different types of networks (electronics and automobiles being the most advanced industries in the diffusion of this organizational pattern). These five types of networks are:

- *Supplier networks* which are defined to include subcontracting, OEM (Original Equipment Manufacturing) and ODM (Original Design Manufacturing) arrangements between a client (the "focal company") and its suppliers of intermediate production inputs.
- *Producer networks* which are defined to include all co-production arrangements that enable competing producers to pool their production capacities, financial, and human resources in order to broaden their product portfolios and geographic coverage.
- *Customer networks* which are defined as the forward linkages of manufacturing companies with distributors, marketing channels, value-added resellers and end users, either in the major export markets or in domestic markets.
- *Standard coalitions* which are initiated by potential global standard setters with the explicit purpose of locking-in as many firms as possible into their proprietary product or interface standards.
- *Technology cooperation networks* which facilitate the acquisition of product design and production technology, enable joint production and process development, and permit generic scientific knowledge and R&D to be shared.[130]

---

[127]   De Anne (1990); Dunning (1992); Enderwick (ed.) (1989).
[128]   Ghoshal and Westney (1993).
[129]   Ohmae (1990).
[130]   Ernst (1994b: 5–6).

However, the formation of these networks does not imply the demise of the multinational enterprise. Ernst, concurring with a number of observers on this matter,[131] considers that networks are either centered on a major multinational enterprise or are formed on the basis of alliances and cooperation between such enterprises. Cooperative networks of small and medium enterprises do exist (for example, in Italy and in East Asia), but they play a minor role in the global economy, at least in the key industries. Oligopolistic concentration seems to have been maintained or increased in most sectors of major industries, not only in spite of but because of the networked form of organization. This is because entry into the strategic networks requires either considerable resources (financial, technological, market share) or an alliance with a major player in the network.

Multinational enterprises seem to be still highly dependent on their national basis. The idea of transnational corporations being "citizens of the world economy" does not seem to hold. Yet the networks formed by multinational corporations do transcend national boundaries, identities, and interests.[132] My hypothesis is that, as the process of globalization progresses, organizational forms evolve from *multinational enterprises* to *international networks*, actually bypassing the so-called "transnationals" that belong more to the world of mythical representation (or self-serving image-making by management consultants) than to the institutionally bounded realities of the world economy.

Furthermore, as mentioned above, multinational enterprises are not only engaged in networking, but are increasingly organized themselves in decentralized networks. Ghoshal and Bartlett, after summarizing evidence on the transformation of multinational corporations, define the contemporary multinational as "an inter-organizational network," or, more precisely, as "a network that is embedded within an external network."[133] This approach is critical to our understanding because, so the argument goes, the characteristics of the institutional environments where the various components of the corporation are located actually shape the structure and dynamics of the corporation's internal network. Thus, multinational corporations are indeed the power-holders of wealth and technology in the global economy, since most networks are structured around such corporations. But at the same time, they are internally differentiated in decentralized networks, and externally dependent on their

[131]   Harrison (1994).
[132]   Imai (1990a).
[133]   Ghoshal and Bartlett (1993: 81).

membership in a complex, changing structure of interlocked networks, cross-border networks in Imai's formulation.[134] Besides, each one of the components of such networks, internal and external, is embedded in specific cultural/institutional environments (nations, regions, locales) that affect the network in varying degrees. Overall, the networks are asymmetrical, but each single element of the network can hardly survive by itself or impose its diktat. The logic of the network is more powerful than the powers in the network. The management of uncertainty becomes critical in a situation of asymmetrical interdependency.

Why are networks central in the new economic competition? Ernst argues that two factors are foremost sources in this process of organizational transformation: globalization of markets and inputs; dramatic technological change that makes equipment constantly obsolete and forces firms to be relentlessly updated with information on processes and products. In such a context, cooperation is not only a way of sharing costs and resources, but also an insurance policy against a bad technological decision: the consequences of such a decision would also be suffered by the competitors, since networks are ubiquitous and intertwined.

Interestingly enough, Ernst's explanation for the emergence of the international network enterprise echoes the argument of market theorists, that I have tried to personalize in Chandler, for the classics, and in Williamson, for the new wave of neoclassical economists. Market characteristics and technology are suggested to be the key variables. However, in Ernst's analysis, the organizational effects are exactly the opposite of those expected by the traditional economic theory: whilst market size was supposed to induce the formation of the vertical, multi-unit corporation, the globalization of competition dissolves the large corporation in a web of multidirectional networks, that become the actual operating unit. The increase of transaction costs, because of added technological complexity, does not result in the internalization of transactions within the corporation but in the externalization of transactions and sharing of costs throughout the network, obviously increasing uncertainty, but also making possible the spreading and sharing of uncertainty. Thus, either the mainstream explanation of business organization, based on neoclassical market theory, is wrong, or else available evidence on the emergence of business networks is faulty. I am inclined to think the former.

Thus, the network enterprise, a predominant form of business

[134] Imai (1990a).

organization in East Asia, seems to be flourishing in various institu-
tional/cultural contexts, in Europe,[135] as in the United States,[136] while
the large, multi-unit corporation, hierarchically organized around
vertical lines of command seems to be ill-adapted to the informa-
tional/global economy. Globalization and informationalization seem
to be structurally related to networking and flexibility. Does this trend
mean that we are shifting to an Asian model of development that
would replace the Anglo-Saxon model of the classical corporation? I
do not think so, in spite of the diffusion of work and management
practices across countries. Cultures and institutions continue to shape
the organizational requirements of the new economy, in an interaction between the logic of production, the changing technological
basis, and the institutional features of the social environment. A
survey of business cultures in Europe shows the variation within
Europe of organizational patterns, particularly *vis-à-vis* the relationships between governments and firms.[137] The architecture and
composition of business networks being formed around the world are
influenced by the national characteristics of societies where such
networks are embedded. For instance, the content and strategies of
electronic firms in Europe are highly contingent on the policies of the
European Union, regarding the reduction of technological dependency on Japan and the US. But, on the other hand, the alliance of
Siemens with IBM and Toshiba in microelectronics is dictated by technological imperatives. The formation of high-technology networks
around defense programs in the US is an institutional characteristic
of the American industry, and one that tends to exclude foreign partnership. The gradual incorporation of Northern Italian industrial
districts by major Italian firms was favored by agreements between
government, large firms, and labor unions concerning the convenience of stabilizing and consolidating the productive base formed
during the 1970s, with the support of regional governments that were
dominated by left-wing parties. In other words, the network enterprise
is increasingly international (not transnational), and its conduct will
result from the managed interaction between the global strategy of
the network and the nationally/regionally rooted interests of its
components. Since most multinational firms participate in a variety
of networks depending on products, processes, and countries, the
new economy cannot be characterized as being centered any longer
on multinational corporations, even if they continue to exercise

[135] Danton de Rouffignac (1991).
[136] Bower (1987); Harrison (1994).
[137] Randlesome et al. (1990).

jointly oligopolistic control over most markets. This is because corpo-rations have transformed themselves into a web of multiple networks embedded in a multiplicity of institutional environments. Power still exists, but it is randomly exercised. Markets still trade, but purely economic calculations are hampered by their dependency on unsolv-able equations overdetermined by too many variables. The market's hand that institutional economists tried to make visible has returned to invisibility. But this time, its structural logic is not only governed by supply and demand but also influenced by hidden strategies and untold discoveries played out in the global information networks.

The Spirit of Informationalism

Max Weber's classic essay on *The Protestant Ethic and the Spirit of Capitalism*, originally published in 1904–5[138] still remains the method-ological cornerstone of any theoretical attempt at grasping the essence of cultural/institutional transformations that in history usher in a new paradigm of economic organization. His substantive analysis of the roots of capitalist development has certainly been challenged by historians, who have pointed at alternative historical configura-tions that sustained capitalism as effectively as the Anglo-Saxon culture did, albeit in different institutional forms. Furthermore, the focus of this chapter is not so much on capitalism, which is alive and well in spite of its social contradictions, as on informationalism, a new mode of development that alters, but does not replace, the dominant mode of production. Yet the theoretical principles proposed by Max Weber almost a century ago still provide a useful guideline to make sense of the series of analyses and observations I have presented in this chapter, bringing them together to highlight the new cultural/institutional configuration underlying the organizational forms of economic life. In homage to one of sociology's founding fathers, I shall call this configuration "the spirit of informationalism."
Where to start? How to proceed? Let us read Weber again:

> The spirit of capitalism. What is to be understood by it? . . . If any object can be found to which this term can be applied with any understandable meaning, it can only be an historical individual, i.e. a complex of elements associated in historical reality which we unite into a conceptual whole from the standpoint of their cultural significance. Such an historical concept, however, since it refers in its content to a phenomenon significant for its unique

[138] Weber (1958).

> individuality . . . must be gradually put together out of the indi-
> vidual parts which are taken from historical reality to make it up.
> Thus the final and definitive concept cannot stand at the begin-
> ning of the investigation, but must come at the end.[139]

We are at the end, at least of this chapter. Which are the elements of
historical reality we have uncovered as being associated in the new
organizational paradigm? And how can we unite them in a conceptual whole of historical significance?

They are, first of all, *business networks*, under different forms, in
different contexts, and from different cultural expressions. Family-
based networks in Chinese societies and Northern Italy;
entrepreneurial networks emerging from technological seedbeds in
the milieux of innovation, as in Silicon Valley; hierarchical,
communal networks of the Japanese *keiretsu* type; organizational
networks of decentralized corporate units from former vertically integrated corporations forced to adapt to the realities of the time; and
cross-border networks resulting from strategic alliances between
firms.

There are also *technological tools*: new telecommunication networks;
new, powerful desktop computers; new, adaptive, self-evolving software; new, mobile communication devices that extend on-line
linkages to any space at any time; new workers and managers,
connected to each other around tasks and performance, able to speak
the same language, the digital language.

There is *global competition*, forcing constant redefinitions of
products, processes, markets, and economic inputs, including capital
and information.

And there is, as always, *the state*: developmental in the take-off stage
of the new economy, as in East Asia; agent of incorporation when
economic institutions have to be rebuilt, as in the process of European
unification; coordinating when territorially based networks need the
nurturing support of local or regional governments to generate
synergistic effects that will set up milieux of innovation; and mission-
oriented messenger when it steers a national economy, or the world
economic order, into a new historical course, scripted in the technology but not fulfilled in the business practice, as in the US
Government's design to built the twenty-first century's information
superhighway, notwithstanding the budget deficit. All these elements
come together to give rise to the network enterprise.

The *emergence and consolidation of the network enterprise*, in all its
different manifestations, may well be the answer to the "productivity

---

[139] Weber (1958: 47).

enigma" that cast such a long shadow on my analysis of the informational economy in the preceding chapter. Because, as Bar and Borrus argue in their study on the future of networking:

> One reason Information Technology investments have not translated into higher productivity is that they have primarily served to automate existing tasks. They often automate inefficient ways of doing things. Realizing the potential of Information Technology requires substantial re-organization. The ability to re-organize tasks as they become automated rests largely on the availability of a coherent infrastructure, i.e. a flexible network able to interconnect the various computer-based business activities.

They go on to establish a historical parallel with the impact of decentralization of small electrical generators to the shop floor of industrial factories, to conclude;

> These decentralized computers are only now [1993] being interconnected, so as to allow and support re-organization. Where this has been effectively accomplished, there are corresponding gains in productivity.[140]

Yet, while all these elements are ingredients of the new developmental paradigm, they still lack the cultural glue that brings them together. Because, as Max Weber wrote:

> The capitalism of today, which has come to dominate economic life, educates and selects the economic subjects which it needs through a process of economic survival of the fittest. But here one can easily see the limits of the concept of selection as a means of historical explanation. In order that a manner of life so well adapted to the peculiarities of capitalism could be selected at all, i.e. should come to dominate others, it had to originate somewhere, and not in isolated individuals alone, but as a way of life common to a whole group of men. This origin is what really needs explanation . . . In the country of Benjamin Franklin's birth . . . the spirit of capitalism was present before the capitalistic order.

And he adds:

> The fact to be explained historically is that in the most highly capitalistic centre of that time, in Florence of the fourteenth and fifteenth centuries, the money and capital market of all the great

---

[140]   Bar and Borrus (1993: 6).

political Powers, this attitude [Benjamin Franklin's defense of profit-searching] was considered ethically unjustifiable, or at best to be tolerated. But in the backwoods small bourgeois circumstances of Pennsylvania in the eighteenth century, where business threatened for simple lack of money to fall back into barter, where there was hardly a sign of large enterprise, where only the earliest beginnings of banking were to be found, the same thing was considered the essence of moral conduct, even commanded in the name of duty. To speak here of a reflection of material conditions in the ideal superstructure would be patent nonsense. What was the background of ideas which could account for the sort of activity apparently directed toward profit alone as a calling toward which the individual feels himself to have an ethical obligation? For it was this idea which gave the way of life of the new entrepreneur its ethical foundation and justification.[141]

What is the ethical foundation of informationalism? And does it need an ethical foundation at all? I should remind the patient reader that in the historical period of the rise of informationalism, capitalism, albeit in new, profoundly modified forms *vis-à-vis* the time of Weber's writing, is still operating as the dominant economic form. Thus, the corporate ethos of accumulation, the renewed appeal of consumerism, are driving cultural forms in the organizations of informationalism. Additionally, the state and the affirmation of national/cultural collective identity have been shown to muster decisive force in the arena of global competition. Families, in their complexity, continue to thrive and reproduce by the means of economic competition, accumulation, and heritage. But while all these elements seem to account, together, for the cultural sustainment of renewed capitalist competition, they do not seem to be specific enough to distinguish the new agent of such capitalist competition: the network enterprise.

   For the first time in history, the basic unit of economic organization is not a subject, be it individual (such as the entrepreneur, or the entrepreneurial family) or collective (such as the capitalist class, the corporation, the state). As I have tried to show, **the unit is the network**, made up of a variety of subjects and organizations, relentlessly modified as networks adapt to supportive environments and market structures. What glues together these networks? Are there purely instrumental, accidental alliances? It may be so for particular networks, but the networking form of organization must have a

---

[141] Weber (1958: 55 and 75).

cultural dimension of its own. Otherwise, economic activity would be performed in a social/cultural vacuum, a statement that can be sustained by some ultrarationalist economists, but that is fully belied by the historical record. What is, then, this *"ethical foundation of the network enterprise"* this *"spirit of informationalism?"*

It is certainly not a new culture, in the traditional sense of a system of values, because the multiplicity of subjects in the network and the diversity of networks reject such unifying "network culture." Neither is it a set of institutions, because we have observed the diverse development of the network enterprise in a variety of institutional environments, to the point of being shaped by such environments into a broad range of forms. But there is indeed a common cultural code in the diverse workings of the network enterprise. It is made of many cultures, many values, many projects, that cross through the minds and inform the strategies of the various participants in the networks, changing at the same pace as the network's members, and following the organizational and cultural transformation of the units of the network. It is a culture, indeed, but a culture of the ephemeral, a culture of each strategic decision, a patchwork of experiences and interests, rather than a charter of rights and obligations. It is a *multifaceted, virtual culture,* as in the visual experiences created by computers in cyberspace by rearranging reality. It is not a fantasy, it is a material force because it informs, and enforces, powerful economic decisions at every moment in the life of the network. But it does not stay long: it goes into the computer's memory as raw material of past successes and failures. The network enterprise learns to live within this virtual culture. Any attempt at crystallizing the position in the network as a cultural code in a particular time and space sentences the network to obsolescence, since it becomes too rigid for the variable geometry required by informationalism. The "spirit of informationalism" is the culture of "creative destruction" accelerated to the speed of the optoelectronic circuits that process its signals. Schumpeter meets Weber in the cyberspace of the network enterprise.

As for the potential social consequences of this new economic history, the voice of the master resonates with force 100 years later:

> The modern economic order . . . is now bound to the technical and economic conditions of machine production which today determine the lives of all individuals who are born into this mechanism, not only those directly concerned with economic acquisition, with irresistible force . . . The care for external goods should only lie on the shoulders of the "saint like a light cloak, which can be thrown aside at any moment." But fate decreed that

the cloak should become an iron cage . . . Today the spirit of religious asceticism . . . has escaped from the cage. But victorious capitalism, since it rests on mechanical foundations, needs its support no longer . . . No one knows who will live in this cage in the future, or whether at the end of this tremendous development, entirely new prophets will arise, or there will be a great rebirth of old ideas, or, if neither, mechanized petrification, embellished with a sort of convulsive self-importance. For of the last stage of this cultural development, it might well be truly said: "Specialists without spirit, sensualists without heart; this nullity imagines that it has attained a level of civilization never before achieved."[142]

[142]   Weber (1958: 180–2).

— 4 —

The Transformation of Work and Employment: Networkers, Jobless, and Flextimers

The process of work is at the core of social structure. The techno-logical and managerial transformation of labor, and of production relationships, in and around the emerging network enterprise is the main lever by which the informational paradigm and the process of globalization affect society at large. In this chapter I shall analyze this transformation on the basis of available evidence, while attempting to make sense of contradictory trends observed in the changes of work and employment patterns over the last decades. I shall first address the classic question of secular transformation of employment struc-ture that underlies theories of postindustrialism, by analyzing its evolution in the main capitalist countries between 1920 and 2005. Next, to reach beyond the borders of OECD countries, I shall consider the arguments on the emergence of a global labor force. I shall then turn to analyze the specific impact of new information technologies on the process of work itself, and on the level of employment, trying to assess the widespread fear of a jobless society. Finally, I shall treat the potential impacts of the transformation of work and employment on the social structure, by focusing on processes of social polarization that have been associated with the emergence of the informational paradigm. In fact, I shall suggest an alternative hypothesis that, while acknowledging these trends, will place them in the broader frame-work of a more fundamental transformation: the individualization of work and the fragmentation of societies.[1] All along such an

I want to acknowledge the significant input to this chapter from Martin Carnoy and Harley Shaiken. I have also relied extensively on data and material provided by the International Institute of Labour Studies, International Labour Office. For this, I am particularly grateful to Padmanabha Gopinath and to Gerry Rodgers.
[1]   To understand the transformation of work in the informational paradigm it is necessary to root this analysis in a comparative and historical perspective. For this, I have relied on what I consider to be the best available source of ideas and

intellectual itinerary, I shall use data and research findings from a flurry of monographs, simulation models, and standard statistics that have treated these questions with minute attention over many years in many countries. Yet the purpose of my inquiry, as for this book in general, is analytical: it aims at raising new questions rather than answering old concerns.

The Historical Evolution of Employment and Occupational Structure in Advanced Capitalist Countries: The G-7, 1920–2005

In any process of historical transition one of the most direct expressions of systemic change is the transformation of employment and occupational structure. Indeed, theories of postindustrialism and informationalism use as the strongest empirical evidence for the change in historical course the coming into being of a new social structure, characterized by the shift from goods to services, by the rise of managerial and professional occupations, by the demise of agricultural and manufacturing jobs, and by the growing information content of work in the most advanced economies. Implicit in much of these formulations is a sort of natural law of economies and societies, that should follow a single path along a trajectory of modernity in which American society has led the way.

I take a different approach. I contend that while there is a common trend in the unfolding of the employment structure characteristic of informational societies, there is also a historical variation of employment patterns according to specific institutions, culture, and political environments. In order to assess both the commonality and the variation of employment structures in the informational paradigm I have examined the evolution of employment structure between 1920 and 1990 for the major capitalist countries that constitute the core of the global economy, the so-called G-7 countries. All of them are in an advanced stage of transition to the informational society, thus can be used to observe the emergence of new employment patterns. They also represent very distinct cultures and institutional systems, allowing us to examine historical variety. In conducting this analysis I am not implying that all other societies, at different levels of development,

---

research on the matter: Pahl (ed.) (1988). The central thesis of this chapter on the transition toward individualization of work, inducing potentially fragmented societies, is also related, although from a very different analytical perspective, to an important book that builds on Polanyi's theory, and relies on empirical analysis of Italian social structure: Mingione (1991).

will conform to one or another of the historical trajectories represented by these countries. As I have argued in the general introduction to this book, the new, informational paradigm interacts with history, institutions, levels of development, and position in the global system of interaction along the lines of different networks. The analysis presented in the following pages has a more precise purpose: to unveil the interaction between technology, economy, and institutions in the patterning of employment and occupation, in the process of transition between agricultural, industrial, and informational modes of development.

By differentiating the internal composition of service employment, and by analyzing the differential evolution of the employment and occupational structure in each one of the seven countries (United States, Japan, Germany, France, Italy, the United Kingdom and Canada) between *circa* 1920 and *circa* 1990, the analysis presented here introduces an empirically grounded discussion on the cultural/institutional diversity of the informational society. To proceed in such a direction, I shall introduce the analytical issues researched in this section, define the concepts, and describe briefly the methodology I have used in this study. [2]

Postindustrialism, the service economy, and the informational society

The classical theory of postindustrialism combined three statements and predictions that ought to be analytically differentiated:[3]

(1) The source of productivity and growth lies in the generation of knowledge, extended to all realms of economic activity through information processing.
(2) Economic activity would shift from goods production to services delivery. The demise of agricultural employment would be followed by the irreversible decline of manufacturing jobs, to the benefit of service jobs which would ultimately form the overwhelming proportion of employment. The more advanced an economy, the more its employment and its production would be focused on services.
(3) The new economy would increase the importance of occupations

---

[2]   The analysis of the evolution of employment structure of G-7 countries was conducted with considerable help from Dr Yuko Aoyama, formerly my research assistant at Berkeley, particularly for the construction of the international, comparative data base on which this analysis is grounded.
[3]   Bell (1976); Dordick and Wang(1993).

with a high information and knowledge content in their activity. Managerial, professional, and technical occupations would grow faster than any other occupational position and would constitute the core of the new social structure.

Although various interpretations would extend the theory of postindustrialism in different versions to the realm of social classes, politics, and culture, the preceding three interrelated statements anchor the theory at the level of the social structure, the level where, in Bell's thinking, the theory belongs.

Each one of these major assertions deserves qualification. In addition, the historical linkage between the three processes has still to be submitted to empirical verification.

First, as we argued in chapter 2, knowledge and information seem indeed to be major sources of productivity and growth in advanced societies. However, as we also mentioned above, it is important to notice that theories of postindustrialism based their original assertion on research by Solow and by Kendrick, both referring to the first half of the twentieth century in America, at the height of the industrial era. This is to say that the knowledge base of productivity growth has been a feature of the industrial economy, when manufacturing employment was at its peak in the most advanced countries. Thus, although the late twentieth-century economies are clearly different from the pre-World War II economies, the feature that distinguishes these two types of economies does not seem to be rooted primarily in the source of their productivity growth. **The appropriate distinction is not between an industrial and a postindustrial economy, but between two forms of knowledge-based industrial, agricultural, and services production.** As I have argued in the opening chapters of this book, what is most distinctive, in historical terms, between the economic structures of the first half and of the second half of the twentieth century is the revolution in information technologies, and its diffusion in all spheres of social and economic activity, including its contribution in providing the infrastructure for the formation of a global economy. Therefore, I propose to shift the analytical emphasis from *postindustrialism* (a relevant question of social forecasting still without an answer at the moment of its formulation) to *informationalism*. In this perspective, societies will be informational, not because they fit into a particular model of social structure, but because they organize their production system around the principles of maximizing knowledge-based productivity through the development and diffusion of information technologies, and by fulfilling the prerequisites for their utilization (primarily human resources and communications infrastructure).

The second criterion of postindustrialist theory by which to consider a society as postindustrial concerns the shift to service activities and the demise of manufacturing. It is an obvious fact that most employment in advanced economies is in services, and that the service sector accounts for the largest contribution to GNP. Yet it does not follow that manufacturing industries are disappearing or that the structure and dynamics of manufacturing activity are indifferent to the health of a service economy. Cohen and Zysman,[4] among others, have forcefully argued that many services depend on their direct linkage to manufacturing, and that manufacturing activity (distinct from manufacturing employment) is critical to the productivity and competitiveness of the economy. For the United States, Cohen and Zysman estimate that 24% of GNP comes from the value added by manufacturing firms, and another 25% of GNP comes from the contribution of services directly linked to manufacturing. Thus, they argue that the postindustrial economy is a "myth," and that we are in fact in a different kind of industrial economy.

Furthermore, the notion of "services" is often considered to be ambiguous at best, misleading at worst.[5] In employment statistics, it has been used as a residual notion that embraces all that is not agriculture, mining, construction, utilities, or manufacturing. Thus, the category of services includes activities of all kinds, historically originated from various social structures and productive systems. The only common feature for these service activities is what they are not. Attempts at defining services by some intrinsic characteristics, such as their "intangibility," opposed to the "materiality" of goods, have been definitely voided of meaning by the evolution of the informational economy. Computer software, video production, microelectronics design, biotechnology-based agriculture, and so on, and many other critical processes characteristic of advanced economies, merge inextricably their information content with the material support of the product, making it impossible to distinguish the boundaries between "goods" and "services." To understand the new type of economy and social structure, we must start by characterizing different types of "services," in order to establish clear distinctions between them. In understanding the informational economy, each one of the specific categories of services becomes as important a distinction as was the old borderline between manufacturing and services in the preceding type of industrial economy. As economies become more complex, we must diversify the concepts through which we categorize economic

---

[4]   Cohen and Zysman (1987).
[5]   Gershuny and Miles (1983); Castells (1976); Daniels (1993); Cohen and Zysman (1987); De Bandt (ed.) (1985); Stanback (1979).

activities, and ultimately abandon Colin Clark's old paradigm based on the primary/secondary/tertiary sectors distinction. Such a distinction has become an epistemological obstacle to the understanding of our societies.

The third major prediction of the original theory of postindustrialism refers to the expansion of information-rich occupations, such as managerial, professional, and technical positions, as the core of the new occupational structure. This prediction also requires qualification. A number of analysts have argued that this trend is not the only characteristic of the new occupational structure. Simultaneous to this trend there is also the growth of low-end, unskilled, service occupations. These low-skilled jobs, despite their slower growth rate, may represent a substantial proportion of the postindustrial social structure in terms of their absolute numbers. In other words, advanced, informational societies could also be characterized by an increasingly polarized social structure, where the top and the bottom increase their share at the expense of the middle.[6] In addition, there is a widespread challenge in the literature to the notion that knowledge, science, and expertise are the critical components in most of the managerial/professional occupations. A harder, closer look must be taken at the actual content of such general statistical classifications before we jump to characterizing our future as the republic of the learned elite.

Yet the most important argument against a simplistic version of postindustrialism is the critique of the assumption according to which the three features we have examined coalesce in the historical evolution, and that such an evolution leads to a single model of the informational society. This analytical construct is in fact similar to the formulation of the concept of capitalism by classical political economists (from Adam Smith to Marx) exclusively based on the experience of English industrialization, only to find continuous "exceptions" to the pattern throughout the diversity of economic and social experience in the world. Only if we start from the analytical separation between the structural logic of the production system of the informational society and its social structure can we observe empirically if a specific techno-economic paradigm induces a specific social structure and to what extent. And only if we open up the cultural and institutional scope of our observation can we separate what belongs to the structure of the informational society (as expressing a new mode of development) from what is specific to the historical trajectory

---

[6]   Kuttner (1983); Rumberger and Levin (1984); Bluestone and Harrison (1988); Leal et al. (1993); Sayer and Walker (1992).

of a given country. To make some tentative steps in such a direction, I have compiled and made somewhat comparable basic statistics for the seven largest market economies in the world, the so-called G-7 countries. Thus I can compare, with reasonable approximation, the evolution of their employment and occupational structure over the last 70 years. I have also considered some employment projections for Japan and the United States through the early twenty-first century. The empirical core of this analysis consists in an attempt at differentiating between various service activities. To do so, I have followed the well-known typology of services employment constructed by Singelmann almost 20 years ago.[7] Singelmann's conceptualization is not without flaws, but has a fundamental merit: it is well adapted to the usual statistical categories, as shown in Singelmann's own doctoral dissertation that analyzed the change of employment structure in various countries between 1920 and 1970. Since the main purpose of this book is analytical I decided to build on Singelmann's work, to compare the 1970–90 period with his findings for the 1920–79 period. Thus, I constructed a similar typology of sectoral employment, and processed the statistics of the G-7 countries along roughly comparable categories, extending Singelmann's analysis to the critical period of development of informational societies, from the 1970s onwards. Because I cannot ensure the absolute equivalence of my decisions in classifying activities with those taken earlier by Singelmann, I present our data separately for the two periods: they must not be read as a statistical series, but as two distinct statistical trends made roughly equivalent in terms of the analytical categories used to compile the data. I did find considerable methodological difficulties in establishing equivalent categories among different countries. The appendix to this chapter provides details on the procedures followed in building this data base. In analyzing these data I have used the simplest statistical procedures, always trying to show the actual trends in the social structure, rather than using analytical methods that would be unnecessarily sophisticated for the current level of elaboration of the data base. I have opted for using descriptive statistics that would simply suggest lines of new theoretical understanding.

By adopting Singelmann's categories of service activities I have embraced a structuralist view of employment, dividing it up according to the place of the activity in the chain of linkages that starts from the production process. Thus, distributive services refer both to communication and transportation activities, as well as to commercial distribution networks (wholesale and retail). Producer services refer

[7]   Singelmann (1978).

more directly to those services that appear to be critical inputs in the economy, although they also include auxiliary services to business that may not be necessarily highly skilled. Social services include a whole realm of government activities, as well as collective consumption-related jobs. Personal services are those related to individual consumption, from entertainment to eating and drinking places. Although these distinctions are admittedly broad, they do allow us to think differentially about the evolution of the employment structure across countries, at least with greater analytical depth than the usual statistical accounts. I have also tried to establish a difference between the services/goods dichotomy and the classification of employment between information-processing and goods-handling activities, since each one of these distinctions belongs to a different approach in the analysis of social structure. To do so, I built two elementary indexes of service-delivery employment/goods-producing employment, and of information-processing employment/goods-handling employment, and calculated these indexes for the countries and periods under consideration. Finally, I also calculated a simplified typology of occupations across countries, building the various countries' categories around those used by American and Japanese statistics. Although I have serious concerns about the definitions of such occupational categories which mix, in fact, occupational positions and types of activities, using standard statistics that are widely available gives us the opportunity of looking at the evolution of occupational structures in roughly comparative terms. The purpose of this exercise is to recast the sociological analysis of informational societies by assessing in a comparative framework the differences in the evolution of their employment structure as a fundamental indicator for both their commonality and their diversity.

The transformation of employment structure, 1920–70 and 1970–90

The analysis of the evolution of employment structure in the G-7 countries must start from the distinction between two periods that, by sheer luck, match our two different data bases: *circa* 1920–70 and *circa* 1970–90. *The major analytical distinction between the two periods stems from the fact that during the first period the societies under consideration became postagricultural, while in the second period they did become postindustrial.* I understand obviously by such terms the massive decline of agricultural employment in the first case and the rapid decline of manufacturing employment in the second period. Indeed, *all G-7 countries maintained or increased (in some cases substantially) the percentage of their employment in transformative activities and in manufacturing between*

1920 and 1970. Thus, if we exclude construction and utilities in order to have a sharper view of the manufacturing labor force, England and Wales decreased only slightly the level of their manufacturing labor force from 36.8% in 1921 to 34.9% in 1971; the United States increased manufacturing employment from 24.5% in 1930 to 25.9% in 1970; Canada from 17.0% in 1921 to 22.0% in 1971; Japan saw a dramatic increase in manufacturing from 16.6% in 1920 to 26.0% in 1970; Germany (although with a different national territory) increased its manufacturing labor force from 33.0% to 40.2%; France, from 26.4% to 28.1%; and Italy, from 19.9% to 27.4%. Thus, as Singelmann argues, the shift in the structure of employment in this half century (1920–70) was from agriculture to services and construction, not out of manufacturing.

The story is a very different one in the 1970–90 period, when the process of economic restructuring and technological transformation that took place during these two decades led to a reduction of manufacturing employment in all countries (See tables 4.1 to 4.14 in Appendix A). However, while this trend was general, the shrinkage of manufacturing employment was uneven, clearly indicating the fundamental variety of social structures according to differences in economic policies and in firms' strategies. Thus, while the United Kingdom, the United States, and Italy experienced rapid deindustrialization (reducing the share of their manufacturing employment in 1970–90 from 38.7% to 22.5%; from 25.9% to 17.5%; from 27.3% to 21.8%, respectively), Japan and Germany reduced their share of manufacturing labor force moderately: from 26.0% to 23.6% in the case of Japan, and from 38.6% to a still rather high level of 32.2% in 1987 in the case of Germany. Canada and France occupy an intermediate position, reducing manufacturing employment from 19.7% (in 1971) to 14.9%, and from 27.7% to 21.3%, respectively.

In fact, England and Wales had already become a postagricultural society in 1921, with only 7.1% of their labor force in agriculture. The United States, Germany, and Canada still had a sizable agricultural population (from a quarter to a third of total employment), and Japan, Italy, and France were, by and large, societies dominated by agricultural and commercial occupations. From this differential starting point in the historical period under study, trends converged toward an employment structure characterized by simultaneous growth of manufacturing and services at the expense of agriculture. Such a convergence is explained by very rapid processes of industrialization in Germany, Japan, Italy, and France, that distributed the surplus of agricultural population between manufacturing and services.

Thus, if we calculate the employment ratio of services to industry (our indicator of the "service economy") it shows only a moderate increase for most countries between 1920 and 1970. Only the United States (change from 1.1 to 2.0) and Canada (1.3 to 2.0) witnessed a significant increase of the relative proportion of service employment during the period that I call postagricultural. In this sense, it is true that the United States was the standard-bearer of the employment structure characteristic of the service economy. Thus, when the trend toward service employment accelerated and generalized in the post-industrial period, the United States and Canada increased even more their service predominance, with indexes of 3.0 and 3.3 respectively. All other countries followed the same tendency, but at different speeds, thus reaching different levels of deindustrialization. While the United Kingdom, France, and Italy seem to be on the same path, North America, Japan, and Germany clearly stand out as strong indus- trial economies, with lower rates of increase of service employment, and lower service to industry employment ratios: 1.8 and 1.4 respec- tively in 1987–90. This is a fundamental observation that deserves careful discussion below. Yet, as a trend, in the 1990s the majority of the population in all G-7 countries is employed in services.

Is employment also concentrating on information processing? Our ratio of information-processing to goods-handling employment provides some interesting clues for the analysis. First, we must put aside Japan for further consideration.

For all other countries there has been a trend toward a higher percentage of information-processing employment. Although Italy and Germany had no or only slow increase in 1920–70, their share of information employment grew considerably in the last two decades. The United States holds the highest information employment ratio among the seven countries, but the United Kingdom, Canada, and France are almost at the same level. Thus, the trend toward informa- tion processing is clearly not a distinctive feature of the United States: the American employment structure is more clearly set apart from the others as a "service economy" than as an "information economy." Germany and Italy have a significantly lower rate of information employment, but they have doubled it in the last two decades, thus displaying the same trend.

The data on Japan are most interesting. They show only a moderate increase of information employment in 50 years (from 0.3 to 0.4), and an even slower increase in the last 20 years, from 0.4 to 0.5. Thus, what is probably the society to put the strongest emphasis on information technologies, and in which high technology plays a most significant role in productivity and competitiveness, also appears to have the lowest level of information-processing employment, and the lowest rate of progression of such employment. The expansion of information employment and the development of an "information society" (*johoka shakai*, in the Japanese concept) seem to be different, although interrelated, processes. It is indeed interesting, and problematic for some interpretations of postindustrialism, that Japan and Germany, the two most competitive economies among major economies in the 1970s and 1980s, are those with the strongest manufacturing employment, the lowest service to industry employment ratio, the lowest information to goods employment ratio, and, for Japan (which has experienced the fastest productivity growth), the lowest rate of increase in information employment throughout the century. I suggest the idea that information processing is most productive when it is embedded in material production or in the handling of goods, instead of being disjointed in a stepped-up technical division of labor. After all, most of automation refers precisely to the integration of information processing in goods handling.

This hypothesis may also help to interpret another important observation: none of the seven countries had a ratio of information employment over 1 in 1990, and only the United States was approaching that threshold. Thus, if information is a critical component in the functioning of the economy and in the organization of society, it does not follow that most jobs are or will be in information processing. The march toward information employment is proceeding at a significantly slower pace, and reaching much lower levels, than the trend toward service employment. Thus, to understand the actual profile of the transformation of employment in advanced societies we must now turn to the differential evolution of each type of services in the G-7 countries.

To do so, I shall first comment on the evolution of each category of services in each country; then I shall compare the relative importance of each type of service *vis-à-vis* each other in each country; finally, I shall consider the trends of evolution of employment in those services that have been identified in the literature as characteristic of "postindustrial" societies. In proceeding with this analysis I must remind the reader that the further we go into the fine-grain analysis of specific categories of employment, the less solid the data base becomes. The inability to obtain reliable data for some categories, countries, and periods will make it difficult to be systematic in our analysis across the board. Yet the observation of the tables presented here still suggests that there are some features that merit closer analysis and further elaboration on country-specific data bases.

Let us start with *producer services*. They are considered in the literature to be the strategic services of the new economy, the providers of information and support for the increase in the productivity and efficiency of firms. Thus, their expansion should go hand in hand with the increasing sophistication and productivity of the economy. Indeed, we observe throughout the two periods (1920–1970, 1970–1990) a significant expansion of employment in these activities in all countries. For instance, in the United Kingdom employment in producer services shot up from 5% in 1970 to 12% in 1990; in the United States, for the same period, from 8.2% to 14%; in France, it doubled, from 5% to 10%. It is significant that Japan increased dramatically its producer services employment between 1921 (0.8%) and 1970 (5.1%), most of this increase taking place during the 1960s, the moment when the Japanese economy internationalized its scope. On the other hand, focusing on 1970–90 on a different data base, the increase of Japanese employment in producer services between 1971 and 1990 (from 4.8% to 9.6%), while substantial, still leaves Japan in the lower tier of employment in producer services among the advanced economies. This could suggest that a significant proportion of producer services are internalized in Japan in manufacturing companies, which could appear to be a more efficient formula, if we consider the competitiveness and productivity of the Japanese economy.

This hypothesis receives additional support from the observation of data concerning Germany. While increasing significantly the share of employment in producer services from 4.5% in 1970 to 7.3% in 1987, Germany still displays the lowest level of producer services employment of the G-7 countries. This could imply a great degree of internalization of service activities in German firms. If these data were confirmed, we must emphasize that the two most dynamic economies (Japan and Germany) have also the lowest rate of employment in producer services, while it is obvious that their firms do use such services in great amount, yet probably with a different organizational structure that links up more closely producer services to the production process.

While it is evident that producer services are strategically crucial in an advanced economy, they still do not represent a substantial proportion of employment in most advanced countries, in spite of their rapid rate of growth in several of them. With the unknown position of Italy, the proportion of employment varies between 7.3% and 14% in the other countries, of course putting them well ahead of agriculture, but far behind in manufacturing. The battalions of professionals and managers have indeed swelled the ranks of employment in advanced economies, but not always, and not predominantly, in the visible spots of the management of capital and the control of information. It seems that the expansion of producer services is linked to the processes of vertical disintegration and outsourcing that characterize the informational corporation.

Social services form the second employment category which, according to the postindustrial literature, should characterize the new society. And indeed it does. With, again, the exception of Japan, employment in social services represents between one-fifth and one-quarter of total employment in the G-7 countries. But the interesting observation here is that the major increase in social services took place during the roaring sixties, actually linking their expansion with the impact of social movements rather than with the advent of post-industrialism. Indeed, the United States, Canada, and France had very moderate rates of growth of employment in social services in the 1970–90 period, while in Germany, Japan, and Britain it grew at a robust rate.

Overall, it would seem that the expansion of the welfare state has been a secular trend since the beginning of the century, with moments of acceleration in periods that vary for each society, and a tendency to slow down in the 1980s. Japan is the exception because it appears to be catching up. It maintained a very low level of employment in social services until 1970, probably linked to a greater decentralization of social support both by the firm and the family. Then, when Japan became a major industrial power, and when more traditional forms of support could not be maintained, Japan engaged in forms of social redistribution similar to the other advanced economies, providing services and creating jobs in the social services sector. Overall, we can say that although the expansion of social services employment at a very high level is a feature of all advanced societies, the pace of such expansion seems to be directly dependent on the relationship between the state and society, rather than on the stage of development of the economy. Indeed, the expansion of social services employment (except in Japan) is more characteristic of the 1950–70 period than of the 1970–90 period, at the dawn of the informational society.

Distributive services combine transportation and communication, relational activities of all advanced economies, with wholesale and retail trade, the supposedly typical service activities of less industrialized societies. Is employment declining in these low-productivity, labor-intensive activities, as the economy progresses toward the automation of work, and toward the modernization of commercial shops? In fact, employment in distributive services remains at a very high level in advanced societies, also oscillating between one-fifth and one-quarter of total employment, with the exception of Germany, which stood at 17.7% in 1987. This level of employment is substantially higher than that of 1920, and has only declined slightly in the last 20 years in the United States (from 22.4% to 20.6%). Thus employment in distributive services is roughly double that in producer services, considered typical of advanced economies. Japan, Canada, and France have increased the share of such employment in the 1970–90 period. About half of employment in distributive services in the G-7 countries corresponds to retail services, although it is often impossible to differentiate the data between wholesale and retail trade. Overall, retail employment has not significantly declined over a 70-year period. In the United States, for instance, it grew from 1.8% in 1940 to 12.8% in 1970, later declining slightly from 12.9% in 1970 to 11.7% in 1991. Japan has increased retail employment from 8.9% in 1960 to 11.2% in 1990, and Germany, while having a lower level of employment in such activity (8.6% in 1987) has actually increased it over its 1970 figure. Thus, there is a large sector of employment still engaged in distribution, as the movements of the employment structure are in fact very slow in the so-called service activities.

Personal services are viewed, at the same time, as the remnants of a proto-industrial structure, and as the expression (at least for some of them) of the social dualism that, according to observers, characterizes the informational society. Here also, the observation of the long-term evolution in the seven countries invites the introduction of a word of caution. They continue to represent a sizable proportion of employment in 1990: with the exception of Germany (6.3% in 1987), they vary in the range between 9.7% and 14.1%, that is roughly equivalent to the quintessential postindustrialist producer services. Overall, they have increased their share since 1970. Focusing on the famous/ infamous "eating and drinking places" jobs, a favorite theme of the literature critical of postindustrialism, we do find a significant expansion of such jobs in the last two decades, particularly in the United Kingdom and in Canada, although the data often mix restaurants and bars with hotel employment which could also be considered as characteristic of the "leisure society." In the United States, eating and drinking places employment stood at 4.9% of total employment in 1991 (up from 3.2% in 1970), which is about twice the size of agricultural employment, but still less than we are asked to believe by the essays elaborating on the notion of the "hamburger society." The main remark to be made on employment in personal services is that it is not fading away in the advanced economies, thus providing ground for the argument that the changes in the social/economic structure concern more the type of services and the type of jobs than the activities themselves.

Let us try now to evaluate some of the traditional theses on postindustrialism in the light of the evolution of employment structure since 1970, more or less at the moment when Touraine, Bell, Richta, and other early theorists of the new, information society were publishing their analyses. In terms of activity, producer services and social services were considered to be typical of postindustrial economies, both as sources of productivity and as responses to social demands and changing values. If we aggregate employment in producer services and social services, we do observe a substantial increase in what could be labeled the "postindustrial services category" in all countries between 1970 and 1990: from 22.8% to 39.2% in the United Kingdom; from 30.2% to 39.5% in the United States; from 28.6% to 33.8% in Canada; from 15.1% to 24.0% in Japan, from 20.2% to 31.7% in Germany; from 21.1% to 29.5% in France (Italian data in our data base do not allow any serious evaluation of this trend). Thus, the trend is there, but it is uneven since it starts from a very different base in 1970: the Anglo-Saxon countries had already developed a strong basis in advanced services employment, while Japan, Germany, and France kept much higher employment in manufacturing, as well as in agriculture. Thus, we observe two different paths in the expansion of "postindustrial" services' employment: one, the Anglo-Saxon model, that shifts from manufacturing to advanced services, maintaining employment in the traditional services; the other, the Japanese/German model, that both expands advanced services and preserves a manufacturing basis, while internalizing some of the service activities in the industrial sector. France is in-between, although leaning toward the Anglo-Saxon model.

In sum, the evolution of employment during what we called the "postindustrial" period (1970–90) shows, at the same time, a general pattern of shifting away from manufacturing jobs, and two different paths regarding manufacturing activity: the first amounts to a rapid phasing away of manufacturing, coupled with a strong expansion of employment in producer services (in rate) and in social services (in size), while other service activities are still kept as sources of employment. A second, different path more closely links manufacturing and producer services, more cautiously increases social services employment, and maintains distributive services. The variation within this second path is between Japan, with a greater agricultural and retail trade population, and Germany with a significantly higher manufacturing employment.

In the process of transformation of the employment structure there is no disappearance of any major service category with the exception of domestic service as compared to 1920. What happens is an increasing diversity of activities, and the emergence of a set of linkages between different activities that makes the employment categories obsolete. There is indeed a postmanufacturing employment structure emerging in the last quarter of the twentieth century. But there is a great deal of variation in the emerging structures of various countries, and it does not seem that great productivity, social stability, and international competitiveness are directly associated with the highest degree of service-related or information-processing jobs. On the contrary, those societies in the G-7 group that have been at the forefront of economic progress and social stability in recent years (Japan and Germany) seem to have developed a more efficient linkage system between manufacturing, producer services, social services, and distributive services than Anglo-Saxon societies, with France and Italy being at the crossroads between the two paths. In all of these societies, informationalization seems to be more decisive than information processing.

Thus, when societies massively destroy manufacturing jobs in a short period of time, instead of gradually phasing the industrial transformation, it is not necessarily because they are more advanced, but because they follow specific policies and strategies that are based in their cultural, social, and political backdrop. And the options taken to conduct the transformation of the national economy and of the labor force have profound consequences for the evolution of the occupational structure that provides the foundations for the new class system of the informational society.

The new occupational structure

A major statement of theories on postindustrialism is that people, besides being engaged in different activities, also hold new positions in the occupational structure. By and large, it was predicted that as we move into what we call the informational society we would observe an increasing importance of managerial, professional, and technical positions, a decreasing proportion of workers in the craft and operator positions, and a swelling in the numbers of clerical and sales workers. In addition, the "left-wing" version of postindustrialism points at the growing importance of semiskilled (often unskilled) service occupations as a counterpart to the growth of professional jobs.

To examine the accuracy of such predictions in the evolution of G-7 countries over the last 40 years is not an easy task, both because the statistical categories do not always correspond exactly across countries and because dates for the various available statistics do not always coincide. Thus, in spite of our methodological efforts to clean up the data, our analysis on this point remains rather tentative, and should be taken only as a first empirical approach to suggest lines of analysis on the evolution of the social structure.

First, let us start with the *diversity of the occupational profiles across societies*. Table 4.15 in Appendix A brings together the distribution of the labor force in the main occupational categories for each country at the time of the latest available statistical information when we conducted this study (1992–3). The first and most important conclusion of our observation is that there are very strong differences between the occupational structures of societies equally entitled to be considered as informational. Thus, if we take the category that groups managers, professionals, and technicians, the epitome of the informational occupations, it was indeed very strong in the United States and in Canada, amounting to almost one-third of the labor force in the early 1990s. But in early 1990s Japan it was only 14.9%. And in France and Germany in 1989 it was only at about one-quarter of all labor. On the other hand, while crafts and operators have substantially dwindled down in North America, they still represented 31.8% of the labor force of Japan, and they were over 27% in both France and Germany, Similarly, sales workers are not a major category in France (3.8%) but they are still important in the United States (11.9%) and truly significant in Japan (15.1%). Japan had a very low proportion of managers (only 3.8%) in 1990, compared to 12.8% in the United States, which could be an indicator of a much more hierarchical structure. France's distinctive feature is the strong component of technicians in the higher professional groups (12.4% of all labor force), in contrast to Germany's 8.7%. On the other hand, Germany has many more jobs than France in the "professionals" category: 13.9% against 6.0%.

Another factor of diversity is the variation in the proportion of semi-skilled service workers: it is significant in the United States, Canada, and Germany, much lower in Japan and France, precisely the countries that, together with Italy, have preserved somewhat more sizable traditional agricultural and commercial activities.

Overall, **Japan and the United States represent the opposite ends of the comparison, and their contrast emphasizes the need to recast the theory of postindustrialism and informationalism.** The data on the United States fit well with the predominant model in the literature, very simply because the "model" was but a theorization of the evolution of the US employment structure. Meanwhile, Japan appears to combine an increase in the professional occupations with the persistence of a strong craft labor force, linked to the industrial era, and with the durability of the agricultural labor force and of sales workers that witness the continuity, under new forms, of the occupations characteristic of the pre-industrial era. The US model progresses into informationalism by substituting new occupations for the old ones. The Japanese model does equally progress into informationalism but following a different route: by increasing some of the required new occupations while redefining the content of occupations of a previous era, yet phasing out those positions that become an obstacle to increase productivity (particularly in agriculture). In between these two "models," Germany and France combine elements of both: they are closer to the United States in terms of the professional/managerial occupations, but closer to Japan in the slower decline of craft/operators jobs.

The second major observation refers, in spite of the diversity we have shown, to the existence of a **common trend toward the increase of the relative weight of the most clearly informational occupation (managers, professionals, and technicians)**, as well as of the overall "white-collar" occupations (including sales and clerical workers). Having first established my call for diversity I also want to give empirical credit to the notion that there is indeed a tendency toward a greater informational content in the occupational structure of advanced societies, in spite of their diverse cultural/political system, and in spite also of the different historical moments of their processes of industrialization.

To observe such a common trend, we must concentrate on the growth of each occupation in each country over time. Let us compare for instance (see tables 4.16 to 4.21 in Appendix A) the evolution of four critical groups of occupations: craft/operators; technicians, professionals, and managers; sales and clerical workers; farm workers and managers. Calculating the rates of change in share of each occupation and group of occupations, we observe some general trends and some critical differences. The share of the managerial/professional/technical occupations showed strong growth in all countries except France. Crafts and operators declined substantially in the United States, the United Kingdom and Canada, and moderately in Germany, France and Japan. Sales and clericals increased moderately their share in the United Kingdom and France and strongly in the four other countries. Farm workers and managers declined substantially in all countries. And semiskilled service and transportation workers presented clearly different trends: they increased their share strongly in the United States and in the United Kingdom; they increased moderately in France; they declined or stabilized in Japan and Germany.

Of all countries considered, Japan was the one that most dramatically upgraded its occupational structure, increasing its share of managers by 46.2% in a 20-year period, and the share of its professional/technical labor force by 91.4%. The United Kingdom also increased the share of its managers by 96.3%, although the increase of its professional/technical workers was much more moderate (5.2%). Thus, we observe a great diversity of rates of change in the share of its occupational group in the overall employment structure. There is diversity in rates because there is some degree of convergence toward a relatively similar occupational structure. At the same time, the differences in management style and in the importance of manufacturing in each country also introduce some variation in the process of change.

Overall, the tendency toward a predominantly white-collar labor force skewed toward its higher tier seems to be the general trend (in the United States in 1991, 57.3% of the labor force was white collar), with the exceptions of Japan and Germany, whose white-collar labor force still does not exceed 50% of total employment. However, even in Japan and Germany, the rates of growth of the informational occupations have been the highest among the various occupational positions; thus, as a trend Japan will count increasingly on a substantial professional labor force, although still holding onto a broader craft and commercial basis than in other societies.

Thirdly, **the widespread argument concerning the increasing polarization of the occupational structure of informational society does not seem to fit with this data set**, if by polarization we mean the simultaneous expansion in equivalent terms of the top and of the bottom of the occupational scale. If such were the case the managerial–professional–technical labor force and the semiskilled service and transport workers would be expanding at similar rates and in similar numbers. Such is clearly not the case. In the United States, semiskilled service workers have indeed increased their share in the occupational structure but at a lower rate than the managerial/professional labor force, and they only represented 13.7% of the labor force in 1991. By contrast, managers, at the top of the scale, have increased their share between 1950 and 1991 at a rate much higher than that of the semiskilled service workers, increasing their number to 12.8% of the labor force in 1991, almost at the same level as that of semiskilled service workers. Even if we add semiskilled transportation workers, we still reach a mere 17.9% of the labor force in 1991, in sharp contrast with the 29.7% of the top managerial–professional–technical category. Of course, many jobs among clerical and sales workers, as well as among operators, are also semiskilled, so that we cannot truly assess the evolution of the occupational structure in terms of skills. Additionally, we know from other sources that *there has been a polarization of income distribution in the United States and in other countries in the last two decades.*[8] However, here I am objecting to the popular image of the informational economy as providing an increasing number of low-level service jobs at a disproportionately higher rate than the rate of increase in the share of the professional/technical component of the labor force. According to this data base, this is simply not the case. In the United

---

[8]   Esping-Andersen (1993); Mishel and Bernstein (1994).

Kingdom there was however a substantial increase in such semiskilled service jobs between 1961 and 1981, but, even there, the share of the higher occupational level increased faster. In Canada, semi-skilled service workers also increased their share substantially to reach 13.7% in 1992 but managerial–professional–technical jobs progressed even more, almost doubling their representation to account for 30.6% of the labor force in 1992. A similar pattern can be found in Germany: low-end service jobs remained relatively stable and well below the progression in rate and in size of the upper occupational tier. France, while increasing substantially such service jobs during the 1980s, still counted them only as 7.2% of the labor force in 1989. As for Japan, semiskilled service jobs experienced a slow growth, from 5.4% in 1955 to a modest 8.6% in 1990.

Thus, while there are certainly signs of social and economic polarization in advanced societies, they do not take the form of divergent paths in the occupational structure, but of different positions of similar occupations across sectors and between firms. Sectoral, territorial, firm-specific, and gender/ethnic/age characteristics are clearer sources of social polarization than occupational differentiation per se.

Informational societies are certainly unequal societies, but inequalities stem less from their relatively upgraded occupational structure than from the exclusions and discriminations that take place in and around the labor force.

Finally, a view of the transformation of the labor force in advanced societies must also consider the *evolution of its employment status*. Again, the data challenge predominant views of postindustrialism, exclusively based on the American experience. Thus, the hypothesis on the fading away of self-employment in mature, informational economies is somewhat supported by the US experience, where the percentage of self-employment in the total labor force declined from 17.6% in 1950 to 8.8% in 1991 *although it has been almost at a standstill for the last 20 years*. But other countries present different patterns. Germany declined at a slow, steady pace, from 13.8% in 1955 to 9.5% in 1975, then to 8.9% in 1989. France has maintained its share of self-employment in the labor force between 1977 and 1987 (12.8% and 12.7% respectively). Italy, while being the fifth largest market economy in the world, still retained 24.8% of its labor force in self-employment in 1989. Japan, while experiencing a decline in self-employment from 19.2% in 1970 to 14.1% in 1990, still has a significant level of such autonomous employment, to which we must add 8.3% of family workers, which places almost one-quarter of the Japanese labor force outside salaried work. As for Canada and the United Kingdom, they have reversed the supposed secular pattern of corporatization of employment in the last 20 years, as Canada increased the proportion of self-employed in its population from 8.4% in 1970 to 9.7% in 1992, and the United Kingdom increased the share of self-employment and family workers in the labor force from 7.6% in 1969 to 13.0% in 1989: a trend that has continued in the 1990s, as I shall show later in this chapter (pp. 266–7).

Granted, the majority of the labor force in the advanced economies is under salaried conditions. But the diversity of the levels, the unevenness of the process, and the reversal of the trend in some cases calls for a differential view of the patterns of evolution of the occupational structure. We could even formulate the hypothesis that as networking and flexibility become characteristic of the new industrial organization, and as new technologies make it possible for small business to find market niches, we witness a resurgence of self-employment and mixed employment status. Thus, the occupational profile of the informational societies, as they emerge historically, will be far more diverse than that imagined by the quasi-naturalistic vision of postindustrial theories biased by an American ethnocentrism that did not fully represent even the American experience.

The maturing of the informational society: employment projections to the twenty-first century

The informational society, in its historically diverse manifestations, is only taking shape in the twilight of the twentieth century. Thus, an analytical clue for its future direction and mature profile could be provided by employment and occupational projections that forecast the social structure of advanced societies into the early years of the coming century. Such projections are always subject to a number of economic, technological, and institutional assumptions that are hardly established on solid ground. Thus, the status of the data that I shall be using in this section is even more tentative than the analysis of the employment trends up to 1990. Yet, by using reliable sources, such as the US Bureau of Labor Statistics, the Japanese Ministry of Labor, and government data compiled by OECD, and by keeping in mind the approximative nature of the exercise, we may be able to generate some hypotheses on the future path of informational employment.

My analysis of employment projections will be mainly focusing on the United States and Japan, because I want to keep within limits the empirical complexity of the study in order to be able to focus on the main argument of my analysis.[9] Thus, by pinpointing the United

[9]   For employment projections concerning other OECD countries, see OECD (1994a: 71–100).

States and Japan, which appear to be two different models of the informational society, I can better assess the hypotheses on the convergence and/or divergence of the informational society's employment and occupational structure.

For the United States, the US Bureau of Labor Statistics (BLS) published in 1991–93 a series of studies, updated in 1994,[10] that together offer a meaningful overview of the evolution of employment and occupational structure between 1990–2 and 2005. To simplify the analysis, I shall refer to the "moderative alternative projection" of the three scenarios considered by the Bureau.

The American economy is projected to create over 26 million jobs between 1992 and 2005. That is a total increase of 22%, slightly higher than the increase in the previous 13-year period, 1979–92. The most apparent features in the projections are the continuation of the trend toward the decline of agricultural and manufacturing jobs, which in 1990–2005 would decline, respectively, at an average annual rate of -0.4 and -0.2. However, manufacturing output would continue to grow at a slightly higher rate than the economy as a whole, at 2.3% per year. Thus the differential growth rate between employment and output in manufacturing and in services shows a substantial gap in labor productivity in favor of manufacturing, in spite of the introduction of new technologies in information-processing activities. Higher than average manufacturing productivity continues to be the key to sustained economic growth able to provide jobs for all other sectors in the economy.

An interesting observation comes from the fact that although employment in agriculture would decline, to a low 2.5% of total employment, agriculture-related *occupations* are expected to grow: this is because, while farmers are expected to decrease by 231,000, an increase of 311,000 jobs for gardeners and groundskeepers is expected: the surpassing of farming jobs by urban-oriented agricultural service jobs underlines how far informational societies have come in their post-agricultural status.

Although only 1 million of the projected 26.4 million new jobs are expected to be created in the goods-producing industries, decline in manufacturing employment is expected to slow down, and some occupational categories in manufacturing, such as precision production, craft, and repair, are actually expected to increase. Yet the bulk of new job growth in the United States is expected to take place in "service activities." About half of such growth is expected to be contributed by the so-called "services division," whose main components are *health*

[10]   See Kutscher (1991); Carey and Franklin (1991); Silvestri and Lukasiewicz (1991); Braddock (1992); Bureau of Labor Statistics (1994).

services and *business services.* Business services, which were the fastest-growing service sector in 1975–90, will continue to be at the top of the expansion through 2005, although with a slower growth rate of about 2.5% per year. One should be aware, though, that not all business services are knowledge intensive: an important component of them are computer data-processing jobs, but *in the 1975–90 period the fastest growing activity was personnel supply services, linked to the increase of temporary work and of contracting out services by firms.* Other fast-growing services in the coming years are expected to be legal services (particularly para-legal), engineering and architectural services, and educational services (*private schools*). In the BLS categories, finance, insurance, and real estate (FIRE) are not included in business services. Thus, to the strong growth in business services we must add the moderate but steady growth projected for this FIRE category, expected to be at about 1.3% per year, to reach 6.1% of total employment by 2005. When comparing these data with my analysis of "producer services" in the preceding sections, both business services and FIRE should be taken into consideration.

Health services will be among the fastest growing activities, at a rate twice as fast as its own increase for the 1975–90 period. By 2005, health services are projected to count for 11.5 million jobs, that is 8.7% of all nonfarm wage and salary employment. To put this figure into perspective, the comparable number for all manufacturing employment in 2005 is projected to be 14% of the labor force. Home healthcare services, particularly for the elderly, would be the fastest growing activity.

Retail trade, growing at a healthy 1.6% average annual rate, and starting from a high level in absolute numbers of jobs, represents the third major source of potential new growth, with 5.1 million new jobs. Within this sector, eating and drinking places would account for 42% of total jobs in retail in 2005.

State and local government jobs would also add to employment in sizable numbers, rising from 15.2 million in 1990 to 18.3 million by 2005. More than half of this increase is expected to take place in education.

Thus, overall, the projected employment structure for the United States closely fits the original blueprint for the informational society:

- agricultural jobs are being phased out;
- manufacturing employment will continue to decline, although at a lower pace, being reduced to a hard core of craft and engineering workforce. Most of the employment impact of manufacturing production will be transferred to services for manufacturing;

- producer services, as well as health and education, lead employment growth in terms of rate, also becoming increasingly important in terms of absolute numbers;
- retail jobs and service jobs continue to swell the ranks of low-skilled activities of the new economy.

If we now turn to examine the projected occupational structure, at first sight the hypothesis of informationalism seems to be confirmed: the fastest-growing rates among occupational groups are those of professionals (32.3% for the period) and technicians (36.9%). But "service occupations," mostly semiskilled, are also growing fast (29.2%) and they would still represent 16.9% of the occupational structure in 2005. Altogether, managers, professionals, and technicians would increase their share of total occupational employment from 24.5% in 1990 to 28.9% in 2005. Sales and clerical workers, taken as a group, would remain stable at about 28.8% of total employment. Craft workers would actually increase their share, confirming the tendency to stabilize a hard core of manual workers around craft skills.

Let us examine more closely this argument: is the future informational society characterized by an increasing polarization of occupational structure? In the case of the United States, the Bureau of Labor Statistics included in its projections an analysis of the educational level required for the 30 occupations that were expected to grow most rapidly and for the 30 occupations that were expected to decline fastest between 1990 and 2005. The analysis considered both the rate of growth or decline of the occupations and their variation in absolute numbers. The conclusion of the authors of the study is that "in general, a majority of the [growing] occupations require education or training beyond high school. In fact, more than 2 out of 3 of the 30 fastest growing occupations, and nearly half of the 30 with the largest number of jobs added had a majority of workers with education or training beyond high school in 1990."[11] The largest job declines, on the other hand, are expected in manufacturing industries, and in some clerical jobs that will be swept away by office automation, generally in the lower tier of skills. Yet at the aggregate level of new jobs being created in the 1992–2005 period Silvestri foresees only modest changes in the distribution of the educational level of the labor force.[12] The proportion of workers who are college graduates is projected to increase by 1.4 percentage points, and the proportion of those with some college education would increase slightly. Conversely, the proportion of high school graduates

---

[11]   Silvestri and Lukasiewicz (1991: 82).
[12]   Silvestri (1993).

decreases by 1 percentage point and the proportion of the lowest educated decreases slightly. Thus, some trends point at an upgrading of the occupational structure, in line with the predictions of post-industrial theory. However, on the other hand the fact that high-skill occupations tend to grow faster does not mean that society at large necessarily avoids polarization and dualism, because of the relative weight of unskilled jobs when they are counted in absolute numbers. BLS projections for 1992–2005 show that the shares of employment for professionals and for service workers are expected to increase approximately by the same amount, about 1.8 and 1.5 percentage points respectively. Since these two groups account together for about half of total job growth, in absolute numbers they do tend to concentrate jobs at both ends of the occupational ladder: 6.2 million new professional workers, and 6.5 million new service workers, whose earnings in 1992 were about 40% below the average for all occupational groups. As Silvestri writes, "part of the reason [for lower earnings of service workers] is that almost a third of these employees had less than a high school education and twice as many worked part-time than the average for all workers."[13] Trying to provide a synthetic vision of projected changes in the occupational structure, I calculated a simplified stratification model on the basis of the detailed data provided by another study by Silvestri concerning distribution of employment by occupation, education, and earnings, for 1992 (actual data) and 2005 (projection).[14] Using median weekly earnings as a most direct indicator of social stratification, I constructed four social groups: upper class (managers and professionals); middle class (technicians and craft workers); lower middle class (sales, clerical, and operators); and lower class (service occupations and agricultural workers). Recalculating under these categories Silvestri's data, I found for the upper class an increase in its share of employment from 23.7% in 1992 to 25.3% in 2005 (+1.6); a slight decline for the middle class, from 14.7% to 14.3% (-0.3); a decline for the lower middle class, from 42.7% to 40.0% (-2.7); and an increase for the lower class, from 18.9% to 20% (+1.1). Two facts deserve comment: on the one hand, there is at the same time relative upgrading of the stratification system and a moderate trend towards occupational polarization. This is because there are simultaneous increases at both the top and the bottom of the social ladder, although the increase at the top is of greater magnitude.

Let us now turn to examine the projections on the Japanese employment and occupational structure. We have two projections, both from

---

[13]   Ibid.: 85.
[14]   Ibid.: table 9.

the Ministry of Labor. One of them, published in 1991, projects (on the basis of the 1980–85 data) to 1989, 1995, and 2000. The other, published in 1987, projects to 1990, 1995, 2000, and 2005. Both project the employment structure by industry and the occupational structure. I have chosen to elaborate on the basis of the 1987 projection because, while being equally reliable, it is more detailed in its breakdown by industries and reaches out to 2005.[15]

The most significant feature of these projections is the slow decline of manufacturing employment in Japan in spite of the acceleration of the transformation of Japan into an informational society. In the 1987 statistical projection, manufacturing employment stood at 25.9% in 1985 and was projected to remain at 23.9% of total employment in 2005. As a reminder, in the US projection, manufacturing employment was expected to decline from 17.5% in 1990 to 14% in 2005, a much sharper decline from a substantially lower base. Japan achieves this relative stability of manufacturing jobs by compensating declines in the traditional sectors with actual increases in the newest sectors. Thus, while employment in textiles would decline from 1.6% in 1985 to 1.1% in 2005, in the same period employment in electrical machinery would increase from 4.1% to 4.9%. Metalworkers will decline substantially, but jobs in the food processing industry will jump from 2.4% to 3.5%.

Overall, the most spectacular increase in employment in Japan is projected to be in business services (from 3.3% in 1985 to 8.1% in 2005), thus showing the increasing role of information-intensive activities in the Japanese economy. However, the employment share of activities in financial, insurance and real estate is projected to remain stable for the 20-year period of the projection. Coupled with the preceding observation, this seems to imply that these rapidly growing business services are, mainly, services to manufacturing and to other services, that is services which input knowledge and information into production. Health services are projected to grow slightly, and education employment is expected to remain at the same share as in 1985.

On the other hand, agricultural employment is expected to decline sharply, from 9.1% in 1985 to 3.9% in 2005, as if Japan had finally assumed its transition to the postagricultural (not postindustrial) age.

In general terms, with the exception of business services and agriculture, the Japanese employment structure is projected to remain remarkably stable, verifying again this gradual transition to the informational paradigm, reworking the content of existing jobs into the new paradigm without necessarily phasing out such jobs.

---

[15]   Ministry of Labor (1991).

As for the occupational structure, the most substantial change projected would be the increase in the share of professional and technical occupations, which would grow from 10.5% in 1985 to a staggering 17% in 2005. On the other hand, managerial occupations, while growing significantly in their share, will grow at a slower rate, and they still would represent less than 6% of total employment in 2005. This would confirm the tendency toward the reproduction of the lean hierarchical structure of Japanese organizations with power concentrated in the hands of a few managers. The data also seem to indicate the increase in the professionalization of middle-level workers and the specialization of tasks in information processing and knowledge generation. Crafts and operators are expected to decline, but will still represent over one-quarter of the labor force in 2005, about 3 percentage points ahead of the corresponding occupational categories for the United States at the same date. Clerical workers are also expected to increase at a moderate rate, while farming occupations would be reduced by about two-thirds in relationship to their 1985 level.

Thus, the projections of the employment structure in the United States and Japan seem to continue the trends observed for the 1970–90 period. These are clearly two different employment and occupational structures corresponding to two societies which can be equally labeled informational in terms of their sociotechnical paradigm of production, yet with clearly distinct performances in productivity growth, economic competitiveness, and social cohesion. While the United States appears to be emphasizing its tendency to move away from manufacturing jobs, and to concentrate in both producer and social services, Japan is maintaining a more balanced structure, with a strong manufacturing sector and a wide cushion of retail service activities. Japanese emphasis in business services is significantly less concentrated in finance and real estate, and the expansion of employment in social services is also more limited. The projections on the occupational structure confirm different styles of management, with Japanese organizations establishing cooperative structures at the shop-floor and office level while at the same time continuing to concentrate decision-making into a leaner managerial rank. Overall, the general hypothesis of diverse paths to the informational paradigm within a common pattern of employment structure seems to be confirmed by the limited test offered by the projections presented here.

Summing up: the evolution of employment structure and its implications for a comparative analysis of the informational society

The historical evolution of employment structure, at the roots of social structure, has been dominated by the secular trend toward the increasing productivity of human labor. As technological and organizational innovations have allowed men and women to put out more and better product with less effort and resources, work and workers have shifted from direct production to indirect production, from cultivation, extraction, and fabrication to consumption services and management work, and from a narrow range of economic activities to an increasingly diverse occupational universe.

But the tale of human creativity and economic progress throughout history has been often told in simplistic terms, thus obscuring the understanding not only of our past but of our future. The usual version of this process of historical transition as a shift from agriculture, to industry, then to services, as an explanatory framework for the current transformation of our societies, presents three fundamental flaws:

(1) It assumes homogeneity between the transition from agriculture to industry and that from industry to services, overlooking the ambiguity and internal diversity of the activities included under the label of "services."
(2) It does not pay enough attention to the truly revolutionary nature of new information technologies, which, by allowing a direct, on-line linkage between different types of activity in the same process of production, management, and distribution, establish a close, structural connection between spheres of work and employment artificially separated by obsolete statistical categories.
(3) It forgets the cultural, historical, and institutional diversity of advanced societies, as well as the fact that they are interdependent in a global economy. Thus, the shift to the sociotechnical paradigm of informational production takes place along different lines, determined by the trajectory of each society and by the interaction between these various trajectories. It follows a diversity of employment/occupational structures within the common paradigm of the informational society.

Our empirical observation of the evolution of employment in the G-7 countries shows some fundamental common features that seem indeed to be characteristic of informational societies:

• the phasing out of agricultural employment;

- the steady decline of traditional manufacturing employment;
- the rise of both producer services and social services, with the emphasis on business services in the first category, and health services in the second group;
- the increasing diversification of service activities as sources of jobs;
- the rapid rise of managerial, professional, and technical jobs;
- the formation of a "white-collar" proletariat, made up of clerical and sales workers;
- the relative stability of a substantial share of employment in retail trade;
- the simultaneous increase of the upper and lower levels of the occupational structure;
- the relative upgrading of the occupational structure over time, with an increasing share of those occupations that require higher skills and advanced education proportionally higher than the increase of the lower-level categories.

It does not follow that societies at large are upgraded in their skills, education, or income status, nor in their stratification system. The impact of a somewhat upgraded employment structure into the social structure will depend on the ability of the institutions to incorporate the labor demand into the labor force and to reward workers proportionally to their skills.

On the other hand, the analysis of the differential evolution of the G-7 countries clearly shows some variation in their employment and occupational structures. At the risk of oversimplifying, we can propose the hypothesis of two different informational models:

(1) The "Service Economy Model," represented by the United States, the United Kingdom, and Canada. It is characterized by a rapid phasing out of manufacturing employment after 1970, as the pace towards informationalism accelerated. Having already eliminated almost all agricultural employment, this model emphasizes an entirely new employment structure where the differentiation among various service activities becomes the key element to analyze social structure. This model emphasizes capital management services over producer services, and keeps expanding the social service sector because of a dramatic rise in healthcare jobs and, to a lesser extent, in education employment. It is also characterized by the expansion of the managerial category that includes a considerable number of middle managers.

(2) The "Industrial Production Model," clearly represented by Japan and to a considerable extent by Germany, which, while reducing also the share of their manufacturing employment, continues to keep it at a relatively high level (around one-quarter of the labor

force) in a much more gradual movement that allows for the restructuring of manufacturing activities into the new sociotechnical paradigm. Indeed, this model reduces manufacturing jobs while reinforcing manufacturing activity. Partly as a reflection of this orientation, producer services are much more important than financial services, and they seem to be more directly linked to manufacturing firms. This is not to say that financial activities are not important in Japan and Germany: after all, eight of the world's ten largest banks are Japanese. Yet, while financial services are indeed important and have increased their share in both countries, the bulk of service growth is in services to companies, and in social services. However, Japan is also specific in showing a significantly lower level of employment in social services than other informational societies. This is probably linked to the structure of the Japanese family and to the internalization of some social services into the structure of the firms: a cultural and institutional analysis of the variegations of employment structure seems to be a necessity to account for the diversity of informational societies.

In between, France seems to be leaning toward the service economy model, but maintaining a relatively strong manufacturing basis and emphasizing both producer and social services. The close linkage between the French and the German economies in the European Union is probably creating a division of labor between management and manufacturing activities that could ultimately benefit the German component of the emerging European economy. Italy characterizes itself as keeping almost one-quarter of employment in self-employed status, maybe introducing a third model that would emphasize a different organizational arrangement, based on networks of small and medium businesses adapted to the changing conditions of the global economy, thus laying the ground for an interesting transition from proto-industrialism to proto-informationalism.

The different expressions of such models in each one of the G-7 countries are dependent upon their position in the global economy. In other words, for a country to be focused on the "service economy" model means that other countries are exercising their role as industrial production economies. The implicit assumption of postindustrial theory that the advanced countries would be service economies and the less advanced countries would specialize in agriculture and manufacturing has been rejected by historical experience. Throughout the world, many economies are quasi-subsistence economies, while agricultural and industrial activities that thrive outside of the informational core do so on the basis of their close connection to the global economy, dominated by the G-7 countries. Thus, the employment structure of the United States and of Japan reflect their different forms of articulation to the global economy, and not just their degree of advancement in the informational scale. The fact that there is a lower proportion of manufacturing jobs or a higher proportion of managers in the United States is partly due to the offshoring of manufacturing jobs by US firms, and to the concentration of management and information-processing activities in the United States at the expense of production activities generated in other countries by US consumption of these countries' products.

Furthermore, different modes of articulation to the global economy are not only due to different institutional environments and economic trajectories, but to different government policies and firms' strategies. Thus, the observed trends can be reversed. If policies and strategies can modify the service and industrial mix of a given economy it means that the variations of the informational paradigm are as important as its basic structure. It is a socially open, politically managed paradigm, whose main common feature is technological.

As economies rapidly evolve towards their integration and inter-penetration, the resulting employment structure will largely reflect the position of each country and region in the interdependent, global structure of production, distribution, and management. Thus, the artificial separation of social structures by institutional boundaries of different nations (the United States, Japan, Germany, and so on) limits the interest of analyzing the occupational structure of the informational society in a given country in isolation from what happens in another country whose economy is so closely interrelated. If Japanese manufacturers produce many of the cars consumed by the American market and many of the chips consumed in Europe, we are not just witnessing the demise of American or British manufacturing, but the impact on the employment structure of each country of the division of labor among different types of informational societies.

The implications of such an observation for the theory of informationalism are far-reaching: the unit of analysis to comprehend the new society will necessarily have to change. The focus of the theory must shift to a comparative paradigm able to explain at the same time the sharing of technology, the interdependence of the economy, and the variations of history in the determination of an employment structure spread across national boundaries.

Is There a Global Labor Force?

If there is a global economy, it should be a global labor market and a global labor force.[16] Yet, as with many of such obvious statements, taken in its literal sense it is empirically wrong and analytically misleading. While capital flows freely in the electronic circuits of global financial networks, labor is still highly constrained, and will be for the foreseeable future, by institutions, culture, borders, police, and xenophobia. Only about 1.5% of the global labor force (about 80 million workers) worked outside their country in 1993, and half of them were concentrated in Sub-Saharan Africa and the Middle-East.[17] In the European Union, in spite of free movement of their citizens in the member countries, only 2% of its nationals worked in another Union country in 1993, a proportion unchanged for ten years.[18] Notwithstanding the public perception in the North concerning the invasion of immigrants from the South and East, in major West European countries in the late 1980s, the impact of immigration on labor was at a lower level than in 1975. Thus, the percentage of foreign labor in the total labor force in Britain was 6.5% in 1975, and 4.5% in 1985–7; in France, it went down from 8.5% to 6.9%; in Germany from 8% to 7.9%; in Sweden from 6% to 4.9%; and in Switzerland from 24% to 18.2%.[19] In the early 1990s, because of social disruption in Eastern Europe (mainly in Yugoslavia), political asylum increased the number of immigrants, particularly in Germany. Yet overall, in the European Union it is estimated that total foreign population of non-European citizens amounts to about 13 million, of which about one-quarter would be undocumented.[20] For the whole of Western Europe, the proportion of foreigners in the total population in 1990 was 4.5% (see table 4.22 in Appendix A), and France and the UK had a lower proportion in 1990 than in 1982. Furthermore, the proportion of foreigners in the total population, for the five largest countries of the European Union in 1994, only surpassed 5% in Germany (to reach almost 7%); it was actually lower than in 1986 in France; and it was only slightly over the 1986 level in the UK.[21] As for the United States, where a significant new wave of immigration did indeed occur during the 1980s and 1990s, it was always an immigrant society, and current trends are in

---

[16]   Johnston (1991).
[17]   Campbell (1994).
[18]   *Newsweek* (1993).
[19]   Sources collected and elaborated by Soysal (1994: 23); see also Stalker (1994).
[20]   Soysal (1994: 22).
[21]   *Economist* (1994).

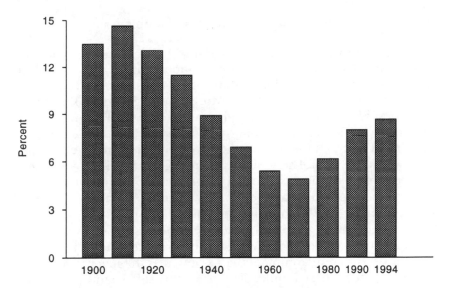

Figure 4.1 Percentage of United States population that is foreign-born
Source: US Census Bureau.

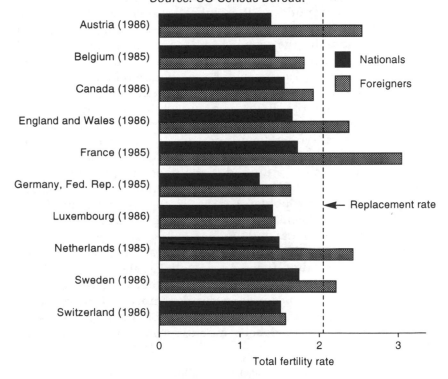

Figure 4.2 Total fertility rates for nationals and foreigners, selected OECD countries
Sources: SOPEMI/OECD; elaborated by Stalker (1994).

the line of historical continuity (see figure 4.1).[22] What has changed, in both contexts, is the ethnic composition of immigration, with a decreasing proportion of immigrants of European stock in America, and with a higher proportion of Muslim immigrants in European countries. What is also happening is that because of differential birth rates between the native population and the residents and citizens of immigrant origin, affluent societies are becoming more ethnically diverse (figure 4.2). The visibility of immigrant workers, and their descendants, has increased because of their concentration in the largest metropolitan areas and in a few regions.[23] As a result of both features, in the 1990s ethnicity and cultural diversity have become a major social problem in Europe, are a new issue in Japan, and continue to be, as they always were, at the top of the American agenda. Yet this is a different argument than saying that the labor market has become global. There is indeed a global market for a tiny fraction of the labor force, concerning the highest-skilled professionals in inno- vative R&D, cutting-edge engineering, financial management, advanced business services, and entertainment, who shift and commute between nodes of the global networks that control the planet.[24] Yet while this integration of the best talent in the global networks is critical for the commanding heights of the informational economy, the overwhelming proportion of labor, in developed as well as in developing countries, remains largely nation-bound. Indeed, for two-thirds of workers in the world, employment still means agricul- tural employment, rooted in the fields, usually in their region.[25] Thus, in the strictest sense, with the exception of the highest level of knowl- edge generators/symbol manipulators (what I call below the *networkers, commanders,* and *innovators*), there is not, and will not be in the foreseeable future, a unified global labor market, in spite of emigration flows to OECD countries, to the Arabian peninsula, and to the booming metropolitan centers in the Asian Pacific. More important for movements of people are massive displacements of population because of war and hunger.

However, there is a historical tendency toward increasing interde- pendence of the labor force on a global scale, through three mechanisms: global employment in the multinational corporations and their associated cross-border networks; impacts of international trade on employment and labor conditions, both in the North and in the South; and effects of global competition and of the new mode of

---

[22]   Bouvier and Grant (1994); Stalker (1994); Borjas et al. (1991).
[23]   Machimura (1994); Stalker (1994).
[24]   Johnston (1991).
[25]   ILO (1994).

flexible management on each country's labor force. In each case, information technology is the indispensable medium for the linkages between different segments of the labor force across national boundaries.

As stated in chapter 2, foreign direct investment has become the driving force of globalization, more significant than trade as a conductor of transborder interdependence.[26] The worldwide stock of FDI tripled from an estimated value of US$500 billion in 1980 to over US$1,500 billion in 1990. While in the early 1970s and early 1980s foreign direct investment grew at the same pace as other economic indicators, from the mid-1980s it accelerated, with annual growth rates for FDI outflows of 33% during 1986–90. The most significant agents of the new pattern of foreign direct investment are multinational corporations and their associated networks: together they organize the core labor force in the global economy. The number of multinational firms increased from 7,000 in 1970 to 37,000 in 1993, with 150,000 affiliates around the world. Although they employ directly "only" 70 million workers, these workers produce one-third of the world's total private output. Global value of their sales in 1992 was US$5,500 billion, a figure 25% greater than the total value of world trade. Labor force located in different countries depends on the division of labor between distinct functions and strategies of such multinational networks. Thus, most of the labor force does not circulate in the network, but becomes dependent on the function, evolution and behavior of other segments in the network. It results in a process of hierarchical, segmented interdependence of the labor force, under the impulse of relentless movements by firms in the circuits of their global network (see figure 4.3).

The second major mechanism of global labor interdependence concerns the impacts of trade on employment, both in the North and in the South.[27] On the one hand, the combination of North-bound exports, foreign direct investment, and growth of domestic markets in the South has triggered a gigantic wave of industrialization in some developing countries.[28] Simply accounting for the direct impact of trade, Wood[29] estimates that between 1960 and 1990 20 million manufacturing jobs have been created in the South. In Guandong province's Pearl River Delta alone, between 5 and 6 million workers have been hired in factories in semirural areas in the last ten years. (Kwok and So (eds) 1995). But while there is agreement on the signif-

---

[26] Bailey et al. (eds) (1993); Tyson et al. (eds) (1988); UNCTAD (1993, 1994).
[27] Rothstein (1993); Mishel and Bernstein (1993).
[28] Patel (1992); Singh (1994); ILO (1993, 1994).
[29] Wood (1994).

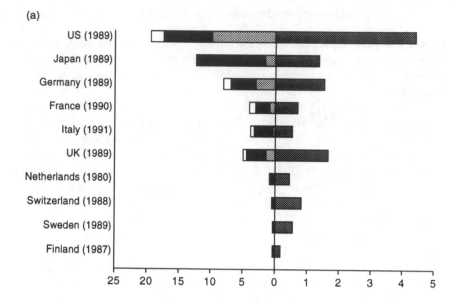

(a)

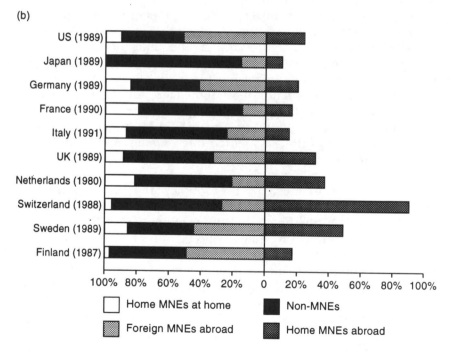

(b)

Home MNEs at home   Non-MNEs

Foreign MNEs abroad   Home MNEs abroad

Figure 4.3   Paid employment in manufacturing firms in selected
industrialized countries by ownership, latest available year
(a) Million employees
(b) Share of domestic paid employment
Source: Bailey et al. (1993).

icance of the new process of industrialization triggered in Asia and Latin America by the new outward orientation of developing economies, an intense debate has raged on the actual impact of trade on employment and labor conditions in OECD countries. The White Paper of the Commission of European Communities (1994) considered global competition to be a significant factor in the rise of unemployment in Europe. In sharp contrast, the 1994 employment study of the OECD Secretariat rejects this relationship, arguing that imports from industrializing countries account only for 1.5% of total demand in the OECD area. Some noted economists, such as Paul Krugman and Robert Lawrence,[30] have proposed empirical analyses according to which the impact of trade on employment and wages in the United States is very small. Yet their analysis has been submitted to serious criticism, both methodological and substantive, by Cohen, Sachs and Shatz, and Mishel and Bernstein, among others.[31] Indeed, the complexity of the new global economy is not easily captured by traditional trade and employment statistics. UNCTAD and ILO estimate that intrafirm trade represents the equivalent of about 32% of world trade. Such exchanges do not take place through the market, but are internalized (through ownership) or quasi-internalized (through networks).[32] It is this kind of trade that affects most directly the labor force in OECD countries. Subcontracting of services by companies around the globe, using telecommunications linkages, further integrates the labor force without displacing it or trading its output. But even using standard trade statistics, it seems that the impact of trade on the labor force has been underestimated by some economic analyses. Perhaps a balanced view of this matter is the empirical study by Adrian Wood on the impact of trade on employment and inequality between 1960 and 1990.[33] According to his calculations (that revise, on the basis of a sound methodological critique, usual estimates), skilled workers in the North greatly benefited from global trade on two grounds: first, they took advantage of higher economic growth brought about by increased trade; second, the new international division of labor gave their firms, and themselves, a comparative advantage in higher value-added products and processes. On the other hand, unskilled workers in the North considerably suffered because of the competition with producers in lower-cost areas. Wood estimates that overall demand for unskilled labor was reduced by 20%. When government and firms could not

[30]   Krugman and Lawrence (1994); Krugman (1994).
[31]   See, for instance, Cohen (1994); Mishel and Bernstein (1994).
[32]   UNCTAD (1993); Bailey et al. (eds) (1993); Campbell (1994).
[33]   Wood (1994).

change the conditions of labor contracts, as in the European Union, unskilled labor became too costly with reference to commodities traded with newly industrializing countries. It followed unemployment of unskilled labor that was, in comparative standards, too expensive for its low skills. Because skilled workers, on the contrary, were still in demand, wage inequality surged in the OECD area.

Yet the new international division of labor theory that underlies the analyses on the differential impact of trade and globalization on the labor force relies on an assumption that has been questioned by empirical observation of production processes in newly industrializing areas, namely the persistence of a productivity gap between workers and factories in the South and the North. The pioneering research by Harley Shaiken on American automobile and computer plants and on Japanese consumer electronic plants in Northern Mexico shows that the productivity of Mexican workers and factories is comparable to that of American plants.[34] Mexican production lines are not at a lower technological level than those in the United States either in process (CAM manufacturing) or products (engines, computers), yet they operate at a fraction of the cost north of the Rio Grande. In another typical example of new labor interdependence, Bombay and Bangalore have become major subcontractors of software for companies around the globe, using the work of thousands of highly skilled Indian engineers and computer scientists who receive about 20% of the wage paid in the United States for similar jobs.[35] Similar trends were taking place in finance and business services in Singapore, Hong Kong and Taipei.[36] In sum, the more the process of economic globalization deepens, the more the interpenetration of networks of production and management expands across borders, and the closer become the links between the conditions of the labor force in different countries, placed at different levels of wages and social protection, but decreasingly distinct in terms of skills and technology.

Thus, a wide range of opportunities opens up for companies in advanced capitalist countries, concerning their strategies toward labor, both skilled and unskilled. They can either:

(a) downsize the firm, keeping the indispensable highly skilled labor force in the North, and importing inputs from low-cost areas; or,
(b) subcontract part of the work to their transnational establishments and to the auxiliary networks whose production can be internalized in the network enterprise system; or,

[34]   Shaiken (1990).
[35]   Balaji (1994).

(c) use temporary labor, part-time workers, or informal firms as suppliers in the home country; or,

(d) automate or relocate tasks and functions for which the standard labor market prices are considered too high *vis-à-vis* alternative formulae; or,

(e) obtain from their labor force, including the core labor force, acquiescence to more stringent conditions of work and pay as a condition for the continuation of their jobs, thus reversing social contracts established under circumstances more favorable for labor.

In the real world, this range of possibilities translates into the actual use of all of them, depending upon firms, countries, and periods of time. Thus, although global competition may not affect directly the majority of the labor force in OECD countries, its indirect effects entirely transform the condition of labor and labor institutions everywhere.[37] Furthermore, the alignment of labor conditions across countries does not take place only because of competition from low-cost areas: it also forces Europe, America, and Japan to converge. The pressures toward greater flexibility of the labor market and toward the reversal of the welfare state in Western Europe come less from the pressures derived from East Asia than from the comparison with the United States.[38] It will become increasingly difficult for Japanese firms to continue life employment practices for the privileged 30% of its labor force if they have to compete in an open economy with American companies practicing flexible employment.[39] Lean production, downsizing, restructuring, consolidation, and flexible management practices are induced and made possible by the intertwined impact of economic globalization and diffusion of information technologies. The indirect effects of such tendencies on the conditions of labor in all countries are far more important than the measurable impact of international trade or cross-border direct employment.

Thus, while there is not a unified global labor market, and therefore not a global labor force, there is indeed global interdependence of the labor force in the informational economy. Such interdependence is characterized by the hierarchical segmentation of labor not between countries but across borders.

The new model of global production and management is

[36] Fouquin et al. (1991); Tan and Kapur (eds) (1986); Kwok and So (eds) (1995).

[37] Rothstein (1994); Sengenberger and Campbell (1994).

[38] Navarro (1994).

[39] Joussaud (1994); NIKKEIREN (1993).

tantamount to the simultaneous integration of work process and disintegration of the workforce. This model is not the inevitable consequence of the informational paradigm but the result of an economic and political choice made by governments and companies selecting the "low road" in the process of transition to the new, informational economy, mainly using productivity increases for short-term profitability. These policies contrast sharply, in fact, with the possibilities of work enhancement and sustained, high productivity opened up by the transformation of the work process under the informational paradigm.

The Work Process in the Informational Paradigm

The maturation of the information technology revolution in the 1990s has transformed the work process, introducing new forms of social and technical division of labor. It took the 1980s for micro-electronics-based machinery to fully penetrate manufacturing, and it is only in the 1990s that networked computers have widely diffused throughout the information-processing activities at the core of the so-called services sector. By the mid-1990s the new informational paradigm, associated with the emergence of the network enterprise, is well in place and set for its unfolding.[40]

There is an old and honorable tradition of sociological and organizational research on the relationship between technology and work.[41] Thus, we know that technology per se is not the cause of the work arrangements to be found in the workplace. Management decisions, systems of industrial relations, cultural and institutional environments, and government policies are such fundamental sources of labor practices and production organization that the impact of technology can only be understood in complex interaction within a social system comprising all these elements. Furthermore, the process of capitalist restructuring decisively marked the forms and outcomes of introducing information technologies into the work process.[42] The means and ways of such a restructuring were also diverse depending upon countries' technological capability, political culture, and labor traditions. Thus, the new informational paradigm of work and labor is not a neat model but a messy quilt, woven from the historical inter-

[40]   For a documented view of developments in the diffusion of information technology in the workplace up to 1995 see *Business Week* (1994a, 1995a).
[41]   For a review of relevant literature, see Child (1986); see also Appelbaum and Schettkat (eds) (1990); Buitelaar (ed.) (1988); Noble (1984).
[42]   Shaiken (1985); Castano (1994a).

action between technological change, industrial relations policy, and conflictive social action. To find patterns of regularity behind this confusing scene, we must have the patience to abstract successive layers of social causation, to first deconstruct, then reconstruct the emerging pattern of work, workers, and labor organization that characterize the new, informational society.

Let us start with information technology. Mechanization first, automation later, have been transforming human labor for decades, always triggering similar debates around issues of workers' displacement, deskilling versus reskilling, productivity versus alienation, management control versus labor autonomy.[43] To follow a French "*filière*" of analysis over the last half-century, George Friedmann criticized "*le travail en miettes*" (piecemeal work) of the Taylorist factory; Pierre Naville denounced the alienation of workers under mechanization; Alain Touraine, on the basis of his pioneering sociological study in the late 1940s on the technological transformation of Renault factories, proposed his typology of work processes as A/B/C (craft, assembly line, and innovation work); Serge Mallet announced the birth of "a new working class" focused on the capacity to manage and operate advanced technology; and Benjamin Coriat analyzed the emergence of a post-Fordist model in the labor process, on the basis of linking up flexibility and integration in a new model of relationships between production and consumption. At the end of this intellectual itinerary, impressive on many grounds, one fundamental idea emerges: automation, which received its full meaning only with the deployment of information technology, increases dramatically the importance of human brain input into the work process.[44] While automated machinery, and later computers, have indeed been used for transforming workers into second-order robots, as Braverman argued,[45] this is not the corollary of technology, but of a social organization of labor that stalled (and still does) the full utilization of the productive capacity generated by the new technologies. As Harley Shaiken, Maryellen Kelley, Larry Hirschhorn, Shoshana Zuboff, and others have shown in their empirical work, the broader and deeper the diffusion of advanced information technology in factories and offices, the greater the need for an autonomous, educated worker able and willing to program and decide entire sequences of work.[46]

[43]   Hirschhorn (1984).
[44]   Friedmann (1956); Friedmann and Naville (eds) (1961); Touraine (1955); Mallet (1963); Coriat (1990).
[45]   Braverman (1973).
[46]   Shaiken (1985, 1993); Kelley (1986, 1990); Hirschhorn (1984); Zuboff (1988); Japan Institute of Labour (1985). For a discussion on the literature, see Adler (1992); for a comparative approach, see Ozaki et al. (1992).

Notwithstanding the formidable obstacles of authoritarian management and exploitative capitalism, information technologies call for
greater freedom for better-informed workers to deliver the full
promise of its productivity potential. The networker is the necessary
agent of the network enterprise made possible by new information
technologies.

In the 1990s several factors accelerated the transformation of the
work process: computer technology, and its applications, progressing
by quantum leaps, became increasingly cheaper and better, thus
being affordable and manageable on a large scale; global competition
triggered a technology/management race between companies all
over the world; organizations evolved and adopted new shapes that
were generally based on flexibility and networking; managers, and
their consultants, finally understood the potential of new technology
and how to use it, although more often than not they constrained such
potential within the limits of the old set of organizational goals (such
as a short-term increase of profits calculated on a quarterly basis).

The massive diffusion of information technologies has caused
rather similar effects in factories, offices, and service organizations.[47]
These effects are not, as was forecasted, the shift towards indirect work
at the expense of direct work which would become automated. On
the contrary: the role of direct work has increased because information technology has empowered the direct worker at the shop floor
level (be it in the process of testing chips or underwriting insurance
policies). What *tends* to disappear through integral automation are
the routine, repetitive tasks, that can be precoded and programmed
for their execution by machines. It is the Taylorist assembly line that
becomes a historic relic (although it is still the harsh reality for
millions of workers in the industrializing world). It should not be
surprising that information technologies do precisely that: replace
work that can be encoded in a programmable sequence and enhance
work that requires analysis, decision, and reprogramming capabilities
in real time at a level that only the human brain can master. Every
other activity, given the extraordinary rate of progress in information
technology and its constant lowering in price per information unit, is
potentially susceptible of automation, and thus the labor engaged in
it is expendable (although workers as such are not, depending upon
their social organization and political capacity).

The informational work process is determined by the characteristics of the informational production process. Keeping in mind the
analyses presented in previous chapters on the informational/global

---

[47]   Quinn (1988); Bushnell (1994).

economy, and on the network enterprise as its organizational form, such process can be summarized as follows:

(1) Value added is mainly generated by innovation, both of process and products. New designs of chips, new software-writing largely condition the fate of the electronics industry. The invention of new financial products (for example, the creation of the "derivatives market" on the stock exchanges during the late 1980s) are at the roots of the boom (however risky) of financial services, and of the prosperity (or collapse) of financial firms, and of their clients.

(2) Innovation is itself dependent upon two conditions: research potential and specification capability. That is, new knowledge has to be discovered, then applied to specific purposes in a given organizational/institutional context. Custom design is critical for microelectronics in the 1990s; instant reaction to macroeconomic changes is fundamental in managing the volatile financial products created in the global market.

(3) Execution tasks are more efficient when they are able to adapt higher-level instructions to their specific application, and when they can generate feedback effects into the system. An optimum combination of worker/machine in the execution tasks is set to automate all standard procedures, and to reserve human potential for adaptation and feedback effects.

(4) Most production activity takes place in organizations. Since the two main features of the predominant organizational form (the network enterprise) are internal adaptability and external flexibility, the two key features for the work process will be: the ability to generate flexible strategic decision-making; and the capacity to achieve organizational integration between all elements of the production process.

(5) Information technology becomes the critical ingredient of the process of work as described because:
   • it largely determines innovation capability;
   • it makes possible the correction of errors and generation of feedback effects at the level of execution;
   • it provides the infrastructure for flexibility and adaptability throughout the management of the production process.

This specific production process introduces a *new division of labor* that characterizes the emerging informational paradigm. The new division of labor can be better understood by presenting a typology constructed around three dimensions. **The first dimension refers to the actual tasks performed in a given work process. The second dimension concerns the relationship between a given organization and its environment, including other organizations. The third** dimension considers the relationship between managers and employees in a given organization or network. I call the first dimension value-making, the second dimension relation-making, and the third dimension decision-making.

In terms of *value-making*, in a production process organized around information technology (be it goods production or service delivery), the following fundamental tasks, and their corresponding workers, can be distinguished:

- strategic decision-making and planning by the *commanders*;
- innovation in products and process by the *researchers*;
- adaptation, packaging, and targeting of innovation by the *designers*;
- management of the relationships between the decision, innovation, design, and execution, taking into consideration the means available to the organization to achieve the stated goals, by the *integrators*;
- execution of tasks under their own initiative and understanding by the *operators*;
- execution of ancillary, preprogrammed tasks that have not been, or cannot be, automated, by what I dare to call the "*operated*" (or human robots).

This typology must be combined with another referring to the need and capacity of each task (and its performer) to link up with other workers in real time, be it within the same organization or in the overall system of the network enterprise. According to this relational capacity we may distinguish between three fundamental positions:

- the *networkers*, who set up connections on their initiative (for example, joint engineering with other departments of companies), and navigate the routes of the network enterprise;
- the *networked*, workers who are on-line but without deciding when, how, why, or with whom;
- the *switched-off* workers, tied to their own specific tasks, defined by non-interactive, one-way instructions.

Finally, in terms of the capacity to input the *decision-making process* we can differentiate between:

- the *deciders*, who make the decision in the last resort;
- the *participants*, who are involved in decision-making;
- the *executants*, who merely implement decisions.

The three typologies do not coincide, and the difference in the relational dimension or in the decision-making process can occur, and indeed does in practice, at all levels of the value-making structure.

This construction is not an ideal type of organization, or some futuristic scenario. It is a synthetic representation of what seems to be emerging as the main task-performing positions in the informational work process, according to empirical studies on the transformation of work and organizations under the impact of information technologies.[48] Yet my argument is certainly not that all or most work processes and workers in our society are reducible to these typologies. Archaic forms of sociotechnical organization do survive, and will for a long, long time remain in many countries, in the same way as pre-industrial, handicraft forms of production were combined with mechanization of industrial production for an extended historical period. But it is critical to distinguish the complex and diverse forms of work and workers in our observation from the emerging patterns of production and management that, because they are rooted in a dynamic sociotechnical system, will tend to become dominant through the dynamics of competition and demonstration effects. My hypothesis is that the work organization sketched in this analytical scheme represents the emerging informational work paradigm. I shall illustrate this emerging paradigm by referring briefly to some case studies on the impacts of computer-aided manufacturing and office automation on work, in order to make somewhat concrete the analytical construction I have proposed.

Thus, Harley Shaiken studied in 1994 the practice of so-called "high performance work organization" in two up-to-date American automobile factories: the GM-Saturn Complex on the outskirts of Nashville, Tennessee, and the Chrysler Jefferson North Plant on the east side of Detroit.[49] Both are cases of successful, highly productive organizations that have integrated the most advanced computer-based machinery in their operation, and have simultaneously transformed the organization of work and management. While acknowledging differences between the two plants, Shaiken points at the critical factors accounting for high performance in both of them, on the basis of new technological tools. The first is the high level of skills of an experienced industrial labor force, whose knowledge of production and products was critical to modifying a complex process when necessary. In order to develop these skills, at the heart of the new work system there is regular work training, on special courses outside the plant and on the job. Saturn workers spent 5% of their

---

[48]   See, among others, Mowery and Henderson (eds) (1989); Wood (ed.) (1989); Hyman and Streeck (eds) (1988); ILO (1988); Carnoy (1989); Wall et al. (1987); Rees (1992); Hartmann (ed.) (1987); Buitelaar (ed.) (1988); Dean et al. (1992).
[49]   Shaiken, personal communication, 1994, 1995; Shaiken (1995).

annual working time in training sessions, most of them in the Work Development Center, a facility adjacent to the plant.

The second factor fostering high performance was increased worker autonomy, as compared to other factories, allowing for shop-floor cooperation, quality circles, and feedback from workers in real time during the production process. Both plants organize production in work teams, with a flat occupational classification system. Saturn eliminated the position of first line supervisor, and Chrysler was moving in the same direction. Workers are able to work with considerable freedom, and are encouraged to increase formal interaction in the performance of their tasks.

Workers' involvement in the upgraded process is dependent on two conditions that were met in both factories: job security and labor union participation in negotiating and implementing the reorganization of work. The building of the new Chrysler plant in Detroit was preceded by a "Modern Operating Agreement," emphasizing managerial flexibility and workers' input. Of course, this is not an ideal world, exempt from social conflicts. Shaiken observed the existence of tensions, and potential sources of labor disputes, between labor and management, as well as between the local union (increasingly behaving as a factory union, in the case of Saturn), and the United Auto Workers leadership. Yet the nature of the informational work process calls for cooperation, team work, workers' autonomy and responsibility, without which new technologies cannot be used up to their potential. The networked character of informational production permeates the whole firm, and requires constant interaction and processing of information between workers, between workers and management, and between humans and machines.

As for office automation, it has gone through three different phases, largely determined by available technology.[50] In the first phase, characteristic of the 1960s and 1970s, mainframe computers were used for batch processing of data; centralized computing by specialists in data-processing centers formed the basis of a system characterized by the rigidity and hierarchical control of information flows; data entry operations required substantial efforts since the goal of the system was the accumulation of large amounts of information in a central memory; work was standardized, routinized, and, in essence, deskilled for the majority of clerical workers, in a process analyzed, and denounced, by Braverman in his classic study. The following stages of automation, however, were substantially different. The second phase, in the early 1980s, was characterized by the

[50]   Zuboff (1988); Dy (ed.) (1990).

emphasis on the use of microcomputers by the employees in charge of the actual work process; although they were supported by centralized data bases, they interacted directly in the process of generating information, although often requiring the support of computer experts. By the mid-1980s, the combination of advances in telecommunications, and the development of microcomputers, led to the formation of networks of workstations and literally revolutionized office work, although the organizational changes required for the full use of new technology delayed the widespread diffusion of the new model of automation until the 1990s. In this third phase of automation, office systems are integrated and networked, with multiple microcomputers interacting among themselves and with mainframes, forming an interactive web that is capable of processing information, communicating, and making decisions in real time.[51] Interactive information systems, not just computers, are the basis of the automated office, and of the so-called "alternative officing" or "virtual offices," networking tasks performed in distant locations. There might be a fourth phase of office automation brewing up in the technological cauldrons of the last years of the century: the mobile office, performed by individual workers provided with portable, powerful information processing/transmitting devices.[52] If it does develop, as seems likely, it will enhance the organizational logic I have described under the concept of the network enterprise, and it will deepen the process of transformation of work and workers along the lines proposed in this chapter.

The effects of these technological changes on office work are not yet fully identified, because empirical studies, and their interpretation, are running behind the fast process of technological change. However, during the 1980s, a number of doctoral students at Berkeley, whose work I followed and supervised, were able to produce a number of detailed monographs documenting the trends of change that seem to be confirmed by the evolution in the 1990s.[53] Particularly revealing was the doctoral dissertation by Barbara Baran on the impact of office automation on the work process in some large insurance companies in the United States.[54] Her work, as well as other sources, showed a tendency for firms to automate the lower end of clerical jobs, those routine tasks that, because they can be reduced to

[51] Strassman (1985).
[52] Thach and Woodman (1994).
[53] Particularly, I relied on work performed in their doctoral dissertations at Berkeley by Barbara Baran (1989), Carol Parsons (1987), Penny Gurstein (1990), Lisa Bornstein (1993), and Lionel Nicol (1985).
[54] Baran (1989).

a number of standard steps, can be easily programmed. Also, data entry was decentralized, gathering the information and entering it into the system as close as possible to the source. For instance, sales accounting is now linked to scanning and storage at the cashier's point-of-sale machine. ATMs (automated teller machines) constantly update bank accounts. Insurance claims are directly stored in memory with regard to all elements that do not call for a business judgement; and so on. The net result of these trends is the possibility of eliminating most of the mechanical, routine clerical work. On the other hand, higher-level operations are concentrated in the hands of skilled clerical workers and professionals, who make decisions on the basis of the information they have stored in their computer files. So, while at the bottom of the process there is increasing routinization (and thus automation), at the middle level there is reintegration of several tasks into an informed decision-making operation, generally processed, evaluated, and performed by a team made up of clerical workers with increasing autonomy in making decisions. In a more advanced stage of this process of reintegration of tasks, middle managers' supervision also disappears, and controls and safety procedures are standardized in the computer. The critical linkage then becomes the one between professionals, evaluating and making decisions on important matters, and informed clerks making decisions on day-to-day operations on the basis of their computer files and their networking capabilities. Thus the third phase of office automation, instead of simply rationalizing the task (as was the case in batch-processing automation) rationalizes the process, because the technology allows the integration of information from many different sources and its redistribution, once processed, to different, decentralized units of execution. So, instead of automating discrete tasks (such as typing, calculating), the new system rationalizes an entire procedure (for example, new business insurance, claims processing, underwriting), and then integrates various procedures by product lines or segmented markets. Workers are then functionally reintegrated instead of being organizationally distributed.

A similar trend has been observed by Hirschhorn in his analyses of American banks, and by Castano in her study of Spanish banking.[55] While routine operations have been increasingly automated (ATMs, telephone information services, electronic banking), the remaining bank clerks are increasingly working as sales persons, to sell financial services to customers, and as controllers of the repayment of the money they sell. In the United States the federal government plans to

[55]   Hirschhorn (1985); Castano (1991).

automate tax and social security payments by the end of the century, thus extending a similar change of the work process to the public sector agencies.

However, the emergence of the informational paradigm in the work process does not tell the whole story of labor and workers in our societies. The social context, and particularly the relationship between capital and labor according to specific decisions by the management of firms, drastically affects the actual shape of the work process and the consequences of the change for workers. This was particularly true during the 1980s when the acceleration of techno-logical change went hand in hand with the process of capitalist restructuring, as I have argued above. Thus, the classic study by Watanabe [56] on the impact of introduction of robots in the automo-bile industry in Japan, the United States, France, and Italy, showed substantially different impacts of a similar technology in the same industry: in the United States and Italy, workers were displaced, because the main goal of introducing new technology was to reduce labor costs; in France, job loss was lower than in the two other countries, because of government policies to cushion the social impacts of modernization; and in Japan, where companies were committed to life-tenured employment, employment actually increased, and productivity shot up, as a result of retraining and higher team-work effort which increased the competitiveness of firms and took market share away from their American counterparts.

Studies conducted on the interaction between technological change and capitalist restructuring during the 1980s also showed that more often than not technologies were introduced, first of all, to save labor, to subdue unions, and to trim costs, rather than to improve quality or to enhance productivity by means other than downsizing. Thus, another of my former students, Carol Parsons, studied in her Berkeley doctoral dissertation the social-technological restructuring of metalworking and apparel industries in America.[57] In the metal-working sector, among the firms surveyed by Parsons, the most-often cited purpose for the introduction of technology was the reduction of direct labor. Furthermore, instead of retooling their factories, firms often closed plants that were unionized and opened new ones, gener-ally without a union, even if firms did not change region for their new location. As a result of the restructuring process, employment fell substantially in all metalworking industries, with the exception of office equipment. In addition, production workers saw their relative

---

[56]   Watanabe (1986).
[57]   Parsons (1987).

numbers reduced *vis-à-vis* managers and professionals. Within production workers there was a polarization between craft workers and unskilled laborers, with assembly line workers being substantially squeezed by automation. A similar development was observed by Parsons in the apparel industry in relation to the introduction of microelectronics-based technology. Direct production workforce was rapidly being phased out, and the industry was becoming a dispatching center connecting the demand of the American market with manufacturing suppliers all over the world. The net result was a bipolar labor force composed of highly skilled designers and telecommunicating sales managers on the one hand, and low-skill, low-paid manufacturing workers, located either offshore or in American, often illegal, domestic sweatshops. This is a strikingly similar model to the one I have described in the preceding chapter for Benetton, the worldwide knitwear networked firm, considered to be the epitome of flexible production.

Eileen Appelbaum[58] found similar trends in the insurance industry, whose dramatic technological changes I have described above on the basis of Barbara Baran's work. Indeed, the story concerning technological innovation, organizational change, and work reintegration in the insurance industry must be completed with the observation of massive layoffs and underpayment of skilled work in the same industry. Appelbaum links the process of rapid technological change in the insurance industry to the impact of deregulation and global competition in the financial markets. As a result, it became critical to ensure the mobility of capital and the versatility of labor. Labor was both trimmed and reskilled. Unskilled data-entry jobs, where ethnic minority women were concentrated, were projected to be all but eliminated by automation by the end of the century. On the other hand, the remaining clerical positions were reskilled, by integrating tasks into multiskilled, multifunctional jobs susceptible of greater flexibility and adaptation to the changing needs of an increasingly diversified industry. Professional jobs were also polarized between less-skilled tasks, taken on by upgraded clerical workers, and highly specialized tasks that generally required college education. These occupational changes were specified by gender, class, and race: while machines mainly replaced ethnic-minority, less-educated women at the bottom of the scale, educated, mainly white women went into replacing white men in the lower professional positions, yet for a lower pay and reduced career prospects *vis-à-vis* those which men used to have. Multiskilling of jobs and individualization of responsibility were often accompanied by ideologically tailored new titles (for example, "assis-

[58] Appelbaum (1984).

tant manager" instead of "secretary"), thus enhancing the potential for commitment of clerical workers without correspondingly increasing their professional rewards.

Thus, new information technology is redefining work processes, and workers, and therefore employment and occupational structure. While a substantial number of jobs are being upgraded in skills, and sometimes in wages and working conditions in the most dynamic sectors, a large number of jobs are being phased out by automation in both manufacturing and services. These are generally jobs that are not skilled enough to escape to automation but are expensive enough to be worth the investment in technology to replace them. Increasing educational qualifications, either general or specialized, required in the reskilled positions of the occupational structure further segregate the labor force on the basis of education, itself a highly segregated system because it roughly corresponds institutionally to a segregated residential structure. Downgraded labor, particularly in the entry positions for a new generation of workers made up of women, ethnic minorities, immigrants, and youth, is concentrated in low-skill, low-paid activities, as well as in temporary work and/or miscellaneous services. The resulting bifurcation of work patterns and polarization of labor is not the necessary result of technological progress or of inexorable evolutionary trends (for example, the rise of the "postindustrial society" or of the "service economy"). It is socially determined and managerially designed in the process of the capitalist restructuring taking place at the shop-floor level, within the framework and with the help of the process of technological change at the roots of the informational paradigm. Under such conditions, work, employment, and occupations are transformed, and the very notion of work and working time may be changed for ever.

The Effects of Information Technology on Employment: Toward a Jobless Society?

The diffusion of information technology in factories, offices, and services has reignited a centuries-old fear by workers of being displaced by machines, thus becoming irrelevant for the productivist logic that still dominates our social organization. While the information age version of the Luddite movement that terrorized English industrialists in 1811 has not appeared yet, increasing unemployment in Western Europe in the 1980s and 1990s has prompted questions about the potential disruption of labor markets, and therefore of the whole social structure, by the massive impact of labor-saving technologies.

The debate on this question has raged over the last decade, and is far from generating a clear-cut answer.[59] On the one hand, it is argued that historical experience shows the secular transfer from one kind of activity to another as technological progress replaces labor with more efficient tools of production.[60] Thus, in Britain, between 1780 and 1988 the agricultural labor force was reduced by half in absolute numbers, and fell off from 50% to 2.2% of the total labor force; yet productivity per capita increased by a factor of 68, and the increase in productivity allowed for the investment of capital and labor in manufacturing, then in services, so as to employ an increasing population. The extraordinary rate of technological change in the American economy during the twentieth century also massively displaced labor from agriculture, but the number of total jobs created by the US economy climbed from about 27 million in 1900 to 124.5 million in 1994. In this view, most traditional manufacturing jobs will know the same fate as agricultural jobs, but new jobs are being created, and will be created, in high-technology manufacturing and, more significantly, in "services."[61] As evidence of the continuity of this technical trend, it is easy to point to the experience of the most technologically advanced industrial economies, Japan and the United States: they are precisely the ones which have created most jobs during the 1980s and 1990s.[62] According to the 1994 White Paper of the European Commission on *Growth, Competitiveness, and Employment*, between 1970 and 1992, the US economy grew in real terms by 70%, and employment by 49%. Japan's economy grew by 173%, and its employment by 25%. While the European Community's economy grew by 81%, but with an employment increase of only 9% (Commission of the European Union 1994: 141). And what the Commission does not say is that almost all of this new employment was created by the public sector: private employment creation in the European Community remained at a standstill during the 1980s. In the 1990s, the gap in employment creation between Europe, on the one hand, and the US, Japan, and South East Asia, on the other hand, has increased (see figure 4.4). Furthermore, between 1993 and 1996, when most of Europe experienced high unemployment, the United States economy, while stepping up technological diffusion in offices and factories, created over eight million new jobs. And the skills profile of

[59]   For a balanced and thorough analysis of unemployment trends in the last two decades, see Freeman and Soete (1994).
[60]   Lawrence (1984); Commission of the European Communities (1994); Cyert and Mowery (eds) (1987); OECD (1994b); Jones (1982); Hinrichs et al. (eds) (1991); Bosch et al. (1994).
[61]   OECD (1994b).
[62]   OECD *Employment Outlook*, several years.

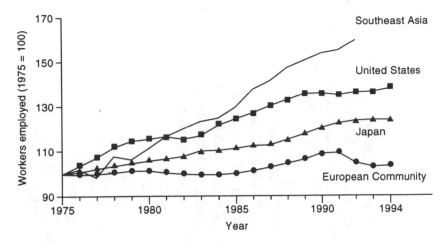

Figure 4.4   Index of employment growth, by region, 1975–94
Sources: ILO, OECD.

the new jobs was, on average, of a higher level than that of the average skills of the overall labor force. Indeed, what characterizes the new labor market of the last two decades is the massive incorporation of women in paid work: the rate of participation of women in the labor force for ages 15–64 increased from 1970 to 1990, from 48.9% to 69.1% in the US; from 55.4% to 61.8% in Japan, from 48.1% to 61.3% in Germany; from 50.8% to 65.3% in the UK; from 47.5% to 59% in France; from 33.5% to 43.3% in Italy; and from 29.2% to 42.8% in Spain (source: OECD, *Main Economic Indicators*, 1995). Yet the pressure of this substantial increase in labor supply did not create high unemployment in the US and Japan as it did in Western Europe.

In a broader context, while the number of manufacturing jobs is declining in OECD countries, it is rapidly growing in developing countries, more than offsetting the losses at world level (see figures 4.5(a) and 4.5(b), and figure 2.5 in chapter 2). All evidence points to the fact that high unemployment is mainly a European problem, caused by mistaken macroeconomic policies and by an institutional environment that discourages private job creation. Thus, in a long-term perspective, between 1960 and 1995, employment has increased at 1.8% per annum in North America, 1.7% in Oceania, 1.2% in Japan, 0.6% in the EFTA countries, but only 0.3% in the European Union.[63] In 1993–4, within the area of the European Union, countries with the highest diffusion of electronic technologies (Austria,

[63]   OECD (1994b: 13).

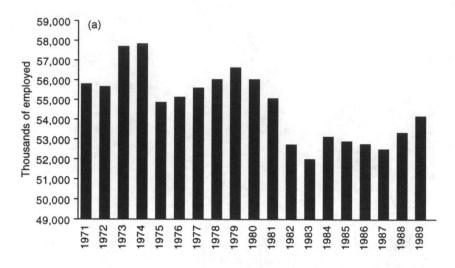

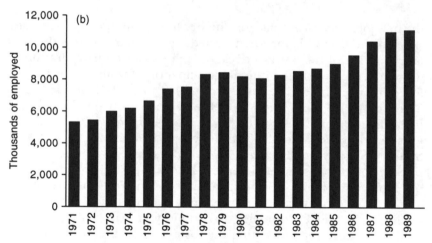

Figure 4.5   Annual progression of employment in manufacturing
(ISIC 3) , 1971–89
(a) In nine industrialized countries
(b) In twelve developing countries
Source: International Labour Office: STAT data base; elaborated by
Wieczorek (1995).

Sweden, Germany) were also those with the lowest unemployment rate, while Spain, a technological laggard, displayed by far the highest rate of unemployment. Yet no rule can be established in the opposite direction: low-tech Portugal had relatively low unemployment, while high-tech Finland had the second largest unemployment rate. As table 4.23 (in Appendix A) indicates, institutional variation seems to account for levels of unemployment, while effects of technological levels do not follow a consistent pattern. If any pattern did emerge from international data it would be in the opposite direction of Luddite predictions: higher technological level is generally associated with lower unemployment rate.

Yet the prophets of massive unemployment, led by the honorable Club of Rome, argue that such calculations are based on a different historical experience that underestimates the radically new impacts of technologies, whose effects are universal and pervasive because they relate to information processing. Thus, so the argument goes, if manufacturing jobs go the way farmers did, there will be not enough service jobs to replace them because service jobs themselves are being rapidly automated and phased out, and the movement is just accelerating in the 1990s.[64] The obvious consequence of this analysis is that our societies will have to choose between massive unemployment, with its corollary, the sharp division of society between the employed and the unemployed/occasional workers, or else a redefinition of work and employment, opening the way to a full restructuring of social organization and cultural values.

Given the importance of the matter, international institutions, governments, and researchers have made extraordinary efforts to assess the impact of new technologies. Dozens of technically sophisticated studies have been conducted in the last 15 years, particularly during the 1980s, when there was still hope that the data could provide the answer. The reading of such studies reveals the difficulty of the search. It is obvious that introducing robots in an assembly line

---

[64] King (1991); Rifkin (1995); Aznar (1993); Aronowitz and Di Fazio (1994). The most salient characteristic of all these writings announcing a jobless society is that they do not provide any consistent, rigorous evidence of their claims, relying on isolated press clippings, random examples of firms in some countries and sectors, and "commonsense" arguments on the "obvious" impact of computers on jobs. There is no serious analysis to explain, for instance, the high rate of job creation in the United States and Japan, as compared to Western Europe; and hardly any reference to the explosion of employment growth, particularly in manufacturing, in East and South-East Asia. Since most of these writers relate themselves to the "political left," their credibility must be challenged before their unfounded theses lead labor and the political left to a new dead end, in the best tradition of ideological self-destructiveness.

reduces human working time for a given level of output. But it does not follow that this reduces employment for the firm or even for the industry. If the superior quality and productivity achieved by introducing electronic machinery increases competitiveness, both the firm and the industry would need to increase employment to supply the broader demand resulting from a larger market share. Thus, the question is raised at the level of the nation: the new growth strategy would imply increased competitiveness at the cost of reducing employment in some sectors, while using the surplus thus generated to invest and create jobs in other sectors, such as business services or environmental technology industries. In the last resort, the net employment results will depend on inter-nation competition. Trade theorists would then argue that there is no zero-sum game, since an expansion of global trade will benefit most of its partners by increasing overall demand. According to this line of argument, there would be a potential reduction of employment as a consequence of the diffusion of new information technologies only if:

- expansion in demand does not offset the increase in labor productivity; *and*
- there is no institutional reaction to such a mismatch by reducing working time, not jobs.

This second condition is particularly important. After all, the history of industrialization has shown a long-term increase in unemployment, production, productivity, real wages, profits, and demand, while significantly reducing working time, on the basis of progress in technology and management.[65] Why should it not be the case in the current stage of techno-economic transformation? Why would information technologies be more destructive for overall employment than mechanization or automation were during the earlier decades of the twentieth century? Let us check the empirical record.

Facing a plethora of studies on different countries and industries in the 1980s, the International Labour Office commissioned some literature reviews that would indicate the state of the knowledge on the relationship between microelectronics and employment in various contexts. Among such reviews two stand out as well documented and analytical: those by Raphael Kaplinsky[66] and by John Bessant.[67] Kaplinsky emphasized the need to distinguish the findings at eight different levels: process level, plant level, firm level, industry

[65] OECD (1994c).
[66] Kaplinsky (1986).
[67] Bessant (1989).

level, region level, sector level, national level, and meta level (meaning the discussion of differential effects related to alternative sociotechnical paradigms). After reviewing the evidence for each one of these levels, he concluded:

> Insofar as the individual studies offer any clear statement on the issue, it would appear that the quantitative macro and micro studies are drawn to fundamentally different conclusions. Process and plant level investigations generally seem to point to a significant displacement of labour. On the other hand, national level simulations more often reach the conclusion that there is no significant employment problem on hand.[68]

Bessant dismisses as excessive what he calls the "repeated scares about automation and employment" that have been stated since the 1950s. Then, after closer examination of the study findings, he writes that "it became increasingly clear that the pattern of employment effects associated with microelectronics would vary widely." According to evidence reviewed by Bessant, on the one hand, microelectronics displaces some jobs in some industries. But, on the other hand, it will also contribute to create jobs, and it will also modify the characteristics of such jobs. The overall equation must take into consideration several elements at the same time:

> new employment generated by new product industries based on microelectronics; new employment in advanced technologies generated in existing industries; employment displaced by process changes in existing industries; employment displaced in industries whose products are being replaced by those based on microelectronics, such as telecommunications equipment; employment lost through a lack of overall competitiveness caused by non-adoption of microelectronics. All things considered, across the whole spectrum the pattern is one of both losses and gains, with overall relatively small change in employment.[69]

Looking at studies of specific countries during the 1980s, the findings are somewhat contradictory although, overall, the same pattern of indetermination seems to emerge. In Japan, a 1985 study of the Japan Institute of Labour, concerning employment and work effects of new electronic technologies in industries as diverse as automobiles, newspaper, electrical machinery, and software, concluded that "in any of

[68] Kaplinsky (1986: 153).
[69] Bessant (1989: 27, 28, 30).

the cases, the introduction of new technologies neither aimed at reducing the size of the work force in practice nor reduced it subsequently."[70]

In Germany, a major research effort, the so-called Meta Study, was commissioned by the Minister of Research and Technology during the 1980s to conduct both econometric and case-study research on the impacts of technological change on employment. Although the diversity of studies included in the research program does not allow a firm conclusion, the synthesis by its authors concluded that it is "the context" that counts for the variation in observed effects. In any case, technological innovation was understood to be an accelerating factor of existing trends in the labor market, rather than its cause. The study forecast that in the short term unskilled jobs would be displaced, although enhanced productivity would probably result in greater job creation in the long term.[71]

In the United States, Flynn analyzed 200 case studies of the employment impacts of process innovations between 1940 and 1982. He concluded that, while process innovations in manufacturing eliminated high-skill jobs and helped to create low-skill jobs, the opposite was true for information-processing in offices, where technological innovation suppressed low-skill jobs and created high-skill ones. Thus, according to Flynn, the effects of process innovation were variable, depending upon specific situations of industries and firms. At the industry level, again in the US, the analysis by Levy et al. of five industries showed different effects of technological innovation: in iron mining, coal mining, and aluminium, technological change increased output and resulted in higher employment levels; in steel and automobiles, on the other hand, growth of demand did not match reduction of labor per unit of output and job losses resulted. Also in the United States, the analysis by Miller in the 1980s of the available evidence on the impact of industrial robotics concluded that most of the displaced workers would be reabsorbed in the labor force.[72]

In the UK, the study by Daniel on the employment impacts of technology in factories and offices concluded there would be a negligible effect. Another study by the London Policy Studies Institute on a sample of 1,200 firms in France, Germany, and the UK estimated that, on average, for the three countries considered, the impact of microelectronics amounted to a job loss equivalent to, respectively, 0.5%, 0.6%, and 0.8% of annual decrease of employment in manufacturing.[73]

[70]   Japan Institute of Labour (1985: 27).
[71]   Schettkat and Wagner (eds) (1990).
[72]   Miller (1989: 80); Flynn (1985); Levy et al. (1984); OTA (1984, 1986).

In the synthesis of studies directed by Watanabe on the impacts of robotization in the automobile industry in Japan, the United States, France, and Italy, the total job loss was estimated at between 2% and 3.5%, but with the additional caveat of the differential effects I mentioned above, namely the increase in employment in Japanese factories because of their use of microelectronics to retrain workers and enhance competitiveness.[74] In the case of Brazil, Silva found no effect of technology on employment in the automobile industry, although employment varied considerably depending on the levels of output.[75]

In the study I directed on the impacts of new technologies on the Spanish economy in the early 1980s we found no statistical relationship between employment variation and technological level in the manufacturing and service sectors. Furthermore, a study within the same research program conducted by Cecilia Castano on the automobile and banking industry in Spain found a trend towards a positive association between the introduction of information technology and employment. An econometric study by Saez on the evolution of employment in Spain, by sector in the 1980s, found also a positive statistical relationship between technological modernization and employment gains, due to increased productivity and competitiveness.[76]

Studies commissioned by the International Labour Office on the UK, on the OECD as a whole, and on South Korea seem also to point to the lack of systematic links between information technology and employment.[77] The other variables in the equation (such as the countries' industrial mix, institutional contexts, place in the international division of labor, competitiveness, management policies, and so on) overwhelm, by and large, the specific impact of technology.

Yet the argument has often been advanced that observed trends during the 1980s did not fully represent the extent of the employment impact of information technologies because their diffusion into the whole economy and society was still to come.[78] Which forces us to

[73]   Daniel (1987); Northcott (1986).
[74]   Watanabe (ed.) (1987).
[75]   Cited in Watanabe (1987).
[76]   Castells et al. (1986); Castano (1994b); Saez et al. (1991).
[77]   Swann (1986); Ebel and Ulrich (1987); Pyo (1986).
[78]   See, for instance, the apocalyptic prophecies of Adam Schaff (1992). It is surprising, to say the least, to see the credit given in the media to books such as Rifkin (1995), announcing "the end of work," published in a country, the United States, where between 1993 and 1996 over 8 million new jobs were created. A different matter is the quality of and pay for these jobs (although their skills profile was higher than that of overall employment structure). Work and employ-

venture onto the shaky ground of projections dealing with two uncertain variables (new information technologies and employment) and their even more uncertain relationship. Nevertheless, there have been a number of fairly sophisticated simulation models that have shed some light on the issues under discussion. One of them is the model built by Blazejczak, Eber, and Horn to evaluate the macroeconomics impacts of investment in R&D in the West German economy between 1987 and 2000. They built three scenarios. Only under the most favorable circumstances does technological change increase employment by enhancing competitiveness. Indeed, they conclude that employment losses are imminent unless compensatory demand effects occur, and this demand cannot be generated only by a better performance in international trade. Yet according to the projections in their model, "at the aggregate level demand effects do in fact compensate a relevant part of the predicted employment decrease."[79] Thus, it is likely that technological innovation will negatively affect employment in Germany, but at a rather moderate level. Here again, other elements such as macroeconomic policies, competitiveness, and industrial relations seem to be much more important as factors determining the evolution of employment.

In the United States, the most widely cited simulation study was that performed in 1984 by Leontieff and Duchin to evaluate the impact of computers on employment for the period 1963–2000 using a dynamic input–output matrix of the US economy.[80] Focusing on their intermediate scenario, they found that 20 million fewer workers would be required in relationship to the number of workers that would have to be employed to achieve the same output while keeping constant the level of technology. This figure, according to their calculations, represents a drop of 11.7% in required labor. However, the impact is strongly differentiated among industries and occupations. Services, and particularly office activities, were predicted to suffer greater job losses than manufacturing as a result of massive diffusion of office

---

ment are indeed being transformed, as this book tries to argue. But the number of paid jobs in the world, notwithstanding the Western European malaise, linked to institutional factors, is at its highest peak in history and going up. And rates of participation of labor force in the adult population are increasing everywhere, because of the unprecedented incorporation of women into the labor market. To ignore these elementary data is to ignore our society.

[79]   One of the most systematic efforts at forecasting the economic and employment effects of new technologies was the "Meta Study" conducted in Germany in the late 1980s. Main findings are presented in Matzner and Wagner (eds) (1990). See especially the chapter "Sectoral and Macroeconomic Impacts of Research and Development on Employment," in Blazejczak et al. (1990: 231).

[80]   Leontieff and Duchin (1985).

automation. Clerical workers and managers would see their prospects
of employment significantly reduced while those for professionals
would increase substantially, and craftsmen and operatives would
maintain their relative position in the labor force. The methodology
of the Leontieff–Duchin study has, however, been strongly criticized,
because it relies on a number of assumptions that, on the basis of
limited case studies, maximize the potential impact of computer
automation while limiting technological change to computers.
Furthermore, as argued by Lawrence, the fundamental flaw in this,
and other models, is that they assumed a fixed level of final demand
and output.[81] *This is precisely what past experience of technological innovation seems to reject as the most likely hypothesis.*[82] If the economy does not
grow, it is obvious that labor-saving technologies will reduce the
amount of working time required (even on this hypothesis by a somewhat limited amount – 11.7%). But in the past, rapid technological
change has generally been associated with an expansionary trend that,
by increasing demand and output, has generated the need for more
working time in absolute terms, even if it represents less working time
per unit of output. However, the key point in the new historical period
is that in an internationally integrated economic system, expansion of
demand and output will depend on the competitiveness of each
economic unit and on their location in a given institutional setting
(also called a nation). Since quality and production costs, the determinants of competitiveness, will largely depend on product and
process innovation, it is likely that faster technological change for a
given firm, industry, or national economy would result in a higher,
not a lower, employment level. This is in line with the findings of
Young and Lawson's study on the effect of technology on employment
and output in US between 1972 and 1984.[83] In 44 of the 79 industries
they examined, the labor-saving effects of new technologies were
more than compensated for by higher final demand, so that, overall,
employment expanded. At the level of national economies, studies on
the newly industrialized countries of the Asian Pacific have also shown
a dramatic increase in employment, particularly in manufacturing,
following the technological upgrading of industries that enhanced
their international competitiveness.[84]

In a more analytical vein, reflecting on the empirical findings
in different European countries, the intellectual leader of the

[81]   See Cyert and Mowery (eds) (1987); Lawrence (1984).
[82]   See Landau and Rosenberg (eds) (1986); OECD (1994b); Lawrence (1984).
[83]   Young and Lawson (1984).
[84]   Rodgers (ed.) (1994).

"regulation school," Robert Boyer, summarizes his argument on the matter in several key points:[85]

(1) All other variables being constant, technological change (measured by R&D density) improves productivity and obviously reduces the level of employment for any given demand.
(2) However, productivity gains can be used to reduce relative prices, thus stimulating demand for a given product. If price elasticities are greater than one, a decline in price parallel to a rise in production will in fact enhance employment.
(3) If prices are constant, productivity increases could be converted into real wage or profit increases. Consumption and/or investment will then be higher with stepped-up technological change. If price elasticities are high, employment losses will be compensated by extra demand from both old and new sectors.
(4) Yet the critical matter is the right mix between process innovation and product innovation. If process innovation progresses faster, a decline in employment will occur, all other factors being equal. If product innovation leads the pace, then newly induced demand could result in higher employment.

The problem with such elegant economic analyses is always in the assumptions: all other factors are never equal . . . Boyer himself acknowledges this fact, and then examines the empirical fit of his model, observing, again, a wide range of variation between different industries and countries. While Boyer and Mistral found a negative relationship between productivity and employment for the OECD as a whole in the 1980–86 period, a comparative analysis by Boyer on OECD countries identified three different patterns of employment in areas with similar levels of R&D density.[86]

(1) In Japan an efficient model of mass production and consumption was able to sustain productivity growth and employment growth, on the basis of enhanced competitiveness.
(2) In the United States, there was an impressive rate of job creation, but by concentrating on generating large numbers of low-wage, low-productivity jobs in traditional service activities.
(3) In Western Europe, most economies entered a vicious circle: to cope with increased international competition, firms introduced labor-saving technologies, thus increasing output but leveling off the capacity to generate jobs, particularly in manufacturing. Technological innovation does *not* increase employment. Given

[85] Boyer (1990).
[86] Boyer and Mistral (1988); Boyer (1988b).

the European characteristics of what Boyer calls "the mode of regulation" (for example, government economic policies and business strategies on labor and technology), innovation is likely to destroy employment in the European context. Yet innovation is increasingly required by competition.

The employment study conducted by the OECD Secretariat in 1994, after examining historical and current evidence on the relationship between technology and employment, concluded that:

> Detailed information, mainly from the manufacturing sector provides evidence that technology is creating jobs. Since 1970 employment in high technology manufacturing has expanded, in sharp contrast to stagnation of medium and low technology sectors and job losses in low-skill manufacturing – at around 1% per year. Countries that have adapted best to new technologies and have shifted production and exports to rapidly growing high tech markets have tended to create more jobs. . . Japan realized a 4% increase in manufacturing employment in the 1970s and 1980s compared with a 1.5% increase in the US. Over the same period the European Community, where exports were increasingly specialized in relatively low-wage, low-tech industries, experienced a 20% drop in manufacturing employment.[87]

In sum, it seems, as a general trend, **that there is no systematic structural relationship between the diffusion of information technologies and the evolution of employment levels in the economy as a whole.** Jobs are being displaced and new jobs are being created, but the quantitative relationship between the losses and the gains varies among firms, industries, sectors, regions, and countries, depending upon competitiveness, firms' strategies, government policies, institutional environments, and relative position in the global economy. The specific outcome of the interaction between information technology and employment is largely dependent upon macroeconomic factors, economic strategies, and sociopolitical contexts. Overall, the employment projections for OECD countries in the early twenty-first century forecast a significant increase in jobs for the US and moderate growth for Japan and the European Community (12 countries): for the 1992–2005 period the projected net increase of jobs would be 24 million (a total increase of 19% over the period) in the US; for Japan, 4 million (an increase of 6%); and for the European Union about 10 million (an increase of between 6% and 7%).[88] However,

[87]   OECD (1994b: 32).
[88]   OECD (194b). For a broader discussion of these data and the policy issues related to the future of work and employment, see Stevens and Michalski (1994).

these projections are highly sensitive to variations in the assumptions on which they are based (such as migration and labor participation rates). This is precisely my argument. The evolution of the level of employment is not a given, which would result from the combination of stable demographic data and a projected rate of diffusion of information technology. It will largely depend on socially determined decisions on the uses of technology, on immigration policy, on the evolution of the family, on the institutional distribution of working time in the lifecycle, and on the new system of industrial relations.

Thus, information technology per se does not cause unemployment, even if it obviously reduces working time per unit of output. But, under the informational paradigm, the kind of jobs change, in quantity, in quality, and in the nature of the work being performed. Thus, a new production system requires a new labor force; those individuals and groups unable to acquire informational skills could be excluded from work or downgraded as workers. Also, because the informational economy is a global economy, widespread unemployment concentrated in some segments of the population (for example, French youth) and in some regions (such as Asturias) could indeed become a threat in the OECD area if global competition is unrestricted, and if the "mode of regulation" of capital–labor relationships is not transformed.

The hardening of capitalist logic since the 1980s has fostered social polarization in spite of occupational upgrading. This tendency is not irreversible: it can be rectified by deliberate policies aimed at rebalancing the social structure. But left to themselves, the forces of unfettered competition in the informational paradigm will push employment and social structure towards dualization. Finally, the flexibility of labor processes and labor markets induced by the network enterprise, and allowed by information technologies, affects profoundly the social relationships of production inherited from industrialism, introducing a new model of flexible work, and a new type of worker: the flex-timer.

Work and the Informational Divide: Flextimers

Linda's new working life is not without its drawbacks. Chief among them is a constant cloud of anxiety about finding the next job. In some ways Linda feels isolated and vulnerable. Fearful of the stigma of having been laid off, for example, she doesn't want her last name to appear in this article.

But the freedom of being her own boss makes up for the insecurity.

Linda gets to build her schedule around her son's. She gets to pick her own assignments. And she gets to be a pioneer of the new work force. (*Newsweek,* June 14 1993: 17)

A new specter haunts Europe (not so much America and Japan): the emergence of a jobless society under the impact of information technologies in factories, offices, and services. Yet, as is usually the case with specters in the electronic age, in a close-up it appears to be more a matter of special effects than a terrifying reality. The lessons of history, current empirical evidence, employment projections in OECD countries, and economic theory do not support these fears in the long term, notwithstanding painful adjustments in the process of transition to the informational paradigm. Institutions and social organizations of work seem to play a greater role than technology in inducing job creation or destruction. However, if technology per se does not create or destroy employment, it does profoundly transform the nature of work and the organization of production. The restructuring of firms and organizations, allowed by information technology and stimulated by global competition, is ushering in a fundamental transformation of work: *the individualization of labor in the labor process.* We are witnessing the reversal of the historical trend of salarization of work and socialization of production that was the dominant feature of the industrial era. The new social and economic organization based on information technologies aims at decentralizing management, individualizing work, and customizing markets, thereby segmenting work and fragmenting societies. New information technologies allow at the same time for the decentralization of work tasks and for their coordination in an interactive network of communication in real time, be it between continents or between floors of the same building. The emergence of lean production methods goes hand in hand with widespread business practices of subcontracting, outsourcing, offshoring, consulting, downsizing, and customizing.

Competition-induced, technology-driven trends towards flexibility underlie the current transformation of working arrangements. The fastest growing categories of work are temporary labor and part-time work. In some countries, such as Italy and the UK, self-employment is becoming again a substantial component of the labor force. Thus, in the UK, the seed-bed of the industrial revolution that spearheaded the historical process of salarization and standardization of labor, the 1993 Labour Force Survey indicated that 38% of people in employment were not employed on a permanent, full-time basis: the bulk of such group is formed by part-timers (85% of whom were women), who accounted for 23.9% of the employed population.[89] Both the OECD and the ILO report that part-time work increased during the 1980s in practically all industrialized countries, rising by about 30% in the decade to reach 50 million workers, of which 40% were in North America.[90] Between 1979 and 1990, part-time work increased from 16.4% to 21.8% of total employment in the UK; from 8.2% to 12% in France; from 11.4% to 13.2% in Germany; from 15.4% to 17.6% in Japan; and from 16.4% to 16.9% in the US.[91]

As shown in table 4.24 (in Appendix A), self-employment as a percentage of total employment largely varies in industrialized countries, in a range that goes between 9.4% (Canada) and 29.1% (Italy) in 1990; temporary work is on the rise in France and Germany, countries with lower part-time work (see figure 4.6). But temporary work is declining in the UK (a country with a high proportion of part-time workers) and in Italy (a country with a high proportion of self-employed). This observation might suggest that the broader category of "flexible work" takes different forms (self-employment, part-time, temporary work) depending on countries' fiscal and labor regulations. Thus, if we add in France in 1990 the self-employed (15.0%), the part-timers (12.0%), and temporary workers (at least 9.2%), we obtain a percentage of non-standard employment close to the British figure (36.2%) – even accounting for some overlapping between these categories. Indeed, in the 1983–88 period, while the full-time employment variation in France was -1.6%, part-time increased by 36.6%. Similar data for Japan, Germany, Italy, and the United Kingdom are shown in table 4.24.

As for the United States, in 1990 self-employment accounted for 10.8% of the workforce, part-time for 16.9%, and "contract" or temporary work for about 2%, adding up to 27.9% of the labor force, although, again, categories overlap to some extent. According to a different estimate, the contingent workforce with no benefits, no job security, and no career amounted in the US in 1992 to about 25% of the labor force, up from 20% in 1982. The projections were for this type of labor to increase to 35% of the US labor force in the year 2000.[92] Outsourcing, facilitated by on-line transactions, concerns not just manufacturing but increasingly services. In a 1994 survey of 392 of America's fastest growing firms, 68% of them were subcontracting

[89]   "Non-standard working under review," *Industrial Relations & Review Report*, no. 565, August 1994: 5–14.
[90]   Robinson (1993).
[91]   OECD (1994b); see also Bosch et al. (eds) (1994): esp. 11–20).
[92]   Jost (1993).

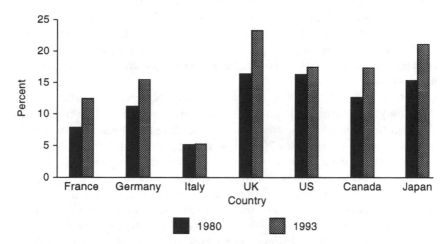

Figure 4.6 OECD countries: part-time employment, 1980–93 (% of total employment)
Source: OECD, *Employment Outlook*, 1994; elaborated by Freeman and Soete (1994).

payroll services, 48% tax compliance services, 46% claim benefits administration, and the like.[93]

The mobility of labor concerns both unskilled and skilled workers. While a core labor force is still the norm in most firms, subcontracting and consulting is a fast-growing form of obtaining professional work. Not only the firm benefits from flexibility. Many professionals add to their main job (full- or part-time) consulting venues which help both their income and their bargaining power. The logic of this highly dynamic work system interacts with the labor institutions of each country: the greater the constraints to such flexibility, and the greater the bargaining power of the labor unions, the lesser will be the impact on wages and benefits, and the greater will be the difficulty for newcomers to enter the core labor force, thus limiting job creation.

While the social costs of flexibility can be high, a growing stream of research emphasizes the transformative value of new work arrangements for social life, and particularly for improved family relationships, and greater egalitarian patterns between genders.[94] A British researcher, P. Hewitt,[95] reports on the growing diversity of

[93] Marshall (1994)
[94] Bielenski (ed.) (1994); for social problems associated with part-time work, see Warme et al. (eds) (1992).
[95] Hewitt (1993). This interesting study is pointedly cited by Freeman and Soete (1994).

working formulae and schedules, and the potential offered by work-sharing between those currently full-time employed and those barely employed *within the same household*. Overall, **the traditional form of work, based on full-time employment, clear-cut occupational assignments, and a career pattern over the lifecycle is being slowly but surely eroded away.**

Japan is different, although not as much as observers usually think. Any analytical framework aimed at explaining new historical trends in the organization of work, and their impact on employment structure, must be able to account for "Japanese exceptionalism:" it is too important an exception to be left aside as an oddity for comparative theory. Therefore, let us consider the matter in some detail.

In May 1995, in spite of economic quasi-stagnation after the prolonged recession that started in 1991, the Japanese unemployment rate, while reaching a record high level for the last two decades, was still at a low 3.2%. Indeed, the main concern of Japanese labor planners is the potential shortage of Japanese workers in the future, given the aging of the demographic structure and Japanese reluctance about foreign immigration.[96] Furthermore, the *Chuki Koyo* system, that provides assurance of long-term employment for the core labor force of large companies, while coming under pressure, did not seem in danger of being dismantled *in the short term*. Thus, it would seem that Japanese exceptionalism belies the general trend towards flexibility of the labor market and the individualization of work that characterizes the other informational, capitalist societies.[97] In fact, I would argue that while Japan has indeed created a highly original system of industrial relations and employment procedures, flexibility has been a structural trend of such a system for the last two decades, and it is increasing along with the transformation of the technological basis and occupational structure.[98]

The Japanese employment structure is characterized by extraordinary internal diversity, as well as by a complex pattern of fluid situations that resist generalization and standardization. The very definition of the *Chuki Koyo* system needs precision.[99] For most workers under such a system it means simply that they can work until retirement in the same company, under normal circumstances, as a matter of custom, not of right. This employment practice is in fact limited to large companies (those with over 1,000 employees), and in most cases concerns only the male, core labor force. In addition to

[96]   NIKKEIREN (1993).
[97]   Kumazawa and Yamada (1989).
[98]   Kuwahara (1989).
[99]   Inoki and Higuchi (eds) (1995).

their regular workers, companies also employ at least three different kinds of workers: part-time workers, temporary workers, and workers sent to the company by another company, or by a recruiting agent ("dispatched workers"). None of these categories has job security, retirement benefits, or is entitled to receive the customary annual bonuses to reward productivity and commitment to the company. In addition, very often workers, particularly older men, are reallocated to other jobs in other companies within the same corporate group (*Shukko*). This includes the practice of separating married men from their families (*Tanshin-Funin*) because of difficulties in finding housing and, most of all, because of the family's reluctance to relocate children to a different school in the middle of their education. *Tanshin-Funin* is said to concern about 30% of managerial employees.[100] Nomura estimates that long-term job security in the same company applies only to about one-third of Japanese employees, including public sector employees.[101] Joussaud provides a similar estimate.[102] Besides, the incidence of job tenure varies widely, even for men, depending on age, level of qualification, and size of the company. Table 4.25 (in Appendix A) provides an illustration of the profile of *Chuki Koyo* in 1991–2.

The critical point in this labor market structure concerns the definition of part-time. According to the government's labor status definitions, 'part-time' workers are those considered as such by the company.[103] In fact, they work almost full-time (6 hours a day, compared to the schedule of 7.5 hours of regular workers), although the number of working days in a month is slightly less than for regular workers. Yet they receive, on average, about 60% of a regular worker's salary, and about 15% of the annual bonus. More importantly, they have no job security, so they are fired and hired according to the company's convenience. Part-timers and temporary workers provide the required labor flexibility. Their role has substantially increased since the 1970s, when the oil shock induced major economic restructuring in Japan. In the 1975–90 period, the number of part-time workers increased by 42.6% for male workers and by 253% for female workers.

Indeed, women account for two-thirds of part-timers. Women are the skilled, adaptable workers that provide flexibility to Japanese labor management practices. This is in fact an old practice in Japanese industrialization. In 1872, the Meiji Government recruited women to work in the nascent textile industry. A pioneer was Wada Ei, daughter of a samurai from Matsuhiro, who went to work in the Tomioka

---

100   Collective Author (1994).
101   Nomura (1994).
102   Joussaud (1994).
103   Shinotsuka (1994); Collective Author (1994).

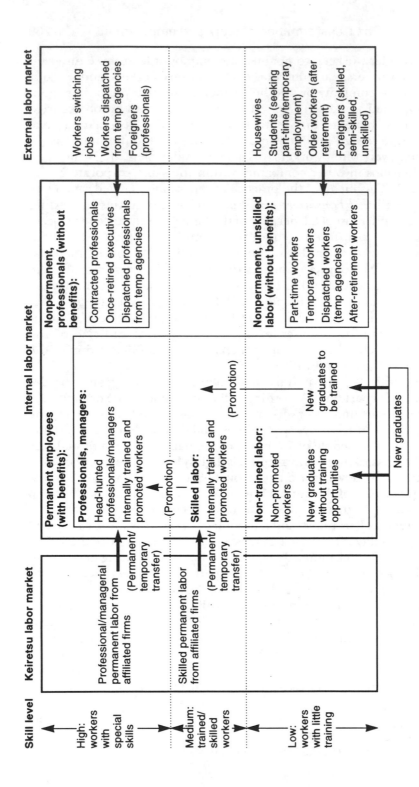

Figure 4.7 The Japanese labor market in the postwar period

Source: Elaborated by Yuko Aoyama, based on information from Japan's Economic Planning Agency, *Gaikokujin rodosha to shakai no shinro*, 1989, p. 99: figure 4.1

Silk-reeling Mill, learned the technology, and helped to train women in other mills. In 1899, women accounted for 70% of workers in spinning mills, and outnumbered male workers in the iron mills. However, at times of crisis women would be fired, while men would be kept as long as possible, emphasizing their role as the last-resort bread-winners of the family. In the last three decades, this historical pattern of gender-based division of labor has hardly changed, although a 1986 Equal Opportunity Law corrected some of the most blatant legal discriminations. Women's participation in the labor force in 1990 features a rate of 61.8% (as compared to 90.2% for men), lower than in the US, but similar to that of Western Europe. Yet their working status varies widely with age and marriage. Thus, 70% of the women who are hired in conditions roughly comparable with men (*sogoshoku*) are under 29 years of age; while 85% of part-timers are married. Women massively enter the labor force in their early twenties, stop working after marriage to raise their children, and return later to the labor force as part-timers. This structure of the occupational lifecycle is reinforced by the Japanese tax code, which makes it more advantageous for women to contribute in a relatively small proportion to the family income than to add a second salary. The stability of the Japanese patriarchal family, with a low rate of divorce and separation and strong intergenerational solidarity,[104] keeps men and women together in the same household, avoiding the polarization of social structure as the result of this obvious pattern of labor market dualism. Uneducated youth and elderly workers of small and medium companies are the other groups accounting for this segment of unstable employees, whose boundaries are difficult to establish because of the fluidity of labor status in Japanese networks of firms.[105] Figure 4.7 attempts to represent schematically the complexity of the Japanese labor market structure.

Thus, it seems that Japan has been practicing for some time the dual labor market logic that is spreading in Western economies. By so doing, it has combined the benefits of the commitment of a core labor force with the flexibility of a peripheral labor market. The former has been essential because it has guaranteed social peace through cooperation between management and company unions; and because it has increased productivity by accumulating knowledge in the firm, and quickly assimilating new technologies. The latter has allowed for quick reaction to changes in labor demand, as well as to competitive pressures from offshored manufacturing in the 1980s. In the 1990s, figures for foreign immigration and day laborers started to

[104] Gelb and Lief Palley (1995).
[105] Takenori and Higuchi (1995).

rise, introducing additional choice and flexibility in the lower-skilled segments of the workforce. Altogether, Japanese firms seemed to be able to cope with competitive pressures by retraining their core labor force and adding technology, while multiplying their flexible labor, both in Japan and in their globalized production networks. However, since this labor practice relies essentially on the occupational subservience of highly educated Japanese women, which will not last for ever, I propose the hypothesis that it is just a matter of time until the hidden flexibility of the Japanese labor market diffuses to the core labor force, calling into question what has been the most stable and productive labor relations system of the late industrial era.[106]

Thus, overall, there is indeed a fundamental transformation of work, workers, and working organizations in our societies, but it cannot be apprehended in the traditional categories of obsolete debates over the "end of work" or the "deskilling of labor." The prevailing model for labor in the new, information-based economy is that of a *core labor force*, formed by information-based managers and by those whom Reich calls "symbolic analysts," and a *disposable labor force* that can be automated and/or hired/fired/offshored, depending upon market demand and labor costs. Furthermore, the networked form of business organization allows outsourcing and subcontracting as forms of externalizing labor in a flexible adaptation to market conditions. Analysts have rightly distinguished between various forms of flexibility in wages, geographical mobility, occupational status, contractual security, and task performance, among others.[107] Often all these forms are lumped together in a self-serving strategy to present as inevitable what is in fact a business or policy decision. Yet it is true that current technological trends foster all forms of flexibility, so that in the absence of specific agreements on stabilizing one or various dimensions of work, the system will evolve into multifaceted, generalized flexibility for workers and working conditions. This transformation has shaken our institutions, inducing a crisis in the relationship between work and society.

Information Technology and the Restructuring of Capital–Labor Relationships: Social Dualism or Fragmented Societies?

The diffusion of information technology in the economy does not directly induce unemployment and may create more jobs in the long

---

[106]   Kuwahara (1989); Whitaker (1990).
[107]   Freeman and Soete (1994).

run. The transformation of management and work upgrades the occupational structure to a greater extent in that it increases the number of low-skill jobs. Increasing global trade and investment do not seem to be, by themselves, major causal factors in eliminating jobs and degrading work conditions in the North, while they contribute to create millions of jobs in newly industrializing countries. And yet the process of historical transition toward an informational society and a global economy is characterized by the widespread deterioration of living and working conditions for labor.[108] This deterioration takes different forms in different contexts: the rise of structural unemployment in Europe; declining real wages, increasing inequality, and job instability in the United States; underemployment and stepped-up segmentation of the labor force in Japan; informalization and downgrading of newly incorporated urban labor in industrializing countries; and increasing marginalization of the agricultural labor force in stagnant, underdeveloped economies. As argued above, these trends do not stem from the structural logic of the informational paradigm, but are the result of the current restructuring of capital–labor relationships, helped by the powerful tools provided by new information technologies, and facilitated by a new organizational form, the network enterprise. Furthermore, although the potential of information technologies could have provided for higher productivity, higher living standards, and higher employment simultaneously, once certain technological choices are in place, technological trajectories are "locked in,"[109] and the informational society could become at the same time (without the technological or historical necessity to be so) a dual society.

Alternative views prevailing in the OECD, IMF, and government circles in major Western countries have suggested that observed trends of rising unemployment, underemployment, income inequality, poverty, and social polarization are by and large the result of a skills mismatch, worsened by the lack of flexibility in the labor markets.[110] According to such views, while the occupational/employment structure is upgraded in terms of the educational content of the skills required for the informational jobs, the labor force is not up to the new tasks, either because of the low quality of the educational system or because of the inadequacy of this system

---

[108]   Harrison (1994); ILO (1994).

[109]   Arthur (1989).

[110]   This is the view usually expressed by Alan Greenspan, chairman of the US Federal Reserve Board, and by the International Monetary Fund and other international expert circles. For an economic discourse articulating this thesis, see Krugman (1994); and Krugman and Lawrence (1994).

to provide the new skills needed in the emerging occupational structure.[111]

In their report to the ILO's research institute, Carnoy and Fluitman have submitted this broadly accepted view to a devastating critique. After extensively reviewing the literature and evidence on the relationship between skills, employment, and wages in the OECD countries, they conclude that

> Despite the apparent consensus around the supply-side, skill mismatch argument, the supporting evidence for it is extremely thin, especially in terms of improved education and more and better training solving either the problem of open unemployment (Europe) or the problem of wage distribution (US). It is much more convincing, we argue, that better education and more training could, in the longer run, contribute to higher productivity and economic growth rates.[112]

In the same sense, David Howell has shown for the US that while there has been an increasing demand for higher skills, this is not the cause of the substantial decline in average wages for American workers between 1973 to 1990 (a fall from a weekly wage of $327 to $265 in 1990, measured in 1982 dollars). Neither is the skill mix the source of increasing income inequality. In his study with Wolff, Howell shows that while the share of low-skilled workers in the US is decreasing across industries, the share of low-wage workers has increased in these same industries. Several studies also suggest that higher skills are in demand, although not in shortage, but higher skills do not necessarily translate into higher wages.[113] Thus, in the US, while decline in real wages was more pronounced for the lowest-educated, salaries for the college-educated also stagnated between 1987 and 1993.[114]

The direct consequence of economic restructuring in the United States is that in the 1980s and 1990s family income has plummeted (see figure 4.8). Wages and living conditions continued to decline in the 1990s in spite of a strong economic recovery in 1993.[115] A study by the US Census Bureau in 1994[116] showed that, in spite of significant

---

[111]   Cappelli and Rogovsky (1994).
[112]   Carnoy and Fluitman (1994).
[113]   Howell (1994); Howell and Wolff (1991); Mishel and Teixeira (1991).
[114]   Center for Budget and Policy Priorities, Washington, D.C., cited by *New York Times*, October 7 1994: 9; see also Murphy and Welch (1993); Bernstein and Adler (1994).
[115]   Mishel and Bernstein (1994).
[116]   Cited by *New York Times*, October 7 1994. See also Newman (1993).

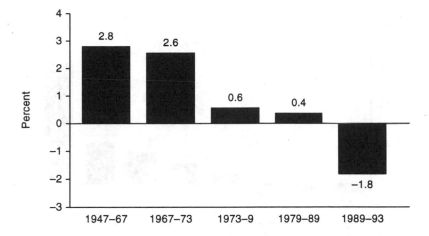

Figure 4.8   United States: annual growth of median family income,
1947–93
Data for 1989 and 1993 were revised using 1990 census weights.
Source: US Bureau of Census (1994); elaborated by Mishel and Bernstein
(1994).

economic growth for the economy as a whole (3%), and an average
increase of 1.8% in the per capita income, median household income
in 1993 declined by 1% in comparison with 1992. From 1989 to 1993
the typical American household lost 7% in annual income. The
percentage of Americans under the poverty line also increased in
1993 to 15.1% (up from 13.1% in 1989), and income inequality
continued to increase to record levels: in 1993, the top fifth of
American households earned 48.2% of total income, while the
bottom fifth earned 3.6%, accentuating the pattern of income
inequality established in the 1980s. According to Thurow (1995: 78),
the median wage for men working full-time began to fall in 1973, and
fell in 20 years from $34,048 to $30,407. In the same period, 1973–93,
the earnings of the top 20% grew steadily and real per capita GDP rose
29%. At the same time, women's wages sustained the family income,
but by the late 1980s they too started to fall in real terms, thus
inducing a decline in household income. By the early 1990s the top
1% of the population owned 40% of all assets, double what it had been
in the mid-1970s, and at the level of the late 1920s, before progressive
taxation. For an illustration of the staggering progression of income
inequality in the US, see figure 4.9. Furthermore, half a century after
Gunnar Myrdal pointed at the "American Dilemma," Martin Carnoy
in a powerful recent book has documented that racial discrimination

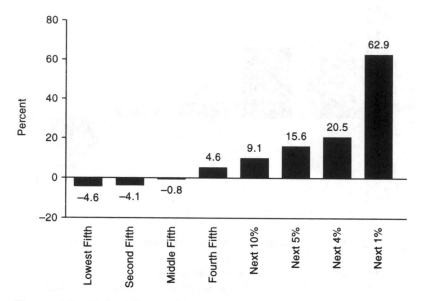

Figure 4.9   United States: income growth, among the top one-fifth
and by fifths, 1980–9
Source: US Congressional Budget Office (1991); compiled by Mishel and
Bernstein (1994).

continues to increase social inequality, contributing to marginalizing
a large proportion of America's ethnic minorities.[117]

While America is an extreme case of income inequality and
declining real wages among the industrialized nations, its evolution is
significant because it does represent the flexible labor market model
at which most European nations, and certainly European firms, are
aiming.[118] And the social consequences of such a trend are similar in
Europe. Thus, in Greater London between 1979 and 1991 real disposable income of households in the lowest decile of income
distribution declined by 14%, and the ratio of real income of the
richest decile over the poorest one almost doubled in the decade,
from 5.6 to 10.2.[119]

The new vulnerability of labor under conditions of unrestrained
flexibility does not concern only the unskilled labor force. The core
labor force, while better paid and more stable, is submitted to mobility
by shortening the working-life period in which professionals are

[117]   Carnoy (1994).
[118]   Sayer and Walker (1992).
[119]   Lee and Townsend (1993: 18–20).

recruited to the core of the enterprise. In American business, the bottom line in the 1990s is the 50/50 rule: those who are over 50 years old and earn over $50,000 have their jobs first in line for any potential downsizing.[120]

The logic of this highly dynamic labor market model interacts with the specificity of labor institutions in each country. Thus, a study of German labor relationships shows that reduction of labor as a result of the introduction of computerized machinery in the 1980s was inversely related to the level of workers' protection provided by the unions in the industry. On the other hand, firms with high levels of protection were also those with the highest change in innovation. This study shows that there is not necessarily a conflict between upgrading the technological basis of the firm and keeping most of the workers, generally retraining them. These firms were also those with the highest level of unionization.[121] The study by Harley Shaiken on Japanese automobile companies in the United States, and on the Saturn automobile plant in Tennessee, reaches similar conclusions, showing the effectiveness of workers' input and unions' participation in the successful introduction of technological innovations, while limiting labor losses.[122]

This institutional variation is what explains the difference we have shown between the United States and the European Union. Social restructuring takes the form of pressuring wages and labor conditions in the US. In the European Union, where labor institutions defend better their historically conquered positions, the net result is increasing unemployment, because of limited entry to young workers and because of the early exit from the labor force for the oldest, or for those trapped in noncompetitive sectors and firms.[123]

As for industrializing countries, they have been featuring for at least three decades a model of articulation between the formal and informal urban labor markets that is tantamount to the flexible forms diffused in the mature economies by the new technological/organizational paradigm.[124]

Why and how has this restructuring of the capital–labor relationship taken place at the dawn of the information age? It resulted from historical circumstances, technological opportunities, and economic imperatives. To reverse the profit squeeze without triggering inflation, national economies and private firms have acted on labor

[120] Byrne (1994).
[121] Warnken and Ronning (1990).
[122] Shaiken (1993, 1995).
[123] Bosch (1995).
[124] Portes et al. (1989); Gereffi (1993)

costs since the early 1980s, either by increasing productivity without employment creation (Europe) or by lowering the cost of a plethora of new jobs (US). Labor unions, the main obstacle to one-sided restructuring strategy, were weakened by their inadaptability to representing new kinds of workers (women, youth, immigrants), to acting in new work places (private sector offices, high-technology industries), and to functioning in the new forms of organization (the network enterprise on a global scale).[125] When necessary, politically induced offensive strategies helped the historical/structural trends working against the unions (for example, Reagan on air traffic controllers, Thatcher on the coal miners). But even socialist governments in France and Spain went on changing the conditions of the labor market, thus weakening the unions, when the pressures of competition made it difficult to depart sharply from the new management rules of the global economy.

What made possible this historical redefinition of the relationship between capital and labor was the use of powerful information technologies and of organizational forms facilitated by the new technological medium. The ability to assemble and disperse labor on specific projects and tasks anywhere, any time, created the possibility for the coming into being of the virtual enterprise as a functional entity. From then on, it was a matter of overcoming institutional resistance to the development of such logic, and/or of obtaining concessions from labor and unions under the potential threat of virtualization. The extraordinary increase in flexibility and adaptability permitted by new technologies opposed the rigidity of labor to the mobility of capital. It followed a relentless pressure to make the labor contribution as flexible as it could be. Productivity and profitability were enhanced, yet labor lost institutional protection and became increasingly dependent on individual bargaining conditions in a constantly changing labor market.

Society became divided, as it was for most of human history, between winners and losers of the endless process of individualized, unequal bargaining. But this time there were few rules about how to win and how to lose. Skills were not enough, since the process of technological change accelerated its pace, constantly superseding the definition of appropriate skills. Membership of corporations, or even countries, ceased to have its privileges, because stepped-up global competition kept redesigning the variable geometry of work and markets. Never was labor more central to the process of value-making.

---

[125]   For assessments of the decline of traditional unionism under new economic/technological conditions, see Carnoy et al. (1993a); see also Gourevitch (ed.) (1984); Adler and Suarez (1993).

But never were the workers (regardless of their skills) more vulnerable to the organization, since they had become lean individuals, farmed out in a flexible network whose whereabouts were unknown to the network itself.

Thus, on the surface, societies were/are becoming dualized, with a substantial top and a substantial bottom growing at both ends of the occupational structure, so shrinking the middle, at a pace and in a proportion that depend on each country's position in the international division of labor and on its political climate. But down in the deep of the nascent social structure, a more fundamental process has been triggered by informational work: the disaggregation of labor, ushering in the network society.

Appendix A: Statistical tables for chapter 4

Table 4.1 United States: percentage distribution of employment by industrial sector and intermediate industry group

Industry	(a) 1920–70						(b) 1970–91				
	1920	1930	1940	1950	1960	1970	1970	1980	1985	1990	1991
I Extractive	28.9	25.4	21.3	14.4	8.1	4.5	4.6	4.5	4.0	3.5	3.5
Agriculture	26.3	22.9	19.2	12.7	7.0	3.7	3.7	3.6	3.1	2.8	2.9
Mining	2.6	2.5	2.1	1.7	1.1	0.8	0.8	1.0	0.9	0.6	0.6
II Transformative	32.9	31.6	29.8	33.9	35.9	33.1	33.0	29.6	27.2	25.6	24.7
Constructive	<	6.5	4.7	6.2	6.2	5.8	6.0	6.2	6.5	6.5	6.1
Utilities	<	0.6	1.2	1.4	1.4	1.4	1.1	1.2	1.2	1.1	1.1
Manufacturing	<	24.5	23.9	26.2	28.3	25.9	25.9	22.2	19.5	18.0	17.5
Food	<	2.3	2.7	2.7	3.1	2.0	1.9	1.9	1.7	1.6	1.5
Textiles	<	4.2	2.0	2.2	3.3	3.0	1.3	0.8	0.7	0.6	0.6
Metal	<	7.7	2.9	3.6	3.9	3.3	3.1	2.7	2.0	1.8	1.7
Machinery	<	^	2.4	3.7	7.5	8.3	5.1	5.2	4.5	3.8	3.7
Chemical	<	1.3	1.5	1.7	1.8	1.6	1.5	1.6	1.3	1.3	1.3
Misc. mfg.	<	9.0	11.8	12.3	8.7	7.7	12.9	10.0	9.4	8.9	8.6
III Distributive services	18.7	19.6	20.4	22.4	21.9	22.3	22.4	21.0	20.9	20.6	20.6
Transportation	7.6	6.0	4.9	5.3	4.4	3.9	3.9	3.7	3.5	3.5	3.6
Communication	<	1.0	0.9	1.2	1.3	1.5	1.5	1.5	1.5	1.3	1.4
Wholesale	11.1	12.6	2.7	3.5	3.6	4.1	4.0	3.9	4.1	3.9	4.0
Retail	<	^	11.8	12.3	12.5	12.8	12.9	11.9	11.9	11.8	11.7
IV Producer services	2.8	3.2	4.6	4.8	6.6	8.5	8.2	10.5	12.7	14.0	14.0
Banking	<	1.3	1.1	1.1	1.6	2.6	2.2	2.6	2.9	2.9	2.8
Insurance	<	1.1	1.2	1.4	1.7	1.8	1.8	1.9	1.9	2.1	2.1
Real Estate	<	0.6	1.1	1.0	1.0	1.0	1.0	1.6	1.7	1.8	1.8
Engineering	<	—	1.3	0.2	0.3	0.4	0.4	0.6	0.7	0.7	0.7

Accounting	<	—	<	0.2	0.3	0.4	0.4	0.5	0.5	0.5	0.6
Misc. business serv.	<	0.1	<	0.6	1.2	1.8	1.8	2.6	4.0	4.9	5.0
Legal services	<	—	<	0.4	0.5	0.5	0.5	0.8	0.9	1.0	1.1
V Social services	8.7	9.2	10.0	12.4	16.3	21.9	22.0	23.7	23.6	24.9	25.5
Medical, health serv.	<	—	2.3	1.1	1.4	2.2	2.4	2.3	3.6	4.3	4.5
Hospital	<	—	<	1.8	2.7	3.7	3.7	5.3	4.0	4.0	4.1
Education	<	—	3.5	3.8	5.4	8.6	8.5	8.3	7.8	7.9	8.0
Welfare, relig. serv.	<	—	0.9	0.7	1.0	1.2	1.2	1.6	2.2	2.6	2.7
Nonprofit org.	<	—	<	0.3	0.4	0.4	0.4	0.5	0.4	0.4	0.4
Postal service	<	0.6	0.7	0.8	0.9	1.0	1.0	0.7	0.7	0.7	0.7
Government	<	2.2	2.6	3.7	4.3	4.6	4.5	4.7	4.7	4.8	4.8
Misc. social services	<	6.3	—	0.1	0.2	0.3	0.3	0.4	0.2	0.2	0.2
VI Personal services	8.2	11.2	14.0	12.1	11.3	10.	10.0	10.5	11.7	11.5	11.7
Domestic serv.	<	6.5	5.3	3.2	3.1	1.7	1.7	1.3	1.2	0.9	0.9
Hotel	<	2.9	1.3	1.0	1.0	1.0	1.0	1.1	1.4	1.5	1.6
Eating, drinking places	<	<	2.5	3.0	2.9	3.3	3.2	4.4	4.9	4.8	4.9
Repair services	<	—	1.5	1.7	1.4	1.3	1.4	1.3	1.5	1.4	1.4
Laundry	<	—	1.0	1.2	1.0	0.8	0.8	0.4	0.4	0.5	0.4
Barber, beauty shops	<	0.9	—		0.8	0.9	0.9	0.7	0.8	0.7	0.7
Entertainment	<	0.9	0.9	1.0	0.8	0.8	0.8	1.0	1.2	1.3	1.3
Misc. personal serv.	<	—	1.6	1.2	0.4	0.3	0.3	0.4	0.4	0.4	0.4
Total	100	100	100	100	100	100	100	100	100	100	100

^ signifies that the figure is included in the above category.

The numbers may not add up due to rounding.

Sources: (a) Singelmann (1978); (b) 1970: Population Census; 1980–1991: Current Population Survey, Bureau of Labor Statistics; Labor statistics: Employment and Earnings, various issues.

Table 4.2 Japan: percentage distribution of employment by industrial sector and intermediate industry group

Industry	(a) 1920–70						(b) 1970–90			
	1920	1930	1940	1950	1960	1970	1970	1980	1985	1990
I Extractive	56.4	50.9	46.3	50.3	34.1	19.6	19.8	11.2	9.5	7.2
Agriculture	54.9	49.9	44.0	48.6	32.9	19.4	19.4	11.0	9.3	7.1
Mining	1.5	1.0	2.2	1.7	1.2	0.3	0.4	0.2	0.2	0.1
II Transformative	19.6	19.8	24.9	21.0	28.5	34.2	34.1	33.7	33.4	33.7
Construction	2.7	3.3	3.0	4.3	6.2	7.6	7.6	9.7	9.1	9.6
Utilities	0.3	0.4	0.4	0.6	0.6	0.6	0.6	0.6	0.6	0.6
Manufacturing	16.6	16.1	21.6	16.1	21.7	26.0	26.0	23.4	23.7	23.6
Food	2.0	1.8	1.4	2.2	2.1	2.1	2.1	2.1	2.2	2.3
Textiles	5.0	4.8	3.9	3.1	3.2	2.7	2.7	1.7	1.5	1.2
Metal	1.0	0.8	1.4	1.6	2.9	1.5	4.0	3.6	3.2	3.2
Machinery	0.4	0.7	2.9	1.6	3.1	4.9	5.0	4.6	5.9	5.9
Chemical	0.4	0.6	1.1	1.2	1.2	1.3	1.3	1.1	1.0	1.1
Misc. mfg.	7.8	7.4	10.9	6.4	9.2	13.5	10.9	10.3	10.0	10.0
III Distributive services	12.4	15.6	15.2	14.6	18.6	22.5	22.4	25.1	24.8	24.3
Transportation	3.5	3.2	3.4	3.5	4.0	5.1	5.1	5.1	5.0	5.0
Communication	0.4	0.7	0.9	1.0	1.1	1.2	1.1	1.2	1.1	1.0
Wholesale	8.5	11.6	10.9	2.3	4.7	6.1	6.1	6.9	7.2	7.1
Retail	^	^	^	7.8	8.9	10.2	10.2	11.9	11.5	11.2
IV Producer services	0.8	0.9	1.2	1.5	2.9	5.1	4.8	7.5	8.6	9.6
Banking	0.4	0.5	0.6	0.7	1.2	1.4	1.4	2.8	3.0	1.9
Insurance	0.1	0.2	0.3	0.2	0.5	0.7	0.7	^	^	1.3
Real Estate	—	—	0.1	0.0	0.2	0.5	0.5	0.8	0.8	1.1
Engineering	0.0	—	0.3	0.3	1.0	0.5	0.5	—	—	0.8

	1	2	3	4	5	6	7	8	9	10
Accounting	—	—	<	<	<	0.2	0.2	—	—	0.3
Misc. business services	0.2	0.2	<	<	<	1.7	1.4	3.9	4.8	4.0
Legal services	0.1	0.0	0.0	0.2	0.1	0.1	0.1	—	—	0.1
V Social services	4.9	5.5	6.0	7.2	8.3	10.1	10.3	12.9	13.5	14.3
Medical, health serv.	0.4	0.3	0.4	1.1	0.3	0.2	0.4	2.9	3.4	1.5
Hospital	0.3	0.5	0.7	<	1.3	1.8	1.8	<	<	2.2
Education	0.9	1.3	1.5	2.2	2.4	2.7	2.9	3.6	3.7	4.5
Welfare, relig. serv.	0.6	0.6	0.6	0.3	0.6	0.7	0.7	1.3	1.3	1.4
Nonprofit org.	0.1	—	0.7	0.2	0.2	0.5	1.0	1.1	1.1	1.1
Postal service	2.2	2.5	1.9	3.3	3.1	3.3	—	—	—	—
Government	<	<	<	<	<	<	3.4	3.6	3.6	3.4
Misc. social services	0.3	0.3	0.3	0.1	0.6	0.9	0.0	0.5	0.4	0.4
VI Personal services	5.7	7.3	6.3	5.3	7.6	8.5	8.5	9.6	10.1	10.2
Domestic serv.	2.5	2.7	2.2	0.8	0.7	0.3	0.3	0.1	0.1	0.1
Hotel	0.5	0.5	0.5	0.5	0.8	0.9	0.9	1.0	1.1	1.1
Eating, drinking places	1.4	2.4	1.8	1.1	2.2	3.1	3.0	4.1	4.3	4.1
Repair services	0.0	0.1	—	0.9	0.7	0.9	0.9	1.1	0.9	1.0
Laundry	0.1	0.2	0.2	0.2	0.4	0.5	0.5	1.6	1.7	0.6
Barber, beauty shops	0.5	0.7	0.6	0.6	1.1	1.1	1.1	<	<	1.1
Entertainment	0.4	0.3	0.8	0.5	0.7	0.7	0.8	0.9	1.0	1.3
Misc. personal serv.	0.2	0.3	0.3	0.7	1.0	1.0	1.0	0.9	0.9	0.9
Unclassifiable	—	—	—	—	—	—	—	—	—	0.6
Total	100	100	100	100	100	100	100	100	100	100

< signifies that the figure is included in the category immediately above.

The numbers may not add up due to rounding.

Source: (a) Singelmann (1978); (b) Population Census, Bureau of Statistics.

Table 4.3 Germany: percentage distribution of employment by industrial sector and intermediate industry group

Industry	(a) 1925-70					(b) 1970-87	
	1925	1933	1950	1961	1970	1970	1987
I Extractive	33.5	31.5	16.1	9.0	5.1	8.7	4.1
Agriculture	30.9	29.1	12.9	6.8	3.8	7.5	3.2
Mining	2.6	2.4	3.2	2.2	1.3	1.2	0.9
II Transformative	38.9	36.3	47.3	51.3	49.0	47.1	40.3
Construction	5.3	6.1	9.3	8.5	8.0	7.7	7.1
Utilities	0.6	0.6	0.8	1.2	0.8	0.8	1.0
Manufacturing	33.0	31.6	37.1	41.6	40.2	38.6	32.2
Food	4.3	5.1	4.6	3.1	3.8	3.6	2.9
Textiles	3.7	3.5	3.5	5.1	2.2	2.4	1.1
Metal	3.7	4.5	2.3	3.7	3.7	4.7	4.3
Machinery	2.9	3.4	3.0	5.0	4.8	9.5	4.9
Chemical	1.1	1.1	1.7	2.4	2.7	2.4	2.7
Misc. mfg.	17.3	14.0	22.0	22.3	23.0	16.0	16.2
III Distributive services	11.9	12.8	15.7	16.4	16.4	17.9	17.7
Transportation	4.0	4.2	5.1	4.5	3.9	5.4	5.9
Communication	—	—	—	0.5	—	^	^
Wholesale	7.9	8.6	10.6	3.9	4.4	4.2	3.2
Retail	^	^	^	7.5	8.6	8.2	8.6
IV Producer services	2.1	2.7	2.5	4.2	5.1	4.5	7.3
Banking	0.7	0.6	0.7	1.2	1.7	1.7	2.4
Insurance	0.4	0.6	0.8	0.7	1.0	0.9	1.0
Real estate	0.0	0.6	0.1	0.3	0.4	0.3	0.4
Engineering	0.1	0.1	0.2	0.4	0.6	0.6	0.7

Accounting	0.5	0.3	0.3	1.0	0.7	—	—
Misc. business serv.	^	^	^	^	^	0.9	2.8
Legal services	0.3	0.6	0.5	0.6	0.8	—	—
V Social services	6.0	6.8	11.1	12.5	17.4	15.7	24.3
Medical, health serv.	0.4	1.3	2.4	2.5	3.2	3.1	5.4
Hospital	0.6	^	^	^	^	—	—
Education	1.1	1.2	1.5	2.1	3.0	3.0	4.9
Welfare, relig. serv.	0.5	0.8	1.0	0.9	0.4	0.9	1.5
Nonprofit org.	—	—	—	—	0.4	0.4	0.2
Postal service	1.1	1.1	1.5	1.7	1.8	—	—
Government	2.1	2.2	4.1	5.3	8.6	7.7	9.5
Misc. social services	0.1	0.2	0.6	—	—	0.5	2.8
VI Personal services	7.7	7.8	6.9	6.4	7.4	6.1	6.3
Domestic serv.	4.4	4.0	3.2	1.5	0.5	0.4	0.2
Hotel	2.1	2.4	2.2	2.6	2.9	2.8	2.7
Eating, drinking places	^	^	^	^	^	^	^
Repair services	—	—	—	—	1.1	1.0	1.1
Laundry	0.2	—	—	0.6	0.5	0.5	0.2
Barber, beauty shops	0.4	0.7	0.8	0.9	0.9	0.9	1.0
Entertainment	0.4	0.5	0.1	—	0.4	0.4	0.9
Misc. personal serv.	0.1	0.2	0.6	0.8	0.4	0.1	0.1
Total	100	100	100	100	100	100	100

^ signifies that the figure is included in the category immediately above.
The numbers may not add up due to rounding.
Sources: (a) Singelmann (1978); (b) Statistisches Bundesamt, Volkszählung.

Table 4.4 France: percentage distribution of employment by industrial sector and intermediate industry group

Industry	(a) 1921–68						(b) 1968–89					
	1921	1931	1946	1954	1962	1968	1968	1970	1975	1980	1985	1989p
I Extractive	43.6	38.3	40.2	30.9	23.0	17.0	15.6	13.5	10.3	8.7	7.6	6.4
Agriculture	42.4	36.6	38.8	28.6	20.6	15.9	14.8	12.9	9.9	8.4	7.4	6.3
Mining	1.2	1.7	1.4	2.3	2.4	1.1	0.2	0.6	0.4	0.3	0.2	0.1
II Transformative	29.7	32.8	29.6	35.2	37.7	39.3	39.4	38.0	37.3	34.8	30.9	29.5
Construction	3.0	4.2	5.1	7.4	8.7	10.3	9.5	9.5	8.9	8.5	7.1	7.2
Utilities	0.2	0.0	0.6	0.7	0.8	0.8	0.8	0.8	0.8	0.9	1.0	1.0
Manufacturing	26.4	28.5	23.8	27.2	28.0	26.0	27.0	27.7	27.6	25.5	22.9	21.3
Food	2.3	2.6	2.2	3.2	3.1	3.0	3.0	3.0	2.9	2.9	2.9	2.8
Textiles	9.4	4.4	2.5	6.0	4.9	2.3	3.8	3.6	3.1	2.5	2.1	1.7
Metal	0.6	2.1	7.3	0.9	1.1	1.5	5.0	5.1	5.0	4.3	3.6	3.5
Machinery	—	—	<	0.9	1.2	1.3	4.9	5.3	5.6	5.2	4.8	4.5
Chemical	0.9	1.1	1.1	1.3	1.4	1.5	1.8	1.9	1.9	1.8	1.7	1.6
Misc. mfg.	13.2	18.3	10.7	14.9	16.3	18.5	8.4	8.8	9.1	8.7	7.7	7.3
III Distributive services	14.4	13.6	15.1	14.2	16.4	15.5	18.8	18.7	19.2	19.9	20.2	20.5
Transportation	5.6	5.1	6.1	4.2	4.3	4.3	4.2	4.1	4.1	4.1	4.2	4.3
Communication	0.7	<	<	1.3	1.7	0.1	1.8	1.8	2.0	2.1	2.3	2.2
Wholesale	8.1	8.5	9.1	2.3	3.2	3.6	3.7	3.8	4.0	4.4	4.4	4.5
Retail	<	<	<	6.5	7.3	7.5	9.1	9.0	9.2	9.3	9.3	9.5
IV Producer services	1.6	2.1	1.9	2.6	3.2	5.5	5.0	5.5	6.5	7.8	8.5	10.0
Banking	0.6	0.9	1.2	0.8	1.1	2.0	1.3	1.4	1.8	2.0	2.8	2.0
Insurance	0.2	0.3	0.4	0.5	0.7	0.8	0.5	0.5	0.6	0.7	0.7	0.8
Real estate	0.0	0.0	0.0	0.4	0.2	0.4	0.1	0.2	0.3	0.3	0.3	0.3
Engineering	0.5	0.7	—	0.9	1.1	0.3	—	—	—	—	—	—
Accounting	<	<	—	<	<	1.6	—	—	—	—	—	—

Misc. business serv.	<	<	—	<	<	<	3.1	3.4	3.8	4.9	5.3	6.9
Legal services	0.3	0.3	0.3	—	—	0.4	—	—	—	—	—	—
V Social services	5.3	6.1	6.8	9.4	12.3	14.5	15.1	15.6	16.4	17.1	19.8	19.5
Medical, health serv.	0.9	1.1	1.2	2.2	2.9	1.0	—	—	—	—	—	—
Hospital	<	<	<	<	<	2.2	—	—	—	—	—	—
Education	1.3	1.4	1.5	2.4	3.5	4.4	—	—	—	—	—	—
Welfare, relig. serv.	0.5	0.5	0.7	0.6	1.1	1.1	—	—	—	—	—	—
Nonprofit org.	—	—	—	—	1.0	0.7	—	—	—	—	—	—
Postal services	2.3	2.8	3.2	4.0	3.4	1.8	—	—	—	—	—	—
Government	<	<	<	<	<	3.3	—	—	—	—	—	—
Misc. social services	0.2	0.2	0.1	0.2	0.4	0.0	—	—	—	—	—	—
VI Personal services	5.6	7.2	6.4	7.4	7.4	7.9	8.2	8.7	10.2	11.6	13.1	14.1
Domestic serv.	3.7	3.8	1.3	3.1	3.0	2.7	—	—	—	—	—	—
Hotel	1.5	2.8	1.4	1.5	1.6	0.9	2.7	2.7	2.7	2.8	3.1	3.5
Eating, drinking places	<	<	<	1.4	1.2	1.8	<	<	<	<	<	<
Repair services	—	—	—	—	0.3	1.1	—	—	—	—	—	—
Laundry	—	—	0.2	1.0	1.2	0.5	—	—	—	—	—	—
Barber, beauty shops	0.3	—	—	<	<	0.7	—	—	—	—	—	—
Entertainment	0.1	0.2	0.3	0.4	0.2	0.2	—	—	—	—	—	—
Misc. personal serv.	0.0	0.5	0.5	—	0.0	0.0	5.6	6.0	7.4	8.8	10.0	10.6
Total	100	100	100	100	100	100	100	100	100	100	100	100

^ signifies the figure is included in the category immediately above.

The numbers may not add up due to rounding.

1989 figures are preliminary. Communication includes postal services. Miscellaneous services includes all non-profit services in 1968–89.

Sources: (a) Singelmann (1978); (b) INSEE, Annuaire statistique de la France.

Table 4.5 Italy: percentage distribution of employment by industrial sector and intermediate industry group.

Industry	(a) 1921–61				(b) 1961–90			
	1921	1931	1951	1961	1961	1971	1981	1990
I Extractive	57.1	48.1	42.9	29.8	29.8	17.2	11.7	9.5
Agriculture	56.7	47.7	42.5	29.1	29.1	17.2	11.4	9.5
Mining	0.4	0.4	0.4	0.7	0.7	—	0.3	—
II Transformative	24.3	29.0	31.8	40.0	39.9	44.3	40.5	29.7
Constructive	4.1	6.0	7.6	12.0	12.0	10.8	9.4	7.0
Utilities	0.3	0.6	0.5	0.6	0.6	0.9	0.9	0.8
Manufacturing	19.9	22.4	23.7	27.4	27.3	32.7	30.2	21.8
Food	1.2	1.5	2.4	2.4	—	—	1.8	1.6
Textiles	3.2	4.2	3.7	3.4	—	—	6.3	5.0
Metal	1.8	4.4	1.2	1.5	—	—	7.0	4.7
Machinery	1.5	<	1.4	1.8	—	—	4.8	3.3
Chemical	0.4	1.0	1.1	1.4	—	—	1.4	1.3
Misc. mfg.	11.8	11.3	13.9	16.9	—	—	8.8	5.9
III Distributive services	8.6	10.1	10.6	13.0	15.3	18.7	16.2	25.8
Transportation	3.9	4.2	3.4	4.1	4.9	5.3	4.9	5.2
Communication	0.4	0.5	0.6	0.8	<	<	1.5	1.3
Wholesale	4.3	5.4	1.2	1.4	10.3	13.4	3.6	17.3
Retail	<	<	5.4	6.7	<	<	6.1	<
IV Producer services	1.2	1.8	1.9	2.0	—	—	4.6	—
Banking	0.2	0.5	0.8	0.9	1.1	1.5	1.7	1.8
Insurance	<	0.1	0.1	0.2	<	<	0.5	<
Real estate	<	<	<	0.0	—	—	0.0	—
Engineering	0.8	<	<	0.0	—	—	1.4	—
Accounting	<	1.0	0.7	0.3	—	—	0.4	—

Misc. business serv.	^	^	^	^	0.1	—	—
Legal services	0.2	0.2	0.3	0.4	0.4	—	—
V Social services	4.1	5.1	7.9	9.3	19.1	—	15.5
Medical, health serv.	0.6	0.8	1.1	0.7	1.7	—	—
Hospital	^	^	^	0.9	2.6	—	—
Education	1.0	1.1	2.0	2.7	7.4	—	—
Welfare, relig. serv.	0.6	0.7	1.2	0.2	0.2	—	—
Nonprofit org.	—	0.1	0.1	—	0.3	—	—
Postal service	1.3	2.1	3.4	4.8	—	—	—
Government	^	^	^	6.9	6.5	6.5	—
Misc. social services	0.6	0.3	0.1	—	0.4	—	—
VI Personal services	4.6	5.6	4.7	5.9	7.9	—	—
Domestic serv.	2.4	3.2	2.2	2.2	1.2	—	—
Hotel	0.2	0.6	1.4	0.7	0.9	—	4.1
Eating, drinking places	0.8	0.7	^	1.4	2.0	—	^
Repair services	—	—	—	—	2.0	—	—
Laundry	0.3	0.2	0.1	0.2	0.3	—	—
Barber, beauty shops	0.4	0.7	0.6	0.9	1.0	—	—
Entertainment	0.0	0.1	0.3	0.3	0.5	—	—
Misc. personal serv.	0.5	0.1	0.1	0.2	0.1	—	—
All other services	—	—	—	7.0	15.6	11.8	15.6
Total	100	100	100	100	100	100	100

^ signifies that the figure is included in the category immediately above.

The numbers may not add up due to rounding.

1990 figures may not be comparable to figures from earlier years due to the difference in sources.

Sources: (a) Singelmann (1978); (b) 1961–81: Istituto Centrale di statistica, Censimento generale della popolazione; 1990: Istituto nazionale di statistica, Annuario Statistico Italiano, 1991.

Table 4.6 United Kingdom: percentage distribution of employment by industrial sector and intermediate industry group

Industry	(a) England and Wales 1921–71					(b) UK (employees) 1970–90					(c) Great Britain (employees) 1970–92						(d) Great Britain (employed) 1971–81	
	1921	1931	1951	1961	1971	1970	1975	1980	1985	1990	1970	1971	1980	1981	1990	1992	1971	1981
I Extractive	14.2	11.8	8.9	6.6	4.3	3.6	3.3	4.7	4.4	3.3	3.6	3.4	4.3	4.9	3.2	1.8	4.3	3.9
Agriculture	7.1	6.1	5.0	3.5	2.6	1.7	1.8	1.6	1.6	1.3	1.7	1.6	1.6	1.6	1.2	1.2	2.7	2.3
Mining	7.1	5.7	3.9	3.1	1.7	1.9	1.6	3.2	2.8	2.0	1.9	1.9	3.2	3.3	2.0	0.5	1.6	1.6
II Transformative	42.2	39.3	45.4	46.0	43.8	46.7	40.3	35.7	29.8	27.3	46.6	45.9	35.7	33.7	27.3	26.3	42.8	35.6
Construction	4.4	5.2	6.5	6.9	7.1	6.3	5.8	5.5	4.8	4.8	6.2	6.0	5.4	5.2	4.8	4.0	7.0	7.0
Utilities	1.0	1.3	1.7	1.7	1.6	1.7	1.6	—	—	—	1.7	1.7	—	—	—	1.2	1.5	1.5
Manufacturing	36.8	32.9	37.2	37.4	34.9	38.7	33.0	30.2	25.0	22.5	38.8	38.2	30.3	28.5	22.5	21.1	34.2	27.1
Food	3.3	3.4	3.0	3.0	3.0	3.9	3.2	3.2	2.8	2.4	3.8	3.8	3.1	3.1	2.9	2.9	3.1	3.0
Textiles	5.9	5.9	4.5	3.4	2.4	3.1	2.1	1.5	1.1	0.9	3.0	2.8	1.5	1.5	0.9	0.8	2.5	1.3
Metal	2.8	2.1	2.7	2.7	2.3	5.4	4.6	6.8	3.6	3.1	5.5	5.3	6.9	6.2	3.2	2.7	4.8	4.1
Machinery	1.6	1.4	3.0	3.2	4.8	9.2	7.7	7.9	6.8	6.1	9.3	9.1	8.0	7.6	6.2	5.8	8.3	7.1
Chemical	1.1	1.1	2.1	2.3	2.0	2.3	2.1	—	1.6	1.4	2.4	2.4	—	—	1.5	1.4	2.2	1.7
Misc. mfg.	22.1	19.0	21.9	22.8	20.4	14.8	13.1	10.8	9.2	8.6	14.8	14.8	10.8	10.2	8.5	8.0	13.4	10.0
III Distributive services	19.3	21.6	19.2	19.7	17.9	18.7	18.9	19.9	20.4	20.6	18.8	18.7	20.2	20.4	20.4	20.7	19.3	20.3
Transportation	7.3	7.0	6.4	5.7	4.8	4.9	4.7	6.5	4.2	4.1	4.9	5.0	6.5	6.6	4.2	4.3	4.8	4.6
Communication	—	—	—	—	—	2.0	2.0	<	2.0	1.9	2.0	2.1	<	<	1.9	1.9	1.8	1.9
Wholesale	12.0	14.6	12.8	14.0	3.4	2.3	3.7	4.0	4.5	4.5	2.3	2.4	4.1	4.2	4.3	4.5	2.1	3.9
Retail	<	<	<	<	9.6	9.5	8.4	9.5	9.7	10.1	9.5	9.3	9.5	9.6	10.1	10.0	10.7	9.8
IV Producer services	2.6	3.1	3.2	4.5	5.6	5.0	5.7	7.5	9.7	12.0	5.1	5.2	7.5	8.0	12.1	12.3	5.6	7.9
Banking	0.8	0.8	0.9	1.2	1.6	1.6	1.9	2.0	2.4	2.8	1.6	1.7	2.0	2.2	2.8	2.8	1.6	2.1
Insurance	0.7	0.9	0.9	1.1	1.2	1.3	1.2	0.9	1.1	1.2	1.3	1.3	1.0	1.0	1.2	1.2	1.2	1.1
Real estate	—	0.3	0.3	0.3	0.4	0.3	0.4	—	0.6	0.6	0.3	0.3	—	—	0.6	0.7	0.4	0.4

	1	2	3	4	5	6	7	8	9	10	11	12	13	14	15	16	17	18
Engineering	0.2	0.2	0.2	—	0.4	0.4	—	—	—	—	—	0.4	—	—	—	—	0.5	—
Accounting	0.0	0.3	0.3	0.4	0.4	0.4	—	—	—	1.1	1.1	1.1	1.0	1.2	—	1.0	0.4	—
Misc. business serv.	0.4	0.2	0.1	1.1	1.0	1.0	4.5	5.6	7.4	—	—	—	—	—	—	—	1.1	4.3
Legal services	0.4	0.4	0.4	0.4	0.5	0.5	—	—	—	0.5	0.5	0.5	0.5	—	—	—	0.5	—
V Social services	8.9	9.7	12.1	14.1	19.4	17.7	22.1	24.2	26.8	27.2	17.7	18.3	23.9	24.9	27.2	28.9	18.9	22.8
Medical, health serv.	1.0	1.1	2.9	3.4	0.8	4.5	5.5	6.8	7.8	8.1	4.4	4.6	6.8	7.1	8.1	8.7	1.0	6.3
Hospital	^	^	^	^	3.1	^	^	^	^	^	^	^	^	^	^	^	3.2	—
Education	2.1	2.2	2.4	3.9	5.8	6.4	8.5	7.6	8.1	8.3	6.4	6.7	7.5	7.8	8.2	8.7	6.2	6.7
Welfare, relig. serv.	0.6	0.6	0.6	0.7	1.0	0.1	0.1	2.5	3.5	3.9	0.1	0.1	2.4	2.6	3.2	3.4	1.1	—
Nonprofit org.	0.1	0.1	^	0.0	0.2	—	—	—	—	—	—	—	—	—	—	—	0.1	—
Postal service	1.1	1.2	1.6	1.6	1.8	—	—	—	—	—	—	—	—	—	—	—	—	—
Government	3.8	4.3	4.2	4.0	6.0	6.2	7.3	7.3	7.4	6.8	6.2	6.4	7.2	7.4	7.0	7.4	6.8	7.2
Misc. social services	0.2	0.2	0.4	0.6	0.6	0.6	0.6	—	—	—	0.6	0.5	—	—	0.6	0.7	0.4	2.6
VI Personal services	12.9	11.3	9.0	9.0	8.1	9.7	8.1	9.0	9.7	8.1	8.1	7.9	8.1	9.8	9.7	8.4	8.4	8.9
Domestic serv.	7.5	8.2	2.4	1.6	1.0	0.4	1.2	1.1	4.3	4.9	5.6	0.4	0.4	4.3	4.4	1.2	1.0	0.4
Hotel	2.4	2.2	2.7	1.6	1.6	1.2	1.1	1.1	2.5	1.9	1.3	1.2	1.3	4.4	4.4	4.0	1.0	4.1
Eating, drinking places	0.8	1.3	^	1.0	1.3	1.3	2.5	1.9	1.9	1.0	1.0	0.9	0.9	1.0	1.0	1.1	1.9	^
Repair services	—	—	^	2.1	1.8	1.8	1.9	0.4	—	0.5	0.5	0.9	0.9	—	—	—	2.1	1.5
Laundry	0.8	0.9	1.8	0.4	0.5	0.5	0.4	0.4	0.4	—	—	—	—	—	—	—	0.4	—
Barber, beauty shops	0.3	0.5	0.7	1.1	0.4	0.4	0.4	0.4	0.4	—	1.1	1.1	1.1	—	—	—	0.6	—
Entertainment	0.7	0.9	1.0	1.1	1.1	1.1	1.3	1.9	2.3	2.3	1.1	1.3	2.1	2.0	2.3	2.3	1.1	1.9
Misc. personal serv.	0.5	0.3	1.0	1.0	1.3	1.3	2.1	1.0	0.9	0.9	1.4	1.4	1.3	0.8	0.9	0.9	0.2	1.1
Unclassifiable	—	—	—	0.5	0.8	0.2	0.0	0.0	—	—	0.3	0.2	—	—	0.0	0.3	0.7	0.6
Total	100	100	100	100	100	100	100	100	100	100	100	100	100	100	100	100	100	100

^ signifies that the figure is included in the category immediately above.

The numbers may not add up due to rounding.

The data for Great Britain are of the employed, while the data for United Kingdom are of employees in employment.

Postal service is included in Communication.

From 1980 UK figures, utilities is included under Mining. Chemical is included in Metal in 1980.

Sources: (a) Singelmann (1978); (b)–(d) 1970–92: Annual Abstract of Statistics, and Employment Gazette; 1971–81: Office of Population Censuses and Surveys, Census Reports.

Table 4.7 Canada: percentage distribution of employment by industrial sector and intermediate industry group.

Industry	(a) 1921–71						(b) 1971–92		
	1921	1931	1941	1951	1961	1971	1971	1981	1992
I Extractive	36.9	34.4	31.7	21.6	14.7	9.1	8.3	7.1	5.7
Agriculture	35.2	32.5	29.5	19.7	12.8	7.4	6.6	5.3	4.4
Mining	1.6	1.9	2.2	1.9	1.9	1.7	1.6	1.8	1.3
II Transformative	26.1	24.7	28.2	33.7	31.1	30.0	27.1	26.8	22.3
Construction	9.0	6.8	5.3	6.9	7.0	6.9	6.3	6.5	6.3
Utilities	—	1.5	0.6	1.2	1.1	1.1	1.0	1.1	1.2
Manufacturing	17.0	16.4	22.3	25.6	23.0	22.0	19.7	19.2	14.9
Food	1.2	2.2	3.4	3.1	3.7	3.2	2.9	2.7	—
Textiles	2.7	2.6	3.7	1.6	1.3	0.9	1.0	0.7	—
Metal	2.9	1.9	2.3	3.9	3.2	1.5	3.0	3.4	—
Machinery	^	0.7	0.9	^	0.8	1.0	2.3	2.2	—
Chemical	0.2	0.4	0.8	1.3	1.4	1.0	1.2	1.1	—
Misc. mfg.	10.0	8.6	11.2	15.7	12.6	14.4	9.3	9.0	14.9
III Distributive services	19.2	18.4	17.7	21.8	23.9	23.0	20.8	22.9	24.0
Transportation	8.5	7.2	5.8	6.8	6.6	5.4	5.0	4.8	4.1
Communication	—	0.9	0.7	1.1	2.1	2.1	1.9	2.1	2.1
Wholesale	10.7	1.6	2.4	3.8	4.7	4.5	4.1	4.8	4.5
Retail	^	8.7	8.8	10.1	10.5	11.0	9.8	11.1	13.2
IV Producer services	3.7	3.3	2.7	3.9	5.3	7.3	6.6	9.7	11.3
Banking	1.2	1.2	0.9	1.3	1.8	2.4	2.2	2.7	3.7
Insurance	^	1.0	0.9	1.1	1.9	2.2	2.0	0.9	^
Real estate	^	0.2	0.3	0.4	^	^	^	1.7	2.2
Engineering	2.3	—	—	0.2	0.4	0.7	0.6	0.9	—
Accounting	^	0.1	0.1	0.2	0.3	0.4	0.4	0.5	—

Misc. business serv.	^	0.4	0.2	0.4	0.5	1.1	1.0	2.3	5.4
Legal services	0.2	0.4	0.3	0.3	0.4	0.5	0.4	0.6	—
V Social services	7.5	8.9	9.4	11.3	15.4	21.1	22.0	24.0	22.6
Medical, health serv.	1.1	1.8	2.2	3.1	0.9	1.0	1.8	2.0	9.1
Hospital	^	^	^	^	3.7	4.7	4.1	4.0	^
Education	2.0	2.7	2.7	2.9	4.4	7.3	6.0	6.6	7.0
Welfare, relig. serv.	0.9	1.0	0.7	1.1	1.3	1.4	1.3	1.9	—
Nonprofit org.	—	—	—	—	—	0.2	0.2	0.2	—
Postal service	3.0	0.5	0.5	0.6	5.1	5.4	—	—	6.5
Government	^	2.6	2.8	3.4	^	^	7.4	7.6	—
Misc. social services	0.5	0.3	0.5	0.2	—	—	1.1	1.6	—
VI Personal services	6.7	10.2	10.2	7.8	9.5	9.6	7.5	9.5	13.5
Domestic serv..	—	4.2	4.5	1.6	1.6	0.7	0.6	0.4	—
Hotel	—	2.8	1.6	1.5	3.9	1.7	1.5	5.7	6.5
Eating, drinking places	—	^	1.3	1.6	^	2.6	2.2	—	^
Repair services	—	0.5	1.1	1.1	1.1	0.9	1.0	1.1	—
Laundry	—	0.5	0.5	0.7	0.6	0.5	0.5	0.3	—
Barber, beauty shops	—	0.6	0.6	0.5	0.7	0.7	0.6	0.5	—
Entertainment	—	0.4	0.4	0.5	0.6	1.0	0.9	1.2	—
Misc. personal serv.	—	1.2	0.2	0.3	1.0	1.5	0.3	0.3	7.0
Unclassifiable	—	—	—	—	—	—	7.3	—	0.7
Total	100	100	100	100	100	100	100	100	100

^ signifies that the figure is included in the category immediately above.

The numbers may not add up due to rounding.

1992 figures may not be comparable to the earlier years due to the difference in sources.

Sources: (a) Singelmann (1978); (b) 1971–81: Population Census; 1992: Statistics Canada (The Labour Force) May.

Table 4.8 United States: employment statistics by industry

	(a) 1920–70						(b) 1970–91				
	1920	1930	1940	1950	1960	1970	1970	1980	1985	1990	1991
Industry	48.0%	43.3%	37.9%	39.2%	38.2%	33.6%	34.0%	30.5%	27.7%	25.8%	24.9%
Services	52.0%	56.7%	62.1%	60.8%	61.8%	66.4%	66.0%	69.5%	72.3%	74.2%	75.1%
Goods handling	73.3%	69.0%	67.4%	69.3%	65.8%	61.1%	61.2%	57.3%	54.7%	52.6%	51.7%
Information handling	26.7%	31.0%	32.5%	30.6%	34.0%	38.9%	39.0%	42.7%	45.3%	47.4%	48.3%
Services: industry	1.1	1.3	1.6	1.6	1.6	2.0	1.9	2.3	2.6	2.9	3.0
Information: goods	0.4	0.5	0.5	0.4	0.5	0.6	0.6	0.7	0.8	0.9	0.9

Industry = mining, construction, manufacturing.

Services = remaining categories.

Goods handling = mining, construction, manufacturing, transportation, wholesale/retail trade.

Information handling = communications; finance, insurance, and real estate (FIRE); services; government.

Services: industry = ratio between services and industry employment.

Information: goods = ratio between information handling and goods handling employment.

Source: See table 4.1.

Table 4.9 Japan: employment statistics by industry

	(a) 1920–70						(b) 1970–91			
	1920	1930	1940	1950	1960	1970	1970	1980	1985	1990
Industry	46.3%	40.7%	47.8%	43.1%	43.4%	42.1%	42.1%	37.4%	36.3%	35.8%
Services	53.7%	59.3%	52.2%	56.9%	56.6%	57.9%	57.9%	62.6%	63.7%	64.2%
Goods handling	76.8%	75.8%	77.3%	72.9%	73.8%	73.2%	73.0%	69.6%	67.9%	65.9%
Information handling	23.2%	24.0%	22.5%	27.1%	26.4%	27.0%	26.9%	30.4%	31.9%	33.4%
Services: industry	1.2	1.5	1.1	1.3	1.3	1.4	1.4	1.7	1.8	1.8
Information: goods	0.3	0.3	0.3	0.4	0.4	0.4	0.4	0.4	0.5	0.5

Industry = mining, construction, manufacturing.
Services = remaining categories.
Goods handling = mining, construction, manufacturing, transportation, wholesale/retail trade.
Information handling = communications; finance, insurance, and real estate (FIRE); services, government.
Services: industry = ratio between services and industry employment.
Information: goods = ratio between information handling and goods handling employment.
Source: See table 4.2.

Table 4.10 Germany: employment statistics by industry

	(a) 1925–70					(b) 1970–87	
	1925	1933	1950	1961	1970	1970	1987
Industry	59.1%	56.6%	57.3%	56.2%	51.2%	51.4%	41.5%
Services	40.9%	43.4%	42.7%	43.8%	48.8%	48.6%	58.5%
Goods handling	78.8%	77.1%	78.1%	76.5%	71.4%	71.6%	60.8%
Information handling	21.2%	22.9%	21.9%	23.5%	29.1%	28.4%	39.2%
Services: industry	0.7	0.8	0.7	0.8	1.0	0.9	1.4
Information: goods	0.3	0.3	0.3	0.3	0.4	0.4	0.6

Industry = mining, construction, manufacturing.
Services = remaining categories.
Goods handling = mining, construction, manufacturing, transportation, wholesale/retail trade.
Information handling = communications; finance, insurance, and real estate (FIRE); services; government.
Services: industry = ratio between services and industry employment.
Information: goods = ratio between information handling and goods handling employment.
Source: See table 4.3.

Table 4.11 France: employment statistics by industry

	(a) 1921–68						(b) 1968–89					
	1921	1931	1946	1954	1962	1968	1968	1970	1975	1980	1985	1989
Industry	53.1%	54.3%	49.7%	51.8%	49.5%	47.3%	43.8%	43.4%	41.0%	37.4%	32.5%	30.6%
Services	46.9%	45.7%	50.3%	48.2%	50.5%	52.7%	56.2%	56.6%	59.0%	62.6%	67.5%	69.4%
Goods handling	79.8%	80.2%	77.8%	73.1%	71.2%	67.7%	67.8%	66.8%	64.1%	60.8%	56.3%	54.9%
Information handling	20.2%	19.8%	22.4%	27.0%	29.0%	32.3%	32.2%	33.2%	35.9%	39.2%	43.7%	45.1%
Services: industry	0.9	0.8	1.0	0.9	1.0	1.1	1.3	1.3	1.4	1.7	2.1	2.3
Information: goods	0.3	0.2	0.3	0.4	0.4	0.5	0.5	0.5	0.6	0.6	0.8	0.8

Industry = mining, construction, manufacturing.

Services = remaining categories.

Goods handling = mining, construction, manufacturing, transportation, wholesale/retail trade, hotels/lodging places.

Information handling = communications; finance, insurance, and real estate (FIRE); services; government.

Services: industry = ratio between services and industry employment.

Information: goods = ratio between information handling and goods handling employment.

Source: See table 4.4.

Table 4.12 Italy: employment statistics by industry

	(a) 1921–61				(b) 1961–90			
	1921	*1931*	*1951*	*1961*	*1961*	*1971*	*1981*	*1990*
Industry	56.5%	55.4%	55.3%	56.6%	56.4%	52.5%	45.0%	31.9%
Services	43.5%	44.6%	44.7%	43.4%	43.6%	47.5%	55.0%	68.1%
Goods handling	76.6%	76.2%	76.1%	75.6%	78.8%	76.1%	63.6%	62.2%
Information handling	23.4%	23.8%	23.9%	24.4%	21.2%	23.9%	36.4%	37.8%
Services: industry	0.8	0.8	0.8	0.8	0.8	0.9	1.2	2.1
Information: goods	0.3	0.3	0.3	0.3	0.3	0.3	0.6	0.6

Industry = mining, construction, manufacturing.
Services = remaining categories.
Goods handling = mining, construction, manufacturing, transportation, wholesale/retail trade, hotels/lodging places.
Information handling = communications; finance, insurance, and real estate (FIRE); services; government.
Services: industry = ratio between services and industry employment.
Information: goods = ratio between information handling and goods handling employment.
1990 figures may not be comparable to figures from earlier years due to the difference in sources.
Source: See table 4.5.

Table 4.13 United Kingdom: employment statistics by industry

	(a) England and Wales, 1921–71					(b) UK, 1970–90				
	1921	1931	1951	1961	1971	1970	1975	1980	1985	1990
Industry	53.0%	47.9%	51.8%	50.9%	46.7%	49.4%	42.6%	39.4%	33.1%	29.6%
Services	47.0%	52.1%	48.2%	49.1%	53.3%	50.6%	57.4%	60.6%	66.9%	70.4%
Goods handling	76.3%	73.3%	76.4%	74.2%	66.6%	67.6%	61.0%	64.0%	56.7%	54.2%
Information handling	23.7%	26.7%	23.6%	25.8%	33.3%	32.2%	39.0%	36.0%	43.3%	45.8%
Services: industry	0.9	1.1	0.9	1.0	1.1	1.0	1.3	1.5	2.0	2.4
Information: goods	0.3	0.4	0.3	0.3	0.5	0.5	0.6	0.6	0.8	0.8

Industry = mining, construction, manufacturing.
Services = remaining categories.
Goods handling = mining, construction, manufacturing, transportation, wholesale/retail trade, hotels/lodging places.
Information handling = communications; finance, insurance, and real estate (FIRE); services; government.
Services: industry = ratio between services and industry employment.
Information: goods = ratio between information handling and goods handling employment.
Source: See table 4.6

Table 4.14 Canada: employment statistics by industry

	(a) 1921–71						(b) 1971–92		
	1921	1931	1941	1951	1961	1971	1971	1981	1992
Industry	42.7%	37.2%	42.3%	42.8%	36.6%	33.0%	29.8%	29.0%	23.5%
Services	57.3%	62.8%	57.7%	57.2%	63.4%	67.0%	70.2%	71.0%	76.5%
Goods handling	72.3%	69.6%	69.6%	71.9%	67.4%	58.6%	52.8%	58.1%	54.3%
Information handling	27.6%	30.4%	30.4%	28.1%	32.6%	41.4%	47.2%	41.9%	45.7%
Services: industry	1.3	1.7	1.4	1.3	1.7	2.0	2.4	2.4	3.3
Information: goods	0.4	0.4	0.4	0.4	0.5	0.7	0.9	0.7	0.8

Industry = mining, construction, manufacturing.
Services = remaining categories.
Goods handling = mining, construction, manufacturing, transportation, wholesale/retail trade, hotels/lodging places.
Information handling = communications; finance, insurance, and real estate (FIRE); services; government.
Services: industry = ratio between services and industry employment.
Information: goods = ratio between information handling and goods handling employment.
1992 figures may not be comparable to figures from previous years due to the difference in sources.
Source: See table 4.7.

Table 4.15 Occupational structure of selected countries (%)

Categories	USA 1991	Canada 1992	UK 1990	France 1989	Germany 1987	Japan 1990
Managers	12.8	13.0	11.0	7.5	4.1	3.8
Professionals	13.7	17.6	21.8	6.0	13.9	11.1
Technicians	3.2	^	^	12.4	8.7	^
Subtotal	29.7	30.6	32.8	25.9	26.7	14.9
Sales	11.9	9.9	6.6	3.8	7.8	15.1
Clerical	15.7	16.0	17.3	24.2	13.7	18.6
Subtotal	27.6	25.9	23.9	28.0	21.5	33.7
Crafts & operators	21.8	21.1	22.4	28.1	27.9	31.8
Semiskilled service workers	13.7	13.7	12.8	7.2	12.3	8.6
Semiskilled transport workers	4.2	3.5	5.6	4.2	5.5	3.7
Subtotal	17.9	17.2	18.4	11.4	17.3	12.3
Farm workers & managers	3.0	5.1	1.6	6.6	3.1	7.2
Unclassified	—	—	1.0	—	3.0	—
Total	100	100	100	100	100	100

1 The figures may not add up due to rounding.
2 the ^ signifies that figure is included in the category immediately above.
Source: Author's elaboration; see Appendix B.

Table 4.16 United States: percentage distribution of employment by occupation, 1960–91 (%)

Occupational category	1960	1970	1980	1985	1990	1990
Managerial	11.1	10.5	11.2	11.4	12.6	12.8
Professional	11.8	14.2	16.1	12.7	13.4	13.7
Technicians	^	^	^	3.0	3.3	3.2
Sales	7.3	6.2	6.3	11.8	12.0	11.9
Clerical	14.8	17.4	18.6	16.2	15.8	15.7
Crafts and operators	30.2	32.2	28.1	23.9	22.5	21.8
Semiskilled service workers	13.0	12.4	13.3	13.5	13.4	13.7
Semiskilled transport workers	4.9	3.2	3.6	4.2	4.1	4.2
Farm workers and managers	7.0	4.0	2.8	3.2	2.9	3.0
Total	100.	100.	100.	100.	100.	100.

^signifies that figure is included in the category immediately above.

Figures are seasonally adjusted annual data except the 1960 data, which are those of December.

Source: Labor Statistics: Employment and Earnings, various issues.

Table 4.17 Japan: percentage distribution of employment by occupation, 1955–90 (%)

Occupational category	1955	1960	1965	1970	1975	1980	1985	1990
Managerial	2.2	2.1	2.8	2.6	4.0	4.0	3.6	3.8
Professional	4.6	5.0	5.0	5.8	7.0	7.9	9.3	11.1
Technicians	^	^	^	^	^	^	^	^
Sales	13.3	13.4	13.0	13.0	14.2	14.4	14.9	15.1
Clerical	9.0	11.2	13.4	14.8	15.7	16.7	17.7	18.6
Crafts and operators	27.0	29.5	31.4	34.2	33.3	33.1	33.2	31.8
Semiskilled service workers	5.4	6.7	7.5	7.6	8.8	9.1	8.7	8.6
Semiskilled transport workers	1.7	2.3	3.7	4.6	4.5	4.5	3.9	3.7
Farm workers and managers	36.7	29.8	23.1	17.3	12.5	10.3	8.7	7.2
Total	100	100	100	100	100	100	100	100

^ signifies that figure is included in the category immediately above.
Sweepers and garbage collectors are included in Semiskilled service category between 1970 and 1980. From 1985, they are included in Crafts & Operators category.
Source: Statistical Yearbook of Japan, 1991.

Table 4.18   Germany: percentage distribution of employment by occupation, 1976–89 (%)

Occupational category	1976	1980	1985	1989
Managerial	3.8	3.2	3.9	4.1
Professional	11.0	11.1	12.6	13.9
Technicians	7.0	7.2	7.8	8.7
Sales	7.6	7.6	7.5	7.8
Clerical	13.1	14.2	12.5	13.7
Crafts & Operators	31.8	32.0	28.3	27.9
Semiskilled service workers	12.5	12.5	15.8	12.3
Semiskilled transport workers	6.3	6.1	5.5	5.5
Farm workers and managers	5.8	4.8	3.9	3.1
Not classifiable	1.1	1.2	2.1	3.0
Total	100	100	100	100

^ signifies that figure is included in the category immediately above.
Source: 1976–89: *Statistisches Bundesamt, Statistisches Jahrbuch*, various issues.

Table 4.19   France: percentage distribution of employment by occupation, 1982–9 (%)

Occupational category	1982	1989
Managerial	7.1	7.5
Professional	4.8	6.0
Technicians	12.3	12.4
Sales	3.3	3.8
Clerical	22.8	24.2
Crafts and operators	30.9	28.1
Semiskilled service workers	6.2	7.2
Semiskilled transport workers	4.6	4.2
Farm workers and managers	8.0	6.6
Not classifiable		
Total	100	100

^ signifies that figure is included in the category immediately above.
Source: 1982: *Enquête sur l'emploi de mars 1982*; 1989: *Enquête sur l'emploi de mars 1989*.

Table 4.20   Great Britain: percentage distribution of employment by occupation, 1961–90 (%)

Occupational category	1961	1971	1981	1990
Managerial	2.7	3.7	5.3	11.0
Professional	8.7	8.6	11.8	21.8
Technicians	^	2.4	2.0	^
Sales	9.7	8.9	8.8	6.6
Clerical	13.3	14.1	14.8	17.3
Crafts and operators	43.1	34.2	27.9	22.4
Semiskilled service workers	11.9	12.7	14.0	12.8
Semiskilled transport workers	6.5	10.0	9.1	5.6
Farm workers and managers	4.0	2.9	2.4	1.6
Not classifiable		2.6	3.8	1.0
Total	100	100	100	100

^ signifies that figure is included in the category immediately above.
Source: Census, 1961, 1971, 1981; 1990: (Spring) *Labour Force Survey 1991*.

Table 4.21   Canada: percentage distribution of employment by occupation, 1950–92 (%)

Occupational category	1950	1970	1980	1985	1992
Managerial	8.4	10.0	7.7	11.4	13.0
Professional	7.0	13.6	15.6	17.1	17.6
Technicians	1.5	^	^	^	^
Sales	6.9	7.1	10.8	9.6	9.9
Clerical	10.6	14.8	17.5	17.3	16.0
Crafts and operators	28.2	29.6	26.0	22.3	21.1
Semiskilled service workers	8.8	12.3	13.1	13.7	13.7
Semiskilled transport workers	6.9	5.3	4.1	3.8	3.5
Farm workers and managers	21.7	7.4	5.3	4.7	5.1
Total	100	100	100	100	100

^ signifies that figure is included in the category immediately above.
1950 figures were taken on March 4 1950; 1980 and 1985 figures are those of January. 1992 figures are those of July.
Source: Statistics Canada, *The Labour Force*, various issues.

Table 4.22 Foreign resident population in Western Europe, 1950–90 (in thousands and as % of total population)

Country	1950		1970		1982ᵃ		1990	
	No.	%	No.	%	No.	%	No.	%
Austria	323	4.7	212	2.8	303	4.0	512	6.6
Belgium	368	4.3	696	7.2	886	9.0	905	9.1
Denmark	—		—		102	2.0	161	3.1
Finland	11	0.3	6	0.1	12	0.3	35	0.9
France	1765	4.1	2621	5.3	3680	6.8	3608	6.4
Germany, Fed. Rep.	568	1.1	2977	4.9	4667	7.6	5242	8.2
Greece	31	0.4	93	1.1	60	0.7	70	0.9
Ireland	—		—		69	2.0	90	2.5
Italy	47	0.1	—		312	0.5	781	1.4
Liechtenstein	3	19.6	7	36.0	9	36.1	—	—
Luxembourg	29	9.9	63	18.4	96	26.4	109	28.0
Netherlands	104	1.1	255	2.0	547	3.9	692	4.6
Norway	16	0.5	—		91	2.2	143	3.4
Portugal	21	0.3	—		64	0.6	108	1.0
Spain	93	0.3	291	0.9	418	1.1	415	1.1
Sweden	124	1.8	411	1.8	406	4.9	484	5.6
Switzerland	285	6.1	1080	17.2	926	14.7	1100	16.3
United Kingdom	—		—		2137	3.9	1875	3.3
Totalᵇ	5100	1.3	10200	2.2	15000	3.1	16600	4.5

ᵃ 1982 is a reference year, rather than 1980 since the data are better for 1982.
ᵇ Includes interpolated figures for the missing (—) data.
Source: Fassman and Münz (1992).

Table 4.23   Unemployment in various countries, 1933–93 (as % of the labour force)

Country	1933	1959–67 average	1982–92 average	1992	1993
Belgium	10.6	2.4	11.3	10.3	12.1
Denmark	14.5	1.4	9.1	11.1	12.1
France	4.5[a]	0.7	9.5	10.4	11.7
Germany	14.8	1.2[b]	7.4	7.7	8.9
Ireland	n.a.	4.6	15.5	17.2	17.6
Italy	5.9	6.2	10.9	10.7	10.2
Netherlands	9.7	0.9	9.8	6.8	8.3
Spain	n.a.	2.3	19.0	18.4	22.7
UK	13.9	1.8	9.7	10.1	10.3
Austria	16.3	1.7	3.5	3.7	4.2
Finland	6.2	1.7	4.8	13.1	18.2
Norway	9.7	2.1	3.2	5.9	6.0
Sweden	7.3	1.3	2.3	5.3	8.2
Switzerland	3.5	0.2	0.7	2.5	4.5
USA	24.7	5.3	7.1	7.4	6.9
Canada	19.3	4.9	9.6	11.3	11.2
Japan	n.a.	1.5	2.5	2.2	2.5
Australia	17.4	2.2	7.8	10.7	10.9

[a] 1936
[b] The Federal Republic for the period 1959–92.
n.a. = not available.
Sources: Freeman and Soete (1994); OECD *Employment Outlook*, 1993.

Table 4.24   Indicators for self-employment and part-time employment, 1990 (%)

	Share of self-employment in total employment		Share of part-time in total employment
	Total economy	Non-agricultural sector	
Canada	9.4	7.5	15.1
France	15.0	9.1	12.0
Germany	11.0	8.0	13.4
Italy	29.1	22.2	5.7
Japan	23.6	11.6	17.6
United Kingdom	14.1	12.4	21.7
United States	10.8	7.7	17.0

Source: OECD *Jobs Study* (1994: 77, table 6.8).

Table 4.25 Percentage of standard workers included in the *Chuki Koyo* system of Japanese firms, according to size of the firm, age of workers and level of education

A. Size of the firm, education of workers and *Chuki Koyo* membership (% calculated on the total of workers in each cell)

	Number of employees		
	>1,000	100–999	10–99
Elementary/new junior high	8.4	4.9	3.9
Old junior high/new high	24.3	11.7	4.8
Professional high/2-year college	14.1	7.2	2.8
University	53.2	35.0	15.7

B. Percentage of workers in firms with over 1,000 employees included in *Chuki Koyo* system, according to their age and education

Education	Age (years)							
	20–24	25–29	30–34	35–39	40–44	45–49	50–54	55–59
Elementary/new junior high	13.1	13.1	27.9	32.5	25.6	17.1	8.4	6.2
Old junior high/new senior high	53.4	50.3	42.9	52.6	41.4	39.1	24.3	14.3
Professional high, 2-year college	50.8	34.1	31.3	37.2	30.9	15.8	14.1	8.6
University	88.9	59.5	57.1	49.9	58.9	53.4	53.2	31.7

Source: Nomura (1994).

Appendix B: Methodological Note and Statistical References for the Analysis of Employment and Occupational Structure of G-7 Countries, 1920–2005

Three sets of statistics have been compiled to illustrate the development of the service and information sectors. Data have been collected for seven countries (Canada, France, Germany, Italy, Japan, the United Kingdom and the United States) beginning from the 1920s up to the most recently available date. The following describes each set of statistics compiled for this exercise.

1 Percentage distribution of employment by industrial sector and intermediate industry group

Employment statistics by industry have been compiled for seven countries. Industries are classified into 6 industrial sectors and 37 intermediate industry groups, according to the classification developed and used by Singelmann (1978). The six industrial sectors are:

I	Extractive
II	Transformative
III	Distributive services
IV	Producer services
V	Social services
VI	Personal services

Within each sector, two to eight intermediate industry groups are included, as shown in table A4.1. Employment statistics with detailed industrial breakdown, from national census or statistical abstracts, have been aggregated and reclassified into these categories.

*This appendix was written by Manuel Castells and Yuko Aoyama.

Classification of industrial sectors and intermediate industry groups

I Extractive	V Social services
Agriculture	Medical, health services
Mining	Hospital
II Transformative	Education
Construction	Welfare, religious services
Utilities	Nonprofit organizations
Manufacturing	Postal service
Food	Government
Textiles	Miscellaneous social
Metal	services
Machinery	VI Personal services
Chemicals	Domestic services
Miscellaneous manufac-	Hotel
turing	Eating, drinking places
III Distributive services	Repair services
Transportation	Laundry
Communication	Barber, beauty shops
Wholesale	Entertainment
Retail	Miscellaneous personal
IV Producer services	services
Banking	
Insurance	
Real estate	
Engineering	
Accounting	
Miscellaneous business	
services	
Legal services	

Source: Singelmann (1978)

Instead of reconstructing the data base from the 1920s, we chose to build upon Singelmann's work by extending his data base beyond 1970. We put the best possible effort into making our classification of industries identical to that used by Singelmann, so that the data base would be comparable in time series.

For the purpose of clarification, table A4.2 shows the industrial breakdown we used in updating the employment distribution by industry. The table lists all detailed industrial categories included in each intermediate industrial group for the seven countries. Any major variations from other countries concerning the classification is noted in each statistical table produced. For all countries, figures that represent annual averages of the number of employed persons (including self-employed, nonsalaried employees) by industry have been used for this analysis.

Note that the sectoral categories (categories I through VI) do not take into account detailed industries which may be included in another sector. For instance, when a country's statistics include eating and drinking places in retail services, but cannot be disaggregated due to the lack of detailed breakdown, the percentage for distributive services (III) becomes overestimated and personal services (VI) becomes underestimated. As a result, proportions for certain industrial sectors may be inflated or deflated.

Also, priority was given to comparability across countries rather than to strict breakdown of detailed industry by our classification. This was done to avoid assigning industries to different categories in each country, which would have disturbed the comparability of the shares of employment in the large categories (I through VI). This was due to the fact that data from some countries combined various sectors and we were unable to disaggregate them. For instance, many countries regarded paper, printing and publishing as one sector, and we have allocated it to miscellaneous manufacturing, although it was theoretically favorable to consider publishing as business services. As a result, we have allocated publishing statistics from all countries under miscellaneous manufacturing, even those countries which provide disaggregated data on publishing, in order to maintain cross-national comparability.

For the same reasons, the following industries are allotted to the following detailed categories.

- products that are made from textile or fabrics, including apparel, shoes and clothing are classified as "miscellaneous manufacturing";
- transport equipment (including automobile, shipbuilding and aerospace industry products) are classified under "miscellaneous manufacturing";
- scientific equipment, including optical, photography, and precision instruments are classified under "miscellaneous manufacturing";
- printing and publishing is classified under "miscellaneous manufacturing";
- depending on the breakdown available in each country, broadcasting (radio and TV) is classified under either "communication" or "entertainment";
- miscellaneous professional and related services may be classified in any miscellaneous services, depending on the country. After

Classification of industries by countries

	Canada	France	Germany	Italy	Japan	United Kingdom	United States
Agriculture	Agriculture, forestry, fishing, trapping	Agriculture, forestry, fisheries	Agriculture, forestry, fisheries, gardening	Agriculture, forestry, fisheries	Agriculture, forestry, fisheries	Agriculture, forestry, fishing	Agriculture, forestry, fisheries
Mining	Mining, quarries oil wells	Solid mineral extraction/coking	Coal mining, ore mining, petroleum/gas extraction	Extraction of combustible solids, liquids	Mining	Coal extraction, solid fuels, electricity/gas	Metal, coal mining, crude petroleum and natural gas extraction
Construction	Construction	Building/civil engineering/agricole	Construction	Construction	Construction	Construction	Construction
Food	Food/beverage, tobacco	Food, meat/milk	Food, beverage, tobacco	Food, beverage, tobacco	Food, beverage, tobacco, feed	Food, drink, tobacco	Food/kindred prods, tobacco manufactures
Textiles	Textiles, knitting mills	Textiles, clothing	Textiles	Textiles	Textiles	Textiles	Textile mill prods
Metal	Primary metal, metal fabricating	Ferrous metals, steel, construction materials, foundry	Foundry, metal, steel	Nonferrous metal, fabricated metal, foundry	Nonferrous metal, fabricated metal, iron/steel	Metal, nonmetallic mineral prods	Primary metal, fabricated metal
Machinery	Machinery, electrical products	Machinery, electric/electronic prods, household appliances	Machinery, electrical, office equipment	Machinery, electrical/electronics machinery	Machinery, electrical/electronic products	Mechanical engineering, data-processing equip., electrical/electronic engineering	Machinery, electrical machinery
Chemical	Chemical petroleum/coal products	Basic chemical/ artificial fibers, pharmaceutical	Chemical/fibers	Chemical	Basic chemical, petroleum/coal prods	Chemical/man-made fibers	Chemical/allied prods, petroleum/coal prods
Miscellaneous manufacturing	Rubber/plastic, leather, clothing, wood, furniture/fixtures, paper, printing/publishing, transp. equipment, nonmetallic mineral products, misc. manufacturing	Automobiles, ship/aerospace/ military equip., apparel, misc. mfg, wood, plastic, glass, paper/printing/ publishing, shoe/leather prods	Stone/clay, rubber, transport equip., aircraft/shipbldg, wood, plastic, glass, paper, printing/publishing, leather, music instr., clothing	Leather, transport equip., clothing/footwear, paper/printing/ publishing, rubber/plastic, misc. mfg	Apparel/other fabric prods, transp. equip., precision instr., misc. mfg, lumber/wood/furni-ture, plastic, rubber, pulp/paper, printing/publishing leather/fur, ceramic/stone/ clay prods	Motor vehicle/parts, other transp. equip., instrument engineering, footwear/clothing, timber/wood furniture/paper/ printing/publishing, rubber/plastics, other mfg	Transportation equip., apparel, prof. photographic equipment/watches, toys/sporting goods, lumber/wood, furniture/fixtures, stone/clay/glass, paper, publishing/ printing, rubber/ plastic, leather, misc. mfg

	Column 1	Column 2	Column 3	Column 4	Column 5	Column 6	Column 7
Utilities	Electric power, gas, water utilities	Electricity production/distrib., gas/water distrib.	Electricity, gas, water supply	Electricity, gas, water	Electricity distr., water/gas/heat supply	Gas/electricity/water	Utilities/sanitary serv.
Transportation	Transportation, storage	Transport	Railways, water transport	Railways, air transport	Railways, road passenger/freight, water/air, other rel. serv., auto. parking	Railways, other inland transport, sea, air transport, supporting serv.	Railroads, bus/urban transit, taxicab trucking, water/air transp., warehousing
Communication	Communications	Telecommunications/postal services	Communications, postal services	Communications	Communication	Communications/postal services	Communications, broadcasting
Wholesale	Wholesale trade	Food wholesale, non-food wholesale	Wholesale	Wholesale	Wholesale, warehousing	Wholesale	Wholesale trade
Retail	Retail trade	Food retail, non-food retail, auto repair/sales	Retail	Retail	Retail	Retail	Retail trade
Banking	Banks, credit agencies, security brokers/dealers	Financial organizations	Financial institutions	Financial institutions, securities	Financing/insurance	Banking/finance	Banking, S&L, credit agencies, security brokerage
Insurance	Insurance carriers/agencies/real estate	Insurance	Insurance	Insurance	Insurance	Insurance, except social security	Insurance
Real estate	n.a.	Real estate rental/finance	Real estate, rental	Real estate	Real estate	Owning/dealing real estate	Real estate, real estate insurance law offices
Engineering	Engineering/scientific services	n.a.	Technical consulting	Technical services	Civil engineering, architecture	n.a.	Engineering/archictectural/survey
Accounting	Accountants	n.a.	n.a.	Accounting	Accounting	Accounting	Accounting/auditing
Misc. business services	Services to business management	Services to enterprises	Legal/accounting/other business services	Other business services, renting	Goods rental/leasing, info. serv./research/advertising, professional serv.	Business services, renting of movables	Advertising, commercial R&D, personnel supply serv., bus. mgmt consulting, computer serv., detective serv., bus. serv.
Legal services	Office of lawyers/notaries	n.a.	n.a.	Legal	Legal services	Legal	Legal serv.

	Canada	France	Germany	Italy	Japan	United Kingdom	United States
Medical, health services	Office of physicians/surgeons, paramedical, dentists, etc.	n.a.	Health/veterinary	Health services, veterinary	Medical/health serv., public health serv.	Medical/other health serv., sanitary serv.	Health serv. except hospitals
Hospital	Hospitals	n.a.	n.a.	Hospitals	Hospitals	n.a.	Hospitals
Education	Education and related services	n.a.	Education, science/research institutions	Education, research, museums, botanical/zoological gardens	Education, science research institutions	Education, research and development	Schools, libraries, vocational schools, educational serv.
Welfare, religious services	Welfare, religious organizations	n.a.	Social serv./employment offices	Religious organizations	Welfare/social insurance, religion	Other serv. incl. social welfare	Religious organizations
Nonprofit organizations	Labor organizations, trade associations	n.a.	Nonprofit organizations	Economic org., professional associations	Co-ops, pol./bus./cultural organizations	n.a.	Membership organizations
Postal service	n.a.	n.a.	n.a..	Postal services	n.a.	n.a.	Postal serv.
Government	Public administration defense	n.a.	Public administration	Public administration, armed forces, international organizations	National gov't serv., local gov't serv., foreign gov'ts/int'l org.	Public administration and defense	Public administration, defense, justice, public order
Misc. social services	Miscellaneous services	n.a.	Trash removal, residential institutions	Other social services	Waste treatment, other services	Other professional/ scientific services	Misc. prof. and related serv.
Domestic services	Private households	n.a.	Private households	Domestic services	Domestic services	n.a.	Private households
Hotel	Hotels/motels lodging houses/residential clubs, camping grounds	Hotels/cafés/ restaurants	Hotels/restaurants	Hotels (with or without restaurants)	Hotels/lodging places	Hotels/catering (restaurants, cafés clubs/canteens)	Hotels/motels, lodging places
Eating drinking places	Restaurants/caterers/ taverns	n.a.	n.a.	Restaurants, camping	Eating/drinking places	Restaurants/cafés/ snack bars	Eating/drinking pl.

Repair services	Repair of shoe, auto, jewelry, electrical appliance	n.a.	Auto/bicycle repair	Repair	Repair services	Repair of consumer goods/vehicles	Auto, electrical, misc. repair
Laundry	Laundries/cleaners/pressor, self-service laundries	n.a.	Laundry/cleaning	Laundry	Laundry	Laundry/dry cleaning	Laundry/cleaning
Barber, beauty shops	Barber/beauty shops	n.a.	Barber/body care businesses	Barber/beauty shops	Barber/beauty shops	Hairdressing/manicure	Beauty shops, barber shops
Entertainment	Amusement/recreational services	n.a.	Culture/sports/entertainment	Entertainment, cinema, broadcasting, sports	Motion pictures, recreation, broadcasting, amusement	Recreation/cultural services	Entertainment, theaters/movies, bowling alleys/billiard/pool places
Misc. personal services	Funeral services misc. personal services	All for-profit personal services	Other personal services	Cemetery administration	Misc. personal services	Personal services	Funeral service/crematories

carefully analyzing the data and finding some further disaggregated data, "other professional services" was classified as "business services" for Japan. For the United States, it is classified as "miscellaneous social services."

In addition, the following specificities should be noted for the countries studied.

Canada

The 1971 figures are based on the census data for persons 15 years and over who worked in 1970. The 1981 figures are based on the 20% sample data from the 1981 census on the labor force 15 years and over. Due to the unavailability of the breakdown of the labor force in detailed industry from the results of the 1991 census as of November 1992, we have used the latest statistics available (May 1992) from Statistics Canada, published in the monthly report, *The Labour Force*. The figures are derived from the sample of about 62,000 representative households across the country (excluding the Yukon and Northwest Territories). The survey has been designed to represent all persons in the population 15 years of age and over residing in the provinces of Canada, with the exception of the following: persons living on Indian reserves; full-time members of the armed forces; and people living in institutions (that is, inmates of penal institutions and patients in hospitals or nursing homes who have resided in the institution for more than six months). The 1992 figures reflect the labor force in May 1992, and have been based on the 1980 Standard Industrial Classification since 1984 (Statistics Canada, 1992).

France

Figures are based on the employed population on December 31 of every year, published in the annual statistical abstract. 1989 figures are preliminary. Problems have been encountered due to the general lack of detailed breakdown of statistics on the service sector employment. Whenever a detailed breakdown of service industries is unavailable, the category "not-for-profit services" is classified as miscellaneous social services, and "for-profit services" is classified as miscellaneous personal services. However, the data from the annual statistical abstract was used instead of the census data since the most recent results currently available to us from the census are those of 1982.

Germany

In this analysis we used the former Federal Republic of Germany prior to unification as a unit of analysis. The figures are based on the census data on the employed for 1970 and 1987. No census was conducted in Germany between these years.

Italy

Figures are based on the census data on labor force in 1971 and 1981; 1990 figures may not be directly comparable to the data in earlier years due to the difference in sources. Since the 1991 census figures are not available at the time of this writing, the 1990 figures have been used as a rough indicator of recent trends.

Japan

Figures are based on the census data from October 1970, 1980 and 1990 on employed persons 15 years of age and over. The 1970 and 1980 figures are that of 20% sample tabulation, and the 1990 figures are that of 1% sample tabulation.

United Kingdom

Figures for England and Wales are used for the years between 1921 and 1971. From 1971 onwards, figures for employees in employment for the entire United Kingdom in June every year are used. These figures are chosen in preference to the census data on employed persons due to the unavailability of 1991 census results at the time of this writing, and the 1971 and 1981 figures available to us do not include the entire United Kingdom. In addition, careful comparisons of the census data on the employed and the Department of Employment data on employees in employment for Great Britain revealed that differences are minor in terms of employment distribution.[126] Thus we have decided that the employees-in-employment figures would serve as a rough estimate of the trends in the United Kingdom between 1970 and 1990. These figures exclude private domestic servants and a small number of employees of agricultural machinery contractors but included seasonal and temporary workers. Family workers are included in the figures for Great Britain but not for Northern Ireland. The figures on the employees in employment also excludes the self-employed. The figures are from censuses of employment conducted in Great Britain by the Department of Employment and for the United Kingdom include information from similar censuses conducted in Northern Ireland by the Department of Manpower Services.

---

[126] There is a tendency, however, for share of agricultural employment to be estimated lower than that of the entire employed population, as shown in table 4.16.

United States

The detailed breakdown of employment from the current population survey for 1970 was not published in the *Employment and Earnings* issues. Thus we have substituted the 1970 data with that of the census, since the intercensal statistics provided by the current population survey are, in general, designed to be comparable with the decennial statistics (see p. VII of 1970 census, volume 2: 7B, Subject Reports: Industrial Characteristics). The US figures are based on all civilians who, during the survey week, did any work at all as paid employees, in their own business, profession, or on their own farm, or who worked 15 hours or more as unpaid workers in an enterprise operated by a member of a family; and all those who were not working but who had jobs or businesses from which they were temporarily absent because of illness, bad weather, vacation, labor–management disputes, or personal reasons, whether they were paid for the time off or were working in other jobs. Members of the armed forces stationed in the United States are also included in the employed total. Each employed person is counted only once. Those who held more than one job are counted in the job at which they worked the greatest number of hours during the survey week. Included in the total are employed citizens of foreign countries who are temporarily in the United States but not living on the premises of an embassy. Excluded are persons whose only activity consisted of work around the house (painting, repairing, or own-home housework) or volunteer work for religious, charitable, and similar organizations (Department of Labor Statistics 1992). Due to the reclassification of the SIC codes for the 1980 census, figures before and after that date may not be strictly comparable.

Employment statistics by industry

Hall proposes two ways of dividing employment sectors: industry versus services, and goods handling versus information handling (Hall 1988). "Industry" includes all mining, construction and manufacturing sectors, and "services"' includes all remaining categories. "Goods handling" sector includes mining, construction, manufacturing, transportation, wholesale/retail trade, and "Information handling" sector includes communications, finance, insurance and real estate (FIRE), all remaining services and government.

In our analysis, employment statistics with Singelmann's classification has been aggregated and reorganized to fit into Hall's classification.[127] Further, the ratio between services and industry

---

[127]   In order to comply with the standard classification of services, eating and drinking places are included in retail trade.

employment, as well as the ratio between information handling and goods handling employment have been derived from the data used in tables 4.10 through 4.17.

Employment by occupations

Standard occupational classifications of most countries habitually confuse sectoral activities with skill levels, and thus are unfavorable for our use. However, after careful consideration based on the available data from the countries, it became clear that a reconfiguration of occupational classifications would be a major project by itself. Since our primary purpose in this appendix excludes such analysis, we decided to use the existing classification as a rough indicator for the occupational breakdown of these countries. As a result, the following rough breakdown of occupations has been determined:

- managerial;
- professional;
- technicians;
- sales;
- clerical;
- crafts and operators;
- semiskilled service workers;
- semiskilled transport workers;
- farm workers and managers.

For most countries, it was impossible to separate professional and technician categories. Also, in some countries, craft workers and operators are mixed, thus we have collapsed these categories into one in order to avoid misleading conclusions from the data. The same applies to the collapse of farm workers and farm managers into one category. "Crafts and operators" also includes laborers, handlers and miners. Those categorized as service workers have been included in semiskilled service workers.

The specificity for each country is described as follows:

Canada

Figures are based on the occupational classification of the employed. Professional and technician categories also include those whose professions are in natural science, social science, teaching, medicine/health and artistic/recreational. Crafts and operators category also included mining/quarrying, machining, processing, construction trades, materials handling, and other crafts/equipment operating. Farm workers and managers also includes agriculture, fishing/hunting/trapping and forestry/logging.

France

Figures are based on the occupational classification of the population aged 15 years and over, excluding unemployed, retired, students, and others who have never worked, according to employment surveys, the results of which are included in the statistical abstract. Managerial category also includes high-level public officials and high-level administrative/commercial workers in business enterprises. Professional category includes professors/scientific occupations, information/art and engineers/technical workers. Technicians includes intermediate professions, workers in religion, and social/health mid-level workers. Clerical category includes civil servants and administrative workers. Crafts and operators category includes qualified and unqualified workers in industries.

Germany

Figures are based on the occupational classification of the employed persons, according to the statistical abstract. Managerial category includes accountants, public officials and entrepreneurs. Professional category includes engineers, scientists, artists, and health service workers. Crafts and operators includes most industrial workers. Technicians includes social workers. Farm workers and managers category includes workers in forestry and fisheries.

Japan

Figures are based on the occupational classification of employed persons, according to Labour Force Survey, the results of which are included in the statistical abstract. Farm workers and managers includes workers in forestry and fisheries. Semiskilled service workers category also includes protective service workers. Semiskilled transport workers includes communications occupations.

United Kingdom

Figures are based on the 10% sample of Great Britain, derived from the censuses. Professional category includes judges, economists, environmental health officers, etc. Technicians includes estimators, welfare occupations, medical technicians, draughtsmen, foremen, tracers, supervisors of tracers, and technician engineers. Crafts and operators includes most industrial workers. Semiskilled transport workers includes warehousemen/storekeepers/packers/bottlers.

Semiskilled service workers includes sport/recreation workers and protective services. The 1990 figures are based on the Labour Force Survey (1990 and 1991) conducted by the Office of Censuses and Surveys. The 1990 figures are not directly comparable to previous years due to the different survey methodology and categories employed. However, since the 1991 census data are not available at the time of this writing, these 1990 figures provide a rough estimate of current employment structure in Great Britain.

United States

Figures are based on the annual averages of employed persons according to the household survey, conducted as part of the Current Population Survey by the Bureau of the Census for the Department of Labor. Managerial category includes executive and administrative occupations. Clerical category includes administrative support. Semiskilled service worker category includes private household and protective services. Crafts and operators category includes precision production, repair, machine operators/assemblers/inspectors, handlers, equipment cleaners, helpers and laborers. Semiskilled transport workers includes material-moving occupations. Farm workers and managers includes forestry and fishing.

Distribution of employment status

The status of the employed persons are broadly categorized as employees, self-employed and family workers. When figures for family workers are not available, they may be included within the self-employed categories. Self-employed generally include employers, unless otherwise noted.

The following lists the specificity for each country.

Canada

Those employers who are paid workers (rather than the self-employed) are included in the employees category.

France

Figures are based on civilian employment, indicated in OECD Labour Force Statistics.

Germany

Figures are based on the annual statistical abstract.

Italy

Figures are based on civilian employment, indicated in OECD Labour Force Statistics.

Japan

Figures are based on the Labour Force Survey on employed persons, included in the annual statistical abstract.

United Kingdom

Figures are based on civilian employment, indicated in OECD Labour Force Statistics.

United States

Figures are based on the annual averages of employed civilians in agriculture and nonagricultural industries.

Statistical references

Canada

Statistics Canada. *1971 Census of Canada*, vol. 3: *Economic Characteristics*, 1973.
———*1981 Census of Canada: Population, Labor Force – Industry by demographic and educational characteristics; Canada, provinces, urban, rural, nonfarm and rural farm*, January 1984.
———*The Labour Force*, various issues.
———*Labour Force: Annual Averages, 1975–1983*, January 1984

France

Institut national de la statistique et des études économiques (INSEE). *Annuaire statistique de la France 1979: résultats de 1978*, Ministère de l'économie, des finances et du budget, Paris: INSEE, 1979.
———*Recensement général de la population de 1982: résultats définitifs*, par Pierre-Alain Audirac, no. 483 des Collections de l'INSEE, série D, no. 103, Ministère de l'économie, des finances et du budget, Paris: INSEE, 1985
———*Enquêtes sur l'emploi de 1982 et 1983: résultats redressés*, no. 120, February 1985.
———*Enquêtes sur l'emploi de mars 1989: résultats détaillés*, no. 28–29, October 1989.
———*Annuaire statistique de la France 1990: résultats de 1989*, vol. 95, nouvelle série no. 37, Ministère de l'économie, des finances et du budget, Paris: INSEE, 1990.

Germany

Statistisches Bundesamt. *Statistisches Jahrbuch 1977: für die Bundesrepublik Deutschland*, Metzler-Poeschel Verlag Stuttgart, 1977
——*Statistisches Jahrbuch 1991: für die Bundesrepublik Deutschland*, Metzler-Poeschel Verlag Stuttgart, 1991.
——*Bevölkerung und Kultur: Volkszählung vom 27. Mai 1970*, Heft 17, Erwerbstätige in wirtschaftlicher Gliederung nach Wochenarbeitszeit und weiterer Tätigkeit, Fachserie A, Stuttgart and Mainz: Verlag W. Kohlhammer.
——*Volkszählung vom 25 Mai 1987*, Bevölkerung und Erwerbstätigkeit, Stuttgart: Metzler-Poeschel, 1989.

Italy

Istituto Centrale di Statistica. *10° Censimento Generale della Popolazione, 15 Ottobre 1961, Vol. IX: Dati Generali Riassuntivi*, Rome, 1969.
——*11° Censimento Generale della Popolazione, 24 Ottobre, 1971*, vol. VI: *Professioni e Attività Economiche*, Tomo 1: *Attività Economiche*, Rome, 1975.
——*12° Censimento Generale della Popolazione, 25 Ottobre, 1981*, vol. II: *Dati sulle caratteristiche strutturali della popolazione e delle abitazioni*, Tomo 3: *Italia*, Rome, 1985.
Istituto Nazionale di Statistica (ISTAT). *Annuario Statistico Italiano*, edizione 1991.

Japan

Statistics Bureau, Management and Coordination Agency (1977) *Japan Statistical Yearbook*, Tokyo.
——(1983) *Japan Statistical Yearbook*, Tokyo.
——(1991) *Japan Statistical Yearbook*, Tokyo.
Bureau of Statistics, Office of the Prime Minister. *Summary of the Results of 1970 Population Census of Japan*, Tokyo: Bureau of Statistics, 1975
——*1980 Population Census of Japan*, Tokyo: Bureau of Statistics, 1980.
——*1990 Population Census of Japan*, Prompt report (results of 1% sample tabulation), Tokyo: Bureau of Statistics, 1990.

United Kingdom

Office of Population Censuses and Surveys, General Registrar Office. *Census 1971: Great Britain, Economic Activity*, Part IV (10% Sample), London: HMSO, 1974.
——*Census 1981: Economic Activity, Great Britain*, London: HMSO, 1984.

——*Labour Force Survey 1990 and 1991: A survey conducted by OPCS and the Department of Economic Development in Northern Ireland on behalf of the Employment Department and the European Community*, Series LFS no. 9, London: HMSO, 1992.

Central Statistical Office. *Annual Abstract of Statistics: 1977*, London: HMSO, 1977.

——*Annual Abstract of Statistics: 1985*, London: HMSO, 1985.

——*Annual Abstract of Statistics: 1992*, no. 128, London: HMSO, 1992.

Department of Employment. *Employment Gazette* vol. 100, no. 8 (August 1992).

United States

United States Department of Labor. *Handbook of Labor Statistics*, Bulletin 2175, Bureau of Labor Statistics, December.

——*Labor Force Statistics: Derived from the current population survey, 1948–87*, Bureau of Labor Statistics, August 1988.

——*Handbook of Labor Statistics*, Bulletin 2340, Bureau of Labor Statistics, March, 1990.

——*Employment and Earnings*, various issues.

Other

Eurostat. *Labour Force Sample Survey*, Luxembourg: Eurostat, various issues.

——*Labour Force Survey*, Theme 3, Series C, *Population and Social Statistics, Accounts, Surveys and Statistics*, Luxembourg: Eurostat, various issues.

Hall, Peter (1988) "Regions in the Transition to the Information Economy," in G. Sternlieb and J.W. Hughes (eds), *America's New Market Geography: Nation, region and metropolis*, Rutgers, N.J.: State University of New Jersey, Center for Urban Policy Research, New Brunswick, pp. 137–59.

Mori, K. (1989) *Hai-teku shakai to rōdō: naniga okite iruka*, Iwanami Shinsho no. 70, Tokyo: Iwanami Shoten.

Organization for Economic Cooperation and Development (OECD) (1991) *OECD Labour Force Statistics: 1969–1989*, Paris: OECD.

——(1992a) *OECD Economic Outlook: Historical Statistics: 1960–90*, Paris: OECD.

——(1992b) *OECD Economic Outlook*, no. 51, June.

— 5 —

The Culture of Real Virtuality: The Integration of Electronic Communication, the End of the Mass Audience, and the Rise of Interactive Networks

Introduction

Around 700BC a major invention took place in Greece: the alphabet. This conceptual technology, it has been argued by leading classics scholars such as Havelock, was the foundation for the development of Western philosophy and science as we know it today. It made it possible to bridge the gap from spoken tongue to language, thus separating the spoken from the speaker, and making possible conceptual discourse. This historical turning point was prepared for by about 3,000 years of evolution in oral tradition and nonalphabetic communication, until Greek society reached what Havelock calls a new state of mind, "the alphabetic mind," that prompted the qualitative transformation of human communication.[1] Widespread literacy did not occur until many centuries later, after the invention and diffusion of the printing press and the manufacturing of paper. Yet it was the alphabet that, in the West, provided the mental infrastructure for cumulative, knowledge-based communication.

However, the new alphabetic order, while allowing rational discourse, separated written communication from the audiovisual system of symbols and perceptions, so critical for the full-fledged expression of the human mind. By implicitly and explicitly establishing a social hierarchy between literate culture and audiovisual expression, the price paid for the foundation of human practice in the written discourse was to relegate the world of sounds and images

---

[1] Havelock (1982: esp. 6–7).

to the backstage of the arts, dealing with the private domain of emotions and with the public world of liturgy. Of course, audiovisual culture took an historical revenge in the twentieth century, first with film and radio, then with television, overwhelming the influence of written communication in the hearts and souls of most people. Indeed, this tension between noble, alphabetic communication and sensorial, nonreflective communication underlies the intellectuals' frustration against the influence of television that still dominates the social critique of mass media.[2]

A technological transformation of similar historic dimensions is taking place 2,700 years later, namely the integration of various modes of communication into an interactive network. Or, in other words, the formation of a Super-Text and a Meta-Language that, for the first time in history, integrates into the same system the written, oral, and audio-visual modalities of human communication. The human spirit reunites its dimensions in a new interaction between the two sides of the brain, machines, and social contexts. For all the science fiction ideology and commercial hype surrounding the emergence of the so-called Information Superhighway, we can hardly underestimate its significance.[3] The potential integration of text, images, and sounds in the same system, interacting from multiple points, in chosen time (real or delayed) along a global network, in conditions of open and affordable access, does fundamentally change the character of communication. And communication decisively shapes culture, because as Postman writes "we do not see . . . reality . . . as 'it' is, but as our languages are. And our languages are our media. Our media are our metaphors. Our metaphors create the content of our culture."[4] Because culture is mediated and enacted through communication, cultures themselves, that is our historically produced systems of beliefs and codes, become fundamentally transformed, and will be more so over time, by the new technological system. At the moment of this writing, such a new system is not fully in place, and its development will occur at uneven pace and with uneven geography in the coming years. Yet it is a certainty that it will develop and embrace at least the dominant activities and the core segments of the population in the whole planet. Furthermore, it already exists in bits and pieces, in the new media system, in the rapidly changing telecommunications

[2]   For a critical presentation of these ideas, see Postman (1985).
[3]   For a documented exposition of the data on the Information Superhighway, as of end of 1994, see Sullivan-Trainor (1994). For an overview of social and economic trends in news media and computer-mediated communication at the international level, see the informed, special supplement of the Spanish news-paper *El Pais/World Media*, "*Habla el Futuro*," March 9 1995.
[4]   Postman (1985: 15).

systems, in the networks of interaction already formed around Internet, in the imagination of people, in the policies of governments, and on the drawing boards of corporate offices. The emergence of a new electronic communication system characterized by its global reach, its integration of all communication media, and its potential interactivity is changing and will change forever our culture. However, the issue arises of the actual conditions, characteristics, and effects of such change. Given the still embryonic development of an otherwise clearly identified trend, how can we assess its potential impact without falling into the excesses of futurology from which this book tries to depart sharply? On the other hand, without analyzing the transformation of cultures under the new electronic communication system, the overall analysis of the information society would be fundamentally flawed. Fortunately, while there is technological discontinuity, there is in history a great deal of social continuity that allows analysis of tendencies on the basis of the observation of trends that have prepared the formation of the new system over the last two decades. Indeed, one of the major components of the new communication system, the mass media of communication, structured around television, have been studied in minute detail.[5] Their evolution towards globalization and decentralization was foreseen in the early 1960s by McLuhan, the great visionary who revolutionized thinking in communications in spite of his unrestrained use of hyperbole.[6] In this chapter I shall first retrace the formation of the mass media, and their interplay with culture and social behavior. Then I shall assess their transformation during the 1980s, with the emergence of decentralized and diversified "new media" that prepared the formation of a multimedia system in the 1990s. I shall later turn my attention to a different system of communication, organized around computer networking, with the emergence of Internet and the surprising, spontaneous development of new kinds of virtual communities. While this is a relatively new phenomenon, we have enough empirical observations, both from France and from the United States, to formulate some hypotheses on reasonable grounds. Finally, I shall try to bring together what we know about the two systems to speculate on the social dimension of their coming merger, and the impact of such a merger on the processes of communication and cultural expression. I argue that through the powerful influence of the new communication system, mediated by social interests, government policies, and business strategies, a new culture is emerging: the *culture of real*

[5]   See the evolution of media research synthesized in Williams et al. (1988).
[6]   For a retrospective of McLuhan's theories, see his posthumous book: McLuhan and Powers (1989).

virtuality, whose content, dynamics, and significance will be presented and analyzed in the following pages.

From the Gutenberg Galaxy to the McLuhan Galaxy: the Rise of Mass Media Culture

The diffusion of television in the three decades following World War II (in different times and with variable intensity depending on countries) created a new Galaxy of communication, if I may use the McLuhanian terminology.[7] Not that other media disappeared, but they were restructured and reorganized in a system whose heart was made of vacuum tubes and whose appealing face was a television screen.[8] Radio lost its centrality but won in pervasiveness and flexibility, adapting modes and themes to the rhythm of people's everyday lives. Films transformed themselves to fit television audiences, with the exceptions of government subsidized art and of special-effects shows on large screens. Newspapers and magazines specialized in deepening their content or targeting their audience, while being attentive to providing strategic information to the dominant TV medium.[9] As for books, they remained books, although the unconscious desire behind many books was to become a TV script; the best sellers' lists soon became filled with titles referring to TV characters or to TV-popularized themes.

Why television became such a prevailing communication mode is still the object of raging debate among scholars and media critics.[10] W. Russell Neuman's hypothesis, which I would rephrase as being the consequence of the basic instinct of a lazy audience, seems to be a plausible explanation in regard to available evidence. In his own words: "The key finding from the realm of research on educational and advertising effects that must be dealt with candidly if we are to understand the nature of low-salience learning in regard to politics and culture is simply that people are attracted to the path of least resistance."[11] He grounds his interpretation in the broader psychological theories by Herbert Simon and Anthony Downs, emphasizing the psychological costs of obtaining and processing information. I would be inclined to place the roots of such logic not in human nature, but in the conditions of home life after long days of strenuous

---

[7]　McLuhan (1964).
[8]　Ball-Rokeach and Cantor (eds) (1986).
[9]　Postman (1985).
[10]　Ferguson (ed.) (1986); Withey and Abeles (eds) (1980).
[11]　Neuman (1991: 103).

work, and in the lack of alternatives for personal/cultural involvement.[12] Yet social conditions in our societies being as they are, the minimum-effort syndrome that seems to be associated with TV-mediated communication could explain the rapidity and pervasiveness of its dominance as a communication medium as soon as it appeared on the historical scene. For instance, according to media studies, [13] only a small proportion of people choose in advance the program they will view. In general, the first decision is to watch television, then programs are scanned until the most attractive is selected or, more often, the least boring.

The TV-dominated system could be easily characterized as mass media.[14] A similar message was simultaneously emitted from a few centralized senders to an audience of millions of receivers. Thus, the content and format of messages were tailored to the lowest common denominator. In the case of private TV, predominant in the original TV country, the US, it was the lowest common denominator of the audience as evaluated by marketing experts. For most of the world, dominated by government television until at least the 1980s, the standard was the lowest common denominator in the minds of bureaucrats in control of broadcasting, although increasingly audience ratings played a role. In both cases, the audience was seen as largely homogeneous, or susceptible to being made homogeneous.[15] The notion of mass culture, arising from mass society, was a direct expression of the media system resulting from the control of new electronic communication technology by governments and corporate oligopolies.[16]

What was fundamentally new in television? The novelty was not so much its centralizing power and its potential as a propaganda instrument. After all, Hitler showed how radio could be a formidable instrument of resonance for one-way single-purpose messages. What TV represented, first of all, was the end of the Gutenberg Galaxy, that is of a system of communication essentially dominated by the typographic mind and the phonetic alphabet order.[17] For all his critics (generally turned off by the obscurity of his mosaic language) Marshall McLuhan struck a universal chord when, in all simplicity, he declared that the "medium is the message":

[12]   Mattelart and Stourdze (1982); Trejo Delarbre (1992).
[13]   Neuman (1991).
[14]   Blumler and Katz (eds) (1974).
[15]   Botein and Rice (eds) (1980).
[16]   Neuman (1991).
[17]   McLuhan (1962).

The mode of TV image has nothing in common with film or photo, except that it offers also a nonverbal gestalt or posture of forms. With TV, the viewer is the screen. He is bombarded with light impulses that James Joyce called "The Charge of the Light Brigade"... The TV image is not a still shot. It is not a photo in any sense, but a ceaselessly forming contour of things limned by the scanning-finger. The resulting plastic contour appears by light through, not light on, and the image so formed has the quality of sculptures and icon, rather than a picture. The TV image offers some three million dots per second to the receiver. From these he accepts only a few dozen each instant, from which to make an image.[18]

Because of the low definition of TV, McLuhan argued, viewers have to fill in the gaps in the image, thus becoming more emotionally involved in the viewing (what he, paradoxically, characterized as a "cool medium"). Such involvement does not contradict the hypothesis of the least effort, because TV appeals to the associative/lyrical mind, not involving the psychological effort of information retrieving and analyzing to which Herbert Simon's theory refers. This is why Neil Postman, a leading media scholar, considers that television represents an historical rupture with the typographic mind. While print favors systematic exposition, TV is best suited to casual conversation. To make the distinction sharply, in his own words:

Typography has the strongest possible bias towards exposition: a sophisticated ability to think conceptually, deductively and sequentially; a high valuation of reason and order; an abhorrence of contradiction; a large capacity for detachment and objectivity; and a tolerance for delayed response.[19]

While for television, "entertainment is the supra-ideology of all discourse on television. No matter what is depicted or from what point of view, the overarching presumption is that it is there for our amusement and pleasure."[20] Beyond the discrepancies in the social/political implications of this analysis, from McLuhan's belief about the universal communitarian potential of television to the Luddite attitudes of Jerry Mander[21] and some of the critics of mass culture,[22] the diagnoses converge toward two fundamental points: a few years after

---

[18] McLuhan (1964: 313).
[19] Postman (1985: 87).
[20] Ibid.
[21] Mander (1978).
[22] Mankiewicz and Swerdlow (eds) (1979).

its development television became the cultural epicenter of our societies;[23] and the television modality of communication is a fundamentally new medium, characterized by its seductiveness, its sensorial simulation of reality, and its easy communicability along the lines of least psychological effort.

Led by television, there has been in the last three decades a communication explosion throughout the world.[24] In the most TV-oriented country, the United States, in the late 1980s TV presented 3,600 images per minute per channel. According to the Nielsen Report the average American home had the TV set on for about seven hours a day, and actual viewing was estimated at 4.5 daily hours per adult. To this had to be added radio, which offered 100 words per minute and was listened to an average of two hours a day, mainly in the car. An average daily newspaper offered 150,000 words, and it was estimated to take between 18 and 49 minutes of daily reading time, while magazines were browsed over for about 6 to 30 minutes, and book reading, including schoolwork-related books, took about 18 minutes per day.[25] Media exposure is cumulative. According to some studies, US homes with cable TV watch more network TV than homes without cable. All in all, the average adult American uses 6.43 hours a day in media attention.[26] This figure can be contrasted (although in rigor it is not comparable) to other data that give the number of 14 minutes per day and per person for interpersonal interaction in the household.[27] In Japan in 1992, the weekly average of television watching time per household was 8 hours and 17 minutes per day, up by 25 minutes from 1980.[28] Other countries seem to be less intensive consumers of media: for example, in the late 1980s French adults watched TV only about three hours a day.[29] Still, the predominant pattern of behavior around the world seems to be that in urban societies media consumption is the second largest category of activity behind work, and certainly the predominant activity at home.[30] This observation must however be qualified to truly understand the role of media in our culture: media watching/listening is by no means an exclusive activity. It is generally mixed with the performance of home tasks, with shared meals, with social interaction. It is the almost constant background presence, the

[23] See Williams (1974); and Martin and Chaudhary (eds) (1983).
[24] Williams (1982).
[25] Data from various sources, reported by Neuman (1991).
[26] Data reported by Sabbah (1985); Neuman (1991).
[27] Sabbah (1985).
[28] Dentsu Institute for Human Studies/DataFlow International (1994: 67).
[29] Neuman (1991); for Japan, see Sato et al. (1995).
[30] Sorlin (1994).

fabric of our lives. We live with the media and by the media. McLuhan used the expression of technological media as staples or natural resources.[31] Rather, the media, particularly radio and television, have become the audiovisual environment with which we interact endlessly and automatically. Very often television, above all, is a presence in the home. A precious feature in a society where increasing numbers of people live alone: in the 1990s, 25% of American households were formed by one single person. Although the situation is not so extreme in other societies, the trend towards decreasing size of households is similar in Europe.

This pervasive, powerful presence of such subliminally provoking messages of sounds and images could be assumed to produce dramatic impacts on social behavior. Yet most available research points to the opposite conclusion. After reviewing the literature, W. Russell Neumann concludes that

> the accumulated findings from five decades of systematic social science research reveal that mass media audience, youthful or otherwise, is not helpless, and the media are not all-powerful. The evolving theory of modest and conditional media effects helps to put in perspective the historical cycle of moral panic over new media.[32]

Furthermore, the barrage of advertising messages received through the media seems to have limited effect. According to Draper,[33] although in the US the average person is exposed to 1,600 advertising messages per day, people respond (and not necessarily positively) to only about 12 of them. Indeed, McGuire,[34] after reviewing accumulated evidence on the effects of media advertising, concluded that there is no substantial evidence of specific impacts by media advertising on actual behavior, an ironic conclusion for an industry that spent at that time US$50 billion a year. Why, then, do companies keep insisting on advertising? For one thing, companies pass on the cost of advertising to consumers: according to *The Economist* in 1993, "free TV" in the US cost every American household $30 per month. Yet a substantive answer to such an important question requires that we first analyze the mechanisms through which television and other media influence behavior.

---

[31]   McLuhan (1964: 21).
[32]   Neuman (1991: 87).
[33]   Roger Draper, "The Faithless Shepard," *New York Review of Books*, June 26, reported by Neuman (1991).
[34]   McGuire (1986).

The key issue is that while mass media are a one-way communication system, the actual process of communication is not, but depends on the interaction between the sender and the receiver in the interpretation of the message. Umberto Eco provided an insightful perspective to interpret media effects in his 1977 seminal paper titled "Does the Audience have Bad Effects on Television?" As Eco wrote:

> There exist, depending on sociocultural circumstances, a variety of codes, or rather of rules of competence and interpretation. The message has a signifying form that can be filled with different meanings . . . So the suspicion grew that the sender organized the televisual image on the basis of his own codes, which coincided with those of the dominant ideology, while the addressees filled it with "aberrant" meanings according to their particular cultural codes.[35]

The consequence of this analysis is that

> One thing we do know is that there doesn't exist a Mass Culture in the sense imagined by the apocalyptic critics of mass communications because this model competes with others (constituted by historical vestiges, class culture, aspects of high culture transmitted through education etc.).[36]

While historians and empirical researchers of the media would find this statement pure common sense, in fact, taking it seriously, as I do, it decisively undermines a fundamental aspect of critical social theory from Marcuse to Habermas. It is one of the ironies of intellectual history that it is precisely those thinkers who advocate social change who often view people as passive receptacles of ideological manipulation, in fact precluding the notions of social movements and social change except under the mode of exceptional, singular events generated outside the social system. If people have some level of autonomy in organizing and deciding their behavior, the messages sent through the media should interact with their receivers, and thus the notion of mass media refers to a technological system, not to a form of culture, the mass culture. Indeed, some experiments in psychology found that even if TV presents 3,600 images per minute per channel, the brain responds consciously to only one sensory stimulus among each million stimuli being sent.[37]

Yet to emphasize the autonomy of human mind and of individual cultural systems in filling in the actual meaning of the messages

[35]   Eco (1977: 90).
[36]   Ibid.: 98.
[37]   Neuman (1991: 91).

received does not imply that the media are neutral institutions, or that their effects are negligible. What empirical studies show is that the media are not independent variables in inducing behavior. Their messages, explicit or subliminal, are worked out, processed by individuals placed in specific social contexts, thus modifying what was the intended effect of the message. But the media, and particularly audiovisual media in our culture, are indeed the basic material of communication processes. We live in a media environment, and most of our symbolic stimuli come from the media. Furthermore, as Cecilia Tichi has shown in her wonderful book *The Electronic Hearth*,[38] the diffusion of television took place in a television environment, that is a culture in which objects and symbols are referred to television, from the shapes of home furniture to acting styles and themes of conversation. The real power of television, as Eco and Postman have also argued, is that it sets the stage for all processes that intend to be communicated to society at large, from politics to business, including sports and art. Television frames the language of societal communication. If advertisers keep spending billions in spite of reasonable doubts about the actual direct impact of advertising on their sales, it may be because an absence of television usually means conceding name recognition in the mass market to those competitors who do advertise. While the effects of television on political choices is highly diverse, politics and politicians that are not on television in advanced societies simply do not stand a chance of obtaining people's support, since people's minds are informed fundamentally by the media, with television being foremost among such media.[39] The social impact of television works in the binary mode: to be or not to be. Once a message is on television, it can be changed, transformed, or even subverted. But in a society organized around mass media, the existence of messages that are outside the media is restricted to interpersonal networks, thus disappearing from the collective mind. However, the price to be paid for a message to be on television is not just money or power. It is to accept being mixed in a multisemantic text whose syntax is extremely lax. Thus, information and entertainment, education and propaganda, relaxation and hypnosis are all blurred in the language of television. Because the context of the viewing is controllable and familiar to the receiver, all messages are absorbed into the reassuring mode of the home or quasi-home situations (for instance, sports bars as one of the few real extended families left . . .).

This normalization of messages, where atrocious images of real war.

---

[38]   Tichi (1991).
[39]   Lichtenberg (ed.) (1990).

can almost be absorbed as part of action movies, does have a fundamental impact: the leveling of all content into each person's frame of images. Thus, because they are the symbolic fabric of our life, the media tend to work on consciousness and behavior as real experience works on dreams, providing the raw material out of which our brain works. It is as if the world of visual dreams (the information/entertainment provided by television) would give back to our consciousness the power to select, recombine, and interpret the images and sounds that we have generated through our collective practices or by our individual preferences. It is a system of feedbacks between distorting mirrors: the media are the expression of our culture, and our culture works primarily through the materials provided by the media. In this fundamental sense, the mass media system fulfilled most of the features suggested by McLuhan in the early 1960s: it was the McLuhan Galaxy.[40] Yet the fact that the audience is not a passive object but an interactive subject opened the way to its differentiation, and to the subsequent transformation of the media from mass communication to segmentation, customization and individualization, from the moment technology, corporations, and institutions allowed such moves.

The New Media and the Diversification of Mass Audience

During the 1980s new technologies transformed the world of media.[41] Newspapers were written, edited and printed at distance, allowing for simultaneous editions of the same newspaper tailored to several major areas (for example, *Le Figaro* in several French cities; *The New York Times* in parallel East Coast/West Coast editions; *International Herald Tribune*, printed daily in several locations in three continents, and so on). Walkman devices made personally selected music a portable audio environment, allowing people, particularly teenagers, to build

[40] I label the mass media electronic communication system the McLuhan Galaxy in homage to the revolutionary thinker who visualized its existence as a distinctive mode of cognitive expression. It should be emphasized, however, that we are entering a new communication system, clearly distinct from the one McLuhan envisaged, as this chapter tries to argue.

[41] This section relies partly on the information and ideas on new developments in the media worldwide provided by Manuel Campo Vidal, leading television journalist in Spain and Latin America, vice-president of Antena-3 Television: see Campo Vidal (1996). For projections on these trends elaborated in the academic world during the 1980s, see also Rogers (1986). For a visionary analysis of media diversification in a historical perspective, I recall De Sola Pool (1983).

walls of sounds against the outside world. Radio became increasingly specialized, with thematic and subthematic stations (such as 24-hour easy-listening music or exclusive dedication to a singer or pop group for several months until the new hit comes in). Radio's hosted talk-shows filled the time of commuters and flexible workers. VCRs exploded all over the world and became in many developing countries a major alternative to boring, official television broadcasting.[42] Although the multiplicity of potential uses of VCRs were not fully exploited, because of lack of consumers' technological skills, and because of rapid commercialization of its use by video rental stores, their diffusion provided a great deal of flexibility to the use of visual media. Films survived in the form of video-cassettes. Music video, accounting for over 25% of total video production, became a new cultural form that shaped the images of a whole generation of youth, and actually changed the music industry. The ability to record TV programs and watch them at selected times changed the habits of TV audiences and reinforced their selective viewing, counteracting the pattern of least resistance that I discussed above. On the basis of VCRs, any future diversification of television offerings was amplified in its effects by the second-step choice of the recording audience, further segmenting it.

People started to tape their own events, from vacation to family celebrations, thus producing their own images beyond the photo album. For all the limits of this self-production of images, it actually modified the one-way flow of images and reintegrated life experience and the screen. In many countries, from Andalusia to Southern India, local community video technology allowed for the blossoming of rudimentary local broadcasting that mixed diffusion of video films with local events and announcements, often on the fringes of communications regulations.

But the decisive move was the multiplication of television channels, leading to their increasing diversification.[43] Development of cable television technologies, to be fostered in the 1990s by fiber optics and digitization, and of direct satellite broadcasting dramatically expanded the spectrum of transmission and put pressure on the authorities to deregulate communications in general and television in particular. It followed an explosion of cable television programming in the United States and of satellite television in Europe, Asia, and Latin America. Soon, new networks were formed that came to challenge the established ones, and in Europe governments lost

[42] Alvarado (ed.) (1988).
[43] Doyle (1992); Dentsu Institute for Human Studies/DataFlow International (1994).

control of much of television. In the US the number of independent TV stations grew during the 1980s from 62 to 330. Cable systems in major metropolitan areas feature up to 60 channels, mixing network TV, independent stations, cable networks, most of them specialized, and pay TV. In the countries of the European Union, the number of TV networks increased from 40 in 1980 to 150 by the mid-1990s, one-third of them being satellite broadcasted. In Japan, the NHK public network has two terrestrial networks and two specialized satellite services; in addition there are five commercial networks. From 1980 to the mid-1990s, the number of satellite-TV stations grew from 0 to 300.

According to UNESCO, in 1992 there were over 1 billion TV sets in the world (35% of which were in Europe, 32% in Asia, 20% in North America, 8% in Latin America, 4% in the Middle East, and 1% in Africa). Ownership of TV sets was expected to grow at 5% per year up to the year 2000, with Asia leading the charge. The impact of such a proliferation of television offerings on the audience was deep in all contexts. In the US, while the three major networks controlled 90% of prime-time audience in 1980, their share went down to 65% in 1990, and the trend has accelerated since: it stands at slightly over 60% in 1995. CNN established itself as the major global news producer worldwide, to the point that in emergency situations in countries around the world politicians and journalists alike turn on CNN full time. In 1995 the embryo of a similar global channel in Spanish, *Telenoticias*, was launched by a consortium of Spanish, Hispanic American, and Latin American television companies. Direct satellite television is making a major penetration in the Asian market, broadcasting from Hong Kong to the whole Asian Pacific. Hubbard Communications and Hughes Corporation launched in 1994 two competing direct satellite broadcasting systems that sell 'à la carte' almost any program from anywhere to anywhere in the US, the Asian Pacific, and Latin America. Chinese communities in the US can watch daily Hong Kong news while Chinese in China may have access to American soap operas (*Falcon Crest* recorded 450 million viewers in China). Thus, as Françoise Sabbah wrote in 1985 in one of the best and earliest assessments of new trends in the media:

> In sum, the new media determine a segmented, differentiated audience that, although massive in terms of numbers, is no longer a mass audience in terms of simultaneity and uniformity of the message it receives. The new media are no longer mass media in the traditional sense of sending a limited number of messages to a homogeneous mass audience. Because of the multiplicity of messages and sources, the audience itself

becomes more selective. The targeted audience tends to choose its messages, so deepening its segmentation, enhancing the individual relationship between sender and receiver.[44]

Youichi Ito, analyzing the evolution of media uses in Japan, has also concluded that there is evolution from a mass society to a "segmented society" (*Bunshu Shakai*), as a result of new communication technologies that focus on diversified, specialized information, so that the audience becomes increasingly segmented by ideologies, values, tastes, and lifestyles.[45]

Thus, because of the diversity of media and the possibility of targeting the audience, we can say that in the new media system, **the message is the medium**. That is, the characteristics of the message will shape the characteristics of the medium. For instance, if feeding the musical environment of teenagers is the message (a very explicit one), MTV will be tailored to the rites and language of this audience, not only in the content but in the whole organization of the station and in the technology and design of image production/broadcasting. Or, again, to produce a 24-hour world news service requires a different setting, programming, and broadcasting, such as weather report shows of global and continental scope. This is indeed the present and future of television: decentralization, diversification, and customization. Within the broader parameters of the McLuhanian language, the message of the medium (still operating as such) is shaping different media for different messages.

Yet diversification of messages and media expressions do not imply loss of control by major corporations and governments over television. Indeed, it is the opposite trend that has been observed during the last decade.[46] Investment has poured into the communications field, as mega-groups have been formed and strategic alliances have been established to carve out market shares in a market in complete transformation. In the 1980–95 period, the three major US TV networks have changed ownership, two of them twice: the merger of Disney and ABC in 1995 was a turning point in integrating TV into the emerging multimedia business. TF1, the leading French channel was privatized. Berlusconi took control of all private TV stations in Italy, organizing them in three private networks. Private television flourished in Spain, with the development of three private networks, including Antena-3, and made significant inroads in the UK and in Germany, always under the control of powerful financial groups, both

[44]   Sabbah (1985: 219).
[45]   Ito (1991b).
[46]   See, for instance, data cited in *The Economist* (1994a); also Doyle (1992); Trejo Delarbre (ed.) (1988); Campo Vidal (1996).

national and international. Russian television became diversified, including private, independent television channels. Latin American television experienced a process of concentration around a few major players. The Asian Pacific became the most hotly contested terrain for new television mavericks, such as Murdoch's Star channel, as well as for "old Television hands" such as the new, global BBC, pitted in competition against CNN. In Japan, the government's NHK was joined in competition by private networks: Fuji TV, NTV, TBS, TV Asahi, and TV Tokyo, as well as by cable and direct satellite broadcasting operations. In 1993–95, about US$80 billion were spent in television programming worldwide, and spending was rising by 10% a year. Between 1994 and 1997 some 70 new communications satellites are expected to be launched, most of them destined for TV broadcasting.

The net result of such business competition and concentration is that while the audience has been segmented and diversified, television has become more commercialized than ever, and increasingly oligopolistic at the global level. The actual content of most programming is not substantially different from one network to the other, if we consider the underlying semantic formulae of most popular programs as a whole. Yet the fact that not everybody watches the same thing at the same time, and that each culture and social group has a specific relationship to the media system, does make a fundamental difference *vis-à-vis* the old system of standardized mass media. In addition, the widespread practice of "surfing" (simultaneously watching several programs) introduces the creation by the audience of their own visual mosaics. While the media have become indeed globally interconnected, and programs and messages circulate in the global network, **we are not living in a global village, but in customized cottages globally produced and locally distributed**.

However, the diversification of the media, because of the conditions of their corporate and institutional control, did not transform the unidirectional logic of their message, nor truly allowed the audience's feedback except in the most primitive form of market reaction. While the audience received more and more diverse raw material from which to construct each person's own image of the universe, the McLuhan Galaxy was a world of one-way communication, not of interaction. It was, and still is, the extension of mass production, industrial logic into the realm of signs, and it fell short, McLuhan's genius notwithstanding, of expressing the culture of the information age. This is because information processing goes far beyond one-way communication. Television needed the computer to be free from the screen. But their coupling, with major potential consequences over society at large, came after a long detour taken by computers in order to be able to talk to television only after learning to talk to each other. Only then could the audience speak up.

Computer-Mediated Communication, Institutional Control, Social Networks, and Virtual Communities

History will recall that the two first large-scale experiments of what Ithiel de Sola Pool labeled "technologies of freedom" were induced by the state: the French MINITEL, as a device to steer France into the information society; the American ARPANET, predecessor of Internet, as a military strategy to enable communication networks to survive a nuclear attack. They were very different, both being deeply rooted in the culture and institutions of their respective societies. Leo Scheer has highlighted their contrasting logic in a synthetic view of each system's features:

> Both announced the information superhighways, but their differences are full of lessons. First of all, Internet links up computers while Minitel links, via Transpac, server centers that can be questioned by terminals with low capacity of memory. Internet is an American initiative of worldwide scope, initiated, with military support, by computer companies, financed by the American government, to create a world club of computer users and data banks. Minitel is a French system that, until now [1994] could never go beyond its national boundaries because of [foreign] regulatory constraints. It is the product of the boldest imagination from high level State technocrats in their effort to remedy the weakness of French electronic industries. On the side of Internet: the random topology of local networks of computer fanatics. On the side of Minitel: the orderly arrangement of the telephone book. Internet: an anarchic tariff system of uncontrollable services. Minitel: a kiosk system that allows for homogeneous tariffs and a transparent sharing of revenues. On the one hand, the uprooting and the phantasm of generalized connections beyond boundaries and cultures; on the other hand, the electronic version of communal roots.[47]

The comparative analysis of the development of these two systems, in relationship to their social and institutional environments, helps to shed some light on the characteristics of the emerging, interactive communication system.[48]

[47] Scheer (1994: 97–8), my translation.
[48] Case (1994).

The Minitel story: *l'état et l'amour*

Teletel, the network feeding Minitel terminals, is a videotex system designed in 1978 by the French Telephone Company and introduced to the market in 1984, after years of localized experiments. The earliest and largest of such systems in the world, in spite of its primitive technology, almost unchanged for 15 years, it won a wide acceptance among French households and grew to phenomenal proportions. By the mid-1990s, it was offering 23,000 services, and billing FFr7 billion to 6.5 million Minitel terminals in service, being used in one out of four French households and by one-third of the adult population.[49]

This success is particularly striking when contrasted to the general failure of videotex systems such as Prestel in Britain and Germany, and Japan's Captain, and to the limited receptivity to Minitel or other videotex networks in the United States.[50] Such success came in spite of very limited video and transmission technology: thus, until the early 1990s it transmitted at 1,200 baud speed, to be compared with typical computer information services in the US operating at 9,600 bauds.[51] Behind the success of Minitel lie two fundamental reasons: the first was the commitment of the French government to the experiment as an element of the challenge presented by the Nora-Minc report on the "informatization of society" prepared in 1978 at the request of the Prime Minister.[52] The second was the simplicity of its use, and the straightforwardness of its kiosk billing system that made it accessible and trustworthy to the average citizen.[53] Still, people needed an extra incentive to use it and this is the most revealing part of the Minitel story.[54]

The government's commitment, through French Telecom, was spectacularly shown in the launching of the program: each household was given the option of the delivery of a free Minitel terminal in place of the usual telephone book. Furthermore, the telephone company subsidized the system until it broke even for the first time in 1995. It was a way of stimulating telecommunications usage, creating a captive market for the troubled French electronics industry and, above all, inducing familiarity with the new medium for both companies and people.[55] However, the most intelligent strategy from French Telecom

---

[49] Thery (1994); Myers (1981); Lehman (1994).
[50] McGowan and Compaine (1989).
[51] Thery (1994); Preston (1994); Rosenbaum (1992).
[52] Nora and Minc (1978).
[53] McGowan (1988).
[54] Mehta (1993).

was to open the system wide to private providers of services, and first of all to French newspapers, which quickly became the defenders and popularizers of Minitel.[56]

But there was a second, major reason for the widespread use of Minitel: the appropriation of the medium by the French people for their personal expression. The first services provided by Minitel were the same that were available via traditional telephone communication: telephone directory, weather reports, transportation information and reservations, advance purchase of tickets for entertainment and cultural events, and so on. As the system and people became more sophisticated, and thousands of providers of services came on line, advertising, tele-shopping, tele-banking, and various business services were offered through Minitel. Yet the social impact of Minitel was limited in the early stages of its development.[57] In terms of volume, the telephone directory accounted for over 40% of total calls; in terms of value, in 1988 36% of Minitel revenues came from 2% of its users, which were businesses.[58] The system caught fire with the introduction of chat-lines or *messageries*, most of which quickly specialized in sex offerings or in sex-related conversations (*les messageries roses*), that by 1990 accounted for more than half of the calls.[59] Some of these services were commercial porno-electronic conversations, equivalent to the phone sex so pervasive in other societies. The main difference was the accessibility of such services over the videotex network, and their massive advertising in public places. But most of the erotic uses of Minitel were initiated by people themselves over the general-purpose chat-lines. Yet there was not a generalized sex bazaar, but a democratized sexual fantasy. More often than not (source: author's participant observation), the on-line exchanges were based on impersonation of ages, genders and physical characteristics, so that Minitel became the vehicle of sexual and personal dreams rather than the substitute for pick-up bars. This infatuation with the intimate use of Minitel was critical to ensure its rapid diffusion among the French people, in spite of the solemn protests of prudish puritans. By the early 1990s, the erotic uses of Minitel dwindled down, as the fashion faded away, and the rudimentary character of the technology limited its sex appeal: chat-lines

[55]   For a comprehensive analysis of the policy that led to the development of Minitel, see Cats-Baril and Jelassi (1994).
[56]   Preston (1994).
[57]   Mehta (1993).
[58]   Honigsbaum (1988).
[59]   Maital (1991); Rheingold (1993).

came to account for less than 10% of the traffic.[60] Once the system was fully settled, the fastest growing services in the 1990s were developed by businesses for their internal use, with the highest growth being that of high value-added services, such as legal services, accounting for over 30% of the traffic.[61] Yet the hooking-up of a substantial proportion of the French people to the system needed the detour through their personal psyche, and the partial fulfillment of their communication needs, at least for a while.

When in the 1990s Minitel emphasized its role as service provider, it also made evident its built-in limitations as a means of communication.[62] Technologically, it was relying on ages-old video and transmission technology whose overhaul would end its basic appeal as a free electronic device. Furthermore, it was not based on personal computing but, by and large, on dumb terminals, thus substantially limiting autonomous capacity for information processing. Institutionally, its architecture, organized around a hierarchy of server networks, with little capacity for horizontal communication, was too inflexible for a society as culturally sophisticated as France, once new realms of communication were available beyond Minitel. The obvious solution adopted by the French system was to offer the option, at a price, of linking up with Internet worldwide. In so doing, Minitel became internally split between a bureaucratic information service, a networked system of business services, and the tributary gateway to the vast communication system of the Internet constellation.

The Internet constellation

The Internet network is the backbone of global computer-mediated communication (CMC) in the 1990s, since it gradually links up most networks. In the mid-1990s it connected 44,000 computer networks and about 3.2 million host computers worldwide with an estimated 25 million users, and it was expanding rapidly (see figure 5.1). According to a survey of the United States conducted in August 1995 by Nielsen Media Research, 24 million people were Internet users, and 36 million had access to it. However, a different survey, conducted by the Emerging Technologies Research Group in November–December 1995 evaluated the number of Americans that used Internet regularly at only 9.5 million, of whom two-thirds signed on only once a week.

[60] Wilson (1991).
[61] Ibid.
[62] Dalloz and Portnoff (1994).

Figure 5.1 The diffusion of the Internet
Source: Batty and Barr (1994).

Number of hosts

1,000,000 to 5,000,000	(1)
100,000 to 1,000,000	(1)
50,000 to 100,000	(3)
20,000 to 50,000	(6)
10,000 to 20,000	(4)
1,000 to 10,000	(19)
1 to 1,000	(18)

July 1992

Figure 5.1 – cont.

Number of hosts

■	1,000,000 to 5,000,000 (1)
▨	100,000 to 1,000,000 (1)
▧	50,000 to 100,000 (3)
▨	20,000 to 50,000 (6)
▨	10,000 to 20,000 (4)
▨	1,000 to 10,000 (19)
□	1 to 1,000 (18)

January 1993

Figure 5.1 – cont.

Number of hosts

1,000,000 to 5,000,000	(1)
100,000 to 1,000,000	(1)
50,000 to 100,000	(3)
20,000 to 50,000	(6)
10,000 to 20,000	(4)
1,000 to 10,000	(19)
1 to 1,000	(18)

July 1993

Figure 5.1 – cont.

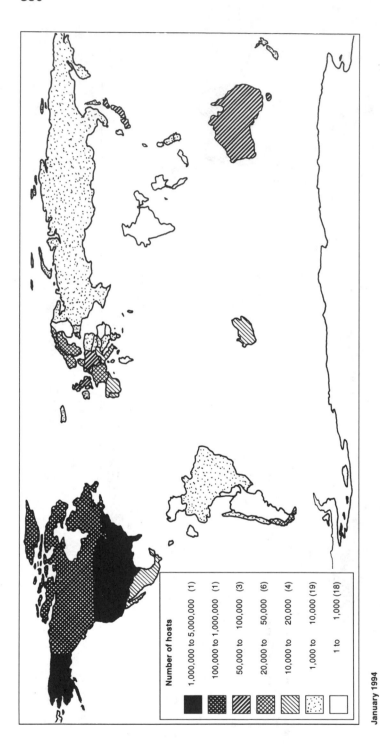

Number of hosts

▓ (black)	1,000,000 to 5,000,000 (1)
▓	100,000 to 1,000,000 (1)
▨	50,000 to 100,000 (3)
▦	20,000 to 50,000 (6)
▨	10,000 to 20,000 (4)
░	1,000 to 10,000 (19)
☐	1 to 1,000 (18)

January 1994

Figure 5.1 – cont.

Yet the projections were for the number of users to double in a year.[63] Overall, while there is wide disagreement about how many users are currently connected to Internet, there is a convergence of opinion that it has the potential to explode into hundreds of millions of users by early in the twenty-first century. Experts consider that, technically, Internet could one day link up 600 million computer networks. This is to be compared with its size in earlier stages of development: in 1973, there were 25 computers in the network; through the 1970s, it could only support 256 computers; in the early 1980s, after substantial enhancement, it was still limited to about 25 networks with only a few hundred primary computers and a few thousand users.[64] The history of Internet's development and of the convergence of other communication networks into the Net provides essential material to understanding the technical, organizational and cultural characteristics of this Net, thus opening the way for assessing its social impacts.[65]

It is indeed a unique blending of military strategy, big science cooperation, and countercultural innovation.[66] At the origins of Internet is the work of one of the most innovative research institutions in the world: the US Defense Department's Advanced Research Projects Agency (DARPA). When in the late 1950s the launching of the first Sputnik alarmed the American high-tech military establishment, DARPA undertook a number of bold initiatives, some of which changed the history of technology and ushered in the information age on a grand scale. One of these strategies, developing an idea conceived by Paul Baran at Rand Corporation, was to design a communications system invulnerable to nuclear attack. Based on packet-switching communication technology, the system made the network independent of command and control centers, so that message units would find their own routes along the network, being reassembled in coherent meaning at any point in the network.

When, later on, digital technology allowed the packaging of all kind of messages, including sound, images, and data, a network was formed that was able to communicate all kinds of symbols without using

---

[63]   McLeod (1996).

[64]   Sullivan-Trainor (1994); *Business Week* (1994a); Hafner and Markoff (1991); *El Pais/World Media* (1995); McLeod (1996).

[65]   For documented and intelligent analyses of the origins, development, and characteristics of Internet and other CMC networks, see Hart et al. (1992); Rheingold (1993). For an empirical study of the growth of Internet, see Batty and Barr (1994). For a discussion of Internet's prospects, see a study by the Rand Corporation available only on-line at the time of this writing: Rand Corporation (1995).

[66]   Hafner and Markoff (1991).

control centers. The universality of digital language and the pure networking logic of the communication system created the technological conditions for horizontal, global communication. Furthermore, the architecture of this network technology is such that it is very difficult to censor or control it. The only way to control the network is not to be into it, and this is a high price to pay for any institution or organization once the network becomes pervasive and channels all kinds of information around the world.

The first such network, named ARPANET after its powerful sponsor, went on-line in 1969. It was opened to research centers cooperating with the US Defense Department, but scientists started to use it for all kinds of communication purposes. At one point it became difficult to separate military-oriented research from scientific communication and from personal chatting. Thus, scientists of all disciplines were given access to the network, and in 1983 there was a split between ARPANET, dedicated to scientific purposes, and MILNET, directly oriented to military applications. The National Science Foundation also became involved in the 1980s in creating another scientific network, CSNET, and – in cooperation with IBM – still another network for non-science scholars, BITNET. Yet all networks used ARPANET as their communication system. The network of networks that formed during the 1980s was called ARPA-INTERNET, then INTERNET, still supported by the Defense Department and operated by the National Science Foundation.

For the network to be able to sustain the fantastic growth in the volume of communication, transmission technology had to be enhanced. In the 1970s, ARPANET was using 56,000 bits-per-second links, In 1987, the network lines transmitted 1.5 million bits per second. By 1992, the NSFNET, backbone network behind Internet, operated at transmission speeds of 45 million bits per second: enough capacity to send 5,000 pages per second. In 1995, gigabit transmission technology was in the prototype stage, with capacity equivalent to transmitting the US Library of Congress in one minute.

However, transmission capacity was not enough to establish a worldwide communication web. Computers had to be able to talk to each other. The obstacle was overcome with the creation of UNIX, an operating system enabling access from computer to computer. The system was invented by Bell Laboratories in 1969, but became widely used only after 1983, when Berkeley researchers (again funded by ARPA) adapted to UNIX the TCP/IP protocol that made it possible for computers not only to communicate but to encode and decode data packages traveling at high speed in the Internet network. Since the new version of Unix was financed with public funds, the software was made available just for the cost of distribution. Networking was born on a large scale as local area networks and regional networks connected to each other, and started to spread anywhere where there were telephone lines and computers were equipped with modems, an inexpensive piece of equipment.

Behind the development of Internet there was the scientific, institutional, and personal networks cutting across the Defense Department, National Science Foundation, major research universities, and specialized technological think-tanks, such as MIT's Lincoln Laboratory, SRI (formerly Stanford Research Institute), Palo Alto Research Corporation (funded by Xerox), ATT's Bell Laboratories, Rand Corporation, BBN (Bolt, Beranek & Newman), the research company where the TCP/IP protocol was invented, and so on. Key technological players in the 1950s–1970s period, such as J.C.R. Licklider, Douglas Engelbart, Robert Taylor, Ivan Sutherland, Lawrence Roberts, Robert Kahn, Alan Kay, Robert Thomas, and the rest, moved back and forth between these institutions, creating a networked milieu of innovation whose dynamics and goals became largely autonomous from the specific purposes of military strategy or supercomputing link-ups. They were technological crusaders, convinced that they were changing the world, as eventually they did.

But this is only one side of the story; because in parallel to the efforts by the Pentagon and Big Science to establish a universal computer network with public access, within "acceptable use" norms, a sprawling computer counterculture emerged in the United States, often mentally associated with the aftershocks of the 1960s movements, in their most libertarian/utopian version. An important element of the system, the modem, was one of the technological breakthroughs emerging from the pioneers of this counterculture, originally labeled "the hackers" before the term took on its malignant connotation. The modem was invented by two Chicago students, Ward Christensen and Randy Suess, in 1978, when they were trying to find a system to transfer microcomputer programs to each other through the telephone to avoid traveling in the Chicago winter between their distant locations. In 1979 they diffused the XModem protocol that allowed computers to transfer files directly without going through a host system. And they diffused the technology at no cost, because their purpose was to spread communication capabilities as much as possible. Computer networks that were excluded from ARPANET (reserved to elite science universities in its early stages) found their way to start communicating with each other on their own. In 1979, three students at Duke University and University of North Carolina, not included in ARPANET, created a modified version of the Unix protocol that made it possible to link up computers over the regular telephone line. They used it to start a forum of on-line computer discussion, Usenet, that quickly became one of the first large-scale electronic conversation systems. The inventors of Usenet News also diffused freely their software in a leaflet circulated at the Unix users conference.

Ironically, this countercultural approach to technology had a similar effect to the military-inspired strategy of horizontal networking: it made available technological means to whoever had the technical knowledge and a computing tool, the PC, which soon would start a spectacular progression of increasing power and decreasing price at the same time. The advent of personal computing and the communicability of networks spurred the development of Bulletin Board Systems (BBS), first in the United States, then world-wide: the electronic protests to the Tian An Men events in China in 1989 via computer networks operated by Chinese students abroad were one of the most notorious manifestations of the potential of the new communication devices. Bulletin Board Systems did not need sophisticated computer networks, just PCs, modems, and the tele-phone line. Thus, they became the electronic notice-boards of all kinds of interests and affinities, creating what Howard Rheingold names "virtual communities."[67]

Thousands and thousands of such micro-networks exist today around the world, covering the whole spectrum of human communi-cation, from politics and religion to sex and research. By the mid-1990s, the majority of them were also connected to Internet, but they were keeping their own identity and enforcing their own rules of behavior. One of the most important rules was (and is) the rejection of the intrusion into BBS of undeclared commercial interests. While it is considered legitimate to create commercial BBS or business-oriented networks, it is not legitimate to invade cyberspaces created for other purposes. The sanction against intruders is devastating: thousands of hostile messages "flame" the bad electronic citizen. When the fault is particularly serious, huge files are dumped onto the guilty system, bringing it to a halt, and usually provoking the expul-sion of the culprit from the network of its host computer. This electronics grass-roots culture marked for ever the evolution and use of the net. While its most heroic tones and its countercultural ideology fade away with the generalization of the medium on a global scale, the technological features and social codes that developed from the original free use of the network have framed its utilization.

In the 1990s, business has realized the extraordinary potential of

[67]   Rheingold (1993).

Internet, as the National Science Foundation decided to privatize some of the major operations of the network to the usual large corporation consortiums (ATT, MCI-IBM, and so on). The commercialization of Internet grew at a fast rate: while in 1991 there were about 9,000 commercial domains (or sub-networks) by the end of 1994 they had increased to 21,700.[68] Several commercial computer services networks were created, providing services on the basis of an organized grid, with adjusted pricing. Yet the capacity of the network is such that the majority of the communication process was, and still is, largely spontaneous, unorganized, and diversified in purpose and membership. In fact, commercial and government interests coincide in favoring the expanding use of the network: the greater the diversity of messages and participants, the higher the critical mass in the network, and the higher the value. The peaceful coexistence of various interests and cultures in the net took the form of the World Wide Web (WWW), a flexible network of networks within the Internet where institutions, businesses, associations, and individuals create their own "sites," on the basis of which everybody with access can produce her/his/its "home page," made of a variable collage of text and images. Helped by software technology first developed in Mosaic (a Web browser software program invented in 1992 by students in Illinois, at the National Center for Supercomputing Applications, the Web allowed for groupings of interests and projects in the net, overcoming the time-costly chaotic browsing of pre-WWW Internet. On the basis of these groupings, individuals and organizations were able to interact meaningfully on what has become, literally, a World Wide Web of individualized, interactive communication.[69] The price to pay for such diverse and widespread participation is to let spontaneous, informal communication flourish at the same time. The commercialization of cyberspace will be closer to the historical experience of merchant streets that sprout out from vibrant urban culture, than to the shopping centers spread in the dullness of anonymous suburbs.

The two sources of the Net, the military/science establishment and the personal computing counterculture, did have a common ground: the university world. The first ARPANET node was set up in 1969 at UCLA, and six other nodes were added in 1970–1 at UC Santa Barbara, SRI, University of Utah, BBN, MIT, and Harvard. From there, they spread primarily over the academic community, with the exception of the internal networks of large electronic corporations. This university origin of the Net has been, and is, decisive for the development and diffusion of electronic communication throughout

[68] *Business Week* (1994).
[69] Markoff (1995).

the world. The large-scale initiation to CMC in the United States took place among graduate students and faculties of universities in the early 1990s. And a similar process took place only a few years later in the rest of the world. In Spain, in the mid-1990s the largest contingent of "internetters" came from the computer networks built around Universidad Complutense de Madrid and Universitat Politécnica de Catalunya. The story seems to be the same around the world. This university-based process of diffusion is significant because it has the highest potential for spreading both the know-how and the habits of CMC. Indeed, against the assumption of social isolation suggested by the image of the ivory tower, universities are major agents of diffusion of social innovation because generation after generation of young people go through them, becoming aware of and accustomed to new ways of thinking, managing, acting, and communicating. As CMC becomes pervasive in the university system on an international scale during the 1990s, the graduates that will take over companies and institutions in the early twenty-first century will bring with them the message of the new medium into the mainstream of society.

The process of the formation and diffusion of Internet, and related CMC networks, in the last quarter of the century shaped for ever the structure of the new medium, in the architecture of the network, in the culture of the networkers, and in the actual patterns of communication. The architecture of the network is, and will remain, technologically open, enabling widespread public access and seriously limiting governmental or commercial restrictions to such access, although social inequality will powerfully manifest itself in the electronic domain, as I shall analyze below. This openness is the consequence, on the one hand, of the original design conceived partly for the above-mentioned military strategic reasons; partly because the scientists managing military research programs wanted to set up such a new system, both to show technological prowess and as a utopian endeavor. On the other hand, the openness of the system also results from the constant process of innovation and free accessibility enacted by early computer hackers and the network hobbyists who still populate the net by the thousands.

This constant, multisided effort to improve the communicability of the network is a remarkable example of how the technological productivity of cooperation through the net ended up enhancing the net itself. Furthermore, the open architecture of the network makes it very difficult to ensure its secrecy against sophisticated intruders. In January 1995 Tsutomu Shimomura, a computer security expert at the San Diego Supercomputer Center, revealed that his security-proof files had been accessed and downloaded onto computers in Rochester University, and that other protected files in several locations have been submitted to similar attacks, providing strong evidence that Internet's network security screens were useless against advanced software invasion. Shimomura took revenge on this professional offense. He went to work to track the hacker and, using strictly electronic means, a few weeks later led the FBI to the housing complex where they made the arrest of Kevin Mitnick, a legendary outlaw of the network frontier. Yet this well-publicized event underscored the difficulty of protecting information in the network. The issue came down to the choice between closing down Internet as it was or finding other communication networks for commercial interests that require protected transmission of information. Given that it would be almost impossible to shut down Internet in its current format (precisely because of the genius of DARPA's researchers), my hypothesis is that, slowly but surely, commercial uses requiring credit card and bank account numbers will develop separate networks, while Internet will expand as an electronic global agora, with its inevitable small dose of psychological deviance.

The culture of first-generation users, with its utopian, communal, and libertarian undercurrents, shaped the Net in two opposite directions. On the one hand, it tended to restrict access to a minority of computer hobbyists, the only people able and willing to spend time and energy living in cyberspace. From this era there remains a pioneering spirit that looks with distrust at the commercialization of the network, and watches with apprehension how the realization of the dream of generalized communication for the people brings with it the limits and misery of humankind as it is. But as the heroics of early computer tribes recedes under the relentless flow of "newbies," what remains from the countercultural origins of the network is the informality and self-directedness of communication, the idea that many contribute to many, and yet each one has her own voice and expects an individualized answer. The multipersonalization of CMC does express to some extent the same tension that arose in the 1960s between the "me culture" and the communal dreams of each individual.[70] In fact, there are more bridges than communication experts usually acknowledge between the countercultural origins of CMC and the mainstream Internetters of the 1990s, as is shown by the business acceptance of *Wired* magazine, created as a countercultural outfit, but to become the hottest expression of Internet culture and how-to advice in the mid-1990s.

Thus, in spite of all efforts to regulate, privatize, and commercialize Internet and its tributary systems, CMC networks, inside and outside Internet, are characterized by their pervasiveness, their multifaceted

[70] Gitlin (1987); Rand Corporation (1995).

decentralization, and their flexibility. They sprawl as colonies of micro-organisms, to follow Rheingold's biological image. They will certainly reflect commercial interests, as they will extend the controlling logic of major public and private organizations into the whole realm of communication. But unlike the mass media of the McLuhan Galaxy, they have technologically and culturally embedded properties of interactivity and individualization. However, do these potentialities translate into new patterns of communication? Which are the cultural attributes emerging from the process of electronic interaction? Let us turn to an examination of the meager empirical record on this matter.

The interactive society

Computer-mediated communication is too recent and has been too narrowly experienced at the time of this writing (1995) to have been the object of rigorous, reliable research. Most of the often-cited evidence is anecdotal, and some of the most accurate sources come in fact from journalists' reports. Furthermore, changes in technology are so fast and the diffusion of CMC is so rapid that most of the available research from the 1980s is hardly applicable to social trends in the 1990s, precisely the historic moment when the new communication culture is taking shape. Yet it is methodologically useful to discuss the social implications of new communication processes within the constraints of reported evidence, in spite of a pattern of somewhat contradictory findings. I shall rely on a nonexhaustive review of social sciences literature on CMC to suggest some tentative lines of interpretation of the relationship between communication and society under the conditions of computer-based interactive technology.[71] First of all, CMC is not a general medium of communication and will not be so in the foreseeable future. While its use expands at phenomenal rates it will exclude for a long time the large majority of humankind, unlike television and other mass media. To be sure, in 1994 more than one-third of American households were equipped with personal computers, and spending on PCs toppled purchases of television sets for the first time. Western Europe also experienced a computer shopping spree by the mid-1990s but rates of household penetration were held at a lower level (less than 20% if we exclude videotex terminals). Japan lags considerably in home computer

---

[71]   I have used extensively an excellent literature review on computer-mediated communication prepared by UC Berkeley graduate student Rod Benson (1994). For some empirical evidence on Japan, based on the analysis of a 1993 survey, see Sato et al. (1995). For an intellectual reflection on the culture of Internet see the insightful book by Turkle (1995).

equipment and computer use outside the work place.[72] And the rest of the world (excluding Singapore), in spite of high rates of growth of computer penetration (with the exception of Africa), was clearly in a different communication age, notwithstanding beepers and pagers relentlessly buzzing all along the Asian Pacific. This will change over time, undoubtedly, but the rate of diffusion of interactive CMC will hardly match that of television for a long historical period.[73]

A different matter, which I shall analyze in the next section, is that of the use of interactive communication in the operation of multimedia systems, which will probably be made available, in extremely simplified versions, to a large proportion of the population in many countries. But CMC as such will remain the domain of an educated segment of the population of the most advanced countries, numbered in tens of millions but still counting as an elite on a global scale. Even the number of Internet users, as cited above, has been challenged by knowledgeable experts on grounds that connection to Internet does not mean actual use of it, even less than the multiplier of ten persons to one link that has been generally used in the estimates.[74] And even among those who use it, only a minority is really active in the medium. A survey of American users of BBSs, published in 1993, indicated that only 18% of them were active on a weekly basis; that the average number of calls was 50 per week and per BBS; that 38% of transactions were uploads of the system; and that 66% of board content was in fact devoted to computer-related matters.[75] As expected, surveys of PC owners show that they are above-average affluent, full-time employed, and single, and less likely to be retired.[76] The large majority of PC users, as well as users of bulletin board systems, are men. As for Internet users, a survey conducted on a national sample in the United States found that 67% of those with Internet access were male, over half of them aged 18–34. Their median household income was between $50,000 and $75,000, and the most frequently mentioned occupations were education, sales, and engineering.[77] A different survey, also for the United States in 1995, again found that 65% of

.[72] See *Business Week* (1994a); *Business Week* (1994e, f, g); *El Pais/World Media* (1995). For data on the diffusion of electronic communication in Japan, see Soumu-cho Toukei-kyoku (Bureau of Statistics, Management and Coordination Agency) (1995); Ministry of Posts and Telecommunications (1994a); Japan Information Processing Center (1994).

[73] Hamelink (1990).

[74] Revised estimates by John S. Quarterman, University of Texas at Austin, reported by *New York Times*, August 10 1994.

[75] Rafaeli and LaRose (1993).

[76] Schweitzer (1995); Sato et al. (1995).

[77] Lohr (1995).

users were male and affluent (average household income $62,000), although older than indicated by other surveys (average age 36).[78] Thus, CMC starts as the medium of communication for the most educated and affluent segment of the population of the most educated and affluent countries, and more often than not in the largest and most sophisticated metropolitan areas.

Clearly, in the near future use of CMC will expand, particularly via the educational system, and will reach substantial proportions of the population *in the industrialized world*: it will not be exclusively an elite phenomenon, although it will be much less pervasive than the mass media. Yet the fact that it will expand through successive waves, starting from a cultural elite, means that it will shape habits of communication through the usages of its first-wave practitioners. Increasingly CMC will be critical in shaping future culture, and increasingly the elites who have shaped its format will be structurally advantaged in the emerging society. Thus, while CMC is truly revolutionizing the process of communication, and through it culture at large, it is a revolution developing in concentric waves, starting from the higher levels of education and wealth, and probably unable to reach large segments of the uneducated masses and poor countries.

On the other hand, within the segment of regular users of CMC, it appears that the medium favors uninhibited communication and stimulates participation from lower-status workers in company-based networks.[79] Along the same line of argument, women, and other oppressed groups of society, seem to be more likely to express themselves openly through the protection of the electronic medium, although we must keep in mind that, as a whole, women are a minority of users up to this point.[80] It works as though the symbolism of power embedded in face-to-face communication has not yet found its language in the new CMC. Because of the historical newness of the medium and the relative improvement of the relative status of power for traditionally subordinated groups, such as women, CMC could offer a chance to reverse traditional power games in the communication process.

Shifting the analysis from the *users* to the *uses*, it must be emphasized that *the overwhelming proportion of CMC activity takes place at work or in work-related situations*. I have discussed above in chapters 3 and 4 the critical importance of the computer medium for the new form of networked organization and for the specific labor conditions of the networkers. In the context of the present analysis on cultural impacts,

[78] McLeod (1996).
[79] Sproull and Kiesler (1991); Rand Corporation (1995).

what should be considered is the symbolic isomorphism in the processes of work, home services, and entertainment in the new structure of communication. Is the relationship to the computer specific enough to connect work, home and entertainment into the same system of symbol processing? Or, on the contrary, does the context determine the perception and uses of the medium? We do not have reliable research on the matter at this point, but some preliminary observations by Penny Gurstein in her doctoral dissertation[81] seem to indicate that while people using computers at home enjoy their self-reliance in the management of time and space, they resent the lack of distinct separation between work and leisure, family and business, personality and function. Let us say, as a hypothesis to be kept in the back of our mind, that the convergence of experience in the same medium blurs somewhat the institutional separation of domains of activity, and confuses codes of behavior.

Beyond the performance of professional tasks, the uses of CMC already reach the whole realm of social activity. While tele-banking has never been a favorite of average people (until they are pushed into it against their will, as will happen), and tele-shopping is dependent on the coming blossoming of virtual reality multimedia, personal communication is exploding in e-mail, the most usual CMC activity outside work.[82] In fact, its widespread use does not substitute for interpersonal communication but for telephone communication, since answering machines and voice-phone services have created a communication barrier that makes e-mail the best alternative for direct communication at a chosen time. Computer sex is another major use of CMC, and is expanding quickly. While there is a fast-growing business market in computerized sexual stimulation, increasingly associated with virtual reality technology,[83] most computer sex takes place on conversation lines, either on specialized BBSs or as a spontaneous derivation of personal interaction. The interactive power of new networks make this activity more dynamic in 1990s California than it was in 1980s French Minitel.[84] Increasingly afraid of contagion and of personal aggression, people scarch for alternatives to express their sexuality, and in our culture of symbolic overstimulation CMC certainly offers avenues to sexual fantasy, particularly as long as the interaction is not visual and identities can be concealed.

---

[80]   Hiltz and Turoff (1993); Sato et al. (1995).
[81]   Gurstein (1990).
[82]   Lanham (1993).; Rand Corporation (1995).
[83]   Specter (1994).
[84]   Armstrong (1994).

Politics is also a growing area of utilization of CMC.[85] On the one hand, e-mail is being used for mass diffusion of targeted political propaganda with the possibility of interaction. Christian fundamentalist groups, the American militia in the US, and the Zapatistas in Mexico are pioneering this political technology.[86] On the other hand, local democracy is being enhanced through experiments in electronic citizen participation, such as the PEN program organized by the City of Santa Monica, California,[87] through which citizens debate public issues and make their feelings known to the city government: a raging debate on homelessness (with electronic participation by the homeless themselves!) was one of the most highly publicized results of this experiment in the early 1990s.

Beyond casual social interaction and instrumental uses of CMC, observers have detected the phenomenon of the formation of virtual communities. By this, in line with Rheingold's argument,[88] is generally understood a self-defined electronic network of interactive communication organized around a shared interest or purpose, although sometimes communication becomes the goal in itself. Such communities may be relatively formalized, as in the case of hosted conferences or bulletin boards systems, or be spontaneously formed by social networks which keep logging into the network to send and retrieve messages in a chosen time pattern (either delayed or in real time).Tens of thousands of such "communities" existed throughout the world in the mid-1990s, most of them based in the US but increasingly reaching out on a global scale. It is still unclear how much sociability is taking place in such electronic networks, and what are the cultural effects of such a new form of sociability. Yet one feature can be highlighted: such networks are ephemeral from the point of view of the participants. While a given conference or BBS can go on for a long time, around a nucleus of dedicated computer users, most of the contributions to the interaction are sporadic, with most people moving in and out of networks as their interests change or their expectations remain unfulfilled. I would advance the hypothesis that two very different populations "live" in such virtual communities: a tiny minority of electronic villagers "homesteading in the electronic frontier,"[89] and a transient crowd for whom their casual incursions into various networks is tantamount to exploring several existences under the mode of the ephemeral.[90]

[85]   Abramson et al. (1988); Epstein (1995).
[86]   Castells, Yazawa and Kiselyova (1996).
[87]   Varley (1991); Ganley (1991).
[88]   Rheingold (1993).
[89]   Ibid.

How specific is the language of CMC as a new medium? To some analysts, CMC, and particularly e-mail, represents the revenge of the written medium, the return to the typographic mind, and the recuperation of the constructed, rational discourse. For others, on the contrary, the informality, spontaneity, and anonymity of the medium stimulates what they call a new form of "orality," expressed by an electronic text.[91] If we can consider such behavior as informal, unconstructed writing in real-time interaction, in the mode of a synchronist chat (a writing telephone . . .), maybe we can foresee the emergence of a new medium, mixing forms of communication that were previously separated in different domains of the human mind.

Overall, when assessing the social and cultural impacts of CMC we must keep in mind the accumulated sociological research on the social uses of technology. More to the point, the masterful work by Claude Fischer on the social history of the telephone in America to 1940 shows the high social elasticity of any given technology.[92] Thus, the Northern California communities he studied adopted the telephone to enhance their existing social networks of communication, and to reinforce their deep-rooted social habits. Telephone was adapted, not just adopted. People shape technology to fit it to their own needs, as I have argued above in relationship to the personal and contextual reception of television messages by the audience, and as is clearly shown by the mass adoption of Minitel by French people to fulfill their sexual fantasy needs. The many-to-many electronic communication mode represented by CMC has been used in different ways and for different purposes, as many as in the range of social and contextual variation among its users. What is common to CMC is that, according to the few existing studies on the matter, it does not substitute for other means of communication nor does it create new networks: it reinforces the preexisting social patterns. It adds to telephone and transportation communication, it expands the reach of social networks, and makes it possible for them to interact more actively and in chosen time patterns. Because access to CMC is culturally, educationally, and economically restrictive, and will be so for a long time, the most important cultural impact of CMC could be potentially the reinforcement of the culturally dominant social networks, as well as the increase of their cosmopolitanism and globalization. This is not because CMC per se is more cosmopolitan: as Fischer showed, early telephone networks favored local over

90 Turkle (1995).
91 John December, "Characteristics of Oral Culture in Discourse on the Net," 1993 unpublished paper, cited and summarized by Benson (1994).
92 Fischer (1992).

long-distance communication. In some of the virtual communities, for instance in the San Francisco Bay Area's SFNET, the majority of their "regulars" are local residents, and some of them periodically celebrate face-to-face parties, in order to nurture their electronic intimacy.[93] Yet for electronic networks at large, they tend to reinforce the cosmopolitanism of the new professional and managerial classes living symbolically in a global frame of reference, unlike most of the population in any country. Thus, CMC may be a powerful medium to reinforce the social cohesion of the cosmopolitan elite, providing material support to the meaning of a global culture, from the chic of an e-mail address to the rapid circulation of fashionable messages.

In contrast, for the majority of the population in all countries, beyond the work place, the experience and uses of CMC will be increasingly intertwined with the new world of communication associated with the emergence of multimedia.

The Grand Fusion: Multimedia as Symbolic Environment

In the second half of the 1990s a new electronic communication system started to be formed out of the merger of globalized, customized mass media and computer-mediated communication. As I mentioned above, the new system is characterized by the integration of different media and by its interactive potential. Multimedia, as the new system was hastily labeled, extend the realm of electronic communication into the whole domain of life, from home to work, from schools to hospitals, from entertainment to travel. By the mid-1990s governments and companies around the world were in a frantic race to position themselves in setting up the new system, considered to be a tool of power, potential source of huge profits, and symbol of hypermodernity. In the US Vice-president Albert Gore launched the National Information Infrastructure program, to renew America's leadership in the twenty-first century.[94] In Japan, the Telecommunications Council proposed the necessary "Reforms toward the Intellectually Creative Society of the Twenty-first Century," and the Ministry of Posts and Telecommunications obliged with a strategy to create a multimedia system in Japan, to overcome the lagging of the nation *vis-à-vis* the United States.[95] The French Prime Minister

[93]   Rheingold (1993).
[94]   Sullivan-Trainor (1994).
[95]   Telecommunications Council (1994).

commissioned a report in 1994 on *"autoroutes de l'information,"* which concluded that it was to the potential advantage of France in the field, building on the society's experience with Minitel and on French advanced technology, to foster the next stage of multimedia, putting emphasis on providing a media content less dependent on Hollywood.[96] European technology programs, particularly Esprit and Eureka, stepped up efforts to develop a European standard of high-definition television, as well as telecommunication protocols that could integrate different communication systems across the borders.[97] In February 1995 the G-7 club held a special meeting in Brussels to jointly address the issues involved in the transition to the "Information Society." And in early 1995, Brazil's new president, distinguished sociologist Fernando Henrique Cardoso, decided, as one of the key measures of his new administration, to overhaul Brazil's communication system, to link up with the emerging global super-highway.

Yet business, not governments, was shaping the new multimedia system.[98] Indeed, the scale of investment in infrastructure prevented any government from acting by itself: for the United States alone, the estimates for the launch phase of the so-called Information Super-highway were $US400 billion. Companies from all over the world were positioning themselves to enter a market that could become, in the early twenty-first century, the equivalent of what the automobile–oil–rubber–highway industrial complex was in the first half of the twentieth century. Furthermore, because the actual technological shape of the system is uncertain, whoever controls its first stages could decisively influence its future evolution, thus acquiring structural competitive advantage. Because of technological convergence between computers, telecommunications, and mass media in all its modalities, global/regional consortia were formed, and dissolved, on a gigantic scale.[99] Telephone companies, cable TV operators, and TV satellite broadcasting were both competing and merging to hedge the risks of the new market. Computer companies were hurrying to provide "the box," this magic device that would embody the potential to hook up the electronic home to a new galaxy of communication, while providing people with a navigating and self-programming capability in a "user-friendly" mode, hopefully by just

---

[96]   Thery (1994).
[97]   Banegas (ed.) (1993).
[98]   See, among a myriad of business sources on the matter, Bunker (1994); Herther (1994); Dalloz and Portnoff (1994); Bird (1994).
[99]   *The Economist* (1994a).
[100]   *Business Week* (1994h).

speaking to "it."[100] Software companies, from Microsoft to Japanese video-games creators such as Nintendo and Saga, were generating the new interactive know-how that would unleash the fantasy of immersion in the virtual reality of the electronic environment.[101] Television networks, music companies, and movie studios were cranking up their production to feed an entire world supposedly hungry for info-entertainment and audiovisual product lines.[102]

The business control over the first stages of development of multimedia systems will have lasting consequences on the characteristics of the new electronic culture. For all the ideology of the potential of new communication technologies in education, health, and cultural enhancement, the prevailing strategy aims at developing a giant electronic entertainment system, considered the safest investment from a business perspective. Indeed, in the pioneer country, the United States, entertainment in all its forms was in the mid-1990s the fastest growing industry, with over $350 billion of consumer spending per year, and about 5 million workers, with employment increasing at 12% per year.[103] In Japan, a 1992 national market survey on the distribution of multimedia software by product category found that entertainment accounted for 85.7% of the value, while education represented only 0.8%.[104] Thus, while governments and futurologists speak of wiring classrooms, doing surgery at a distance, and tele-consulting the *Encyclopedia Britannica*, most of the actual construction of the new system focuses on "video-on-demand," tele-gambling, and virtual reality theme parks. In the analytical vein of this book, I am not opposing the noble goals of new technologies to their mediocre materialization. I am simply indicating that their actual use in the early stages of the new system will considerably shape the uses, perceptions, and ultimately the social consequences of multimedia.

However, the process of formation of the new system is likely to be slower, and more contradictory, than anticipated. In 1994, there were a number of experiments with multimedia interactive systems in a number of areas: in Kansai Science City in Japan; a coordinated program in eight European telecommunication networks, to test the Asymmetrical Digital Subscriber Loop (ASDL);[105] and in several areas of the United States, from Orlando to Vermont, from Brooklyn to

---

[101]   Poirier (1993); *Business Week* (1994d); Elmer-Dewwit (1993).
[102]   *New Media Markets* (1993).
[103]   *Business Week* (1994f).
[104]   Dentsu Institute for Human Studies (1994: 117).
[105]   Ministry of Posts and Telecommunications (1994b); *New Media Markets* (1994).

Denver.[106] The results did not match the expectations. Major techno-logical problems were still unsolved, particularly the ability of the software system to make possible interaction on a very large scale, for thousands of homes and hundreds of communication sources. While "video-on-demand" companies advertise unlimited possibilities, the technological ability to handle requests still does not go too far beyond the range of choice provided by existing cable and satellite-based systems or on-line servers of the Minitel type. While adequate technology will undoubtedly be developed, the investment necessary to speed it up depends on the existence of a mass market which cannot materialize until efficient technology becomes available. Here again, the issue is not if a multimedia system will develop (it will) but when and how, and under what conditions in different countries, because the cultural meaning of the system will be deeply modified by the timing and shape of the technological trajectory.

Furthermore, the expectations of unlimited demand for entertain-ment seem to be overstated and heavily influenced by the ideology of the "leisure society." While entertainment spending appears to be recession-resilient, payment for the full range of possibilities proposed on-line clearly exceeds the expected evolution of house-holds' income in the near future. Time is also a scarce resource. There are indications that in the United States leisure time decreased by 37% between 1973 and 1994. In addition, media viewing time declined in the second half of the 1980s: between 1985 and 1990 total time spent reading and watching TV and movies declined by 45 hours per year; hours spent watching TV declined by 4%; and hours watching network TV declined by 20%.[107] Although decreasing media exposure seems to be linked more to an overworked society (dual-job families) than to lack of interest, multimedia business is betting on another interpretation: lack of sufficiently attractive content. Indeed, most experts of the media industry consider that the real bottleneck for the expansion of multimedia is that content does not follow the technological transformation of the system: the message is lagging the medium.[108] A dramatic expansion of broadcasting capacity, coupled with interactive choice, will fall short of its potential if there is no real choice in terms of the content: the on-line availability of 50 distinct-but-similar sex/violence movies does not justify the dramatic broadening of transmission capacity. This is why the acquisition of Hollywood studios, movie companies, and TV documentary archives

[106]   Wexler (1994); Lizzio (1994); Sellers (1993); Kaplan (1992); Booker (1994); *Business Week* (1994e).
[107]   Martin (1994).
[108]   Bunker (1994); Cuneo (1994); *The Economist* (1994a); *Business Week* (1994f).

is a must for any global multimedia consortium. Entrepreneurial creators, such as Steven Spielberg, seem to have understood that, **in the new system, because of the potential diversity of contents, the message is the message**: it is the ability to differentiate a product that yields the greatest competitive potential. Thus, any conglomerate with enough financial resources could have access to multimedia technology and, in an increasingly deregulated context, could access almost any market. But whoever controls Bogart's films or the capacity to generate the new electronic Marilyn or the next Jurassic Park episode will be in the position to supply the much-needed commodity to whichever communication support.

However, it is not sure that what people want, even if given the time and resources, is more entertainment with an increasingly sophisticated format, from sadistic video-games to endless sports events. Although there is scant evidence on the matter, some indications point to a more complex demand pattern. One of the most complete surveys on multimedia demand, carried out by Charles Piller on a national sample of 600 adults in 1994 in the United States,[109] revealed a much deeper interest in using multimedia for information access, community affairs, political involvement, and education, than in adding television and movies to their choice. Only 28% of consumers considered video-on-demand as highly desirable, and the lack of interest in entertainment was equally strong among Internet users. On the other hand, political uses were highly valued: 57% would like to participate in electronic town-hall meetings; 46% wanted to use e-mail to send messages to their representatives; and about 50% valued the possibility of voting electronically. Additional services in high demand were: educational/instructional courses; interactive reports on local schools; access to reference materials; access to information about government services. Respondents were ready to back up their opinions with their pocket: 34% were ready to pay an additional $10 a month for distant learning, while only 19% were ready to pay that amount for additional entertainment choice. Also, experiments conducted by multimedia companies for video-on-demand in local markets have shown that people are not ready for a substantial increase in their entertainment dose. Thus, the 18-month experiment conducted by US West/ATT video in Littleton, Colorado, in 1993–4, showed that households had indeed switched from standard video viewing to customized video offerings, but they did not increase the number of films they were viewing: it stayed at 2.5 movies per month, priced at $3 per movie.[110]

[109]　Piller (1994).
[110]　Tobenkin (1993); Martin (1994).

Coupled with the large-scale success of French Minitel, offering services rather than entertainment, and the fast diffusion of personal communication in Internet, observation tends to suggest that mass-produced, diversified entertainment on demand may not be the obvious choice for multimedia users, although it is clear that this is the strategic choice of business firms shaping the field. It may result in an increasing tension between infotainment products, guided by the ideology of what people are, as imagined in marketing think-tanks, and the need for personal communication and information enhancement that asserts itself with great determination in CMC networks. It may well also be that this tension is diluted through the social stratification of different multimedia expressions, a critical theme to which I shall return.

Because of the newness of multimedia, it is difficult to assess their implications for the culture of society, beyond acknowledging that fundamental changes are indeed under way. Nevertheless, scattered empirical evidence and informed commentary on the different components of new communications system provide a basis to ground some hypotheses on the emerging social and cultural trends. Thus, a "scanning report" by the European Foundation for the Improvement of Living and Working Conditions on the development of the "electronic home" emphasizes two critical features of the new life style: its "home centredness," and its individualism.[111] On the one hand, the increasing electronic equipment in European homes has increased their comfort and stepped up their self-sufficiency, enabling them to link up with the whole world from the safety of the home. Together with the increase in the size of housing units and the decrease in size of the household, more space per person is available, making home a cozier place. Indeed, time spent at home went up in the early 1990s. On the other hand, the new electronic home and portable communication devices increase the chances of individual members of the family to organize their own time and space. For instance, microwave ovens, allowing for individual consumption of precooked food, has reduced the incidence of collective family dinners. Individual TV dinner sets represent a growing market. VCRs and walkman devices, together with the decrease in the price of TV sets, radio, and CD players, allow a large segment of the population to be individually hooked into selected audiovisual worlds. Family care is also helped/transformed by electronics: children are monitored from a distance through remote control; studies show the increased use of TV as a baby-sitter while parents do their house work; elderly persons

[111] Moran (1993).

living alone are provided with alarm systems for emergency situations. Yet some social features seem to endure beyond the technological revolution: the sharing of home tasks between genders (or, rather, lack of it) is unaffected by the electronic means; VCR use and the handling of remote control devices reflect the authority structure in the family; and the use of electronic devices is differentiated along gender and age lines, with men more often using computers, women handling electrical home maintenance and telematic services, and children obsessed with video-games.

New electronic media do not depart from traditional cultures: they absorb them. A case in point is the Japanese invention of *karaoke*, rapidly diffusing all over Asia in the 1990s, and most likely spreading to the rest of the world in the near future. In 1991, *karaoke* dissemination in Japan reached 100% of recreational hotels and inns, and about 90% of bars and clubs, to which should be added an explosion of specialized *karaoke* rooms, from under 2,000 in 1989 to over 107,000 in 1992. In 1992, about 52% of Japanese participated in *karaoke*, including 79% of all teenage women.[112] At first sight, *karaoke* extends and amplifies the traditional habit of singing together in bars, something as popular in Japan as it was (and is) in Spain or the UK, thus escaping the world of electronic communication. Yet what in fact it does is to integrate this habit into a preprogrammed machine, whose musical rhythms and repertoire have to be followed by the singer, reciting the words that appear on the screen. Indeed, competition with friends to reach a higher score depends on the reward given by the machine to whoever best follows its pace. The *karaoke* machine is not a musical instrument: the singer is swallowed by the machine to supplement its sounds and images. While in the *karaoke* room we become part of a musical hypertext, we physically enter the multimedia system, and we separate our singing from that of our friends waiting their turn to substitute a linear sequence of performance for the disorderly chorus of traditional pub singing.

Overall, in Europe as in America or in Asia, multimedia appear to be supporting, even in their early stage, a social/cultural pattern characterized by the following features. First, *widespread social and cultural differentation*, leading to the segmentation of the users/viewers/readers/listeners. Not only are the messages segmented by markets following senders' strategies, but they are also increasingly diversified by users of the media, acccording to their interests, taking advantage of interactive capacities. As some experts put it, in the new system,

---

[112]   Dentsu Institute for Human Studies (1994: 140–3).

"prime time is my time. "[113] The formation of virtual communities is but one of the expressions of such differentiation.

Secondly, *increasing social stratification among the users*. Not only will choice of multimedia be restrained to those with time and money to access, and to countries and regions with enough market potential, but cultural/educational differences will be decisive in using interaction to the advantage of each user. The information about what to look for and the knowledge about how to use the message will be essential to truly experience a system different from standard customized mass media. **Thus, the multimedia world will be populated by two essentially distinct populations: the** *interacting and the interacted*, meaning those who are able to select their multidirectional circuits of communication, and those who are provided with a restricted number of prepackaged choices. And who is what will be largely determined by class, race, gender, and country. The unifying cultural power of mass television (from which only a tiny cultural elite had escaped in the past) is now replaced by a socially stratified differentiation, leading to the coexistence of a customized mass media culture and an interactive electronic communication network of self-selected communes.

Thirdly, the communication of all kinds of messages in the same system, even if the system is interactive and selective (in fact, precisely because of this), induces an *integration of all messages in a common cognitive pattern*. Accessing audiovisual news, education, and shows on the same medium, even from different sources, takes one step further the blurring of contents that was already taking place in mass television. From the perspective of the medium, different communication modes tend to borrow codes from each other: interactive educational programs look like video-games; newscasts are constructed as audio-visual shows; trial cases are broadcast as soap operas; pop music is composed for MTV; sports games are choreographed for their distant viewers, so that their messages becomes less and less distinguishable from action movies; and the like. From the perspective of the user (both as receiver and sender, in an interactive system), the choice of various messages under the same communication mode, with easy switching from one to the other, reduces the mental distance between various sources of cognitive and sensorial involvement. The issue at stake is not that the medium is the message: messages are messages. And because they keep their distinctiveness as messages, while being mixed in their symbolic communication process, they blur their codes in this process, creating a multifaceted semantic context made of a random mixture of various meanings.

[113]   Negroponte (1995).

Finally, perhaps *the most important feature of multimedia is that they capture within their domain most cultural expressions, in all their diversity.* Their advent is tantamount to ending the separation, and even the distinction, between audiovisual media and printed media, popular culture and learned culture, entertainment and information, education and persuasion. Every cultural expression, from the worst to the best, from the most elitist to the most popular, comes together in this digital universe that links up in a giant, a historical supertext, past, present, and future manifestations of the communicative mind. By so doing, they construct a new symbolic environment. They make virtuality our reality.

The Culture of Real Virtuality

Cultures are made up of communication processes. And all forms of communication, as Roland Barthes and Jean Baudrillard taught us many years ago, are based on the production and consumption of signs.[114] Thus there is no separation between "reality" and symbolic representation. In all societies humankind has existed in and acted through a symbolic environment. Therefore, what is historically specific to the new communication system, organized around the electronic integration of all communication modes from the typographic to the multisensorial, is not its inducement of virtual reality but the construction of real virtuality. I shall explain, with the help of the dictionary, according to which : "*virtual*: being so in practice though not strictly or in name," and "*real*: actually existing."[115] Thus reality, as experienced, has always been virtual because it is always perceived through symbols that frame practice with some meaning that escapes their strict semantic definition. It is precisely this ability of all forms of language to encode ambiguity and to open up a diversity of interpretations that makes cultural expressions distinct from formal/logical/mathematical reasoning. It is through the polysemic character of our discourses that the complexity and even contradictory quality of messages of the human brain manifest themselves. This range of cultural variation of the meaning of messages is what enables us to interact with each other in a multiplicity of dimensions, some explicit, some implicit. Thus, when critics of electronic media argue that the new symbolic environment does not represent "reality," they

[114]   Barthes (1978); Baudrillard (1972).
[115]   *Oxford Dictionary of Current English* (1992).

implicitly refer to an absurdly primitive notion of "uncoded" real experience that never existed. All realities are communicated through symbols. And in human, interactive communication, regardless of the medium, all symbols are somewhat displaced in relationship to their assigned semantic meaning. In a sense, all reality is virtually perceived.

What is then a communication system that, in contrast to earlier historical experience, generates *real virtuality*? **It is a system in which reality itself (that is, people's material/symbolic existence) is entirely captured, fully immersed in a virtual image setting, in the world of make believe, in which appearances are not just on the screen through which experience is communicated, but they become the experience**. All messages of all kinds become enclosed in the medium, because the medium has become so comprehensive, so diversified, so malleable, that it absorbs in the same multimedia text the whole of human experience, past, present, and future, as in that unique point of the Universe that Jorge Luis Borges called "Aleph." Let me give an example.

In the 1992 American presidential campaign, then Vice-president Dan Quayle, wanted to make a stand in defense of traditional family values. Armed with his moral convictions he initiated an unusual debate with Murphy Brown. Murphy Brown, played by a fine actress, Candice Bergen, was the main character of a popular television soap opera who (re)presented the values and problems of a new kind of woman: the single, working professional woman with her own criteria about life. Around the weeks of the presidential campaign, Murphy Brown (not Candice Bergen) decided to have a child out of wedlock. Vice-president Quayle hurried to condemn her behavior as improper, prompting national outrage, particularly among working women. Murphy Brown (not just Candice Bergen) retaliated: in her next episode, she appeared watching the television interview in which Vice-president Quayle was criticizing her, and she spoke up, sharply criticizing politicians' interference with women's life, and defending her right to a new morality. Eventually *Murphy Brown* increased its share of the audience and Dan Quayle's outdated conservatism contributed to the electoral defeat of President Bush, both events being real and, to some extent, socially relevant. Yet a new text of the real and the imaginary had been composed throughout the dialogue. The unsolicited presence of Murphy Brown's imaginary world in the real life presidential campaign induced the transformation of Quayle (or rather, of his "real" television image) into a character of Murphy Brown's imaginary life: a supertext had been made, blending in the same discourse passionately argued messages emitted from both levels of experience. In this case, virtuality (that is Murphy Brown being in practice what many women were, without being so in the name of any woman) had become real, in the sense that it actually interacted, with some significant impact, with the process of election to the most powerful political office on earth. Granted, the example is extreme and unusual, but I believe it illustrates my analysis, helping to reduce the obscurity of its abstraction. Hoping that such is the case, let me be more precise.

What characterizes the new system of communication, based in the digitized, networked integration of multiple communication modes, is its inclusiveness and comprehensiveness of all cultural expressions. Because of its existence, all kinds of messages in the new type of society work in a binary mode: presence/absence in the multimedia communication system. Only presence in this integrated system permits communicability and socialization of the message. All other messages are reduced to individual imagination or to increasingly marginalized face-to-face subcultures. From society's perspective, *electronically-based communication (typographic, audiovisual, or computer-mediated)* is *communication.* Yet it does not follow that there is homogenization of cultural expressions and full domination of codes by a few central senders. It is precisely because of the diversification, multimodality, and versatility of the new communication system that it is able to embrace and integrate all forms of expression, as well as the diversity of interests, values, and imaginations, including the expression of social conflicts. But the price to pay for inclusion in the system is to adapt to its logic, to its language, to its points of entry, to its encoding and decoding. This is why it is so critical for different kinds of social effects that there should be the development of a multinodal, horizontal network of communication, of Internet type, instead of a centrally dispatched multimedia system, as in the video-on-demand configuration. The setting of barriers to entry into this communication system, and the creation of passwords for the circulation and diffusion of messages throughout the system, are critical cultural battles for the new society, the outcome of which predetermines the fate of symbolically mediated conflicts to be fought in this new historical environment. Who are the *interacting* and who are the *interacted* in the new system, to use the terminology whose meaning I suggested above, largely frames the system of domination and the processes of liberation in the informational society.

The inclusion of most cultural expressions within the integrated communication system based in digitized electronic production, distribution, and exchange of signals, has major consequences for social forms and processes. On the one hand, it weakens considerably the symbolic power of traditional senders external to the system, transmitting through historically encoded social habits: religion, morality, authority, traditional values, political ideology. Not that they disappear, but they are weakened unless they recode themselves in the new system, where their power becomes multiplied by the electronic materialization of spiritually transmitted habits: electronic preachers and interactive fundamentalist networks are a more efficient, more penetrating form of indoctrination in our societies than face-to-face transmission of distant, charismatic authority. But by having to concede the earthly coexistence of transcendental messages, on-demand pornography, soap operas, and chat-lines within the same system, superior spiritual powers still conquer souls but lose their suprahuman status. The final step of secularization of society follows, even if it sometimes takes the paradoxical form of conspicuous consumption of religion, under all kinds of generic and brand names. Societies are finally and truly disenchanted because all wonders are on-line and can be combined into self-constructed image worlds.

On the other hand, the new communication system radically transforms space and time, the fundamental dimensions of human life. Localities become disembodied from their cultural, historical, geographic meaning, and reintegrated into functional networks, or into image collages, inducing a space of flows that substitutes for the space of places. Time is erased in the new communication system when past, present, and future can be programmed to interact with each other in the same message. The *space of flows* and *timeless time* are the material foundations of a new culture, that transcends and includes the diversity of historically transmitted systems of representation: the culture of real virtuality where make-believe is belief in the making.

—— 6 ——

The Space of Flows

Introduction

Space and time are the fundamental, material dimensions of human life. Physicists have unveiled the complexity of such notions, beyond their fallacious intuitive simplicity. School children know that space and time are related. And superstring theory, the latest fashion in physics, advances the hypothesis of a hyperspace that articulates ten dimensions, including time.[1] There is of course no place for such a discussion in my analysis, strictly concerned with the *social meaning of space and time*. But my reference to such complexity goes beyond rhetorical pedantry. It invites us to consider social forms of time and space that are not reducible to what have been our perceptions to date, based upon socio-technical structures superseded by current historical experience.

Since space and time are intertwined in nature and in society, so they will be in my analysis, although for the sake of clarity I shall focus sequentially first on space, in this chapter, and then on time in the next one. The ordering in the sequence is not random: unlike most classical social theories, that assume the domination of space by time, I propose the hypothesis that space organizes time in the network society.This statement will hopefully make more sense at the end of the intellectual journey I propose to the reader in these two chapters.

Both space and time are being transformed under the combined effect of the information technology paradigm, and of social forms and processes induced by the current process of historical change, as presented in this book. However, the actual profile of such transformation sharply departs from common-sense extrapolations of technological determinism. For instance, it appears to be obvious

[1] Kaku (1994).

that advanced telecommunications would make location of offices ubiquitous, thus enabling corporate headquarters to quit expensive, congested, and unpleasant central business districts for custom-made sites in beautiful spots around the world. Yet Mitchell Moss' empirical analysis on the impact of telecommunications on Manhattan's business in the 1980s found that these new, advanced telecommunications facilities were among the factors responsible for slowing down corporate relocation away from New York, for reasons that I shall expose below. Or, to use another example on a different social domain, home-based electronic communication was supposed to induce the decline of dense urban forms, and to diminish spatially localized social interaction. Yet the first mass diffused system of computer mediated communication, the French Minitel, described in the previous chapter, originated in the 1980s in an intense urban environment, whose vitality and face-to-face interaction was hardly undermined by the new medium. Indeed, French students used Minitel to successfully stage *street* demonstrations against the government. In the early 1990s tele-commuting, that is working at home on-line, was practiced by a very small fraction of the labor force, in the United States (between 1% and 2% on a given day), Europe, or Japan, if we except the old, customary practice of professionals to keep working at home or to organize their activity in flexible time and space when they have the leisure to do so.[2] While working at home part-time seems to be emerging as a mode of professional activity in the future, it develops out of the rise of the network enterprise and of the flexible work process, as analyzed in preceding chapters, not as the direct consequence of available technology. The theoretical and practical consequences of such precisions are critical. It is this complexity of the interaction between technology, society, and space that I shall address in the following pages.

To proceed in this direction, I shall examine the empirical record on the transformation of location patterns of core economic activities under the new technological system, both for advanced services and for manufacturing. Afterwards, I shall try to assess the scarce evidence on the interaction between the rise of the electronic home and the evolution of the city, and I shall elaborate on the recent evolution of urban forms in various contexts. I shall then synthesize the observed

[2]   For an excellent overview of the interaction between telecommunications and spatial processes, see Graham and Marvin (1996). For evidence on the impact of telecommunications on business districts, see Moss (1987, 1991, 1992:147–58). For summary of evidence on teleworking and telecommuting in advanced societies, see Qvortup (1992); and Korte et al. (1988).

tendencies under a new spatial logic that I label *space of flows*. I shall oppose to such logic the historically rooted spatial organization of our common experience: *the space of places*. And I shall refer to the reflection of such dialectical opposition between the space of flows and the space of places in current debates in architecture and urban design. The purpose of this intellectual itinerary is to draw the profile of this new spatial process, the space of flows, that is becoming the dominant spatial manifestation of power and function in our societies. In spite of all my efforts to anchor the new spatial logic in the empirical record, I am afraid it is unavoidable, towards the end of the chapter, to confront the reader with some fundamentals of a social theory of space, as a way to approach the current transformation of the material basis of our experience. Yet my ability to communicate a rather abstract theorization of new spatial forms and processes will hopefully be enhanced by a brief survey of available evidence on recent spatial patterning of dominant economic functions and social practices.[3]

Advanced Services, Information Flows, and the Global City

The informational/global economy is organized around command and control centers able to coordinate, innovate, and manage the intertwined activities of networks of firms.[4] Advanced services, including finance, insurance, real estate, consulting, legal services, advertising, design, marketing, public relations, security, information gathering, and management of information systems, but also R&D and scientific innovation, are at the core of all economic processes, be it in manufacturing, agriculture, energy, or services of different kinds.[5] They all can be reduced to knowledge generation and

---

[3]   To a large extent, the empirical basis and the analytical foundations of this chapter rely on the research work I did in the 1980s, summarized and elaborated in my book *The Informational City: Information Technology, Economic Restructuring, and the Urban–Regional Process* (Castells 1989). Although this chapter contains updated, additional information on various countries, as well as further theoretical elaboration, I still refer the reader to the cited book for more detailed analysis and empirical support of the analysis presented here. Accordingly, *I shall not repeat here again the empirical sources that have been used and cited in the above-mentioned book.* This note should be considered as a generic reference to the sources and material contained in *The Informational City*. For an up-to-date discussion on these matters, see also Graham and Marvin (1996).
[4]   For an excellent overview of current transformations of spatial forms and processes at the global level, see Hall (1995: 3–32).
[5]   Daniels (1993).

information flows.[6] Thus, advanced telecommunications systems could make possible their scattered location around the globe. Yet more than a decade of studies on the matter have established a different spatial pattern, characterized by the simultaneous dispersion and concentration of advanced services.[7] On the one hand, advanced services have substantially increased their share in employment and GNP in most countries, and they display the highest growth in employment and the highest investment rates in the leading metropolitan areas of the world.[8] They are pervasive, and they are located throughout the geography of the planet, excepting the "black holes" of marginality. On the other hand, there has been a spatial concentration of the upper tier of such activities in a few nodal centers of a few countries.[9] Such concentration follows a hierarchy between tiers of urban centers, with the higher-level functions, in terms of both power and skill, being concentrated in some major metropolitan areas.[10] Saskia Sassen's classic study on the global city has shown the joint dominance of New York, Tokyo, and London in international finance, and in most consulting and business services of international scope.[11] These three centers together cover the spectrum of time zones for the purpose of financial trading, and work largely as a unit in the same system of endless transactions. But other centers are important, and even more preeminent in some specific segments of trade, for example Chicago and Singapore in futures' contracts (in fact, first practiced in Chicago in 1972). Hong Kong, Osaka, Frankfurt, Zurich, Paris, Los Angeles, San Francisco, Amsterdam, and Milan are also major centers both in finance and in international business services.[12] And a number of "regional centers" are rapidly joining the network, as "emergent markets" develop all over the world: Madrid, São Paulo, Buenos Aires, Mexico, Taipei, Moscow, Budapest, among others.

As the global economy expands and incorporates new markets it also organizes the production of advanced services required to manage the new units joining the system, and the conditions of their ever-changing linkages.[13] A case in point that illustrates such process is Madrid, relatively a backwater of the global economy until 1986. In

[6]   Norman (1993).
[7]   Graham (1994).
[8]   Enderwick (ed.) (1989).
[9]   Daniels (1993).
[10] Thrift (1986); Thrift and Leyshon (1992).
[11] Sassen (1991).
[12] Daniels (1993).
[13] Borja et al. (eds) (1991).

that year Spain joined the European Community, opening up fully to
foreign capital investment in the stock exchange markets, in banking
operations, and in acquisition of companies equity, as well as in real
estate. As shown in our study[14], in the 1986–90 period foreign direct
investment in Madrid and in Madrid's stock exchange fueled a
period of rapid regional economic growth, together with a boom in
real estate and a fast expansion of employment in business services.
Acquisitions of stocks in Madrid by foreign investors between 1982
and 1988 jumped from 4,494 million pesetas (pts) to 623,445 million
pts. Foreign direct investment in Madrid went up from 8,000 million
pts in 1985 to almost 400,000 million pts in 1988. Accordingly, office
construction in downtown Madrid, and high-level residential real
estate, went in the late 1980s through the same kind of frenzy experienced in New York and London. The city was deeply transformed
both through the saturation of valuable space in the core city, and
through a process of massive suburbanization that, until then, had
been a somewhat limited phenomenon in Madrid.

Along the same line of argument, the study by Cappelin on services
networking in European cities shows the increasing interdependence
and complementarity between medium-sized urban centers in the
European Union.[15] He concluded that

> The relative importance of the city–region relationships seems
> to decrease with respect to the importance of the relationships
> which interlink various cities of different regions and countries
> . . . New activities concentrate in particular poles and that implies
> an increase of disparities between the urban poles and their
> respective hinterlands.[16]

Thus, the global city phenomenon cannot be reduced to a few
urban cores at the top of the hierarchy. It is a process that connects
advanced services, producer centers, and markets in a global network,
with different intensity and at a different scale depending upon the
relative importance of the activities located in each area *vis-à-vis* the
global network. Inside each country, the networking architecture
reproduces itself into regional and local centers, so that the whole
system becomes interconnected at the global level. Territories
surrounding these nodes play an increasingly subordinate function,
sometimes becoming irrelevant or even dysfunctional) for example,
Mexico City's *colonias populares* (originally squatter settlements) that
account for about two-thirds of the megapolitan population, without

[14] For a summary of the research report, see Castells (1991).
[15] Cappelin (1991).
[16] Ibid.: 237.

playing any distinctive role in the functioning of Mexico City as an international business center).[17] Furthermore, globalization stimulates regionalization. In his studies on European regions in the 1990s, Philip Cooke has shown, on the basis of available evidence, that the growing internationalization of economic activities throughout Europe has made regions more dependent on these activities. Accordingly, regions, under the impulse of their governments and business elites, have restructured themselves to compete in the global economy, and they have established networks of cooperation between regional institutions and between region-based companies. Thus, regions and localities do not disappear, but become integrated in international networks that link up their most dynamic sectors.[18]

An approximation to the evolving architecture of information flows in the global economy has been obtained by Michelson and Wheeler on the basis of data analysis of traffic for one of the leading business couriers, Federal Express Corporation.[19] They studied the 1990s movement of overnight letters, packages, and boxes between US metropolitan areas, as well as between the US major sending centers and international destinations. The results of their analysis, illustrated in figures 6.1 and 6.2 show two basic trends: (a) dominance of some nodes, particularly New York, followed by Los Angeles, increasing over time; (b) selected national and international circuits of connection. As they conclude:

> All indicators point to a strengthening of the hierarchical structure of command-and-control functions and the resulting exchange of information . . . The locational concentration of information results from high levels of uncertainty, driven in turn by technological change, market demassification, deregulation and market globalization. . . . (However) as the current epoch unfolds, the importance of flexibility as a basic coping mechanism, and of agglomeration economies as the preeminent locational force will persist. The importance of the city as a center of gravity for economic transactions thus will not vanish. But with the impending regulation of international markets . . . with less uncertainty about the rules of the economic game and the players involved, the concentration of the information industry will slow and certain aspects of production and distribution will filter into lower levels of an internationalized urban hierarchy.[20]

[17] Davis (1994).
[18] Cooke (1994); Cooke and Morgan (1993).
[19] Michelson and Wheeler (1994).
[20] Ibid.: 102–3.

The space of flows

Figure 6.1 Largest absolute growth in information flows, 1982 and 1990
Source: Federal Express data; elaborated by Michelson and Wheeler (1994).

Indeed, the hierarchy in the network is by no means assured or stable: it is subject to fierce inter-city competition, as well as to the venture of highly risky investments in both finance and real estate. Thus, P.W.Daniels, in one of the most comprehensive studies on the matter, explains the partial failure of the major redevelopment project of Canary Wharf in London's Docklands because of the overextended strategy of its developer, the notorious Canadian firm Olympia & York, unable to absorb the office development glut of the early 1990s, in the wake of retrenchment of financial services employment in both London and New York. He concludes that:

> The expansion of services into the international market place has therefore introduced a greater degree of flexibility, and ultimately competition, into the global urban system than was

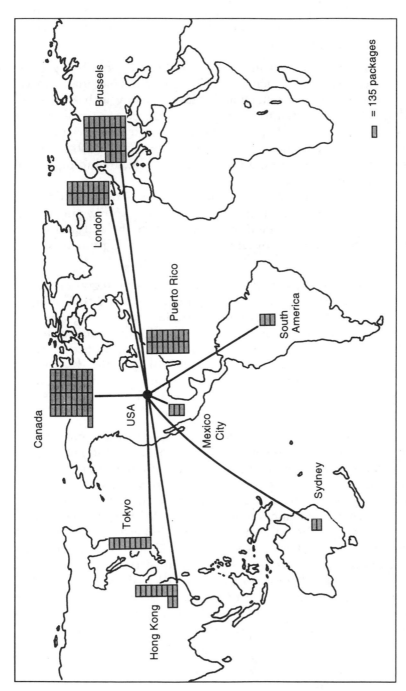

Figure 6.2 Exports of information from the United States to major world regions and centers
Source: Federal Express data, 1990; elaborated by Michelson and Wheeler (1994).

the case in the past. As the experience with Canary Wharf has
shown, it also made the outcome of large-scale planning and
redevelopment within cities a hostage to external international
factors over which they can have limited control.[21]

Thus, in the early 1990s, while business-led explosive urban growth
was experienced in cities such as Bangkok, Taipei, Shanghai, Mexico
D.F., or Bogota, on the other hand, Madrid, along with New York,
London, and Paris, went into a slump that triggered a sharp downturn
in real estate prices and halted new construction. This urban roller
coaster at different periods, across areas of the world, illustrates both
the dependence and vulnerability of any locale, including major
cities, to changing global flows.

But why must these advanced service systems still be dependent on
agglomeration in a few large metropolitan nodes? Here again, Saskia
Sassen, capping years of field work research by herself and other
researchers in different contexts, offers convincing answers. She
argues that:

> The combination of spatial dispersal and global integration has
> created a new strategic role for major cities. Beyond their long
> history as centers for international trade and banking, these
> cities now function in four new ways: first, as highly concentrated
> command points in the organization of the world economy;
> second, as key locations for finance and for specialized service
> firms . . . ; third, as sites of production, including the production
> of innovation in these leading industries; and fourth, as markets
> for the products and innovations produced.[22]

These cities, or rather, their business districts, are information-based,
value production complexes, where corporate headquarters and
advanced financial firms can find both the suppliers and the highly
skilled, specialized labor they require. They constitute indeed
networks of production and management, whose flexibility needs *not*
to internalize workers and suppliers, but to be able to access them
when it fits, and in the time and quantities that are required in each
particular instance. Flexibility and adaptability are better served by
this combination between agglomeration of core networks, and
global networking of these cores and of their dispersed, ancillary
networks, via telecommunications and air transportation. Other
factors seem also to contribute to strengthen concentration of high-
level activities in a few nodes: once they are constituted, heavy

[21]   Daniels (1993: 166).
[22]   Sassen (1991: 3–4).

investment in valuable real estate by corporations explains their reluctance to move because such a move would devalue their fixed assets; also, face-to-face contacts for critical decisions are still necessary in the age of widespread eavesdropping, since, as Saskia Sassen reports a manager confessed to her during an interview, sometimes business deals are, of necessity, marginally illegal.[23] And, finally, major metropolitan centers still offer the greatest opportunities for the personal enhancement, social status, and individual self-gratification of the much-needed upper-level professionals, from good schools for their children to symbolic membership at the heights of conspicuous consumption, including art and entertainment.[24]

Nevertheless, advanced services, and even more so services at large, do indeed disperse and decentralize to the periphery of metropolitan areas, to smaller metropolitan areas, to less-developed regions, and to some less-developed countries.[25] New regional centers of service processing activities have emerged in the United States (for example, Atlanta, Georgia, or Omaha, Nebraska), in Europe (for example, Barcelona, Nice, Stuttgart, Bristol), or in Asia (for example, Bombay, Bangkok, Shanghai). The peripheries of major metropolitan areas are bustling with new office development, be it Walnut Creek in San Francisco or Reading near London. And in some cases, new major service centers have sprung up on the edge of the historic city, Paris' La Défense being the most notorious and successful example. Yet, in almost all instances, decentralization of office work affects "back offices," that is the mass processing of transactions that execute strategies decided and designed in the corporate centers of high finance and advanced services.[26] These are precisely the activities that employ the bulk of semi-skilled office workers, most of them suburbanite women, many of them replaceable or recyclable, as technology evolves and the economic roller coaster goes on.

What is significant about this spatial system of advanced service activities is neither their concentration nor decentralization, since both processes are indeed taking place at the same time throughout countries and continents. Nor is it the hierarchy of their geography, since this is in fact tributary to the variable geometry of money and

[23]   Personal notes, reported by Sassen over a glass of Argentinian wine, Harvard Inn, April 22 1994.
[24]   For an approximation to the differentiation of social worlds in global cities, using New York as an illustration, see the various essays collected in Mollenkopf and Castells (eds) (1991); and Mollenkopf (ed.) (1989); also Zukin (1992).
[25]   For evidence on spatial decentralization of services, see Castells (1989: ch.3); Daniels 1993: ch. 5); and Marshall et al. (1988).
[26]   See Castells (1989b: ch.3); and Dunford and Kafkalas (eds) (1992).

information flows. After all, who could predict in the early 1980s that Taipei, Madrid or Buenos Aires could emerge as important international financial and business centers? I believe that the megalopolis Hong Kong–Shenzhen–Guangzhou–Zhuhai–Macau will be one of the major financial and business capitals in the early twenty-first century, thus inducing a major realignment in the global geography of advanced services.[27] But for the sake of the spatial analysis I am proposing here, it is secondary if I miss my prediction. Because, while the actual location of high-level centers in each period is critical for the distribution of wealth and power in the world, from the perspective of the spatial logic of the new system what matters is the versatility of its networks. The global city is not a place, but a process. A process by which centers of production and consumption of advanced services, and their ancillary local societies, are connected in a global network, while simultaneously downplaying the linkages with their hinterlands, on the basis of information flows.

The New Industrial Space

The advent of high-technology manufacturing, namely microelectronics-based, computer-aided manufacturing, ushered in a new logic of industrial location. Electronic firms, the producers of new information technology devices, were also the first to practice the locational strategy both allowed and required by the information-based production process. During the 1980s, a number of empirical studies conducted by faculty and graduate students at the University of California Berkeley's Institute of Urban and Regional Development provided a solid grasp on the profile of "the new industrial space."[28] It is characterized by the technological and organizational ability to separate the production process in different locations while reintegrating its unity through telecommunications linkages, and microelectronics-based precision and flexibility in the fabrication of components. Furthermore, geographic specificity of each phase of the production process is made advisable by the singularity of the labor force required at each stage, and by the different social and environmental features involved in the living conditions of highly distinct segments of this labor force. This is because high-technology manufacturing presents an occupational composition very different

[27]   See Kwok and So (1992); Henderson (1991); Kwok and So (eds) (1995).
[28]   For an analytical summary of the evidence gathered by these studies on new patterns of manufacturing location see Castells (1988a). See also Scott (1988); Henderson (1989).

from traditional manufacturing: it is organized in a bipolar structure around two predominant groups of roughly similar size; a highly skilled, science- and technology-based labor force, on the one hand; a mass of unskilled workers engaged in routine assembly and auxiliary operations, on the other hand. While automation has increasingly enabled companies to eliminate the lower tier of workers, the staggering increase in the volume of production still employs, and will for some time, a considerable number of unskilled and semi-skilled workers whose location in the same areas as scientists and engineers is neither economically feasible nor socially suitable, in the prevailing social context. In between, skilled operators also represent a distinctive group that can be separated from the high levels of high-technology production. Because of the light weight of the final product, and because of easy communication linkages developed by companies throughout the globe, electronics firms, particularly American, developed from the origins of the industry (as early as Fairchild's plant location in Hong Kong in 1962) a locational pattern characterized by the international spatial division of labor.[29] Roughly speaking, both for microelectronics and computers, four different types of location were sought for each one of the four distinctive operations in the production process:

a)   R&D, innovation, and prototype fabrication were concentrated in highly innovative industrial centers in core areas, generally with good quality of life before their development process degraded the environment to some extent;
b)   skilled fabrication in branch plants, generally in newly industrializing areas in the home country, which in the case of the US generally meant in medium-sized towns in the Western states;
c)   semi-skilled, large-scale assembly and testing work that from the very beginning was located offshore in a substantial proportion, particularly in South East Asia, with Singapore and Malaysia pioneering the movement of attracting factories of American electronics corporations;
d)   customization of devices and aftersales maintenance and technical support, which was organized in regional centers throughout the globe, generally in the area of major electronics markets, originally in America and Western Europe, although in the 1990s the Asian markets rose to equal status.

European companies, used to cozy locations on their protected home turfs, were pushed to decentralize their production systems in

---

[29]   Cooper (ed.) (1994).

a similar global chain, as markets opened up, and they started to feel the pinch of competition from Asian-based operations, and from American and Japanese technological advantage.[30] Japanese companies tried to resist for a long time to quit "fortress Japan," both for reasons of nationalism (at the request of their government) and because of their close dependence on "just in time" networks of suppliers. However, unbearable congestion and skyrocketing prices of operation in the Tokyo–Yokohama area forced first regional decentralization (helped by MITI's Technopolis program) in less-developed areas of Japan, particularly in Kyushu;[31] and then, from the late 1980s, Japanese companies proceeded to follow the locational pattern initiated by their American competitors two decades earlier: offshore production facilities in South East Asia, searching for lower labor costs and looser environmental constraints, and dissemination of factories throughout the main markets in America, Europe, and Asia as a preemption to overcome future protectionism.[32] Thus, the end of Japanese exceptionalism confirmed the accuracy of the locational model that, together with a number of colleagues, we proposed to understand the new spatial logic of high technology industry. Figure 6.3 displays schematically the spatial logic of this model, elaborated on the basis of empirical evidence gathered by a number of researchers in different contexts.[33]

A key element in this location pattern is the decisive importance of technological innovation production complexes for the whole system. This is what Peter Hall and I, as well as the pioneer in this field of research, Philippe Aydalot, called "milieux of innovation."[34] By milieu of innovation I understand a specific set of relationships of production and management, based on a social organization that by and

[30] Chesnais (1994).
[31] Castells and Hall (1994).
[32] Aoyama (1995).
[33] Castells (1989b: ch.2).
[34] The concept of milieu of innovation, as applied to technological/industrial development emerged in the early 1980s in a series of exchanges, in Berkeley, between Peter Hall, the late Philippe Aydalot, and myself. We were also influenced by some economic writings on the matter, around the same time, by B. Arthur, and by A.E. Anderson. Peter Hall and I, in separate papers, attempted formulations of the concept in 1984 and subsequent years; and in Europe the research network originally organized by Philippe Aydalot, the Groupe de Recherche sur les Milieux Innovateurs (GREMI), undertook systematic research on the matter, published in 1986 and subsequent years. Among GREMI researchers, Roberto Camagni provided, in my personal opinion, the most precise analysis on this topic.

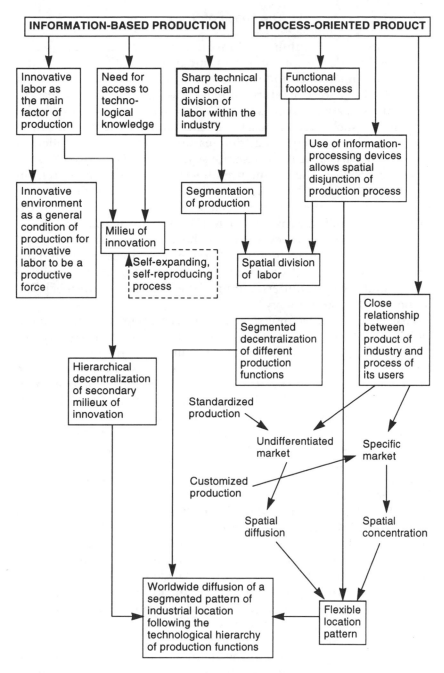

Figure 6.3 System of relationships between the characteristics of information technology manufacturing and the industry's spatial pattern
Source: Elaborated by Castells (1989a).

large shares a work culture and instrumental goals aimed at generating new knowledge, new processes, and new products. Although the concept of milieu does not necessarily include a spatial dimension, I argue that in the case of information technology industries, at least in this century, spatial proximity is a necessary material condition for the existence of such milieux, because of the nature of the interaction in the innovation process. What defines the specificity of a milieu of innovation is its capacity to generate synergy, that is the added value resulting not from the cumulative effect of the elements present in the milieu but from their interaction. Milieux of innovation are the fundamental sources of innovation and of generation of value added in the process of industrial production in the information age. Peter Hall and I studied for several years the formation, structure, and dynamics of the main technological milieux of innovation around the world, both actual and supposed. The results of our inquiry added some elements to the understanding of the locational pattern of information technology industry.[35]

First of all, high-technology-led industrial milieux of innovation, which we called "technopoles," come in a variety of urban formats. Most notably, it is clear that in most countries, with the important exceptions of the United States and, to some extent Germany, the leading technopoles are in fact contained in the leading metropolitan areas: Tokyo, Paris-Sud, London–M4 Corridor, Milan, Seoul–Inchon, Moscow–Zelenograd, and at a considerable distance Nice–Sophia Antipolis, Taipei–Hsinchu, Singapore, Shanghai, São Paulo, Barcelona, and so on. The partial exception of Germany (after all, Munich is a major metropolitan area) relates directly to political history: the destruction of Berlin, the preeminent European science-based industrial center, and the relocation of Siemens from Berlin to Munich in the last months of the Third Reich, under the anticipated protection of American occupation forces and with the subsequent support of the Bavarian CSU party. Thus, against the excessive imagery of upstart technopoles there is indeed continuity in the spatial history of technology and industrialization in the information age: major metropolitan centers around the world continue to cumulate innovation-inducing factors and to generate synergy, in manufacturing as in advanced services.

However, some of the most important innovation centers of information-technology manufacturing are indeed new, particularly in the world's technological leader, the United States. Silicon Valley, Boston's Route 128 (rejuvenating an old, traditional manufacturing

---

[35]   Castells and Hall (1994).

structure), the Southern California Technopole, North Carolina's Research Triangle, Seattle, and Austin, among others, were by and large linked to the latest wave of information-technology-based industrialization. We have shown that their development resulted from the clustering of specific varieties of the usual factors of production: capital, labor, and raw material, brought together by some kind of institutional entrepreneur, and constituted by a particular form of social organization. Their raw material was made up of new knowledge, related to strategically important fields of application, produced by major centers of innovation, such as Stanford University, CalTech, or MIT schools of engineering research teams, and the networks built around them. Their labor, distinct from the knowledge factor, required the concentration of a large number of highly skilled scientists and engineers, from a variety of locally based schools, including those above mentioned but also others, such as Berkeley, San Jose State, or Santa Clara, in the case of Silicon Valley. Their capital was also specific, willing to take the high risks of investing in pioneering high tech: either because of the military imperative on performance (defense-related spending); or else because of the high stakes of venture capital betting on the extra rewards of risk-taking investments. The articulation of these production factors was generally the fact, at the onset of the process, of an institutional actor, such as Stanford University launching the Stanford Industrial Park that induced Silicon Valley; or the Air Force commanders who, relying on Los Angeles boosterism, won for Southern California the defense contracts that would make the new Western metropolis the largest high-technology defense complex in the world. Finally, social networks, of different kinds, powerfully contributed to the consolidation of the milieu of innovation, and to its dynamism, ensuring the communication of ideas, the circulation of labor, and the cross-fertilization of technological innovation and business entrepreneurialism.

What our research on the new milieux of innovation, in the US or elsewhere, shows is that while there is indeed spatial continuity in metropolitan dominance, it can also be reversed given the right conditions. And that the right conditions concern the capacity to spatially concentrate the proper ingredients for inducing synergy. If such is the case, as our evidence seems to support, then we do have a new industrial space marked by fundamental discontinuity: milieux of innovation, new and old, constitute themselves on the basis of their internal structure and dynamics, later attracting firms, capital and labor to the seedbed of innovation they constituted. Once established, milieux of innovation both compete and cooperate between different regions, creating a network of interaction that brings them together in a common industrial structure beyond their geographical discontinuity. Research by Camagni and the research teams organized around the GREMI network[36] shows the growing interdependence of these milieux of innovation all over the globe, while at the same time emphasizing how decisive for their fate is the capacity of each milieu to enhance its synergy. Finally, milieux of innovation command global networks of production and distribution that extend their reach all over the planet. This is why some researchers, such as Amin and Robins, argue that the new industrial system is neither global nor local but "a new articulation of global and local dynamics."[37]

However, to have a clear vision of the new industrial space constituted in the information age we must add some precision. This is because too often the emphasis of the analysis has been placed on the hierarchical spatial division of labor between different functions located in different territories. This is important, but not essential in the new spatial logic. Territorial hierarchies can be blurred, and even reversed, as the industry expands throughout the world, and as competition enhances or depresses entire agglomerations, including milieux of innovation themselves. Also, secondary milieux of innovation are constituted, sometimes as decentralized systems spun off from primary centers, but they often find their niches in competition with their original matrices, examples to the point being Seattle *vis-à-vis* Silicon Valley and Boston in software, or Austin, Texas, *vis-à-vis* New York or Minneapolis in computers. Furthermore, in the 1990s, the development of electronics industry in Asia, mainly under the impulse of American–Japanese competition, has complicated extraordinarily the geography of the industry in its mature stage, as shown in the analyses by Cohen and Borrus and by Dieter Ernst.[38] On the one hand, there has been substantial upgrading of the technological potential of American multinationals' subsidiaries, particularly in Singapore, Malaysia, and Taiwan, and this upgrading has trickled down to their local subsidiaries. On the other hand, Japanese electronics firms, as mentioned above, have massively decentralized their production in Asia, both to export globally and to supply their onshore parent plants. In both cases, a substantial supply base has been built in Asia, thus rendering obsolete the old spatial division of labor in which South East and East Asian subsidiaries occupied the bottom level of the hierarchy.

Furthermore, on the basis of the review of available evidence up to 1994, including his own company surveys, Richard Gordon con-

---

[36] Camagni (1991).
[37] Amin and Robins (1991).
[38] Cohen and Borrus (1995a); Ernst (1994c).

vincingly argues for the emergence of a new spatial division of labor, one characterized by its variable geometry, and its back and forth linkages between firms located in different territorial complexes, including the leading milieux of innovation. His detailed analysis of developments in 1990s' Silicon Valley shows the importance of extra-regional relationships for the most technologically sophisticated and transaction-intensive interactions of regional high technology firms. Thus he argues that

> in this new global context, localized agglomeration, far from constituting an alternative to spatial dispersion, becomes the principal basis for participation in a global network of regional economies . . . Regions and networks in fact constitute interdependent poles within the new spatial mosaic of global innovation. Globalization in this context involves not the leavening impact of universal processes but, on the contrary, the calculated synthesis of cultural diversity in the form of differentiated regional innovation logics and capabilities.[39]

The new industrial space does not represent the demise of old, established metropolitan areas and the rising sun of new, high-tech regions. Nor can it be apprehended under the simplistic opposition between automation at the center and low-cost manufacturing at the periphery. It is organized in a hierarchy of innovation and fabrication articulated in global networks. But the direction and architecture of these networks are submitted to the endless changing movements of cooperation and competition between firms and between locales, sometimes historically cumulative, sometimes reversing the established pattern through deliberate institutional entrepreneurialism. What does remain as the characteristic logic of the new industrial location is its geographical discontinuity, paradoxically made up of territorial production complexes. The new industrial space is organized around flows of information that bring together and separate at the same time – depending upon cycles or firms, – their territorial components. And as the logic of information technology manufacturing trickles down from the producers of information technology devices to the users of such devices in the whole realm of manufacturing, so the new spatial logic expands, creating a multiplicity of global industrial networks whose intersections and exclusions transform the very notion of industrial location from factory sites to manufacturing flows.

---

[39]   Gordon (1994: 46).

Everyday Life in the Electronic Cottage: the End of Cities?

The development of electronic communication and information systems allows for an increasing disassociation between spatial proximity and the performance of everyday life's functions: work, shopping, entertainment, healthcare, education, public services, governance, and the like. Accordingly, futurologists often predict the demise of the city, or at least of cities as we have known them until now, once they are voided of their functional necessity. Processes of spatial transformation are of course much more complicated, as history shows. Therefore, it is worthwhile to consider the scant empirical record on the matter.[40]

A dramatic increase of teleworking is the most usual assumption about the impact of information technology on cities, and the last hope for metropolitan transportation planners before surrendering to the inevitability of the mega-gridlock. Yet, in 1988, a leading European researcher on telecommuting could write, without the shadow of a joke, that "There are more people doing research on telework than there are actual teleworkers."[41] In fact, as pointed by Qvortup, the whole debate is biased by the lack of precision in defining telework, leading to considerable uncertainty when measuring the phenomenon.[42] After reviewing available evidence, he adequately distinguishes between three categories; (a) "Substitutors, those who substitute work done at home for work done in a traditional work setting." These are telecommuters in the strict sense; (b) self-employed, working on-line from their homes; (c) supplementers, "bringing supplementary work home from their conventional office." Furthermore, in some cases this "supplementary work" takes most of the working time; for example, according to Kraut,[43] in the case of university professors. By most reliable accounts the first category, telecommuters *stricto sensu* employed regularly to work on-line at home, is very small overall, and is not expected to grow substantially in the foreseeable future.[44] In the United States the highest estimates evaluated in 1991 about 5.5 million home-based telecommuters, but of this total only 16% telecommuted 35 hours or more per week, 25% telecommuted less than one day a week, with two days a week being

---

[40] For sources on topics covered in this section, see Graham and Marvin (1996).
[41] Steinle (1988:8).
[42] Qvortup (1992:8).
[43] Kraut (1989).
[44] Rijn and Williams (eds) (1988); Nilles (1988); Huws et al. (1990).

the most common pattern. Thus, the percentage of workers who on any given day are telecommuting ranges, depending on estimates, between 1% and 2% of total labor force, with major metropolitan areas in California displaying the highest percentages.[45] On the other hand, what seems to be emerging is telecommuting from telecenters, that is networked computer facilities scattered in the suburbs of metropolitan areas for workers to work on-line with their companies.[46] If these trends are confirmed, homes would not become workplaces, but work activity could spread considerably throughout the metropolitan area, increasing urban decentralization. Increase of home work may also result as a form of electronic outworking by temporary workers, paid by the piece of information processing under an individualized subcontracting arrangement.[47] Interestingly enough, in the United States, a 1991 national survey showed that fewer than a half of home telecommuters used computers: the rest worked with a telephone, pen, and paper.[48] Examples of such activities are social workers and welfare fraud investigators in Los Angeles County.[49] What is certainly significant, and on the rise, is the development of self-employment, and of "supplementers," either full-time or part-time, as part of the broader trend toward the disaggregation of labor and the formation of virtual business networks, as indicated in previous chapters. This does not imply the end of the office, but the diversification of working sites for a large fraction of the population, and particularly for its most dynamic, professional segment. Increasingly mobile tele-computing equipment will enhance this trend toward the office-on-the-run, in the most literal sense.[50]

How do these tendencies affect cities? Scattered data seem to indicate that transportation problems will get worse, not better, because increasing activity and time compression allowed by new networking organization translate into higher concentration of markets in certain areas, and into greater physical mobility for a labor force that was previously confined to its working sites during working hours.[51] Work-related commuting time is kept at a steady level in the US metropolitan areas, not because of improved technology, but because of a more decentralized location pattern of jobs and residences that

---

[45]   Mokhtarian (1991a, 1991b); Handy and Mokhtarian (1995).
[46]   Mokhtarian (1991b).
[47]   See Lozano (1989); Gurstein (1990).
[48]   "Telecommuting Data form Link Resources Corporation", cited by Mokhtarian (1991b).
[49]   Mokhtarian (1992:12).
[50]   "The New Face of Business," in *Business Week* (1994a: 99ff).
[51]   I have relied on a balanced evaluation of impacts by Vessali (1995).

allows easier, suburb-to-suburb traffic flows. In those cities, particularly in Europe, where a radioconcentric pattern still dominates daily
commuting (such as Paris, Madrid, or Milan), commuting time is
sharply up, particularly for stubborn automobile addicts.[52] As for the
new, sprawling metropolises of Asia, their coming into the information age is parallel to their discovery of the most awesome traffic jams
in history, from Bangkok to Shanghai.

Teleshopping is also slow to live up to its promise. While it is
increasing in most countries, in fact it is mainly substituting for traditional mail catalog orders, rather than for actual presence in
shopping malls and merchant streets. As with other on-line activities
of everyday life, it supplements rather than replaces commercial
areas.[53] A similar story can be told of most on-line consumer services.
For instance, telebanking[54] is spreading fast, mainly under the
impulse of banks interested in eliminating branch offices and
replacing them by on-line customer services and automated teller
machines. However, the consolidated bank branches continue as
service centers, to sell financial products to their customers through
a personalized relationship. Even on-line, cultural features of
localities may be important as locational factors for information-
oriented transactions. Thus, First Direct, the telephone banking
branch of Midland Bank in Britain, located in Leeds because its
research "showed West Yorkshire's plain accent, with its flat vowel
sounds but clear diction and apparent classlessness, to be the most
easily understood and acceptable throughout the UK – a vital element
of any telephone-based business."[55] Thus, it is the system of branch
office sellers, automated tellers, customer service-by-telephone, and
on-line transactions that constitutes the new banking industry.

Health services offer an even more interesting case of the emerging
dialectics between concentration and centralization of people-
oriented services. On the one hand, expert systems, on-line
communications, and high-resolution video transmission allow for
the distant interconnection of medical care. For instance, in a practice that has become usual, if not yet routine, in 1995, highly skilled
surgeons supervise by videoconference surgery performed at the
other end of the country or of the world, literally guiding the less-
expert hand of another surgeon into a human body. Regular health
checks are also conducted via computer and telephone on the basis
of patients' computerized, updated information. Neighborhood

[52]   Cervero (1989, 1991); Bendixon (1991).
[53]   Miles (1988); Schoonmaker (1993); Menotti (1995).
[54]   Silverstone (1991); Castano (1991).
[55]   Fazy (1995).

healthcare centers are backed by information systems to improve the quality and efficiency of their primary-level attention. Yet, on the other hand, in most countries major medical complexes emerge in specific locales, generally in large metropolitan areas. Usually organized around a big hospital, often connected to medical and nursing schools, they include in their physical proximity private clinics headed by the most prominent hospital doctors, radiology centers, test laboratories, specialized pharmacists, and, not infrequently, gift shops and mortuaries, to cater to the whole range of possibilities. Indeed, such medical complexes are a major economic and cultural force in the areas and cities where they are located, and tend to expand in their surrounding vicinity over time. When forced to relocate, the whole complex moves together.[56]

Schools and universities are paradoxically the institutions least affected by the virtual logic embedded in information technology, in spite of the foreseeable quasi-universal use of computers in the classrooms of advanced countries. But they will hardly vanish into the virtual space. In the case of elementary and secondary schools, this is because they are as much childcare centers and/or children's warehouses as they are learning institutions. In the case of universities, this is because the quality of education is still and will be for a long time, associated with the intensity of face-to-face interaction. Thus, the large-scale experiences of "distant universities," regardless of their quality (bad in Spain, good in Britain), seem to show that they are second-option forms of education which could play a significant role in a future, enhanced system of adult education, but which could hardly replace current higher education institutions.

On the other hand, computer-mediated communication is diffusing around the world, although with an extremely uneven geography, as mentioned above in chapter 5. Thus, some segments of societies across the globe, invariably concentrated in the upper professional strata, interact with each other, reinforcing the social dimension of the space of flows.[57]

There is no point in exhausting the list of empirical illustrations of the actual impacts of information technology on the spatial dimension of everyday life. What emerges from different observations is a similar picture of simultaneous spatial dispersion and concentration via information technologies. People increasingly work and manage services from their home, as the 1993 survey of the European Foundation for the Improvement of Living Conditions shows.[58] Thus,

[56]   Lincoln et al. (1993); Moran (1990); Miller and Swensson (1995).
[57]   Batty and Barr (1994); Graham and Marvin (1996).
[58]   Moran (1993).

"home centeredness" is an important trend of the new society. Yet it does not mean the end of the city. Because workplaces, schools, medical complexes, consumer services outlets, recreational areas, commercial streets, shopping centers, sports stadiums, and parks still exist and will exist, and people will shuttle between all these places with increasing mobility precisely because of the newly acquired looseness of working arrangements and social networking: as time becomes more flexible, places become more singular, as people circulate among them in an increasingly mobile pattern.

However, the interaction between new information technology and current processes of social change does have a substantial impact on cities and space. On the one hand, the urban form is considerably transformed in its layout. But this transformation does not follow a single, universal pattern: it shows considerable variation depending upon the characteristics of historic, territorial, and institutional contexts. On the other hand, the emphasis on interactivity between places breaks up spatial patterns of behavior into a fluid network of exchanges that underlies the emergence of a new kind of space, the space of flows. On both counts, I must tighten the analysis and raise it to a more theoretical level.

The Transformation of Urban Form: the Informational City

The information age is ushering in a new urban form, the informational city. Yet, as the industrial city was not a worldwide replica of Manchester, the emerging informational city will not copy Silicon Valley, let alone Los Angeles. On the other hand, as in the industrial era, in spite of the extraordinary diversity of cultural and physical contexts there are some fundamental common features in the transcultural development of the informational city. I shall argue that, because of the nature of the new society, based upon knowledge, organized around networks, and partly made up of flows, the informational city is not a form but a process, a process characterized by the structural domination of the space of flows. Before developing this idea, I think it is first necessary to introduce the diversity of emerging urban forms in the new historical period, to counter a primitive technological vision that sees the world through the simplified lenses of endless freeways and fiber optic networks.

America's last suburban frontier

The image of a homogeneous, endless suburban/exurban sprawl as the city of the future is belied even by its unwilling model, Los Angeles, whose contradictory complexity is revealed by Mike Davis' marvelous *City of Quartz*.[59] Yet it does evoke a powerful trend in the relentless waves of suburban development in the American metropolis, West and South as well as North and East, toward the end of the millennium. Joel Garreau has captured the similarities of this spatial model across America in his journalistic account of the rise of *Edge City*, as the core of the new urbanization process. He empirically defines Edge City by the combination of five criteria:

> Edge City is any place that: a) Has five million square feet or more of leasable office space – the work place of the Information Age. . . b) Has 600,000 square feet or more of leasable retail space . . . c) Has more jobs than bedrooms. d) Is perceived by the population as one place . . . e) Was nothing like 'city' as recently as thirty years ago.

He reports the mushrooming of such places around Boston, New Jersey, Detroit, Atlanta, Phoenix, Texas, Southern California, San Francisco Bay Area, and Washington, D.C. They are both working areas and service centers around which mile after mile of increasingly dense, single-family dwelling residential units, organize the "home centeredness" of private life. He remarks that these exurban constellations are

> tied together not by locomotives and subways, but by freeways, jetways, and rooftop satellite dishes thirty feet across. Their characteristic monument is not a horse-mounted hero, but the atria reaching for the sun and shielding trees perpetually in leaf at the core of corporate headquarters, fitness centers, and shopping plazas. These new urban areas are marked not by the penthouses of the old urban rich or the tenements of the old urban poor. Instead, their landmark structure is the celebrated single-family detached dwelling, the suburban home with grass all around that made America the best housed civilization the world has ever known.[60]

Naturally, where Garreau sees the relentless frontier spirit of American culture, always creating new forms of life and space, James Howard Kunstler sees the regrettable domination of the "geography

[59] Davis (1990).
[60] Garreau (1991).

of nowhere,"[61] thus reigniting a decades-long debate between partisans and detractors of America's sharp spatial departure from its European ancestry. Yet, for the purpose of my analysis, I will retain just two major points of this debate.

First, the development of these loosely interrelated exurban constellations emphasizes the functional interdependence of different units and processes in a given urban system over very long distances, minimizing the role of territorial contiguity, and maximizing the communication networks in all their dimensions. Flows of exchange are at the core of the American Edge City.[62]

Second, this spatial form is indeed very specific to the American experience. Because, as Garreau acknowledges, it is embedded in a classic pattern of American history, always pushing for the endless search for a promised land in new settlements. While the extraordinary dynamism that this represents did indeed build one of the most vital nations in history, it did so at the price of creating, over time, staggering social and environmental problems. Each wave of social and physical escapism (for example, the abandonment of inner cities, leaving the lower social classes and ethnic minorities trapped in their ruins) deepened the crisis of American cities,[63] and made more difficult the management of an overextended infrastructure and of an overstressed society. Unless the development of private "jails-for-rent" in Western Texas is considered a welcome process to complement the social and physical disinvestment in American inner cities, the *"fuite en avant"* of American culture and space seems to have reached the limits of refusing to face unpleasant realities. Thus, the profile of America's Informational City is not fully represented by the "Edge City" phenomenon, but by the relationship between fast exurban development, inner-city decay, and obsolescence of the suburban built environment.[64]

European cities have entered the information age along a different line of spatial restructuring linked to their historical heritage, although finding new issues, not always dissimilar to those emerging in the American context.

[61]   Kunstler (1993).
[62]   See the collection of papers gathered in Caves (1994).
[63]   Goldsmith and Blakely (1992).
[64]   Fainstein et al. (eds) (1992); Gottdiener (1985).

The fading charm of European cities

A number of trends constitute together the new urban dynamics of major European metropolitan areas in the 1990s.[65]

The business center is, as in America, the economic engine of the city, networked in the global economy. The business center is made up of an infrastructure of telecommunications, communications, advanced services, and office space, based upon technology-generating centers and educational institutions. It thrives upon information processing and control functions. It is usually complemented by tourism and travel facilities. It is a node of the inter-metropolitan network.[66] Thus, the business center does not exist by itself but by its connection to other equivalent locales organized in a network that forms the actual unit of management, innovation, and work.[67]

The new managerial–technocratic–political elite does create exclusive spaces, as segregated and removed from the city at large as the bourgeois quarters of the industrial society, but, because the professional class is larger, on a much larger scale. In most European cities (Paris, Rome, Madrid, Amsterdam), unlike in America – if we except New York, the most un-American of US cities – the truly exclusive residential areas tend to appropriate urban culture and history, by locating in rehabilitated or well-preserved areas of the central city. By so doing, they emphasize the fact that when domination is clearly established and enforced (unlike in nouveau-riche America) the elite does not need to go into suburban exile to escape the populace. This trend is however limited in the case of the UK where the nostalgia for the life of the gentry in the countryside translates into up-scale residence in selected suburbs of metropolitan areas, sometimes urbanizing charming historic villages in the vicinity of a major city.

The suburban world of European cities is a socially diversified space, that is segmented in different peripheries around the central city. There are the traditional working-class suburbs, often organized around large, public housing estates, lately in home ownership. There are the new towns, French, British, or Swedish, inhabited by a younger population of the middle classes, whose age made it difficult for them to penetrate the housing market of the central city. And there are also the peripheral ghettos of older public housing estates, exemplified by Paris' La Courneuve, where new immigrant populations and poor

[65] For developments on European cities, see Hall (1995); Martinotti (1993); Borja et al. (eds) (1991); Siino (1994); Deben et al. (eds) (1993).
[66] Dunford and Kafkalas (eds) (1992); Robson (1992).
[67] Tarr and Dupuy (eds) (1988).

working families experience exclusion from their "right to the city."
Suburbs are also the locus of manufacturing production in European
cities, both for traditional manufacturing and for new, high-technology industries that locate in the newest and environmentally most
desirable peripheries of metropolitan areas, close enough to the
communication centers but removed from old industrial districts.

Central cities are still shaped by their history. Thus, traditional
working-class neighborhoods, increasingly populated by service
workers, constitute a distinctive space, a space that, because it is the
most vulnerable, becomes the battleground between the redevelopment efforts of business and the upper middle class, and the invasion
attempts of countercultures (Amsterdam, Copenhagen, Berlin)
trying to reappropriate the use value of the city. Thus, they often
become defensive spaces for workers who only have their home to
fight for, being at the same time meaningful popular neighborhoods
and likely bastions of xenophobia and localism.

The new professional middle class in Europe is torn between the
attraction to the peaceful comfort of boring suburbs and the excitement of a hectic, and often too expensive, urban life. The trade-offs
between the differential spatial patterns of work of dual-job families
often determine the location of their household.

The central city, in Europe as well, is also the focus for the ghettos
of immigrants. However, unlike American ghettos, most of these areas
are not so economically deprived, because immigrant residents are
generally workers, with strong family ties, thus counting on a very
strong support structure that makes European ghettos family-
oriented communities, unlikely to be taken over by street crime.
England again seems exceptional in this regard, with some ethnic-
minority neighborhoods in London (for example, Tower Hamlets, or
Hackney) being closer to the American experience than to Paris' La
Goutte d'Or. Paradoxically, it is in the core administrative and entertainment districts of European cities, be it Frankfurt or Barcelona,
where urban marginality makes itself present. Its pervasive occupation
of the busiest streets and public transportation nodal points is a
survival strategy destined to be present, so that they can receive public
attention or private business, be it welfare assistance, a drug transaction, a prostitution deal, or the customary police attention.

Major European metropolitan centres present some variation
around the urban structure I have outlined, depending upon their
differential role in the European network of cities. The lower their
position in the new informational network, the greater the difficulty
of their transition from the industrial stage, and the more traditional
will be their urban structure, with old established neighborhoods and
commercial quarters playing the determinant role in the dynamics of

the city. On the other hand, the higher their position in the competitive structure of the new European economy, the greater the role of their advanced services in the business district, and the more intense will be the restructuring of urban space.

The critical factor in the new urban processes, in Europe as elsewhere, is the fact that urban space is increasingly differentiated in social terms, while being functionally interrelated beyond physical contiguity. It follows the separation between symbolic meaning, location of functions, and the social appropriation of space in the metropolitan area. This is the trend underlying the most important transformation of urban forms worldwide, with particular force in the newly industrializing areas: the rise of megacities.

Third millennium urbanization: megacities

The new global economy and the emerging informational society have indeed a new spatial form, which develops in a variety of social and geographical contexts: megacities.[68] Megacities are, certainly, very large agglomerations of human beings, all of them (13 in the United Nations classification) with over 10 million people in 1992 (see table 6.1 and figure 6.4), and four of them projected to be well over 20 million in 2010. But size is not their defining quality. They are the nodes of the global economy, concentrating the directional, productive, and managerial upper functions all over the planet; the control of the media; the real politics of power; and the symbolic capacity to create and diffuse messages. They have names, most of them alien to the still dominant European/North American cultural matrix: Tokyo, São Paulo, New York, Ciudad de Mexico, Shanghai, Bombay, Los Angeles, Buenos Aires, Seoul, Beijing, Rio de Janeiro, Calcutta, Osaka. In addition, Moscow, Jakarta, Cairo, New Delhi, London, Paris, Lagos, Dacca, Karachi, Tianjin, and possibly others, are in fact members of the club.[69] Not all of them (for example Dacca or Lagos) are dominant centers of the global economy, but they do connect to this global system huge segments of the human population. They also function as magnets for their hinterlands, that is the whole country or regional area where they are located. Megacities cannot be seen only in terms of their size, but as a function of their gravitational power toward major regions of the world. Thus, Hong

[68] The notion of megacities has been popularized by several urban experts on the international arena, most notably by Janice Perlman, founder and director of the New York-based "Megacities Project." For a journalistic account of her vision, see *Time* (1993), which also offers basic data on the topic.
[69] See Borja and Castells (1996).

Table 6.1 World's largest urban agglomerations, 1992

Rank	Agglomeration	Country	Population (millions)
1	Tokyo	Japan	25,772
2	São Paulo	Brazil	19,235
3	New York	United States of America	16,158
4	Mexico City	Mexico	15,276
5	Shanghai	China	14,053
6	Bombay	India	13,322
7	Los Angeles	United States of America	11,853
8	Buenos Aires	Argentina	11,753
9	Seoul	Republic of Korea	11,589
10	Beijing	China	11,433
11	Rio de Janeiro	Brazil	11,257
12	Calcutta	India	11,106
13	Isaka	Japan	10,535

Source: United Nations (1992).

Kong is not just its six million people, and Guangzhou is not just its six and a half million people: what is emerging is a megacity of 40 to 50 million people, connecting Hong Kong, Shenzhen, Guangzhou, Zhuhai, Macau, and small towns in the Pearl River Delta, as I shall develop below. Megacities articulate the global economy, link up the informational networks, and concentrate the world's power. But they are also the depositories of all these segments of the population who fight to survive, as well as of those groups who want to make visible their dereliction, so that they will not die ignored in areas bypassed by communication networks. Megacities concentrate the best and the worst, from the innovators and the powers that be to their structurally irrelevant people, ready to sell their irrelevance or to make "the others" pay for it. Yet what is most significant about megacities is that they are connected externally to global networks and to segments of their own countries, while internally disconnecting local populations that are either functionally unnecessary or socially disruptive. I argue that this is true of New York as well as of Mexico or Jakarta. **It is this distinctive feature of being globally connected and locally disconnected, physically and socially, that makes megacities a new urban form.** A form that is characterized by the functional linkages it establishes across vast expanses of territory, yet with a great deal of discontinuity in land use patterns. Megacities' functional and social hierarchies are spatially blurred and mixed, organized in retrenched encampments, and unevenly patched by unexpected pockets of

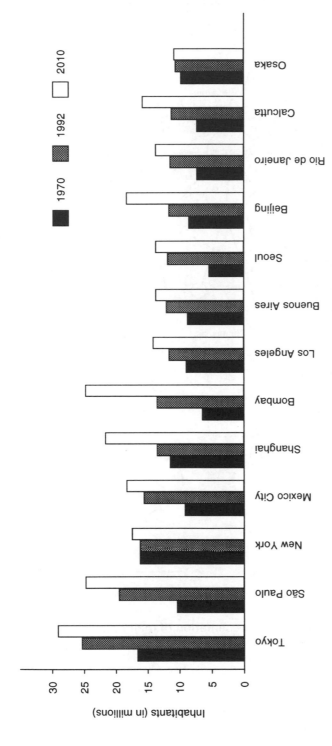

Figure 6.4 The world's largest urban agglomerations (> 10 million inhabitants in 1992)
Source: United Nations (1992).

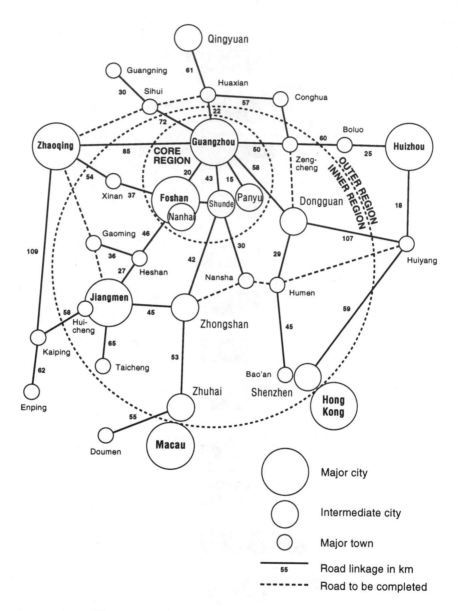

Figure 6.5   Diagrammatic representation of major nodes and links in
the urban region of the Pearl River Delta
Source: Elaborated by Woo (1994).

un-desirable uses. Megacities are discontinuous constellations of spatial fragments, functional pieces, and social segments.[70]

To illustrate my analysis I shall refer to a megacity in the making that is not even yet on the map but that, in my opinion, will be one of the preeminent industrial, business, and cultural centers of the twenty-first century, without indulging in futurology: the Hong Kong–Shenzhen–Canton–Pearl River Delta–Macau–Zhuhai metropolitan regional system.[71] Let us look at the mega-urban future from this vantage point (see figure 6.5). In 1995, this spatial system, still without a name, extended itself over 50,000 km^2, with a total population of between 40 and 50 million, depending on where boundaries are defined. Its units, scattered in a predominantly rural landscape, were functionally connected on a daily basis, and communicated through a multimodal transportation system that included railways, freeways, country roads, hovercrafts, boats, and planes. New super-highways were under construction, and the railway was being fully electrified and double-tracked. An optic fiber telecommunications system was in process of connecting the whole area internally and with the world, mainly via earth stations and cellular telephony. Five new airports were under construction in Hong Kong, Macau, Shenzhen, Zhuhai, and Guangzhou, with a projected passenger traffic capacity of 150 million per year. New container ports were also being built in North Lantau (Hong Kong), Yiantian (Shenzhen), Gaolan (Zhuhai), Huangpo (Guangzhou) and Macau, adding up to the world's largest port capacity in a given location. At the heart of such staggering metropolitan development are three interlinked phenomena:

1. The economic transformation of China, and its link-up to the global economy, with Hong Kong being one of the nodal points in such connection. Thus, in 1981–91, Guandong province's GDP grew at 12.8% per year in real terms. Hong Kong-based investors accounted at the end of 1993 for US$40 billion invested in China, representing two-thirds of total foreign direct investment. At the same time, China was also the largest foreign investor in Hong Kong, with about US$25 billion a year (compared with Japan's US$12.7 billion). The management of these capital flows was

[70] Mollenkopf and Castells (eds) (1991).
[71] My analysis on the emerging Southern China Metropolis is based, on the one hand, on my personal knowledge of the area, particularly of Hong Kong and Shenzhen, where I conducted research in the 1980s; on the other hand, particularly for developments in the 1990s, on a number of sources of which the most relevant are the following: Sit (1991); Hsing (1995); Lo (1994); Leung (1993); Ling (1995); Kwok and So (eds) (1995).

dependent upon the business transactions operated in, and inbetween, the various units of this metropolitan system. Thus, Guanghzou was the actual connecting point between Hong Kong business and the governments and enterprises not only of Guandong province, but of inland China.

2. The restructuring of Hong Kong's economic basis in the 1990s led to a dramatic shrinkage of Hong Kong's traditional manufacturing basis, to be replaced by employment in advanced services. Thus, manufacturing workers in Hong Kong decreased from 837,000 in 1988 to 484,000 in 1993, while employees in trading and business sectors increased, in the same period, from 947,000 to 1.3 million. Hong Kong developed its functions as a global business center.

3. However, Hong Kong's manufacturing exports capacity did not fade away: it simply modified its industrial organization and its spatial location. In about ten years, between the mid-1980s and the mid-1990s, Hong Kong's industrialists induced one of the largest-scale processes of industrialization in human history in the small towns of the Pearl River Delta. By the end of 1994, Hong Kong investors, often using family and village connections, had established in the Pearl River Delta 10,000 joint ventures and 20,000 processing factories, in which were working about 6 million workers, depending upon various estimates. Much of this population, housed in company dormitories in semi-rural locations, came from surrounding provinces beyond the borders of Guandong. This gigantic industrial system was being managed on a daily basis from a multilayered managerial structure, based in Hong Kong, regularly traveling to Guangzhou, with production runs being supervised by local managers throughout the rural area. Materials, technology, and managers were being sent from Hong Kong and Shenzhen, and manufactured goods were generally exported from Hong Kong (actually surpassing the value of Hong Kong-made exports), although the building of new container ports in Yiantian and Gaolan aimed at diversifying export sites.

This accelerated process of export-oriented industrialization and business linkages between China and the global economy led to an unprecedented urban explosion. Shenzhen Special Economic Zone, on the Hong Kong border, grew from zero to 1.5 million inhabitants between 1982 and 1995. Local governments in the whole area, full of cash from overseas Chinese investors, embarked on the construction of major infrastructural projects, the most amazing of which, still in the planning stage at the time of this writing, was the decision by

Zhuhai's local government to build a 60 km bridge over the South China Sea to link by road Zhuhai and Hong Kong.

The Southern China Metropolis, still in the making but a sure reality, is a new spatial form. It is not the traditional Megalopolis identified by Gottman in the 1960s on the north-eastern seaboard of the United States. Unlike this classical case, the Hong Kong–Guandong metropolitan region is not made up of the physical conurbation of successive urban/suburban units with relative functional autonomy in each one of them. It is rapidly becoming an interdependent unit, economically, functionally, and socially, and it will be even more so after Hong Kong becomes formally part of China in 1997, with Macau joining the flag in 1999. But there is considerable spatial discontinuity within the area, with rural settlements, agricultural land, and undeveloped areas separating urban centers, and industrial factories being scattered all over the region. The internal linkages of the area and the indispensable connection of the whole system to the global economy via multiple communication links are the real backbone of this new spatial unit. Flows define the spatial form and processes. Within each city, within each area, processes of segregation and segmentation take place, in a pattern of endless variation. But such segmented diversity is dependent upon a functional unity marked by gigantic, technology-intensive infrastructures, which seem to know as their only limit the amount of fresh water that the region can still retrieve from the East River area. The Southern China Metropolis, only vaguely perceived in most of the world at this time, is likely to become the most representative urban face of the twenty-first century.

Current trends point in the direction of another Asian megacity on an even greater scale when, in the early twenty-first century, the corridor Tokyo–Yokohama–Nagoya (already a functional unit) links up with Osaka–Kobe–Kyoto, creating the largest metropolitan agglomeration in human history, not only in terms of population, but in economic and technological power.

Thus, in spite of all their social, urban and environmental problems, megacities will continue to grow, both in their size and in their attractiveness for the location of high-level functions and for people's choice. The ecological dream of small, quasi-rural communes will be pushed away to countercultural marginality by the historical tide of megacity development. This is because megacities are:

a) centers of economic, technological, and social dynamism, in their countries and on a global scale. They are the actual development engines. Their countries' economic fate, be it the United States

or China, depends on megacities' performance, in spite of the
small-town ideology still pervasive in both countries;
b)   they are centers of cultural and political innovation;
c)   they are the connecting points to the global networks of every
     kind. Internet cannot bypass megacities: it depends on the
     telecommunications and on the "telecommunicators" located in
     those centers.

To be sure, some factors will slow down their pace of growth,
depending on the accuracy and effectiveness of policies designed to
limit megacities' growth. Family planning is working, in spite of the
Vatican, so we can expect a continuation of the decline in the
birthrate already taking place. Policies of regional development may
be able to diversify the concentration of jobs and population to other
areas. And I foresee large-scale epidemics, and disintegration of social
control that will make megacities less attractive. However, overall,
megacities will grow in size and dominance, because they keep
feeding themselves on population, wealth, power, and innovators,
from their extended hinterland. Furthermore, they are the nodal
points connecting to the global networks. Thus, in a fundamental
sense, the future of humankind, and of each megacity's country, is
being played out in the evolution and management of these areas.
Megacities are the nodal points, and the power centers of the new
spatial form/process of the information age: the space of flows.
     Having laid out the empirical landscape of new territorial
phenomena, we now have to come to grips with the understanding of
such a new spatial reality. This requires an unavoidable excursus
through the uncertain trails of the theory of space.

The Social Theory of Space and the Theory of the Space of Flows

Space is the expression of society. Since our societies are undergoing
structural transformation, it is a reasonable hypothesis to suggest that
new spatial forms and processes are currently emerging. The purpose
of the analysis presented here is to identify the new logic underlying
such forms and processes.
     The task is not an easy one, because the apparently simple acknowl-
edgement of a meaningful relationship between society and space
hides a fundamental complexity. This is because space is not a reflection of society, it is its expression. In other words: space is not a
photocopy of society, it is society. Spatial forms and processes are
formed by the dynamics of the overall social structure. This includes

contradictory trends derived from conflicts and strategies between social actors playing out their opposing interests and values. Furthermore, social processes influence space by acting on the built environment inherited from previous socio-spatial structures. Indeed, **space is crystallized time**. To approach in the simplest possible terms such a complexity, let us proceed step by step.

What is space? In physics, it cannot be defined outside the dynamics of matter. In social theory it cannot be defined without reference to social practices. This area of theorizing being one of my old trades, I still approach the issue under the assumption that "space is a material product, in relationship to other material products – including people – who engage in [historically] determined social relationships that provide space with a form, a function, and a social meaning."[72] In a convergent and clearer formulation, David Harvey, in his recent book *The Condition of Postmodernity*, states that

> from a materialist perspective, we can argue that objective conceptions of time and space are necessarily created through material practices and processes which serve to reproduce social life . . . It is a fundamental axiom of my enquiry that time and space cannot be understood independently of social action.[73]

Thus, we have to define, at a general level, what space is, from the point of view of social practices; then, we must identify the historical specificity of social practices, for example those in the informational society that underlie the emergence and consolidation of new spatial forms and processes.

From the point of view of social theory, **space is the material support of time-sharing social practices.** I immediately add that any material support bears always a symbolic meaning. By time-sharing social practices I refer to the fact that space brings together those practices that are simultaneous in time. It is the material articulation of this simultaneity that gives sense to space *vis-à-vis* society. Traditionally, this notion was assimilated to contiguity. Yet it is fundamental that we separate the basic concept of material support of simultaneous practices from the notion of contiguity, in order to account for the possible existence of material supports of simultaneity that do not rely on physical contiguity, since this is precisely the case of the dominant social practices of the information age.

I have argued in the preceding chapters that our society is

---

[72]   Castells (1972: 152) (my own translation).
[73]   Harvey (1990: 204).

constructed around flows: flows of capital, flows of information, flows of technology, flows of organizational interaction, flows of images, sounds, and symbols. Flows are not just one element of the social organization: they are the expression of processes *dominating* our economic, political, and symbolic life. If such is the case, the material support of the dominant processes in our societies will be the ensemble of elements supporting such flows, and making materially possible their articulation in simultaneous time. Thus, I propose the idea that there is a new spatial form characteristic of social practices that dominate and shape the network society: the space of flows. **The space of flows is the material organization of time-sharing social practices that work through flows.** By flows I understand purposeful, repetitive, programmable sequences of exchange and interaction between physically disjointed positions held by social actors in the economic, political, and symbolic structures of society. Dominant social practices are those which are embedded in dominant social structures. By dominant structures I understand those arrangements of organizations and institutions whose internal logic plays a strategic role in shaping social practices and social consciousness for society at large.

The abstraction of the concept of the space of flows can be better understood by specifying its content. The space of flows, as the material form of support of dominant processes and functions in the informational society, can be described (rather than defined) by the combination of at least three layers of material supports that, together, constitute the space of flows. **The first layer, the first material support of the space of flows, is actually constituted by a circuit of electronic impulses** (microelectronics, telecommunications, computer processing, broadcasting systems, and high-speed transportation – also based on information technologies) that, together, form the material basis for the processes we have observed as being strategically crucial in the network of society. This is indeed a material support of simultaneous practices. Thus, it is a spatial form, just as it could be "the city" or "the region" in the organization of the merchant society or of the industrial society. The spatial articulation of dominant functions does take place in our societies in the network of interactions made possible by information technology devices. In this network, no place exists by itself, since the positions are defined by flows. Thus, the network of communication is the fundamental spatial configuration: places do not disappear, but their logic and their meaning become absorbed in the network. The technological infrastructure that builds up the network defines the new space, very much like railways defined "economic regions" and "national markets" in the industrial economy; or the boundary-specific, institutional rules of citizenry (and their technologically advanced armies) defined "cities" in the merchant origins of capitalism and democracy. This technological infrastructure is itself the expression of the network of flows whose architecture and content is determined by the powers that be in our world.

The second layer of the space of flows is constituted by its nodes and hubs. The space of flows is not placeless, although its structural logic is. It is based on an electronic network, but this network links up specific places, with well-defined social, cultural, physical, and functional characteristics. Some places are exchangers, communication hubs playing a role of coordination for the smooth interaction of all the elements integrated into the network. Other places are the nodes of the network, that is the location of strategically important functions that build a series of locality-based activities and organizations around a key function in the network. Location in the node links up the locality with the whole network. Both nodes and hubs are hierarchically organized according to their relative weight in the network. But such hierarchy may change depending upon the evolution of activities processed through the network. Indeed, in some instances, some places may be switched off the network, their disconnection resulting in instant decline, and thus in economic, social and physical deterioration. The characteristics of nodes are dependent upon the type of functions performed by a given network.

Some examples of networks, and their corresponding nodes, will help to communicate the concept. The easiest type of network to visualize as representative of the space of flows is the network constituted by decision-making systems of the global economy, particularly those relative to the financial system. This refers to the analysis of the global city as a process rather than a place, as presented in this chapter. The analysis of the "global city" as the production site of the informational, global economy has shown the critical role of these global cities in our societies, and the dependence of local societies and economies upon the directional functions located in such cities. But beyond the main global cities, other continental, national, and regional economies have their own nodes that connect to the global network. Each one of these nodes requires an adequate technological infrastructure, a system of ancillary firms providing the support services, a specialized labor market, and the system of services required by the professional labor force.

As I showed above, what is true for top managerial functions and financial markets is also applicable to high-technology manufacturing (both to industries producing high technology and to those using high technology, that is all advanced manufacturing). The spatial division of labor that characterizes high-technology manufacturing

translates into the worldwide connection between the milieux of innovation, the skilled manufacturing sites, the assembly lines, and the
market-oriented factories, with a series of intra-firm linkages between
the different operations in different locations along the production
lines; and another series of inter-firm linkages among similar functions of production located in specific sites that become production
complexes. Directional nodes, production sites and communication
hubs are defined along the network and articulated in a common
logic by communication technologies and programmable, micro-
electronic-based, flexible integrated manufacturing.

The functions to be fulfilled by each network define the characteristics of places that become their privileged nodes. In some cases, the
most unlikely sites become central nodes because of historical
specificity that ended up centering a given network around a particular locality. For instance, it was unlikely that Rochester, Minnesota,
or the Parisian suburb of Villejuif would become central nodes of a
world network of advanced medical treatment and health research,
in close interaction with each other. But the location of the Mayo
Clinic at Rochester and of one of the main centers for cancer treatment of the French Health Administration at Villejuif, in both cases
for accidental, historical reasons, have articulated a complex of knowledge generation and advanced medical treatment around these two
odd locales. Once established they attracted researchers, doctors, and
patients from around the world: they became a node in the world's
medical network.

Each network defines its sites according to the functions and
hierarchy of each site, and to the characteristics of the product or
service to be processed in the network. Thus, one of the most powerful
networks in our society, narcotics production and distribution
(including its money-laundering component), has constructed a
specific geography that has redefined the meaning, structure, and
culture of societies, regions, and cities connected in the network.[74]
Thus, in cocaine production and trade, the coca production sites of
Chapare or Alto Beni in Bolivia or Alto Huallanga in Peru are
connected to the refineries and management centers in Colombia,
which were subsidiary, until 1995, to the Medellin or Cali headquarters, themselves connected to financial centers such as Miami,
Panama, the Cayman Islands, and Luxembourg, and to transportation centers, such as the Tamaulipas or Tijuana drug traffic networks
in Mexico, then finally to distribution points in the main metropolitan
areas of America and Western Europe. None of these localities can
exist by itself in such network. The Medellin and Cali cartels, and their

[74]   Arrieta et al. (1991); Laserna (1995).

close American and Italian allies, would soon be out of business without the raw materials produced in Bolivia or Peru, without the chemicals (precursors) provided by Swiss and German laboratories, without the semi-legal financial networks of free-banking paradises, and without the distribution networks starting in Miami, Los Angeles, New York, Amsterdam or La Coruña.

Therefore, while the analysis of global cities provides the most direct illustration of the place-based orientation of the space of flows in nodes and hubs, this logic is not limited by any means to capital flows. The main dominant processes in our society are articulated in networks that link up different places and assign to each one of them a role and a weight in a hierarchy of wealth generation, information processing, and power making that ultimately conditions the fate of each locale.

The third important layer of the space of flows refers to the spatial organization of the dominant, managerial elites (rather than classes) that exercise the directional functions around which such space is articulated. The theory of the space of flows starts from the implicit assumption that societies are asymmetrically organized around the dominant interests specific to each social structure. The space of flows is not the only spatial logic of our societies. It is, however, the dominant spatial logic because it is the spatial logic of the dominant interests/functions in our society. But such domination is not purely structural. It is enacted, indeed conceived, decided, and implemented by social actors. Thus, the technocratic–financial–managerial elite that occupies the leading positions in our societies will also have specific spatial requirements regarding the material/spatial support of their interests and practices. The spatial manifestation of the informational elite constitutes another fundamental dimension of the space of flows. What is this spatial manifestation?

The fundamental form of domination in our society is based on the organizational capacity of the dominant elite that goes hand in hand with its capacity to disorganize those groups in society which, while constituting a numerical majority, see their interests partially (if ever) represented only within the framework of the fulfillment of the dominant interests. Articulation of the elites, segmentation and disorganization of the masses seem to be the twin mechanisms of social domination in our societies.[75] Space plays a fundamental role in this mechanism. In short: elites are cosmopolitan, people are local. The space of power and wealth is projected throughout the world, while people's life and experience is rooted in places, in their culture,

---

[75] See Zukin (1992).

in their history. Thus, the more a social organization is based upon ahistorical flows, superseding the logic of any specific place, the more the logic of global power escapes the socio-political control of historically specific local/national societies.

On the other hand, the elites do not want and cannot become flows themselves, if they are to preserve their social cohesion, develop the set of rules and the cultural codes by which they can understand each other and dominate the others, thus establishing the "in" and "out" boundaries of their cultural/political community. The more a society is democratic in its institutions, the more the elites have to become clearly distinct from the populace, so avoiding the excessive penetration of political representatives into the inner world of strategic decision-making. However, my analysis does not share the hypothesis about the improbable existence of a "power elite" *à la* Wright Mills. On the contrary, the real social domination stems from the fact that cultural codes are embedded in the social structure in such a way that the possession of these codes opens the access to the power structure without the elite needing to conspire to bar access to its networks.

The spatial manifestation of such logic of domination takes two main forms in the space of flows. On the one hand, the elites form their own society, and constitute symbolically secluded communities, retrenched behind the very material barrier of real estate pricing. They define their community as a spatially bound, interpersonally networked subculture. I propose the hypothesis that the space of flows is made up of personal micro-networks that project their interests in functional macro-networks throughout the global set of interactions in the space of flows. This is a well-known phenomenon in the financial networks: major strategic decisions are taken over business luncheons in exclusive restaurants, or in country house week-ends over golf playing, as in the good old times. But such decisions will be executed in instant decision-making processes over telecommunicated computers which can trigger their own decisions to react to market trends. Thus, the nodes of the space of flows include residential and leisure-oriented spaces which, along with the location of headquarters and their ancillary services, tend to cluster dominant functions in carefully segregated spaces, with easy access to cosmopolitan complexes of arts, culture, and entertainment. Segregation happens both by location in different places and by security control of certain spaces open only to the elite. From the pinnacles of power and their cultural centers, a series of symbolic socio-spatial hierarchies are organized, so that lower levels of management can mirror the symbols of power and appropriate such symbols by constructing second-order spatial communities that will also tend to isolate themselves from the rest of society, in a succession of hierarchical segregation processes that, together, are tantamount to socio-spatial fragmentation.

A second major trend of cultural distinctiveness of the elites in the informational society is to create a lifestyle and to design spatial forms aimed at unifying the symbolic environment of the elite around the world, thus superseding the historical specificity of each locale. Thus, there is the construction of a (relatively) secluded space across the world along the connecting lines of the space of flows: international hotels whose decoration, from the design of the room to the color of the towels, is similar all over the world to create a sense of familiarity with the inner world, while inducing abstraction from the surrounding world; airports' VIP lounges, designed to maintain the distance *vis-à-vis* society in the highways of the space of flows; mobile, personal, on-line access to telecommunications networks, so that the traveler is never lost; and a system of travel arrangements, secretarial services, and reciprocal hosting that maintains a close circle of the corporate elite together through the worshipping of similar rites in all countries. Furthermore, there is an increasingly homogeneous lifestyle among the information elite that transcends the cultural borders of all societies: the regular use of SPA installations (even when traveling), and the practice of jogging; the mandatory diet of grilled salmon and green salad, with *udon* and *sashimi* providing a Japanese functional equivalent; the "pale chamois" wall color intended to create the cozy atmosphere of the inner space; the ubiquitous laptop computer; the combination of business suits and sportswear; the unisex dressing style, and so on. All these are symbols of an international culture whose identity is not linked to any specific society but to membership in the managerial circles of the informational economy across a global cultural spectrum.

The call for cultural connectedness of the space of flows between its different nodes is also reflected in the tendency toward the architectural uniformity of the new directional centers in various societies. Paradoxically, the attempt by postmodern architecture to break the molds and patterns of architectural discipline has resulted in an over-imposed postmodern monumentality which became the generalized rule of new corporate headquarters from New York to Kaoshiung during the 1980s. Thus, the space of flows includes the symbolic connection of homogeneous architecture in the places that constitute the nodes of each network across the world, so that architecture escapes from the history and culture of each society and becomes captured into the new imaginary, wonderland world of unlimited possibilities that underlies the logic transmitted by multimedia: the culture of electronic surfing, as if we could reinvent all forms in any place, on the sole condition of leaping into the cultural indefinition of the flows of power. The enclosure of architecture into a historical abstraction is the formal frontier of the space of flows.

The Architecture of the End of History

Nomada, sigo siendo un nomada.   Ricardo Bofill[76]

If the space of flows is truly the dominant spatial form of the network society, architecture and design are likely to be redefined in their form, function, process, and value in the coming years. Indeed, I would argue that all over history, architecture has been the "failed act" of society, the mediated expression of the deeper tendencies of society, of those that could not be openly declared but yet were strong enough to be cast in stone, in concrete, in steel, in glass, and in the visual perception of the human beings who were to dwell, deal, or worship in such forms.

Panofsky on the Gothic cathedrals, Tafuri on the American skyscrapers, Venturi on the surprisingly kitsch American city, Lynch on city images, Harvey on postmodernism as the expression of time/space compression by capitalism, are some of the best illustrations of an intellectual tradition that has used the forms of the built environment as one of the most signifying codes to read the basic structures of society's dominant values.[77] To be sure, there is no simple, direct interpretation of the formal expression of social values. But as research by scholars and analysts has revealed, and as works by architects have demonstrated, there has always been a strong, semiconscious connection between what society (in its diversity) was saying and what architects wanted to say.[78]

Not any more. My hypothesis is that the coming of the space of flows is blurring the meaningful relationship between architecture and society. Because the spatial manifestation of the dominant interests takes place around the world, and across cultures, the uprooting of experience, history, and specific culture as the background of meaning is leading to the generalization of ahistorical, acultural architecture.

[76]   Opening statement of Ricardo Bofill's architectural autobiography, *Espacio y Vida* (Bofill 1990).
[77]   Panofsky (1957); Tafuri (1971); Venturi et al. (1977); Lynch (1960); Harvey (1990).
[78]   See Burlen (1972).

Figure 6.6   Downtown Kaoshiung (photograph: Professor Hsia
Chu-joe)

Some tendencies of "postmodern architecture," as represented for
instance by the works of Philip Johnson or Charles Moore, under the
pretext of breaking down the tyranny of codes, such as modernism,
attempt to cut off all ties with specific social environments. So did
modernism in its time, but as the expression of a historically rooted
culture that asserted the belief in progress, technology and rationality.
In contrast, postmodern architecture declares the end of all systems
of meaning. It creates a mixture of elements that searches formal
harmony out of transhistorical, stylistic provocation. Irony becomes
the preferred mode of expression. Yet, in fact what most postmodernism does is to express, in almost direct terms, the new dominant
ideology: the end of history and the supersession of places in the space
of flows.[79] Because only if we are at the end of history can we now mix
up everything we knew before (see figure 6.6: Downtown Kaoshiung).
Because we do not belong any longer to any place, to any culture, the
extreme version of postmodernism imposes its codified code-
breaking logic anywhere something is built. The liberation from
cultural codes hides in fact the escape from historically rooted

[79]   I find my own understanding of postmodernism and postmodern architecture very close to David Harvey's analysis. But I shall not take responsibility for
using his work in support of my position.

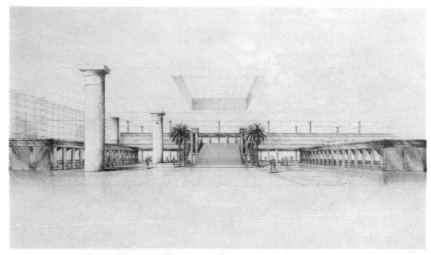

Figure 6.7 The entrance hall of Barcelona airport.
Source: Original drawing by Ricardo Bofill; reproduced by kind
permission of Ricardo Bofill.

societies. In this perspective, postmodernism could be considered the
architecture of the space of flows.[80]

The more that societies try to recover their identity beyond the
global logic of uncontrolled power of flows, the more they need an
architecture that exposes their own reality, without faking beauty
from a transhistorical spatial repertoire. But at the same time, over-
significant architecture, trying to give a very definite message or to
express directly the codes of a given culture, is too primitive a form to
be able to penetrate our saturated visual imaginary. The meaning of
its messages will be lost in the culture of "surfing" that characterizes
our symbolic behavior. This is why, paradoxically, the architecture
that seems most charged with meaning in societies shaped by the logic
of the space of flows is what I call "the architecture of nudity." That is,
the architecture whose forms are so neutral, so pure, so diaphanous,
that they do not pretend to say anything. And by not saying anything
they confront the experience with the solitude of the space of flows.
Its message is the silence.

For the sake of communication, I shall use two examples drawn
from Spanish architecture, an architectural milieu that is widely

[80] For a balanced, intelligent discussion of the social meaning of postmodern
architecture, see Kolb (1990); for a broader discussion of the interaction between
globalization/informationalization processes and architecture, see Saunders,
(ed.) (1996).

recognized as being currently at the forefront of design. Both concern, not by accident, the design of major communication nodes, where the space of flows materializes ephemerally. The Spanish festivities of 1992 provided the occasion for the construction of major functional buildings designed by some of the best architects. Thus, the new Barcelona airport, designed by Bofill, simply combines beautiful marble floor, dark glass facade, and transparent glass separating panels in an immense, open space (see figure 6.7). No cover up of the fear and anxiety that people experience in an airport. No carpeting, no cozy rooms, no indirect lighting. In the middle of the cold beauty of this airport passengers have to face their terrible truth: they are alone, in the middle of the space of flows, they may lose their connection, they are suspended in the emptiness of transition. They are, literally, in the hands of Iberia Airlines. And there is no escape.

Let us take another example: the new Madrid AVE (high speed train) station, designed by Rafael Moneo. It is simply a wonderful old station, exquisitely rehabilitated, and made into an indoor palm-tree park, full of birds that sing and fly in the enclosed space of the station. In a nearby structure, adjacent to such a beautiful, monumental space, there is the real station with the high-speed train. Thus, people go to the pseudo-station, to visit it, to walk through its different levels and paths, as they go to a park or a museum. The too-obvious message is that we are in a park, not in a station; that in the old station, trees grew, and birds nested, operating a metamorphosis. Thus, the high-speed train becomes the oddity in this space. And this is in fact the question everybody in the world asks: what is a high-speed train doing there, just to go from Madrid to Seville, with no connection whatsoever with the European high-speed network, at a cost of US$4 billion? The broken mirror of a segment of the space of flows becomes exposed, and the use value of the station recovered, in a simple, elegant design that does not say much but makes everything evident.

Some prominent architects, such as Rem Koolhas, the designer of the Lille Grand Palais Convention Center, theorize the need to adapt architecture to the process of de-localization, and to the relevance of communication nodes in people's experience: Koolhas actually sees his project as an expression of the "space of flows." Or, in another instance of a growing self-awareness of architects about the structural transformation of space, the American Institute of Architects' award-winning design of D.E. Shaw & Company's offices by Steven Holl in New York's West 45th Street

> offers – in Herbert Muschamp's words – a poetic interpretation
> of . . . the space of flows. . . . Mr Holl's design takes the Shaw
> offices to a place as novel as the information technology that

Figure 6.8   The waiting room at D.E. Shaw & Company: no ficus
trees, no sectional sofas, no corporate art on the walls
Source: Muschamp (1992).

paid to build them. When we walk in the door of D.E. Shaw [see
figure 6.8] we know we are not in 1960s Manhattan or Colonial
New England. For that matter, we have left even much of present
day New York far below on the ground. Standing inside the Holl
atrium we have got our head in the clouds and our feet firmly
planted on solid air.[81]

Granted we may be forcing Bofill, Moneo, and even Holl into discourses that are not theirs.[82] But the simple fact that their

[81]   Muschamp (1992).
[82]   For Bofill's own interpretation of the Barcelona airport (whose formal
antecedent, I believe, is in his design of Paris' Marché St Honoré), see his book
(Bofill 1990). However, in a long personal conversation, after reading the draft
of my analysis, he did not disagree with my interpretation of the project of an
"architecture of nudity," although he conceived it rather as an innovative attempt
to bring together high-tech and classic design. We both agreed that the new architectural monuments of our epoch are likely to be built as "communication
exchangers" (airports, train stations, intermodal transfer areas, telecommunication infrastructures, harbors, and computerized trading centers).

architecture would allow me, or Herbert Muschamp, to relate forms to symbols, to functions, to social situations, means that their strict, retained architecture (in rather formally different styles) is in fact full of meaning. Indeed, architecture and design, because their forms either resist or interpret the abstract materiality of the dominant space of flows, could become essential devices of cultural innovation and intellectual autonomy in the informational society through two main avenues. Either the new architecture builds the palaces of the new masters, thus exposing their deformity hidden behind the abstraction of the space of flows; or it roots itself into places, thus into culture, and into people.[83] In both cases, under different forms, architecture and design may be digging the trenches of resistance for the preservation of meaning in the generation of knowledge. Or, what is the same, for the reconciliation of culture and technology.

Space of Flows and Space of Places

The space of flows does not permeate down to the whole realm of human experience in the network society. Indeed, the overwhelming majority of people, in advanced and traditional societies alike, live in places, and so they perceive their space as place-based. **A place is a locale whose form, function and meaning are self-contained within the boundaries of physical contiguity.** A place, to illustrate my argument, is the Parisian *quartier* of Belleville.

Belleville was, as for so many immigrants throughout its history, my entry point to Paris, in 1962. As a 20-year-old political exile, without much to lose except my revolutionary ideals, I was given shelter by a Spanish construction worker, an anarchist union leader, who introduced me to the tradition of the place. Nine years later, this time as a sociologist, I was still walking Belleville, working with immigrant workers' committees, and studying social movements against urban renewal: the struggles of what I labeled *"La Cité du Peuple,"* reported in my first book.[84] Thirty years after our first encounter, both Belleville and I have changed. But Belleville is still a place, while I am afraid I look more like a flow. The new immigrants (Asians, Yugoslavs) have joined a long-established stream of Tunisian Jews, Maghrebian Muslims, and Southern Europeans, themselves the successors of the intra-urban exiles pushed into Belleville in the nineteenth century by

[83]   For a useful debate on the matter, see Lillyman et al. (eds) (1994).
[84]   Castells (1972: 496ff).

Figure 6.9   An Urban Place: Rambla de les Flors, Barcelona, 1996,
Photograph by Olga Torres.

the Hausmannian design of building a bourgeois Paris. Belleville itself
has been hit by several waves of urban renewal, intensified in the
1970s.[85] Its traditional physical landscape of a poor but harmonious
historic *faubourg* has been messed up with plastic postmodernism,
cheap modernism, and sanitized gardens on top of a still somewhat
dilapidated housing stock. And yet, Belleville in 1995 is a clearly iden-
tifiable place, both from the outside and from the inside. Ethnic
communities that often degenerate in hostility toward each other
coexist peacefully in Belleville, although keeping track of their own
turf, and certainly not without tensions. New middle-class households,
generally young, have joined the neighborhood because of its urban
vitality, and powerfully contribute to its survival, while self-controlling
the impacts of gentrification. Cultures and histories, in a truly plural
urbanity, interact in the space, giving meaning to it, linking up with
the "city of collective memory," *à la* Christine Boyer.[86] The landscape
pattern swallows and digests substantial physical modifications, by
integrating them in its mixed uses and active street life. Yet Belleville

---

[85]   For an updated social and spatial, illustrated history of Belleville, see the
delightful book: Morier (ed.) (1994); on urban renewal in Paris in the 1970s, see
Godard et al. (1973).
[86]   Boyer (1994).

is by no means the idealized version of the lost community, which probably never existed, as Oscar Lewis demonstrated in his revisit of Tepoztlan. Places are not necessarily communities, although they may contribute to community-building. But the life of their inhabitants is marked by their characteristics, so they are indeed good and bad places depending on the value judgement of what a good life is. In Belleville, its dwellers, without loving each other, and while certainly not being loved by the police, have constructed throughout history a meaningful, interacting space, with a diversity of uses and a wide range of functions and expressions. They actively interact with their daily physical environment. In between home and the world, there is a place called Belleville.

Not all places are socially interactive and spatially rich. It is precisely because their physical/symbolic qualities make them different that they are places. Thus Allan Jacobs, in his great book about "great streets".[87] examines the difference in urban quality between Barcelona and Irvine (the epitome of suburban Southern California) on the basis of the number and frequency of intersections in the street pattern: his findings go even beyond what any informed urbanist could imagine (see figures 6.10 and 6.11). So Irvine is indeed a place, although a special kind of place, where the space of experience shrinks inward toward the home, as flows take over increasing shares of time and space.

The relationships between the space of flows and the space of places, between simultaneous globalization and localization are not predetermined in their outcome. For instance, Tokyo has undergone a substantial process of urban restructuring during the 1980s, to live up to its role as "a global city," a process fully documented by Machimura. The city government, sensitive to the deep-seated Japanese fear about the loss of identity, added to its business-oriented restructuring policy an image-making policy of singing the virtues of old Edo, Pre-Meiji Tokyo. A historical museum (*Edo-Tokyo Hakubutsukan*) was opened in 1993, a public relations magazine was published, exhibitions regularly organized. As Machimura writes:

> Although these views seem to go in totally different directions, both of them seek for redefinition of the Westernized image of the city in more domestic ways. Now, "Japanization" of the Westernized city provides an important context for the discourse about "global city" Tokyo after modernism.[88]

[87]   Jacobs (1994).
[88]   Machimura (1995:16). See his book on the social and political forces under-lying the restructuring of Tokyo: Machimura (1994).

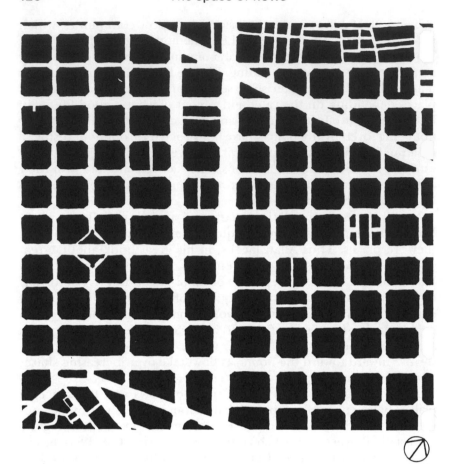

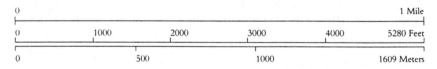

Figure 6.10   Barcelona: Paseo de Gracia
Source: Jacobs (1993).

Yet Tokyo citizens were not complaining just about the loss of historical essence, but about the reduction of their everyday life's space to the instrumental logic of the global city. A project symbolized this logic: the celebration of a World City Fair in 1997, a good occasion to build another, major business complex on reclaimed land in Tokyo Harbor. Large construction companies happily obliged, and work was

Figure 6.11 Irvine, California: business complex
Source: Jacobs (1993).

well under way in 1995. Suddenly, in the 1995 municipal election, an independent candidate, Aoshima, a television comedian without backing from political parties or financial circles, campaigned on a one-issue program: to cancel the World City Fair. He won the election by a large margin, and became Governor of Tokyo. A few weeks later, he kept his campaign promise and canceled the World City Fair, to the disbelief of the corporate elite. The local logic of civil society was catching up with, and contradicting, the global logic of international business.

Thus, people do still live in places. But because function and power in our societies are organized in the space of flows, the structural domination of its logic essentially alters the meaning and dynamic of places. Experience, by being related to places, becomes abstracted from power, and meaning is increasingly separated from knowledge. It follows a structural schizophrenia between two spatial logics that threatens to break down communication channels in society. The dominant tendency is toward a horizon of networked, ahistorical space of flows, aiming at imposing its logic over scattered, segmented places, increasingly unrelated to each other, less and less able to share cultural codes. Unless cultural *and physical* bridges are deliberately built between these two forms of space, we may be heading toward life in parallel universes whose times cannot meet because they are warped into different dimensions of a social hyperspace.

— 7 —

The Edge of Forever:
Timeless Time

Introduction

We are embodied time, and so are our societies, made out of history. Yet the simplicity of this statement hides the complexity of the concept of time, one of the most controversial categories in the natural and social sciences alike, whose centrality is underlined by current debates in social theory.[1] Indeed, the transformation of time under the information technology paradigm, as shaped by social practices, is one of the foundations of the new society we have entered, inextricably linked to the emergence of the space of flows. Furthermore, according to the illuminating essay by Barbara Adam on time and social theory, recent research in physics and biology seems to converge with social sciences in adopting a contextual notion of human time.[2] All time, in nature as in society, seems to be specific to a given context: time is local. Focusing on the emerging social structure, I argue, in the tradition of Harold Innis, that "the fashionable mind is the time-denying mind,"[3] and that this new "time regime" is linked to the development of communication technologies. Thus, in

---

[1]   The analysis of time plays a central role in the thought of Anthony Giddens, one of the leading sociological theorists of our intellectual generation. See, particularly, Giddens (1981, 1984). An extremely stimulating theorization of the relationship between time, space, and society is the work by Lash and Urry (1994); see also Young (1988). For a more traditional, empirical approach to social analysis of time, see Kirsch et al.(eds)(1988). For recent debates, see Friedland and Boden (eds)(1994). Of course, for sociologists, the classic references on social time continue to be Durkheim (1912) and Sorokin and Merton (1937). See also, the pioneering work by Innis (1950, 1951, 1952) on regimes of time and space as defining historical epochs.

[2]   Adam(1990: 81, 87-90).

[3]   Innis (1951: 89ff); see also Innis (1950).

order to appreciate the transformation of human time under the new social socio-technical context it may be helpful to introduce briefly a historical perspective on the changing relationship between time and society.

Time, History, and Society

In a classic book, Whitrow has shown how conceptions of time have varied considerably throughout history, from the determination of human fate under the Babylonian horoscopes, to the Newtonian revolution of absolute time as an organizing principle of nature.[4] And Nigel Thrift has reminded us of the fact that time in medieval societies was a loose notion, with some major events (religious celebrations, market fairs, the coming of the seasons) becoming time markers around which most of the daily life went by without precise timing.[5] To illustrate the wide contextual variation of such an apparently simple fact of life, let us recall in a few paragraphs the transformation of the notion of time in Russian culture in two critical historical periods: the reforms of Peter the Great, and the rise and fall of the Soviet Union.[6]

Traditional, popular Russian culture viewed time as eternal, without beginning or end. Writing in the 1920s, Andrey Platonov emphasized this deep-seated notion of Russia as a timeless society. Yet Russia was periodically shaken by statist modernization efforts to organize life around time. The first deliberate attempt at timing life came from Peter the Great. Upon his return from a long trip abroad to educate himself about ways and means in more advanced countries, he decided to bring Russia, literally, to a new departure, by shifting to the Western European (Julian) calendar, and starting the new year in January instead of September, as had been the case until then. On

[4]   Whitrow (1988). For a good example of cultural/historical variation of time and time measures, see the fascinating book by Zerubavel (1985).
[5]   Thrift (1990).
[6]   The plural source for this analysis of the evolution of time in the Russian culture is the set of unpublished presentations and discussions at the Conference on Time and Money in the Russian Culture, organized by the University of California at Berkeley's Center for Slavic and Eastern European Studies, and the Stanford University's Center for Russian and East European Studies, held at Berkeley on March 17 1995 (personal notes and summary of the proceedings by Emma G. Kiselyova). Among the various significant contributions to this conference, I have used Zhivov (1995). Additionally, for the time implications of Peter the Great's reforms, see Waliszewski (1990); Kara-Murza and Polyakov (1994); Anisimov (1993).

December 19 and 20 1699, he issued two decrees that would start the eighteenth century in Russia a few days later. He prescribed detailed instructions about celebrating the new year, including the adoption of the Christmas tree, and adding a new holiday to entice the traditionalists. While some people marveled at the Czar's power to alter the course of the sun, many were concerned about offending God: was not September 1 the day of the Creation in 5508BC? And was it not supposed to be so because the daring act of Creation had to take place in warm weather, an occurrence extremely unlikely in the Russian January? Peter the Great argued personally with his critics, in his customary pedagogic mode, indulging in teaching them about global time geography. His stubbornness was rooted in his reformist motivation to homogenize Russia with Europe, and to emphasize time-measured obligations of people towards the state. Although these decrees focused strictly on calendar changes, Peter the Great's reforms, in broader terms, introduced a distinction between the time of religious duty and secular time to be given to the state. Measuring and taxing people's time, and giving his own personal example of an intense, timed work schedule, Peter the Great inaugurated a centuries-old tradition of associating service to the country, submission to the state, and the timing of life.

In the early stage of the Soviet Union, Lenin shared with Henry Ford the admiration for Taylorism and the "scientific organization of work," based on measuring working time to the smallest movement in the assembly line. But time compression under communism came with a decisive ideological twist.[7] While under Fordism the speeding up of work was associated with money, by increasing pay, under Stalinism not only was money evil, in line with the Russian tradition, but time should be accelerated by ideological motivation. Thus, Stakhanovism meant working more per unit of time as a service to the country, and five-year plans were fulfilled in four years as a proof of the ability of the new society to revolutionize time. In May 1929, at the Fifth Congress of the Soviets of the Union which marked the triumph of Stalin, an even more extreme acceleration of time was attempted: the uninterrupted (*nepreryvka*) work week. Although increase in production was the explicit goal of the reform, the destruction of the weekly rhythm of religious observance was an even greater motivation, in the tradition of the French Revolution. So, in November 1931, a resting day was introduced every sixth day, but the traditional seven-

[7]   For analysis of time in the Soviet Union, see Hanson (1991); Castillo (1994); on developments related to "uninterrupted workweek" under Stalin, see Zerubavel (1985: 35–43).

day cycle was still denied. Protests arising from families separated by differences in schedules between their members brought the seven-day week back in 1940, particularly after it was realized that cities were on the six-day pattern, but most of the countryside was still observing the traditional week, introducing a dangerous cultural cleavage between peasants and industrial workers. Indeed, while forced collectivization of agriculture aimed at eliminating the communal notion of slow-paced time, rooted in nature, family, and history, the social and cultural resistance to such brutal imposition was widespread, showing the depth of the time foundation of social life. Yet, while compressing time at the workplace, the time horizon of communism was always in the long term and to some extent eternal, as expressed in Lenin's embodied immortality, and in Stalin's attempt to make an idol of himself during life. Accordingly, in the 1990s, the collapse of communism shifted Russians, and particularly the new professional classes, from the long-term horizon of historical time to the short term of monetized time characteristic of capitalism, thus ending the centuries-old statist separation between time and money. By so doing Russia joined the West at the very moment advanced capitalism was revolutionizing its own time frame.

Contemporary societies are still by and large dominated by the notion of clock time, a mechanical/categorical discovery that E.P. Thompson,[8] among others, considers to be critical to the constitution of industrial capitalism. Modernity can be conceived, in material terms, as the dominance of clock time over space and society, a theme that has been developed by Giddens, Lash and Urry, and Harvey. Time as repetition of daily routine, as Giddens proposes,[9] or as "the mastery of nature, as all sorts of phenomena, practices and places become subjected to the disembedding, centralizing and universalizing march of time," in the words of Lash and Urry,[10] is at the core of both industrial capitalism and statism. Industrial machinism brought the chronometer to the assembly lines of Fordist and Leninist factories almost at the same moment.[11] Long-distance travel in the West became organized by the late nineteenth century around Greenwich Mean Time, as the materialization of the hegemony of the British Empire. While, half a century later, the constitution of the Soviet Union was marked by the organization of an immense territory around Moscow time, with time zones arbitrarily decided by the bureaucrats' convenience without proportion to geographical

[8]   Thompson (1967).
[9]   Giddens (1984).
[10] Lash and Urry (1994: 229).

distance. Significantly the first act of defiance of the Baltic Republics during Gorbachev's *perestroyka* was to vote for the adoption of Finland's time zone as the official time in their territories.

This linear, irreversible, measurable, predictable time is being shattered in the network society, in a movement of extraordinary historical significance. But we are not just witnessing a relativization of time according to social contexts or alternatively the return to time reversibility as if reality could become entirely captured in cyclical myths. The transformation is more profound: it is the mixing of tenses to create a forever universe, not self-expanding but self-maintaining, not cyclical but random, not recursive but incursive: timeless time, using technology to escape the contexts of its existence, and to appropriate selectively any value each context could offer to the ever-present. I argue that this is happening now not only because capitalism strives to free itself from all constraints, since this has been the capitalist system's tendency all along, without being able fully to materialize it.[12] Neither is it sufficient to refer to the cultural and social revolts against clock time, since they have characterized the history of the last century without actually reversing its domination, indeed furthering its logic by including clock time distribution of life in the social contract.[13] Capital's freedom from time and culture's escape from the clock are decisively facilitated by new information technologies, and embedded in the structure of the network society.

Having said the words, I shall proceed with the specification of their meaning, so that by the end of this chapter sociological analysis has a chance to replace metaphorical statements. To do so without annoying repetition I shall rely on the empirical observations presented in other chapters of this book on the transformation of various domains of social structure, while adding illustrations or analyses when necessary to complete our understanding. Thus, I shall sequentially explore the effects on time of transformations occurring in the economic, political, cultural, and social spheres, and end with an attempt at reintegrating time and space in their new, contradictory relationship. In this exploration of ongoing transformation of time in very different social spheres, I shall be somewhat schematic in my statements, since it is materially impossible to develop fully in a few pages the analysis of domains as complex and diverse as global finance, working time, the life-cycle, death, war-making, and the media. However, by dealing with so many and different matters I try to extract, beyond such diversity, the shared logic of new temporality

[11]   Castillo (1994).
[12]   As Harvey (1990) shows.
[13]   Hinrichs et al. (eds) (1991); see also Rifkin (1987).

manifesting itself in the whole range of human experience. Thus, the
purpose of this chapter is not to summarize the transformation of
social life in all its dimensions, but, rather, to show the consistency of
patterns in the emergence of a new concept of temporality, that I call
timeless time.

Another word of caution must be added. The transformation of
time as surveyed in this chapter does not concern all processes, social
groupings, and territories in our societies, although it does affect the
entire planet. What I call *timeless time* is only the emerging, *dominant*
form of social time in the network society, as the space of flows does
not negate the existence of places. It is precisely my argument that
social domination is exercised through the selective inclusion and
exclusion of functions and people in different temporal and spatial
frames. I shall return to this theme at the end of the chapter after
having explored the profile of time in its new, dominant form.

Time as the Source of Value: the Global Casino

David Harvey adequately represents current transformations in capitalism under the formula of "time-space compression."[14] Nowhere is
this logic more evident than in the circulation of capital at the global
level. As we analyzed in chapter 2, during the 1980s the convergence
of global deregulation of finance and the availability of new information technologies and new management techniques transformed the
nature of capital markets. For the first time in history, a unified global
capital market, *working in real time,* has emerged.[15] The explanation,
and the real issue, of the phenomenal volume of transborder financial flows, as shown in chapter 2, lies in the *speed* of the transactions.[16]
The same capital is shuttled back and forth between economies in a
matter of hours, minutes, and some times seconds.[17] Favored by
deregulation, disintermediation, and the opening of domestic financial markets, powerful computer programs and skillful financial
analysts/computer wizards sitting at the global nodes of a selective
telecommunications network play games, literally, with billions of
dollars.[18] The main card room in this electronic casino is the currency
market, which has exploded in the last decade, taking advantage of
floating exchange rates. In 1995, US$1.2 trillion were exchanged

[14]   See Harvey (1990: 284–5).
[15]   Chesnais (1994); O'Brien (1992).
[16]   Reynolds (1992), Javetski and Glasgall (1994).
[17]   Shirref (1994); Breeden (1993).
[18]   *Time* (1994); Jones (1993). For a revealing "financial fiction" allegory, enjoy
the reading of Kimsey (1994).

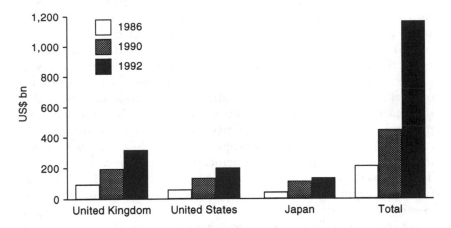

Figure 7.1   Average daily transactions on stock exchanges, 1986–92
(US$bn)
Source: Chesnais and Serfati (1994), quoted in Chesnais (1994); based on
triennial reports of the Bank for International Settlement.

every day in the currency market (see figure 7.1).[19] These global
gamblers are not obscure speculators, but major investment banks,
pension funds, multinational corporations (of course including
manufacturing corporations), and mutual funds organized precisely
for the sake of financial manipulation.[20] François Chesnais identified
about 50 major players in the global financial markets.[21] Yet, as argued
above, once turbulences are generated in the market, flows take over,
as central banks have repeatedly learned to their heavy cost. Time is
critical to the profit-making of the whole system. It is the speed of the
transaction,   sometimes   automatically   preprogrammed   in
the computer to make quasi-instantaneous decisions, that generates the gain – or the loss. But it is also the time circularity of the
process, a relentless sequence of buying and selling which characterizes the system. The architecture of global finance is indeed
constructed around time zones, with London, New York, and Tokyo
anchoring the three shifts of capital, and a number of financial
maverick centers working on the slight discrepancies between market
values at their opening and closing times.[22] Furthermore, a significant
and growing number of financial transactions are based on making

19   *Economist* (1995b).
20   Heavey (1994).
21   Chesnais (1994).
22   Lee and Schmidt-Marwede (1993).

value out of the capture of future time in present transactions, as in the futures, options, and other derivative capital markets.[23] Together these new financial products dramatically increase the mass of nominal capital *vis-à-vis* bank deposits and assets, so that it can be said properly that time creates money, as everybody bets on and with future money anticipated in computer projections.[24] The very process of marketing future development affects these developments, so that the time frame of capital is constantly dissolved into its present manipulation after being given a fictitious value for the purpose of monetizing it. Thus capital not only compresses time: it absorbs it, and lives out of (that is, generates rent) its digested seconds and years.

The material consequences of this apparently abstract disgression on time and capital are increasingly felt in economies and daily lives around the world: recurrent monetary crises, ushering in an era of structural economic instability and actually jeopardizing European integration; the inability of capital investment to anticipate the future, thus undermining incentives for productive investment; the wrecking of companies, and of their jobs, regardless of performance because of sudden, unforeseen changes in the financial environment in which they operate; the increasing gap between profits in the production of goods and services and rents generated in the sphere of circulation, thus shifting an increasing share of world savings to financial gambling; the growing risks for pension funds and private insurance liabilities, thus introducing a question mark into the hard-bought security of working people around the world; the dependence of entire economies, and particularly those of developing countries, on movements of capital largely determined by subjective perception and speculative turbulence; the destruction in the collective experience of societies of the deferred-gratification pattern of behavior, in favour of the "quick buck" common ideology, emphasizing individual gambling with life and the economy; and the fundamental damage to the social perception of the correspondence between production and reward, work and meaning, ethics and wealth. Puritanism seems to have been buried in Singapore in 1995 along with the venerable Barings Bank.[25] And Confucianism will last in the new economy only as long as "blood is thicker than water,"[26] that is while family ties still provide social cohesion beyond pure speculation in the brave new world of gambling finance. The annihilation and manipulation of

[23] Lee et al. (1994); *Asian Money, Asian Issuers & Capital Markets Supplement* (1993-4); Fager (1994).
[24] Chesnais (1994).
[25] *Economist* (1995a).
[26] Hsing (1994).

time by electronically managed global capital markets are at the source of new forms of devastating economic crises, looming into the twenty-first century.

Flextime and the Network Enterprise

The supersession of time is also at the core of new organizational forms of economic activity that I have identified as the *network enterprise*. Flexible forms of management, relentless utilization of fixed capital, intensified performance by labor, strategic alliances, and inter-organizational linkages, all come down to shortening time per operation and to speeding up turnover of resources. Indeed, the "just in time" inventory management procedure has been the symbol of lean production, even if, as I mentioned above, it belongs to a pre-electronic age of manufacturing technology. Yet, in the informational economy, this time compression does not primarily rely on extracting more time from labor or more labor from time under the clock imperative. Because the value-making potential of labor and organizations is highly dependent on the autonomy of informed labor to make decisions in real time, traditional disciplinary management of labor does not fit the new production system.[27] Instead, skilled labor is required to manage its own time in a flexible manner, sometimes adding more work time, at other times adjusting to flexible schedules, in some instances reducing working hours, and thus pay. This new time-oriented management of labor could be called, as John Urry suggests, "just-in-time labor."

For the networked firm, the time frame of its adaptability to market demand and technology changes is also at the roots of its competitiveness. Thus, the showcase of networking production, the Italian knitwear multinational firm Benetton, was overtaken in 1995 by its American competitor Gap mainly because of its inability to follow Gap's speed in introducing new models according to evolving consumer taste: every two months, as compared to twice a year for Benetton.[28] Another example: in the software industry in the mid-1990s firms started to give away their products for free, over the line, in order to attract customers at a faster pace.[29] The rationale behind this final dematerialization of software products is that profits are to be made in the long term, mainly out of customized relationships with users over development and improvements of a given program. But

---

[27]   See the discussion of the matter in Freeman (ed.) (1994).
[28]   *Business Week* (1995d).
[29]   *Business Week* (1995c).

Table 7.1 Annual hours worked per person, 1870–1979

	1870	1880	1890	1900	1913	1929	1938	1950	1960	1970	1979
Canada	2,964	2,871	2,789	2,707	2,605	2,399	2,240	1,967	1,877	1,805	1,730
France	2,945	2,852	2,770	2,688	2,588	2,297	1,848	1,989	1,983	1,888	1,727
Germany	2,941	2,848	2,765	2,684	2,584	2,284	2,316	2,316	2,083	1,907	1,719
Italy	2,886	2,795	2,714	2,634	2,536	2,228	1,927	1,997	2,059	1,768	1,556
Japan	2,945	2,852	2,770	2,688	2,588	2,364	2,391	2,272	2,432	2,252	2,129
United Kingdom	2,984	2,890	2,807	2,725	2,624	2,286	2,267	1,958	1,913	1,735	1,617
United States	2,964	2,871	2,789	2,707	2,605	2,342	2,062	1,867	1,794	1,707	1,607

For Italy, 1978 figure is used for 1979.
Source: Maddison (1982); Bosch et. al. (eds) (1994: 8, table 1).

Table 7.2 Potential lifelong working hours, 1950–85

	1950	1960	1979	1980	1985
France	113,729	107,849	101,871	92,708	77,748
West Germany	114,170	104,076	93,051	87,367	85,015
East Germany	108,252	n.a.	97,046	93,698	93,372
Hungary	97,940	96,695	92,918	85,946	78,642
Italy	n.a.	n.a.	n.a.	n.a.	82,584
Japan	109,694	109,647	100,068	95,418	93,976
United Kingdom	n.a.	n.a.	n.a.	n.a.	82,677
USA	n.a.	n.a.	n.a.	n.a.	93,688
USSR	n.a.	n.a.	n.a.	n.a.	77,148

n.a. = not available
Source: Schuldt (1990: 43).

the initial adoption of such a program depends on the advantage of solutions offered by a product over other products in the market, thus putting a premium on the quick availability of new breakthroughs, as soon as they are generated by a firm or an individual. The flexible management system of networked production relies on flexible temporality, on the ability to accelerate or slow down product and profit cycles, on the time-sharing of equipment and personnel, and on the control of time lags of available technology *vis-à-vis* the competition. Time is managed as a resource, not under the linear, chronological manner of mass production, but as a differential factor in reference to the temporality of other firms, networks, processes or products. Only the networked form of organization and increasingly powerful and mobile information-processing machines are able to ensure the flexible management of time as the new frontier of high-performance firms.[30] Under such conditions time is not only compressed: it is processed.

The Shrinking and Twisting of Life Working Time

Work is, and will be for the foreseeable future, the nucleus of people's life. More specifically in modern societies, *paid working time* structures social time. Working time in industrialized countries has experienced a secular decline in the last 100 years, measured in annual working hours *per person*, as shown in the study by Maddison[31] (see table 7.1). I should remind the reader that this reduction in working time hides in fact a substantial increase in total labor, as a result of the increase in the number of jobs since, as I showed in chapter 4, aggregate employment is less a function of technology than of the expansion of investment and demand, depending on social and institutional organization. Calculations on the potential lifelong working hours per person also show a significant reduction in the last four decades, although with important variations in the number of hours between countries[32] (see table 7.2).

The number of working hours and their distribution in the lifecycle and in the annual, monthly, and weekly cycles of people's lives, are a central feature of how they feel, enjoy, and suffer. Their differential evolution in various countries and historical periods reflects

---

[30] Benveniste (1994).
[31] Maddison (1982).
[32] K. Schuldt, *Soziale und ökonomische Gestaltung der Elemente der Lebensarbeitszeit der Werktätigen*, Dissertation, Berlin (GDR), 1990; cited in Bosch et al. (eds) (1994:15).

Table 7.3 Duration and reduction of working time, 1970–87

	Agreed working hours	Reduction of agreed hours (%)		Actual working hours per employee			Working hours per person, working age 55–64 years			Working hours per person
		1970–80	1980–7	1980	1987	Change (%) 1980–7	1980	1987	Change (%) 1980–7	
Sweden	1,796 (9)	-8.2(3)	0(8)	1,438 (1)	1,482 (1)	+3.1 (10)	1,133 (7)	1,188 (6)	+4.9 (8)	770 (6)
Norway	1,714 (2)	-6.2(4)	-6.6(3)	1,563 (2)	1,537 (2)	-1.7 (7)	1,131 (6)	1,210 (7)	+7.0 (9)	788 (7)
Denmark	1,733 (4)	-2.6(6)	-6.0(4)	1,720 (4)	1,596 (4)	-7.2 (2)	1,246 (8)	1,211 (8)	-2.8 (4)	812 (8)
Finland	1,720 (3)	0 (8)	-7.5(1)	1,818 (8)	1,782 (10)	-2.0 (6)	1,299 (9)	1,305 (10)	+0.5 (6)	890 (10)
Germany	1,712 (1)	-5.9(5)	-4.7(6)	1,736 (7)	1,672 (6)	-3.7 (4)	1,090 (3)	1,020 (4)	-6.4 (2)	712 (4)
Netherlands	1,744 (5)	-9.1(2)	-7.0(2)	1,720 (4)	1,645 (5)	-4.5 (3)	881 (1)	864 (1)	-1.9 (5)	603 (2)
Belgium	1,759 (6)	-9.2(1)	-5.0(5)	1,590 (3)	1,550 (3)	-3.0 (5)	925 (2)	875 (2)	-5.4 (3)	601 (1)
France	1,767 (7)	0 (8)	-4.6(7)	1,850 (9)	1,696 (7)	-3.3 (1)	1,122 (5)	1,001 (3)	-10.8 (1)	672 (5)
United Kingdom	1,782 (8)	-2.1(7)	-4.6(7)	—	1,730 (8)	—	—	1,183 (5)	—	765 (5)
USA	1,916 (10)	0 (8)	0 (8)	1,735 (6)	1,770 (9)	+2.0 (9)	1,106 (4)	1,231 (9)	+11.3 (10)	832 (9)
Japan	2,121 (11)	-5.9(5)	0 (8)	2,113 (10)	2,085 (11)	-1.3 (8)	1,446 (10)	1,469 (11)	+1.6 (7)	1,020 (11)

The table is based on Eurostat figures. It is assumed that hours of part-timers are 25% lower than those of full-time employees and that hours outside industry are 2.5% longer than in industry.

Figures in brackets are rankings.

Source: Pettersson (1989).

economic organization, the state of technology, the intensity of social struggles, and the outcomes of social contracts and institutional reforms.[33] French workers were the first in Europe to conquer the 40-hour week and the right to paid vacation, after bitter social struggles and the election to government of the Popular Front in 1936. The UK, the USA, and Japan have been the bastions of business-imposed Stakhanovism, with workers having half or one-third less vacation time than workers in Germany, France, or Spain, with no apparent effect on productivity (actually, in terms of productivity growth in the last 30 years, if we except Japan, vacation time seems to correlate positively with growth in labor productivity). Yet overall, for more than one century, between 1870 and 1980, we could observe two related trends in industrialized economies toward decreasing labor time per person and per worker, and toward increasing homogenization and regulation of working time as part of the social contract underlying the welfare state. However, recently these trends have been modified toward an increasingly complex and variable pattern[34] (see table 7.3). The key phenomenon seems to be the increasing diversification of working time and working schedules, reflecting the trend toward the disaggregation of labor in the work process, as analyzed in chapter 4. Thus the 1994 ILO study on the evolution of working time in 14 industrialized countries synthesizes its observations as follows:

> In the long term, the reduction of working time obviously is the dominant trend. Also, in the last 20 years working hours were reduced in most countries, but by very different combinations of increasing part time work, reducing agreed and actual weekly and yearly working hours and lifetime hours. However, in analyzing this main trend one easily overlooks some manifest tendencies towards an extension of hours at least in some countries and for some groups of workers within different countries. *These tendencies may indicate the increasing differentiation of the duration of working hours between and within countries after a long period of standardization and harmonization of working hours.*[35]

What are the sources of such diversity? On the one hand, institutional differences in the regulation of labor markets, with the US, Japan, and the European Union displaying clear-cut contrasting logics. On the other hand, within countries, longer working hours are concentrated in two groups: high-level professionals and unskilled service workers. The former, because of their value-making contribu-

---

[33]   Hinrichs et al. (eds) (1991).
[34]   Bosch et al. (eds) (1994).
[35]   Ibid.:19 (my added emphasis).

tion, the latter because of their weak bargaining power, often associated with immigrant status or informal work arrangements. As for
shorter working time and atypical schedules, they are linked to part-
time and temporary work, and concern mainly women and
low-educated youth. The massive entry of women into the labor force
is, to some extent, associated with the diversification of work status
and working schedules. As a result, as shown above in chapter 4,
between one-quarter and one-third of the employed population of
major industrialized countries (including self-employment) does not
follow the classic pattern of a full-time job with a regular working
schedule. The number of workers in variable job assignments is
rapidly increasing everywhere. In addition, a considerable proportion
of full-time workers (probably a majority of the professional labor
force) are heading toward flexible time schedules, generally
increasing their work load. The technological ability to reintegrate in
a network of stored information contributions from various workers
at various times induces the constant variation of the actual time of
work performance, undermining the structuring capacity of working
time over everyday life. Thus, in his insightful analysis on the transformation of work and firms in France, Frederic de Conninck focuses
on the fact that "the enterprise is affected by plural and divergent
temporalities," "the economy is dominated more and more by the
search for flexibility, or organized around short run time," with the
result that "today, the individual is overwhelmed by the various temporalities he has to confront;" thus, while work remains integrated,
society tends toward its *éclatement,* out of the unmanageable development of contradictory temporalities within the same structure.[36]

Therefore, the real issue in our societies is not so much that technology allows us to work less for the same unit of output: it does so,
but the impact of this technological fact on actual working time and
schedules is undetermined. What is at stake, and what appears to be
the prevailing trend in most advanced sectors of most advanced societies, is the general diversification of working time, depending on
firms, networks, jobs, occupations, and characteristics of the workers.
Such diversity ends up, in fact, being measured in terms of each
worker's and each job's differential capacity to manage time. Without
anticipating my analysis on the evolution of the family (in volume II),
it seems that the heterogeneity of working schedules in a society with
similar participation by the genders in the labor force, imposes a
dramatic readjustment of household arrangements. Not necessarily
for the worse, since in fact added work-time flexibility could provide

---

[36] De Conninck (1995); quotes are, in sequential order, from pp.200, 193, and
193 (my translation).

the basis for time-sharing in the household. Yet new household partnerships would have to be built on the ruins of patriarchal family
rules.[37] Since flex-time and part-time have penetrated the contractual
structures of working time on the basis of women's work, largely to
accommodate women's needs to combine their child-rearing
endeavors and their working lives, the extension of this logic to men
and to other domains of social life other than child-rearing could actually introduce (it is in fact already introducing in many instances)[38] a
new articulation of life time and work time at different ages and under
different conditions, for both men and women. Thus, under such new
arrangements, working time may lose its traditional centrality
throughout the lifecycle.

A convergent trend pointing in the same direction comes from the
dramatic shortening of actual working *years* in major industrialized
countries, precisely at the moment of a substantial increase in life
expectancy. This is, on the one hand, because the age of entry into
the labor force, both for men and women, is increasingly higher, as a
greater proportion of the population attends universities: a trend that
results from cultural expectations, the tightening of labor markets,
and employers' increasing requirement for higher education creden-
tials in the labor force.[39] On the other hand, Anne Marie Guillemard
has conducted comparative studies that show the dramatic decline of
actual employment for the labor force over 50 years, and specially over
55 years.[40] As figure 7.2 shows, the rate of activity of men between 55
and 65 has declined precipitously in the last 20 years in major industrialized economies, and in 1991 was down to 65% in the US, 64% in
the UK, 54% in Germany, and 43% in France. For these countries, be
it by early retirement, disability, permanent unemployment, attrition,
or discouragement, between one-third and over one-half of the male
labor force *permanently* quits the labor market in their early fifties.
Guillemard puts forward a solid argument in the sense that this
tendency is not temporary but rooted in shortsighted government
and business policies, and in the belief of the inability of the aged
worker to adapt to the current speed of technological and organizational innovation.[41] Under such circumstances, the actual working
lifetime could be shortened to about 30 years (from 24 to 54), out of
a real lifetime span of about 75–80 years. Then, not only working time

---

[37]   Martin Carnoy and I have jointly elaborated on this theme in Carnoy and
Castells (1996).
[38]   Hewitt (1993).
[39]   Carnoy and Levin (1985).
[40]   Guillemard (1993).
[41]   Guillemard and Rein (1993).

444

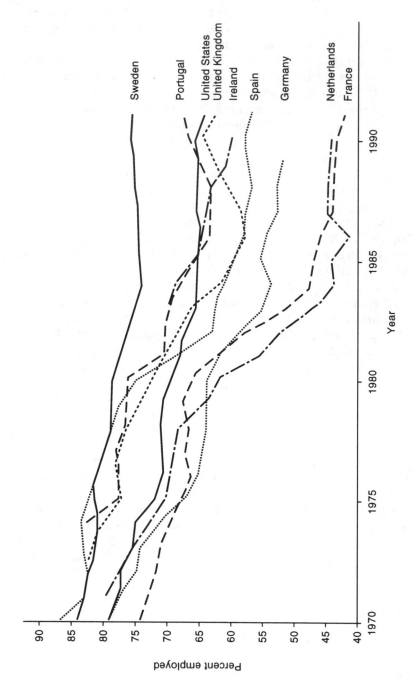

Figure 7.2 Labor force participation rate (%) for men 55–64 years old in nine countries, 1970–91
Source: Guillemard (1993).

loses its centrality *vis-à-vis* life in general, but the accounting system on which pensions and healthcare are calculated collapses, not because there are too many elderly persons, but because the proportion between contributing workers and nonworking recipients becomes unbearable, unless productivity increases are dramatic and society accepts a massive intergenerational redistribution.[42]

Thus, the real challenge of the new relationship between work and technology does not concern mass unemployment, as I tried to discuss in chapter 4, but the overall shortening of life working time for a substantial proportion of the population. Unless the basis of calculation for social benefits is modified through a new social contract, the shrinkage of valuable working time and the accelerated obsolescence of labor will bring to an end the institutions of social solidarity, ushering in the age wars.

The Blurring of Lifecycle: Toward Social Arrhythmia?

It seems that all living beings, including us, are biological clocks.[43] Biological rhythms, be it individual, related to the species, or even cosmic, are essential in human life. People and societies ignore them at their peril.[44] For millennia human rhythmicity was constructed in close relationship to the rhythms of nature, generally with little bargaining power against hostile natural forces, so that it seemed reasonable to go with the flow, and to model the lifecycle in accordance with a society where most babies would die as infants, where women's reproductive power had to be used early, where youth was ephemeral (Ronsard), where growing elderly was such a privilege that it brought with it the respect due to a unique source of experience and wisdom, and where plagues would periodically wipe out a sizable share of the population.[45] In the developed world, the industrial revolution, the constitution of medical science, the triumph of Reason, and the affirmation of social rights has altered this pattern in the last two centuries, prolonging life, overcoming illness, regulating births, alleviating death, calling into question the biological determination of roles in society, and constructing the lifecycle around social categories, among which education, working time, career patterns, and the right to retirement became paramount. However, although the principle of a sequential life shifted from being bio-social to becoming

---

[42]   Lenoir (1994).
[43]   Berger (1984), cited by Adam (1990).
[44]   Schor (1991).
[45]   McNeill (1977).

socio-biological, there was (indeed, there still is) a lifecycle pattern to which advanced societies tend to conform, and toward which developing countries try to evolve. Now, organizational, technological, and cultural developments characteristic of the new, emerging society, are decisively undermining this orderly lifecycle without replacing it with an alternative sequence. **I propose the hypothesis that the network society is characterized by the breaking down of rhythmicity, either biological or social, associated with the notion of a lifecycle.**

I have already examined one of the reasons for this new trend, namely the variable chronology of working time. But an even more important development is the increasing ability to control, within obvious limits, the reproduction of our species, and the average duration of the life of its individuals (see chapter 1). Although the upper limit of longevity has a biological boundary, the prolongation of the average duration of life to the late seventies (early eighties for women), and the increasing share of the population reaching well beyond the average, into the eighties age group, has considerable consequences for our societies and for the ways we conceive of ourselves. While old age was once considered a homogeneous last stage of life, in fact dominated by "social death," as demonstrated in the French study that Anne Marie Guillemard conducted many years ago with my collaboration,[46] it is now a highly diverse universe, made up of early retirees, average retirees, able elders, and elders with various degrees and forms of disability. So, suddenly, the "third age" is extended toward younger and older groups, and substantially redefines the lifecycle in three ways: it denies the exit from the labor market as the defining criterion, since for a substantial proportion of the population about one-third of their life may occur after this event; it differentiates the elderly fundamentally in terms of their level of disability, not always correlating with age, thus assimilating to some extent their disabled condition to other disabled groups of a younger age, thus inducing new social category; and it compels the distinction between several age groups, whose actual differentiation will greatly depend on their social, cultural, and relational capital accumulated throughout their lives.[47] Depending on each one of these variables, the social attributes of these distinct old ages will differ considerably, thus breaking down the relationship between social condition and biological stage at the roots of the lifecycle.

Simultaneously, this relationship is being called into question at the other end: reproduction is coming under increasing control around the world. In advanced societies the norm is birth control, although

[46]   Guillemard (1972); Castells and Guillemard (1971).
[47]   Guillemard (1988).

social marginality and religious beliefs constitute areas of resistance to planned motherhood. In close interaction with the cultural and professional emancipation of women, the development of reproductive rights has altered the demographic structure and biological rhythms of our societies in just two decades (see table 7.4). Overall, the most industrialized countries have entered an era of low birth rates (below the reproduction rate for the native population), of delayed time for marriage and reproduction, and of variable stages for women to have children throughout their lifecycle, as they strive to combine education, work, personal life, and children in an increasingly individualized pattern of decision-making (see table 7.5). Together with the transformation of the family and the increasing diversification of lifestyles (see volume II) we observe a substantial modification of the time and forms for mothering and fathering in the lifecycle, where the new rule is, increasingly, that there are few rules. Furthermore, new reproductive technologies and new cultural models make it possible, to a considerable extent, to disassociate age and biological condition from reproduction and from parenthood. In strictly technical terms it is possible today to differentiate the legal parent(s) of a child; whose is the sperm; whose is the egg; where and how the fertilization is performed, in real or delayed time, even after the death of the father; and whose is the womb which gives birth to the child. *All combinations are possible and are socially decided.* Our society has already reached the technological capacity to separate social reproduction and biological reproduction of the species. I am obviously referring to exceptions to the rule, but to tens of thousands of exceptions throughout the world. Some of them are showcases of the possibility for aged women (in their late fifties or early sixties) actually to give birth. Others are soap opera happenings about a dead lover whose frozen sperm is fought by irate heirs. Most are secluded events often whispered over dinner in high-tech California or in gossipy Madrid. Since these developments are related to very simple reproductive technologies which do not involve genetic engineering, it is plausible to imagine a much greater range for the possible manipulation of reproductive ages and reproduction conditions when human genetic engineering ends up finding a legal and ethical accommodation in society, as all technologies do in the long term.

Since I am not speculating on future projections but elaborating on well-known facts of our everyday life, I believe it is legitimate to think about the on-going consequences of these developments for human life, and particularly for the lifecycle. It is very simple: they lead to the final blurring of the biological foundation of the lifecycle concept. Sixty-year-old parents of infants; children of different marriages enjoying brothers and sisters 30 years older with no intermediate age

Table 7.4(a) Principal demographic characteristics by main regions of the world, 1970–95[a]

	Total fertility rate			Life expectancy at birth			Infant mortality rate		
	1970–5	1980–5	1990–5	1970–5	1980–5	1990–5	1970–5	1980–5	1990–5
World	4.4	3.5	3.3	57	60	65	93	78	62
More-developed regions	2.2	2.0	1.9	71	73	75	22	16	12
Less-developed regions	5.4	4.1	3.6	54	57	62	104	88	69
Africa	6.5	6.3	6.0	46	49	53	142	112	95
Asia	5.1	3.5	3.2	56	59	65	97	83	62
Europe	2.2	1.9	1.7	71	73	75	24	15	10
Americas	3.6	3.1	—	64	67	68	64	49	—
Latin	—	—	3.1	—	—	—	—	—	47
Northern	—	—	2.0	—	—	—	—	—	8
Oceania	3.2	2.7	2.5	66	68	73	39	31	22
USSR	2.4	2.4	2.3	70	71	70	26	25	21

[a] Data for 1990–5 all projections.

Sources: United Nations, World Population Prospects. Estimates and Projections as Assessed in 1984; United Nations, World Population at the Turn of the Century, 1989, p. 9, table 3; United Nations Population Fund, The State of World Population: Choices and Responsibilities, 1994.

Table 7.4(b) Total fertility rates of some industrialized countries, 1901–85

	Denmark	Finland	France	Germany[a]	Italy	Netherlands	Portugal	Sweden	Switzerland	United Kingdom	United States
1901–05	4.04	4.22	2.78	4.74	—	4.48	—	3.91	3.82	3.40	—
1906–10	3.83	4.15	2.59	4.25	—	4.15	—	3.76	3.56	3.14	—
1911–15	3.44	3.68	2.26	3.19	—	3.79	—	3.31	3.02	2.84	—
1916–20	3.15	3.49	1.66	2.13	—	3.58	—	2.94	2.46	2.40	3.22
1921–25	2.85	3.33	2.43	2.49	—	3.47	—	2.58	2.43	2.39	3.08
1926–30	2.41	2.88	2.29	2.05	—	3.08	—	2.08	2.10	2.01	2.65
1931–35	2.15	2.41	2.18	1.86	3.06	2.73	3.88	1.77	1.91	1.79	2.21
1936–40	2.17	2.38	2.07	2.43	3.00	2.58	3.45	1.82	1.80	1.80	2.14
1941–45	2.64	2.60	2.11	2.05	2.56	2.85	3.43	2.35	2.38	2.00	2.45
1946–50	2.75	2.86	2.99	2.05	2.78	3.48	3.29	2.45	2.52	2.38	2.97
1951–55	2.55	2.99	2.73	2.09	2.30	3.05	3.05	2.23	2.30	2.19	3.27
1956–60	2.54	2.78	2.70	2.34	2.32	3.11	3.02	2.24	2.40	2.52	3.53
1961–65	2.59	2.58	2.83	2.50	2.56	3.15	3.10	2.33	2.61	2.83	3.16
1966–70	2.20	2.06	2.60	2.33	2.50	2.74	2.91	2.12	2.29	2.56	2.41
1971–75	1.96	1.62	2.26	1.62	2.31	1.99	2.64	1.89	1.82	2.06	1.84
1976–80	1.65	1.67	1.88	1.41	1.88	1.59	2.32	1.66	1.51	1.76	1.69
1981–85	1.38	1.74	1.82	1.32	1.53	1.47	1.97	1.61	1.50	1.75	1.66

Note: [a] German figures include both FRG and GDR.

Sources: J. Bourgeois-Pichat, "Comparative fertility trends in Europe," in *Causes and Consequences of Non-Replacement Fertility* (Hoover Institution, 1985); United Nations, *World Population at the Turn of the Century,* 1989, p. 90, table 21.

Table 7.5   First live births per 1,000 women, USA, by age-group of
mother (30–49 years) and by race, 1960 and 1990

	Age group			
	30–34 years	35–39 years	40–44 years	45–49 years
Total				
1960	8.6	3.2	0.8	0.0
1990	21.2	6.7	1.0	0.0
White				
1960	8.9	3.3	0.8	0.0
1990	21.6	6.8	1.0	0.0
All other				
1960	6.9	2.9	0.7	0.1
1990	19.1	6.3	1.1	0.1
Black				
1964	5.4	2.2	0.6	0.0
1990	12.9	4.0	0.7	0.0

Note the dramatic increase in the first live birth rate between 1960
and 1990: an increase of 146.5% for the 30–34 year age group, and of
109% for the 35–39 year age group.
Sources: US Bureau of Census, *Historical Statistics of the United States:
Colonial Times to 1970,* vol. 1, p. 50, Series B 11–19, 1975; US Dept of Health
and Human Services. *Vital Statistics of the United States: 1990*, vol. 1, section
1, table 1.9, 1994.

groups; men and women deciding to procreate, with or without
coupling, at whichever age; grandmothers giving birth to the baby
originated in her daughter's egg (also cases in real life); posthumous
babies; and an increasing gap between social institutions and reproductive practices (children out of wedlock represent about 25% of all
births in Sweden, and about 50% of African Americans). It is essential that we do not include a value judgement in this observation. What
for traditionalists amounts to challenging the divine wrath, for
cultural revolutionaries is the triumph of individual desire, and
indeed the ultimate affirmation of women's rights to their bodies and
their lives. Yet what is essential is that we are not on the fringes of
society, even if these are still embryos of a new relationship between
our social and biological condition. These are growing social trends,
whose technological and cultural diffusion seems unstoppable,
except under conditions of a new theocracy. And their direct impli-
cation is another form of the annihilation of time, of human
biological time, of the time rhythm by which our species has been
regulated since its origins. Regardless of our opinion, we may have to
live without the clock that told our parents when they were supposed

to procreate us, and that told us when, how, and if, to pass our life on to our children. A secular biological rhythm has been replaced by a moment of existential decision.

Death Denied

The belief in the probability of death with dignity is our, and society's attempt to deal with the reality of what is all too frequently a series of destructive events that involve by their very nature the disintegration of the dying person's humanity. I have not often seen much dignity in the process by which we die. The quest to achieve true dignity fails when our bodies fail . . . The greatest dignity to be found in death is the dignity of the life that preceded it.   Sherwin B. Nuland[48]

Time in society and life is measured by death. Death is and has been the central theme of cultures throughout history, either revered as God's will or defied as the ultimate human challenge.[49] It has been exorcised in the rites destined to calm the living, accepted with the resignation of the serene, tamed in the carnivals of the simple, fought with the desperation of the romantics, but never denied.[50] It is a distinctive feature of our new culture, the attempt to exile death from our lives. Although the matrix of this attempt lies in the rationalist belief in all mighty progress, it is the extraordinary breakthroughs of medical technology and biological research in the last two decades that provide a material basis for the oldest aspiration of humankind: to live as if death did not exist, in spite of its being our only certainty. By so doing, the ultimate subversion of the lifecycle is accomplished, and life becomes this flat landscape punctuated by chosen moments of high and low experiences, in the endless boutique of customized feelings. So when death does happen it is simply an additional blip on the screen of distracted spectators. If it is true that, as Ionesco said, "each of us is the first one to die,"[51] social mechanisms make sure that we are also the last, namely that the dead are truly alone, and do not take away the vital energy of the living. Yet this old, and healthy, aspiration to survival, documented by Philippe Aries as being present in Western culture since the Middle Ages,[52] takes a new turn under the biological revolution. Because we are so close to unveiling the secrets

[48]   Nuland (1994: xvii, 242).
[49]   Morin, (1970).
[50]   Thomas (1988, 1985).
[51]   Quoted by Thomas (1988: 17).
[52]   Aries (1977, 1983).

of life, two major trends have diffused from the medical sciences towards the rest of the society: obsessive prevention, and the fight to the end.

According to the first trend, every biological study, every medical exploration relating human health to the environment becomes quickly translated into hygienic advice or mandatory prescription (for example, the anti-smoking crusade in the US, the same country where submachine guns can be purchased by mail) which increasingly transforms society into a symbolically sanitized environment, with the full cooperation of the media. Indeed, newscasters have found in the health crusade an endless source of public attention, more so since the results of studies are periodically refuted and replaced by new specific instructions. A whole "healthy living" industry is directly related to this crusade, from hygienized food to fashionable sportswear and to mainly irrelevant vitamin pills. This perverted use of medical research is particularly pathetic when contrasted to the indifference of health insurance companies and mainstream business towards primary care and occupational safety.[53] Thus, an increasing proportion of people in advanced societies, and the professional classes throughout the world, spend considerable time, money, and psychological energy all through their lives pursuing health fashions in ways and with outcomes only slightly different from traditional shaman rites. For instance, while recent studies show that weight is largely linked to genetically programmed metabolism, and that people oscillate in a 10–15% range around their age and size average regardless of their efforts,[54] diet is a social obsession, either real or manipulated. True, personal aesthetics and the relationship to the body is also linked to the culture of individualism and narcissism, but the hygienist view of our societies adds a decisive instrumental twist to it (indeed, it is often linked with rejecting the objectification of woman's body). It aims at delaying and fighting death and aging every minute of life, with the support of medical science, the health industry, and media information.

Yet the real offensive against death is the good-faith, all-out medical struggle to push back the ineluctable as much as humanly possible. Sherwin B. Nuland, a surgeon and historian of medicine, writes in his soul-shaking book *How We Die:*

> Every medical specialist must admit that he has at times convinced patients to undergo diagnostic or therapeutic measures at a point in illness so far beyond reason that The

[53]   Navarro (1994).
[54]   Kolata (1995).

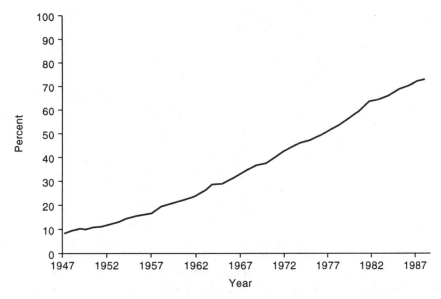

Figure 7.3   Ratio of hospitalized deaths to total deaths (%), by year,
1947–87
Source: Koichiri Kuroda, "Medicalization of Death: Changes in Site of
Death in Japan after World War Two," Hyogo: Kobe College, Department
of Intercultural Studies, 1990, unpublished research paper.

Riddle might better have remained unsolved. Too often near the
end, were the doctor able to see deeply within himself, he might
recognize that his decisions and advice are motivated by his
inability to give up The Riddle and admit defeat as long as there
is any chance of solving it. Though he be kind and considerate
of the patient he treats, he allows himself to push his kindness
aside because the seduction of The Riddle is so strong and the
failure to solve it renders him so weak.[55]

This medical impulse to repulse death has nothing to do with capitalism. In fact, some insurance companies would rather welcome
euthanasia, and would like to send patients home as soon as possible,
a cynical view daily fought against by doctors. Without this relentless
will to reject the inevitable, valuable lessons would be lost, and our
collective ability to survive and overcome suffering would be
hampered. Yet the societal impact of such efforts, along with less-noble
enterprises of using terminal patients as experimental subjects, is
tantamount to the denial of death until its very last act. So strong is

[55]   Nuland (1994: 249).

the temporal and spatial confinement of death that the overwhelming majority of deaths (80% in the US, and a growing proportion in all countries: see figure 7.3 for Japan, a society with a strong family culture) take place in the hospital, very often in special intensive care units, with the bodies already removed from their social and emotional environments. In spite of some limited movements in defense of humane hospices for terminal patients, and even more limited tendencies towards bringing the dying back home, our last episode is increasingly sanitized, and our loved ones do not have the courage to object: it is too messy, too dirty, too painful, too inhuman, too degrading in fact. Life is interrupted at the threshold of the last possible smile, and death becomes visible only for a brief, ceremonial moment, after specialized image-makers perform their soothing *mise-en-scène*. Afterwards, mourning is becoming out of fashion in our societies, both as a reaction against traditional social hypocrisy, and as a down-to-earth philosophy of survival. Yet psychoanalysts and anthropologists have shown the social functions and individual benefits of mourning, both in its ritual and in its feeling.[56] But forfeiting mourning is the price to pay for accessing eternity in our lifetime through the denial of death.

The dominant trend in our societies, as an expression of our technological ambition, and in line with our celebration of the ephemeral, is to erase death from life, or to make it meaningless by its repeated representation in the media, always as the other's death, so that our own is met with the surprise of the unexpected. By separating death from life, and by creating the technological system to make this belief last long enough, we construct eternity in our life span. Thus, eternal we become except for that brief moment when embraced by the light.

Instant Wars

Death, war, and time are secular historical associates. It is one of the most striking characteristics of the emerging technological paradigm that this association is essentially altered, at least for the decisive warfare of dominant powers. Indeed, the advent of nuclear technology, and the possibility of planetary holocaust had the paradoxical effect of canceling large-scale, global warfare between major powers, superseding a condition that marked the first half of the twentieth century as the most destructive, lethal period in history.[57] However,

[56]   Thomas (1975).
[57]   Van Creveld (1989); Tilly (1995).

geopolitical interests and societal confrontations continue to fuel international, inter-ethnic, and ideological hostility to the limit of aiming at physical destruction:[58] the roots of war, we must acknowledge, are in human nature, at least as historically experienced.[59] Yet in the last two decades, democratic, technologically advanced societies, in North America, Western Europe, Japan, and Oceania, have come to reject warfare and to oppose extraordinary resistance to governments' calling their citizens to the ultimate sacrifice. The Algerian war in France, the Vietnam war in the United States, and the Afghanistan war in Russia[60] were turning points in the capacity of states to commit their societies to destruction for not so compelling

[58] For some useful information, of questionable conceptualization, see US House of Representatives, Committee on Armed Services, Readiness Subcommittee (1990). See also Gurr (1993); Harff (1986).

[59] I have to confess that my understanding of war, and of the social context of warfare, is influenced by what is probably the oldest military treatise on strategy: Sun Tzu's *On the Art of War* (c.505–496BC). If the reader suspects that I indulge in exoticism, I invite her or him to its reading, on the condition of having the patience to extract the logic embedded in the analysis from its historical context. Read a sample of it:

> The art of war is of vital importance to the State. It is a matter of life and death, a road either to safety or ruin. Hence it is a subject of inquiry which can on no account be neglected. The art of war, then, is governed by five constant factors, to be taken into account in one's deliberations, when seeking to determine the conditions obtaining in the field. These are (1) The Moral Law (2) Heaven (3) Earth (4) The Commander (5) Method and Discipline. The Moral Law causes the people to be in complete accord with their ruler, so that they will follow him regardless of their lives. Heaven signifies night and day, cold and heat, times and seasons. Earth comprises distances, great and small; danger and security; open ground and narrow passes; the chances of life and death. The Commander stands for the virtues of wisdom, sincerity, benevolence, courage, and strictness. By Method and Discipline are to be understood the marshalling of the army in its proper subdivisions, the gradations of rank among the officers, the maintenance of roads by which supplies may reach the army, and *the control of military expenditure.* (pp.1–3; my emphasis)

[60] Public opinion in Russia is probably, with Japan and Germany, one of the most pacifist in the world, since in the twentieth century Russian people have suffered more from war than anyone else in the world. This pacifism could not express itself in the open until the 1980s for obvious reasons, but widespread discontent with the war in Afghanistan was an important factor in inducing Gorbachev's *perestroyka*. Furthermore, although the war in Chechnya in 1994 seemed to belie this statement, in fact it provoked the disaffection of a large proportion of the population *vis-à-vis* Yeltsin's policies, and precipitated the split between the Russian President and many of the democrats who had supported him in the past. On the basis of my personal knowledge of Russia and of some

reasons. Since warfare, and the credible threat of resorting to it, is still at the core of state power, since the end of the Vietnam war strategists have been busy finding ways still to make war. Only under this condition can economic, technological, and demographic power be translated into domination over other states, the oldest game in humankind. Three conclusions were rapidly reached in advanced, democratic countries, regarding the conditions necessary to make war somewhat acceptable to society:[61]

1   It should not involve common citizens, thus being enacted by a professional army, so that the mandatory draft should be reserved for truly exceptional circumstances, perceived as unlikely.
2   It should be short, even instantaneous, so that the consequences would not linger on, draining human and economic resources, and raising questions about the justification for military action.
3. It should be clean, surgical, with destruction, even of the enemy, kept within reasonable limits and as hidden as possible from public view, with the consequence of linking closely information-handling, image-making, and war-making.

Dramatic breakthroughs in military technology in the last two decades provided the tools to implement this socio-military strategy. Well-trained, well-equipped, full-time, professional armed forces do not require the involvement of the population at large in the war effort, except for viewing and cheering from their living rooms a particularly exciting show, punctuated with deep patriotic feelings.[62] Professional management of news reporting, in an intelligent form that understands the needs of the media while monitoring them, can bring the war live to people's homes with limited, sanitized

---

survey data, I would propose the admittedly optimistic hypothesis that Russia's military lobby will face in the future as serious a popular opposition to war-making as Western countries do, thus inducing a shift to technological emphasis in warfare.

[61]   See the reassessment of American military strategy, in fact initiated in the late 1970s, in an important report from a blue-ribbon Commission for the US Defense Department: Ikle and Wohlsletter (1988). See my elaboration on the impact of technology on military strategy, in Castells and Skinner (1988).

[62]   Most Western European countries still had no strictly professional armed forces in the mid-1990s. Yet, although a time-limited draft (less than a year in general) was still practiced, actual military operations were in the hands of a core of professional soldiers with appropriate technological training and ready to fight. Indeed, given widespread opposition to risk life for the sake of the country, the more an army relies on the draft the less these troops are likely to be engaged in combat. The overall trend points clearly to a purely symbolic military service for the large majority of the population in advanced, democratic societies.

perception of killing and suffering, a theme that Baudrillard has elaborated thoroughly.[63] Most importantly, communications and electronic weapons technology allow for devastating strikes against the enemy in extremely brief time spans. The Gulf War was of course the general rehearsal for a new type of war, and its 100 hours' denouement, against a large, and well-equipped Iraqi army, was a demonstration of the decisiveness of new military powers when an important issue is at stake (the West's oil supply in that case).[64] Of course, this analysis, and the Gulf War itself, would require some lengthy qualifications. The US and its allies did send half a million soldiers for several months to launch a ground attack, although many experts suspect that this was in fact due to internal politics in the Defense Department, not yet ready to concede to the Air Force that wars can be won from the air and the sea. This was indeed the case, since land forces did not in practice meet much resistance after the punishment inflicted on the Iraqis at a distance. True, the allies did not press their drive into Baghdad, yet this decision was not because of serious military obstacles, but because of their political calculation in keeping Iraq as a military power in the area, to check Iran and Syria. The lack of support from a major state (Russia or China) made the Iraqis particularly vulnerable, so that other major wars are not potentially so easy for the Western powers' coalition. Technologically equivalent powers would have greater difficulty going after each other. However, given the mutual cancellation of nuclear exchange between major military powers, their potential wars, and the wars between their surrogate states, are likely to depend on rapid exchanges that set the real state of technological imbalance between the warring forces.Massive destruction, or a quick demonstration of its possibility, in minimum time seems to be the accepted strategy to fight advanced wars in the information age.

However, this military strategy can only be pursued by dominant technological powers, and it contrasts sharply with numerous, endless internal and international violent conflicts that have plagued the world since 1945.[65] This temporal difference in war-making is one of the most striking manifestations of the difference in temporality that characterizes our segmented global system, a theme on which I shall elaborate below.

In dominant societies, this new age of warfare has considerable impact on time, and on the notion of time, as experienced in history. Extraordinarily intense moments of military decision-making will

[63]   Baudrillard (1991).
[64]   See, for instance, Morrocco (1991).
[65]   Tilly (1995); Carver (1980); Holsti (1991).

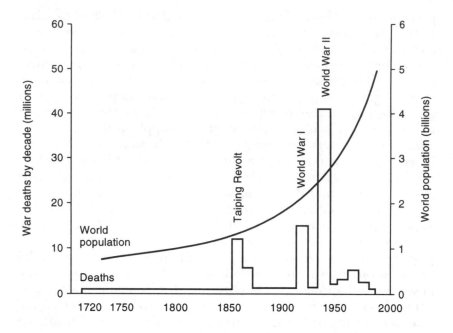

Figure 7.4   War deaths relative to world population, by decade,
1729–2000
Source: Kaye et al. (1985).

emerge as shaping instants over long periods of peace or restrained
tension. For instance, according to a historical quantitative study on
armed conflicts, conducted for the Canadian Defense Ministry, the
duration of conflicts in the first half of the 1980s was reduced, on
average, by more than half in comparison to the 1970s, and by more
than two-thirds with reference to the 1960s.[66] Relying on the same
source, figure 7.4 displays the decrease in the scale of death as the
result of war *in recent years,* particularly when compared to the size of
world population. However, observation of the same figure shows the
extent to which war has been historically a way of life, with particular
intensity in the first half of the twentieth century. Other sources indicate that per capita deaths from war in Western Europe, North
America, Japan, and Latin America were much lower in 1945–89 than
in 1815–1913.[67] Under the new warfare temporality, induced by the
convergence of technology and the pressure from civil societies in

[66]   Kaye et al. (1985).
[67]   Tilly (1995), citing Derriennic (1990).

advanced countries, it seems likely that war will recede to the background of these dominant societies, to flare up from time to time in a sudden reminder of human nature.

In several societies, this disappearance of war from the lifecycle of most people has already decisively impacted culture and behavior. In industrialized, democratic countries, if we except a minority of the population for a short period of time in France, in Portugal, and in the United States, the generations born after the Second World War are the first in history not to have experienced war in their lifetime, with the exception of the lucky Swedes and Swiss. This is a fundamental discontinuity in the human experience. Indeed, this essentially affects masculinity and the culture of manhood, for instance. Up to these generations, in the life of all men it was assumed that at one point something terrible would happen: they would be sent to be killed, to be killers, to live with death and the destruction of bodies, to experience dehumanization on a large scale, and yet be proud of it, or else be banned from the esteem of their society and, frequently, of their families. It is impossible to understand the women's extraordinary patience in the traditional, patriarchal family without a reference to this moment of truth, to this male's atrocious fate, to which mothers, wives, and daughters did pay their respect, a recurrent theme in the literature of all countries.[68] Anyone who has grown up, as in my case, in the first generation without war in their life, knows how decisive the experience of war was for our fathers, how much childhood and the life of the family was filled with the wounds and the reconstructed memories of those years, sometimes only months, but still shaping men's personality for ever, and with it, the personality of their families throughout the lifecycle. This acceleration of time by cohabitation with death, regularly experienced by generation over generation for most of human history, is now over in some societies.[69] And this truly ushers in a new age in our experience.

However, we must be strongly reminded that instant, surgical, secluded, technology-driven wars are the privilege of technologically dominant nations. All around the world, half-ignored, cruel wars linger on for years and years, often fought with primitive means,

[68] This theme has been elaborated by French feminist writer Annie Leclerc. Although I discovered this idea through our personal conversations, it is also present in some of her essays; see especially Leclerc (1975).

[69] In his cultural study of post-War World II Japanese youth, Inoue Syun found that the "non-war" generation differed sharply from its fathers by thinking of life apart from death. He writes: "We might very loosely label the war-time generation as death-acceptors and the non-war generation as death-defiers" (Syun 1975). For a broader analysis on the matter, see Freud (1947).

although global diffusion of high-tech weaponry is also catching up in this market. In the 1989–92 period alone the United Nations counted 82 armed conflicts in the world, of which 79 were internal to a nation.[70] The Indian guerrillas of Guatemala, the endless revolutionary struggles in Colombia and Peru, the Christian rebellion of Southern Sudan, the liberation struggles of Kurdish people, the Muslim rebellion of Mindanao, the mixing of drug traffic and national struggles in Myanmar and Thailand, the tribal/ideological wars in Angola, the warlords' confrontations in Somalia or Liberia, the ethnic civil wars of Rwanda and Burundi, the Sahara resistance to Morocco, the civil war in Algeria, the civil war in Afghanistan, the civil war in Sri Lanka, the civil war in Bosnia, the decades-old Arab–Israeli wars and struggles, the wars in the Caucasus, and so many other armed confrontations and wars that last for years and decades, clearly demonstrate that slow-motion, debilitating wars are still, and will be for the foreseeable future, the hideous sign of our destructive capacity.[71] It is precisely the asymmetry of various countries in their relationship to power, wealth, and technology that determines different temporalities, and particularly the time of their warfare. Furthermore, the same country may shift from slow-motion wars to instant wars depending on its relationship to the global system and to the interests of dominant powers. Thus, Iran and Iraq fought for seven years an atrocious war, carefully fed by Western countries supporting both sides of the carnage (US and France helping Iraq, Israel helping Iran, Spain selling chemical weapons to both), so that their reciprocal destruction would undermine the capacity of either of them to jeopardize the oil supply. When Iraq, with a well-equipped, combat-hardened army, went on to affirm its leadership in the region (indeed, counting on the acquiescence of Western powers), it found itself confronted by instant war technology, in a demonstration of force that was intended as a warning of future world disorder. Or elsewhere, the lingering, atrocious war in Bosnia, the shame of the European Union, was transformed in a few days, and a peace process was imposed at Dayton, Ohio, in August 1995, once the NATO countries settled their differences, and shifted the technological mode to a few days of selective, devastating strikes that crippled the Bosnian Serbs' fighting capacity. When and if a conflict becomes included in the high-priority plans of world powers, it shifts to a different tempo.

To be sure, even for dominant societies, the end of war does not mean the end of violence and of violent confrontation with political

---

[70]   *Economist* (1993).
[71]   Tillema (1991).

apparatuses of various kinds. The transformation of war ushers in new forms of violent conflict, terrorism being foremost among them. Potential nuclear, chemical, and bacteriological terrorism, in addition to indiscriminate massacres and hostage-taking, with the media as the focus of the action, are likely to become the expressions of warfare in advanced societies. Yet even these violent acts, susceptible to affecting everybody's psyche, are experienced as discontinuous instants in the course of peaceful normality. This is in striking contrast to the pervasiveness of state-induced violence in much of the planet.[72]

Instant wars, and their technologically induced temporality, are an attribute of informational societies, but, as with other dimensions of the new temporality, they characterize the forms of domination of the new system, to the exclusion of countries and events that are not central to the emerging, dominant logic.

Virtual Time

The culture of real virtuality associated with an electronically integrated multimedia system, as argued in chapter 5, contributes to the transformation of time in our society in two different forms: simultaneity and timelessness.

On the one hand, instant information throughout the globe, mixed with live reporting from across the neighborhood, provides unprecedented temporal immediacy to social events and cultural expressions.[73] To follow minute by minute in real time the collapse of the Soviet state in August 1991, with simultaneous translation of Russian political debates, introduced a new era of communication, when the making of history can be directly witnessed, provided it is deemed interesting enough by the controllers of information. Also, computer-mediated communication makes possible real-time dialogue, bringing people together around their interests, in interactive, multilateral chat writing. Time-delayed answers can be easily overcome, as new communication technologies provide a sense of immediacy that conquers time barriers, as much as the telephone did but with greater flexibility, with the communicating parties able to lapse for a few seconds, or minutes, to bring in other information, to expand the realm of communication, without the pressure of the telephone, ill-adapted to long silences.

[72] Tilly (1995).
[73] Wark (1994); Campo Vidal (1996).

On the other hand, the mixing of times in the media, within the same channel of communication and at the choice of the viewer/interactor, creates a temporal collage, where not only genres are mixed, but their timing becomes synchronous in a flat horizon, with no beginning, no end, no sequence. The timelessness of multimedia's hypertext is a decisive feature of our culture, shaping the minds and memories of children educated in the new cultural context. History is first organized according to the availability of visual material, then submitted to the computerized possibility of selecting seconds of frames to be pieced together, or split apart, according to specific discourses. School education, media entertainment, special news reports or advertising organize temporality as it fits, so that the overall effect is a nonsequential time of cultural products available from the whole realm of the human experience. If encyclopedias have organized human knowledge by alphabetical order, electronic media provide access to information, expression, and perception according to the impulses of the consumer or to the decisions of the producer. By so doing, the whole ordering of meaningful events loses its internal, chronological rhythm, and becomes arranged in time sequences depending upon the social context of their utilization. Thus, **it is a culture at the same time of the eternal and of the ephemeral.** It is eternal because it reaches back and forth to the whole sequence of cultural expressions. It is ephemeral because each arrangement, each specific sequencing, depends on the context and purpose under which any given cultural construct is solicited. We are not in a culture of circularity, but in a universe of undifferentiated temporality of cultural expressions.

I have discussed the relationship between the ideology of the end of history, the material conditions created under the logic of the space of flows, and the emergence of postmodern architecture, where all cultural codes can be mixed without sequencing or ordering, since we are in a world of finite cultural expressions. Eternal/ephemeral time also fits in this particular cultural mode, as it transcends any particular sequencing. David Harvey, along similar lines of argument, has brilliantly shown the interaction between postmodern culture, be it in architecture, cinema, art, or philosophy, and what he calls the "post-modern condition" induced by space-time compression. Although I believe that he gives to capitalist logic more responsibility than it deserves for current processes of cultural transformation, his analysis unveils the social sources of the sudden convergence of cultural expressions towards the negation of meaning and the affirmation of irony as the supreme value.[74] Time is compressed and

[74]   Harvey (1990: 284ff).

ultimately denied in culture, as a primitive replica of the fast turnover in production, consumption, ideology, and politics on which our society is based. A speed only made possible because of new communication technologies.

Yet culture does not simply reproduce in all its manifestations the logic of the economic system. The historical correspondence between the political economy of signs and the signs of political economy is not a sufficient argument to characterize the emergence of timeless time in postmodernism. I think we must add something else: the specificity of new cultural expressions, their ideological and technological freedom to scan the planet and the whole history of humankind, and to integrate, and mix, in the supertext any sign from anywhere, from the rap culture of American ghettoes, mimicked a few months later in the pop groups of Taipei or Tokyo, to Buddhist spiritualism transformed in electronic music. The eternal/ephemeral time of the new culture does fit with the logic of flexible capitalism and with the dynamics of the network society, but it adds its own, powerful layer, installing individual dreams and collective representations in a no-time mental landscape.

Perhaps New Age music, so characteristic of the taste of today's professionals throughout the world, is representative of the timeless dimension of the emerging culture, bringing together reconstructed Buddhist meditation, electronic sound-making, and sophisticated Californian composition. The electric harp of Hillary Staggs, modulating the range of elementary notes in an endless variation of a simple melody, or the long pauses and sudden volume alterations of Ray Lynch's painful serenity, combine within the same musical text a feeling of distance and repetition with the sudden surge of restrained sentiment, as blips of life in the ocean of eternity, a feeling often underscored by background sound of ocean waves or of the desert's wind in many New Age compositions. Assuming, as I do, that New Age is the classic music of our epoch, and observing its influence in so many different contexts but always among the same social groups, it can be suggested that the manipulation of time is the recurrent theme of new cultural expressions. A manipulation obsessed with the binary reference to instantaneity and eternity: me and the universe, the self and the net. Such reconciliation, actually fusing the biological individual into the cosmological whole, can only be achieved under the condition of the merger of all times, from the creation of ourselves to the end of the universe. Timelessness is the recurrent theme of our age's cultural expressions, be it in the sudden flashes of video clips or in the eternal echoes of electronic spiritualism.

Time, Space, and Society: the Edge of Forever

So, in the end, what is time, this elusive notion that bewildered St Augustine, misled Newton, inspired Einstein, obsessed Heidegger? And how is it being transformed in our society?

For the sake of my exploration, I find it helpful to call upon Leibniz, for whom time is the order of succession of "things," so that without "things" there would be no time.[75] Current knowledge on the concept of time in physics, biology, history, and sociology does not seem to be contradicted by such clear, synthetic conceptualization. Furthermore, we may better understand the on-going transformation of temporality by reference to the Leibnizian notion of time. I propose the idea that **timeless time,** as I label the dominant temporality of our society, **occurs when the characteristics of a given context, namely, the informational paradigm and the network society, induce systemic perturbation in the sequential order of phenomena performed in that context.** This perturbation may take the form of compressing the occurrence of phenomena, aiming at instantaneity, or else by introducing random discontinuity in the sequence. Elimination of sequencing creates undifferentiated time, which is tantamount to eternity.

The specific analyses presented in this chapter provide illustrations of the substantive issues involved under such abstract characterization. Split-second capital transactions, flex-time enterprises, variable life working time, the blurring of the lifecycle, the search for eternity through the denial of death, instant wars, and the culture of virtual time, all are fundamental phenomena, characteristic of the network society, that systemically mix tenses in their occurrence.

However, this characterization does not refer to all time in human experience. In fact, in our world, most people and most spaces live in a different temporality. I mentioned the dramatic contrast between

---

[75]   Although the analysis of space and time is embedded in the whole philosophical vision of Leibniz, one of the most clear formulations of his thinking is the following paragraph, extracted from his correspondence with Clark (1715–16):

> I have more than once stated that I held *space* to be something purely relative, like *time; space being an order of co-existences as time is an order of successions.* For space denotes in terms of possibility an order of things which exist at the same time, in so far as they exist together, and is not concerned with their particular ways of existing: and when we see several things together we perceive this order of things among themselves . . . The same is true of time . . . *Instants apart from things are nothing, and they only consist in the successive order of things.*   (Quoted from Parkinson (ed.) 1973: 211–12, my added emphasis)

instant wars and the elimination of war in the life horizon of most people in the dominant countries, on the one hand, and the endless, daily war-making in places scattered all over the planet, on the other hand. A similar argument may be extended to each instance associated with the new temporality. Infant mortality rates in Uruguay and in the former USSR are more than twice the average of those in the US, but so are the rates for infant mortality in Washington, D.C. (see table 7.6). Although death and illness are being pushed back throughout the world, yet in 1990 people from the least-developed countries were expected to live 25 years less than those in the most advanced areas. Flex-time, networked production, and self-management of time in Northern Italy or Silicon Valley have very little meaning for the millions of workers brought into the clock-run assembly lines of China and South-East Asia. Flexible schedules still mean for the vast majority of the world's urban population their survival in unpredictable work patterns of the informal economy, where the notion of unemployment is strange to a system where you work or you die. For instance, mobile telephony adds time/space flexibility to personal and professional connections, but in the streets of Lima, in 1995, it spurred a new form of informal business, nicknamed *cholular*,[76] in which street communication vendors wandered around carrying cellular phones, offering rental calls to people walking by: maximum flexibility in endless working days of unpredictable future. Or, again, virtual culture is still associated for a large segment of people with passive TV viewing at the end of exhausting days, with the mind captured in images of soap operas about Texas millionaires, strangely equally familiar to youngsters in Marrakech and to housewives in Barcelona where, naturally proud of their identity, they watch it in Catalan.

Timeless time belongs to the space of flows, while time discipline, biological time, and socially determined sequencing characterize places around the world, materially structuring and destructuring our segmented societies. Space shapes time in our society, thus reversing a historical trend: flows induce timeless time, places are time-bounded.[77] The idea of progress, at the roots of our culture and society for the last two centuries, was based on the movement of

[76] "Cholo" is the common language name received by the people of the coast in Peru. "Cholular" plays with the linguistic integration between cellular telephony and Lima's identity.
[77] This conceptualization has some similarity with the construction of space-time regimes proposed by Innis (1950, 1951). I do not claim, however, an intellectual lineage with his theory, since I believe he would probably have disagreed with my overall analysis of time.

Table 7.6 Comparisons of infant mortality rates, selected countries, 1990–5 estimates

	Deaths per 1,000 live births
United States Total	9
White	8
Other	16
Black	18
Counties and cities	
Norfolk City, VA	20
Portsmouth City, VA	19
Suffolk City, VA	25
New York City, NY	12
Bronx	13
Orleans, LA	17
Los Angeles Co., CA	8
Wayne Co. (Detroit), MI	16
Washington, DC	21
Africa	95
Algeria	61
Egypt	57
Kenya	66
Morocco	68
Nigeria	96
South Africa	53
Tanzania	102
Zaire	93
Asia	62
Europe	10
Latin America	47
Northern America	8
Oceania	22
USSR (former)	21
Other countries	
Bulgaria	14
Canada	7
Chile	17
China	27
Costa Rica	14
France	7
Germany	7
Hong Kong	6
Jamaica	14
Japan	5
Korea	21
Malaysia	14
Poland	15
Singapore	8
Thailand	26
Ukraine	14
Uruguay	20
United Kingdom	7

Sources: United Nations Population Fund, *The State of World Population*, 1994; US Dept of Health and Human Services, *Vital Statistics of the United States: 1990*, vol. II section 2, table 2-1, 1994.

history, indeed on the predetermined sequence of history under the lead of reason and with the impulse of productive forces, escaping the constraints of spatially bounded societies and cultures. The mastery of time, the control of rhythmicity colonized territories and trans- formed space in the vast movement of industrialization and urbanization accomplished by the twin historical processes of forma- tion of capitalism and statism. *Becoming* structured *being*, time conformed space.

The dominant trend in our society displays the historical revenge of space, structuring temporality in different, even contradictory logics according to spatial dynamics. The space of flows, as analyzed in the preceding chapter, dissolves time by disordering the sequence of events and making them simultaneous, thus installing society in eternal ephemerality. The multiple space of places, scattered, frag- mented, and disconnected, displays diverse temporalities, from the most primitive domination of natural rhythms to the strictest tyranny of clock time. Selected functions and individuals transcend time,[78] while downgraded activities and subordinate people endure life as time goes by. While the emerging logic of the new social structure aims at the relentless supersession of time as an ordered sequence of events, most of society, in a globally interdependent system, remains on the edge of the new universe. Timelessness sails in an ocean surrounded by time-bound shores, from where still can be heard the laments of time-chained creatures.

Furthermore, the logic of timelessness is not displayed without resistance in society. As places and localities aim at regaining control over the social interests embedded in the space of flows, so time- conscious social actors try to bring under control the ahistorical domination of timelessness. Precisely because our society reaches the understanding of material interactions for the whole environment, science and technology provide us with the potential to foresee a new kind of temporality, also placed within the framework of eternity, but taking into account historical sequences. This is what Lash and Urry call "glacial time," a notion in which "the relation between humans and nature is very long-term and evolutionary. It moves back out of immediate human history and forwards into a wholly unspecifiable

---

[78] It would seem counterintuitive to argue that the professional elite in our soci- eties is time-transcendent. Are not they (we) constantly running against the clock? My argument is that this behavioral pattern is precisely the consequence of aiming at the relentless supersession of time and of the rhythmicity of the life- cycle (aging, career advancement), induced by our culture/organization, and apparently facilitated by new technological means. What can be more time stressful than the daily battle against time?

future."[79] In fact, the opposition between the management of glacial time and the search for timelessness anchors in contradictory positions in the social structure the environmentalist movement and the powers that be in our society, as I shall elaborate further in volume II. What must be retained from the discussion at this point is the conflictive differentiation of time, understood as the impact of opposed social interests on the sequencing of phenomena. Such differentiation concerns, on the one hand, the contrasting logic between timelessness, structured by the space of flows, and multiple, subordinate temporalities, associated with the space of places. On the other hand, the contradictory dynamics of society opposes the search for human eternity, through the annihilation of time in life, to the realization of cosmological eternity, through the respect of glacial time. Between subdued temporalities and evolutionary nature the network society rises on the edge of forever.

[79] Lash and Urry (1994: 243).

Conclusion:
The Network Society

Our exploration of emergent social structures across domains of human activity and experience leads to an overarching conclusion: as a historical trend, dominant functions and processes in the information age are increasingly organized around networks. Networks constitute the new social morphology of our societies, and the diffusion of networking logic substantially modifies the operation and outcomes in processes of production, experience, power, and culture. While the networking form of social organization has existed in other times and spaces, the new information technology paradigm provides the material basis for its pervasive expansion throughout the entire social structure. Furthermore, I would argue that this networking logic induces a social determination of a higher level than that of the specific social interests expressed through the networks: the power of flows takes precedence over the flows of power. Presence or absence in the network and the dynamics of each network *vis-à-vis* others are critical sources of domination and change in our society: a society that, therefore, we may properly call the network society, characterized by the preeminence of social morphology over social action.

To clarify this statement, I shall try to link up the main lines of analysis presented in this volume with the broader theoretical perspective outlined in the Prologue. It should, however, be kept in mind that I cannot address the full range of theoretical questions introduced at the onset of this inquiry until after examining (in volumes II and III) fundamental issues such as gender relationships, the construction of identity, social movements, the transformation of political process, and the crisis of the state in the information age. It is only after treating these matters, and observing their actual expression in the macro-processes reshaping societies in this end of millennium, that I shall try to propose some exploratory hypotheses to interpret the new society in the making. Nevertheless, enough information and ideas have been submitted to the reader's attention in this volume to be able to reach some provisional conclusions concerning the new structure of dominant functions and processes, a necessary starting point to understand the overall dynamics of society.

I shall first define the concept of network, since it plays such a central role in my characterization of society in the information age.[1] A network is a set of interconnected nodes. A node is the point at which a curve intersects itself. What a node is, concretely speaking, depends on the kind of concrete networks of which we speak. They are stock exchange markets, and their ancillary advanced services centers, in the network of global financial flows. They are national councils of ministers and European Commissioners in the political network that governs the European Union. They are coca fields and poppy fields, clandestine laboratories, secret landing strips, street gangs, and money-laundering financial institutions, in the network of drug traffic that penetrates economies, societies, and states throughout the world. They are television systems, entertainment studios, computer graphics milieux, news teams, and mobile devices generating, transmitting, and receiving signals, in the global network of the new media at the roots of cultural expression and public opinion in the information age. The topology defined by networks determines that the distance (or intensity and frequence of interaction) between two points (or social positions) is shorter (or more frequent, or more intense) if both points are nodes in a network than if they do not belong to the same network. On the other hand, within a given network flows have no distance, or the same distance, between nodes. Thus, distance (physical, social, economic, political, cultural) for a given point or position varies between zero (for any node in the same network) and infinite (for any point external to the network). The inclusion/exclusion in networks, and the architecture of relationships between networks, enacted by light-speed operating information technologies, configurate dominant processes and functions in our societies.

Networks are open structures, able to expand without limits, integrating new nodes as long as they are able to communicate within the network, namely as long as they share the same communication codes (for example, values or performance goals). A network-based social structure is a highly dynamic, open system, susceptible to innovating without threatening its balance. Networks are appropriate instru-

[1]   I am indebted for my conceptualization of networks to my on-going intellectual dialogue with François Bar.

ments for a capitalist economy based on innovation, globalization, and decentralized concentration; for work, workers, and firms based on flexibility, and adaptability; for a culture of endless deconstruction and reconstruction; for a polity geared towards the instant processing of new values and public moods; and for a social organization aiming at the supersession of space and the annihilation of time. Yet the network morphology is also a source of dramatic reorganization of power relationships. Switches connecting the networks (for example, financial flows taking control of media empires that influence political processes) are the privileged instruments of power. Thus, the switchers are the power holders. Since networks are multiple, the interoperating codes and switches between networks become the fundamental sources in shaping, guiding, and misguiding societies. The convergence of social evolution and information technologies has created a new material basis for the performance of activities throughout the social structure. This material basis, built in networks, earmarks dominant social processes, thus shaping social structure itself.

So observations and analyses presented in this volume seem to indicate that the new economy is organized around global networks of capital, management, and information, whose access to technological know-how is at the roots of productivity and competitiveness. Business firms and, increasingly, organizations and institutions are organized in networks of variable geometry whose intertwining supersedes the traditional distinction between corporations and small business, cutting across sectors, and spreading along different geographic clusters of economic units. Accordingly, the work process is increasingly individualized, labor is disaggregated in its performance, and reintegrated in its outcome through a multiplicity of interconnected tasks in different sites, ushering in a new division of labor based on the attributes/capacities of each worker rather than on the organization of the task.

However, this evolution towards networking forms of management and production does not imply the demise of capitalism. The network society, in its various institutional expressions, is, for the time being, a capitalist society. Furthermore, for the first time in history, the capitalist mode of production shapes social relationships over the entire planet. But this brand of capitalism is profoundly different from its historical predecessors. It has two fundamental distinctive features: it is global, and it is structured to a large extent, around a network of financial flows. Capital works globally as a unit in real time; and it is realized, invested, and accumulated mainly in the sphere of circulation, that is as finance capital. While finance capital has generally been among the dominant fractions of capital, we are witnessing the emergence of something different: capital accumulation proceeds, and its value-making is generated, increasingly, in the global financial markets enacted by information networks in the timeless space of financial flows. From these networks, capital is invested, globally, in all sectors of activity: information industries, media business, advanced services, agricultural production, health, education, technology, old and new manufacturing, transportation, trade, tourism, culture, environmental management, real estate, war-making and peace-selling, religion, entertainment, and sports. Some activities are more profitable than others, as they go through cycles, market upswings and downturns, and segmented global competition. Yet whatever is extracted as profit (from producers, consumers, technology, nature, and institutions) is reverted to the meta-network of financial flows, where all capital is equalized in the commodified democracy of profit-making. In this electronically operated global casino specific capitals boom or bust, settling the fate of corporations, household savings, national currencies, and regional economies. The net result sums to zero: the losers pay for the winners. But who are the winners and the losers changes by the year, the month, the day, the second, and permeates down to the world of firms, jobs, salaries, taxes, and public services. To the world of what is sometimes called "the real economy," and of what I would be tempted to call the "unreal economy," since in the age of networked capitalism the fundamental reality, where money is made and lost, invested or saved, is in the financial sphere. All other activities (except those of the dwindling public sector) are primarily the basis to generate the necessary surplus to invest in global flows, or the result of investment originated in these financial networks.

Financial capital needs, however, to rely for its operation and competition on knowledge and information generated and enhanced by information technology. This is the concrete meaning of the articulation between the capitalist mode of production and the informational mode of development. Thus, capital that would remain purely speculative is submitted to excessive risk, and ultimately washed out by simple statistical probability in the random movements of the financial markets. It is in the interaction between investment in profitable firms and using accumulated profits to make them fructify in the global financial networks that the process of accumulation lies. So it depends on productivity, on competitiveness, and on adequate information on investment and long-term planning in every sector. High-technology firms depend on financial resources to go on with their endless drive toward innovation, productivity, and competitiveness. Financial capital, acting directly through financial institutions or indirectly through the dynamics of stock exchange markets, conditions the fate of high-technology industries. On the other hand, technology and information are decisive tools in generating profits and in appropriating market shares. Thus, financial capital and high-technology, industrial capital are increasingly interdependent, even if their modes of operation are specific to each industry. Hilferding and Schumpeter were both right, but their historical coupling had to wait until it was dreamed of in Palo Alto and consummated in Ginza.

Thus, capital is either global or becomes global to enter the accumulation process in the electronically networked economy. Firms, as I have tried to show in chapter 3, are increasingly organized in networks, both internally and in their relationship. So capital flows, and their induced production/management/distribution activities are spread in interconnected networks of variable geometry. Under these new technological, organizational, and economic conditions, who are the capitalists? They are certainly not the legal owners of the means of production, who range from your/my pension fund to a passer-by in a Singapore ATM suddenly deciding to buy stock in Buenos Aires' emergent market. But this has been to some extent true since the 1930s, as shown by Berle and Means' classic study on control and ownership in United States corporations. Yet neither are the corporate managers, as suggested in their study, and, thereafter, by other analysts. For managers control specific corporations, and specific segments of the global economy, but do not control, and do not even know about, the actual, systemic movements of capital in the networks of financial flows, of knowledge in the information networks, of strategies in the multifaceted set of network enterprises. Some actors at the top of this global capitalist system are indeed managers, as in the case of Japanese corporations. Others could still be identified under the traditional category of bourgeoisie, as in the overseas Chinese business networks, who are culturally bonded, often family or personally related, share values and, sometimes, political connections. In the United States, a mixture of historical layers provides to the capitalist characters a colorful array of traditional bankers, nouveau riche speculators, self-made geniuses-turned-entrepreneurs, global tycoons, and multinational managers. In other cases, public corporations (as in French banking or electronics firms) are the capitalist actors. In Russia, survivors of communist *nomenklatura* compete with wild young capitalists in recycling state property in the constitution of the newest capitalist province. And all over the world, money-laundering from miscellaneous criminal businesses flows toward this mother of all accumulations that is the global financial network.

So all these are capitalists, presiding over all sorts of economies, and people's lives. But a capitalist class? There is not, sociologically and economically, such a thing as a global capitalist class. But there is an integrated, global capital network, whose movements and variable logic ultimately determine economies and influence societies. Thus, above a diversity of human-flesh capitalists and capitalist groups there is a faceless collective capitalist, made up of financial flows operated by electronic networks. This is not simply the expression of the abstract logic of the market, because it does not truly follow the law of supply and demand: it responds to the turbulences, and unpredictable movements, of noncalculable anticipations, induced by psychology and society, as much as by economic processes. This network of networks of capital both unifies and commands specific centers of capitalist accumulation, structuring the behavior of capitalists around their submission to the global network. They play their competing, or converging, strategies by and through the circuits of this global network, and so they are ultimately dependent upon the nonhuman capitalist logic of an electronically operated, random processing of information. It is indeed capitalism in its pure expression of the endless search for money by money through the production of commodities by commodities. But money has become almost entirely independent from production, including production of services, by escaping into the networks of higher-order electronic interactions barely understood by its managers. While capitalism still rules, capitalists are randomly incarnated, and the capitalist classes are restricted to specific areas of the world where they prosper as appendixes to a mighty whirlwind which manifests its will by spread points and futures options ratings in the global flashes of computer screens.

What happens to labor, and to the social relationships of production, in this brave new world of informational, global capitalism? Workers do not disappear in the space of flows, and, down to earth, work is plentiful. Indeed, belying apocalyptic prophecies of simplistic analyses, there are more jobs and a higher proportion of working-age people employed than at any time in history. This is mainly because of the massive incorporation of women in paid work in all industrialized societies, an incorporation that has generally been absorbed, and to a large extent induced, by the labor market without major disruptions. So the diffusion of information technologies, while certainly displacing workers and eliminating some jobs, has not resulted, and it does not seem that it will result in the foreseeable future, in mass unemployment. This in spite of the rise of unemployment in European economies, a trend that is related to social institutions rather than to the new production system. But, if work, workers, and working classes exist, and even expand, around the world, the social relationships between capital and labor are profoundly transformed.

At its core, capital is global. As a rule, labor is local. Informationalism, in its historical reality, leads to the concentration and globalization of capital, precisely by using the decentralizing power of networks. Labor is disaggregated in its performance, fragmented in its organization, diversified in its existence, divided in its collective action. Networks converge toward a meta-network of capital that integrates capitalist interests at the global level and across sectors and realms of activity: not without conflict, but under the same overarching logic. Labor loses its collective identity, becomes increasingly individualized in its capacities, in its working conditions, and in its interests and projects. Who are the owners, who the producers, who the managers, and who the servants, becomes increasingly blurred in a production system of variable geometry, of teamwork, of networking, outsourcing, and subcontracting. Can we say that the producers of value are the computer nerds who invent new financial instruments to be dispossessed from their work by corporate brokers? Who is contributing to value creation in the electronics industry: the Silicon Valley chip designer, or the young woman on the assembly line of a South-East Asian factory? Certainly both, albeit in quite substantially different proportions. Thus, are they jointly the new working class? Why not include in it the Bombay computer consultant subcontracted to program this particular design? Or the flying manager who commutes or telecommutes between California and Singapore customizing chip production and electronics consumption? There is unity of the work process throughout the complex, global networks of interaction. But there is at the same time differentiation of work, segmentation of workers, and disaggregation of labor on a global scale. So while capitalist relationships of production still persist (indeed, in many economies the dominant logic is more strictly capitalist than ever before), capital and labor increasingly tend to exist in different spaces and times: the space of flows and the space of places, instant time of computerized networks versus clock time of everyday life. Thus, they live by each other, but do not relate to each other, as the life of global capital depends less and less on specific labor, and more and more on accumulated, generic labor, operated by a small brains trust inhabiting the virtual palaces of global networks. Beyond this fundamental dichotomy a great deal of social diversity still exists, made up of investors' bids, workers' efforts, human ingenuity, human suffering, hirings and layoffs, promotions and demotions, conflicts and negotiations, competition and alliances: working life goes on. Yet, at a deeper level of the new social reality, social relationships of production have been disconnected in their actual existence. Capital tends to escape in its hyperspace of pure circulation, while labor dissolves its collective entity into an infinite variation of individual existences. Under the conditions of the network society, capital is globally coordinated, labor is individualized. The struggle between diverse capitalists and miscellaneous working classes is subsumed into the more fundamental opposition between the bare logic of capital flows and the cultural values of human experience.

Processes of social transformation summarized under the ideal type of the network society go beyond the sphere of social and technical relationships of production: they deeply affect culture and power as well. Cultural expressions are abstracted from history and geography, and become predominantly mediated by electronic communication networks that interact with the audience and by the audience in a diversity of codes and values, ultimately subsumed in a digitized, audiovisual hypertext. Because information and communication circulate primarily through the diversified, yet comprehensive media system, politics becomes increasingly played out in the space of media. Leadership is personalized, and image-making is power-making. Not that all politics can be reduced to media effects, or that values and interests are indifferent to political outcomes. But whoever the political actors and whatever their orientations, they exist in the power game through and by the media, in the whole variety of an increasingly diverse media system, that includes computer-mediated communication networks. The fact that politics has to be framed in the language of electronically based media has profound consequences on the characteristics, organization, and goals of political processes, political actors, and political institutions. Ultimately, the powers that are in the media networks take second place to the power of flows embodied in the structure and language of these networks.

At a deeper level, the material foundations of society, space and time are being transformed, organized around the space of flows and timeless time. Beyond the metaphorical value of these expressions, supported by a number of analyses and illustrations in preceding chapters, a major hypothesis is put forward: dominant functions are organized in networks pertaining to a space of flows that links them up around the world, while fragmenting subordinate functions, and people, in the multiple space of places, made of locales increasingly segregated and disconnected from each other. Timeless time appears to be the result of the negation of time, past and future, in the networks of the space of flows. Meanwhile clock time, measured and valued differentially for each process according to its position in the network, continues to characterize subordinate functions and specific locales. The end of history, enacted in the circularity of computerized financial flows or in the instantaneity of surgical wars, overpowers the biological time of poverty or the mechanical time of industrial work. The social construction of new dominant forms of space and time develops a meta-network that switches off nonessential functions, subordinate social groups, and devalued territories. By so doing, infinite social distance is created between this meta-network and most individuals, activities, and locales around the world. Not that people, locales, or activities disappear. But their structural meaning does, subsumed in the unseen logic of the meta-network where value is produced, cultural codes are created, and power is decided. The new social order, the network society, increasingly appears to most people as a meta-social disorder. Namely, as an automated, random sequence of events, derived from the uncontrollable logic of markets, technology, geopolitical order, or biological determination.

In a broader historical perspective, the network society represents a qualitative change in the human experience. If we refer to an old sociological tradition according to which social action at the most fundamental level can be understood as the changing pattern of relationships between Nature and Culture, we are indeed in a new era.

The first model of relationship between these two fundamental poles of human existence was characterized for millennia by the domination of Nature over Culture. The codes of social organization almost directly expressed the struggle for survival under the uncontrolled harshness of Nature, as anthropology taught us by tracing the codes of social life back to the roots of our biological entity.

The second pattern of the relationship established at the origins of the Modern Age, and associated with the Industrial Revolution and with the triumph of Reason, saw the domination of Nature by Culture, making society out of the process of work by which Humankind found both its liberation from natural forces and its submission to its own abysses of oppression and exploitation.

We are just entering a new stage in which Culture refers to Culture, having superseded Nature to the point that Nature is artificially revived ("preserved") as a cultural form: this is in fact the meaning of the environmental movement, to reconstruct Nature as an ideal cultural form. Because of the convergence of historical evolution and technological change we have entered a purely cultural pattern of social interaction and social organization. This is why information is the key ingredient of our social organization and why flows of messages and images between networks constitute the basic thread of our social structure. This is not to say that history has ended in a happy reconciliation of Humankind with itself. It is in fact quite the opposite: history is just beginning, if by history we understand the moment when, after millennia of a prehistoric battle with Nature, first to survive, then to conquer it, our species has reached the level of knowledge and social organization that will allow us to live in a predominantly social world. It is the beginning of a new existence, and indeed the beginning of a new age, the information age, marked by the autonomy of culture *vis-à-vis* the material bases of our existence. But this is not necessarily an exhilarating moment. Because, alone at last in our human world, we shall have to look at ourselves in the mirror of historical reality. And we may not like the vision.

   To be continued.

Summary of the Contents of Volumes II and III

Throughout this volume reference has been made to the themes to be presented in the subsequent volumes of this work (to be published by Blackwell Publishers in 1997). An outline of their contents is given below.

Volume II: *The Power of Identity*

Introduction: Our lives, our world

1 Communal Heavens: Identity and meaning in the network society

2 The end of patriarchalism: the transformation of gender, family, sexuality, and personality

3 Social movements and social change in a world of flows

4 The powerless state

5 Informational politics and the crisis of democracy

Conclusion: The subjects of social change in the network society

Volume III: *End of Millennium*

Introduction: Social theory and processes of historical transformation

1   The crisis of industrial statism and the end of communism: the collapse of the Soviet Union

2   The black holes of informational capitalism: social exclusion and the rise of the Fourth World

3   The perverse connection: the global criminal economy and the new world disorder

4   Forward to the past: the reunification of Europe

5   Toward the Pacific era? The multicultural foundation of techno-economic interdependence

General conclusion: Connections: making sense of our world

Bibliography

Abegglen, J.C. and Stalk, G. (1985) *Kaisha: The Japanese Corporation*, New York: Basic Books.

Abolaffia, Michael Y. and Biggart, Nicole W. (1991) "Competition and markets: an institutional perspective." In Amitai Etzioni and Paul R. Lawrence (eds), *Socio-economics: Towards a New Synthesis*, Armonk, NY: M.E. Sharpe, pp. 211–31.

Adam, Barbara (1990) *Time and Social Theory*, Cambridge: Polity Press.

Adler, Glenn and Suarez, Doris (1993) *Union Voices: Labor's Responses to Crisis*, Albany, NY: State University of New York Press.

Adler, Paul S. (1992) *Technology and the Future of Work*, New York: Oxford University Press.

African Development Bank (1990) *The Social Dimensions of Adjustment in Africa: A Policy Agenda*, Washington D.C.: World Bank.

Agence de l'Informatique (1986) *L'Etat d'informatisation de la France*, Paris: Economica.

Aglietta, Michel (1976) *Régulation et crise du capitalisme: l'expérience des Etats-Unis*, Paris: Calmann-Levy.

Allen, G.C. (1981a) *The Japanese Economy*, New York: St Martin's Press.

—— (1981b) *A Short Economic History of Modern Japan*, London: Macmillan.

Allen, Jane E. (1995) "New computers may use DNA instead of chips." *San Francisco Chronicle*, May 13: B2.

Alvarado, Manuel (ed.) (1988) *Video World-wide*, London and Paris: John Libbey.

Amin, Ash and Robins, Kevin (1991) "These are not Marshallian times." In Roberto Camagni (ed.) *Innovation Networks: Spatial Perspectives*, London: Belhaven Press, pp. 105–20.

Amsdem, Alice (1979) "Taiwan's economic history: a case of étatisme and a challenge to dependency theory," *Modern China*, 5(3): 341–80.

—— (1985) "The state and Taiwan's economic development." In Peter B.

Evans, Dietrich Rueschemeyer and Theda Skocpol (eds), *Bringing the State Back in*, Cambridge: Cambridge University Press.

—— (1989) *Asia's Next Giant: South Korea and Late Industrialization*, New York: Oxford University Press.

—— (1992) "A theory of government intervention in late industrialization." In Louis Putterman and Dietrich Rueschemeyer (eds), *State and Market in Development: Synergy or Rivalry?*, Boulder, CO: Lynne Rienner.

Anderson, A.E. (1985) *Creativity and Regional Development*, Laxenburg: International Institute for Applied Systems Analysis, Working Paper 85/14.

Andrieu, Michel, Michalski, Wolfgang and Stevens, Barrie (eds) (1992) *Long-term Prospects for the World Economy*, Paris: OECD.

Anisimov, Evgenii (1993) *The Reforms of Peter the Great: Progress Through Coercion in Russia*, Armonk, NY: M.E. Sharpe.

Aoki, Masahiko (1988) *Information, incentives, and bargaining in the Japanese economy*, Cambridge: Cambridge University Press.

Aoyama, Yuko (1995 in progress) "Locational strategies of Japanese multi-national corporations in electronics," University of California, PhD dissertation in city and regional planning.

Appelbaum, Eileen (1984) *Technology and the Redesign of Work in the Insurance Industry*, Research Report, Stanford, CA: Stanford University Institute of Research on Educational Finance and Governance.

—— and Schettkat, Ronald (eds) (1990) *Labor Markets, Adjustments to Structural Change and Technological Progress*, New York: Praeger.

Appelbaum, Richard P. and Henderson, Jeffrey (eds) (1992) *States and Development in the Asian Pacific Rim*, London: Sage.

Arancibia, Sergio (1988) *Dependencia y deuda externa*, Lima: Taller Popular.

Aries, Philippe (1977) *L'homme devant la mort*, Paris: Seuil.

—— (1983) *Images de l'homme devant la mort*, Paris: Seuil.

Armstrong, David (1994) "Computer sex: log on; talk dirty; get off." *San Francisco Examiner*, April 10.

Aron, Raymond (1963) *Dix-huit leçons sur la société industrielle*, Paris: Idées-Gallimard.

Aronowitz, Stanley and Di Fazio, Williams (1994) *The Jobless Future*, Minneapolis: University of Minnesota.

Arrieta, Carlos G. et al. (1991) *Narcotrafico en Colombia. Dimensiones politicas, economicas, juridicas e internacionales*, Bogota: Tercer Mundo Editores.

Arthur, Brian (1985) *Industry Location and the Economics of Agglomeration: Why a Silicon Valley?*, Stanford, CA: Stanford University Center for Economic Policy Research, Working Paper.

—— (1986) *Industry Location Patterns and the Importance of History*, Stanford, CA: Stanford University Food Research Institute, Research Paper.

—— (1989) "Competing technologies, increasing returns, and lock-in by historical events." *Economic Journal*, 99 (March): 116–31.

Ashton, Thomas S. (1948) *The Industrial Revolution, 1760–1830*, Oxford: Oxford University Press.

Asian Money, Asian Issuers & Capital Markets Supplement (1993/1994) "Derivatives: making more room to manoeuvre," Dec.–Jan.: 30–2.

Aslund, Anders (1995) *How Russia Became a Market Economy,* Washington D.C.: Brookings Institution.

Aydalot, Philippe (1985) "L'aptitude des milieux locaux a promouvoir innovation technologique," communication au symposium *Nouvelles technologies et regions en crise,* Association de science régionale de langue française, Brussels, April 22–23.

Aznar, Guy (1993) *Travailler moins pour travailler tous,* Paris: Syros.

Baghwati, J. and Srinivasan, T.M. (1993) *Indian Economic Reforms,* New Delhi: Ministry of Finance.

Bailey, Paul, Parisotto, Aurelio and Renshaw, Geoffrey (eds) (1993) *Multinationals and Employment: The Global Economy of the 1990s,* Geneva: International Labour Organization.

Baker, Hugh (1979) *Chinese Family and Kinship,* New York: Columbia University Press.

Balaji, R. (1994) "The formation and structure of the high technology industrial complex in Bangalore, India," Berkeley, CA: University of California, PhD dissertation in City and Regional Planning (in progress).

Baldwin-Evans, Martin and Schain, Martin (eds) (1995) *The Politics of Immigration in Western Europe,* London: Frank Cass.

Ball-Rokeach, Sandra J. and Cantor, Muriel (eds) (1986) *Media, Audience and Social Structure,* Beverly Hills, CA: Sage.

Banegas, Jesus (ed.) (1993) *La industria de la información. Situación actual y perspectivas,* Madrid: Fundesco.

Bar, François (1990) *Configuring the Telecommunications Infrastructure for the Computer Age: The Economics of Network Control,* Berkeley, CA: University of California, PhD dissertation.

—— (1992) "Network flexibility: a new challenge for telecom policy." *Communications and Strategies,* special issue, June: 111–22.

—— and Borrus, M. (1993) *The Future of Networking,* Berkeley, CA: University of California, BRIE Working Paper.

—— and —— with Coriat, Benjamin (1991) *Information Networks and Competitive Advantage: Issues for Government Policy and Corporate Strategy Development,* Brussels: Commission of European Communities, DGIII-BRIE-OECD Research Program.

Baran, Barbara (1985) "Office automation and women's work: the technological transformation of the insurance industry." In Manuel Castells (ed.), *High Technology, Space, and Society,* Beverly Hills, CA: Sage, pp. 143–71.

—— (1989) *Technological Innovation and Deregulation: The Transformation of the Labor Process in the Insurance Industry,* Berkeley, CA: University of California, PhD dissertation in City and Regional Planning.

Baranano, Ana M. (1994) "La empresa española en los programas europeos de cooperación tecnológica," Madrid: Universidad Autonoma de Madrid, unpublished doctoral thesis in Business Economics.

Barglow, Raymond (1994) *The Crisis of the Self in the Age of Information: Computers, Dolphins, and Dreams*, London: Routledge.

Barthes, Roland (1978) *Leçon inaugurale de la chaire de sémiologie littéraire du Collège de France, prononcée le 7 Janvier 1977*, Paris: Seuil.

Bassalla, George (1988) *The Evolution of Technology*, Cambridge: Cambridge University Press.

Batty, Michael and Barr, Bob (1994) "The electronic frontier: exploring and mapping cyberspace," *Futures*, 26(7): 699–712.

Baudrillard, Jean (1972) *Pour une critique de l'économie politique du signe*, Paris: Gallimard.

—— (1991) *La Guerre du Golfe n'a pas eu lieu*, Paris: Fayard.

Baumgartner, Peter and Payr, Sabine (eds) (1995) *Speaking Minds: Interviews with Twenty Eminent Cognitive Scientists*, Princeton, NJ: Princeton University Press.

Baumol, W.J., Blackman S.A.B. and Wolf, E.N. (1989) *Productivity and American Leadership: The Long View*, Cambridge, MA: MIT Press.

Bayart, Jean-François (1992) *The State in Africa: The Politics of the Belly*, London: Longman.

Beasley, W.G. (1990) *The Rise of Modern Japan*, London: Weidenfeld & Nicolson.

Bedi, Hari (1991) *Understanding the Asian Manager*, Sydney: Allen & Unwin.

Bedoui, Mongi (1995) *Bibliographie sur l'exclusion dans les pays arabes du Mahgreb et du Machreq*, Geneva: International Institute of Labour Studies, Discussion paper 80/1995.

Bell, Daniel (1976) *The Coming of Post-industrial Society: A Venture in Social Forecasting*, New York: Basic Books. (First published 1973.)

Belussi, Fiorenza (1992) "La flessibilita si fa gerarchia: la Benetton." In F. Belussi (ed.), *Nuovi Modelli d'Impresa, Gerarchie Organizzative e Imprese Rete*, Milan: Franco Angeli.

Bendixon, Terence (1991) "El transporte urbano." In Jordi Borja et al., pp 427–53. *Las grandes ciudades en la decada de los noventa*, Madrid: Editorial Sistema.

Beniger, James R. (1986) *The Control Revolution: Technological and Economic Origins of the Information Society*, Cambridge, MA: Harvard University Press.

Bennett, A. (1990) *The Death of Organization Man*, New York: William Morrow.

Benson, Rod (1994) "Telecommunications and society: a review on the research literature on computer-mediated communication," Berkeley, CA: University of California, Berkeley Roundtable on the International Economy, Compuscript.

Benveniste, Guy (1994) *Twenty-first Century Organization: Analyzing Current Trends, Imagining the Future*, San Francisco, CA: Jossey Bass.

Berger, J. (1984) *And Our Faces, My Heart, Brief as Photos*, London: Writers & Readers.

Berger, Peter (1987) *The Capitalist Revolution*, London: Wildwood.

Berger, Peter and Hsiao, M. (eds) (1988) *In Search of an East Asian Development Model*, New Brunswick, NJ: Transaction Books.

Bergsten, C. Fred and Noland, Marcus (eds) (1993) *Pacific Dynamism and the*

International Economic System, Washington D.C.: Institute for International Economics.

Bernstein, Michael A. and Adler, David E. (1994) *Understanding American Economic Decline*, New York: Cambridge University Press.

Bertazzoni, F. et al. (1984) *Odissea Informatica. Alle soglie della nuova era: intinerario nelle societa informatiche*, Milan: Istituto A. Gemelli per I Problemi della Comunicazione, Gruppo Editoriale Jackson.

Bertrand, O. and Noyelle, T.J. (1988) *Corporate and Human Resources: Technological Change in Banks and Insurance Companies in Five OECD Countries*, Paris, OECD.

Bessant, John (1989) *Microelectronics and Change at Work*, Geneva: International Labour Organization.

Bettinger, Cass (1991) *High Performance in the 1990s: Leading the Strategic and Cultural Revolution in Banking*, Homewood, IL: Business One Irwin.

Bianchi, Patrizio, Carnoy, Martin and Castells, Manuel (1988) *Economic Modernization and Technology Policy in the People's Republic of China*, Stanford, CA: Stanford University Center for Education Research, Research Monograph.

Bielenski, Harald (ed.) (1994) *New Forms of Work and Activity: Survey of Experience at Establishment Level in Eight European Countries*, Dublin: European Foundation for the Improvement of Living and Working Conditions.

Biggart, Nicole Woolsey (1990a) *Charismatic Capitalism*, Chicago, IL: University of Chicago Press.

—— (1990b) "Institutionalized patrimonialism in Korean business." *Comparative Social Research*, 12: 113–33.

—— (1991) "Explaining Asian economic organization: toward a Weberian institutional perspective." *Theory and Society*, 20: 199–232.

—— (1992) "Institutional logic and economic explanation." In Jane Marceau (ed.), *Reworking the World: Organizations, Technologies, and Cultures in Comparative Perspective*, Berlin: Walter de Gruyter, pp. 29–54.

—— and Hamilton, G.G. (1992) "On the limits of a firm-based theory to explain business networks: the western bias of neoclassical economics." In Nitin Nohria and Robert G. Ecckles (eds), *Networks and Organizations: Structure, Form, and Action*, Boston, MA: Harvard Business School Press.

Bijker, Wiebe E., Hughes, Thomas P. and Pinch, Trevor (eds) (1987) *The Social Construction of Technological Systems: New Directions in the Sociology and History of Technology*, Cambridge, MA: MIT Press.

Birch, David L. (1987) *Job Generation in America*, New York: Free Press.

Bird, Jane (1994) "Dial M for multimedia." *Management Today*, July: 50–3.

Bishop, Jerry E. and Waldholz, Michael (1990) *Genome*, New York: Simon & Schuster.

Blakely, Edward, Scotchmer, S. and Levine, J. (1988) *The Locational and Economic Patterns of California's Biotech Industry*, Berkeley, CA: University of California Institute of Urban and Regional Development, Biotech Industry Research Group Report.

Blazejczak, Jurgen, Eber, Georg and Horn, Gustav A. (1990) "Sectoral and

macroeconomic impacts of research and development on employment."
In Egon Matzner and Michael Wagner (eds), *The Employment Impact of New Technology: The Case of West Germany*, Aldershot, Hants: Avebury, pp. 221–33.

Bluestone, Barry and Harrison, Bennett (1988) *The Great American Job Machine: The Proliferation of Low-wage Employment in the U.S. Economy*, New York: Basic Books.

Blumler, Jay G. and Katz, Elihu (eds) (1974) *The Uses of Mass Communications*, Newport Beach, CA: Sage.

Bofill, Ricardo (1990) *Espacio y Vida*, Barcelona: Tusquets Editores.

Booker, Ellis (1994) "Interactive TV comes to public broadcasting." *Computerworld*, 28(3): 59.

Borja, Jordi and Castells, Manuel (1996) *The Local and the Global: Cities in the Information Age*, report commissioned by the United Nations Habitat Center for Habitat II – United Nations Conference *The City Summit*, Istanbul, 1996; to be published by Earthscan, London.

Borja, Jordi et al. (eds) (1991) *Las grandes ciudades en la decada de los noventa*, Madrid: Editorial Sistema.

Borjas, George F., Freeman, Richard B. and Katz, Lawrence F. (1991) *On the Labour Market Effects of Immigration and Trade*, Cambridge, MA: National Bureau of Economic Research.

Bornstein, Lisa (1993) "Flexible production in the unstable state: the Brazilian information technology industry." Unpublished PhD dissertation, University of California, Berkeley, Department of City and Regional Planning.

Borrus, Michael G. (1988) *Competing for Control: America's Stake in Microelectronics*, Cambridge, MA: Ballinger.

—— and Zysman, John (1992) "Industrial competitiveness and American national security." In W. Sandholtz et al., *The Highest Stakes: The Economic Foundations of the Next Security System*, New York: Oxford University Press.

Bosch, Gerhard (1995) *Flexibility and Work Organization: Report of Expert Working Group*, Brussels: European Commission, Directorate General for Employment, Industrial Relations, and Social Affairs.

——, Dawkins, Peter and Michon, François (eds) (1994) *Times Are Changing: Working Time in 14 Industrialised Countries*, Geneva: International Labour Organization.

Botein, Michael and Rice, David M. (eds) (1980) *Network Television and the Public Interest*, Lexington, MA: Lexington Books.

Boureau, Allain et al. (1989) *The Culture of Print: Power and the Uses of Print in Early Modern Europe*, ed. Roder Chartier, Princeton, NJ: Princeton University Press.

Bouvier, Leon F. and Grant, Lindsay (1994) *How Many Americans? Population, Immigration, and the Environment*, San Francisco, CA: Sierra Club Books.

Bower, J.L. (1987) *When Markets Quake*, Boston, MA: Harvard Business School Press.

Boyer, Christine (1994) *The City of Collective Memory*, Cambridge, MA: MIT Press.

Boyer, Robert (1988a) "Is a new socio-technical system emerging?" Paper prepared for a conference on *Structural Change and Labour Market Policy*, Var, Gard, 6–9 June.

—— (1988b) "Technical change and the theory of regulation." In G. Dosi, et al., *Technical Change and Economic Theory*, London: Pinter, pp. 67–94.

—— (1990) "Assessing the impact of R&D on employment: puzzle or consensus?" In E. Matzner and M. Wagner (eds), *The Employment Impact of New Technology: The Case of West Germany*, Aldershot, Hants: Avebury, pp. 234–54.

—— (ed.) (1986) *Capitalismes fin de siècle*, Paris: Presses Universitaires de France.

Boyer, R. and Mistral, J. (1988) "Le bout du tunnel? Stratégies conservatrices et nouveau régime d'accumulation," paper delivered at the International Conference on the Theory of Regulation, Barcelona, June 16–18.

—— and Ralle, P. (1986a) "Croissances nationales et contrainte extérieure avant et après 1973." *Economie et société*, no. P29.

—— and —— (1986b) "L'Insertion internationale conditionne-t-elle les formes nationales d'emploi? Convergences ou différentiations des pays européens." *Economie et société*, no. P29

Boyett, Joseph H. and Conn, Henry P. (1991) *Workplace 2000: The Revolution Reshaping American Business*, New York: Dutton.

Braddock, D.J. (1992) "Scientific and technical employment, 1900–2005." *Monthly Labor Review*, February: 28–41.

Bradford, Colin I. (ed.) (1992) *Strategic Options for Latin America in the 1990s*, Paris: OECD Development Center.

—— (1994) *The New Paradigm of Systemic Competitiveness: Toward More Integrated Policies in Latin America*, Paris: OECD Development Center.

Braudel, Fernand (1967) *Civilisation matérielle et capitalisme. XVe–XVIIe siècle*, Paris: Armand Colin.

Braun, Ernest and Macdonald, Stuart (1982) *Revolution in Miniature: The History and Impact of Semiconductor Electronics Re-explored*, 2nd edn, Cambridge: Cambridge University Press.

Braverman, Harry (1973) *Labor and Monopoly Capital*, New York: Monthly Review Press.

Breeden, Richard C. (1993) "The globalization of law and business in the 1990s." *Wake Forest Law Review*, 28(3): 509–17.

BRIE (1992) *Globalization and Production*, Berkeley, CA: University of California, BRIE Working Paper 45.

Broad, William J. (1985) *Star Warriors*, New York: Simon & Schuster.

Brooks, Harvey (1971) "Technology and the ecological crisis," lecture given at Amherst, May 9.

Brown, Richard P.C. (1992) *Public Debt and Private Wealth: Debt, Capital Flight and the IMF in Sudan*, London: Macmillan.

Brusco, S. (1982) "The Emilian model: productive decentralization and social integration." *Cambridge Journal of Economics* 6(2): 167–84.

Buitelaar, Wout (ed.) (1988) *Technology and Work: Labour Studies in England, Germany and the Netherlands*, Aldershot, Hants: Avebury.

Bunker, Ted (1994) "The multimedia infotainment I-way: telephone, cable, and media companies are pursuing video-on-demand, interactive education, multimedia politicking, and more." *LAN Magazine*, 9(10): S24.

Bureau of Labor Statistics (1994) *Occupational Projections and Training Data*, Statistical and Research Supplement to the 1994–5 *Occupational Outlook Handbook*, Bulletin 2451, May.

Burlen, Katherine (1972) "La réalisation spatiale du désir et l'image spatialisée du besoin." *Espaces et sociétés*, n.5: 145–59.

Bushnell, P. Timothy (1994) *The Transformation of the American Manufacturing Paradigm*, New York: Garland.

Business Week (1993) "The horizontal corporation." October 28.

—— (1993b) "Asia's wealth: special report." November 29.

—— (1994a) "The information technology revolution: how digital technology is changing the way we work and live." Special Issue.

—— (1994b) "The new face of business." In Special issue on "The Information Revolution," pp. 99ff.

—— (1994c) "China: birth of a new economy." January 31: 42–8.

—— (1994d) "Sega: it's blasting beyond games and racing to build a high-tech entertainment empire." February 21: cover story.

—— (1994e) "Interactive TV: not ready for prime time." March 14: 30.

—— (1994f) "The entertainment economy." March 14: 58–73.

—— (1994g) "How the Internet will change the way you do business." November 14.

—— (1994h) "Home computers: sales explode as new uses turn PCs into all-purpose information appliances." November 28: 89ff.

—— (1995a) "The networked corporation." Special issue.

—— (1995b) "Mexico: can it cope?" January 16.

—— (1995c) "Software industry." February 27: 78–86.

—— (1995d) "Benetton's new age." April 14.

—— (1995e) "The gene kings." May 8: 72ff.

—— (1995f) "The networked corporation." June 26: 85ff.

—— (1996) "Sun's rise." January 22.

Byrne, John H. (1994) "The pain of downsizing." *Business Week*, May 9.

Calderon, Fernando and Dos Santos, Mario (directors) (1989) *Hacia un nuevo orden estatal? Democratizacion, modernizacion y actores socio-politicos*, 4 vols, Buenos Aires: CLACSO.

—— and —— Mario R. (1995) *Sociedades sin atajos. Cultura politica y restructuracion económica en America Latina*, Buenos Aires: Paidos.

—— and Laserna, Roberto (1994) *Paradojas de la modernidad. Sociedad y cambios en Bolivia*, La Paz: Fundacion Milenio.

Calhoun, Craig (ed.) (1994) *Social Theory and the Politics of Identity*, Oxford: Blackwell.

Camagni, Roberto (1991) "Local milieu, uncertainty and innovation networks: towards a new dynamic theory of economic space." In Roberto Camagni (ed.), *Innovation Networks: Spatial Perspectives*, London: Belhaven Press, pp. 121–44.

Campbell, Duncan (1994) "Foreign investment, labor immobility and the quality of employment." *International Labour Review*, 2: 185–203.

Campo Vidal, Manuel (1996) "La transición audiovisual." Madrid: Antena-3 TV (unpublished).

Campos Alvarez, Tostado (1993) *El Fondo Monetario y la dueda externa mexicana*, Mexico: Plaza y Valdes Editores.

Canby, E.T. (1962) *A History of Electricity*, Englewood Cliffs, NJ: Prentice-Hall.

Cappelin, Riccardo (1991) "International networks of cities." In Roberto Camagni (ed.), *Innovation Networks: Spatial Perspectives*, London: Belhaven Press.

Cappelli, Peter and Rogovsky, Nicolai (1994) "New work systems and skill requirements." *International Labour Review*, 133(2): 205–20.

Cardoso, Fernando H. (1993) "New North/South relations in the present context: a new dependency?" In Martin Carnoy et al., *The New Global Economy in the Information Age*, University Park, PA: Penn State University Press, pp. 149–59.

—— and Faletto, Enzo (1969) *Desarrollo y dependencia en America Latina*, Mexico D.F.: Siglo XXI Editores; English trans. in expanded edition, Berkeley, CA: University of California Press, 1979.

Carey, M. and Franklin, J.C. (1991) "Outlook: 1990–2005 industry output and job growth continues slow into next century." *Monthly Labor Review*, Nov.: 45–60.

Carnoy, Martin (1989) *The New Information Technology: International Diffusion and Its Impact on Employment and Skills. A Review of the Literature*, Washington D.C.: World Bank, PHREE.

—— (1994) *Faded Dreams: The Politics and Economics of Race in America*, New York: Cambridge University Press.

—— and Castells, Manuel (1996) "Sustainable flexibility: work, family, and society in the information age," Berkeley: University of California, Center for Western European Studies.

—— and Fluitman, Fred (1994) "Training and the reduction of unemployment in industrialized countries," Geneva: International Labour Organization, unpublished report.

—— and Levin, Henry (1985) *Schooling and Work in the Democratic State*, Stanford, CA: Stanford University Press.

——, Pollack, Seth and Wong, Pia L. (1993a) *Labor Institutions and Technological Change: A Framework for Analysis and Review of the Literature*, Stanford, CA: Stanford University International Development Education Center, report prepared for the International Labour Organization, Geneva.

—— et al. (1993b) *The New Global Economy in the Information Age*, University Park, PA: Penn State University Press.

Carre, Jean-Jacques, Dubois, Paul and Malinvaud, Edmond (1984) *Abrégé de la croissance française: un essai d'analyse économique causale de l'après guerre*, Paris: Editions du Seuil.

Carver, M. (1980) *War since 1945*, London: Weidenfeld & Nicolson.

Case, Donald O. (1994) "The social shaping of videotex: how information services for the public have evolved." *Journal of the American Society for Information Science*, 45(7): 483–9.

Castano, Cecilia (1991) *La Informatizacion de la banca en Espana*, Madrid: Ministerio de Economia/Universidad Autónoma de Madrid.

—— (1994a) *Nuevas Tecnologias, Trabajo y Empleo en Espana*, Madrid: Alianza Editorial.

—— (1994b) *Tecnologia, empleo y trabajo en Espana*, Madrid: Alianza Editorial.

Castells, Manuel (1972) *La Question urbaine*, Paris: François Maspero.

—— (1976) "The service economy and the postindustrial society: a sociological critique." *International Journal of Health Services*, 6(4): 595–607.

—— (1980) *The Economic Crisis and American Society*, Princeton, NJ: Princeton University Press, and Oxford: Blackwell.

—— (1988a) "The new industrial space: information technology manufacturing and spatial structure in the United States." In G. Sternlieb and J. Hughes (eds), *America's New Market Geography: Nation, Region and Metropolis*, New Brunswick, NJ: Rutgers University.

—— (director) (1988b) *The State and Technology Policy: A Comparative Analysis of U.S. Strategic Defense Initiative, Informatics Policy in Brazil, and Electronics Policy in China*, Berkeley, CA: University of California, Berkeley Roundtable on the International Economy (BRIE), Research Monograph.

—— (1989a), "High technology and the new international division of labor." *Labour Studies*, October.

—— (1989b) *The Informational City: Information Technology, Economic Restructuring, and the Urban–Regional Process*, Oxford: Blackwell.

—— (1989c), "Notes of field work in the industrial areas of Taiwan," unpublished.

—— (1990) "Die zweigeteilte Stadt. Arm und Reich in den Stadten Lateinamerikas, der USA and Europas." In Tilo Schabert (ed.), *Die Weldt der Stadt*, Munich: Piper, pp. 199–216.

—— (1991) "Estrategias de desarrollo metropolitano en las grandes ciudades españolas: la articulación entre crecimiento economico y calidad de vida." In Jordi Borja et al. (eds), *Las grandes ciudades en la decada de los noventa*, Madrid: Editorial Sistema, pp. 17–64.

—— (1992), "Four Asian tigers with a dragon head: a comparative analysis of the state, economy, and society in the Asian Pacific Rim." In Richard Appelbaum and Jeffrey Henderson (eds), *States and Development in the Asian Pacific Rim*, Newbury Park, CA: Sage, pp. 33–70.

—— (1994) "Paths towards the informational society: employment structure in G-7 countries, 1920–1990." *International Labour Review*, 133(1): 5–33 (with Yuko Aoyama).

—— (1996) "The net and the self: working notes for a critical theory of informational society." *Critique of Anthropology*, 16(1): 9–38.

—— (ed.) (1985) *High Technology, Space and Society*, Beverly Hills, CA: Sage.

—— and Guillemard, Anne Marie (1971) "Analyse sociologique des pratiques sociales en situation de retraite." *Sociologie du travail*, 3: 282–307.

—— and Hall, Peter (1994) *Technopoles of the World: The Makings of 21st Century Industrial Complexes*, London: Routledge.

—— and Laserna, Roberto (1989) "The new dependency: technology and social change in Latin America." *Sociological Forum,* Fall.

—— and Natalushko, Svetlana (1993) "La modernizacion tecnologica de las empresas de electrónica y telecomunicaciónes en Rusia: un estudio de Szelenograd," Madrid: Universidad Autónoma de Madrid, Programa de Estudios Rusos, unpublished research monograph.

—— and Skinner, Rebecca (1988) "State and technological policy in the U.S.: the SDI program." In Manuel Castells (director) *The State and Technological Policy: A Comparative Analysis,* Berkeley, CA: University of California, BRIE Research Monograph.

—— and Tyson, Laura d'Andrea (1988) "High technology choices ahead: restructuring interdependence." In John W. Sewell and Stuart Tucker (eds), *Growth, Exports, and Jobs in a Changing World Economy,* New Brunswick, NJ: Transaction Books.

—— and —— (1989) "High technology and the changing international division of production: Implications for the U.S. economy." In Randall B. Purcell (ed.), *The Newly Industrializing Countries in the World Economy: Challenges for U.S. Policy,* Boulder, CO: Lynne Rienner, pp. 13–50.

—— et al. (1986) *Nuevas tecnologias, economia y sociedad en España,* 2 vols, Madrid: Alianza Editorial.

——, Goh, Lee and Kwok, R.W.Y. (1990) *The* Shek Kip Mei *Syndrome: Economic Development and Public Housing in Hong Kong and Singapore,* London: Pion.

—— (director), Gamella, Manuel, De la Puerta, Enrique, Ayala, Luis and Matias, Carmen (1991) *La industria de las tecnologias de informacion (1985–90). España en el contexto mundial,* Madrid: Fundesco.

——, Granberg, Alexander and Kiselyova, Emma (1996a – in progress) *The Development of Siberia and the Russian Far East and its Implications for the Pacific Economy,* Berkeley, CA: University of California Pacific Rim Research Program and Institute of Urban and Regional Development, Research Monograph.

——, Yazawa, Shujiro and Kiselyova, Emma (1996b), "Insurgents against the global order: a comparative analysis of Chiapas Zapatistas, American militia movement, and Aum Shinrikyo." *Berkeley Journal of Sociology,* forthcoming.

Castillo, Gregory (1994) "Henry Ford, Lenin, and the scientific organization of work in capitalist and soviet industrialization," Berkeley, CA: University of California Department of City and Regional Planning, Seminar paper for CP 275, unpublished.

Cats-Baril, William L. and Jelassi, Tawfik (1994) "The French videotex system Minitel: a successful implementation of a national information technology infrastructure." *MIS Quarterly,* 18(1): 1–20.

Caves, Roger W. (1994) *Exploring Urban America,* Thousand Oaks, CA: Sage.

Cecchini, Paolo (1988) *The European Challenge, 1992: The Benefits of a Single Market,* Aldershot, Hants: Gower.

Centre d'Etudes Prospectives et d'Informations Internationales (CEPII) (1992) *L'Economie mondiale 1990–2000: l'impératif de la croissance,* Paris: Economica.

—— and OFCE (1990) Mimosa: une modelisation de l'économie mondiale, *Observations et diagnostics économiques*, 30 January.

CEPAL (Comision Economica para America Latina, Naciones Unidas) (1986) *El desarrollo fruticola y forestal en Chile y sus derivaciones sociales*, Santiago, Chile: Informe CEPAL.

—— (1990a) *La apertura financiera de Chile y el comportamiento de los bancos transnacionales*, Santiago, Chile: Informe CEPAL.

—— (1990b) *Transformacion productiva con equidad*, Santiago de Chile: Naciones Unidas, CEPAL.

—— (1994) *El crecimiento economico y su difusion social: el caso de Chile de 1987 a 1992*, Santiago de Chile: CEPAL, Division de Estadisticas y Proyecciones.

Cervero, Robert (1989) *America's Suburban Centers: The Land Use–Transportation Link*, Boston, MA: Unwin Hyman.

—— (1991) "Changing live-work spatial relationships: implications for metropolitan structure and mobility." In John Brotchie et al. (eds), *Cities in the 21st Century: New Technologies and Spatial Systems*, Melbourne: Longman & Cheshire, pp. 330–47.

Chandler, Alfred D. (1977) *The Visible Hand: The Managerial Revolution in American Business*, Cambridge, MA: Harvard University Press.

—— (1986) "The evolution of modern global competition." In M.E. Porter (ed.), *Competition in Global Industries*, Boston, MA: Harvard Business School Press, pp. 405–48.

Chen, Edward K.Y. (1979) *Hypergrowth in Asian Economies: A Comparative Analysis of Hong Kong, Japan, Korea, Singapore and Taiwan*, London: Macmillan.

Chesnais, François (1994) *La Mondialisation du capital*, Paris: Syros.

Chida, Tomohei and Davies, Peter N. (1990) *The Japanese Shipping and Shipbuilding Industries: A History of Their Modern Growth*, London: Athlone Press.

Child, John (1986) "Technology and work: An outline of theory and research in the western social sciences." In Peter Grootings (ed.), *Technology and Work: East–West Comparison*, London: Croom Helm, pp. 7–66.

Chin, Pei-Hsiung (1988) *Housing Policy and Economic Development in Taiwan*, Berkeley, CA: University of California, IURD.

Chion, Miriam (1995) "Recent process of globalization in Peru," Berkeley, CA: University of California Department of City and Regional Planning, unpublished research paper for CP229.

Chizuko, Ueno (1987) "The position of Japanese women reconsidered." *Current Anthropology*, 28(4): 75–84.

—— (1988) "The Japanese women's movement: the counter-values to industrialism." In Grakan McCormack and Yoshio Sugimoto (eds), *Modernization and Beyond: The Japanese Trajectory*, Cambridge: Cambridge University Press, pp. 167–85.

Choucri, Nazli (1986) "The hidden economy: a new view of remittances in the Arab World." *World Development Report*, 14: 702–9.

Chung, K.H., Lee H.C. and Okumura, A. (1988) "The managerial practices of Korean, American, and Japanese firms." *Journal of East and West Studies*, 17: 45–74.

Clark, R. (1979) *The Japanese Company*, New Haven, CT: Yale University Press.

Clegg, Stewart (1990) *Modern Organizations: Organization Studies in the Postmodern World*, London: Sage.

—— (1992) "French bread, Italian fashions, and Asian enterprises: modern passions and postmodern prognoses." In Jane Marceau (ed.), *Reworking the World*, Berlin: Walter de Gruyter, pp. 55–94.

—— and Redding, S. Gordon (eds) (1990) *Capitalism in Contrasting Cultures*, Berlin: Walter de Gruyter.

Clow Archibald and Clow, Nan L. (1952) *The Chemical Revolution*, London: Batchworth Press.

Coclough, Christopher and Manor, James (eds) (1991) *States or Markets? Neoliberalism and the Development Policy Debate*, Oxford: Clarendon Press.

Cohen Stephen (1990) "Corporate nationality can matter a lot," testimony before the US Congress Joint Economic Committee, September.

—— (1993) "Geo-economics: lessons from America's mistakes." In Martin Carnoy et al., *The New Global Economy in the Information Age*, University Park, PA: Penn State University Press, pp. 97–147.

—— (1994) "Competitiveness: a reply to Krugman." *Foreign Affairs*, 73: 3.

—— and Borrus, Michael (1995a) *Networks of American and Japanese Electronics Companies in Asia*, Berkeley, CA: University of California, BRIE Research Paper.

—— and —— (1995b) *Networks of Companies in Asia*, Berkeley, CA: University of California, BRIE Research Paper.

—— and Guerrieri, Paolo (1995) "The variable geometry of Asian trade." In Eileen M. Doherty (ed.), *Japanese Investment in Asia*, proceedings of a conference organized with Berkeley Roundtable on the International Economy, San Francisco: Asia Foundation, pp. 189–208.

—— and Zysman, John (1987) *Manufacturing Matters: The Myth of Postindustrial Economy*, New York: Basic Books.

—— et al., (1985) *Global Competition: The New Reality*, vol. III of John Young (chair), *Competitiveness. The Report of the President's Commission on Industrial Competitiveness*, Washington D.C.: Government Printing Office, p. 1.

Cohendet, P. and Llerena, P. (1989) *Flexibilité, information et décision*, Paris: Economica.

Colas, Dominique (1992) *La Glaive et le fléau. Généalogie du fanatisme et de la société civile*. Paris: Grasset.

Collado, Cecilia (1995) "Unsustainable development: environmental policy and regional development in Chile," Berkeley, University of California: Department of City and Regional Planning, PhD dissertation, in progress.

Collective Author (1994) *The State of Working Women: 1994 Edition*, Tokyo: 21 Seiki Zoidan (in Japanese).

Coloquio de Invierno (1992) *Los grandes cambios de nuestro tiempo: la situación internacional, America Latina y Mexico*, 3 vols, Mexico DF: Universidad Nacional Autónoma de Mexico/Fondo de Cultura Economica.

Comision Economica para America Latina, Naciones Unidas, *see* CEPAL.

Commersant Weekly (1995) "Survey on commercial crime in Russia." June 13.

Commission of the European Union (1994) *Growth, Competitiveness, Employment: The Challenges and Ways Forward into the 21st Century, White Paper,* Luxembourg: Office of the European Communities.

Conference on Time and Money in the Russian Culture (1995), organized by the University of California at Berkeley's Center for Slavic and Eastern European Studies, and the Stanford University's Center for Russian and Eastern European Studies, held at Berkeley on March 17 1995, unpublished presentations and discussions (personal notes and summary of the proceedings by Emma G. Kiselyova).

Cooke, Philip (1994) "The cooperative advantage of regions," paper prepared for Harold Innis Centenary Celebration Conference *Regions, Institutions and Technology,* University of Toronto, September 23–25.

—— and Morgan, K. (1993) "The network paradigm: new departures in corporate and regional development." *Society and Space,* 11: 543–64.

Cooper, Charles (ed.) (1994) *Technology and Innovation in the International Economy,* Aldershot, Hants.: Edward Elgar and United Nations University Press.

Cooper, James C. (1995) "The new golden age of productivity." *Business Week,* September 26: 62.

Coriat, Benjamin (1990) *L'Atelier et le robot,* Paris: Christian Bourgois Editeur.

—— (1994) "Neither pre- nor post-fordism: an original and new way of managing the labour process." In K. Tetsuro and R. Steven (eds), *Is Japanese Management Post-Fordism?,* Tokyo: Mado-sha, p. 182.

Council of Economic Advisers (1995) *Economic Report to the President of the United States. Transmitted to the Congress, February 1995,* Washington D.C.: Government Printing Office, pp. 95–127.

Coutrot, T. and Husson, M. (1993) *Les Destins du tiers monde,* Paris: Nathan.

Crick, Francis (1994) *The Astonishing Hypothesis: The Scientific Search for the Soul,* New York: Charles Scribner's Sons.

Cuneo, Alice (1994) "Getting wired in the Gulch: creative and coding merge in San Francisco's multimedia community." *Advertising Age,* 65(50).

Cusumano, M. (1985) *The Japanese Automobile Industry: Technology and Management at Nissan and Toyota,* Cambridge, MA: Harvard University Press.

Cyert, Richard M. and Mowery, David C. (eds) (1987) *Technology and Employment: Innovation and Growth in the U.S. Economy,* Washington D.C.: National Academy Press.

Dahlman, C., Ross-Larsen, B. and Westphal, L.E. (1987) "Managing technological development: lessons from newly industrialising countries." *World Development,* 15(6).

Dalloz, Xavier and Portnoff, Andre-Yves (1994) "Les promesses de l'unimedia." *Futuribles,* n. 191: 11–36.

Daniel, W. (1987) *Workplace Survey of Industrial Relations,* London: Policy Studies Institute.

Daniels, P.W. (1993) *Service Industries in the World Economy,* Oxford: Blackwell.

Danton de Rouffignac, Peter (1991) *Europe's New Business Culture*, London: Pitman.

Darbon, Pierre and Robin, Jacques (eds) (1987) *Le Jaillissement des biotechnologies*, Paris: Fayard-Fondation Diderot.

David, Paul (1989) *Computer and Dynamo: The Modern Productivity Paradox in Historical Perspective*, Stanford, CA: Stanford University Center for Economic Policy Research, Working Paper No. 172.

David, P.A. (1975) *Technical Choice Innovation and Economic Growth: Essays on American and British Experience in the Nineteenth Century*, London: Cambridge University Press.

—— and Bunn, J.A. (1988) "The economics of gateways' technologies and network evolution: lessons from the electricity supply industry." *Information Economics and Policy*, 3 (April): 165–202.

Davidson, Basil (1992) *The Black Man's Burden: Africa and the Curse of the Nation-state*, London: James Currey.

Davis, Diane (1994) *Urban Leviathan: Mexico in the 20th Century*, Philadelphia, PA: Temple University Press.

Davis, Mike (1990) *City of Quartz*, London: Verso.

Dean, James W., Yoon, Se Joon and Susman, Gerald I. (1992) "Advanced manufacturing technology and organization structure: empowerment or subordination?" *Organization Science*, 3(2): 203–29.

De Anne, Julius (1990) *Global Companies and Public Policy: The Growing Challenge of Foreign Direct Investment*, New York: Council of Foreign Relations Press.

De Bandt, J (ed.) (1985) *Les Services dans les sociétés industrielles avancées*, Paris: Economica.

Deben, Leon et al. (eds) (1993) *Understanding Amsterdam: Essays on Economic Vitality, City Life, and Urban Form*, Amsterdam: Het Spinhuis.

De Conninck, Frederic (1995) *Société éclatée. Travail intégré*, Paris: Presses Universitaires de France.

Denison, Edward F. (1967) *Why Growth Rates differ: Postwar Experience in Nine Western Countries*, Washington D.C.: Brookings Institution.

—— (1974) *Accounting for United States Economic Growth, 1929–69*, Washington D.C.: Brookings Institution.

—— (1979) *Accounting for Slower Economic Growth: The United States in the 1970s*, Washington D.C.: Brookings Institution.

Denisova, L.I. (1995) "Fondovyi rynok i inostrannye investitsii [Stock exchange market and foreign investment]." *EKO*, no. 4: 65–73.

Dentsu Institute for Human Studies/DataFlow International (1994) *Media in Japan*, Tokyo: DataFlow International.

Derriennic, J.P. (1990) "Tentative de polémologie nécrométrique," Quebec: Université Laval, unpublished paper.

Deyo, Frederick (ed.) (1987) *The Political Economy of New Asian Industrialism*, Ithaca, NY: Cornell University Press.

Dicken, Peter (1992) *Global Shift: The Internationalization of Economic Activity*, New York: Guilford Press.

Dickens, William T., Tyson, Laura D'Andrea and Zysman, John, (eds) (1988) *The Dynamics of Trade and Employment*, Cambridge, MA: Ballinger Press.

Dickinson, H.W. (1958) "The steam engine to 1830." In C. Singer (ed.), *A History of Technology*, vol. 4: *The Industrial Revolution, 1750–1850*, Oxford: Oxford University Press, pp. 168–97.

Dizard, Wilson P. (1982) *The Coming Information Age*, New York: Longman.

Dodgson, M. (ed.) (1989) *Technology Strategy and the Firm: Management and Public Policy*, Harlow, Essex: Longman.

Doherty, Eileen M. (ed.) (1995) *Japanese Investment in Asia: International Production Strategies in a Rapidly Changing World*, proceedings of a conference organized with Berkeley Roundtable on the International Economy, San Francisco: Asia Foundation.

Dohse, K., Jurgens, V. and Malsch, T. (1985) "From Fordism to Toyotism? The social organization of the labour process in the Japanese automobile industry." *Politics and Society*, 14(2): 115–46.

Dondero, George (1995) "Information, communication, and vehicle technology," Berkeley, CA: University of California Department of City and Regional Planning, Spring, unpublished seminar paper for CP-298I.

Dordick, Herbert S. and Wang, Georgette (1993) *The Information Society: A Retrospective View*, Newbury Park, CA: Sage.

Dosi, Giovanni (1988) "The nature of the innovative process." In G. Dosi et al., *Technical Change and Economic Theory*, London: Pinter, 221–39.

—— and Soete, Luc (1983), "Technology, competitiveness, and international trade." *Econometrica*, 3.

—— Pavitt, K and Soete, L. (1988a) *The Economics of Technical Change and International Trade*, Brighton, Sussex: Wheatsheaf.

——, Freeman, Christopher, Nelson, Richard, Silverberg, Gerald and Soete Luc (eds) (1988b) *Technical Change and Economic Theory*, London: Pinter.

Dower, John W. (ed.) (1975) *Origins of the Modern Japanese State: Selected Writings of E.H. Norman*, New York: Pantheon Books.

Doyle, Marc (1992) *The Future of Television: A Global Overview of Programming, Advertising, Technology and Growth*, Lincolnwood, IL: NTC Business Books.

Drexler, K. Eric and Peterson, Chris (1991) *Unbounding the Future: The Nanotechnology Revolution*, New York: Quill/William Morrow.

Drucker, Peter F. (1988) "The coming of the new organization." *Harvard Business Review*, 88: 45–53.

Dubois, Pierre (1985) "Rupture de croissance et progrès technique." *Economie et statistique*, 181.

Dunford, M. and Kafkalas, G. (eds) (1992) *Cities and Regions in the New Europe: The Global–Local interplay and Spatial Development Strategies*, London: Belhaven Press.

Dunning, John (ed.) (1985) *Multinational Enterprises, Economic Structure, and International Competitiveness*, New York: John Wiley.

—— (1992) *Multinational Enterprises and the Global Economy*, Reading, MA: Addison-Wesley.

—— (1993) *Multinational Enterprises and the Global Economy*, Reading, MA: Addison Wesley.

Durlabhji, Subhash and Marks, Norton (eds) (1993) *Japanese Business: Cultural Perspectives*, Albany, NY: State University of New York Press.

Durufle, G. (1988) *L'Ajustement structurel en Afrique (Sénégal, Côte d'Ivoire, Madagascar*, Paris: Karthala.

Dy, Josefina (ed.) (1990) *Advanced Technology in Commerce, Offices, and Health Service*, Aldershot, Hants: Avebury.

Ebel, K. and Ulrich, E. (1987) *Social and Labour Effects of CAD/CAM*, Geneva: International Labour Organization.

Eco, Umberto (1977) "Dalla periferia dell'impero," cited in the English translation as Eco, Umberto, "Does the audience have bad effects on television?" In Umberto Eco, *Apocalypse Postponed*, Bloomington: Indiana University Press, 1994, pp. 87–102.

Economist, (1993) 7 July 27.

—— (1994a) "Feeling for the future: survey of television." February 12: special report.

—— (1994b) "Sale of the century." May 14: 67–9.

—— (1995a) "The bank that disappeared." February 27.

—— (1995b) "Currencies in a spin." March 11: 69–70.

—— (1995c) "A survey of Brazil: half-empty or half-full?" April 29.

—— (1995d) "A survey of Vietnam: the road to capitalism." July 8.

Economist Intelligence Unit (1995) "Country report: Russian Federation, 2nd quarter."

Edquist, Charles and Jacobsson, Stefan (1989) *Flexible Automation: The Global Diffusion of New Technologies in the Engineering Industry*, Oxford: Blackwell.

Egan, Ted (1995) "The development and location patterns of software industry in the U.S.," Berkeley, CA: University of California, PhD dissertation in City and Regional Planning (in progress).

Elkington, John (1985) *The Gene Factory: Inside the Business and Science of Biotechnology*, New York: Carroll & Graf.

Elmer-Dewwit, Philip (1993) "The amazing video game boom." *Time*, September 27: 67–72.

El Pais/World Media (1995) "Habla el futuro." March 9: supplement.

Enderwick, Peter (ed.) (1989) *Multinational Service Firms*, London: Routledge.

Epstein, Edward (1995) "Presidential contender's campaign online." *San Francisco Chronicle*, November 27.

Ernst, Dieter (1994a) *Carriers of Regionalization? The East Asian Production Networks of Japanese Electronics Firms*, Berkeley, CA: University of California, BRIE Working Paper 73.

—— (1994b) *Inter-Firms Networks and Market Structure: Driving Forces, Barriers and Patterns of Control*, Berkeley, CA: University of California, BRIE Research Paper.

—— (1994c) *Networks in Electronics*, Berkeley, CA: University of California, BRIE Research Monograph.

—— (1995) "International production networks in Asian electronics: how do they differ and what are their impacts?" Unpublished paper presented at the Berkeley Roundtable on the International Economy/Asia Foundation

Conference on Competing Production Networks in Asia, San Francisco, 27–28 April.

—— and O'Connor, David (1992) *Competing in the Electronics Industry: The Experience of Newly Industrializing Economies*, Paris: OECD, Development Centre Studies.

Esping-Andersen, G (ed.) (1993) *Changing Classes*, London: Sage.

Evans, Peter (1987) "Class, state and dependence in East Asia: lessons for Latin Americanists." In Frederic Deyo (ed.), *The Political Economy of East Asian Industrialism*, Ithaca, NY: Cornell University Press.

—— (1995) *Embedded Autonomy: States and Industrial Transformation*, Princeton, NJ: Princeton University Press.

Fager, Gregory (1994) "Financial flows to the major emerging markets in Asia." *Business Economics*, 29(2): 21–7.

Fainstein, Susan S., Gordon, Ian and Harloe, Michael (eds.) (1992) *Divided Cities*, Oxford: Blackwell.

Fajnzylber, Fernando (1983) *La industrialización truncada de America Latina*, Mexico: Nueva Imagen.

—— (1988) "Competitividad internacional, evolución y lecciónes." *Revista de la CEPAL*, no. 36.

—— (1990) *Unavoidable Industrial Restructuring in Latin America*, Durham, NC: Duke University Press.

Faria, Vilmar E. (1995) "Social exclusion and Latin American analyses of poverty and deprivation." In Gerry Rodgers, Charles Gore and Jose B. Figueredo (eds), *Social Exclusion: Rhetoric, Reality, Responses*, Geneva: International Institute of Labor Studies and United Nations Development Programme.

Fassmann H. and Münz, R. (1992) Patterns and trends of international migration in Western Europe. *Population and Development Review*, 18(3).

Fazy, Ian Hamilton (1995) "The superhighway pioneers." *The Financial Times*, June 20.

Feldstein, Martin et al. (1987) *Restructuring Growth in the Debt-laden Third World*, New York: Trilateral Commission.

Ferguson, Marjorie (ed.) (1986) *New Communications Technologies and the Public Interest: Comparative Perspectives on Policies and Research*, Newbury Park, CA: Sage.

Feuerwerker, Albert (1984) "The state and economy in late imperial China." *Theory and Society*, 13: 297–326.

Fischer, Claude (1985) "Studying technology and social life." In Manuel Castells (ed.), *High Technology, Space, and Society*, Beverly Hills, CA: Sage (*Urban Affairs Annual Reviews*, 28: 284–301).

—— (1992) *America Calling: A Social History of the Telephone to 1940*, Berkeley, CA: University of California Press.

Flynn, P.M. (1985) *The Impact of Technological Change on Jobs and Workers*, paper prepared for the US Department of Labor, Employment Training Administration.

Fontaine, Arturo (1988) *Los economistas y el Presidente Pinochet*, Santiago de Chile: Zig-Zag.

Fontana, Josep (1988) *La fin de l'Antic Regim i l'industrialitzacio, 1787–1868*, vol. V of Pierre Vilar (director), *Historia de Catalunya*, Barcelona: Edicions 62.

Foray, Dominique and Freeman, Christopher (eds) (1992) *Technologie et richesse des nations*, Paris: Economica.

Forbes, R.J. (1958) "Power to 1850." In C. Singer (ed.), *A History of Technology*, vol. 4: *The Industrial Revolution, 1750–1850*, Oxford: Oxford University Press.

Forester, Tom (1987) *High-tech Society*, Oxford: Blackwell.

—— (1993) *Silicon Samurai: How Japan Conquered the World Information Technology Industry*, Oxford: Blackwell.

—— (ed.) (1980) *The Microelectronics Revolution*, Oxford: Blackwell.

—— (ed.) (1985) *The Information Technology Revolution*, Oxford: Blackwell.

—— (ed.) (1988) *The Materials Revolution*, Oxford: Blackwell Business.

—— (ed.) (1989) *Computers in the Human Context*, Oxford: Blackwell.

Fouquin, Michel, Dourille-Feer, Evelyne and Oliveira-Martins, Joaquim, (1992) *Pacifique: le recentrage asiatique*, Paris: Economica.

Foxley, Alejandro (1995) *Los objetivos economicos y sociales en la transicion a la democracia*, Santiago: Universidad de Chile.

Frank, Andre Gunder (1967) *Capitalism and Underdevelopment in Latin America*, New York: Monthly Review Press.

Frankel, Robert et al. (1990) "Growth and structural reform in Latin America." *Cuadernos CEDES* (Buenos Aires).

Freeman, Christopher (1982) *The Economics of Industrial Innovation*, London: Pinter.

—— (ed.) (1986) *Design, Innovation, and Long Cycles in Economic Development*, London: Pinter.

—— (ed.) (1990) *The Economics of Innovation*, Aldershot, Hants.: Edward Elgar.

—— and Soete, Luc (1994) *Work for All or Mass Unemployment?* London: Pinter.

——, Sharp, Margaret and Walker, William (eds) (1991) *Technology and the Future of Europe*, London: Pinter.

Freeman, Richard (ed.) (1994) *Working Under Different Rules*, Cambridge, MA: Harvard University Press.

French-Davis, Ricardo (ed.) (1983) *Relaciones financieras externas: su efecto en la economia latinoamericana*, Mexico: Fondo de Cultura Economica – CIEPLAN.

Freud, Sigmund (1947) "Thoughts for the times on war and death." In his *On War, Sex, and Neurosis*, New York: Arts and Science Press, pp. 243–76.

Friedland, Roger and Boden, Deirdre (eds) (1994) *Nowhere: Space, Time, and Modernity*, Berkeley, CA: University of California Press.

Friedman, D. (1988) *The Misunderstood Miracle* Ithaca, NY: Cornell University Press.

Friedman, Milton (1968) *Dollars and Deficits: Living with America's economic problems*, Englewood Cliffs, N.J.: Prentice-Hall.

Friedmann, Georges (1956) *Le Travail en miettes*, Paris: Gallimard.

—— and Naville, Pierre (eds) (1961) *Traité de sociologie du travail*, Paris: Armand Colin.

—— (1957) *Countries in the World Economy: Challenges for US Policy*, Boulder, CO: Lynne Reinner, pp. 159–86.

Frischtak, Claudio (1989) "Structural change and trade in Brazil and in the newly industrializing Latin American economies." In Randall B. Purcell (ed.), *The Newly Industrializing.*

Froebel, Friedrich, Henricks, Jurgen and Kreye, Otto (1980) *The New International Division of Labor*, Cambridge: Cambridge University Press.

Fulk, J. and Steinfield, C. (eds) (1990) *Organizations and Communication Technology*, Newbury, CA: Sage.

Ganley, Gladys D. (1991) "Power to the people via electronic media." *Washington Quarterly*, Spring: 5–22.

Garcia-Sayan, Diego (ed.) (1989) *Coca, cocaina y narcotrafico. Laberinto en los Andes*, Lima: Comision Andina de Juristas.

Garratt, G.R.M. (1958) "Telegraphy." In C. Singer (ed.), *A History of Technology*, vol. 4: *The Industrial Revolution, 1750–1850*, Oxford: Oxford University Press, pp. 644–62.

Garreau, Joel (1991) *Edge City: Life on the New Frontier*, New York: Doubleday.

GATT (General Agreement on Tariffs and Trade) (1994) *International Trade*, Geneva: GATT, Trends and Statistics.

Gelb, Joyce and Lief Palley, Marian (eds) (1994) *Women of Japan and Korea: Continuity and Change*, Philadelphia, PA: Temple University Press.

Gelernter, David (1991) *Mirror Worlds*, New York: Oxford University Press.

Gereffi, Gary (1989) "Rethinking development theory: insights from East Asia and Latin America." *Sociological Forum*, 4: 505–35.

—— (1993) *Global Production Systems and Third World Development*, Madison: University of Wisconsin Global Studies Research Program, Working Paper Series, August.

—— and Wyman, Donald (eds) (1990) *Manufacturing Miracles: Paths of Industrialization in Latin America and East Asia*, Princeton, NJ: Princeton University Press.

Gerlach, Michael L. (1992) *Alliance Capitalism: The Social Organization of Japanese Business*, Berkeley, CA: University of California Press.

Gershuny, J.I. and Miles, I.D. (1983) *The New Service Economy: The Transformation of Employment in Industrial Societies*, London: Pinter.

Ghai, Dharam and Rodwan, Samir (eds) (1983) *Agrarian Policies and Rural Poverty in Africa*, Geneva: International Labour Organization.

Ghoshal, Sumantra and Bartlett, Christopher (1993) "The multinational corporation as an inter-organizational network." In Sumantra Ghoshal and D. Eleanor Westney (eds), *Organization Theory and Multinational Corporations*, New York: St Martin's Press, pp. 77–104.

—— and Westney, E. Eleanor (eds) (1993) *Organization Theory and Multinational Corporations*, New York: St Martin's Press.

Gibson, David G. and Rogers, Everett (1994) *R&D: Collaboration on Trial. The Microelectronics Computer Technology Corporation*, Boston, MA: Harvard Business School Press.

Giddens, A. (1981) *A Contemporary Critique of Historical Materialism*, Berkeley, CA: University of California Press.

—— (1984) *The Constitution of Society: Outline of a Theory of Structuration*, Cambridge: Polity Press.

Gill, Bertrand (1978) *Histoire des techniques: technique et civilisations, technique et sciences*, Paris: Gallimard.

Gitlin, Todd (1987) *The Sixties: Years of Hope, Days of Rage*, Toronto and New York: Bantam Books.

Gleick, James (1987) *Chaos*, New York: Viking Penguin.

Glewwe, Paul and de Tray, Dennis (1988) *The Poor During Adjustment: A Case Study of Côte d'Ivoire*, Washington D.C.: World Bank.

Glickman, Norman J. and Woodward, Douglas P. (1987) *Regional Patterns of Manufacturing Investment in the United States*, Special Project Report for the US Department of Commerce, Austin, TX: University of Texas, Lyndon B. Johnson School of Public Affairs.

Godard, Francis et al. (1973) *La Renovation urbaine à Paris*, Paris: Mouton.

Gold, Thomas (1986) *State and Society in the Taiwan Miracle*, Armonk, NY: M.E. Sharpe.

Goldenstein, Lidia (1994) *Repensando a Dependencia*, Rio de Janeiro: Paz e Terra.

Goldsmith, William W. and Blakely, Edward J. (1992) *Separate Societies: Poverty and Inequality in U.S. cities,* Philadelphia, PA: Temple University Press.

Goodman, P.S., Sproull, L.S. and Associates (1990) *Technology and Organization*, San Francisco, CA: Jossey-Bass.

Gordon, Richard (1994) *Internationalization, Multinationalization, Globalization: Contradictory World Economies and New Spatial Divisions of Labor*, Santa Cruz, CA: University of California Center for the Study of Global Transformations, Working Paper 94.

Gorgen, Armelle and Mathieu, Rene (1992) "Developing partnerships: new organizational practices in manufacturer–supplier relationships in the French automobile and aerospace industry." In Jane Marceau (ed.) *Reworking the World: Organizations, Technologies, and Cultures in Comparative Perspective*, Berlin: Walter de Gruyter, pp. 171–80.

Gottdiener, Marc (1985) *The Social Production of Urban Space*, Austin TX: University of Texas Press.

Gould, Stephen J. (1980) *The Panda's Thumb: More Reflections on Natural History*, New York: W.W. Norton.

Gourevitch, Peter A. (ed.) (1984) *Unions and Economic Crisis: Britain, West Germany and Sweden*, Boston, MA: Allen & Unwin.

Graham, Stephen (1994) "Networking cities: telematics in urban policy – a critical review." *International Journal of Urban and Regional Research*, 18(3): 416–31.

—— and Marvin, Simon (1996) *Telecommunications and the City: Electronic Spaces, Urban Places*, London: Routledge.

Granovetter, M. (1985) "Economic action and social structure: the problem of embeddedness." *American Journal of Sociology*, 49: 323–34.

Greenhalgh, S. (1988) "Families and networks in Taiwan's economic development." In E.A. Winckler and S. Greenhalgh (eds), *Contending Approaches to the Political Economy of Taiwan*, Armonk, NY: M.E. Sharpe.

Griffith-Jones, Stephany (ed.) (1988) *Managing Third World Debt*, New York: St Martin's Press.

Guerrieri, Paolo (1991) *Technology and International Trade Performance in the Most Advanced Countries*, Berkeley, CA: University of California BRIE Working Paper 49.

—— (1993) "Patterns of technological capability and international trade performance: an empirical analysis." In M. Kreinin (ed.), *The Political Economy of International Commercial Policy: Issues for the 1990s*, London: Taylor & Francis.

—— (1994) "International competitiveness, trade integration and technological interdependence." In Colin I. Bradford (ed.), *The New Paradigm of Systemic Competitiveness: Toward More Integrated Policies in Latin America*, Paris: OECD Development Centre, pp. 171–206.

Guile, Bruce R. (ed.) (1985) *Information Technologies and Social Transformation*, Washington D.C.: National Academy of Engineering, National Academy Press.

—— and Brooks, Harvey (eds) (1987) *Technology and Global Industry: Companies and Nations in the World Economy*, Washington D.C.: National Academy of Engineering.

Guillemard, Anne Marie (1972) *La Retraite: une mort sociale*, Paris: Mouton.

—— (1988) *Le Déclin du social*, Paris: Presses Universitaires de France.

—— (1993) "Travailleurs vieillissants et marché du travail en Europe." *Travail et emploi*, Sept.: 60–79.

—— and Rein, Martin (1993) "Comparative patterns of retirement: recent trends in developed societies." *Annual Review of Sociology*, 19: 469–503.

Gurr, T.R. (1993) *Minorities at Risk: A Global View of Ethnopolitical Conflicts*, Washington D.C.: US Institute of Peace Press.

Gurstein, Penny (1990) "Working at home in the live-in office: computers, space, and the social life of household," Berkeley, CA: University of California, unpublished PhD dissertation.

Gwin, Catherine and Feinberg, Richard (eds) (1989) *Pulling Together: The IMF in a Multipolar World*, New Brunswick, NJ: Transaction Books.

Hafner, Katie and Markoff, John (1991) *Cyberpunk: Outlaws and Hackers in the Computer Frontier*, New York: Touchstone.

Haggard, Stephan and Kaufman, Robert R. (eds) (1992) *The Politics of Economic Adjustment: International Constraints, Distributive Conflicts, and the State*, Princeton, NJ: Princeton University Press.

Hall, Nina (ed.) (1991) *Exploring Chaos: A Guide to the New Science of Disorder*, New York: W.W. Norton.

Hall, Peter (1995) "Towards a general urban theory." In John Brotchie et al. (eds), *Cities in Competition: Productive and Sustainable Cities for the 21st Century*, Sydney: Longman Australia, pp. 3–32.

—— and Preston, Pascal (1988) *The Carrier Wave: New Information Technology and the Geography of Innovation, 1846–2003*, London: Unwin Hyman.

—— et al. (1987) *Western Sunrise: The Genesis and Growth of Britain's Major High Technology Corridor*, London: Allen & Unwin.

——, Bornstein, Lisa, Grier, Reed and Webber, Melvin (1988) *Biotechnology: The Next Industrial Frontier*, Berkeley, CA: University of California Institute of Urban and Regional Development, Biotech Industry Research Group Report.

Hall, Stephen S. (1987) *Invisible Frontiers: The Race to Synthesize a Human Gene*, New York: Atlantic Monthly Press.

Hamelink, Cees (1990) "Information imbalance: core and periphery." In C. Downing et al., *Questioning the Media*, Newbury Park: Sage, pp. 217–28.

Hamilton, Gary G. (1991) *Business Networks and Economic Development in East and Southeast Asia*, Hong Kong: University of Hong Kong, Centre of Asian Studies.

—— and Biggart, N.W. (1988) "Market, culture, and authority: a comparative analysis of management and organization in the Far East." In C. Winship and S. Rosen (eds), *Organization and Institutions: Sociological Approaches to the Analysis of Social Structure*, Chicago, IL: University of Chicago Press, American Journal of Sociology Supplement, pp. S52–S95.

——, Zeile, W. and Kim, W.J. (1990) "The networks structures of East Asian economies." In Stewart R. Clegg and S. Gordon Redding (eds), *Capitalism in Contrasting Cultures*, Berlin: Walter de Gruyter.

Hamilton, Gary G. (1984) "Patriarchalism in Imperial China and Western Europe." *Theory and Society*, 13: 293–426.

—— (1985) "Why no capitalism in China? Negative questions in historical comparative research." *Journal of Asian Perspectives*, 2: 2.

—— and Kao, C.S. (1990) "The institutional foundation of Chinese business: the family firm in Taiwan." *Comparative Social Research*, 12: 95–112.

Handelman, Stephen (1995) *Comrade Criminal: Russia's New* Mafiya, New Haven, CT: Yale University Press.

Handinghaus, Nicolas H. (1989) "Droga y crecimiento economico: el narcotrafico en las cuentas nacionales." *Nueva Sociedad* (Bogota), no. 102.

Handy, Susan and Mokhtarian, Patricia L. (1995) "Planning for telecommuting." *Journal of the American Planning Association*, 61(1): 99–111.

Hanks, Roma S. and Sussman, Marvin B. (eds) (1990) *Corporations, Businesses and Families*, New York: Haworth Press.

Hanson, Stephen E. (1991) "Time and Soviet industrialization," Berkeley, CA: University of California, unpublished PhD dissertation.

Harff, B. (1986) "Genocide as state terrorism." In Michael Stohl and George A. Lopez, *Government Violence and Repression*, Westport, CT: Greenwood Press.

Harrington, Jon (1991) *Organizational Structure and Information Technology*, New York: Prentice-Hall.

Harris, Nigel (1987) *The End of the Third World*, Harmondsworth, Middx.: Penguin.

Harrison, Bennett (1994) *Lean and Mean: The Changing Landscape of Corporate Power in the Age of Flexibility*, New York: Basic Books.

Hart, Jeffrey A., Reed, Robert R. and Bar, François (1992) *The Building of Internet*, Berkeley, CA: University of California, BRIE Working Paper.

Hartmann, Heidi (ed.) (1987) *Computer Chips and Paper Clips: Technology and Women's Employment*, Washington D.C.: National Academy Press.

Harvey, David (1990) *The Condition of Postmodernity*, Oxford: Blackwell.

Havelock, Eric A. (1982) *The Literate Revolution in Greece and its Cultural Consequences*, Princeton, NJ: Princeton University Press.

Heavey, Laurie (1994) "Global integration." *Pension World*, 30(7): 24–7.

Henderson, Jeffrey (1989) *The Globalisation of High Technology Production: Society, Space and Semiconductors in the Restructuring of the Modern World*, London: Routledge.

—— (1990) *The American Semiconductors Industry and the New International Division of Labor*, London: Routledge.

—— (1991) "Urbanization in the Hong Kong–South China region: an introduction to dynamics and dilemmas." *International Journal of Urban and Regional Research* 15(2): 169–79.

Herman, Robin (1990) *Fusion: The Search for Endless Energy*, Cambridge: Cambridge University Press.

Herther, Nancy K. (1994) "Multimedia and the 'information superhighway'." *Online*, 18(5): 24.

Hewitt, P. (1993) *About Time: The Revolution in Work and Family Life*, London: IPPR/Rivers Oram Press.

Hiltz, Starr Roxanne and Turoff, Murray (1993) *The Network Nation: Human Communication via Computer*, Cambridge, MA: MIT Press.

Hinrichs, Karl, Roche, William and Sirianni, Carmen (eds) (1991) *The Political Economy of Working Hours in Industrial Nations*, Philadelphia, PA: Temple University Press.

Hirschhorn, Larry (1984) *Beyond Mechanization: Work and Technology in a Postindustrial Age*, Cambridge, MA: MIT Press.

—— (1985) "Information technology and the new services game." In Manuel Castells (ed.), *High Technology, Space and Society*, Beverly Hills, CA: Sage, pp. 172–90.

Ho, H.C.Y. (1979) *The Fiscal System of Hong Kong*, London: Croom Helm.

Hohenberg, Paul (1967) *Chemicals in Western Europe, 1850-1914*, Chicago, IL: Rand-McNally.

Holsti, K.J. (1991) *Peace and War: Armed Conflicts and International Order, 1648–1989*, Cambridge: Cambridge University Press.

Honigsbaum, Mark (1988) "Minitel loses fads image, moves toward money." *MIS Week*, 9(36): 22.

Howell, David (1994) "The skills myth." *American Prospect*, 18 (Summer): 81–90.

—— and Wolff, Edward (1991) "Trends in the growth and distribution of skills in the U.S. workplace, 1960–85." *Industrial and Labor Relations Review*, 44(3): 486–502.

Hsing, You-tien (1994) "Blood thicker than water: networks of local Chinese officials and Taiwanese investors in Southern China." Paper delivered at the conference sponsored by the University of California Institute on

Global Conflict and Cooperation, *The Economies of the China Circle*, Hong Kong, September 1–3.

—— (1995) *Migrant Workers, Foreign Capital, and Diversification of Labor Markets in Southern China*, Vancouver: University of British Columbia, Asian Urban Research Networks, Working Paper Series.

—— (1996) *Making Capitalism in China: The Taiwan Connection*, New York: Oxford University Press.

Humbert, M. (ed.) (1993) *The Impact of Globalisation on Europe's Firms and Industries*, London: Pinter.

Huws, U., Korte, W.B. and Robinson, S. (1990) *Telework: Towards the Elusive Office*, Chichester, Sussex: John Wiley.

Hyman, Richard and Streeck, Wolfgang (eds) (1988) *New Technology and Industrial Relations*, Oxford: Blackwell.

Ikle, Fred C. and Wohlsletter, Albert (co-chairmen) (1988) *Discriminate Deterrence: Report of the Commission on Integrated Long-term Strategy to the Secretary of Defense*, Washington D.C.: US Government Printing Office.

Illife, John (1987) *The African Poor*, Cambridge: Cambridge University Press.

ILO-ARTEP (1993) *India: Employment, Poverty, and Economic Policies*, New Delhi: ILO-ARTEP.

Imai, Ken'ichi (1980) *Japan's Industrial Organization and its Vertical Structure*, Kunitachi: Hitotsubashi University, Institute of Business Research, Discussion paper no. 101.

—— (1990a) *Joho netto waku shakai no tenbo* [The information network society], Tokyo: Chikuma Shobo.

—— (1990b) *Jouhon Network Shakai no Tenkai* [The development of information network society], Tokyo: Tikuma Shobou.

—— and Yonekura, Seiichiro (1991) "Network and network-in strategy," paper presented at the international conference between Bocconi University and Hitotsubashi University, Milan, September 20.

Innis, Harold A. (1950) *Empire and Communications*, Oxford: Oxford University Press.

—— (1951) *The Bias of Communication*, Toronto: University of Toronto Press.

—— (1952) *Changing Concepts of Time*, Toronto: University of Toronto Press.

Inoki, Takenori and Higuchi, Yoshio (eds) (1995) *Nihon no Koyou system to lodo shijo* [Japanese employment system and labor market], Tokyo: Nihon Keizai Shinbunsha.

International Labor Organization (ILO) (1993 and 1994) *World Labor Report*, Geneva: International Labor Organization.

—— (1988) *Technological Change, Work Organization and Pay: Lessons from Asia*, Geneva: ILO Labor-Management Relations Series, no. 68.

Islam, Rizwanul (1995) "Rural institutions and poverty in Asia." In Gerry Rodgers and Rolph van der Hoeven, (eds), *The Poverty Agenda: Trends and Policy Options*, Geneva: International Institute of Labour Studies, pp. 33–58.

Ito, Youichi (1991a) "Birth of *Joho Shakai* and *Johoka* concepts in Japan and their diffusion outside Japan." *Keio Communication Review*, no. 13: 3–12.

—— (1991b) "*Johoka* as a driving force of social change." *Keio Communication Review*, no. 12: 33–58.

—— (1993) "How Japan modernised earlier and faster than other non-western countries: an information sociology approach." *Journal of Development Communication*, 4(2).

—— (1994) "Japan." In Georgette Wang (ed.), *Treading Different Paths: Informatization in Asian Nations*, Norwood, NJ: Ablex, pp. 68–97.

Jackson, John H. (1989) *The World Trading System*, Cambridge, MA: MIT Press.

Jacobs, Allan (1993) *Great Streets*, Cambridge, MA: MIT Press.

Jacobs, N. (1985) *The Korean Road to Modernization and Development*, Urbana, IL: University of Illinois Press.

Jacoby, S. (1979) "The origins of internal labor markets in Japan." *Industrial Relations*, 18: 184–96.

Jamal, Vali (1995) "Changing poverty and employment patterns under crisis in Africa." In Gerry Rodgers and Rolph van der Hoeven (eds), *The Poverty Agenda: Trends and Policy Options*, Geneva: International Institute of Labour Studies, pp. 59–88.

James, William E., Naya, Seiji and Meier, Gerald M. (1989) *Asian Development: Economic Success and Policy Lessons*, Madison, WIS: University of Wisconsin Press.

Janelli, Roger with Yim, Downhee (1993) *Making Capitalism: The Social and Cultural Construction of a South Korean Conglomerate*, Stanford, CA: Stanford University Press.

Japan Informatization Processing Center (1994) *Informatization White Paper*, Tokyo: JIPDEC.

Japan Institute of Labour (1985) *Technological Innovation and Industrial Relations*, Tokyo: JIL.

Jarvis, C.M. (1958) "The distribution and utilization of electricity." In Charles Singer et al., *A History of Technology*, vol.5: *The Late Nineteenth Century*, Oxford: Clarendon Press, pp. 177–207.

Javetski, Bill and Glasgall, William (1994) "Borderless finance: fuel for growth." *Business Week*, Nov. 18: 40–50.

Jewkes, J., Sawers, D. and Stillerman, R. (1969) *The sources of invention*, New York: W.W. Norton.

Jia, Qingguo (1994) "Threat or opportunity? Implications of the growth of the China Circle for the distribution of economic and political power in the Asia-Pacific region." Beijing: Beijing University, Department of International Politics, unpublished discussion paper.

Johnson, Chalmers (1982) *MITI and the Japanese Miracle*, Stanford, CA: Stanford University Press.

—— (1985) "The institutional foundations of Japanese industrial policy." *California Management Review*, 27(4).

—— (1987) "Political institutions and economic performance: the government–business relationship in Japan, South Korea, and Taiwan." In Frederick Deyo (ed.), *The Political Economy of New Asian Industrialism*, Ithaca, NY: Cornell University Press, pp. 136–64.

—— (1995) *Japan: Who Governs? The Rise of the Developmental State*, New York: W.W. Norton.

——, Tyson, L. and Zysman, J. (eds) (1989) *Politics and Productivity: How Japan's Development Strategy Works*, New York: Harper Business.

Johnston, Ann and Sasson, Albert (1986) *New Technologies and Development*, Paris UNESCO.

Johnston, William B. (1991) "Global labor force 2000: the new world labor market." *Harvard Business Review*, March–April.

Jones, Barry (1982) *Sleepers, Wake! Technology and the Future of Work*, Melbourne: Oxford University Press (references are to the 1990 rev. edn).

Jones, David (1993) "Banks move to cut currency dealing costs." *Financial Technology International Bulletin*, 10(6): 1–3.

Jones, Eric L. (1981) *The European Miracle*, Cambridge: Cambridge University Press.

—— (1988) *Growth Recurring: Economic Change in World History*, Oxford: Clarendon Press.

Jones, L.P. and Sakong, I. (1980) *Government Business and Entrepreneurship in Economic Development: The Korean Case*, Cambridge, MA: Council on East Asian Studies.

Jorgerson, Dale W. and Griliches, Z. (1967) "The explanation of productivity growth." *Review of Economic Studies*, 34 (July): 249–83.

Jost, Kennet (1993) "Downward mobility." *CQ Researcher*, 3(27): 627–47.

Joussaud, Jacques (1994) "Diversité des statuts des travailleurs et flexibilité des entreprises au Japon." *Japan in Extenso*, no.31: 49–53.

Kaiser, M., Klingspor, V., Millan, J. de R., Accami, M., Wallner, F. and Dillman, R. (1995) "Using machine learning techniques in real-world mobile robots." *IEEE Expert*, 10(2).

Kaku, Michio (1994) *Hyperspace: A Scientific Odyssey Through Parallel Universes, Time Warps, and the 10th Dimension*, New York: Oxford University Press.

Kamatani, Chikatoshi (1988) *Gijutsu Taikoku Hyakunen no Kei: Nippon no Kindaika to Kokuritsu Kenkyu Kikan* [The road to techno-nationalism: Japanese modernization and national research institutes from the Meiji era], Tokyo: Heibonsha.

Kaplan, Rachel (1992) "Video on demand." *American Demographics*, 14(6): 38–43.

Kaplinsky, Raphael (1986) *Microelectronics and Work Revisited: A Review*, report prepared for the International Labor Organization, Brighton: University of Sussex Institute of Development Studies.

Kara-Murza, A.A. and Polyakov, L.V. (1994) *Reformator. Opyt analiticheskoy antologii*, Moscow: Institut Filosofii Rossiiskoi Akademii Nauk, Flora.

Katz, Jorge (1994) "Industrial organization, international competitiveness and public policy." In Colin I. Bradford (ed.), *The New Paradigm of Systemic Competitiveness: Toward More Integrated Policies in Latin America*, Paris: OECD Development Center.

Katz, Jorge (ed.) (1987) *Technology Generation in Latin American Manufacturing Industries*, London: Macmillan.

Katz, Raul L. (1988) *The Information Society: An International Perspective*, New York: Praeger.

Kaye, G.D., Grant, D.A. and Emond, E.J. (1985) *Major Armed Conflicts: A Compendium of Interstate and Intrastate Conflict, 1720 to 1985*, Ottawa: Operational Research and Analysis Establishment, Report to National Defense, Canada.

Kelley, Maryellen (1986) "Programmable automation and the skill question: a re-interpretation of the cross-national evidence." *Human Systems Management*, 6.

—— (1990) "New process technology, job design and work organization: a contingency model." *American Sociological Review*, 55 (April): 191–208.

Kelly, Kevin (1995) *Out of Control: The Rise of Neo-biological Civilization*, Menlo Park, CA: Addison-Wesley.

Kendrick, John W. (1961) *Productivity Trends in the United States*, National Bureau of Economic Research, Princeton, NJ: Princeton University Press.

—— (1973) *Postwar Productivity Trends in the United States, 1948–69*, National Bureau of Economic Research New York: Columbia University Press.

—— (1984) *International Comparisons of Productivity and Causes of the Slowdown*, Cambridge, MA: Ballinger.

—— and Grossman, E. (1980) *Productivity in the United States: Trends and Cycles*, Baltimore, MD: Johns Hopkins University Press.

Kenney, Martin (1986) *Biotechnology: The University–Industrial Complex*, New Haven, CT: Yale University Press.

Kepel, G. (ed.) (1993) *Les Politiques de Dieu*, Paris: Seuil.

Khanin, Gregory I. (1994) "Nachalo Krakha [Beginning of collapse]." *EKO*, no. 7.

Khoury, Sarkis and Ghosh, Alo (1987) *Recent Developments in International Banking and Finance*, Lexington, MA: D.C. Heath.

Kim, E.M. (1989) "From domination to symbiosis: state and chaebol in Korea." *Pacific Focus*, 2: 105–21.

Kim, Kyong-Dong (ed.) (1987) *Dependency Issues in Korean Development*, Seoul: Seoul National University Press.

Kimsey, Stephen (1994) "The virtual flight of the cyber-trader." *Euromoney*, June: 45–6.

Kincaid, A. Douglas and Portes, Alejandro (eds) (1994) *Comparative National Development: Society and Economy in the New Global Order*, Chapel Hill, NC: University of North Carolina Press.

Kindleberger, Charles (1964) *Economic Growth in France and Britain, 1851–1950*, Cambridge, MA: Harvard University Press.

King, Alexander (1991) *The First Global Revolution: A Report by the Council of the Club of Rome*, New York: Pantheon Books.

Kirsch, Guy, Nijkamp, Peter and Zimmermann, Klaus (eds) (1988) *The Formulation of Time Preferences in a Multidisciplinary Perspective*, Aldershot, Hants: Gower.

Koike, Kazuo (1988) *Understanding Industrial Relations in Modern Japan*, London: Macmillan.

Kolata, Gina (1995) "Metabolism found to adjust for a body's natural weight." *New York Times*, March 9: A 1/A 11.

Kolb, David (1990) *Postmodern Sophistications: Philosophy, Architecture and Tradition*, Chicago, IL: University of Chicago Press.

Koo, H. and Kim, E.M. (1992) "The developmental state and capital accumulation in South Korea." In Richard P. Appelbaum and Jeffrey Henderson (eds), *States and Development in the Asian Pacific Rim*, London: Sage, pp. 121–49.

Korte, W.B., Robinson, S. and Steinle, W.K. (eds) (1988) *Telework: Present Situation and Future Development of a New Form of Work Organization*, Amsterdam: North-Holland.

Kotter, John P. and Heskett, James L. (1992) *Corporate Culture and Performance*, New York: Free Press.

Kovalyova, Galina (1995) *Sibir' na mirovom rynke: Tekyshchyi obzor vneshney torgovli* [Siberia in the world market: current survey of foreign trade], Novosibirsk: Institute of Economics and Industrial Engineering, Russian Academy of Sciences, Siberian Branch, Research Report.

Kranzberg, M. (1985) "The information age: evolution or revolution?" In Bruce R. Guile (ed.), *Information Technologies and Social Transformation*, Washington D.C.: National Academy of Engineering.

—— (1992) "The scientific and technological age." *Bulletin of Science and Technology Society*, 12: 63–5.

—— and Pursell, Carroll W. Jr (eds) (1967) *Technology in Western Civilization*, 2 vols, New York: Oxford University Press.

Kraut, R.E. (1989) "Tele-commuting: the trade-offs of home-work." *Journal of Communications*, 39: 19–47.

Krugman, Paul (1990) *The Age of Diminished Expectations*, Cambridge, MA: MIT Press.

—— (1994a) *Peddling Prosperity: Economic Sense and Nonsense in the Age of Diminished Expectations*, New York: W.W. Norton.

—— (1994b) "Competitiveness: a dangerous obsession." *Foreign Affairs*, 73(2): 28–44.

—— (ed.) (1986) *Strategic Trade Policy and the New International Economics*, Cambridge, MA: MIT Press.

—— and Lawrence, Robert Z. (1994) "Trade, jobs and wages." *Scientific American*, April: 44–9.

Krykov, Valery (1994) "Polnye kanistry i pystyye karmany [Full jerricans and empty pockets]." *EKO*, 1: 53–62.

Kuhn, Thomas (1962) *The Structure of Scientific Revolutions*, Chicago, IL: University of Chicago Press.

Kuleshov, Valery I. (1994) "Perekhodnaya economika: proidennye etapy, nametivshiyesya tendentsii [Transition economy: past stages, emerging trends]." *EKO*, 12: 54–63.

Kumazawa, M. and Yamada, J. (1989) "Jobs and skills under the lifelong Nenko employment practice." In Stephen Wood (ed.), *The Transformation of Work?: Skill, Flexibility and the Labour Process*, London: Unwin Hyman.

Kunstler, James Howard (1993) *The Geography of Nowhere: The Rise and Decline of America's Man Made Landscape*, New York: Simon & Schuster.

Kuo, Shirley W.Y. (1983) *The Taiwan Economy in Transition*, Boulder,CO: Westview Press.

Kur'yerov, V.G. (1994) "Ekonomika Rossii: Obshchiye Tendentsii [Russian economy: general trends]." *EKO*, no. 5: 2–7.

—— (1995a) "Vneshneekonomicheskiye svyazi [Foreign economic relations]." *EKO*, no. 3: 77–98.

—— (1995b) "Vneshneekonomicheskiye svyazi [Foreign economic relations." *EKO*, no. 9: 51–75.

Kutscher, R.E. (1991) "Outlook 1990–2005. New BLS projections: findings and implications." *Monthly Labor Review*, November: 3–12.

Kuttner, Robert (1983) "The declining middle." *Atlantic Monthly*, July: 60–72.

Kuwahara, Yasuo (1989) *Japanese Industrial Relations System: A New Interpretation*, Tokyo: Japan Institute of Labour.

Kuwayama, M. (1992) "America Latina y la internacionalizacion de la economia mundial." *Revista de la CEPAL*, no. 46.

Kwok, R. Yin-Wang and So, Alvin (1992) *Hong Kong–Guandong Interaction: Joint Enterprise of Market Capitalism and State Socialism*, Manoa: University of Hawaii, Research paper.

Kwok and So (eds) (1995) *The Hong Kong–Guandong Link: Partnership in Flux*, Armouk, NY: M.E. Sharpe.

Lachaud, Jean-Pierre (1994) *The Labour Market in Africa*, Geneva: International Institute of Labour Studies, Research Series.

Lafay, Gerard and Herzog, Colette (1989) *Commerce international: la fin des avantages acquis*, Paris: Economica/Centre d'Etudes Prospectives et d'Informations Internationales.

Landau, Ralph and Rosenberg, Nathan (eds) (1986) *The Positive Sum Strategy: Harnessing Technology for Economic Growth*, Washington D.C.: National Academy Press.

Landes, David (1969) *The Unbound Prometheus: Technical Change and Industrial Development in Western Europe from 1750 to the Present*, London: Cambridge University Press.

Lanham, Richard A. (1993) *The Electronic Ward*, Chicago, IL: University of Chicago Press.

Laserna, Roberto (1995) "Regional development and coca production in Cochabamba, Bolivia," Berkeley, CA: University of California, unpublished PhD dissertation in City and Regional Planning.

—— (1996) "El circuito coca-cocaine y sus implicaciones," La Paz: ILDIS.

Lash, Scott (1990) *Sociology of Postmodernism*, London: Routledge.

—— and Urry, John (1994) *Economies of Signs and Space*, London: Sage.

Lawrence, Robert Z. (1984) "The employment effects of information technologies: an optimistic view," paper delivered at the OECD *Conference on the Social Challenge of Information Technologies*, Berlin, November: 28–30.

Leal, Jesus (1993) *La desigualdad social en España*, 10 vols, Madrid: Universidad

Autonóma de Madrid, Instituto de Sociologia de Nuevas Tecnologias, Research Monograph.

Leclerc, Annie (1975) *Parole de femme*, Paris: Grasset.

Lee, Peter and Townsend, Peter (1993) *Trends in Deprivation in the London Labour Market: A Study of Low-Incomes and Unemployment in London between 1985 and 1992*, Geneva: International Institute of Labour Studies, Discussion paper 59/1993.

Lee, Peter, King, Paul, Shirref, David and Dyer, Geof (1994) "All change." *Euromoney*, June: 89–101.

Lee, Roger and Schmidt-Marwede, Ulrich (1993) "Interurban competition? Financial centres and the geography of financial production." *International Journal of Urban and Regional Research*, 17(4): 492–515.

Lehman, Yves (1994) "Videotex: a Japanese lesson." *Telecommunications*, 28(7): 53–4.

Lenoir, Daniel (1994) *L'Europe sociale*, Paris: La Découverte.

Leo, P.Y. and Philippe, J. (1989) "Réseaux et services aux entreprises. Marchés locaux et développement global," papers of Seminar 32, 1989-II, CEP, pp. 79–103.

Leontieff, Wassily and Duchin, Faye (1985) *The Future Impact of Automation on Workers*, New York: Oxford University Press.

Lethbridge, Henry J. (1978) *Hong Kong: Stability and Change*, Hong Kong: Oxford University Press.

Leung, Chi Kin (1993) "Personal contacts, subcontracting linkages, and development in the Hong Kong–Zhujiang Delta Region." *Annals of the Association of American Geographers*, 83(2): 272–302.

Levy, Pierre (1994) *L'Intelligence collective: pour une anthropologie du cyberspace*, Paris: La Découverte.

Levy, R.A., Bowes, M. and Jondrow, J.M. (1984) "Technical advance and other sources of employment change in basic industry." In E.L. Collins and L.D. Tanner (eds), *American Jobs and the Changing Industrial Base*, Cambridge, MA: Ballinger, pp. 77–95.

Levy, Stephen (1984) *Hackers: Heroes of the Computer Revolution*, Garden City, NY: Doubleday.

Leys, Colin (1987) "The state and the crisis of simple commodity production in Africa." *Institute of Development Studies Bulletin*, 8(3): 45–8.

—— (1994) "Confronting the African tragedy." *New Left Review*, no. 204: 33–47.

Lichtenberg, Judith (ed.) (1990) *Democracy and Mass Media*, New York: Cambridge University Press.

Lillyman, William, Moriarty, Marilyn F. and Neuman, David J. (eds) (1994) *Critical Architecture and Contemporary Culture*, New York: Oxford University Press.

Lim, Hyun-Chin (1982) *Dependent Development in Korea (1963–79)*, Seoul: Seoul National University Press.

Lin, T.B., Mok, V. and Ho, Y.P. (1980) *Manufactured Exports and Employment in Hong Kong*, Hong Kong: Chinese University Press.

Lincoln, Edward J. (1990) *Japan's Unequal Trade*, Washington, DC: Brookings Institution.

Lincoln, Thomas L. and Essin, Daniel J. (1993) "The electronic medical record: a challenge for computer science to develop clinically and socially relevant computer systems to coordinate information for patient care and analysis." *Information Society*, 9:157–88.

——, —— and Ware, Willis H. (1993) "The electronic medical record." *Information Society*, 9(2): 157–88.

Ling, K.K. (1995) "A case for regional planning: the Greater Pearl River Delta: a Hong Kong perspective," unpublished Research Seminar Paper, CP 229, Berkeley, CA: University of California Department of City and Regional Planning.

Lizzio, James R. (1994) "Real-time RAID storage: the enabling technology for video on demand." *Telephony*, 226(21): 24–32.

Lo, C.P. (1994) "Economic reforms and socialist city structure: a case study of Guangzhou, China." *Urban Geography*, 15(2) 128–49.

Lohr, Steve (1995) "Who uses Internet?" *New York Times*, September 22.

Lorenz, E. (1988) "Neither friends nor strangers: informal networks of subcontracting in French industry." In D. Gambetta, (ed.), *Trust: Making and Breaking Cooperative Relations*, Oxford: Blackwell, pp. 194–210.

Lovins, Amory B. and Lovins, L. Hunter (1995) "Reinventing the wheels." *Atlantic Monthly*, January: 75–86.

Lozano, Beverly (1989) *The Invisible Work Force: Transforming American Business with Outside and Home-based Workers*, New York: Free Press.

Lustig, Nora (1995) "Coping with austerity: poverty and inequality in Latin America." In Gerry Rodgers and Rolph van der Hoeven (eds), *The Poverty Agenda: Trends and Policy Options*, Geneva: International Institute of Labour Studies, pp. 89–126.

Lynch, Kevin (1960) *The Image of the City*, Cambridge, MA: MIT Press.

Lyon, David (1988) *The Information Society: Issues and Illusions*, Cambridge: Polity Press.

—— (1995) *Postmodernity*, Oxford: Blackwell.

Lyon, Jeff and Gorner, Peter (1995) *Altered Fates: Gene Therapy and the Retooling of Human Life*, New York: W.W. Norton.

Machimura, T. (1994) *Sekai Toshi Tokyo no Kozo* [The structural transformation of a global city Tokyo], Tokyo: Tokyo University Press.

—— (1995) *Symbolic Use of Globalization in Urban Politics in Tokyo*, Kunitachi: Hitotsubashi University Faculty of Social Sciences, Research Paper.

Machlup, Fritz (1962) *The Production and Distribution of Knowledge in the United States*, Princeton, NJ: Princeton University Press.

—— (1980) *Knowledge: Its Creation, Distribution, and Economic Significance*, vol. I: *Knowledge and Knowledge Production*, Princeton, NJ: Princeton University Press.

—— (1982) *Knowledge: Its Creation, Distribution and Economic Significance*, vol. II: *The Branches of Learning*, Princeton, NJ: Princeton University Press.

—— (1984) *Knowledge: Its Creation, Distribution and Economic Significance*, vol.

III, *The Economics of Information and Human Capital*, Princeton, NJ: Princeton University Press.

Mackie, J.A.C. (1992a) "Changing patterns of Chinese big business in Southeast Asia." In Ruth McVey (ed.), *Southeast Asian Capitalists*, Ithaca, N.Y.: Cornell University, Southeast Asian Program.

—— (1992b) "Overseas Chinese entrepreneurship." *Asian Pacific Economic Literature*, 6(1): 41–64.

Maddison, A. (1982) *Phases of Capitalised Development*, New York: Oxford University Press.

Maddison, Angus (1984) "Comparative analysis of the productivity situation in the advanced capitalist countries." In John W. Kendrick (ed.), *International Comparisons of Productivity and Causes of the Slowdown*, Cambridge, MA: Ballinger.

Maital, Shlomo (1991) "Why the French do it better." *Across the Board*, 28(11): 7–10.

Malinvaud, Edmond et al. (1974) *Fresque historique du système productif français*, Paris: Collections de l'INSEE, Séries E, 27 (October).

Mallet, Serge (1963) *La Nouvelle Classe ouvrière*, Paris: Seuil.

Malone, M.S. (1985) *The Big Score: The Billion-dollar Story of Silicon Valley*, Garden City, NY: Doubleday.

Mander, Jerry (1978) *Four Arguments for the Elimination of Television*, New York: William Morrow.

Mankiewicz, Frank and Swerdlow, Joel (eds) (1979) *Remote Control: Television and the Manipulation of American Life*, New York: Ballantine.

Mansfield, Edwin (1982) *Technology Transfer, Productivity, and Economic Policy*, Englewood Cliffs, NJ: Prentice-Hall.

Marceau, Jane (ed.) (1992) *Reworking the World: Organisations, Technologies, and Cultures in Comparative Perspective*, Berlin: Walter De Gruyter.

Markoff, John (1995) "If the medium is the message, the message is the Web." *New York Times*, 20 November: A1, C5.

Marshall, Alfred (1919) *Industry and Trade*, London: Macmillan.

Marshall, Jonathan (1994) "Contracting out catching on: firms find it's more efficient to farm out jobs." *San Francisco Chronicle*, August 22: D2–D3.

Marshall, J.N. et al. (1988) *Services and Uneven Development*, Oxford: Oxford University Press.

Martin, L. John and Chaudhary, Anja Grover (eds) (1983) *Comparative Mass Media Systems*, New York: Longman.

Martin, Linda G. (1987) *The ASEAN Success Story: Social, Economic, and Political Dimensions*, Honolulu: University of Hawaii Press.

Martin, Patricia (1994) "The consumer market for interactive services: observing past trends and current demographics." *Telephony*, 226(18): 126–30.

Martinez, Gabriel and Farber, Guillermo (1994) *Desregulacion economica 1989–93*, Mexico DF: Fondo de Cultura Economica.

Martinotti, Guido (1993) *Metropoli. La Nuova morfologia sociale della citta*, Bologna: Il Mulino.

Marx, Jean L. (ed.) (1989) *A Revolution in Biotechnology*, Cambridge:

Cambridge University Press for the International Council of Scientific Unions.

Massad, Carlos (1991) "El financiamiento del desarrollo industrial en un continente empobrecido." In *Industrializacion y desarrollo tecnologico*, Santiago, Chile: Joint ECLAC/UNIDO Industry and Technology Division, Informe no.11, August.

—— and Eyzaguirre, N. (1990) *Ahorro y formacion de capital. Experiencias latinoamericanas: Argentina, Brasil, Chile, El Salvador y Mexico*, Buenos Aires: CEPAL/PNUD, Grupo Editor Latinoamericano.

Matsumoto, Miwao and Sinclair, Bruce (1994) "How did Japan adapt itself to scientific and technological revolution at the turn of the 20th Century?" *Japan Journal for Science, Technology, and Society*, 3: 133–55.

Mattelart, Armand and Stourdze, Yves (1982) *Technologie, culture et communication*, Paris: La Documentation française.

Matzner, Egon and Wagner, Michael (eds) (1990) *The Employment Impact of New Technology: The Case of West Germany*, Aldershot, Hants.: Avebury.

Mazlish, Bruce (1993) *The Fourth Discontinuity: The Co-evolution of Humans and Machines*, New Haven, CT: Yale University Press.

McGowan, James (1988) "Lessons learned from the Minitel phenomenon." *Network World*, 5(49): 27.

—— and Compaine, Benjamin (1989) "Is Minitel a good model for the North American market?" *Network World*, 6(36).

McGuire, William J. (1986) "The myth of massive media impact: savagings and salvagings." In George Comstock (ed.), *Public Communication and Behavior*, Orlando, FLA: Academic Press, pp. 173–257.

McKinsey Global Institute (1992) *Service Sector Productivity*, Washington D.C.: McKinsey Global Institute.

—— (1993) *Manufacturing Productivity*, Washington D.C.: McKinsey Global Institute.

McLeod, Roger (1996) "Internet users abandoning TV, survey finds." *San Francisco Chronicle*, 12 January: 1, 17.

McLuhan, Marshall (1962) *The Gutenberg Galaxy: The Making of Typographic Man*, Toronto: University of Toronto Press.

—— (1964) *Understanding Media: The Extensions of Man*, New York: Macmillan.

—— and Powers, Bruce R. (1989) *The Global Village: Transformations in World Life and Media in the 21st Century*, New York: Oxford University Press.

McMillan, C. (1984) *The Japanese Industrial System*, Berlin: De Gruyter.

McNeill, William H. (1977) *Plagues and People*, New York: Doubleday.

Mehta, Suketu (1993) "The French connection." *LAN Magazine*, 8(5).

Menotti, Val (1995) "The transformation of retail social space: an analysis of virtual shopping's impact on retail centers." Unpublished research paper for seminar CP298I, University of California, Berkeley, Department of City and Regional Planning.

Michelson, Ronald L. and Wheeler, James O. (1994) "The flow of information in a global economy: the role of the American urban system in 1990." *Annals of the Association of American Geographers*, 84 (1): 87–107.

MIDEPLAN (1994) *Integracion al Desarrollo: Balance de la Politica Social 1990–93, Santiago de Chile: Ministerio de Desarrollo y Planificacion.*

Miles, Ian (1988) *Home Informatics: Information Technology and the Transformation of Everyday Life*, London: Pinter.

Millan, Jose del Rocio (1996) "Rapid, safe, and incremental learning of navigation strategies." *IEEE Transactions on Systems, Man, and Cybernetics*, 26(6).

Miller, Steven, M. (1989) *Impacts of Industrial Robotics: Potential Effects of Labor and Costs within the Metalworking Industries*, Madison, WIS: University of Wisconsin Press.

Miller, Richard L. and Swensson, Earl S. (1995) *New Directions in Hospital and Health Care Facility Design*, New York: McGraw-Hill.

Miners, N. (1986) *The Government and Politics of Hong Kong*, Hong Kong: Oxford University Press.

Mingione, Enzo (1991) *Fragmented Societies*, Oxford, Blackwell.

Ministry of Labor [Japan] (1991) *Statistical Yearbook*, Tokyo: Government of Japan.

Ministry of Posts and Telecommunications [Japan] (1994a) *1994 White Paper: Communications in Japan*, Tokyo: Ministry of Posts and Telecommunications.

—— (1994b) *Communications in Japan 1994*, Part 3: *Multimedia: Opening up a New World of Info-communication*, Tokyo: Ministry of Posts and Telecommunications.

—— (1995) *Tsushin Hakusho Heisei 7 nenban* [White Paper on Communication in Japan], Tokyo: Yusei shou.

Mishel, Lawrence and Bernstein, Jared (1993) *The State of Working America*, New York: M.E. Sharpe.

—— and —— (1994) *The State of Working America 1994–95*, Washington D.C.: Economic Policy Institute.

—— and Teixeira, Ruy A. (1991) *The Myth of the Coming Labor Shortage: Jobs, Skills, and Incomes of America's Workforce 2000*, Washington, D.C.: Economic Policy Institute Report.

Mokhtarian, Patricia L. (1991a) "Defining telecommuting." *Transportation Research Record*, 1305: 273–81.

—— (1991b) "Telecommuting and travel: state of the practice, state of the art." *Transportation*, 18: 319–42.

—— (1992) "Telecommuting in the United States: letting our fingers do the commuting." *Telecommuting Review: the Gordon Report*, 9(5): 12.

Mokyr, Joel (1990) *The Lever of Riches: Technological Creativity and Economic Progress*, New York: Oxford University Press.

—— (ed.) (1985) *The Economics of the Industrial Revolution*, Totowa, NJ: Rowman & Allanheld.

Mollenkopf, John (ed.) (1989) *Power, Culture, and Place: Essays on New York City*, New York: Russell Sage Foundation.

—— and Castells, Manuel (eds) (1991) *Dual City: Restructuring New York*, New York: Russell Sage Foundation.

Monk, Peter (1989) *Technological Change in the Information Economy*, London: Pinter.

Moran, R. (1990) "Health environment and healthy environment." In R. Moran, R. Anderson and P. Paoli, *Building for People in Hospitals, Workers, and Consumers*, Dublin: European Foundation for the Improvement of Living and Working Conditions.

—— (1993) *The Electronic Home: Social and Spatial Aspects. A Scoping Report*, Dublin: European Foundation for the Improvement of Living and Working Conditions.

Morier, Françoise (ed.) (1994) *Belleville, Belleville. Visages d'un planète*, Paris: Editions Creaphis.

Morin, Edgar (1970) *L'homme et la mort*, Paris: Seuil.

Morrocco, John D. (1991) "Gulf War boosts prospects for high-technology weapons." *Aviation Week & Space Technology*, 134(11): 45–7.

Mortimore, Michael (1992) "A new international industrial order." *CEPAL Review*, no. 48: 39–59.

Moss, Mitchell (1987) "Telecommunications, world cities, and urban policy." *Urban Studies*, 24: 534–46.

—— (1991) "The new fibers of economic development." *Portfolio*, 4: 11–18.

—— (1992) "Telecommunications and urban economic development." In OECD, *Cities and New Technologies*, Paris: OECD, pp. 147–58.

Mowery, David (ed.) (1988) *International Collaborative Ventures in U.S. Manufacturing*, Cambridge, MA: Ballinger.

—— and Henderson, Bruce E. (eds) (1989) *The Challenge of New Technology to Labor–Management Relations*, Washington D.C.: Dept of Labor, Bureau of Labor Management Relations.

Mowshowitz, Abbe (1986) "Social dimensions of office automation." In *Advances in Computers*, vol. 25, New York: Academic Press.

Mulgan, G.J. (1991) *Communication and Control: Networks and the New Economies of Communication*, New York: Guilford Press.

Murphy, Kevin M. and Welch, Finis (1993) "Inequality and relative wages." *American Economic Review*, May.

Muschamp, Herbert (1992) "A design that taps into the 'Informational City'." *Sunday New York Times*, August 9, Architecture View Section: 32.

Mushkat, Miron (1982) *The Making of the Hong Kong Administrative Class*, Hong Kong: University of Hong Kong Centre of Asian Studies.

Myers, Edith (1981) "In France it's Teletel." *Datamation*, 27(10): 78–88.

Nadal, Jordi and Carreras, Albert (eds) (1990) *Pautas regionales de la industrializacion española. Siglos XIX y XX*, Barcelona: Ariel.

National Science Board (1991) *Science and Engineering Indicators, 1991*, 10th edn (NSB 91–1), Washington, D.C.: US Government Printing Office.

Naughton, Barry (1994) "Increasing economic interaction in the China Circle in the context of East Asian Growth," paper delivered at the Conference sponsored by the University of California Institute on Global Conflict and Cooperation, *The Economics of the China Circle*, Hong Kong, September 1–3.

Navarro, Vicente (1994a) *The Politics of Health Policy*, Oxford: Blackwell.

—— (1994b) "La economia y el Estado de bienestar," unpublished paper presented at the 10th Meeting on the Future of the Welfare State, Madrid.

Nayyar, Deepak (1994) *Macroeconomic Adjustment, Liberalization and Growth: The Indian Experience*, Geneva: International Institute of Labour Studies, Discussion paper 73/1994.

Needham, Joseph (1954–88) *Science and Civilization in China*, Cambridge: Cambridge University Press.

—— (1969) *The Grand Titration*, Toronto: Toronto University Press.

—— (1981) *Science in Traditional China*, Cambridge, MA: Harvard University Press.

Negroponte, Nicholas (1995) *Being Digital*, New York: Alfred A. Knopf.

Nelson, Joan M. (ed.) (1990) *Economic Crisis and Policy Choice: The Politics of Adjustment in the Third World*, Princeton, NJ: Princeton University Press.

Nelson, Richard (1980) "Production sets, technological knowledge, and R&D: fragile and overworked constructs for analysis of productivity growth?" *American Economic Review*, 70(2): 62–7.

—— (1981) "Research on productivity growth and productivity differences: dead ends and new departures." *Journal of Economic Literature*, 19(3): 1029–64.

—— (1984) *High Technology Policies: A Five Nations Comparison*, Washington D.C.: American Enterprise Institute.

—— (1988) "Institutions supporting technical change in the United States." In G. Dosi et al. *Technical Change and Economic Theory*, London: Pinter, pp. 312–29.

—— (1994) "An agenda for formal growth theory," New York: Columbia University Department of Economics, unpublished paper (communicated by the author).

—— and Winter, S.G. (1982) *An Evolutionary Theory of Economic Change*, Cambridge, MA: Harvard University Press.

Neuman, W. Russell (1991) *The Future of Mass Audience*, New York: Cambridge University Press.

New Media Markets (1993) "Video on demand will provide Hollywood studios with much-needed boost." 11(10): 13–15.

—— (1994) "Video-on-demand trials planned across Europe." 12(1): 8.

Newman, Katherine S. (1993) *Declining Fortunes: The Withering of the American Dream*, New York: Basic Books.

Newsweek (1993) "Jobs." Special issue, June 14.

Nicol, Lionel (1985) Communications technology: economic and social impacts. In Manuel Castells (ed.), *High Technology, Space and Society*, Beverly Hills, CA: Sage.

NIKKEIREN [Japan Federation of Employers Associations] (1993) *The Current Labor Economy in Japan*, Tokyo: NIKKEIREN, Information Report.

Nilles, J.M. (1988) "Traffic reduction by telecommuting: a status review and selected bibliography." *Transportation Research A*, 22A(4): 301–17.

Noble, David F. (1984) *Forces of Production: A Social History of Industrial Automation*, New York: Alfred A. Knopf.

Nolan, Peter and Furen, Dong (eds) (1990) *The Chinese Economy and its Future: Achievements and Problems of Post-Mao Reform*, Cambridge: Polity Press.

Nomura, Masami (1994) *Syushin Koyo*, Tokyo: Iwanami Shoten.

Nonaka, Ikujiro (1990) *Chisiki souzou no keiei* [Knowledge creation: episte-mology of the Japanese firms], Tokyo: Nikkei shinbunsha.
—— (1991) "The knowledge-creating company." *Harvard Business Review,* Nov.–Dec.: 96–104.
—— and Takeuchi, Hirotaka (1994) *The Knowledge-creating Company: How Japanese Companies Created the Dynamics of Innovation,* New York: Oxford University Press.
"Non-standard working under review." (1994) *Industrial Relations & Review Report,* no. 565: 5–14.
Nora, Simon and Minc, Alain (1978) *L'Informatisation de la société.* Paris: La Documentation française.
Norman, Alfred Lorn (1993) *Informational Society: An Economic Theory of Discovery, Invention and Innovation,* Boston/Dordrecht/London: Kluwer Academic Publishers.
Norman, E. Herbert (1940) *Japan's Emergence as a Modern State: Political and Economic Problems of the Meiji Period,* New York: Institute of Pacific Relations.
North, Douglas (1981) *Structure and Change in Economic History,* New York: W.W. Norton.
Northcott, J. (1986) *Microelectronics in Industry,* London: Policy Studies Institute.
Nuland, Sherwin B. (1994) *How We Die: Reflections on Life's Final Chapter,* New York: Alfred A. Knopf.
O'Brien, Richard (1992) *Global Financial Integration: The End of Geography,* London: Pinter.
OECD (Organization for Economic Cooperation and Development) *Cities and New Technologies,* Paris: OECD.
—— (1994a) *Employment Outlook,* July, Paris: OECD.
—— (1994b) *Employment/Unemployment Study: Policy Report,* Paris: OECD, document for Council at ministerial level, May.
—— (1994c) *The OECD Jobs Study,* Paris: OECD.
—— (1995) *Economic Outlook,* June, Paris: OECD.
Office of Technology Assessment (OTA) (US Congress) (1984) *Computerized Manufacturing Automation: Employment, Education, and the Workplace,* Washington D.C.: US Government Printing Office.
—— (1986) *Technology and Structural Unemployment,* Washington D.C.: US Government Printing Office.
Ohmae, Kenichi (1985) *Triad Power: The Coming Shape of Global Competition,* New York: Free Press.
—— (1990) *The Borderless World: Power and Strategy in the Interlinked Economy,* New York: Harper.
Okimoto, Daniel (1984), "Political context." In Daniel Okimoto, Takuo Sugano and Franklin B. Weinstein (eds), *Competitive Edge,* Stanford, CA: Stanford University Press.
Ozaki, Muneto et al. (1992) *Technological Change and Labour Relations,* Geneva: International Labour Organization.
Pahl, Ray (ed.) (1988) *On Work: Historical, Comparative, and Theoretical Approaches,* Oxford: Blackwell.

Panofsky, Erwin (1957) *Gothic Architecture and Scholasticism*, New York: Meridian Books.

Park, Young-bum (1992) *Wage-fixing Institutions in the Republic of Korea*, Geneva: International Institute of Labour Studies, Discussion paper 51/1992.

Parkinson, G.H.R. (ed.) (1973) *Leibniz: Philosophical Writings*, London: J.M. Dent.

Parsons, Carol A. (1987) *Flexible Production Technology and Industrial Restructuring: Case Studies of the Metalworking, Semiconductor, and Apparel Industries*, PhD dissertation, Berkeley, University of California.

Patel, S.J. (1992) "In tribute to the Golden Age of the South's development." *World Development*, 20(5): 767–77.

Payer, Cheryl (1974) *The Debt Trap*, New York: Monthly Review Press.

Perez, Carlotta (1983) "Structural change and the assimilation of new technologies in the economic and social systems." *Futures*, 15: 357–75.

Petrella, Ricardo (1993) *Un techno-monde en construction. Synthèse des résultats et des recommandations FAST 1989–1992/93*, Brussels: European Commission: FAST Programme.

Petterson, L.O. (1989) "Arbetstider i tolv Lander." *Statens offentliga utredningar*, 53: cited in Bosch et al. (eds) (1994).

Piller, Charles (1994) "Dreamnet." *Macworld* 11(10): 96–9.

Piore, Michael J. and Sabel, Charles F. (1984) *The Second Industrial Divide: Possibilities for Prosperity*, New York: Basic Books.

Poirier, Mark (1993) "The multimedia trail blazers." *Catalog Age*, 10(7): 49.

Pool, Ithiel de Sola (1983) *Technologies of Freedom: On Free Speech in the Electronic Age*, Cambridge, MA: Belknap Press of Harvard University Press.

—— (1990) *Technologies Without Boundaries*, ed. Eli M. Noam, Cambridge, MA: Harvard University Press.

Porat, Marc (1977) *The Information Economy: Definition and Measurement*, Washington D.C.: US Department of Commerce, Office of Telecommunications, publication 77–12 (1).

Porter, Michael (1990) *The Competitive Advantage of Nations*, New York: Free Press.

Portes, Alejandro and Rumbault, Ruben (1990) *Immigrant America: A Portrait*, Berkeley, CA: University of California Press.

——, Castells, Manuel and Benton, Lauren (eds) (1989) *The Informal Economy: Studies on Advanced and Less Developed Countries*, Baltimore, MD: Johns Hopkins University Press.

Postman, Neil (1985) *Amusing Ourselves to Death: Public Discourse in the Age of Show Business*, New York: Penguin Books.

—— (1992) *Technopoly*, New York: Pantheon.

Poulantzas, Nicos (1978) *L'Etat, le pouvoir, le socialisme*, Paris: Presses Universitaires de France.

Powell, Walter W. (1990) "Neither market nor hierarchy: network forms of organization." In Barry M. Straw and Larry L. Cummings (eds), *Research in Organizational Behavior*, Greenwich, CT: JAI Press, pp. 295–336.

Pozas, Maria de los Angeles (1993) *Industrial Restructuring in Mexico*, San Diego: University of California Center for US–Mexican Studies.

Preston, Holly H. (1994) "Minitel reigns in Paris with key French connection." *Computer Reseller News*, no. 594: 49–50.

Pyo, H. (1986) *The Impact of Microelectronics and Indigenous Technological Capacity in the Republic of Korea*, Geneva: International Labour Organization.

Qian, Wen-yuan (1985) *The Great Inertia: Scientific Stagnation in Traditional China*, London: Croom Helm.

Qingguo Jia (1994) "Threat or opportunity? Implications of the growth of the China Circle for the distribution of economic and political power in the Asia Pacific Region," paper delivered at the conference sponsored by the University of California Institute on Global Conflict and Cooperation, *The Economics of the China Circle*, Hong Kong, September 1–3.

Quinn, James Brian (1987) "The impacts of technology in the services sector." In Bruce R. Guile and Harvey Brooks (eds), *Technology and Global Industry: Companies and Nations in the World Economy*, Washington D.C.: National Academy of Engineering: National Academy Press, pp. 119–159.

—— (1988) "Technology in services: past myths and future challenges." In Bruce R. Guile and James B. Quinn (eds), *Technology in Services*, Washington D.C.: National Academy Press, pp. 16–46.

Quiroga Martinez, Layen (ed.) (1994) *El tigre sin selva: consecuencias ambientales de la transformacion economica de Chile, 1974–1993*, Santiago de Chile: Instituto de Ecologia Politica.

Qvortup, Lars (1992) "Telework: visions, definitions, realities, barriers." In OECD *Cities and New Technologies*, Paris: OECD, pp. 77–108.

Rafaeli, Sheifaz and LaRose, Robert J. (1993) "Electronic bulletin boards and public goods explanations of collaborative mass media." *Communications Research*, 20(2): 277–97.

Ramamurthy, K. (1994) "Moderating influences of organizational attitude and compatibility on implementation success from computer-integrated manufacturing technology." *International Journal of Production Research*, 32(10):2251–73

Rand Corporation (1995) *Universal Access to E-Mail: Feasibility and Social Implications*, World Wide Web, ttp://www.rand.org/publications/MR/MR650/

Randall, Stephen J. (ed.) (1992) *North America Without Borders?*, Calgary: University of Calgary Press.

Randlesome, Collin, Brierly, William, Bruton, Kevin, Gordon, Colin and King, Peter (1990) *Business Cultures in Europe*, Oxford: Heinemann.

Redding, S. Gordon (1990) *The Spirit of Chinese Capitalism*, Berlin: Walter de Gruyter.

Rees, Teresa (1992) *Skill Shortages, Women, and the New Information Technologies*, Report of the Task Force of Human Resources, Education, Training, and Youth, Brussels: Commission of the European Communities, January.

Reich, Robert (1991) *The Work of Nations*, New York: Random House.

Reynolds, Larry (1992) "Fast money: global markets change the investment game." *Management Review*, 81(2): 60–1.

Rheingold, Howard (1993) *The Virtual Community*, Reading, MA: Addison-Wesley.

Rice, Ronald E. "Issues and concepts on research on computer-mediated communication systems." *Communication Yearbook*, 12: 436–76.

Rifkin, Jeremy (1987) *Time Wars: The Primary Conflict in Human History*, New York: Henry Holt.

—— (1995) *The End of Work*, New York: Putnam.

Rijn, F.V. and Williams, R. (eds) (1988) *Concerning Home Telematics*, Amsterdam: North-Holland.

Roberts, Edward B. (1991) *Entrepreneurs in High Technology: MIT and Beyond*, New York: Oxford University Press.

Robinson, Olive (1993) "Employment in services: perspectives on part-time employment growth in North America." *Service Industries Journal*, 13(3): 1–18.

Robson, B. (1992) "Competing and collaborating through urban networks." *Town and Country Planning*, Sept: 236–8.

Rodgers, Gerry (ed.) (1994) *Workers, Institutions, and Economic Growth in Asia*, Geneva: International Institute of Labour Studies.

—— (ed.) (1995) *The Poverty Agenda and the ILO: Issues for Research and Action. A Contribution to the World Summit for Social Development*, Geneva: International Institute of Labour Studies.

——, Gore, Charles and Figueiredo, Jose B. (eds) (1995) *Social Exclusion: Rhetoric, Reality, Responses*, Geneva: International Institute of Labour Studies.

Rogers, Everett M. (1986) *Communication Technology: The New Media in Society*, New York: Free Press.

—— and Larsen, Judith K. (1984) *Silicon Valley Fever: Growth of High Technology Culture*, New York: Basic Books.

Rogozinski, Jacques (1993) *La privatizacion de las empresas estatales*, Mexico DF: Fondo de Cultura Economica.

Rosenbaum, Andrew (1992) "France's Minitel has finally grown up." *Electronics*, 65(6).

Rosenberg, Nathan (1976) *Perspectives on Technology*, Cambridge: Cambridge University Press.

—— (1982) *Inside the Black Box: Technology and Economics*, Cambridge: Cambridge University Press.

—— and Birdzell, L.E. (1986) *How the West Grew Rich: The Economic Transformation of the Industrial World*, New York: Basic Books.

Rostow, W.W. (1975) *How It All Began*, New York: McGraw Hill.

Roszak, Theodore (1986) *The Cult of Information*, New York: Pantheon.

Rothchild, Donald and Chazan, Naomi (eds) (1988) *The Precarious Balance: State and Society in Africa*, Boulder, CO: Westview Press.

Rothstein, Richard (1993) *Workforce Globalization: A Policy Response*, Washington D.C.: Economic Policy Institute, Report prepared for the Women's Bureau of the US Department of Labor.

—— (1994) "The global hiring hall: why we need worldwide labor standards."
American Prospect, no. 17: 54–61.

Rumberger, R.W. and Levin, H.M. (1984) *Forecasting the Impact of New Technologies on the Future Job Market*, Stanford, CA: Stanford University School of Education, Research Report.

Russell, Alan M. (1988) *The Biotechnology Revolution: An International Perspective*, Brighton, Sussex: Wheatsheaf Books.

Sabbah, Françoise (1985) "The new media." In Manuel Castells (ed.), *High Technology, Space, and Society*, Beverly Hills, CA: Sage.

Sabel, C. and Zeitlin, J. (1985) "Historical alternatives to mass production: politics, markets, and technology in 19th century industrialization." *Past and Present*, 108 (August): 133–76.

Saez, Felipe et al. (1991) *Tecnologia y empleo en España: situación y perspectivas*, Madrid: Universidad Autónoma de Madrid–Instituto de Sociologia de Nuevas Tecnologias y Ministerio de Economia–Instituto de Estudios de Prospectiva.

Sagasti, Francisco and Araoz, Alberto (eds) (1988) *La planificacion científica y tecnologica en los paises en desarrollo. La experiencia del proyecto STPI*, Mexico: Fondo de Cultura Economica.

—— et al. (1988) *Conocimiento y desarrollo: ensayos sobre ciencia y tecnologia*, Lima: GRADE.

Sainz, Pedro and Calcagno, Alfredo (1992) "In search of another form of development." *CEPAL Review*, 48 (December): 7–38.

Salomon, Jean-Jacques (1992) *Le Destin technologique*, Paris: Editions Balland.

Salvaggio, Jerry L. (ed.) (1989) *The Information Society: Economic, Social, and Structural Issues*, Hillsdale, NJ: Lawrence Erlbaum Associates.

Sandbrook, Richard (1985) *The Politics of Africa's Economic Stagnation*, Cambridge: Cambridge University Press.

Sandholtz, Wayne et al. (1992) *The Highest Stakes: The Economic Foundations of the Next Security System*, New York: Oxford University Press (a BRIE Project).

Sandkull, Bengdt (1992) "Reorganizing labour: the Volvo experience." In Jane Marceau (ed.), *Reworking the World: Organisations, Technologies, and Cultures in Comparative Perspective*, Berlin: Walter de Gruyter, pp. 399–409.

Sassen, Saskia (1988) *The Mobility of Labor and Capital*, Cambridge: Cambridge University Press.

—— (1991) *The Global City: New York, London, Tokyo*, Princeton, NJ: Princeton University Press.

Sato, Takeshi et al. (1995) *Johoza to taisyu bunka* [Informationalization and mass culture], Kunitachi: Hitotsubashi University Department of Social Psychology, Research Report.

Saunders, William (ed.) (1996) *Architectural Practices in the 1990s*, Princeton, NJ: Princeton University Press.

Sautter, Christian (1978) "L'efficacité et la rentabilité de l'économie française de 1954 à 1976." *Economie et statistique*, 68.

Saxby, Stephen (1990) *The Age of Information*, London: Macmillan.

Saxenian, Anna L. (1994) *Regional Advantage: Culture and Competition in Silicon Valley and Route 128*, Cambridge, MA: Harvard University Press.

Sayer, Andrew and Walker, Richard (1992) *The New Social Economy: Reworking the Division of Labor*, Oxford: Blackwell.

Schaff, Adam (1992) *El Socialismo del Futuro*, no. 4: special issue on the future of labor.

Schatan, Jacobo (1987) *World Debt: Who is to Pay?*, London: Zed Books.

Scheer, Leo (1994) *La Démocratie virtuelle*, Paris: Flammarion.

Schettkat, R. and Wagner, M. (eds) (1990) *Technological Change and Employment Innovation in the German Economy*, Berlin: Walter De Gruyter.

Schiatarella, R. (1984) *Mercato di Lavoro e struttura produttiva*, Milan: Franco Angeli.

Schiffer, Jonathan (1983) *Anatomy of a Laissez-faire Government: The Hong Kong Growth Model Reconsidered*, Hong Kong: University of Hong Kong Centre for Asian Studies.

Schoonmaker, Sara (1993) "Trading on-line: information flows in advanced capitalism." *Information Society*, 9(1): 39–49.

Schor, Juliet (1991) *The Overworked American*, New York: Basic Books.

Schuldt, K. (1990) *Soziale und ökonomische Gestaltung der Elemente der Lebensarbeitzeit der Werktätigen*, Dissertation, Berlin; cited in Bosch et al. (eds) (1994).

Schumpeter, J.A. (1939) *Business Cycles: A Theoretical, Historical, and Statistical Analysis of the Capitalist Process*, New York: McGraw-Hill.

Schweitzer, John C. (1995) "Personal computers and media use." *Journalism Quarterly*, 68(4): 689–97.

Schwitzer, Glenn E. (1995) "Can research and development recover in Russia?" *Business World of Russia Weekly*, May 15–20: 10–12; reprinted from *Journal of Technology and Society*, 17(2).

Scott, Allen (1988) *New Industrial Spaces*, London: Pion.

SEADE Foundation (1995) *Survey of Living Conditions in the Metropolitan Area of São Paulo*, Geneva: International Institute of Labour Studies, Research Series.

Seidman, Steven and Wagner, David G. (eds) (1992) *Postmodernism and Social Theory*, Oxford: Blackwell.

Seki, Kiyohide (1988) *Summary of the National Opinion Survey of Family in Japan*, Tokyo: Nihon University Research Center, Research Paper.

Sellers, Patricia (1993) "The best way to reach buyers." *Fortune*, 128(13): 14–17.

Sengenberger, Werner and Campbell, Duncan (eds) (1992) *Is the Single Firm Vanishing? Inter-enterprise Networks, Labour, and Labour Institutions*, Geneva: International Institute of Labour Studies.

—— and —— (eds) (1994) *International Labour Standards and Economic Interdependence*, Geneva: International Institute of Labour Studies.

——, Loveman, Gary and Piore, Michael (eds) (1990) *The Re-emergence of Small Enterprises: Industrial Restructuring in Industrialized Countries*, Geneva: International Institute for Labour Studies.

Shaiken, Harley (1985) *Work Transformed: Automation and Labor in the Computer Age*, New York: Holt, Rinehart & Winston.

—— (1990) *Mexico in the Global Economy: High Technology and Work*

Organization in Export Industries, La Jolla, CA: University of California at San Diego, Center for US–Mexican Studies.

—— (1993) "Beyond lean production." *Stanford Law & Policy Review,* 5(1): 41–52.

—— (1995) "Experienced workers and high performance work organization: a case study of two automobile assembly plants," unpublished paper presented at the Industrial Relations Research Association Annual Meetings, Washington D.C., January 6.

Shapira, Phillip (1990) *Modernizing Manufacturing,* Washington D.C.: Economic Policy Institute.

Sharlin, Harold I. (1967) "Electrical generation and transmission." In Melvin Kranzberg and Carroll W. Pursell Jr (eds), *Technology in Western Civilization,* 2 vols, New York: Oxford University Press, vol. 2, pp. 578–91.

Shin, E.H. and Chin S.W. (1989) "Social affinity among top managerial executives of large corporations in Korea." *Sociological Forum,* 4: 3–26.

Shinotsuka, Eiko (1994) "Women workers in Japan: past, present, and future." In Joyce Gelb and Marian Lief Palley (eds), *Women of Japan and Korea: Continuity and Change,* Philadelphia, PA: Temple University Press, pp. 95–119.

Shirref, David (1994) "The metamorphosis of finance." *Euromoney,* June: 36–42.

Shoji, Kokichi (1990) *Le Nipponisme comme méthode sociologique. Originalité, particularité, universalité,* Tokyo: Tokyo University Department of Sociology, Discussion paper.

Shujiro Urata (1993) "Changing patterns of direct investment and its implications for trade and development." In C. Fred Bergsten and Marcus Noland (eds), *Pacific Dynamism and the International Economic System,* Washington, D.C.: Institute for International Economics, pp. 273–99.

Siddell, Scott (1987) *The IMF and Third World Political Instability,* London: Macmillan.

Siino, Corinne (1994) "La ville et le chomage." *Revue d'économie régionale et urbaine,* no. 3: 324–52.

Silverstone, R. (1991) *Beneath the bottom line: households and information and communication technologies in the age of the consumer,* London: Brunel University Center for Research on Innovation, Culture, and Technology.

Silvestri, George T. (1993) "The American work force, 1992–2005: occupational employment, wide variations in growth." *Monthly Labor Review,* November: 58–86.

—— and Lukasiewicz, J. (1991) "Outlook 1990–2005: occupational employment projections." *Monthly Labor Review,* November:

Singleman, Joachim (1978) *The Transformation of Industry: From Agriculture to Service Employment,* Beverly Hills, CA: Sage.

Singer, Charles et al. (1957) *A History of Technology,* vol. 3: *From the Renaissance to the Industrial Revolution,* Oxford: Clarendon Press.

——, Holmyard, E.J., Hall, A.R. and Williams, Trevor I. (eds) (1958) *A History of Technology,* vol. 4: *The Industrial Revolution, c.1750 to c.1850,* Oxford: Clarendon Press.

Singh, Ajit (1994) "Global economic changes, skills, and international competitiveness." *International Labour Review*, 133(2): 107–83.

Sit, Victor Fueng-Shuen (1991) "Transnational capital flows and urbanization in the Pearl River Delta, China." *Southeast Asian Journal of Social Science*, 19(1–2): 154–79.

—— and Wong, S.L. (1988) *Changes in the Industrial Structure and the Role of Small and Medium Industries in Asian Countries: The Case of Hong Kong*, Hong Kong: University of Hong Kong Centre of Asian Studies.

Sit, Victor F.S., Wong, Sin Lun and Kiang, Tsiu-Sing (1979) *Small-scale Industry in a Laissez-faire Economy: A Hong Kong Case Study*, Hong Kong: University of Hong Kong, Centre of Asian Studies.

Skezely, Gabriel (1993) "Mexico's international strategy: looking east and north." In Barbara Stallings and Gabriel Skezely (eds), *Japan, the United States, and Latin America*, Baltimore, MD: Johns Hopkins University Press.

Smith, Merrit Roe and Marx, Leo (eds) (1994) *Does Technology Drive History? The Dilemma of Technological Determinism*, Cambridge, MA: MIT Press.

Soesastro, Hadi and Pangetsu, Mari (eds) (1990) *Technological Challenge in the Asia–Pacific Economy*, Sydney: Allen & Unwin.

Soete, Luc (1987) "The impact of technological innovation on international trade patterns: the evidence reconsidered." *Research Policy*, 16.

—— (1991) "Technology and economy in a changing world," background paper prepared for the OECD International Policy Conference on *Technology and the Global Economy*, Montreal, February.

Solow, Robert M. (1956) "A contribution to the theory of economic growth." *Quarterly Journal of Economics*, 70 (Feb.): 65–94.

—— (1957) "Technical change and the aggregate production function." *Revue of Economics and Statistics*, 39 (Aug.): 214–31.

Sorlin, Pierre (1994) *Mass Media*, London: Routledge.

Sorokin, P.A. and Merton, R.K. (1937) "Social time: a methodological and functional analysis." *American Journal of Sociology*, 42: 615–29.

Soumu-cho Toukei-kyoku (Bureau of Statistics, Management and Coordination Agency, Japan) (1995) *Nihon no Toukei*, Tokyo.

Southern, R.W. (1995) *Scholastic Humanism and the Unification of Europe*, vol. 1: *Foundations*, Oxford: Blackwell Publishers.

Soysal, Yasemin Nuhoglu (1994) *Limits of citizenship: Migrants and Postnational Membership in Europe*, Chicago, IL: University of Chicago Press.

Specter, Michael (1994) "Russians' newest space adventure: cyberspace." *New York Times*, March 9: C1–C2.

—— (1995) "Plunging life expectancy puzzles Russia." *New York Times*, August 2: 1.

Spence, Michael and Hazard, Heather A. (eds) (1988) *International Competitiveness*, Cambridge, MA: Ballinger.

Sproull, Lee and Kiesler, Sara (1991) *Connections: New Ways of Working in the Networked Organization*, Cambridge, MA: MIT Press.

Stalker, Peter (1994) *The Work of Strangers: A Survey of International Labour Migration*, Geneva: International Labour Organization.

Stallings, Barbara (1992) "International influence on economic policy: debt, stabilization and structural reform." In Stephen Haggard and Robert R. Kaufman (eds), *The Politics of Adjustment*, Princeton, NJ: Princeton University Press, pp. 41–88.

—— (1993) *The New International Context of Development*, Madison, WIS: University of Wisconsin, Working Paper Series on the New International Context of Development, no. 1.

—— and Kaufman, Robert (eds) (1989) *Debt and Democracy in Latin America*, Boulder, CO: Westview Press.

Stanback, T.M. (1979) *Understanding the Service Economy: Employment, Productivity, Location*, Baltimore, MD: Johns Hopkins University Press.

Steers, R.M., Shin, Y.K. and Ungson, G.R. (1989) *The Chaebol*, New York: Harper & Row.

Steinle, W.J. (1988) "Telework: opening remarks and opening debate." In W.B. Korte, S. Robinson and W.K. Steinle (eds), *Telework: Present Situation and Future Development of a New Form of Work Organization*, Amsterdam: North-Holland.

Stevens, Barrie and Michalski, Wolfgang (1994) *Long-term Prospects for Work and Social Cohesion in OECD Countries: An Overview of the Issues*, Paris: Report to the OECD Forum for the Future.

Stevenson, Richard W. (1994) "Foreign capitalists brush risks aside to invest in Russia." *New York Times*, October 11: c1, p. 4.

Stonier, Tom (1983) *The Wealth of Information*, London: Methuen.

Stourdze, Yves (1987) *Pour une poignée d'électrons*, Paris: Fayard.

Stowsky, Jay (1992) "From spin-off to spin-on: redefining the military's role in American technology development." In Wayne Sandholtz, Michael Borrus and John Zysman et al., *The Highest Stakes: The Economic Foundations of the Next Security System*, New York: Oxford University Press.

Strassman, Paul A. (1985) *Information Payoff: The Transformation of Work in the Electronic Age*, New York: Free Press.

Sugihara, Kaoru et al. (1988) *Taisho, Osaka, and the Slum: Another Modern History of Japan*, Tokyo: Shinhyoron.

Sukhotin, Iurii (1994) "Stabilization of the economy and social contrasts." *Problems of Economic Transition*, November: 44–61.

Sullivan-Trainor, Michael (1994) *Detour: The Truth about the Information SuperHighway*, San Mateo, CA: IDG Books.

Sun Tzu (*c.* 505–496BC) *On the Art of War*, trans. from Chinese with critical notes by Lionel Giles, Singapore: Graham Brash, 1988 (first published in English in 1910).

Sung, Yun-Wing (1994) "Hong Kong and the economic integration of the China Circle." Paper delivered at the conference sponsored by the University of California Institute on Global Conflict and Cooperation, *The Economies of the China Circle*, Hong Kong, September 1–3.

Sunkel, Osvaldo (ed.) (1993) *Development from Within: Toward a Neostructuralist Approach for Latin America*, Boulder, CO: Lynne Reiner.

Swann, J. (1986) *The Employment Effects of Microelectronics in the UK Service Sector*, Geneva: International Labour Organization.

Syun, Inoue (1975) The loss of meaning in death. *Japan Interpreter*, 9(3): 336.

Tafuri, Manfredo (1971) *L'urbanistica del riformismo*, Milan: Franco Angeli.

Takenori, Inoki and Higuchi, Yoshio (eds) (1995) *Nihon no Koyou system to lodo shijo* [Japanese employment system and labour market], Tokyo: Nihon Keizai Shinbunsha.

Tan, Augustine H.H. and Kapur, Basant (eds) (1986) *Pacific Growth and Financial Interdependence*, Sydney: Allen & Unwin.

Tan Kong Yam (1994) "China and ASEAN: competitive industrialization through foreign direct investment," paper delivered at the conference sponsored by the University of California Institute on Global Conflict and Cooperation, *The Economics of the China Circle*, Hong Kong, September 1–3.

Tarr, J. and Dupuy, G. (eds) (1988) *Technology and the Rise of the Networked City in Europe and North America*, Philadelphia, PA: Temple University Press.

Tchernina, Natalia (1993) *Employment, Deprivation, and Poverty: The Ways in which Poverty is Emerging in the Course of Economic Reform in Russia*, Geneva: International Institute of Labour Studies, Discussion Paper no. 60/1993.

Teitelman, Robert (1989) *Gene Dreams: Wall Street, Academia, and the Rise of Biotechnology*, New York: Basic Books.

Teitz, Michael B., Glasmeier, Amy and Shapira, Philip (1981) *Small Business and Employment Growth in California*, Berkeley, CA: Institute of Urban and Regional Development, Working Paper no. 348.

Telecommunications Council (Japan) (1994) *Reforms Toward the Intellectually Creative Society of the 21st Century: Program for the Establishment of High-performance Info-communications Infrastructure*, Report–response to Inquiry no. 5, 1993, Tokyo: May 31 (unofficial translation, July 1994).

Tetsuro, Kato and Steven, Rob (eds) (1994) *Is Japanese Management Post-Fordism?*, Tokyo: Mado-sha.

Thach, Liz and Woodman, Richard W. (1994) "Organizational change and information technology: managing on the edge of cyberspace." *Organizational Dynamics*, 1: 30–46.

Thery, Gérard (1994) *Les autoroutes de l'information. Rapport au Premier Ministre*, Paris: La Documentation française.

Thomas, Hugh (1993) *The Conquest of Mexico*, London: Hutchinson.

Thomas, Louis-Vincent (1975) *Anthropologie de la mort*, Paris: Payot.

—— (1985) *Rites de mort pour la paix des vivants*, Paris: Fayard.

—— (1988) *La Mort*, Paris: Presses Universitaires de France.

Thompson, E.P. (1967) "Time, work-discipline, and industrial capitalism." *Past and Present*, 36: 57–97.

Thrift, Nigel J. (1986) *The "Fixers": The Urban Geography of International Financial Capital*, Lampeter: University of Wales Department of Geography.

—— (1990) "The making of capitalism in time consciousness." In J. Hassard (ed.), *The Sociology of Time*, London: Macmillan, pp. 105–29.

—— and Leyshon, A. (1992) "In the wake of money: the City of London and the accumulation of value." In L. Budd and S. Whimster (eds), *Global Finance and Urban Living: A Study of Metropolitan Change*, London: Routledge, pp. 282–311.

Thurow, Lester (1992) *Head to Head: The Coming Economic Battle among Japan, Europe, and America*, New York: William Morrow.

—— (1995) "How much inequality can a democracy take?" *New York Times Magazine*, special issue: *The Rich*, November 19: 78.

Tichi, Cecilia (1991) *Electronic Hearth: Creating an American Television Culture*, New York: Oxford University Press.

Tillema, H.K. (1991) *International Armed Conflict Since 1945: A Bibliographic Handbook of Wars and Military Intervention*, Boulder, CO: Westview Press.

Tilly, Charles (1995) "State-incited violence, 1900–1999." *Political Power and Social Theory*, 9: 161–79.

Time (1993) Special issue on Megacities, January 11.

—— (1994) "Risky business in Wall Street: high-tech supernerds are playing dangerous games with money." Special report, April 11: 24–35.

Tirman, John (ed.) (1984) *The Militarization of High Technology*, Cambridge, MA: Ballinger.

Tobenkin, David (1993) "Customers respond to video on demand." *Broadcasting & Cable*, 123(48): 16.

Touraine, Alain (1955) *L'Evolution du travail ouvrier aux usines Renault*, Paris: Centre National de la Recherche Scientifique.

—— (1959) "Entreprise et bureaucratie." *Sociologie du travail*, no. 1: 58–71.

—— (1969) *La Société post-industrielle*, Paris: Denoel.

—— (1987) *La Parole et le sang. Politique et société en Amerique Latine*, Paris: Odile Jacob.

—— (1991) "Existe-t-il encore une société française?" *Contemporary French Civilization*, 15: 329–52.

—— (1992) *Critique de la modernité*, Paris: Fayard.

—— (1994) *Qu'est-ce que la démocratie?*, Paris: Fayard.

Trejo Delarbre, Raul (1992) *La Sociedad Ausente. Comunicacion, democracia y modernidad*, Mexico: Cal y Arena.

—— (ed.) (1988) *Las Redes de Televisa*, Mexico: Como/Rotativo.

Turkle, Sherry (1995) *Life on the Screen: Identity in the Age of the Internet*, New York: Simon & Schuster.

Tyson, Laura D'Andrea (1992) *Who's Bashing Whom? Trade Conflict in High-technology Industries*, Washington D.C.: Institute of International Economics.

—— and Zysman, John (1983) *American Industry in International Competition*, Ithaca, N.Y.: Cornell University Press.

——, Dickens, William T. and Zysman, John (eds) (1988) *The Dynamics of Trade and Employment*, Cambridge, MA: Ballinger.

Ubbelhode, A.R.J.P. (1958) "The beginnings of the change from craft mystery to science as a basis for technology." In C. Singer et al., *A History of Technology*, vol. 4: *The Industrial Revolution, 1750–1850*, Oxford: Clarendon Press.

Uchida, Hoshimi (1991) "The transfer of electrical technologies from the U.S. and Europe to Japan, 1869–1914." In David J. Jeremy (ed.), *International Technology Transfer: Europe, Japan, and the USA, 1700–1914*, Aldershot, Hants: Edward Elgar, pp. 219–41.

Ungar, Sanford J. (1985) *Africa: The People and Politics of an Emerging Continent*, New York: Simon & Schuster.

United Nations Center on Transnational Corporations (1991) *Transnational Banks and the External Indebtedness of Developing Countries*, New York: United Nations, UNCTC Current Studies, Series A, No.22.

United Nations Conference on Trade and Development (UNCTAD), Programme on Transnational Corporations (1993) *World Investment Report 1993: Transnational Corporations and Integrated International Production*, New York: United Nations.

—— (1994) *Transnational Corporations and Employment*, report by the UNCTAD Secretariat to the Commission on Transnational Corporations, 2–11 May.

US Congress, Office of Technology Assessment (1991) *Biotechnology in a Global Economy*, Washington D.C.: US Government Printing Office.

US House of Representatives, Committee on Armed Services, Readiness Subcommittee (1990) *U.S. Low-intensity Conflicts, 1899–1990*, a study by the Congressional Research Service, Library of Congress, Washington D.C.: US Government Printing Office.

US National Science Board (1991) *Science and Engineering Indicators: 1991*, 10th edn, Washington D.C.: US Government Printing Office.

Vaill, P.B. (1990) *Managing as a Performing Art: New Ideas for a World of Chaotic Change*, San Francisco, CA: Jossey-Bass.

Van Creveld, Martin (1989) *Technology and War from 2000 BC to the Present*, New York: Free Press.

Van Tulder, Rob and Junne, Gerd (1988) *European Multinationals in Core Technologies*, New York: John Wiley.

Vaquero, Carlos (ed.) (1994) *Desarrollo, probreza y medio ambiente. FMI, Banco Mundial, GATT al final del siglo*, Madrid: Talasa Ediciones.

Varley, Pamela (1991) "Electronic democracy." *Technology Review*, Nov/Dec: 43–51.

Velloso, Joao Paulo dos Reis (1994) "Innovation and society: the modern bases for development with equity." In Colin I. Bradford (ed.), *The New Paradigm of Systemic Competitiveness: Toward More Integrated Policies in Latin America*, Paris: OECD Development Center, pp. 97–118.

Venturi, Robert et al. (1977) *Learning from Las Vegas: The Forgotten Symbolism of Architectural Form*, Cambridge, MA: MIT Press.

Vessali, Kaveh V. (1995) "Transportation, urban form, and information technology," Berkeley, CA: University of California, unpublished seminar paper for CP 298 I.

Voshchanov, Pavel (1995) "Mafia godfathers become fathers of the nation." *Business World of Russia Weekly*, May 25–30: 13–14.

Wade, Richard (1990) *Governing the Market: Economic Theory and the Role of Government in East Asian Industrialization*, Princeton, NJ: Princeton University Press.

Waldrop, M. Mitchell (1992) *Complexity: The Emerging Science at the Edge of Order and Chaos*, New York: Simon & Schuster.

Waliszewski, Kasimierz (1900) *Peter the Great*, New York: D. Appleton and Co.

Wall, Toby D. et al. (eds) (1987) *The Human Side of Advanced Manufacturing Technology*, Chichester, Sussex: John Wiley.

Wallerstein, Immanuel (1974) *The Modern World System*, New York: Academic Press.

Wang, Georgette (ed.) (1994) *Treading Different Paths: Informatization in Asian Nations*, Norwood, NJ: Ablex.

Wang, Yeu-fain (1993) *China's Science and Technology Policy, 1949–1989*, Brookfield, VT: Avebury.

Wark, McKenzie (1994) *Virtual Geography: Living with Global Media Events*, Bloomington, IND: Indiana University Press.

Warme, Barbara et al. (eds) (1992) *Working Part-time: Risks and Opportunities*, New York: Praeger.

Warnken, Jurgen and Ronning, Gerd, "Technological change and employment structures." In R. Schettkat and M. Wagner (eds), *Technological Change and Employment Innovation in the German Economy*, Berlin: Walter De Gruyter, pp. 214–53.

Watanabe, Susumu (1986) "Labour-saving versus work-amplifying effects of microelectronics." *International Labour Review*, 125(3): 243–59.

—— (ed.) (1987) *Microelectronics, Automation, and Employment in the Automobile Industry*, Chichester, Sussex: John Wiley.

Watanuki, Joji (1990) *The Development of Information Technology and its Impact on Japanese Society*, Tokyo: Sophia University Institute of International Relations, Research Paper.

Weber, Marx (1958) *The Protestant Ethic and the Spirit of Capitalism*, trans. Talcott Parsons, New York: Charles Scribner's Sons. First published 1904–5.

Webster, Andrew (1991) *Science, Technology, and Society: New Directions*, London: Macmillan.

Weiss, Linda (1988) *Creating Capitalism: The State and Small Business since 1945*, Oxford: Blackwell.

—— (1992) "The politics of industrial organization: a comparative view." In Jane Marceau (ed.), *Reworking the World: Organizations, Technologies, and Cultures in Comparative Perspective*, Berlin: Walter De Gruyter, pp. 95–124.

Wexler, Joanie (1994) "ATT preps service for video on demand." *Network World*, 11(25): 6.

Whightman, D.W. (1987) "Competitive advantage through information technology." *Journal of General Management*, 12(4).

Whitaker, D.H. (1990) "The end of Japanese-style employment." *Work, Employment & Society*, 4(3): 321–47.

Whitley, Richard (1993) *Business Systems in East Asia: Firms, Markets, and Societies*, London: Sage.

Whitrow, G.J. (1988) *Time in History: The Evolution of our General Awareness of Time and Temporal Perspective*, Oxford: Oxford University Press.

Wieczorek, Jaroslaw (1995) *Sectoral Trends in World Employment*, Working Paper 82, Geneva: International Labour Organization, Industrial Activities Branch.

Wieviorka, Michel (1993) *La Démocratie a l'épreuve. Nationalisme, populisme, ethnicité*, Paris: La Découverte.

Wilkinson, B. (1988) "A comparative analysis." In *Technological Change, Work, Organization and Pay: Lessons from Asia*, Geneva: International Labour Organization.

Wilkinson, Barry, Morris, Jonathan and Nich, Oliver (1992) "Japanizing the world: the case of Toyota." In Jane Marceau (ed.), *Reworking the World: Organizations, Technologies, and Cultures in Comparative Perspective*, Berlin: Walter de Gruyter, pp. 133–50.

Williams, Frederick (1982) *The Communications Revolution*, Beverly Hills, CA: Sage.

—— (1991) *The New Telecommunications: Infrastructure for the Information Age*, New York: Free Press.

—— (ed.) (1988) *Measuring the Information Society*, Beverly Hills, CA: Sage.

——, Rice, Ronald E. and Rogers, Everett M. (1988) *Research Methods and the New Media*, New York: Free Press.

Williams, Raymond (1974) *Television: Technology and Cultural Form*, New York: Schocken Books.

Williamson, Oliver E. (1975) *Markets and Hierarchies: Analysis and Anti-trust Implications*, New York: Free Press.

—— (1985) *The Economic Institutions of Capitalism*, New York: Free Press.

Willmott, W.E. (ed.) (1972) *Economic Organization in Chinese Society*, Stanford, CA: Stanford University Press.

Wilson, Carol (1991) "The myths and magic of Minitel." *Telephony*, 221(23): 52.

Wilson, Ernest J. (1991) "Strategies of state control of the economy: nationalization and indigenization in Africa." *Comparative Politics*, July: 411.

Withey, Stephen B. and Abeles, Ronald P. (eds) (1980) *Television and Social Behavior*, Hillsdale, NJ: Lawrence Erlbaum.

Wong, Siulun (1988) *Emigrant Entrepreneurs: Shanghai Industrialists in Hong Kong*, Hong Kong: Oxford University Press.

Wong, S.L. (1985) "The Chinese family firm: a model." *British Journal of Sociology*, 36: 58–72.

Woo, Edward S.W. (1994) Urban development. In Y.M. Yeung and David K.Y. Chu, *Guandong: Survey of a Province Undergoing Rapid Change*, Hong Kong: Chinese University Press.

Wood, Adrian (1994) *North–South Trade, Employment and Inequality*, Oxford: Clarendon Press.

Wood, Stephen (ed.) (1989) *The Transformation of Work*, London: Unwin Hyman.

Woodward, Kathleen (ed.) (1980) *The Myths of Information: Technology and Postindustrial Culture*, London: Routledge & Kegan Paul.

World Bank (1994a) *Adjustment in Africa: Reforms, Results and the Road Ahead*, New York: Oxford University Press.

—— (1994b) *World Development Report: Infrastructure for Development. World Development Indicators*, Washington D.C.: World Bank.

—— (1995) *World Development Report, 1995*, Washington, D.C.: World Bank.

Ybarra, Josep-Antoni (1989) "Informationalization in the Valencian economy: a model for underdevelopment." In A. Portes, M. Castells and L. Benton *The Informal Economy*, Baltimore, MD: Johns Hopkins University Press.

Yoo, S. and Lee, S.M. (1987) "Management style and practice in Korean chaebols." *California Management Review*, 29: 95–110.

Yoshihara, K. (1988) *The Rise of Ersatz Capitalism in South East Asia*, Oxford: Oxford University Press.

Yoshino, Kosaku (1992) *Cultural Nationalism in Contemporary Japan*, London: Routledge.

Yoshino, M.Y. and Lifson, T.B. (1986) *The Invisible Link: Japan's Sogo Shosha and the Organization of Trade*, Cambridge, MA: MIT Press.

Young, K. and Lawson, C. (1984) "What fuels U.S. job growth? Changes in technology and demand on employment growth," paper prepared for the Panel on Technology and Employment of the National Academy of Sciences, Washington D.C.

Young, Michael (1988) *The Metronomic Society*, Cambridge, Mass.: Harvard University Press.

Youngson, A.J. (1982) *Hong Kong: Economic Growth and Policy*, Hong Kong: Oxford University Press.

Zaldivar, Carlos Alonso and Castells, Manuel (1992) *España, fin de siglo*, Madrid: Alianza Editorial.

Zerubavel, Eviatar (1985) *The Seven Day Circle: The History and Meaning of the Week*, New York: Free Press.

Zhivov, Victor M. (1995) "Time and money in Imperial Russia." Unpublished paper delivered at the conference on *Time and Money in the Russian Culture*, University of California at Berkeley, Center for Slavic and Eastern European Studies, March 17.

Zuboff, Shoshana (1988) *In the Age of the Smart Machine*, New York: Basic Books.

Zukin, Sharon (1992) *Landscapes of Power*, Berkeley, CA: University of California Press.

Index